AF322721

SPEAKEASY

A NOVEL

BY

ROBERT JAMES ALLEN

Speakeasy: A Novel

Copyright © 2024 by ROBERT JAMES ALLEN. All rights reserved.

This title is also available at Amazon. Visit https://www. Amazon.com for more information.

No part of this publication may be reproduced, stored in a retrieval system or transmitted in any way by any means, electronic, mechanical, photocopy, recording or otherwise without the prior permission of the author except as provided by USA copyright law.

This novel is a work of fiction. Names, descriptions, entities, and incidents included in the story are products of the author's imagination. Any resemblance to actual persons, events, and entities is entirely coincidental.

Published by Robert James Allen

Book design copyright © 2024 by Robert James Allen. All rights reserved.

TABLE OF CONTENTS

PREFACE: 1932, GREENWICH VILLAGE, NEW YORK CITY

It's been twelve years since the 18th Amendment was passed, banning the selling and consuming of alcohol nationwide. Now an economic strife known as the great depression has rendered the once prosperous and industrious citizens of New York to succumb to lives of waiting in long and dismal breadlines and frantically selling bootleg alcohol in any way, shape, or form. Greenwich Village has now become a boiling pot of duplicitous characters and indulgent poisons. Disenfranchised workers, downtrodden immigrants, and the constant resurgence of speakeasies have now grown throughout the languishing city. These surreptitious establishments cater to man's every pleasure, and the most desired of all pleasures is undoubtedly the sweet numbing effect of alcohol.

We begin by following the proprietor of a popular speakeasy. This man has taken it upon himself to stop at nothing when it comes to providing all of his many friends with every creature comfort known to man.

... I'm only being facetious, for men like Jack have no friends.

CHAPTER 1:
BRIDGES BURNED
- JACK -

"Get out. I never want to see you again. You're nothing but a whore with no disregard for anyone or anything but your own filthy desires!" I shouted at Dezerae, as I threw a rag into her flushed face as she sat upon the lap of Johnny "the Hammer" O'Connor, the mobster who beat me to within an inch of my life a few nights back.

"Go drink yourself to death, Jack," Dezerae said to me with a laugh, and then continued kissing Johnny.

"Oh you don't want to do that, Jack," Johnny said to me with a snicker, as he averted his bourbon soaked mouth from Dezerae to me.

"I don't fucking care who you work for," I said to Johnny in a stern tone, as I swiftly pulled out my shotgun from underneath the bar and pointed it at him.

"No ... we'll leave. This watering hole is beneath us anyways. Come on, Dez," Johnny pronounced with a whistle, as he raised his hands and gestured for his crew to leave my bar. "He will satisfy her in ways you could only imagine, Jack.

"You should be happy for her," one of Johnny's associates said to me with a grin, as he walked past me.

"Take your misbegotten daughter with you!" I shouted at Dezerae, as she hiked up her drab burgundy dress so that it covered up her cleavage.

"Hayley, Hayley we're leaving!" Dezerae shouted, as she reached out her hand towards Hayley who sat at a corner table of the bar, as she wrote in a small, leather-bound book. Hayley then scampered over to her mother's side, as Johnny put on his pinstripe-jacket and fedora.

"Goodbye Uncle Jack," Hayley, said to me in a somber tone and slight wave, as I stared intently at Dezerae and Johnny with a fire of hatred burning in my eyes just before the three of them exited the bar.

*****

"That was five years ago," I said to Bernadette with a scoff, as I shook my head, and then took a shot of bourbon with a grimace.

"Heaven's me, Jack. I can't believe you really treated your sister and niece in such a ruthless manner," Bernadette said to me, as the lethargic jazz band picked up their pace with an upbeat piano solo.

"Now wait sweetheart, a deal's a deal. You promised me that if I bared my soul to you, then you would bare your chest to me," I said to Bernadette with a smirk, as I pulled her in close to me as she began to walk away in a flouting manner.

"After that story, I'm in no mood to humor your indulgences," Bernadette said to me, as she pried my hands off her waist with a scoff.

"This is my establishment. You either service me and my fellow patrons or you can join the nearest breadline around the corner," I said to Bernadette in a stern tone, as I swiftly grasped her wrist.

"Well, well, just like five years ago, huh, Jack. You would think a man like you would learn from the past," Bernadette said to me in a stern tone, and then grabbed my glass of bourbon from the bar and tossed it into my face.

The jazz band then ceased their tune, as all the eyes of all the patrons in the speakeasy became instantly fixed upon me. I then swiftly back-handed Bernadette in the face with no hesitation, and the band then instantly began to play their rousing tune again. Bernadette then lay crying upon the hardwood floor with her hand upon her cheek.

"Oh no, sweetheart, I've learned a great deal from the past. I've learned not to let women like you shackle my pride," I said to Dezerae with a smirk.

"You're a heartless bastard, Jack Dansby. One of these days you're going to get what you deserve," Bernadette remarked in a distressed tone.

"Toss her out. She's worn out her welcome here. Besides, *Jack of All Trades* will not miss a common whore like her," I said in a stern tone and then took a shot of bourbon, as Bernadette was dragged out of the speakeasy by Samson kicking and screaming.

"Aren't you worried that dame will talk?" Samson inquired, as he locked the front door of the speakeasy.

"I won't lose any sleep over that. She wouldn't dare rat us out," I replied with a scoff, as the lights dimmed in the speakeasy for a few moments.

"You know what they say; hell hath no fury like a woman scorned," Samson said to me with a smirk.

"If you're worried that Bernadette will talk to the police, then you can put those fears to bed right now. She depends too much on our patrons for survival," I said to Samson, as I wiped down the bar with a rag.

"Does Bernadette have the password?" Samson inquired.

"No, you damn fool. She only gains entry from us personally. She's nothing but a decoration, now stop fucking quivering over the possibility of her talking to the police. That's exactly what a woman like her wants," I replied in a stern tone. "Very well, Jack. You haven't led me astray yet," Samson said to me.

Samson Monaghan was one of my associates at the *Jack of All Trades*, and one tough son of a bitch at that. I once saw the man head butt a belligerent, drunken Italian, sending him flying off the barstool, but then again, those Irish have some of the shortest tempers out of any race of people that walk into my speakeasy. The man was a means to an end during a time where you needed a fist more than a heart. The only thing a heart has ever gotten me in this day and age was a black eye and the copper taste of blood in my mouth.

"Caroline, you're on!" I shouted, as I snapped my fingers and pointed to the stage.

"Those negroes sure have a knack for the song and dance," Samson remarked, as Caroline Jenkins took a long drag from her cigarette and then began to sing a recycled jazz tune which you could hear in any speakeasy throughout Manhattan.

"She's no Bessie Smith, but she'll do for now," I remarked with a snicker, while shaking my head.

"Bessie Smith… boy you sure are a fan of that vaudeville movement. I for one say it's nothing but brash Negroes tossing bread crumbs to us immigrants," Samson said to me.

"Now what would an ignorant Irishman like you know about good music," I said to Samson with a scoff.

"Easy now, Jack, you're not exactly a scholar yourself," Samson remarked.

"Go check on Maurice and that dame who's draped around him," I said to Samson in a stern tone.

Maurice Caldor used to be a wealthy man of prominence in the village, but now he's nothing but a lowlife wretch with mere pennies to his name. There was a time when he once owned a club on every block from Carmine Street to the Meatpacking District. Now the man has fallen from his lofty perch of decadence as a result of this prohibition and depression, and where do all pitiful souls go when they have not a joy left in their life, to the *Jack of All Trades* of course. I was in no way like Maurice. For the prohibition law took the life out of him. The manner of which he carried himself was completely transformed. I, for one, took the heavy blow of the prohibition law like a prize fighter. Sure my once thriving bar was shut down, but I wasn't about to let such bullshit laws dictate how I run my life, I never have, and I never will. So I set my sights on a new business endeavor to continue to serve alcohol and any other vice which man needs in this day and age. Right here on Minetta Street was where I invested the last of my finances into a dilapidated wine cellar from some restaurateur who up and split to greener pastures. I breathed new life into a once dead street, for it's always been my nature to capitalize from strife in any way it chooses to present itself to me.

*****

It was 8:25 PM in the speakeasy.

"Mr. Jack, can I go home now. These men have grown awfully ugly towards me?" Caroline inquired, as she walked up to the bar with a sigh.

"They're always ugly, Caroline, but your job is to entertain them," Samson said to Caroline, as he prepared an expensive looking drink in such an unrefined manner.

"Samson is right, Caroline. You entertain our patrons, but if you want to leave in the middle of happy hour, then your pay will be cut," I told Caroline in a stern tone.

"I've worked for you for a year now and you still treat me like that?" Caroline inquired in a distressed tone, as she slammed her hands upon the bar.

"You watch your tongue, Caroline," Samson said to Caroline in a stern tone, as he pointed at her with that familiar Irish furor burning in his eyes.

"If you want to follow in Bernadette's footsteps, then go right on ahead. There's the door," I said to Caroline with a smirk, as I pointed to the front door of the speakeasy.

"I … I need a break, please," Caroline said to me.

"You have three minutes. Any longer and I'm cutting your pay," I said to Caroline in a stern tone.

"Thank you, sir," Caroline said to me with a nod, and then scampered behind the burgundy curtains of the stage, while the rest of the band smoked their cigarettes in a fiendish manner.

"Play my song," I said to Samson in a stern tone, as I snapped my fingers and pointed to the victrola on a stand situated next to the band.

"Of course, Bessie Smith "Nobody Knows You When You're Down and Out" coming right up, Jack," Samson said to me with a smirk, as he adjusted his black vest and tie before placing the record in the victrola with a smile to the handful of patrons sitting at the tables in front of the stage.

*****

It was 2:14 AM in the speakeasy.

"Even if I was a rat I wouldn't spend my days and nights lingering in this filthy hole in the ground. You live a truly pitiful life, Jack," Allie May said to me with a scoff, as she walked away from the bar.

"Don't kid yourself, sweetheart, you are a rat, just a rat in a shiny dress, but a rat nonetheless, and don't for one second act like you're superior to the likes of me. You're banned from this establishment. I don't need another pompous whore with delusions of grandeur in my speakeasy," I said to Allie May in a stern tone, as I pointed to the front door. Allie May then walked towards the front door of the speakeasy in a flouting manner. I then snapped my fingers and pointed at Allie May, as Samson scampered over to the front door and quickly unlocked it.

"That's the third dame you cast out of here, Jack. You keep up that pace and not a single lady will set foot in here," Samson said to me, as he walked over to the bar.

"Go home Samson. I don't need your input on how to run this establishment," I said to Samson in a stern tone, as I took off my black vest, and tie in an aggressive manner.

"Aye, very well, you're lucky Mickey has more patience with you, praise that boy and his timid nature," Samson said to me, as he put on his jacket and hat.

"Luck is a fallacy, Samson. If you live your life by luck, then you will find yourself in the gutter fighting over scraps of bread," I said to Samson.

"If not luck then what else is there? I for one welcome luck in all its forms," Samson said to me.

"Then it's a fucking miracle that a bullheaded Irishman like you is still breathing in this day and age," I remarked with a snicker, and then took a shot of bourbon.

"It's not a miracle, its luck … goodnight Jack," Samson said to me.

"What a fool," I spoke aloud, as Samson exited the front door of the speakeasy, leaving me alone in the dimly-lit glow of an old night.

The speakeasy is where I laid my head down every night. You could say I was a squatter here, but I consider myself to be a soldier, a sole proprietor of joy. I awoke and fell asleep in an establishment outlawed by the very men who partake in the same vices behind the closed doors of their lavish apartments. I've always been as blatantly honest man; perhaps that's why I'm alone. Nobody wants to hear the truth, and I sure as hell won't tell a dame anything less.

"Take me away Calloway," I spoke, aloud, as I placed a record on the victrola and then laid my head down upon my bed with a bottle of bourbon in hand.

*****

I awoke at 8:30 AM to a knock on the front door.

"Give me a goddamn minute!" I shouted, as I stood out of bed and turned off the victrola. I then turned on the lights of the speakeasy, as they flickered at first, but then glowed in a steady manner.

"Who's there?" I inquired in a stern tone, as I stood up against the front door of the speakeasy with my hand grasping the lock of the thin iron window slot.

"It's me, Mickey. I have your mail just like we arranged, sir," a timid voice replied.

Why did I even care anymore about the post? I was basically an outlaw in the eyes of the police. What exactly was I expecting to be delivered to me by that boy Mickey?

"Get in here, Mickey. Did anybody follow you?" I inquired in a stern tone, as I unlocked the front door of the speakeasy and then swiftly pulled Mickey inside by his scrawny arm.

"Not to my knowledge, sir," Mickey replied.

Mickey Sullivan was a young lad at the end of his rope when he started working for me just a little over a month ago. The boy carried himself in the manner of an orphan, and he may very well be one, but I couldn't give a damn about his personal strife.

"Now what could this be?" I inquired with a sigh, as I sat down at the bar and stared intently at the letter Mickey handed me in a quivering manner.

"You get more mail than I do, Jack," Mickey remarked with a smirk, and then began to get dressed in his uniform which hung upon a hook in the back room behind the bar.

"I get mostly propaganda from Hoover, Mickey. The very man who supports this unjust outlaw of alcohol," I said to Mickey in a stern tone, as I opened up the letter.

"Well let's hope that President Hoover decides to –"

"Shut up," I said to Mickey in a stern tone, as I read the letter in a brooding manner, while Mickey studiously got the speakeasy ready for patrons.

Dear Mr. Dansby,

We regret to inform you with the deepest of sorrows that your sister Dezerae Carmona was found dead in her apartment in Mercer Street, *SoHo* on June 5th, 8:45 PM. The NYPD was called to the scene shortly after by the daughter of Dezerae who found her mother lying motionless soon thereafter with a pillow over her face. The NYPD have deduced that Dezerae was murdered by a gunshot to the head by her boyfriend Johnny O'Connor who now has a warrant out for his arrest.

The funeral services for Dezerae Carmona will be held on June 6th, 10 AM at the Frank E. Campbell Funeral Chapel on 1076 Madison Avenue. We strongly implore you to attend the funeral services of Dezerae Carmona so that you can disclose to the NYPD any information that would help us in the arrest of your sister's murderer Johnny O'Connor.

On the matter regarding your fifteen year old niece, she currently resides at the New York Foundling Hospital on 590 Avenue of the Americas. Being her only living relative; you are now henceforth the sole legal guardian of this child. Whether or not you choose to adopt Ms. Carmona, is your decision.

Detective, Alabaster Simmons New York City Police Department
   Police Precinct, 153 E 67th St, Manhattan

CHAPTER 2:
NEXT OF KIN
- HAYLEY -

This must be what hell feels like. I knew Johnny would be the death of her, but my countless pleas for her to break up with him fell on deaf ears, and now, she's gone. In this already cruel world, I now no longer had a mother, but I suppose she was never truly there to protect me from all the evil men who have left their mark on me. I felt cold whenever the image of my bloody mother lying still upon the same chair she used to give me life affirmations as I sat upon her lap many mornings flashed in my mind. So I now remain here at this hospital full of kids of all shapes, sizes, and colors, who I'm sure, have suffered their fair share of loss as well. I can't stop shaking. My mother always told me to project myself in the manner of a queen when I'm around other men, for that's how she lived her life, but I just cannot bring myself to look another man in the eye without a sense of fear pulsing in my heart.

Will Jack come for me, or will he show me the same cruelness and disregard as he's shown me and my mother in the past? My last memory of him was not a pleasant one. He was always such an angry man who would lash out at my mother over the slightest thing. I remember that day clearly, that day my mother and I parted ways from Uncle Jack

*****

I want to go home, this place where Uncle Jack works is scary, but my mom always brings me here with her every weekend to meet him. I'll just stay quiet right here in the corner and continue to write in my diary while Jack and my mom talk. "You crossed the line, Jack, mom taught you better than that," my mom said to Uncle Jack in a stern tone, as she pointed at him.

"Who on earth are you to judge me? I thought you would support me and my bar, but you look at me as if I was just some two-timing bootlegger," Jack said to my mom, as his voice rose to an angry level, which made me cover my ears in fear of what he might say next.

"I've had it with you and your desperate ways," my mom said to Uncle

Jack, as she put on her jacket.

"Don't you fucking walk away from me," Uncle Jack shouted, as he grabbed my mom's wrist.

"What are you going to do, smack me down like you do with the rest of these poor women who stumble in and out of this godforsaken bar?" my mom inquired, as Jack stared at her with such anger in his eyes.

"So now you're going to betray me too. Just like everybody else," Jack said to my mother, as he pulled her in close to him. "Take your hand off that dame, Jack," a tall man wearing a pinstripe hat and suit said to Uncle Jack, as he walked up to him and my mom.

"Mind your own goddamn business or—it's you, who let you back in here?" Jack inquired, as he stared at the tall man in the suit with a scared look in his eyes.

"No doors in this city are locked for me and my associates," the tall man replied with a smirk, as three other men dressed just like him stood beside him.

"Let's get out of this rat's nest. I'll show you how a woman of your beauty should be treated," the tall man said to my mother, as he reached out his black-gloved hand towards her.

"I'll take that offer big guy," my mom said to the tall man, as she freed herself from Jack's grasp and then took the tall man's hand.

"Come now Hayley," we're leaving," my mom shouted. I didn't know this tall man, but he showed my mother more kindness in that short time than Uncle Jack ever has, so I ran over to him and my mom with my diary in hand.

"Dez … if you leave this bar with that man, then don't bother ever coming back," Uncle Jack said to my mom in a stern tone, while shaking his head.

"Let's get out of here, Hayley," my mom said to me, as she grabbed my hand.

"Goodbye Uncle Jack," I said to Uncle Jack just before me, my mom, and the tall man exited the bar, but Uncle Jack just stared back at me with such anger in his eyes.

*****

Would my mother still be alive today if she chose not to leave Uncle Jack's bar with Johnny? When I look back at that moment it taught me that during times of hatred we make choices that turn us into somebody else, and although at that moment five years ago I didn't fear Johnny the way I feared Uncle Jack, I still sensed that my mother chose to leave with him just to spite Uncle Jack.

"Do you need anything sweetheart?" an elderly nurse inquired, as she walked up to my bed with a smile.

"What if my uncle doesn't come, then what will happen to me," I replied in a somber tone, as I wrapped my quivering arms around my quivering legs.

"Then you will remain here until an orphanage has vacancy for you, but it pains me to say that this depression has only increased the number of orphans, while decreasing the number of employed workers. I'm sorry child," the nurse said to me and then walked away to attend to another girl around my age who was crying in the bed across from mine.

Yes this had to be hell, for I felt no warmth here. Tears then began to stream from my eyes, as I rocked myself back and forth; joining in on the symphony of sorrow which emanated from the floor of the hospital I was on.

*****

It was 3:47 PM in the Foundling Hospital.

"All right where is she, Nurse Haggard," a voice proclaimed, as I drew a picture of a bouquet of roses in my dairy. How I wish a boy would give me such beautiful roses as a gift.

"My name is Hargrim, sir, and I ask that you please be patient with us, for there are many children on this floor," the elderly nurse said to a man wearing a tan newsboy hat and a brooding look upon his face.

My heart then raced at the possibility of that brooding man being Uncle Jack. I haven't seen him in five years. Could his appearance have changed so much?

"You two must have a lot of catching up to do, call me if you need anything," the elderly nurse proclaimed, as she walked up to me with the brooding man beside her.

"Hayley is that you … you sure have grown kid," the brooding man remarked as he stared at me in the manner of a man staring at a stray puppy.

"Oh my god Uncle Jack," I pronounced, as tears welled up in my eyes. I then quickly stood up and wrapped my arms around Jack so tightly, which made him grunt.

"Easy, kid, don't go jumping to conclusions now. I'm not here to adopt you. I'm only here to take you to your mother's funeral tomorrow morning. The man who killed your mother nearly killed me five years ago, and if I can help the NYPD track him down and lock him up, then justice will be served," Jack said to me, as he pried my arms off his waist.

"Oh … of course, I should've known. You never showed her respect in life so why show her any now," I said to Jack in a distressed tone, as tears began to stream from my eyes once more.

"Is there a problem?" the elderly nurse inquired, as she scampered over to me and Jack, while I sat back down on the bed and wrapped my arms back around my legs.

"Everything's fine, Nurse Haggard, now go attend to those orphans over there and leave us be with our family matters," Jack said to the elderly nurse in a stern tone.

"Horrible man," the elderly nurse remarked, as she shook her head and walked away from me and Jack.

"Listen kid. What happened to your mother was terrible, but I must do my duty and help the NYPD lock up that lowlife mobster. He may have already left town, so time is of the essence," Jack said to me, as he sat down beside me on the bed, which made me instinctively move away from him towards the far end of the bed.

"This is all about revenge for you, isn't it? You don't care about my mother at all, you never did," I said to Jack in a distressed tone, as he stared back at me with the same stern eyes of Johnny when he fought with my mother.

"You're too young, you wouldn't understand my daily strife," Jack said to me in a stern tone and scoff, and then lit a cigarette and took a puff.

"Excuse me, sir, but you can't smoke in a hospital," the elderly nurse said to Jack, as she scampered over to us.

"Can you believe this, kid, another law that takes away our god given pleasures in life," Jack pronounced in a stern tone, and then dropped his cigarette on the floor and smashed it with his foot in an aggressive manner.

"I have some documents for you to sign, if you would come with me," the elderly nurse said to Jack.

"I'm not signing anything. I told her this. I will take her to her mother's funeral, then after that she's out of my hands," Jack said to the elderly nurse, as she stared at me with somber eyes.

I hated Jack. He was a vile man who only cared about his own self interest, but I suppose I shouldn't be surprised that Jack didn't greet me warmly, for all my memories of him where just as cruel. He was my only relative in this world, and now I had a terrible choice to make. I could either remain here at the Foundling Hospital and eventually be sent to an even worse orphanage where I will be treated no better than a stray puppy, or I could leave this hospital now with Jack. Jack made me nervous and afraid just as Johnny did, but would he really treat me the same way Johnny did?

*****

"This is my bar, well they call it a speakeasy now," Jack said to me, as we entered the speakeasy, to the sight of dozens of men and women indulging in alcohol, music and themselves. I then stared at the empty corner table of the speakeasy, which is where I sat every time I would visit this wretched place with my mother. I miss her so much now. I miss her voice, her touch, and her smile.

"Who's the girl, Jack?" a brutish looking man inquired with a grin, as he pointed at me.

"That's my niece, Hayley," Jack replied and then whispered into the man's ear for a few moments and then walked to the back room of the bar.

"The names Samson and you definitely bear no resemblance to Jack, little lady," the brutish man remarked with a snicker.

"Good," I said to Samson with a scowl, as I brushed off my black dress and sat down at the bar.

Jack was loud, brash, and had no patience for the people around him who were struggling. The smoke was so thick in this wretched place I could barely see two feet in front of me. I didn't belong here. My mother always told me that Jack's bar was a means to an end. At the time, I didn't fully understand what she meant by that remark, but now I'm beginning to understand. This speakeasy which Jack runs is a means to an end of suffering from unpopular laws. Every time a stared at Jack's brooding eyes I saw no love, not even a glint of compassion for a fleeting moment. He was a man who could only care for himself alone, and those kinds of men were growing by the numbers in this day and age. I felt so alone in this crowded speakeasy, but perhaps this place could help numb my pain for the time being. I then took a half empty glass of liquor from the bar and quickly drunk it down in one gulp without anyone seeing me.

"Are you all right sweetie?" a woman in a sparkling gold dress inquired, as the quick shot of hard liquor brought forth sharp coughs from within my chest.

"I'm fine," I replied in a somber tone, as I wiped my nose with my handkerchief, and brushed back a strand of my hair into my black bonnet.

"You don't seem fine. Are you sure you're allowed to be in a place like this. You look awfully young?" the woman inquired, as she stared at herself in a pocket mirror.

"I'm Jack's niece," I said to the woman in a somber tone.

"Well by god, I had no idea that man had any family he cares for. I'm Caroline," the woman said to me with a smile, as she extended her black, velvet-gloved hand towards me.

"I'm Hayley, and Jack doesn't have any family he cares for, only himself," I said to Caroline in a somber tone, as I quickly shook her hand.

"Toss that bastard out, Samson, he's worn out his welcome here," Jack shouted in a stern tone, as he pointed to a large man in a weathered beige suite.

"They're barbaric, aren't they," Caroline remarked with a scoff.

"Are they always like this?" I inquired in a timid tone, as I leaned away from the brutish man named Samson who grabbed the large man by the arm and collar of his suit and aggressively escorted him to the front door like he was the size of a child.

"Jack and Samson ... ever since I can remember, sweetie," Caroline replied.

"I saw you singing with the band. Are you the entertainment here?" I inquired, as Caroline blew cigarette smoke into my burning eyes. I didn't talk to many colored women in my life, but Caroline seemed friendly, the kind of woman I could confide in with no fear of being judged harshly, just like my mother was.

"I sure am. One of many forms of entertainment your uncle employs and then treats lower than a rat in a gutter," Caroline replied with a scoff.

"He's not my uncle," I said to Caroline in a distressed tone, and then grabbed another half empty glass of liquor and drunk it down in one gulp.

"Easy, honey. A child of your fairness shouldn't be poisoning herself like that," Caroline said to me, as the liquor washed over my body like a warm bath, suppressing my quivering which began the moment I saw my mother dead with a pillow covering her vacant, bloody face.

"Caroline, get back to work or—,"

"I know you will cut my pay. Right away, sir," Caroline interjected, as Jack pointed to the band.

"Sorry sweetie. I'll see you when I see you. Keep your chin up," Caroline said to me with a warm smile.

Caroline then put out her cigarette and then scampered over to the stage, as the band perked up by her return.

"She's crying again, Jack," the man known as Samson said to Jack, as the tears began to stream from my eyes once again. I didn't think there could be this many tears inside of me. Every time I cried, it was a release, but the eyes which then fixed upon me made me feel even more alone.

"She's always crying. She was crying when I first met her. What do you want me to do about it, Samson?" Jack inquired in a stern tone.

"Your sister's dead Jack. Don't you feel any grief?" Samson inquired

"She died in my mind five years ago, Samson. Now go clean those empty tables before I cut your pay!" Jack shouted, which made me recoil off the barstool.

I then grabbed my diary and ran past Jack to the back room behind the bar. I then ripped off my bonnet from my flushed head and unbuttoned the first two buttons of my dress.

"This is my bed. I'm still trying to figure out where you're going to sleep tonight," Jack said to me, as he entered the back room.

"Why not in the gutter with the rats, you treat me no better than them," I said to Jack in a distressed tone

"You've been talking to Caroline haven't you? That arrogant broad should be thanking her lucky stars that I employ here at the speakeasy, and as for you, wallowing in your self- pity won't bring your mother back. Her funeral service is tomorrow morning. If you want to avenge your mother's death by helping the NYPD lock up that son of a bitch mobster who killed her, then you do as I say, understand?" Jack inquired in a stern tone.

I didn't respond to Jack, as he stared intently at me, as he's done to my mother many times. Jack then exited the kitchen, I then lay down upon the floor where I belong and tried to cry myself to sleep.

*****

I awoke at 8:24 AM upon a blanket on the kitchen floor of the speakeasy.

My ginger hair was now tinted with the filth from the grimy blanket, but I supposed I should get used to not feeling or looking beautiful any more.

Jack was already awake and shouting obscenities at that brutish man known as Samson. I tried to gather the little shred grace and dignity had left as I looked into the partially cracked mirror above the kitchen sink before I entered the bar.

"Are you ready, kid?" Jack inquired, as I walked up beside him in a timid manner.

"Excuse me," I replied, as I ran back to the kitchen.

My stomach was in flames from drinking last night and I couldn't suppress the overwhelming urge any longer. I then vomited into the sink, as I tried to hold my own hair back with no gentleman around to do it for me in my time of need. I was in no condition to attend my mother's funeral, but I needed any semblance of closure I could get, even if it meant I had to go with Jack.

"Have you been drinking, kid?" Jack inquired, as I walked back to him at the bar while wiping my mouth.

"Just a little," I replied in a somber tone and sniff.

"What ever gets you through the night," Jack remarked with a smirk.

"I need to eat something," I said to Jack, as I brushed the tinted gray ginger strands of hair away from my eyes.

"How do I know you won't just vomit again in my Pontiac?" Jack inquired in a stern tone, "Please, Jack, I feel like I may faint at any moment," I said to Jack in a distressed tone, as I clutched my arms tightly to keep myself from shaking.

"Samson, fix her something quick, we have to go in ten minutes," Jack said to Samson in a stern tone and sigh, before car.

"Which are?" I inquired, as I sat down beside Jack and then he went into the back room of the bar.

"Here, this is what I eat whenever the poison lingers in my stomach the morning after," Samson said to me as he slid a plate upon the bar towards me.

"Thank you. So how long have you worked for Jack?" I inquired in a timid tone, and then took a small bite out of a thick piece of bread with some sort of gray meat mixed within it.

"Two years. Consider yourself grateful you haven't been as close to Jack day by day as I have," Samson replied, with a scoff, as he dried a glass mug.

"Why is that," I inquired, as I took a bigger bite of the minced meat toast.

"Let me just say that men like Jack are wanted during this time, but never needed," Samson replied, and then scampered over to a table in front of the stage while adjusting his tie and vest.

"All right let's go. Samson, we'll be back in a couple of hours. Hopefully you can keep this place running for that long," Jack pronounced.

"Aye, Mickey will be here soon to assist me anyways," Samson said to Jack. Jack then snapped his fingers at me with a whistle, gesturing for me to follow him like a sick little puppy, but perhaps that's the very image I projected myself to him.

How was jack any better of a man than Johnny? He was solely inspired by his own emotions, and those emotions were that of vengeance upon Johnny, not for killing my mother, but for nearly killing Jack. Jack's pride was overwhelming. Now I see why my mother changed the subject whenever I mentioned his name. Jack died in my mother's mind just as my mother died in his, but now Jack and I were forced upon each other, by my mother's death.

"How could you afford such a car during these times," I inquired, as I stared at the black and beige Pontiac parked in the back alley leading to the speakeasy.

"It's quite simple kid. Four easy installment plans," Jack replied with a snicker, as he lit a cigarette before entering the leaned against the door making sure I was an arm's distance from Jack when he started up the car.

"Installment one, identify a wealthy Wall Street wretch looking to drown his sorrows at my speakeasy. Installment two, befriend the pretentious blowhard, while he prattles on and on about how the market crashed and took everything away from him but his prized car. Installment three, make sure the Wall Street wretch is liquored up to the point where he can't walk or see straight before you pick pocket his car keys, while you hail him a cab and insist that he takes it easy for the remainder of the night. Installment four, my favorite part, you reap the spoils of the wealthy as you take the man's car, giving him no reason left to live," Jack replied with a laugh and cough, as we drove down a boulevard lined with people waiting in long breadlines on both sides of the street.

"You stole this car, but aren't you worried the man will return with the police," I inquired, as Jack rested his arm out the driver's side window.

"He never did. Samson and I put the fear of god into his quivering eyes. We told him that we would take much more than his car from him if he ever alerted the cops about my speakeasy. Long story short, he never returned," Jack replied with a laugh, and then took a swig from a flask most likely filled with liquor. Jack was a criminal who preyed off of people's desperate state of minds. He may have never killed anyone like Johnny has, but I don't doubt by the look in his stark eyes that he could very well take a life without hesitation.

"Where are we going again … oh right, Frank E. Campbell Funeral Chapel on 1076 Madison Avenue," Jack said to me, as he read the letter, which rested upon the steering wheel. Jack then handed the letter to me before tossing his cigarette out the window and shouting an obscenity at an elderly man crossing the street.

"I feel sick again," I said to Jack in a weary tone as I held my stomach.

"Vomit out the window. I'll be damned if I'm going to miss this funeral service," Jack said to me in a stern tone. Jack drove like a madman, nearly hitting three people on the way to my mother's funeral. I didn't feel safe with Jack. He was the kind of man who would sacrifice the safety of the ones around him in the blink of an eye just for his own personal gain.

"I'm fine now. Are we almost there?" I inquired, as we drove past a group of protestors holding signs and chanting '*Save our jobs, save or lives*' outside of what appeared to be a factory.

"Depending on traffic we should arrive at the funeral home in ten minutes, but then again with the unemployment rate at twenty-three percent, there hasn't been much traffic these days," Jack replied with a scoff.

"Where will I go after my mother's funeral," I inquired in a somber tone, as we drove into a parking lot.

"That's none of my concern," Jack replied, as he parked the car.

"You said it yourself. Like it or not, you're my legal guardian and only blood relative left," I said to Jack in a distressed tone, as he sighed.

"All right kid. Then for the time being, as your guardian, I want you to put your dingy hair up and cover it with that spare bonnet in the back seat," Jack said to me in a stern tone.

"No, my mother always loved my hair down. She told me my true beauty shined when my hair was down, so this is how I will attend her funeral," I said to Jack in a distressed tone as my eyes began to well up with tears.

"If you want to attend your mother's funeral looking like a rat in a gutter then so be it. Let's go!" Jack shouted as he exited the car and slammed the door shut in an aggressive manner which caused me to recoil.

Jack and I entered the funeral home to the sight of only a few people dressed in black gathered around a casket.

"Good afternoon how may I help you?" an elderly woman dressed in a stark black dress inquired, as she walked up to Jack.

"I'm here—we're here for the services of Dezerae Carmona," Jack replied.

"Yes of course and who might you two be?" the elderly woman inquired.

"She was my sister and her mother," Jack replied, as he pointed at me.

"You have my condolences. The services of Ms. Carmona will be held momentarily. You two may pay your respects as you see fit," the elderly woman said as she gestured towards the casket.

"Why are there no flowers decorating her casket, or even a portrait of her," I inquired in a somber tone, as the tears began to stream from my eyes once again.

"Your mother's funeral service was basically run by the NYPD and don't assume for one second that I would spend a large amount of money lavishing your mother in death when she wouldn't spend a dime on me in life," Jack replied with a scowl, as he sat down in one of the chairs in front of my mother's casket and lit a cigarette.

"I miss you so much. Why did you leave me with him?" I spoke aloud in a tearful tone, as I placed my hand upon the cold, smooth wood of the casket. No flowers, no smiling portrait, and nobody around to hold me. I then dropped to the ground, as my crying rose to such a level, as if all the sorrows of my life had now erupted from within me. I could see Jack out of the corner of my tear-flooded eyes staring at me with a stern visage, as he continued to smoke as if he was waiting for food at a diner. How could a man be so detached, so cold, so cruel to his own family?

It was 10:45 AM at the Frank E, Campbell Funeral Home.

I sat two chair spaces away from Jack, as the priest spoke for no longer than fifteen minutes before concluding the wake. That's all my mother's life was worth, only fifteen minutes?

"Good afternoon, I'm Detective Simmons of the NYPD. Us three have much to talk about if you would follow me," a man with a thin black beard wearing a long trench coat pronounced, as he walked up to me and Jack.

"We do indeed detective," Jack said with a sigh, as he stood up from the chair.

"Ms. Carmona," the detective said to me.

It would always make me nervous whenever adults spoke in formalities. It was a precursor of something awful to come, and as I followed Jack and the detective down a hallway of the funeral home into an office I knew I would be given even more devastating news.

"Do you have any leads?" Jack inquired in a stern tone. "What leads," the detective replied.

"Leads on the whereabouts of that mobster son of a bitch Johnny O'Connor," Jack said to the detective in a stern tone.

They talked amongst themselves as if I wasn't even in the room. They didn't even acknowledge me when talking about the man who killed my mother.

"Mr. Dansby are you familiar with the Five Points Gang?" the detective, inquired, as he read through some papers on his desk.

"Of course I am, but not too familiar with them if I see what you're getting at," Jack replied.

"We have on good authority and information that Johnny O'Connor, the mobster who killed your sister, is part of the Five Points Gang of lower Manhattan," the detective said to Jack, as I continued to make fleeting glances at both of them with somber eyes.

"Shit, I knew Johnny was a mobster, but I had no idea he was part of the most powerful crime organization currently operating in New York," Jack said to the detective.

"He's not hiding," I pronounced.

"Who's not hiding, Ms Carmona?" the detective inquired. "Johnny. He's not hiding or fleeing from this town. It's just as you said. Why would a man who is part of the most powerful crime organization in New York fear anyone?" I replied. "The kid has a good point," Jack said to the detective.

"Ah yes of course, Johnny O'Connor wouldn't run if he felt the presence of the Five Points Gang wherever he did his dealings in this city," the detective said to Jack.

"I'm surprised the Five Points Gang would let an Irishman into their gang, I thought they were made up of mostly Italians," Jack said to the detective.

"Johnny is known as an enforcer. He silences people who could be a threat," the detective said.

"Like my mother," I said in a somber tone.

"Yes Ms. Carmona. Do you have any idea of why Johnny killed her? Did she have incriminating information on the Five Points Gang?" the detective inquired.

"All I heard was shouting. From when I woke up to when I tried to fall asleep. I feared for my mother's safety, but I was too afraid to talk back to Johnny. I suppose if I alerted the police sooner, then my mother would still be alive," I replied in a distressed tone, as tears began to stream from my eyes.

"Do not blame yourself Mr. Carmona. Johnny O'Connor is an extremely dangerous mobster. The fact that he got close with your mother was bad luck," the detective said.

"No it was her own nature that got her killed. I remember that day five years ago. She could've stayed with me, but she chose to leave with that bastard," Jack said while shaking his head.

"She left with him because she couldn't stand your abuse!"
I shouted at Jack.

"I never once laid a hand on your mother, but I see she has an attraction for men who beat her something fierce. Don't you remember your father before he died? Johnny silenced him and then took his place," Jack said to me in a stern tone.

"I was only six years old when he left my mother," I said to Jack in a distressed tone.

"Who are you talking about?" the detective inquired.

"Her father, Fernando Carmona, the man was a lowlife Italian immigrant fresh off the boat who her mother married so hastily. Then when she grew tired of all the beatings, she enlisted the services of Johnny "the Hammer" O'Connor. Johnny silenced that man all right, but then continued to give her the same shiners Fernando did," Jack said to the detective in a stern tone.

"Shut up, just shut up. I hate you," I shouted, as the tears streamed from my eyes, but Jack just continued to stare back at me with such a brooding detachment emanating from his stark brown eyes.

"If this was all the information you have for me on Johnny then I'll be in the parlor. You've got five minutes, kid," Jack said to me in a stern tone, as he pointed aggressively at me before exiting the office.

"Ms, Carmona … Ms, Carmona. I must give you something before you leave here," the detective said to me, as I wiped the tears from my face with my damp handkerchief.

"What? There's nothing that could bring me comfort now," I said to the detective in a somber tone.

"Here … this is your mother's will, written two weeks before she was killed by Johnny. I thought that you should be the first one to read it," the detective said to me in a somber tone.

I then quickly grabbed the paper from the detective's hand and began to read my mother's will with widened eyes, hoping that her words would bring me some closure.

Dear Hayley,

I write you this letter as my last will and testament, and if you're reading this now, it means that Johnny has silenced me for good. I couldn't stand his abuse any longer, but I felt trapped with him in or apartment. You are my precious angel Hayley, and I will not let him hurt you. I now see the only way to protect you is to potentially leave you. Men like Johnny have such power in this city, a power which is far beyond the likes of a woman like me.

I managed to gather information on Johnny's boss. That's right, the boss of the Five Points Gang. The man has made millions from bootlegging alcohol and preying off the poor and desperate people of this city. Every Friday night Johnny and his boss do their dealings at Pier 45 *Hudson River* Park.

When I told Johnny I would rat him out to the police if he ever laid a hand on me again he was furious. I thought I had put an end to his abuse, but something tells me that Johnny would never let a woman like me get the upper hand on a man like him.

I wish I had more to leave you with in my passing. Right now I hear you singing in your bedroom. You have such a beautiful voice, and don't you let any man put a muzzle on it.

Your Uncle Jack is now your only living blood relative. So he will now be your legal guardian, if he chooses so. Jack is not a perfect man, but deep down I know that there's good in him. He just needs a beautiful heart like yours to awaken it. I remember Jack would always defend me from bullies at school when we were your age. Remember Hayley, no matter how cruel Jack may seem, no matter how awful he may treat you; know that he is suffering on the inside. He's barely keeping his head above water with his speakeasy and he feels like this world doesn't see him. It won't be easy for you and Jack, but he is still my older brother and your uncle, and during these unforgiving times you two will need each other more than ever. Stay strong my angel.

Love,
Dezerae Carmona

CHAPTER 3:
BOURBON AND BEDFELLOWS
- JACK -

Everything about her reminded me of her mother. Her eyes, her voice, the way she carried herself, and most of all, the way she talked down to me, and that's why I couldn't stand being around the kid. Was I now stuck with her, or is there some way to pass her on to an orphanage or hospital? The kid now knows where I live, so she would most likely come crawling back to my speakeasy for compassion, a compassion which her mother never showed me when I needed it most in my life.

"Jack, quit daydreaming and serve the gentleman at table 4, we don't want him sobering up," Samson said to me in a stern tone, as he snapped his fingers and pointed to a dapperly- dressed man with two lose broads draped over his shoulders.

"Did you just snap your goddamn fingers at me Samson, remember who you work for, you Irish lout," I said to Samson in a stern tone and glare. I often wondered who would win if me and Samson were to finally come to blows and go at it. Sure the man is bigger and stronger than me, but he lacks agility, so I would go for his legs first before he tries to throttle me into submission.

Hayley remained sitting at that same corner table in the speakeasy writing in the same leather-bound book she wrote in five years ago. What could the kid be writing so studiously day after day? She was a mystery, one which I didn't care solve for the time being. As long as she remained out of my hair, then I would be able to tolerate her.

"Mon chéri Jack, you must get out of this hole in the ground. It's bad for your mental health," Faye said to me with a grin, as she leaned over the bar and caressed my chin with her finger. Ms. Faye Dubois was a very alluring young woman who I propositioned to do her business in my speakeasy to replace Bernadette, because the way I see it, all women are replaceable. The dame was willowy with snow-white skin, dark smoky eyes, and straight black hair which ended at her chin. Her come hither lips always seemed to be pouting, which never failed to drive me wild.

"Do you have another place in mind, Ms, Dubois?" I inquired with a grin, as I wiped down the bar.

"Anywhere but here, *Washington Square Park* est si charmant this time of year," Faye replied, and then began to reapply lipstick, while looking into her silver compact mirror.

"English doll, try to speak English when you speak to me, not that I don't find that language of yours pleasing to the ear, I just want to know every word that comes out of those pouty lips of yours," I said to Faye with a grin.

"Nature mon chéri, the countryside in my homeland of *Loire Valley* was how you say ... taking ones breath from them," Faye said to me with a smile.

"You mean breathtaking," I said to Faye with a snicker. "Oui oui breathtaking," Faye said to me with a giggle as she placed her hand upon mine.

"Eh I'm not one for nature. What can I get from being in the woods that I cannot get from here?" I inquired while shaking my head.

"Tranquillité d'esprit, how you say ... peace of mind," Faye replied with a smile.

"Miss Dubois," the dapperly-dressed man at table four shouted, as he snapped his fingers, and gestured for Faye to join him.

"Jusqu'à ce que nous revoyions, Jack" Faye said to me with a grin, and then scampered over to table 4.

"I think she's sweet on you, Jack," Samson said to me with a grin.

"Who are you talking about?" I inquired.

"That flapper broad over there charming that man at table 4 out of his last dollar I'm sure. Is she French American?" Samson inquired.

"She's more French than American, but I'm not complaining about that," I replied with a grin.

"Indeed you're not, Jack. You looked like a smitten young lad when she was talking to you," Samson remarked, with a snicker.

"She's just a decoration, like Bernadette," I remarked. "Yes but unlike Bernadette, Ms, Dubois is a flapper broad. I though her kind was scattered to the winds, but it appears those kinds of women still exist in this day and age," Samson said to me.

"Why wouldn't they exist during these times of oppression?" I inquired in a stern tone, and then snapped my fingers at the band that appeared to be half-asleep on the stage. The band then perked up and began to play an upbeat jazz tune, as Faye and my eyes locked for a fleeting but intense moment from across the speakeasy.

It was 12:45 PM in the speakeasy.

"Let's go, Samson. We're late," I shouted, as Samson was talking up some drunk broad at the bar who appeared to be rather wealthy judging by her upscale attire.

"I'm coming, Jack," Samson said to me, as he escorted the drunken women to the front door of the speakeasy.

"Have a goodnight," Samson said to the woman, as I unlocked the front door with a smile.

The drunken woman then exited the speakeasy in the manner of a woman who just got beaten by a man, but managed to compose herself enough to walk down the back alley and hail a cab.

"Who the hell was she," I inquired, as I took a glance at Hayley still sitting at the corner table, before Samson and I exited the speakeasy.

"That was Mrs. Carmichael. She's just some sad old barfly widow at the end of her rope," Samson replied, as we entered my Pontiac.

"Oh, thank god. By the way she dresses I would've figured her for a mobster's dame," I remarked.

"Ah don't worry, Jack. I make sure to thoroughly sniff out anyone who could potential overthrow our establishment," Samson said to me, as I started up my Pontiac and slowly drove out the shady back alley of Minetta Street.

"Our establishment, I founded the *Jack of All Trades*, and don't you forget that," I said to Samson in a stern tone, as I tucked my pistol into the waistband of my pants.

"Aye, Jack, but no man is an island," Samson said to me. "Just don't lose your nerve this time. We need this liquor dealing to go smoothly," I said to Samson in a stern tone, as I drove down the once thriving but now pitiful *Perry St.* and then took a left to arrive at Pier 45.

"If only the weather was this fair every day we did our dealings then I wouldn't be so inclined to lurk in the shadows," I said to Samson with a scoff.

"I would've thought you'd be used to lurking in the shadows by now, Jack," Samson remarked with a grin.

"Once you see the light, you can never truly get used to the shadows," I said to Samson, as I parked the Pontiac in a discreet location.

Samson and I have done our bootleg dealings with a pair of small time distributors known as the Rivelli brothers. They were a nervous pair, but then again so were Samson and I. Are dealings with them went fairly well considering how difficult it was for us to meet up, but we managed nonetheless. By any means necessary I would keep my speakeasy running. It is my legacy and I will endure this storm known as the prohibition act which has loomed over me for the past seven years now.

"They're they are," Samson said to me, as we exited my Pontiac and then walked across the street to Pier 45.

"Late as usual Jack, this better not be a common occurrence with you and your associate here," Marco said to me, as he leaned up against a stack of crates partially covered by a torn tarp which I assumed was the alcohol.

"We have your money Marco, now let's see the payload," I said to Marco, as I waved the $350 dollars in my hand. The Rivelli brothers then swiftly pulled off the tarp revealing the fifty crates of various liquors.

"Samson, you know the drill," I sad to Samson as I snapped and pointed to the crates of alcohol, gesturing for him to count all the alcohol for our records. Samson may be an ignorant Irishman, but I noticed over the years that he is rather good when it comes to numbers.

"Aye of course, Jack," Samson said to me with a dismissive wave, as he took out a crumpled up piece of paper from his vest and then began to count the alcohol in a hasty manner.

"So Jack, word on the street is that "the Hammer" is looking for you," Patricio said to me with a grin as he lit a cigarette and took a smoke.

"Why on earth would that ape be looking for me now?" I inquired in a stern tone, as Marco helped Samson count the crates of alcohol.

"To tie up loose ends of course, I heard through the ranks of the Five Points Gang that he killed your sister, is this true?" Patricio inquired.

"He did, but he knows where I live, and if he wanted me dead, then I'm sure I wouldn't be talking to your ugly mug right now," I replied in a stern tone.

"I also heard that your sister's daughter is a potential threat to him, for she could have insider information on the Five Points Gang," Patricio said to me.

"You sure hear a lot of bullshit, don't you Patricio. Now why on earth would the most prominent crime organization in New York want to silence some miserable orphan?" I inquired with a snicker, as Samson took a glance back at me.

"I don't claim to know all the details, I'm just a runt," Patricio replied, and then flicked his cigarette into the water, as a ship at the docks blew its horn.

"Indeed you are. You and your brother should just keep your mouths shut before someone shuts them for good, capisci?" I inquired in a stern tone.

"It's all accounted for, Jack. Pay the man and let's get out of here," Samson shouted, as he loaded the last crate of alcohol onto a wagon and then scampered over to my Pontiac, as I tossed him the keys.

"Marco, riesci a credere al coraggio di quest'uomo," Patricio said with a laugh, as he and his brother walked up close to me.

"I would think twice before you threaten us, Jack. You're a wanted man, and I have no doubt there's a price on your head," Marco said to me, as he pressed his lit cigarette into my chest.

I then grimaced as both the Rivelli brothers laughed in unison. These upstart brothers were far too arrogant. They disrespected me, Samson, and most of all they threatened the future of my speakeasy as if they weren't just some independent bootleggers, but I would not stand for it. I then stared back at Samson who was in the driver's seat of my Pontiac, as he shook his head at me, but I nodded at him with such a stern look, a look he was all too familiar with.

"Capisco, oh boys, if you see Johnny, tell him this," I pronounced in a stern tone and then swiftly punched the younger brother Marco in his smiling mug, knocking him down into a barrel of crude oil.

"Sei un uomo morto!" Patricio shouted, as I ran towards the Pontiac. I then dove head-first into the open passenger' side window, as the Rivelli brothers pulled out their guns and began to fire at me and Samson.

"Drive goddamn it!" I shouted, as Samson peeled out of Pier 45 into a back alley, as I pulled out my pistol and fired back at the Rivelli brothers.

"So much for this deal going smoothly," Samson said to me in a stern tone, as he drove down the narrow back alleys of Greenwich Village, making sure not to take a single main street along our way back to the speakeasy.

"Don't give me that fucking look. I know you would've done the same damn thing if you were in my position," I said to Samson in a heaving tone, as I loosened my tie and took off my vest.

"Are they still chasing us?" Samson inquired in a distressed tone, as he swerved back and forth trying not to crash into numerous dumpsters which lined the shady back alleys on our way back to Minetta Street.

"No … I think we lost them, for now," I replied with a sigh.

"Did you at least pay the brothers, before you slugged one of them?" Samson inquired in a stern tone.

"Oh I forgot," I replied as I took out the $350 dollars from the tattered pocket of my vest.

"Holy fuck, Jack, as if we didn't have enough desperate men in this city trying to take us out, now you can add the Rivelli brothers to that list," Samson said to me in a stern tone. "Let's just get this alcohol unloaded. People will want to drown all there miseries at this hour seeing as that they have no jobs," I said to Samson, as he parked the Pontiac in the back alley beside the speakeasy.

*****

It was 2:40 PM in the speakeasy.

"Just perfect, Samson, because of your goddamn swerving we lost five crates of bourbon," I said to Samson in a stern tone, as I counted the last crate of alcohol containing 8 pints of dark rum.

"Well if you hadn't slugged Patricio then we wouldn't have lost a drop of liquor now would we," Samson said to me in a stern tone.

"We've done these dealing dozens of times and you still drive like a fucking madman. You have to be more careful with our valuable payload, a payload which pays for the food you eat and the clothes you wear, you Irish lout!" I shouted, as Samson wiped down the bar in an aggressive manner, while staring at me with such fervor burning in his eyes.

"I would've driven much more calmly if I wasn't being shot at by two bloodthirsty Italians. Your ignorance never fails to amaze me, Jack," Samson remarked in a stern tone.

"Then take a walk, Samson, we've had this discussion before. If you believe you can make it out there, then there's the door," I said to Samson in a stern tone, and then adjusted my burned vest and tie.

"What happened?" Hayley inquired in a timid tone as she entered the bar from the kitchen.

"None of your business," I replied with a scoff. "Jack, I'm hungry, can I—"

"Then go feed yourself, kid. Goddamn didn't your mother teach you that before she died," I interjected in a stern tone.

Hayley then burst out crying once again, as she covered her face with her hands and ran back into the kitchen. She was nothing but a nuisance to me, a reminder of the past which no longer existed, a past which even if I wanted to, I couldn't return to.

"You sure have a way with children, Jack. I'm getting some air," Samson said to me in a stern tone, while shaking his head, and then exited the speakeasy.

"Many days it felt like it was me, Samson, and Mickey against the world. Could I depend on them to uphold the creed of my speakeasy, or will they inevitably rat me out to either a mobster or the police? Were the Rivelli brothers telling the truth when they told me that Johnny was looking for me? If that bastard was looking to silence me and Hayley just to tie up loose ends, then so be it. I, for one, will not run or hide from that man. Or perhaps I could give him Hayley, like tossing meat to a hungry dog. That may very well keep the hammer from silencing me. For the time being I will now have to look over my shoulder with every step I take.

"Compose yourself. We're opening in five minutes," I said to Samson, as he entered the speakeasy with a sigh.

A knock on the front door of the speakeasy then averted my attention from Samson, as I scampered over to the front door with my pistol in hand.

"Please I need a drink more now than ever," a man wearing a weathered gray suit said to me as I slid open the iron window of the front door.

"Ah don't we all, but I don't recognize your face, what's the password?" I inquired in a stern tone, as I stared intently at the disheveled man.

"Uhm … Delilah," the disheveled man replied.

"Welcome to the *Jack of All Trades*, where your pleasure is our business," I said to the man, as I unlocked and opened the door of the speakeasy.

"Do you know him?" I whispered, as I walked up to Samson behind the bar.

"Can't say that I do," Samson replied.

"Then it appears that the password to this speakeasy is spreading throughout the city," I said to Samson.

"Aye that can either be good or bad for us," Samson said to me.

"Yes let's hope tonight fills our wallets with money rather than our bodies with bullets," I said to Samson, as I smiled at the disheveled man who sat down at the bar with a groan.

It was 8:15 PM in the speakeasy.

"We haven't gotten business this good since the first week the prohibition law went into effect," I shouted at Samson with a smile across the speakeasy, as I served a group of gentlemen at table 6 who were playing what appeared to be a high stakes game of Texas Holdem. Samson then gestured for me to come over to the bar, as I noticed the gentleman wearing a pinstripe fedora and suite to match had a three-of-a-kind hand.

"What is it Samson?" I inquired with a sigh, as Caroline began to sing a song at the stage which I haven't heard before. "Word is that three speakeasies in *Gramercy Park* got shut down yesterday," Samson replied.

"Ah that would explain our booming business tonight. We are an endangered species, Samson, one which the police want dead," I said to Samson.

"This is good news indeed, Jack, our profits will now triple from the shut downs of our neighboring speakeasies. We may even be able to afford one of those Jukeboxes I see in all those upscale restaurants, not that I could afford to ever dine in one of those places," Samson said to me with a scoff.

"Why on earth would we replace a live jazz band with recorded music," I inquired.

"Well, we could let go of that band that is draining our profits. That's six members of that mediocre jazz band we have continued to pay for the last two years. Just think of the extra money we would have then," Samson said to me.

"Not a terrible idea, Samson, I'll mull it over," I said to Samson with a grin, as Hayley entered the speakeasy from the kitchen while closely clutching that leather-bound book of hers as if it was a life jacket keeping her afloat at sea.

"I've never seen it so crowded in here. Is there a special occasion?" Hayley inquired, as she sat at the bar.

"There is no special occasion. This speakeasy has just become rarer," I replied, as I served a flushed-faced man at the bar a double bourbon on the rocks.

"We could change the password to keep us from becoming too popular," Samson whispered, as he walked up to me.

"No we've already changed it three times. Let's for once relish in our popularity, however fleeting it may be," I said to Samson with a smile.

I then noticed a bloodstain on the white sheets where Hayley slept. *What on earth was that girl doing last night?* I thought to myself as I took a closer look at the bloodstain. I then scoffed and exited the kitchen in a staggering manner.

It was just me and Hayley in the speakeasy this morning. The kid was once again studiously writing in that leather-bound book of hers, as I prepared my prairie oyster cocktail at the bar. I noticed Hayley glancing at me from across the speakeasy, while brushing her hair out of her gray-tinted face.

"There's a shower in this speakeasy," I shouted.

"I didn't know that. Where is it?" Hayley inquired, as she walked over to the bar and sad down in a timid manner, as if I was some wild animal that would either run from her or attack her.

*****

It was 1:45 AM in the speakeasy.

Samson had just left for the night, as I just finished bussing the last table.

"What a profitable night," I spoke aloud with a grin, and then turned off the lights of the speakeasy and entered the kitchen. I now had to share the sleeping quarters AKA the kitchen with Hayley, but it appeared that the kid was asleep so I wouldn't have to suffer any of her self-loathing for the remainder of the night.

I awoke at 4:26 AM to the sound of Hayley crying, but I was too damn drunk from the bourbon to even tell her to shut her mouth and go to sleep. So I continued to lay awake, as Hayley continued to cry for another hour until the kid's cries finally ended. *I have to get rid of her,* I thought to myself with a grimace, as I tried to fall asleep with a throbbing headache.

*****

I awoke at 8:15 AM with a groan, as I stood out of bed and opened the fridge in the kitchen. I then took out one egg, a bottle of hot sauce, a bottle of tomato juice, and a tumbler.

"It's that locked door in the kitchen. Here, wash up. I'm tired of seeing you looking like a chimney sweeper," I replied, as I tossed the key to the shower upon the bar and then continued to prepare my cocktail.

"Thank you," Hayley said to me with a sniff.

I then noticed several cut marks on Hayley's pale arm, as she reached for the key to the shower on the bar. Hayley then pulled up the sleeve of her black dress and scampered into the kitchen. This kid was troubled and I wanted nothing to do with all her demons. I then took my shot of the prairie oyster cocktail in one grimacing gulp before putting on my hat and jacket. I then heard the shower from the other room, as I slowly walked into the kitchen. The shower door was open, as I peered through and saw Hayley's bare, tinted gray body slowly turned to ivory and glisten, as she washed herself in such a slow and miserable manner. The dark cut marks on the kids arm remained as she continued to wash herself. I was still hung over from the bourbon and my mind took a backseat to my body, as I continued to watch Hayley wash herself. I had to clear my head. I couldn't stare at this kid any longer! I then exited the kitchen and scampered towards the front door of the speakeasy. I then took one last glance at the steam from the shower slowly finding its way into the bar before I exited the speakeasy.

Sal's Diner on the corner of 3rd and *MacDougal Street* was where I would go whenever the weight of the speakeasy began to bare down on me. The fresh air hit my lungs as soon as I stepped out into the back alley of Minetta Street, as I lit a cigarette and took a smoke. I decided to take a walk even though my hangover felt like a hammer pounding down on my head, but I would take the hammer of a hangover any day over Johnny the hammer, who most likely could be following me this very moment. It was a warm and sunny spring day in Greenwich Village. The kind of day that almost makes your forget about the depression and prohibition act. If I was a wanted man, then maybe I should hide in plain sight. Johnny was used to tracking down squealers and silencing them, but as long as I surrounded myself with people, then maybe that would turn off Johnny from silencing me. Judging by what the Rivelli brothers told me, it seems that Hayley could be Johnny's number one target. What kind of information could that miserable kid have that would provoke such a killer like Johnny?

I entered *Sal's Diner* and sat down at a stool with a sigh, as Blanch scoffed and entered the kitchen.

What'll you have, Jack," Blanch inquired in a sulking tone, as if she was taking the order of a man who was about to eat his last meal. Blanch was a haggard waitress at *Sal's Diner*, one which I scowled at whenever I saw her weathered bag of a face. "Listen carefully … Two eggs, two, pieces of bacon, hash browns, and black coffee," I replied with a groan, as I placed my hand on my forehead.

"We're out of eggs and bacon," Blanch said to me in a stern tone.

"For fuck's sake, and you call this a diner … fine I'll just have hash browns and black coffee then," I said to Blanch in a stern tone.

Blanch then glared at me, as she entered the kitchen, as the radio behind the counter blared a news report which I for one supported.

"Meanwhile in Greenwich Village, Mayor James J. Walker continues his outright opposition to the prohibition act, thus giving more fuel to these wretched speakeasies which appear to be remerging soon after they're shut down. When we questioned Mayor Walker on how his actions could be promoting crime, and destitution throughout New York he replied with the following statement 'neither I nor any struggling man can make it in a city governed by such an unjust law. The Prohibition act paired with this economic depression are a one two punch to a man who is on his death bed."

"That man needs to run for president," I said to Blanch, as I pointed to the radio beside her.

"Jimmy Walker is nothing but a crook," Blanch remarked with a scoff, as she poured my cup of coffee and placed it upon the counter.

"What would you know about politics? Now where are my hash browns?" I inquired in a stern tone.

I always felt a bond with Mayor Walker, as if we could be brothers. The man wasn't part of Wall Street. Sure he lived a fast and loose life, but all of the investments he has made to the crumbling utilities of this city are a breath of fresh air in a sea of smoke.

"Here you go, hun," Blanch said to me in a raspy voice, as she served me my hash browns in such a dull manner.

I then took a large bite of the greasy hash browns with a slight grimace, as I quickly reached for the ketchup bottle.

"These are awful. A goddamn orphan eats better food than this," I remarked, while shaking my head, as Blanch gave me a dismissive wave before entering the kitchen.

"You should try the pie; I hear its top notch at this diner," A man wearing a long beige trench coat and fedora said to me with a grin, as he sat down on the stool beside me at the counter. "It used to be top notch, just like everything else in this city," I said to the man with a scoff, as I flooded the hash browns with ketchup.

"You really slipped up, Jack. I don't think I can look the other way this time," the man said to me, which caused me to choke on a spoonful of the awful hash browns for a moment, before I cleared my throat with a sip of coffee.

"Who the hell are you?" I inquired in a stern tone, as I gripped my pistol tucked between the waist-band of my pants. "Take you hand off that side arm, unless you want more blood on your hands," the man said to me in a stern tone.

"You don't dress like a mobster, so who do you work for?" I inquired, as I stared intently at the man, trying to identify just who he was, and if he had any power over me.

"You don't remember me, Jack. I'm not surprised. A man like you needs to have a short memory, it helps keep you from going mad, doesn't it," the man said to me with a snicker and smirk towards Blanch, as she poured him a cup of coffee.

"Who are you? This is the last time I'm going to ask you, and then you will see how mad I can be," I said to the man in a stern tone.

"Alabaster Simmons, I've been tailing you for the past couple of days, Jack," the man said to me, as he showed me his badge.

"Detective Simmons … you were the one at my sister's funeral who gave me that briefing on Johnny. Why are you following me now, what do you want from a man like me?" I inquired.

"Listen, Jack, I know you are the proprietor of a bustling speakeasy. I know you just recently stiffed a pair of two-bit bootleggers on Pier 45, but most of all, I know how vital of a role you can play in reeling in the hammer for me," Detective Simmons replied.

"So are you going to turn me in and shut down my speakeasy, Detective? Leaving me nothing more than a handful of salt and bread to survive in this city?" I inquired in a distressed tone.

"Come here," Detective Simmons said to me in a stern tone, as he stood up from the stool at the counter and pulled me over to an empty booth of the diner by the collar of my shirt in the manner of a father reprimanding his unruly son.

"Speak fast, Detective. I may be a wanted man by the Five Points Gang. So if you want me to squeal, then you better give me some incentive," I said to Detective Simmons, as I put out my cigarette in the ash tray.

"You're nothing, Jack, you're not worth a dime to anybody, but how's this for incentive, that poor niece of yours has information, information that has put a price on her head, and she will most likely be silenced by the Five Points Gang in the coming week if you don't work hand in hand with me," Detective Simmons said to me in a stern tone, as he took darting glances out the window.

"Now what information could she have that would prompt a hit on that little ginger head of hers?" I inquired with a scoff. "Information that could lock up an entire criminal organization, you're in over your head, Jack, unless you cooperate with me," Detective Simmons replied.

"Well be that as it may, Detective, that's still no incentive for me. I never wanted to cross paths with that miserable girl in the first place. In fact, this is my chance to finally be rid of her," I said to Detective Simmons with a grin.

"You will do no such thing to Ms. Carmona, or I will shut down your speakeasy so fast the mere memory of her will haunt you forever, in prison," Detective Simmons said to me in a stern tone.

"Very well, Detective, You sure know how to threaten a desperate man, but that seems to be how the NYPD operates. The way I see it, you boys and the Five Points Gang are two sides of the same coin in this city," I said to Detective

Simmons in a stern tone

"If it wasn't for the NYPD you and your associates would be—,"

"Drinking happily right now with no fear of being arrested," I interjected in a stern tone, as I stared intently at Detective Simmons with such a deep hatred burning in my eyes.

"You need to get your facts straight, Jack. It's either me or Johnny. I have no doubt that you wouldn't be talking to the hammer for as long as you have with me, before he silences that obnoxious mug of yours for good," Detective Simmons said to me in a stern tone, as he pointed his finger at me, before gesturing for Blanch to join us at the booth.

"What'll you have, hun?" Blanch inquired, as she walked up to the booth in a dull manner.

"I'll have the polenta and a cup of black coffee. I haven't had an Italian dish in awhile," Detective Simmons replied with a grin, as he handed Blanch the menu.

"Coming right up," Blanch said to Detective Simmons, and then walked away towards the kitchen.

"You should've taken your own advice and ordered the pie," I said to Detective Simmons, as I noticed an entire family begging for change on the street corner, most likely caused by this depression.

"I've kept this very close to the chest, Jack. Nobody else in my office knows about this operation," Detective Simmons said to me, as Blanch walked up to the booth and poured the Detective his black coffee with a smile. Why did that old bag not smile when she served me? Was I so different from Detective Simmons, or perhaps Blanch was just paying him respect just because she noticed he worked with the NYPD.

"Thank you," Detective Simmons said to Blanch, as she nodded at him with another smile which was the polar opposite demeanor of hers when she was serving me.

"You don't trust the other men in your office, do you," I said to Detective Simmons with a grin, "I trust them to a certain degree, but I know the Five Points Gang has paid off some men in my office," Detective Simmons said to me.

"Ah so you too are a lone wolf on a mission to take out an entire pack. What makes you think you can do battle with the Five Points Gang and your own office and come out of it alive?" I inquired.

"I have a snake in the grass like you who will help me, well … you're more like a rat in a gutter, but either way you will serve as a pawn which neither the crooks in my office or the Five Points Gang will suspect," Detective Simmons replied, as Blanch walked up to the booth and placed the dish of polenta on the table in front of the Detective with a smile.

"Get this straight, Detective, I'm not a pawn, snake, or rat. If I'm going to die then it will be on my terms," I said to Detective Simmons in a stern tone.

"Not bad," Detective Simmons remarked, as he took a bite of the steaming polenta.

"I work for me, myself and I. This is how I've managed to survive during this prohibition, and now you want me to basically serve as a bullet proof vest for you," I said to Detective Simmons, as he continued to eat the polenta in a hasty manner. "You work for me now, Jack. For once in your goddamn life, try thinking about someone other than yourself, like Ms. Carmona," Detective Simmons said to me, as he shook his head, while wiping his mouth with a napkin.

"You're putting me between a rock and a hard place, Detective. I'll need time to mull this over," I said to Detective Simmons with a sigh.

"Where is she now, Jack?" Detective Simmons inquired in a stern tone.

"Where's who?" I inquired.

"Katherine Hepburn, who do you think, your niece goddamn it," Detective Simmons replied in a stern tone, as he smacked his hand down upon the table.

"Right where I left her, at the speakeasy, most likely writing in that book of hers while she cries her eyes out," I replied.

"You pay your bill and get back to her now. Johnny edges closer to Ms. Carmona with every minute that passes. I will contact you tomorrow on your decision," Detective Simmons said to me.

"What decision. I have no choice in the matter now," I said with a scoff, as I tossed a couple of dollars upon the table.

"Oh and Jack," Detective Simmons shouted, as I stood up from the booth and began to walk away.

"What now?" I inquired, as I turned around with a glare towards Detective Simmons who was now eating the polenta in the manner of a pig eating from a trough.

"Don't even think about leaving town," Detective Simmons said to me with a grin.

"I wouldn't dream of it, Detective," I said to Detective Simmons with a grin, and then exited *Sal's Diner*.

*****

It was 2:43 PM when arrived at the speakeasy to a light rain which washed over but failed to clean the scum which tinted every building on Minetta Street.

That son of a bitch Detective, how dare he gamble my life all for the sake of his own ambitions. Furthermore, how dare he say the life of that miserable girl at my speakeasy is worth far more than mine. Men like him have continued to abuse their power over men like me who claw and scrap for what little power I have. My walk back to the speakeasy was nerve-racking to say the least. I now had to look over my shoulder with each step I took in fear of Johnny silencing me for good. If I could just make it back to the speakeasy in one piece then I could regroup mentally and physically. I felt safe in the speakeasy. In many ways I considered it to be a bunker protecting me from all the unjust bastards who seek to impose their power over people like me, but now I had to share that bunker with another. Hayley will be the death of me; Johnny will most likely use me to get to her, while Detective Simmons is using me to get to Johnny. *Was there any way out of this?* I thought to myself as I arrived at the speakeasy with a sigh. I then unlocked the door and entered with my hand on my pistol.

"Where were you?" Hayley inquired in a timid tone, as I surveyed the speakeasy with wide eyes.

"I was just informed by Detective Simmons that you have very dangerous information, kid," I replied, as I walked behind the bar and poured myself a double bourbon on the rocks.

"What are you talking about," Hayley inquired, in a distressed tone.

"Don't play innocent. You know damn well what I'm talking about ... it was her will, wasn't it? Your mother told you something in her will that has now put a price on your head and mine, well, a higher price on your head than mine, but you now might as well be a magnet attracting all the mobsters of the Five Points Gang to you," I replied with a scoff and grin, and then took a sip of bourbon with a grimace.

"No, I don't believe you. You're just trying to scare me," Hayley said to me in a distressed tone, while shaking her head. "Here I thought your mother dying would bring me some peace of mind, but even in her death she continues to haunt me in the form of Johnny and that son of a bitch Detective," I said to Hayley in a stern tone, as I finished the last of my bourbon in one gulp and slammed the glass tumbler down on the bar.

"My mother defied Johnny, which made him see her as a threat, and now you see me as a threat to your life. You're projecting all your fears onto me," Hayley said to me in a distressed tone, as tears began to well up in her eyes.

"Tell me what your mother told you in her will," I said to Hayley in a stern tone, as I stared intently at her, while she began to cry.

I wanted to throttle her little neck. Her very presence here was putting my life in danger. I could no longer breathe a sigh of relief every day knowing that my very breath could immediately be stifled by the Hammer. I saw great fear in the kid's eyes, but also great ignorance. If Hayley didn't fully understand the danger she was in, then perhaps I could knock some sense into that dense little head of hers.

"No, my mother's will was meant for my eyes only," Hayley said to me in a distressed tone, as she stood up from the barstool and took a couple steps away from me.

"Damn it, kid! Tell me the information your mother has on the Five Points Gang before we both have bullets in our heads!" I shouted, as I walked towards Hayley, while she continued to back away from me, while clutching that leather book of hers.

"I won't be a victim to me like you. My mother always taught me to be strong in the face of abusive men," Hayley said to me in a distressed tone, as she pulled out a knife from the black sleeve of her dress and pointed it at me with a shaking hand.

"Your mother was nothing but a whore who slept with one of the most dangerous mobsters in New York. Now you want to threaten me today just like that fucking Detective at the diner. I can only take so much insolence from you!" I shouted, as I threw the glass tumbler at Hayley's feet. Hayley then recoiled as the glass tumbler shattered.

"I won't have you disrespect my mother's name in death as you have in life so many times. Don't pretend that you're different from Johnny or Fernando. You three have that same look in your eyes. That same ruthless look that my mother feared until she managed to gather up all the strength she had left and—"

"Die, that's what all of your mother's strength amounted to, a bullet to the head," I interjected with a snicker.

"She was wrong. You're a truly evil man," Hayley remarked in a stern tone and wide-eyes.

"Nobody pulls a knife on me in my speakeasy. You know how to use that, kid?" I inquired, as I slowly walked towards Hayley, while she slowly walked backwards towards the front door of the speakeasy.

"Don't come any closer or I'll—,"

"You'll what, stab me? Now I see your mother in you? That fiery temper I couldn't tolerate, but I suppose that runs in the family," I interjected.

"Stop, get away from me!" Hayley shouted, as tears streamed from her eyes. Hayley then stepped back into the front door of the speakeasy, as I stood face to face with the insolent kid.

"I'm only going to ask you this once more before I force the words out of you. What information did your mother give you on the Five Points Gang?" I shouted, as I punched the front door of the speakeasy.

A sudden knock then broke the lock of me and Hayley's dagger wielding eyes to the front door of the speakeasy. Hayley continued to cry while pointing that small knife at me, as I continued to impose myself onto her, as well as the knocking at the front door continued, as all three forces struggled for dominance in such a critical moment.

"Who is it?" I shouted, as Hayley's frightened breaths echoed in the background.

"It's Mickey, sir. Please open the door," a voice replied. "Move," I said to Hayley in a stern tone, as I opened the iron window of the front door.

"Password," I said in a stern tone as I stared at Mickey who appeared to be shaking in his boots.

"Delilah," Mickey said to me, as his eyes darted from side to side.

I then unlocked and opened the front door of the speakeasy, as Mickey scampered inside. I then noticed Hayley tuck her knife back underneath the black sleeve of her dress before she sat back down at the corner table near the stage with her head in her hands.

"Why are you out of breath, Mickey, did you run all the way here?" I inquired with a grin, as Mickey sat down at the bar and took off his tan jacket and newsboy hat.

"I was being followed, but I managed to lose them," Mickey replied.

"Who was following you, did they look like mobsters or Detectives," I inquired in a stern tone, as Hayley stood up from the corner table and slowly walked towards Mickey, while clutching her leather book against her chest.

"I couldn't tell who they worked for, sir, but they had their eyes on me no matter which street I took," Mickey replied, as Hayley sat down beside him in a timid manner.

"Goddamn it!" I shouted, as I placed my hand on my forehead with a groan.

"Hi, I'm Mickey, Mickey Sullivan," Mickey said to Hayley. "I'm Hayley," Hayley said to Mickey.

"Do you work for Jack now at the speakeasy?" Mickey inquired, as he reached over the bar and poured himself a glass of water.

"No, she's just my niece, and she was just leaving," I replied in a stern tone.

"It was nice to meet you," Hayley said to Mickey, and then entered the kitchen before glaring at me on the way.

"Nice to meet you, too ... she seems nice," Mickey remarked.

"Forget about her. Now, listen carefully, kid, describe to me as much as you can what they looked like.

"There were two of them, one man had a mustache and wore suspenders, while the other man dressed like either a mobster or a Detective. I'm sorry, I don't know how Detectives dress," Mickey said to me.

"If they're undercover, then they can dress in any style they deem suitable to infiltrate, but if that man in the suit was a mobster, then I sure as hell hope you lost them," I said to Mickey.

"I'm positive I lost them, sir. When I started running, they began to run as well, but they were slow and couldn't keep up with me," Mickey said to me.

"Mickey, this speakeasy will be a target now more than ever. My worthless niece in the kitchen has information about the Five Points Gang which is putting us all in danger," I said to Mickey, as I paced back and forth behind the bar.

"She seems scared. What's the information," Mickey inquired.

"She won't talk. Wait ... maybe you could get her to talk," I said to Mickey, as I gestured for him to lean closer to me.

"We just met. Why would she tell me?" Mickey whispered.

"You're around her age, Mickey. Befriend her, do whatever it takes to get that information out of her and I will give you a 25 cent raise," I whispered, as I pointed to the kitchen.

"I don't know, sir. What if she—,"

"Our lives and the future of this speakeasy depend on it," I interjected, as I grabbed Mickey by the collar and pulled him over the bar.

"I'll try my best, sir," Mickey said to me.

"Good ... now let's clean this place up. We're opening in ten minutes," I said to Mickey, as I lit a cigarette and took a smoke, before wiping down the bar in a frantic manner.

*****

It was 5:30 PM in the speakeasy.

Caroline arrived with the band, along with Samson who appeared to already be drunk off his ass, but I needed as much muscle around at all times if I was to defend myself from Johnny. The speakeasy was making better business due to the last three speakeasies in the Meatpacking District being shut down, but the cost of such revenue would most likely bring dangerous men into the *Jack of All Trades*, men who are hellbent on silencing me and that miserable kid in the kitchen. I didn't know what to do, so for the time being, I did the only thing I knew how to do during such dangerous times.

"Entertain," that's our purpose," I said to Caroline, as I snapped my fingers, and pointed at the stage.

"Do you think I could go one on one with Johnny?" Samson inquired with a grin

"You're a tough son of a bitch, Samson, but Johnny didn't get that nickname 'the hammer' for nothing," I said to Samson. "We both have that Irish fighting blood in us. Which makes me think he might give even me a run for my money," Samson said to me with a grin.

"The man is a killer, Samson. Don't make light of the situation as a common brawl in a bar. I for one will not trade blows with the man, he's as tall as an oak tree and just as dense. If I have the opportunity, then my pistol will silence him not my fists," I said to Samson, as the lights in the speakeasy dimmed for a few moments which always made me think that someone has cut our power for good.

"*Breaking news in Greenwich Village, a cop was found dead in an alleyway on Minetta Street at 3:37 PM this afternoon,*" the radio sounded, catching my ear through Caroline and the jazz band's lethargic song.

"Turn that up!" I shouted to Samson from one end of the bar, as I pointed to the radio.

"*Upon examination, the NYPD has deduced the identity of the cop to be Detective Alabaster Simmons of the NYPD. 'Detective Simmons didn't die quickly. Someone wanted information out of him before they put a bullet between his eyes,' Detective Langston Price reported during a short interview on the scene of the murder. Services for one of the NYPD's finest will be held tomorrow morning at 10:00 AM at the Frank E. Campbell Funeral Chapel on 1076 Madison Avenue,*" the radio sounded.

I was then immediately hit by an array of emotions from the news on the radio. It appeared that Detective Simmons was closely tailing me after I left the diner this afternoon. The diligent man may have been protecting me from the very man who killed him. Some weight was lifted off my shoulders from the Detective being killed by Johnny, for I no longer was a pawn in his game and I could then willingly give Hayley over to Johnny without being locked up by the now dead Detective. Johnny knew I was talking to the Detective, so he took him out before he would inevitably come for me and Hayley. I will not get the NYPD involved in my family squabbles once again. I will deal with Johnny one way and one way alone. The first time I dealt with the Hammer he beat me half to death and I have yet to regain half my life back ever since.

"I heard the news on the radio, what are we going to do?" Hayley inquired in a distressed tone, as she scampered over to me from the kitchen.

"'We', there's no 'we', kid, you and your mother brought all of this on us," I replied in a stern tone.

"Take it easy, Jack," Samson said to me, as he placed his hand on my shoulder.

"Take your fucking hand off me and go back to serving the party at table five before I cut your pay," I said to Samson in a stern tone and glare, as I pushed away his muscular arm from my shoulder.

"Johnny and his associates will not set foot in this speakeasy. I have reinforced the front door with 3 inches of iron plating. That enough to defend against any firearm him and his associates wield in their attempts to silence you and me," I said to Hayley, as I walked over to the front door.

"What if he blows the door open with dynamite? Those hinges won't hold then," Hayley inquired in a distressed tone, as she pointed to the hinges of the front door.

"Then you better pray to whatever god you believe in, because I'm not about to risk my life for a kid who won't tell me information that can save us both," I replied, as I walked behind the bar.

"How do you know Johnny and his gang won't kill us both even after we tell him the information?" Hayley inquired in a distressed tone.

"Aye she's right Jack. It wouldn't be in Johnny's best interest to leave you both alive, especially knowing such vital information that could bring down the Five Points Gang," Samson said to me.

"I don't even know what this goddamn information is. It could be that linguini is Johnny's favorite pasta for all I know," I said to Samson in a stern tone and then snapped my fingers at Caroline and the band that were dragging out their smoke break for far too long on the stage.

"What hope do we have without help from the NYPD?" Hayley inquired in a distressed tone, as Caroline and the band began to play a song which mirrored my chaotic state of mind. "Detective Simmons told me that his fellow boys in blue are being paid off by the Five Points Gang, so we cannot depend on them for protection," I replied.

I had a plan, but I first needed Mickey to pry that information out of Hayley as soon as possible. I hated the fact that my very life is now in the hands of a timid bumbling boy like Mickey, but I still place more trust in him than that sobbing ginger mess who refuses to talk to me.

The lights dimmed once again in the speakeasy, but during the darkness three loud knocks on the front door echoed throughout the speakeasy, silencing everyone, as we all stared at the front door.

"Everyone shut up," I shouted, as I took out my pistol and slowly walked towards the front door, as the lights began to flicker.

"Samson, get over here," I said as I gestured for the Irish brute to possibly be a human shield for me.

Samson then took out his pistol; as I slid open the iron window of the front door as Samson and I quickly moved to each side of the door. The lights of the speakeasy then turned back on, as all the patrons began to cheer and continue their drinking.

"What is that?" Samson inquired, as what appeared to be a letter was shoved in between the iron slots of the window. I then tucked my pistol back between the waist-band of my pants, as I walked over to the bar with Samson and Hayley standing closely beside me.

"Don't open it," Hayley said to me in a distressed tone.

"I have to open it. Now would you two quit breathing down my neck," I pronounced, and then opened the envelope and began to read the letter.

JACKIE BOY

THERE'S NOBODY LEFT IN THIS CITY TO PROTECT YOU AND HAYLEY FROM ME NOW, BUT IF YOU HAND THE GIRL OVER TO ME WILLINGLY AT THE NYPD ON 153rd E 67th St, THEN I PROMISS NOT TO HARM A SINGLE HAIR ON HER PRETTY RED HEAD. MAKE THE RIGHT CHOICE, OR I WILL MAKE ANOTHER PROMISS THAT WILL HAVE YOU AND HAYLEY JOINING DEZERAE AND THE DETECTIVE.

UNTIL WE MEET AGAIN

CHAPTER 4:
THE DAME TALKED
- HAYLEY -

"What does it say?" I inquired in a zealous tone, as I tried my hardest to peer over Jack's shoulders and read the letter, but he kept turning around so I could only make out one word from the letter being *Jackie Boy*.

"This is a threat from Johnny, or should I say, a promise" Jack replied with a stern look, as I clamored to read more of the letter he held.

"Why won't you let me read it? Johnny wrote about me in the letter, didn't he?" I inquired in a distressed tone. I could tell by Jack's demeanor that he was keeping information about me. This information could very well take my life, or perhaps that's exactly what Jack wants.

"You want this letter, kid. Then give me your mother's will. That's the only way you're going to read this," Jack said to me, as he folded up the letter and tucked it into the pocket of his vest.

"How could you gamble my life like this, how could—,"

"How could I, how could I, how could you and your mother put my life in danger. If you want to know what Johnny wrote about you in this letter, then you know what to do," Jack said to me in a stern tone, as he walked behind the bar.

I then scampered back into the kitchen, as tears began to well up in my eyes. I didn't feel safe when I was around Jack. I saw him staring at me through the kitchen doorway when I was in the shower this afternoon, and for a brief moment, I feared what he could have done next. At that moment when I was at my most vulnerable, washing the filth off my body, Jack stared at me with the same eyes as Johnny and Fernando, the eyes of a predator. Jack has shown me no signs that he would protect me from Johnny, and this makes me doubt my mother's will even more. Despite what my mother said, I saw no good in Jack. What happened to Jack to make him treat me so cruel? Was it all simply his hatred towards my mother which he now projects onto me, or was is something much deeper in his life that has continued to fester inside of him?

"I'm sorry about Jack. If it makes you feel any better, he treats me just as cruel as he treats you," Mickey said to me, as he entered the kitchen.

"Why do you work for him?" I inquired, and then wiped my nose with the ragged handkerchief from the pocket of my dress.

"I had no other choice in my life when I met Jack. 'How'd you like to work for me, kid. I promise that your life of clawing and scraping for survival on the streets will end'. That's what Jack said to me with a smile, as I was panhandling on the pier," Mickey replied, as he sat more than an arm's distance away from me on Jack's small bed.

"He lied to you. He's a sinister man who swindles people during their most desperate times and I feel ashamed to be related to such a man," I said to Mickey.

"Why don't you just give Jack your mother's will in exchange for Johnny's letter," Mickey inquired in a timid tone. "My mother wrote that will for my eyes only. I've never felt regarded as a girl of significance in my entire life, but the information about the Five Points Gang which my mother wrote to me in her will now makes me feel like so much more than just a girl with no parents. My mother's will gave me a sense of importance over such dangerous men in this city who could so easily smack me down to the ground for so much as looking at them wrong and not suffer any consequences. I will not hand over the only significance I have in my life to Jack," I replied to Mickey in a stern tone.

"You could die. You and Jack could be killed by Johnny. Are you really willing to take that risk?" Mickey inquired.

"Mickey … I need your help. You must get me Johnny's letter, which Jack keeps in the pocket of his vest. My uncle is a wretched man who will betray me, you, and anybody who breaths just to save his own life. Please … I need a friend now more than ever," I said to Mickey in a somber tone, as I reached out and placed my hand upon his.

Mickey was a timid boy, but I saw a heart in his light brown eyes. I needed to plea to that sense of humanity I saw within Mickey before Jack bares down on him with such anger, just as he did to me this afternoon when I so desperately pointed my make-shift knife at him in fear of my life.

"I don't know if I can do that. I mean … Jack will sure as day—,"

"It's a matter of life and death, just as you said. Don't you want to save my life Mickey, or will you just let Johnny kill me as he killed my mother," I interjected in a distressed tone, as tears began to pour from my eyes.

Mickey knew Jack far longer than me. Did he have such a loyalty to my uncle, or was it all based in fear? Mickey was a gentle boy, and I didn't shake when I was around him as I did with all the other men in my life, but could a gentle boy such as Mickey really get the upper hand over such a cruel man like Jack? Cruelty seems to be how the world is run right now, and I could never hope to survive in a world dominated by such cruel men all alone. I needed Mickey, but I understand his fear of Jack.

"I'm sorry, but if I were to betray Jack he would surely toss me out of the speakeasy. I've seen him and Samson do it to all kinds of people. Is there any other way I can help?" Mickey inquired in a somber tone.

"No … I'm afraid not. You may be my only hope," I replied. "I'll … I'll see what I can do," Mickey said to me in a timid tone, as he stood up from the bed and walked away from me.

"Thank you Mickey," I said to Mickey in a somber tone, just before he exited the kitchen. I then lay down upon the bed and began to drift off, as I could hear more people entering the speakeasy in a cheerful manner.

*****

"Get the hell out of my bed!" a voice shouted, as I awoke to the sight of Jack standing over me with such a stern look upon his face.

"The blankets on the floor hurt my back," I said to Jack in weary tone, as I brushed my hair behind my ears, and then quickly stood out of Jack's bed.

"Business is great tonight. If you and I are going to die, at least we will die in great company," Jack said to me with snicker, as he opened the freezer and took out what appeared to be a steel keg.

Was Jack really making light of our possible deaths by the hand of Johnny, or was he so drunk at the moment that the thought of being killed struck no fear into him? I for one needed to stop myself from shaking, so I decided to numb my senses, just as everyone else in the speakeasy is doing right now.

"Miss double vodka on the rocks," a man at the bar said to me with a smile.

"Oh … I …uhm—,"

"She doesn't work here. Coming right up, sir," Samson interjected in a stern tone, as I recoiled from his brutish presence towering behind me.

"Why so low in the face Miss Hayley?" Caroline inquired, as she walked up to the bar and lit a cigarette.

"You mean you haven't heard? Jack and I are wanted by the Five Points Gang, well me more than Jack," I replied in a somber tone, as I sat down at the bar beside Caroline.

"Now why would gangsters be after a sweet child like you?" Caroline inquired in an incredulous tone, as she stared intently at me with a sense of disbelief.

"It all has to do with the information in my mother's will. That information could very well bring down their entire criminal organization," I replied.

"Oh boy Miss Hayley, you may be in a world of trouble, but you are also a very important young woman right now. You do what my mother always told me to do in trying times," Caroline said to me.

"What did your mother say to you?" I inquired.

"She told me to always listen to my heart before my head. Sure my head may think logically, but my heart knows how   to comfort me more than any logic," Caroline replied, as she pointed to her head and then heart with a grin.

"My mother always told me that my voice was beautiful, and to never let a man silence it," I said to Caroline.

"Ah she was a wise woman. My voice is my life, and I use it to bring about peace. Will I make millions from being a two- bit jazz singer in a speakeasy, hell no, but as long as I speak from my heart then no man can keep me in line, especially your uncle," Caroline said to me with a smile.

"I'm afraid to leave this speakeasy now. I could be killed the very moment I step foot out that front door," I said to Caroline. "I'm so sorry child. You deserve all the attention from those men, but none of the danger," Caroline said to me, as she shook her head.

"What if I ran away, far away from this town, far away from the Five Points Gang?" I inquired in a zealous tone.

"Running from your problems is always a choice which seems the most pleasing to the heart, but let me tell you something from a woman who knows more than most, when you run from your problems you simply make them stronger. Problems are like sheep, they follow you wherever you may run to," Caroline replied.

"Sheep are nice and gentle though," I remarked with a smile.

"They are Miss Hayley, but I wouldn't want a heard of sheep following me wherever I run to. Take your uncle for instance—,"

"I'd rather not," I interjected in a stern tone.

"I know that man is staring me down at the moment and will soon bark orders at me to go back on stage and sing, but I don't run from him, I confront the bastard so he knows that there's no fear in my heart. When a man senses fear in the heart of a woman he knows child, he knows he has power over her," Caroline said to me.

"How can I not show fear from Jack and the Five Points Gang?" I inquired

"By what you told me Miss Hayley, you seem to hold all the cards, not those men. You are so much stronger and wiser than you know," Caroline replied.

"Caroline, get back on stage, you've gabbed long enough," Jack said to Caroline in a stern tone, as he exited the kitchen, while holding two dusty bottles of wine.

"Stay strong Miss Hayley. I have faith in you," Caroline said to me, as she stood up from the barstool with a smile and then scampered to the stage.

"Are you ready to talk, kid, or do you want to continue this stand off?" Jack inquired in a stern tone.

Caroline's comforting and uplifting words were just what I needed at this moment. Jack knew I had information which many dangerous men, including him, where out to get.

I then grabbed Caroline's half empty glass of whiskey and took a swig, and slammed the glass down upon the bar, as I stared intently at Jack.

"We both have a price on our heads, but you will not lay eyes on my mother's will until you start treating me with the respect I deserve," I replied in a stern tone.

"You impudent little girl, what makes you think for one moment that you—,"

"Did you miss me Jack," a blonde woman dressed in a white fur coat over a shear amber dress interjected as she sat down at the bar beside me. The woman looked sweet and smelled even sweeter with a fragrance of roses wafting off her hair like a beguiling spell cast by a beautiful sorceress. The woman was everything I wanted to be, but nothing I projected to the world, but that's not what surprised me about her. It was the look of bewilderment in Jack's eyes as he stared at the beautiful woman which kept my eyes intently focused on her. Who was she?"

"Bernadette ... what are you doing here? I banned you from this speakeasy," Jack said to the woman known as Bernadette, as I stared at the both of them staring daggers at each other, like two ex-lovers.

"Oh is that any way to treat me after all this time. I would watch your tone considering the grave circumstances you're in," Bernadette replied with a smile.

"Samson ... Samson!" Jack shouted, as he gestured for Samson to no doubt toss out the beautiful woman who sat beside me, as she flouted Jack with every bat of her alluring blue eyes.

"Aye what is it Jack?" Samson inquired, as he walked up to the bar with a sigh.

"I banned her for life. Who let her back in here?" Jack inquired in a stern tone, as he and Bernadette continued to stare daggers at each other, but I could tell that the woman known as Bernadette had affected Jack, for she was smiling, as Jack was seething with anger. Samson then whispered into Jack's ear, as Bernadette lit a cigarette and blew the smoke into Jack's stern face with a giggle.

"What's wrong," I inquired, as I stared intently at Jack, as he stared intently at Bernadette with wide eyes.

"It was you ... you ran to Johnny that day I banned you from this speakeasy. You're the reason me and this kid are wanted by the Five Points Gang. Where is he now? I know you wouldn't be bold enough to flout me in my own speakeasy all by yourself?" Jack inquired in a stern tone, as he placed his handgun upon the bar and stared frantically around the speakeasy.

"I told you one of these days you would get what you deserve, Jack, and now Johnny and his associates know your every move. Maybe next time you'll think twice before you smack a woman to the ground. Oh wait ... there won't be a next time for you when Johnny shuts that mouth of your for good," Bernadette said to Jack with a smile.

"You stupid—,"

"No Jack. Don't make the same mistake twice," Samson interjected, as he clutched Jack's arm before it could strike the smiling Bernadette from across the bar, "Is it true, are you the reason Johnny and the Five Points Gang want me dead?" I inquired in a timid tone, as Bernadette continued to blow smoke into Jack's face in such a flouting manner.

"Darling, I have no idea who you are, but if you affiliate yourself with this man right here, then you're as good as dead," Bernadette replied, as she pointed at Jack who continued to stare daggers at Bernadette, while Samson continued to restrain him from striking her.

"Well well, look at you Bernadette. So you're a made woman now. Was it worth the cost of your soul?" Samson inquired.

"Don't act self-righteous with me, honey. You and Jack are the lowest of the low in this town and if you so much as raise a finger at me, then Johnny will make you both wish you were dead. You remember don't you, *Jackie boy*. That story you regaled me with of Johnny beating you to within an inch of your life.

Well don't you forget that pain," Bernadette pronounced in a stern tone.

"I now noticed Samson begin to seethe with rage, as Bernadette giggled. It amazed me how one woman could have such power over two domineering men like Jack and Samson, but according to Bernadette, Jack got what he deserved by smacking her. It was of no consequence any more over who was to blame for Johnny and the Five Points Gang wanting Jack and I dead, Jack blames this beautiful flouting woman, my mother, and me for all the dangerous men who are trying to kill us, but I place no such blame on anybody. Nothing can change what my mother said to Johnny which provoked his mad mind into killing her, as I'm sure nothing would change Jack's cruel temperament regarding women in general.

"I need some air," Jack pronounced, and then whispered into Samson's ear, as he pointed at me and Bernadette, before storming out of the front door of the speakeasy.

"Hayley, come here," Samson said to me in a stern tone, as he gestured for me to follow him into the kitchen. Samson frightened me. He was the kind of brutish man who could easily overpower me with one finger if he wanted to, just as Fernando and Johnny did to me and my mother.

"Sit down … Stay away from that woman. I know her kind, and she will try to make a deal with you. She's now on the arm of Johnny just as your mother was, so she now has a false sense of pride and power," Samson said to me in a stern tone, as I sat down on the far side of Jack's bed in a timid manner.

"Are you saying my mother was just like her?" I inquired in a distressed tone.

"I won't make that judgment call just yet, but your mother didn't die for nothing, Hayley. And that's why, you must show me and Jack her last will if we ever hope to survive Johnny and the Five Points Gang," Samson replied.

"You're just like Jack, and don't you dare speak for my mother. You only care about the preservation of this hole in the ground," I said to Samson in a stern tone, as I stood up from the bed.

"I'm not like Jack. I've never hit a woman before in my life, despite the stereotype of a typical Irishman makes me out to be. I cannot force you to do what I believe to be right, but you will eventually have to make a choice that will not only save your life, but the lives of others around you, then you can ask yourself what your mother would do, god rest her soul," Samson said to me and then exited the kitchen.

I didn't feel safe in the speakeasy, nor did I feel safe if I set one foot outside. Would Johnny and the Five Points Gang really kill me, as they killed my mother, or would Johnny torture me for the information in my mother's will, which he believes could bring the downfall of the Five Points Gang? Why are men in power never satisfied, why do they continue they're cruelty no matter what the cost, to gain even more power? I've never felt power a day in my life, but in my mother's death, she gave me power, a power which I will not relinquish to any cruel man.

It was 8:47 PM in the speakeasy.

There were no windows in this establishment of liquor which Jack holds so dearly, more dearly than his own flesh and blood. I couldn't see the sunlight or the moon while I sat at the corner table drawing a picture of Mickey in my diary. Would Mickey help me acquire that letter from Johnny which Jack kept on himself? There's no doubt that Jack trusted Mickey over me, his own niece, and I didn't know what more I could do to make Jack see the truth. I have a feeling that Jack will only appeal to reason at the very moment before the end, I just hope that feeling is wrong.

The speakeasy was so busy tonight that I could barely hear my own thoughts, but perhaps that's all for the best. My thoughts always lead me down a dark alley where I'm cold and alone. To feel alone in this crowded speakeasy is a feeling I'm all too familiar with, but I fear that I will easily fall prey to any one of these men if they see fit to advance on me.

Jack was talking to a woman at the bar, but his entire mood was that of a young smitten boy, as he smiled and laughed, whenever the woman talked to him. This woman did not carry herself in a flouting manner like Bernadette, for she had an air of class, yet light-hearted grace, not to mention her beauty which was apparent from across the far end of the speakeasy where I observed her and Jack. She had black hair and pouty red lips, which seemed to shine even brighter every time she spoke. There was a word for her kind, but I forgotten what society calls her. Jack was indeed smitten with her, the likes of which I've never seen him before. He was kind, charming, cordial, and respectful when he talked to that mystery woman, but why, what power did she have over Jack, what made her so special in his eyes? I just had to find out for myself. So I waited for Jack to enter the kitchen, and then I walked over to the mystery woman at the bar who had Jack utterly enthralled by her charm and beauty.

"Do you know my uncle Jack?" I inquired in a timid tone as I sat down at the bar beside the mystery woman, who was applying lipstick in an alluring manner, nothing like the clumsy way in which I put on lipstick.

"Oui, you can say that, so how are you related to Monsieur Jack?" the mystery woman replied with a smile. I could already understand why Jack was smitten with the mystery woman, for she was charming, beautiful, kind, and had a way of making me feel special as she spoke to me.

"I'm Hayley Carmona, Jack's niece, nice to meet you Miss—,"

"Dubois, Faye Dubois and it's a pleasure to meet you mon chéri. Jack has told me about you," the mystery woman interjected, as she extended her slender hand towards me with a smile.

"What did Jack tell you about me?" I inquired in a timid tone, as I shook Faye's hand.

"He told me that you were a … how you say, burden to him. I then told Jack to never speak of a child in such a way, especially one as beautiful as you," Fay replied, as she lit a cigarette and then took smoke.

How could a woman as incredibly beautiful as Faye really think that I'm beautiful? I thought to myself with a smile.

"He likes you. I cannot remember the last time I saw him treat a woman with such respect and kindness in the way he does with you," I remarked.

"Ah Jack is a tortured man indeed, but if you look deep beyond the façade, then you will see a heart crying out. I knew this from the first moment I laid eyes on him," Faye said to me. "My mother told me the same thing in her will. She said that no matter how cruel he may treat me, that there's still good in him, but I saw a glimmer of kindness in his eyes when he was speaking to you a moment ago," I said to Faye.

"Mon chéri Hayley, with men like Jack, it is like a seed planted underneath a war-torn farmland. The surface may be covered in ash, but if you continue to show love, then that seed will grow into a flower and make its appearance above the ash where it once lived in darkness for so long," Faye said to me, as she gestured the entire process of a seed growing underneath the earth and then blooming into a flower.

"I've never seen Jack in such a way," I said to Faye.

"Perhaps you need to see with your heart and not with your eyes," Faye said to me with a smile and then took a sip from a glass of red wine, which Samson just poured for he from behind the bar.

"You're a flapper girl, isn't that what men call you?" I inquired.

"Qui, but men call me many things. I am simply a woman trying to find happiness," Faye replied with a giggle.

"My mother would be friends with you if she was still alive," I remarked, in a somber tone, as visions of my mother flashed before my tearful eyes.

"Jack told me what happened to your mother. My mother died when I was not much older than you," Faye said to me in a somber tone, as she placed her hands upon mine.

"How did you cope with the loss? Every day I hear her voice in my ear, then I wish it was more than just her voice, I wish that she—,"

"Was there to hold you until all the tears inside of you are emptied," Faye interjected

"She was my strength and now I fear that I won't be able to survive without her," I said to Faye in a sobbing tone.

"No, no, no, mon chéri, ta mère is still with you. My mother died during the war on a sunny afternoon from a stray bullet shot by a French battalion patrolling our village. So now whenever the sun shines so warmly upon my skin I feel my mother's love as if she was holding me in her arms," Faye said to me with a warm smile.

"I just killed the biggest rat you've ever seen in the kitchen. Let that be a lesson to any rat in here," Jack pronounced with a grin.

"How charming of you, Jack," Faye said to Jack with a look of disgust on her face, and then took a smoke.

"It was a pleasure to meet you Ms. Hayley," Faye said to me, as she stood up from the barstool with a sigh.

"It was a pleasure to meet you too Ms. Dubois," I said to Faye with a smile. Faye then scampered over to a table with a finely dressed couple who appeared to know Faye, or perhaps they were just drunk enough to welcome anybody who sat down at their table, especially a woman as kind and beautiful as Faye. "Did I scare her off again," Jack inquired with a sigh, as he wiped down the bar.

"Talking about killing a giant rat will do that," I replied with a smile.

"Faye isn't just any woman," Jack remarked with a grin.

"You like her ... don't you?" I inquired with a grin.

"I like the atmosphere and business she brings to my speakeasy," Jack replied.

"No don't do that. Don't disregard that look in your eyes when you talk to her. I know she's much more special to you than just a decoration for business," I said to Jack.

"Don't claim to know my emotions, kid," Jack said to me in a stern tone.

"The only thing I claim to know about you Jack is that you're a cruel man, but Faye told me in such flowery words that she likes you as well," I said to Jack in a stern tone, as I stood up from the barstool and entered the kitchen.

Faye was far too good for Jack. He should be on his hands and knees professing his heart to her or she might give up on him and find a true gentleman who treats her right. I needed fresh air from all the smoke in the speakeasy, but I was afraid to set foot outside.

"Jack, could you open the front door, I need fresh air?" I inquired.

"One moment, kid ... all right what do you want now?" Jack inquired, as he uncorked a wine bottle with a grimace.

"My eyes and throat are irritated from the smoke, I need fresh air," I replied with a cough, as Jack stared at me in the manner of a master staring at his weary dog yelping at his feet. That's what I felt like whenever Jack would stare at me in such a stern manner.

"Fine, make it quick," Jack said to me, as he unlocked the front door with a grin.

"Wait ... you're going to let me back in, right Jack?" I inquired, as Jack stood with his hand on the iron handle of the door, ready to let me out of his sight for good, like a dog who he could no longer tolerate.

"Just give her the damn key, Jack," Samson said to Jack in a stern tone.

"Why? So she can come and go as she pleases and possibly bring in more stray children into my speakeasy," Jack inquired in a stern tone.

Samson then swiftly snatched the key out of Jack's hand and handed it to me.

"Thank you," I said to Samson, as Jack stood face-to-face with him furious over him helping me.

"Just for that Samson, I'm cutting your pay by 25 cents. You better pray that kid doesn't run off with the only copy of keys I have to this speakeasy or you're out of here you stupid Irish—,"

Jack and Samson's argument was cut short, as Jack slammed the door behind me. I felt guilty over Samson's pay being cut by Jack, all so I could get a breath of fresh air, but in all honesty, the quality of air in the back alley wasn't much better than the speakeasy. The world outside of the speakeasy was just as loud, but not as crowded. The spring night was warm with a slight breeze which blew the stench of smoke away from my personal space.

"He's a heartless bastard, isn't he," a woman's voice remarked, as my eyes darted in every direction hoping to spot who exactly was in the back alley with me.

"Who's there?" I inquired in a distressed tone, as I walked backwards towards the safety of the speakeasy front door.

"Do you remember me, honey?" I was the one your uncle almost took a swing at a couple hours ago?" a woman inquired, as she stepped into the glow of the nearest flickering light.

"Yes. You're the woman who's now with the man who killed my mother," I replied.

"I'm Bernadette Saunders, and let's not make this personal, honey. I had nothing to do with your mother's death," Bernadette said to me, as she shook her head.

"Why are you here, is Johnny with you now?" I inquired in a distressed tone, as Bernadette walked closer towards me with a grin.

"Honey, that uncle of yours in there is the scum of the earth, and the world would be better off without men like him … I know you agree with me," Bernadette remarked.

"Don't claim to know me. Just tell me what you want from me," I said to Bernadette in a stern tone, as she stood face-to- face with me, blowing smoke into my already red eyes with a snicker.

"If you break your bonds with that heartless bastard in there, then you may very well have a happy future, but if you continue to do his bidding, then Johnny says he will have to silence the both of you. A sweet girl like you who has lost so much should know by now the cost of survival versus the cost of living happily," Bernadette said to me, as she reached out and stroked my hair with a smile.

"What do you mean?" I inquired in a timid tone, as Bernadette pressed her buxom chest against mine.

"He didn't show you the letter Johnny delivered here, did he?" Bernadette inquired, as she continued to press herself against me in such a domineering manner.

"No he didn't," I replied.

"Of course he didn't. If you want to stay alive, then Johnny and I can protect you from men like Jack. My car is parked just down the alley; you can leave this hole in the ground and be rid of that bastard once and for all. Just take my hand, honey," Bernadette said to me, as she reached out her velvet-gloved hand towards me.

"My mother always told me to trust my heart. Jack may be cruel, but I trust him now more than a conniving mobster broad like you," I said to Bernadette in a stern tone.

"You dumb little bitch, either Johnny will silence you, or I will!" Bernadette shouted, as she clutched my wrist and pulled me away from the speakeasy front door.

"Let go of me!" I shouted as I pulled out my make-shift knife and swiftly slashed Bernadette's wrist, which made her release me with a grimace and gasp.

"Ah! How dare you! I was hoping not to use this, but you leave me no choice!" Bernadette shouted.

As Bernadette reached into her purse, the front door of the speakeasy opened and there stood Samson pointing a shotgun at her, as he extended his other muscular arm in front of me.

"You would really kill a child just to live a life of wealth Bernadette," Samson said to Bernadette in a stern tone, as she kept her hand in her purse.

"Stay out of Johnny's business, Samson, or you too will have a price on your head," Bernadette said to Samson in a venomous tone, as the blood from her wrist dripped upon the pavement.

"What in god's name happened to you, lass?" Samson inquired, while shaking his head, as I nervously observed the standoff which he and Bernadette were locked in.

"Johnny and I will silence you and Jack, mark my words! That little bitch won't go blabbing to the cops about the Five Points Gang. Not like it matters any way, those boys in blue are all in our pockets now," Bernadette, pronounced in a venomous tone, as she pointed at me in an aggressive manner.

"You got some real delusions of grandeur. Oh tell Johnny that if he ever wants to spare with me hand to hand, then I will be more than willing to teach him a lesson!" Samson shouted, as Bernadette scampered down the alley, entered her car, and peeled out of Minetta Street.

"What happened, who was that?" Jack inquired in a stern tone, as Samson and I entered the speakeasy.

"That was Bernadette. She tried to proposition Hayley," Samson replied, as he, Jack and I entered the kitchen.

"Son of a bitch, what did you tell her?" Jack inquired in a stern tone, as he placed his hand on his forehead.

"I didn't tell her anything," I replied in a distressed tone, as I sat down upon Jack's bed. Jack then whispered something into Samson's ear, as they both stared at me in that same manner as an owner staring at a dog they no longer care for.

"No quite, the opposite. She actually injured that crazy broad, I saw her wrist bleeding," Samson said to Jack.

"Is this true," Jack inquired with a grin.

"Yes. She grabbed me and then I cut her with this," I replied in a timid tone, as I showed Jack my make-shift knife still covered in Bernadette's blood.

"Well I'll be damned," Jack remarked with a snicker. "I'm sorry. I thought she was going to—,"

"Kill you. Yes she was about to. She no doubt had a pistol in that handbag of hers," Samson said to me.

"Thank you for intervening. A couple of seconds later and I would be dead, but like she said, either she will silence me, or Johnny will," I said to Samson in a somber tone, as Jack began to pace back and forth from one end of the kitchen to the other. "No problem. I told you she would try to make a deal with you," Samson said to me with a dismissive wave.

"This speakeasy may be an incredibly safe stronghold against the Five Points Gang, but I sure as hell won't be spending the remainder of my days locked away in here. The Five Points Gang has bootleggers from all around New York working for them. How do you propose we conduct our business henceforth?" Samson inquired in a stern tone, as Jack lit a cigarette and took a smoke, while continuing to pace back and forth.

"Since you pulled that shotgun on Bernadette, all three of us may have a price on our heads now, but Mickey doesn't," I said to Samson.

"You want to use that poor stammering boy to do our business … not a bad idea, but He could very well get shot in an instant if he blows his cover during a liquor dealing," Jack said to me.

"Aye that lad may be our only hope now," Samson said with a groan.

"Like it or not we three are in this together," Jack pronounced.

"That's more like it Jack. A little solidarity will keep us alive, as for Mickey, I don't know if the boy has it in him to do liquor dealings by himself," Samson remarked.

"No, forget I said anything. I don't want Mickey to get hurt as well," I pronounced, as I shook my head.

What was happening to me? I can't believe that thought of using Mickey to do the work of the speakeasy even crossed my mind. Perhaps Jack's cruel nature is rubbing off on me.

"No, Samson's right. That boy may be our only hope now," Jack pronounced with a sigh. Jack then dropped his cigarette on the floor and put it out with his foot, before exiting the kitchen. "Try to get some sleep. We will be closing up in fifteen minutes," Samson said to me, and then exited the kitchen, leaving me frozen upon Jack's bed with a sense of disbelief which only a life threatening occurrence could provoke.

*****

"Wake up kid. Mickey's here!" Jack shouted at 9:05 AM, as I gripped my make-shift knife in response to his aggressive shout.

"Mickey," I whispered, and then sat upright from upon the floor with a moan. I can't remember the last time I felt beautiful around a boy I liked. I didn't care how I looked around Jack and Samson, but Mickey brought out such a sense of vanity within me.

"We're counting on you, lad," Samson said to Mickey as I exited the kitchen to the sight of Jack and Samson standing around him with stern faces.

"You don't have to do this, Mickey. I don't want you to risk your life because of me and Jack," I said to Mickey, as I scampered over to him and placed my hand on his shoulder.

"Mickey already said he would do it. Don't go trying to persuade him otherwise, kid," Jack said to me in a stern tone. "It's all right, Hayley. I can manage the liquor dealings from here on out to keep the speakeasy alive. It's the least I could do," Mickey said to me.

"You're going alone?" I inquired in a distressed tone, as Mickey put on his newsboy hat and weathered beige jacket.

"Jack says I will be less conspicuous that way," Mickey said to me.

"Here's the pick-up point, kid. Now project a sense of authority when you're dealing, or else you will be taken advantage of within the blink of an eye," Jack said to Mickey, as he handed him a folded up piece of paper.

"If push comes to shove just think what would Jack do, then do the opposite," Samson said to Mickey with a snicker.

"Excuse me. My dealings are what have kept this establishment flourishing," Jack said to Samson in a stern tone. "What about the last dealing with the Rivelli Brothers. You stole from them and now they too want us dead," Samson said to Jack in a stern tone.

"Don't act like you wouldn't have done the same thing if you were in my position, Samson. I know you all too well and you would have probably taken one or two more swings at the Rivelli's than I did," Jack said to Samson in a stern tone, as he shook his head.

"Don't worry. I'll try to stay calm during the deal," Mickey pronounced.

I could tell by the look in Mickey's eyes that he was scared to make a deal all by himself, but I for one wasn't going to use him as a pawn like Jack and Samson.

"Any damage you make to my Pontiac, I will make to you, understand?" Jack said to Mickey in a stern tone, as he handed him the keys and an envelope which I could only assume had the money for the liquor deal inside of it, then whispered into Samson's ear, as they both looked at me.

"I'll be back soon," Mickey pronounced, as Jack unlocked and opened the front door of the speakeasy for him.

"Good luck, kid," Jack said to Mickey, as he placed his hand upon his shoulder.

"Aye, we're counting on you, lad, come back in one piece," Samson said to Mickey.

I had a bad feeling about all of this. Why did it feel to me as if Jack and Samson were sending Mickey off to his death? If this was the case, then I wouldn't allow it. I wouldn't allow a sweet boy like Mickey to die all because I, Jack, and Samson all have prices on our heads. I had to follow Mickey, and make sure he was safe during his deal, but how could I exit the speakeasy and trail Mickey without being noticed by Jack or Samson?

"Where do you think you're going?" Jack inquired in a stern tone, as Mickey exited the speakeasy.

"I just need some fresh air, that's all," I replied in a timid tone, as Jack stared intently at me.

"Every time you've gone out for fresh air it has always been bad for this establishment. You will remain here at least until Mickey returns," Jack said to me in a stern tone, as he placed his arm across the front door of the speakeasy.

"Sorry, lass, but I agree with Jack. You would only jeopardize the deal we have in motion," Samson said to me.

"Jeopardize, big word for an Irishman," Jack said to Samson with a snicker.

I then scampered into the kitchen, as Jack and Samson once again began to argue, but all I could think about was how endanger Mickey was. There had to be a way out of this hole in the ground other than the front door. So I frantically searched every inch of the kitchen in hopes to find some sort of passage that would lead me out of this prison where Jack and Samson act as my guards. I then noticed a chrome-colored square behind the shelves where all of the kitchen supplies were stored. If this was what I thought it was, then I could use it to escape the speakeasy!

I then pushed the tall shelves of kitchen supplies away from the wall with all my might, and stared intently at the chrome- colored square on the wall.

"It's a dumbwaiter," I spoke aloud with a smile.

I then slid open the chrome door of the dumbwaiter and climbed inside in a stealthy manner. This was my only chance to escape the speakeasy and watch out for Mickey during his deal. The elevator wasn't operational on the dumbwaiter which explains why it was covered up by the shelves of kitchen supplies. So I then began to brace my back against one side of the shaft, while my feet were braced against the opposing side and then climbed my way up the shaft.

I was almost at the top of the shaft when I felt my quivering legs begin to give out. I then grabbed onto the edge of the door at the top of the dumbwaiter shaft, as my heart raced in fear of plummeting to the bottom, but I had to escape, I had to make sure Mickey was safe! So I pulled myself up onto the thin ledge and then pushed the chrome door of the dumbwaiter open and crawled out.

I was filthy, covered in every kind of grease, grime, soot, and dust imaginable, but my ordeal wasn't over. The first story of the restaurant that is now Jack's speakeasy was boarded up and I lacked the tools to break free, or did I? The handle of the dumbwaiter door was very loose, so I pulled back on it with all my might and broke it off the door, giving me a make- shift crowbar which I could use to pry the boards from off the window. As I pried off the last board from over the window, I could hear Mickey starting up the Pontiac

"Mickey, wait!" I shouted, as I smashed the window with the dumbwaiter handle and quickly escaped into the alley, while tearing the skirt of my dress upon the shards of broken glass, but Mickey didn't hear my plea as he drove away.

"Taxi!" I shouted, as I ran down the alley and waved down a taxicab passing by.

"Where to lady?" the cab driver inquired, as I entered the cab in a hasty manner.

"Quick, follow that beige and black Pontiac," I replied, as I pointed to Mickey driving down Minetta Street.

"Oh that one. You got it," The cab driver said, as he closely tailed Mickey on his route to the liquor deal.

I tried to compose myself, as the cab driver continued to follow Mickey through midday traffic. I'm sure my appearance resembled gutter a rat from climbing up that filthy dumbwaiter, but my looks were the least of importance now. I saw fear in Mickey's eyes just after Jack warned him not to damage his Pontiac. That must be why he was driving so slowly to the meet up point.

"Damn gridlock traffic as usual," the cab driver pronounced, as the cab came to a stop. I realized I didn't have any money to pay my cab fare, so this was a perfect time to flee the cab.

"Hey where are you going lady? Your fare is $0.85," The cab driver said to me in a stern tone, as I opened the door of the cab.

"Sorry!" I shouted, as I ran past the cab driver, to Mickey who began to drive left to the Pier.

"Get back here, you thieving broad!" the cab driver shouted, as he exited the cab and then slammed his fist upon the hood.

It's a good thing that the cab driver was and old rather heavy-set man, or else he wouldn't hesitate to chase me down the street for his fare, but I still felt bad over taking advantage of him.

I was out of breath, but I noticed Mickey parking the Pontiac in a back alley across from the pier, before exiting the car in a nervous manner. I needed to find a place to hide where I could watch over Mickey during the liquor deal, but where?

"Good afternoon ... uhm, you two must be the Rivelli brothers," Mickey pronounced, as he walked up to a pair of smirking men who appeared as if they had the most sinister of intentions in mind for him.

"We are indeed, but don't tell me you're the one we're doing business with on this bellissimo afternoon?" one of the Rivelli brothers inquired with a snicker.

"I am, sir. Uhm ...s-shall we get down to business?" Mickey replied in a timid tone as the once authoritative tone of his voice quickly began to diminish.

I slowly walked as close as I could to Mickey and the Rivelli brothers at the pier and then stealthily hid behind a mass of crates which were stacked no more than ten feet away from the three of them, as the brothers continued to laugh, as they stood face-to-face with the now cowering Mickey. I hate to say it, but Jack may be right, it appears that the Rivelli brothers have already detected the fear in Mickey and will soon take advantage of him. So I continued to watch the deal unfold with wide-eyes through an opening on the stack of crates.

"You mean to tell me you have no other associates to help you with this deal, giovane ragazzo?" one of the Rivelli brothers inquired with a snicker.

I wish I understood Italian so I could know what those sinister men have in store, but I remained just as oblivious as poor Mickey.

"Yes sir, but I am more than capable of loading the liquor by myself," Mickey replied.

"Oh no, now they now he's alone," I spoke aloud, as I searched for anything around the pier that I could use as a weapon, but those two sinister men would most likely be armed with handguns, so how could I distract them long enough for Mickey to escape?

"Questo bambino non ci guarderà nemmeno negli occhi, Patricio," one of the brothers said with a snicker, as he pointed to Mickey who stood with his hands in his pockets, staring down at the pier.

"Here's the money, now … w-where is the liquor?" Mickey inquired in a timid tone, as the Rivelli brothers continued to snicker.

The Rivelli brothers then whispered among themselves, as Mickey's eyes darted all around the pier in a nervous manner.

Mickey was in danger. I could feel it in my gut, but what could I do to protect him, I'm just a girl? There must be something I could do, anything to give Mickey a fighting chance against those sinister, snickering brothers.

"We have your precious liquor right here, uno momento, ragazzo," one of the Rivelli brothers said to Mickey, as they walked over to a stack of crates right on the edge of the docks. "Great, I'll be quick in counting it all. Then I'll be on my way," Mickey pronounced, as he walked over to the crates of liquor.

"Oh just one more thing, bambino," one of the Rivelli brothers said to Mickey.

"Yes what is it?" Mickey inquired, as he studiously counted the bottles of liquor in the crates, while the Rivelli brothers stood smirking on either side of him.

"Tell Jack we said hello," one of the Rivelli brothers said to Mickey, which caused him to freeze in the middle of his counting.

"Uh … I-I'm afraid I don't know who you're talking about, sir," Mickey said to one of the Rivelli brothers who both began to snicker in response to Mickey's transparent lying.

The Rivelli brothers knew Mickey works for Jack, but how? Did they follow him back to the speakeasy? If this was the case, then they were about to get revenge on poor Mickey just because Jack and Samson stole from them.

"What should we do with him, Patricio," one of the Rivelli brothers inquired with a snicker, as he walked behind Mickey.

"Grab him," the Rivelli brother known as Patricio, replied. The other brother then locked his arms around Mickey in a swift motion.

"What are you doing? I told you I don't know Jack," Mickey pronounced in a distressed tone, as he struggled to break free from the other brother.

"Oh no," I spoke aloud with wide eyes, as Patricio threw a series of punches at Mickey, two to his stomach and one to his face.

"Hold him up, I'm not done with this bambino yet," Patricio, said to the other Rivelli brother who was now keeping Mickey from collapsing to the ground.

"Please … I thought we had a deal?" Mickey inquired in dismay, as he slowly raised his head which hung low in anguish, while the Rivelli brothers continued to laugh their obnoxious laughs.

"I had to help Mickey, but I was just a lone girl, what could I do against two full grown men.

"Think Hayley, think," I spoke aloud, as Mickey fell to the ground.

"You mean to tell me you don't remember me, bambino?" Patricio inquired.

"I do … you and that bulking man in the suit were the ones who were following me last week until I gave you both the slip," Mickey replied, and then wiped his bloody mouth with a sniff.

"Ha ha, that bulking man was 'the Hammer' O'Connor and you didn't give us the slip one bit. We found your destination of so-called solitude," Patricio said to Mickey.

"The *Jack of All Trades* speakeasy, you led us right to Jack and that pretty little rag-doll of a niece of his who Johnny wants dead as well," Patricio said to Mickey, as he grasped his hair and raised his head to meet his stern eyes.

"Do what you must with Jack, but please spare Hayley, she is innocent in all of this," Mickey pronounced.

"Oh look Patricio, the bambino quit stuttering and stumbling over his words," one of the Rivelli brothers remarked with a smirk, as Mickey slowly stood straight up with a stern look upon his bruised and bloodied face.

Infatti Marco, perhaps the mere mention of that niece gives him courage," Patricio remarked.

I then searched the docks for anything I could use as a weapon or distraction against the Rivelli brothers, while they continued to physically and mentally torment poor Mickey. Time was running out, and I feared the Rivelli brothers were just playing with Mickey before they silence him for good.

"What can I do, what can I do," I spoke aloud with my hands on my head, as the Rivelli's sinister laughter echoed through the docks.

"All right Marco enough. Let's plug this bambino and be on our way. Johnny will be pleased when we inform him that one of Jack's associates is now at the bottom of the *Hudson River*," Patricio said to the other Rivelli brother known as Marco, as he pulled out his handgun.

At that moment, a heartbreaking reality then dawned on me. I wasn't strong enough to save Mickey, just as I wasn't strong enough to save my mother, but could I really watch Mickey die, after I came all this way just to try and protect him? There must be something I could do for Mickey. I know he would do the same for me. Then I saw it just above me, a small crane which held a mass of crates by a netting of ropes. I alone stood no chance against the Rivelli brothers, but my mother always told me that 'a man never fails to underestimate the mind of a woman' and this crane was my weapon now. I then quickly climbed into the crane and stared at all the levers in front of me with wide eyes.

"Say goodnight bambino, but don't worry, Jack and that niece of his will be joining you soon," Patricio said to Mickey, as he pointed his hand gun at him.

"Mickey, run!" I shouted, as I pulled a lever which made the crane turn to the left.

"Hayley!" Mickey shouted, and then dove to the ground, narrowly dodging the mass of crates which knocked both of the Rivelli brothers off the dock and into the river in one swift motion.

"Who's operating the crane?" one of the Rivelli brothers shouted, as I began to climb up the dock.

"Hayley!" Mickey shouted, as I ran up to him as fast as my heart would allow me to. "Hurry, let's get out of here," Mickey said to me in a heaving tone, as he grabbed my hand. I've never held a boy's hand before, but what better time to hold the hand of someone you care for than when you're both protecting each other from a life threatening event.

"Are you all right?" I inquired in a distressed tone, as Mickey quickly started up the Pontiac and peeled out of the alley.

"I am now, thanks to you," Mickey replied with a smile, as he drove in the manner of a man trying to evade the cops, but this danger that Mickey and I were in was much worse than that.

"Are you sure you want to drive so fast, remember Jack said if you damage his Pontiac then he will damage you," I said to Mickey, as I placed my hand upon his shoulder.

"I don't give a damn about the condition of this car any more. All I care about is your safety. Besides, I've already stood face-to-face with the Rivelli brothers, so I'm not afraid of Jack anymore," Mickey said to me.

"I was so worried I was going to have to watch you die … I didn't think—"

"You saved my life, Hayley. It's the most compassion anybody has shown to an orphan like me," Mickey interjected. "I didn't know you were an orphan," I said to Mickey, as he drove down Minetta Street.

"I am … I thought I would find comfort working with your uncle at the speakeasy, but over the years, him and Samson have continued to treat me like nothing more than a desperate orphan who will carry out any life threatening task for them and perhaps that's what I am. They will no doubt be furious that I blew this deal," Mickey said to me.

"No, you're so much more than an orphan, Mickey, and you can always find comfort with me," I said to Mickey with a smile, as he smiled back at me, before parking the Pontiac in the shady lot beside the speakeasy.

"Are you ready," Mickey inquired with a sigh.

"Could we just stay parked here for awhile until my heart calms down," I replied, as I brushed a strand of my hair behind my ear.

"Of course, I could use the time to compose myself as well before I face Jack," Mickey said to me and then turned on the car radio, as a news report blared loudly before Mickey quickly lowered the volume.

"Kansas born Aviator Amelia Earhart made history today when she became the first woman to fly solo across the Atlantic. The woman pilot's flight was faster than her male predecessors, Wiley Post and Harold Gatty, clocking in at 15 hours and 39 minutes," the radio sounded.

"It's all right. We're safer here from the Rivelli brothers," Mickey said to me, as I began to cry.

"No, it's not that. The radio, my mother spoke so highly of that woman. My mother told me that I should never live in the shadows of a man's successes, but to soar beyond them, like Mrs. Earhart has done. I still here her voice … I just miss her so much," I said to Mickey in a weeping tone.

"Mrs. Earhart sure is brave, but so are you. You took out two members of the Five Points Gang. If it wasn't for you, I would be at the bottom of the *Hudson River* right now full of led," Mickey said to me, as he stared at me intently.

"We make a good team … don't we," I remarked, as I gently grabbed Mickey's hand which was still shaking from the Rivelli brothers torments.

"We sure do. I … I trust you more than anybody," Mickey said to me in a timid tone and grin, as I continued to gaze into his kind downcast eyes.

My heart raced as Mickey leaned in closer to me. Was he about to kiss me? I've never kissed a boy before, but if this was to be my first kiss, then I was very pleased that it was with Mickey. I then closed my eyes, as my lips pouted with anticipation of Mickey kissing me.

CHAPTER 5:
LONG WALK, SHORT PIER
- JACK -

"How the hell did you get out of the speakeasy?" I inquired in a stern tone and bewildered stare, as I slammed my hands on the hood of the Pontiac, which made the two kids recoil from each other.

"She used the dumbwaiter, no doubt. It's the only way out other than the front door," Samson pronounced, as the kids exited my Pontiac.

"Goddamn it! I don't know where to begin … both of you get inside now," I pronounced in a stern tone, as I pointed to the front door of the speakeasy.

*****

It was 12:35 PM at the speakeasy.

"They were going to kill him!" Hayley shouted in a distressed tone, as I paced back and forth, while Samson wiped down the bar.

"I have so many questions right now I feel like my head is going to explode.

"Jack … here," Samson said to me, as he slid a shot of bourbon across the bar.

I then took the shot of bourbon with a sigh and stared at both of the unruly kids who sat at the bar in front of me, staring back at me with wide-eyes, as if they were just a pair of innocent kids. Hayley was a bad influence on Mickey, I could tell that as much already. The boy was always good at following my orders, but now it seems that he is more worried about pleasing that grease and soot covered girl than me, the very man who pays his way in life. I had to put an end to this attraction Mickey has with my niece. I had to teach the boy that when you think with your heart, you end up dead.

"Talk some sense into Hayley, while I talk to Mickey," I said to Samson, as I gestured for him and Hayley to go into the kitchen.

"So not only did you blow the deal which this speakeasy was relying on to stay afloat, but you also managed to drag Hayley into your failure as well. What do you have to say for yourself, son?" I inquired in a stern tone, as I stared intently at Mickey, but something was different about the boy, as he stared back at me with stern eyes.

"Jack … the Rivelli brothers knew I worked for you from the start. They had no intentions of doing business with me, rather than filling me with led and tossing my body into the Hudson. They beat me down, and just when I thought it was all over for me, Hayley's quick thinking saved my life," Mickey said to me in a stern tone.

"I wasn't going to let him die like you and Jack were," Hayley shouted at Samson in the kitchen, as he tried to talk some sense into the hysterical kid.

"Oh Mickey … we're all wanted by the Five Points Gang now, all four of us. I don't know how long this speakeasy can stay afloat, but mark my words, If we're going down, by either, the police or the Five Points Gang, then we're all going down together," I said to Mickey in a stern tone, as I pointed at him in an aggressive manner, before taking another shot of bourbon with a grimace and cough.

"Maybe we can ride it out, you said yourself this speakeasy is built like a fortress," Mickey said to me.

"If that kid in there can get out of this speakeasy without the key, then the Five Points Gang can sure as hell get in, and don't think for one moment that they don't know where you live. They will stop at nothing to ensure the future of their organization," I said to Mickey in a stern tone.

Mickey had changed, perhaps the Rivelli brothers beat the timid boy right out of him, because he continued to talk and look at me in the manner of a stern man, a man who nearly died, a man who could die at any moment in the near future.

"Holy fuck, that sure is impressive, young lady," Samson remarked with a cackle from the kitchen.

Our situation was grim any way you slice it. All four of us now had a price on our heads by the Five Points Gang. Was this the end of my speakeasy? How could I keep the liquor flowing without my weekly dealings? Either the *Jack of All Trades* would die first, or one of the four of us would die trying to keep it alive and running. I was working with incompetent, arrogant, fools, but sadly they were all I had.

"I just got done with our liquor inventory, Jack," Samson said to me with a sigh, as he entered the bar from the kitchen.

"Where is that conniving niece of mine?" I inquired, as I stared around the bar.

"She's taking a shower now," Samson replied.

"She looked like a chimney sweeper when I saw her in my Pontiac," I remarked with a scoff, as I began to clean up each table before I open up the speakeasy in 10 minutes.

"Do you have any idea what that niece of yours did to save that lad Mickey?" Samson inquired.

"Whatever she did, she did with a recklessness that could have gotten the both of them killed," I replied.

"Ah then she's acting more like her uncle every day then," Samson said to me, with a grin, as the first knock upon the front door resonated throughout the quiet, but tense atmosphere of the speakeasy.

"Mickey, go see who's at the door," I said to Mickey in a stern tone, as I pointed to the front door.

"It appears the demand for liquor is still high," Samson remarked.

"Indeed ... so how is our liquor inventory?" I inquired, as I buttoned up my black vest to appear presentable to whoever should enter the speakeasy.

"We have enough liquor to keep this place running for another week tops, then we will be dry," Samson replied.

"Do you know of anyone other than the Five Points Gang who is currently bootlegging liquor?" I inquired.

"No, I wish I did. That gang seems to be at the top of the bootlegging empire in New York City," Samson replied, while shaking his head, as a disheveled man in a worn olive-colored suit sat down at the bar with his head in his hands.

"Then we may have to take matters into our own hands then," I said to Samson.

"What do you have to do for service in this hole in the ground?" the man at the bar inquired.

"You can talk to us more politely, pal," I said to the man in a stern tone.

"I'm sorry, I 'm just at the end of my rope," the man said to me in a distressed tone.

"Well you came to the right place then. What'll you have, friend?" Samson inquired with a grin.

"Rum, and keep the bottle right here," the man replied, as he pointed at a spot at the bar right in front of him.

"Samson, I need some time to think over our dire situation. Can you and Mickey handle things while I step out for a couple of hours?" I inquired.

"Sure Jack, but why can't you think here?" Samson replied.

"I need perspective, and this speakeasy continues to play the same song on repeat day after day," I replied.

"It's not safe Jack. The Five Points Gang will sure enough threaten your life the very moment you set foot outside of this speakeasy," Samson said to me, as he shook his head.

"Don't treat me like that kid in the kitchen, Samson. Just do your job, while I do mine," I said to Samson in a stern tone. "Very well, Jack. I hope you return in one piece," Samson said to me.

I then unlocked and opened the front door of the speakeasy, before tucking my pistol between the waist-band of my pants. Just before I exited the speakeasy, I saw Hayley staring intently at me through the crack of the kitchen door wearing nothing but a beige towel and her hair sopping wet.

*****

It was 1:27 PM in Greenwich Village, as I drove down 2nd Avenue through the slum that was the *Ukrainian Village*, but I suppose most of New York City was a slum in this day and age. All these European immigrants are like rats fleeing a sinking ship that was their homeland to only find out that they have arrived at another sinking ship known as New York City.

I didn't know where I was driving exactly, but I knew I couldn't return to the speakeasy until I had a plan that would secure the future of the bar I've risked my life on a daily basis to keep that bar up and running. That bar was my legacy, and I wasn't about to let some psychopathic, Irish fuck known as the hammer take it all away from me. I found myself grasping my pistol at every red light in fear of Johnny rolling up beside me and plugging me in the head before the light turns green. Perhaps I should take a page from Miss Dubois and try some of that nature she speaks so fondly of. So I decided to drive west to *Washington Square Park*.

The traffic down E 4th St. was like being in a maze of rats, just as filthy and wild in every way. I always wondered why the traffic in New York City was so terrible when most New Yorkers had no jobs to go to everyday.

"Get the fuck out of the street you bum," a cab driver shouted at a man chanting, while holding a sign that read *I WANT WHISKEY*!

"You and me both pal," I shouted at the man, as he walked past my Pontiac with a nod.

I didn't know what my plan was to keep the speakeasy afloat, but I just had to get away from Samson, Mickey, and that niece of mine for a couple of hours. I could hire on another worker and have them do the liquor dealings. The Rivelli brothers wouldn't know any new worker I hire in the confines of the speakeasy. That is unless the Five Points Gang has spies in my speakeasy right now.

My mind was racing as I drove past numerous billboards depicting happy people living out their happy lives. It was all false advertising, and it was a way for the capitalist elites to flaunt all of the money they're making, while 99% of New Yorkers waited in bread lines. So I then rolled up the windows and turned the radio to Charles Coughlin's broadcast. I agreed with most of what Father Coughlin preached regarding the economy, civil rights corruption in Washington, and racism, however, the man was a radio giant who was listened to by millions of people every week, so he knew what the people wanted to hear.

"Remember my children. The hands of fascism and capitalism have been working together for centuries. We need merely amputate that evil capitalist hand so that we may better prosper as a society. Godspeed and god bless. This is Father Charles Edward Coughlin signing off," the radio sounded.

"Amen," I spoke aloud with a scoff, as I turned off the radio and parked in an alley across from *Washington Square Park*. I don't know why Faye was so in love with nature and all of its aspects. I, for one, found it to be dull, as I sat down on a bench and lit a cigarette. There were many homeless people camped out throughout the park, which sullied the view of the scenery for me, as I tried to stare past their misery, but there was misery everywhere you looked in this city. I remember reading when I was around Hayley's age that the grounds of this park were once used as gallows for executions, and now the homeless have taking up residents here, completing a circle of despair which only New York could create.

There wasn't much nature to be seen in this park anyway. I'd much rather hear Faye speak of nature in that enticing voice of hers than actually be in it.

"Mister, spare change please," a young boy said to me with a somber look on his grimy face, as he held out his hands towards me.

"I'm no charity. There's a breadline just across the street, kid," I said to the boy, as I pointed to the breadline.

There was no peace of mind to be found here in this park of despair. The only peace of mind for me was at the bottom of a bottle of bourbon, so I got back in my Pontiac and drove west back to the speakeasy.

*****

It was 2:55 PM as I arrived at the speakeasy.

I then unlocked and opened the front door of the speakeasy to the sight of something unexpected.

"Where's Caroline and the rest of the band?" I inquired, as I stared at the empty stage.

"She and the rest of her band quit," Samson replied. "Don't tell me she was demanding another raise," I said to Samson while shaking my head.

"No, I simply told her that we couldn't afford to pay her and her band any longer. Then that feisty Negro up and left. Good riddance, right, Jack," Samson replied with a scoff.

"What are we going to do for live entertainment now you fucking imbecile!" I shouted, as all the patrons sitting at the bar averted their bleary-eyed gaze from their liquor to me, and then quickly back to their liquor.

"Easy Jack, I thought you hated that two-bit jazz singer," Samson said to me.

"I've told you before, Samson, live entertainment is the cornerstone of this speakeasy," I said to Samson in a stern tone. "Ah think of it this way. We can now keep the speakeasy running for at least another two weeks now that we don't have to pay Caroline and her band, and maybe we could purchase one of those Jukeboxes," Samson said to me.

"Fine, just put on some Armstrong," I said to Samson in a stern tone, as I pointed to the victrola beside the empty stage.

"I take it you don't have a plan," Hayley said to me, as she sat down at the bar with leather book in hand.

"Leave me alone, kid. I'm in no mood to deal with you," I said to Hayley in a stern tone, as I took a shot of bourbon with a grimace.

"You said it yourself. If one of us goes down, then we all go down, but if one of us can find a way to succeed, then perhaps we can all be saved," Hayley said to me.

"You're so naïve. How on earth did you manage to take out the Rivelli brothers anyway?" I inquired with a scoff.

"I saw my opportunity in the form of a crane. I then used the crane to knock those two terrible men into the river," Hayley replied.

"I think the Rivelli brothers will no doubt think twice before doing any bootlegging after the beatings we handed them," I said to Hayley with a snicker.

"I hope so. Next time I won't be so lucky," Hayley said to me.

"Now just what are you so busy with writing in that book of yours, kid?" I inquired.

"Just my thoughts of a life less lived," Hayley replied in a somber tone.

"Think of it this way, kid, It's just as that detective said to me just hours before Johnny killed him. The Five Points Gang wants you dead more than me. So you can say that your life right now is—,"

"Worth more than yours, I don't feel special because dangerous men are trying to kill me, I feel hunted," Hayley interjected in a distressed tone.

"Johnny knows something about you that I don't know, doesn't he. Why else would he be trying to lure you back to him with the promise of a made life like he did with that crazy broad Bernadette?" I inquired.

"I don't want to talk about my home life living with him, it's too painful to even think about," Hayley replied.

"You believe your mother's will is only intended for your eyes, well guess what kid, If you continue to keep that information in your mother's will a secret from the world, then you will share her fate," I said to Hayley in a stern tone.

"What will happen next if I give you my mother's will?" Hayley inquired in a somber tone and sigh.

Was I finally getting through to the stubborn little kid? I now had to speak to Hayley in a manner that I wasn't comfortable with if I was to ever persuade her into giving me her mother's will, but would it work? As much as I hate to admit it, Hayley was indeed an intelligent and competent young lady. She was smarter than Samson and Mickey combined, but her pride seems to always be the one at the wheel.

"Hayley … you have your whole life ahead of you. Your mother wouldn't want her will to be the death of you. I'm sure she didn't write you that will, so you would take the information to the grave," I said to Hayley with a sigh.

"Jack …why did you choose my mother's middle name for the password of this speakeasy," Hayley inquired.

"What are you talking about?" I inquired in a stern tone and stare.

"*Delilah*. I heard Mickey tell you that name, when you asked him for the password at the front door," Hayley replied.

"You really think your mother's middle name inspired that password?" I inquired with a scoff.

"It's all right to miss her. Every day I can hear her—," "Listen kid! Your mother never gave a damn about me! All I did my entire life was protect her from lowlifes like Johnny, but she saw fit to take his side over mine. She fucking betrayed me, and the mere memory of her is a thorn in my side. Get out of my sight and take your book with you!" I shouted, as I pointed to the kitchen.

Hayley then grabbed her book and scampered to the kitchen, as tears welled up in her eyes. She was so ignorant to who her mother really was. If she could only see her mother through my eyes, then she wouldn't be so quick to defend her. I was tired of trying to persuade the kid to give up her mother's will. Perhaps it's time to escort the kid by force to the NYPD, just as Johnny instructed me to in his letter. The way I see it, either Hayley dies or we all die.

"Samson!" I shouted, as I gestured for the dense Irish brute to come over to the bar.

"Aye what is it, Jack?" Samson inquired, as he walked over to the bar, while adjusting his vest.

"That niece of mine is going to get all of us killed unless we offer her up to the NYPD," I whispered to Samson.

"Bernadette told me the Five Points Gang has the entire NYPD in their pockets," Samson whispered to me.

"I don't fucking care anymore. I will not die for the pride of an ignorant little girl," I whispered to Samson.

"If you do this … then you're no better than Johnny. You're sending your own flesh and blood to her death," Samson whispered to me.

"What would you have me do then, Samson?" I inquired.

"This situation is not cut or dry, Jack. It's very complicated, and many players are involved. For once in your goddamn life try to see through the eyes of someone other than yourself," Samson said to me in a stern tone, as he picked up a tray full of cocktails and then walked over to table five.

I knew Samson wouldn't support my plan, but sometimes in life, a bad decision may only seem bad at the moment, then later down the road you find yourself happy with that decision you made. Samson believes I'm a selfish man unable to see any point of view other than my own. Where the hell does that Irish brute get off acting all self righteous with me. When I first met the man fresh off the boat that brought his kind to Ellis Island, he told me he was in a street gang in Belfast before he up a fled to America, and now another gang threatens his life. If I ever believed in karma then that would be a perfect example of it. It was all settled in my mind now. One way or another, I'm taking that kid to the NYPD.

"Do you want to take a drive with me and get some fresh air?" I inquired, as I entered the kitchen to the sight of Hayley sobbing on the floor.

"Where are you going?" Hayley inquired, and then wiped her nose with a black handkerchief, as she sat upright from the floor.

"I thought we'd take a drive through *Midtown* and take a gander at all of those *Broadway* lights," I replied with a grin, as I spun my keys around my finger.

"All right, I've never been to a Broadway show before," Hayley said to me, as she stood up from the floor and began to primp herself in the mirror.

"Whoa hold your horses there, kid. I said we can look at all the lights, not go to a Broadway show. I'm not made out of money," I said to Hayley.

"Oh … all right, I'll be ready in five minutes then," Hayley said to me.

"I'll be waiting in the car. Don't take too long," I said to Hayley, and then exited the kitchen.

"Where are you off to?" Samson inquired, as I walked to the front door of the speakeasy.

"I'm going to show the kid some sights," I replied. Samson then quickly scampered over to the front door, blocking me from exiting the speakeasy.

"What are you doing, Samson?" I inquired in a stern tone. "I won't let you send that poor niece of yours to her death," Samson replied in a stern tone, as he firmly stood in front of the front door.

"This is family business, Samson. Now get the hell out of my way," I said to Samson in a stern tone.

"For fuck's sake, Jack, your family business has put a price on all of our heads," Samson said to me in a stern tone.

"I'm doing what must be done. Later on down the road, you will thank me for this choice I had to make. Now you either move or I will shoot that kneecap of yours full of led. Do you really want to walk with a limp for the rest of your life," I inquired in a stern tone, as I gripped my pistol tucked between the waistband of my pants. That Irish temper I was all too familiar with began to burn intensely in Samson's eyes, as we stood face-to-face with each other.

"I'm ready, Jack," Hayley said to me, as she scampered out of the kitchen to the front door with a smile.

"Very well, Jack. I hope this decision haunts you for the rest of your goddamn life, just like your sister does," Samson said to me in a stern tone.

"Let's go, kid," I said to Hayley, as I stared intently at Samson. Hayley and I then exited the speakeasy, as Samson shook his head in condemnation.

*****

It was 7:15 PM as Hayley and I drove through *Midtown* just as the sun began to set.

"It's all so glamorous. It's hard to believe some people actually live these lifestyles," Hayley remarked, as she gazed out the car window at all the lit up billboards of *Midtown*.

"Some people don't get squeezed as much by this bullshit prohibition act. Those people live their lives blissfully unaware of the turmoil which surrounds them," I said to Hayley with a scoff.

"I remember my mother once drove me through Broadway after the war had ended and before this prohibition act," Hayley said to me as she continued to stare wide-eyed out the window. "That moment in time was a brief respite before this city entered a new hell," I said to Hayley.

"Well ... she told me that Broadway was built for woman like me to shine," Hayley said to me, as we drove northeast down *5th Avenue* passing by *Rockefeller Center*. It always seemed that no matter where you are in the world, the further north you go, the better life is, and this was no exception for New York City.

"I don't see any breadlines here," Hayley remarked.

"You're right, kid. The way of life in this part of town is populated by the elite," I said to Hayley with a scoff.

"If they have all this money to spare then they should give back to all of those who are unemployed and living on the streets," Hayley said to me.

"I'll give you a blow horn so you can shout that message atop the *Empire State Building*," I said to Hayley in a sarcastic tone and snicker.

"Jack … Have you given up on this town," Hayley inquired in a somber tone.

"New York City gave up on me long before I gave up on her. There will come a time in your life when those rose-tinted glasses which you kids see the world through begin to fade. Then all you will see is gray," I replied.

Hayley appeared unaware that we were about five minutes from the NYPD Precinct, and yet she continued to smile, which pulled at an emotion from deep within me, an emotion I no longer believed I was capable of feeling in this day and age. I had to push though. The kid's very presence around the speakeasy will only bring death in the form of the Five Points Gang, and I'm not about to die twice.

"Well Jack … as long as we stick together, I believe we can overcome all of this," Hayley said to me, as she averted her gaze out the window towards me.

My eyes then widened in response to what Hayley just said to me as a memory rushed to my mind

*****

"I miss dad too, Jack, but mom says he will return from the war. She told me he promised he would return," Dezerae said to me in a somber tone, as she played Hopscotch in the alley next to our apartment.

"I don't need him for anything!" I shouted, as my eyes began to well up with tears.

"You two give us all your money now," a smirking boy pronounced, as he stood with two other smirking boys with their fists clenched.

"Just look at us, does it look like we have money," Dezerae inquired in a stern tone.

"Every tenant we've robbed from this apartment has had a heavy wallet, now I won't ask you again doll," the snickering boy said to Dezerae in a stern tone, as I slowly grabbed a led pipe I noticed laying on the ground behind Dezerae.

"All right, grab her!" the snickering boy shouted. The two boys then reached for Dezerae, but she didn't recoil from them, my sister would never cower from bullies, but I still had to protect her.

"Don't touch my sister!" I shouted, as I swiftly swung the led pipe at both of the boys who were about to grab Dezerae.

I hit both of the boys in the head, as they cringed and hissed in pain, while the third boy stared at me intently, before pulling out a knife.

"Jack, be careful," Dezerae said to me in a distressed tone, as the knife wielding boy slowly walked towards me.

"You little bastard, I'm going to cut you to ribbons for that," the knife wielding boy said in a stern tone, as the two other boys pressed their hands against their bleeding heads.

"Uh oh," Dezerae pronounced while shaking her head. "What did you call me?" I inquired in a stern tone and wide-eyed stare.

"What, a bastard," the knife wielding boy replied with a snicker. I then swung the led pipe with such fury, first knocking the knife out of the boy's hand, and then hitting his shoulder and knee, which sent the boy to the ground.

"Stop Jack, you'll kill him!" Dezerae shouted, as she grabbed my arm.

"Get out of here!" I shouted in a heaving tone, as I stood over the three boys who now lay in pain upon the ground.

"We'll be back," one of the boys pronounced as the three of them limped away down the alley.

"Cowards!" I shouted, as I spit on the ground towards the fleeing boys.

"Jack, are you all right?" Dezerae inquired with a wide-

eyed stare, as she hugged me tightly.

"I'm fine. I just ... I just—,"

"Jack look at me ... breathe," Dezerae interjected, as she cupped my cheeks with both her hands.

"I just miss dad so much, where is he?" I inquired in a distressed tone, as my eyes began to well up with tears.

"I miss him too, Jack, but I believe we can overcome all of this pain, as long as we stick together," Dezerae said to me in a weeping tone, as she began to cry along with me in the alley.

*****

"Jack ... Jack are you all right?"

"I'm fine ... I'm just worn out."

"Where are we going now?" Hayley inquired, as I drove up to the NYPD Precinct.

"Home ... we're going home, kid," I replied as I stared intently at Hayley, as she stared out the window with wide eyes.

*****

It was 9:45 PM as I parked the car in the shady lot beside the speakeasy.

"We're here!" I shouted, as I exited the Pontiac.

"Oh ... thanks, Jack," Hayley said to me, as she rubbed her bleary eyes.

"For what?" I inquired, as I unlocked the front door of the speakeasy.

"For giving me some peace of mind," Hayley replied, as we entered the speakeasy to the sight of only a few men drinking at the bar.

Samson then smiled and nodded at me from behind the bar, as he saw Hayley.

"I'm going to take a shower then go to bed," Hayley said to me, as I nodded at her before she scampered into the kitchen. "Well, well, it appears Jack does have a heart after all. I can't say I'm not surprised that you returned with Hayley," Samson said to me, as I walked up to him with a sigh. "Don't look at me like that," I said to Samson. "Like what?" Samson inquired with a snicker.

"I wanted to Samson. I wanted to drop her off at the Precinct," I said to Samson, as I rubbed my bleary eyes.

"Aye then why didn't you?" Samson inquired.

"Why should I confide in you? You're just going use whatever I blab to you about against me in the future," I said to Samson with a scoff.

"Fine, leave it be then. All that matters is that you didn't send that poor niece of yours to her death," Samson said to me. "It was a memory of my sister," I said to Samson in a stern tone.

"That niece of yours is the incarnation of your sister. I'm not surprised she brought a memory of your sister to that dense head of yours. So was it a good memory?" Samson inquired.

"Yes … and no. It's complicated and I'm far too tired to explain it to you," I replied, as I turned off the victrola beside the empty stage.

"You know we can always buy that Jukebox I mentioned and step into the twentieth century. Those victrolas are a thing of the past in this day and age," Samson said to me.

"I'll consider it now that we have no live band, but remember Samson, the past can be quite comforting to a man at the end of his rope, goodnight," I said to Samson, as I took off my vest and then entered the kitchen.

Perhaps Samson was right when he said that Hayley was the incarnation of her mother. Well of course she was in the literal sense, but whenever I stared at the kid I would see Dezerae in her eyes. That same strength and kindness would glimmer in her eyes just as her mother's eyes would whenever I needed her. That memory of Dezerae was like a blow to the head. I spent most of my days trying to drown my past with bourbon after I moved out of that apartment in *SoHo* where I, Dezerae, and my mother lived. Now it looks like I may have a second chance to protect Hayley, where I failed to protect her mother. I then heard the shower turn off, as Hayley entered the kitchen with a beige towel wrapped tightly around her.

"Oh … are you going to bed early too?" Hayley inquired in a timid tone, as she recoiled slightly from my presence, as I sat on my bed with my hand upon my forehead.

"Delilah, I chose your mother's middle name for the password of this speakeasy because I was afraid," I said to Hayley in a somber tone.

"What were you afraid of?" Hayley inquired in a somber tone, as she sat down on the bed beside me.

"I was afraid of starting my own business, but whenever I heard your mother's middle name it would always lift my spirits," I replied with a smirk.

"It's a beautiful name," Hayley remarked in a somber tone as her flushed face quivered.

"You're more like her than you know, kid," I said to Hayley as I stood up from the bed with a sigh.

"Jack … here," you deserve to read it," Hayley said to me in a somber tone, as she pried open a loose floorboard and took out a piece of paper.

"What's this?" I inquired, as Hayley handed me the folded up piece of paper.

"It's my mother's will. Her last words should live on through you as well as me," Hayley replied.

"Thanks kid. I'm glad you finally came to your senses," I said to Hayley as I stared pensively at the will.

"I thought the kid would take this information to her grave, but I finally have it," I said to Samson as I walked to the front door of the speakeasy

"What may that be?" Samson inquired, as he put on his jacket and newsboy hat.

"It's my sister's will. Hayley just gave it to me," I replied.

"I've never seen someone so happy while holding the last will and testament of a relative," Samson said to me.

"It's not like that. We may have the upper hand on the Five Points Gang now. If the information my sister has on them is indeed worth killing for," I said to Samson.

"Well go on then read it, unless you're afraid what the truth entails," Samson said to me with a snicker, as he sat down at the bar.

"… Well I'll be damned. They've been doing their business right under our noses this entire time," I spoke aloud with bewildered eyes, as I finished reading my sisters will.

"What does it say?" Samson inquired.

"Every Friday night at Pier 45 *Hudson River* Park the leader of the Five Points Gang himself does business," I replied to Samson.

"Now you see why I was reluctant to give up this information to you," Hayley said to me, as she walked up to me behind the bar.

"What do you propose we do with this information?" Samson inquired.

"Well judging by Johnny's letter to me, that lug head believes that Hayley is the only one who knows this information. "What did Johnny say to you in the letter?" Hayley inquired. "He wanted me to give you up to him, but I'm not threatened by that cop killing bastard. We all now know where the Mafia Don does his business, but the question is, how we stop him," I replied with a sigh.

"Aye that deranged broad Bernadette told me they have every NYPD Precinct in their pockets," Samson said to me while shaking his head.

"If this is true, then we have no hope in stopping them," Hayley pronounced in a distressed tone.

"No hope huh, kid. Let me tell you something about those two words. When I first opened this establishment after my old bar got shut down because of that bullshit prohibition law, every fiber of my being was telling me I had no hope of ever becoming a profitable proprietor of liquor, that I would be living in the gutter in no less than a week. Then the demand for liquor skyrocketed and all of the sudden my bold business endeavor paid off. Hope is a delusion. This fire right here inside all of us is what we must keep burning. If the Five Points Gang has the entire NYPD in their pockets, then we will look elsewhere for help into bringing them down," I pronounced in a stern tone, as I paced back and forth behind the bar with Dezerae's will in my hand.

"Bringing down the Five Points gang sounds like a fantasy, Jack. You may as well tell me that we can set up our speakeasy on the moon while you're at it," Samson said to me with a scoff. "They underestimate us. We're just the proprietors of a speakeasy to them," I pronounced.

"Aye and just look what Miss Hayley did to the Rivelli brothers all by herself," Samson remarked with a snicker, as Hayley smiled.

"All our lives people like us have been counted out, beaten down, walked over, and bullied by men like Johnny, but no more. If Johnny will stop at nothing to kill us four, then we will stop at nothing to bring him down to hell with us," I pronounced, as I firmly placed my hand upon Samson's broad shoulder.

"I like your spirit Jack, but we need a plan, and a bulletproof one at that. The Five Points Gang has resources across every borough of Manhattan. They are vast and have been dominant for twelve years now," Samson said to me.

"I'm going to bed … goodnight," Hayley pronounced, and then entered the kitchen.

"I would think of all people you would understand Samson. To cut the head off a snake you don't go in headfirst or you die quickly.

"Are you suggesting we try to infiltrate the Five Points Gang?" Samson inquired.

"That may be are only option for now," I replied with a sigh.

"The Five Points Gang knows what we all look like Jack. That plan will only get us a couple rounds of led to our chests," Samson said to me.

"You have any bright ideas Samson, by all means speak up. Out of the four of us you have the most gang experience," I said to Samson in a stern tone.

"Aye but I left that piece of me back in Belfast … along with the two men I killed," Samson said to me in a somber tone. "So you are a killer after all. I knew it," I said to Samson with a scoff.

"I was a young lad back then who was constantly fueled by rage, and our leader Marcus Macready capitalized on that young fervor. Our gang was king in Belfast, until I slipped up and made the mistake of having a heart. One night we went to collect on this local pub owner who had been stiffing us for weeks. Macready said to me and my fellow associates that if he stiffs us once more then we would burn down his pub. Long story short, when me and my two associates let ourselves into the pub, the owners we lad of a boy immediately grabbed his father's rifle. My associate cared not of the boy's sanguine age, for he was ready to kill him. So I shot him before he could shoot the lad. When my other associate rushed in to see what just occurred, I panicked and shot him as well. The pub owner's family was frightened, but grateful to me for having a change of heart and protecting them. I thank you, my good sir, but you will be hunted now. You must flee Belfast and never look back' those were the words the pub owner spoke to me before I fled to this so-called land of opportunity known as America," Samson said to me, as he poured himself a shot of whiskey.

"I knew your past had to have been a bloody one, but I'm going to need you to find that young lad who was full of rage within you once again, if we ever have a chance in taking down a far more powerful crime organization than the one you fled from in your home country. You're a killer, plain and simple, Samson, but so is Johnny. Like it or not, you two are cut from the same cloth," I said to Samson.

"Stop comparing me to Johnny. Just because we're both Irish doesn't mean we share the same moral compass you racist bastard!" Samson shouted, as he slammed his fist down upon the bar.

"Take it easy Samson. I'm not the one trying to kill you," I said to Samson, as I slightly recoiled from his outburst.

Was I afraid of Samson? I knew now what the man was capable of. The question is will Samson ever revert back to that young man in Belfast who was full of rage, or is that part of him gone for good?

"I will let you ponder on all of this tonight. Don't drink yourself into too much of a stupor Jack," Samson said to me with a sigh, as he walked to the front door of the speakeasy.

"Samson wait … I don't think of you the same as Johnny. That man killed my sister. I just need all the help I can get right now. I know I haven't treated you fairly over the past year, but you have always been loyal to me and the speakeasy," I said to Samson.

"Wow you really must be drunk if you're getting this sentimental with me," Samson said to me with a grin.

"I mean it goddamn it. You, me, Hayley, and Mickey must stick together if we're to ever overcome the Five Points Gang and this prohibition law," I said to Samson.

At that moment I could see humanity in Samson's eyes as he stared intently at me. Samson may have killed two men, but he did so to save a kid's life. Perhaps I needed a noble man more than a killer right now.

"I'm worn to the bone Jack. I'll see you tomorrow morning. Then we can discuss how exactly we plan on thwarting the Five Points Gang," Samson said to me, as he patted my shoulder in a hearty manner.

"Thwarting, that's a big word for an Irishman," I said to Samson in a facetious tone and grin.

"Next time I'll speak slower for you. Goodnight Jack," Samson said to me with a snicker and then exited the speakeasy. I then staggered into the kitchen to the sight Hayley once again sleeping in my bed, but I was far too drunk and tired to tell her to move. So I then collapsed onto the blankets on the floor were Hayley slept.

"Jack, are you all right … Jack?" Hayley inquired in a weary tone just before my heavy eyelids shut.

*****

It was 9:45 AM in the speakeasy as I awoke from the floor with a throbbing headache.

I could hear Hayley talking to Mickey at the bar, as I opened the fridge and prepared a prairie oyster to help my hangover.

"Good morning," Hayley said to me, as I walked behind the bar with all the ingredients for the prairie oyster in hand.

"Mickey … did you notice anybody follow you here," I inquired with a grimace, as I clumsily prepared the cocktail.

"I don't know, Jack. I wish I had eyes in the back of my head considering that I'm marked by the Five Points Gang as well," Mickey replied.

"We must infiltrate their organization, but they could very well be trying to infiltrate this speakeasy as well. Samson, you must board up the dumbwaiter from this little adventurers excursion last week. Both doors must be covered by either brick or sheet metal," I said to Samson, as I cracked the egg into the tumbler.

"Aye, I already did Jack. Both doors of the dumbwaiter are now sealed with a sheet of metal," Samson said to me.

"Good man. You would've done well in the war," I remarked with a snicker, and then took the shot of the prairie oyster with a grimace.

"It feels like we're in a war right now," Hayley remarked in a somber tone.

"Women are the cause of all wars. From Helena of Troy to … well your mother," I said to Hayley with a scoff, and then took a swig of water.

"How could you say that? Last night you spoke so fondly of her," Hayley inquired in a distressed tone as she stared at me with those all too familiar eyes about to well up with tears.

"All I remember from last night was that surpassed my limit when it comes to bourbon, kid," I said to Hayley, as I slowly put on my vest.

"That's not true. That couldn't be just the liquor talking last night," Hayley said to me in a distressed tone, as she quickly stood up from the bar.

"Lower your goddamn voice. I need time to recover from last night. Mickey, make yourself useful and sweep the speakeasy before we open in fifteen minutes," I said to Mickey, as I pinched the bridge of my nose.

"I won't believe it, I can't believe it," Hayley said to me in a distressed tone, and then scampered into the kitchen.

"There she goes again," Samson said to me.

"Does she ever leave a room quietly?" I inquired with a snicker.

A knock on the front door of the speakeasy then averted, me, Samson, and Mickey's attention from our daily routines to the front door. We used to love the sound of a knock on the front door. Now a knock on the front door could very well mean the death of us.

I then walked over to the front door with my pistol in hand as Samson grabbed the rifle and Mickey pointed his pistol in a shaking manner.

"What's the password?" I inquired in a stern tone, as I slid open the iron window of the front door, and then quickly moved to the side.

"Uhm … oh shit. It s-starts with a *D* I-I know that," the balding man replied in a stammering manner, as I stared intently at his every move.

"If you don't know the password to this speakeasy then I suggest you come back at another time, I don't much care for loiterers around the entrance to my speakeasy," I said to the stammering balding man in a stern tone.

"Wait, is it … Delilah," the balding stammering man said to me, as I was about to shut the iron window of the front door. "Welcome to the *Jack of All Trades*. I said to the man with a sigh, as I unlocked and opened the front door of the speakeasy. "Mickey, attend to this gentleman's every need," I said to Mickey, as I snapped my fingers and pointed to the balding man who sat down at the bar.

"We must now thoroughly vet every patron who enters this speakeasy. Having the password isn't enough during these times," I said to Samson.

"Aye … what do you make of that man? He sure looks shady," Samson inquired, as he pointed to the balding man at the bar.

"I don't know, but we're about to find out," I replied.

The Five Points Gang could very well send in a stooge to infiltrate this speakeasy and gather vital information us, but this man who sat before Samson and me at the bar appeared as a nervous wreck, a stumbling and stammering man who was afraid of his own shadow. I would find out if this man worked for the Five Points Gang one way or another.

"So are you from around here?" I inquired, as I wiped down the bar.

"What does it matter," the balding man replied in a dismissive manner and then took a shot of whiskey.

"It matters to me. Where are you from and how did you find out about this speakeasy. Tell me now or you will be tossed out of here," I said to the balding man in a stern tone.

"Do you always give your patrons the third degree, what kind of place is this," the balding man replied in a stern tone.

"We're waiting. If you want to continue to drink here then you will answer our questions," Samson said to the balding man in a stern tone as he stood behind him.

"Fine, I'm from the lower east side and I heard of this speakeasy from a buddy of mine who told me this is the only speakeasy currently in business in Greenwich Village," the balding man pronounced.

"So we're the only speakeasy in business right now, I find that hard to believe," I said to the balding man.

"Believe it. I'm surprised you're business is so slow right now. Are you looking for a supplier," the balding man inquired. "We may be in the need of someone to do our dealings. What are you offering exactly," I inquired.

Either this balding shady man was a stooge for the Five Points Gang, or he was just another desperate fool at the end of his rope looking to make a few bucks. If this man is in league with the Five Points Gang and I hire him, then I could perhaps use him, as he is trying to extract information from us. I had to invite the snake into our den if I was to ever extract his venom. "Any job you see fit for me at your speakeasy. Before the stock market crash I worked on Wall Street. So I am very good at calculations. If you want to double your sales within this month then I'm your man," the balding man said to me.

"One moment, sir, my associate and I need to have a discussion on the matter of your potential employment at the *Jack of All Trades*," I said to the balding man.

"Mickey, Samson, we need to talk in about that man's potential employment at this speakeasy. Don't take your eyes off that man while we're in the kitchen, understand," I said to Mickey in a hush tone as I pulled him in close to me by his arm. "Sure thing, Jack, I won't let him out of my sight," Mickey said to me.

"Take your time, I'll be here," the balding man pronounced with a grin, as he raised his glass of whiskey.

"Ah it's hard to tell whether or not that man is in league with the Five Points Gang. I've seen men who look like him every day in the speakeasy," Samson said to me, as we entered the kitchen to the sight of Hayley writing in her book.

"Go keep Mickey company at the bar, Samson and I have vital matters to discuss," I said to Hayley in a stern tone as I pointed to the bar.

"Fine, but whatever decision you both make will no doubt affect all of us," Hayley said to me with a sigh.

"You're not my mother kid so don't talk like one," I said to Hayley in a stern tone and dismissive wave as she exited the kitchen.

"I want to hire this man. If he is a stooge sent by the Five Points Gang to infiltrate our speakeasy then we can use him while he thinks he's using us, and if he isn't a stooge sent by the Five Points Gang then we have just hired a new man to do our dealings. It's a win, win scenario in my book" I said to Samson. "Aye, but that man could be a hitman just waiting to pump a couple rounds of led into us when our backs are turned," Samson said to me.

"There's no way that man is a hitman," I said to Samson. "What makes you so sure?" Samson inquired.

"It's his shifty eyes. No hitman has shifty eyes like that. I remember Johnny's eyes and how cold and calm they always seemed to be even when he was beating me half to death," I replied.

"Very well, Jack, we will use this man, but keep your hand on your pistol whenever you're around him," Samson said to me.

"Same goes for you. Now go inform the man of his immediate employment at this speakeasy and then tell Hayley I need to speak with her," I said to Samson.

"Is something wrong, Jack?" Hayley inquired in a timid tone as she entered the kitchen with her leather book in hand. "That shady looking bald man at the bar is going to be working for us. Now he could very well be working with the Five Points Gang, so we need to be subtle when we're around him," I said to Hayley and then took a smoke.

"What if he tries to kill us?" Hayley inquired in a distressed tone.

"I guarantee you that man is no killer. The way he stammers his words would indicate a nervous rat, not a cold and calm killer. Either way, this goes without saying, but do not tell him anything about your mother's will or your family in general.

"I wasn't going to. What's the man's name?" Hayley inquired.

"Oh I forgot to get his name. Well Samson will get his name sure enough when he hires him.

"Are we really that desperate?" Hayley inquired.

"All four of our faces are known to every bootlegger working for the Five Points Gang, kid, but this man is a nobody. So he will do our liquor dealings for us, after we train him how to conduct himself during said dealings," I said to Hayley.

"The way he looks at me makes me feel uncomfortable," Hayley remarked.

"Just deal with it. I don't want to blow this opportunity we have to bring down the Five Points Gang," I said to Hayley as I put out my cigarette and exited the kitchen.

"This is Chip Benowitz and he will be working with us at the speakeasy," Samson said to me as I walked up to the balding man known as Chip who was already half in the bag.

"Well Mr. Benowitz let's get started. Samson and I have a lot to teach you about our fine establishment and how it runs. Now your salary will depend on a percentage of sales we make every week. So you must learn how to sell liquor," I said to Chip with a grin, as I nodded to Samson.

"How hard could that be? I saw a man on the street yesterday stab another man just for the bottle of beer he was drinking," Chip pronounced while shaking his head.

"Desperate times call for desperate measures Mr. Benowitz. The demand for alcohol in general is at an all time high in New York. Therefore we must capitalize on that desperate demand which has us killing each other over something that should've never been outlawed in the first place," I said to Chip.

"Amen to that. I'm just looking to make enough money to get by each week. It seems that all the women in this city are gainfully employed, but when I applied for a job at a bank last week I was turned down," Chip pronounced with a scoff.

"Aye you're right about that. Women do seem to be doing well during this depression," Samson remarked.

"At least someone is doing well. All right let's begin with your training Mr. Benowitz," I said to Chip with a sigh.

"I'm ready, and please call me Chip," Chip said to me with a grin as he stood up from the bar.

"We'll start with cleaning the speakeasy, inventory, bartender training, and then the most important, our liquor dealings," I said to Chip as I patted his shoulder.

*****

It was 2:45 PM as I waited for Chip to return to the meet up point in the back alley across from Pier 45.

It had been two weeks since I hired that stammering man, and although he failed on his promise to double our sales this month, he had still executed successful dealings every week. I was pleased with Chip's competence when it came to working at the speakeasy, but I still couldn't get a clear read on the man. At times Chip seemed to be the most nervous man in New York, but then there were brief moments where he would speak with the confidence of Mayor James Walker. I wore a disguise of sun glasses and a trench coat buttoned up above my chin as I waited in the Pontiac for Chip to return with the cart of liquor. This was so that the Rivelli brothers wouldn't find out my true identity and kill me as they tried to kill Mickey.

"I got the liquor Rick. Here's the money," Chip said to me in a heaving tone as he pulled the cart of liquor up to the Pontiac.

"I made it a rule that I would go by the name Rick when I'm doing dealings, you never know who could be listening and my real name is unfortunately well known by the Five Points Gang.

"Good work…now load up all the liquor in the trunk so we can get back to the speakeasy, happy hour is near," I said to Chip as I counted the money in the envelope.

"We're all set," Chip said to me in a heaving tone as he entered the Pontiac and sat down in the passenger's side seat with a sigh.

"You have any family, Chip?" I inquired, as I slowly drove down the back alleys of Minetta Street.

"I have a wife and son. They would be ashamed of me by the path I have chosen now," Chip replied, as roaring thunder signaled a rainstorm which quickly began to downpour.

"Ah think nothing of it. You provide for them during these trying times. That's all that matters," I said to Chip as I took off my hat, sunglasses, and then unbuttoned my trench coat.

"W-What about you Jack. D-do you have any family?" Chip inquired in a stammering manner.

"That's another story. One that I don't tell to outsiders," I replied in a stern tone as I parked in the shady lot beside the speakeasy.

"F-Fair enough … All right, let's unload all of this demon rum before we get soaked to our breeches," Chip said to me, as we exited the Pontiac.

"This speakeasy will stay in business for at least another week on account of Chip's successful dealings," I pronounced as Chip and I entered the speakeasy with crates of liquor in hand.

"Aye but what if some down on his luck drunk wants to numb himself to death. It's happened before and you don't toss them out, you just let them drink to where they can no longer keep their eyes open," Samson said to me with a grin as he wiped down the bar.

"One down on his luck drunk is very profitable for this speakeasy. Now go make yourself useful and help Chip and I unload the crates of liquor before someone steals them off the wagon," I said to Samson in a stern tone.

"Where's Mickey?" I inquired, as I walked up to Hayley sitting at the bar, as she wrote in her book.

"He left. He told me he wasn't feeling well," Hayley replied.

"None of us are a portrait of perfect health. If he leaves in the middle of his shift again tell him I'm cutting his pay, this is a business I'm trying to run," I said to Hayley in a stern ton, but she didn't respond, as she stared back at me with a brooding look on her face.

"Don't give me that look kid. You should be happy we made another deal. It appears that Chip succeeded where Mickey failed," I said to Hayley.

"I don't trust him," Hayley said to me as she brushed a strand of her red hair behind her ear.

"Neither do I kid, but it's as I told Samson, if this man is a rat, snake, mole, or any other fucking animal I'm disgusted by, then we must use him so that we can be one step ahead of his associates," I said to Hayley.

"You're talking about Johnny and the Five Points Gang. When Chip talked to me yesterday it was like he was a different man. He talked in such a suave and articulate manner," Hayley said to me as she leaned in close.

"Sometimes when he talks to me he begins to stutter and stammer over his words like he's being interrogated by the police," I said to Hayley.

"So which one do you think is the real Chip, the nervous stammering man or the suave articulate man?" I inquired.

"I think the suave man is just an act. The stammering man is the real him. I can see it in his nervous eyes," Hayley replied.

"No, I think the stammering man is the act. He wants us to think of him as a timid sap so he will be unassuming to our eyes," I said to Hayley.

"My mother always told me to trust my intuition," Hayley said to me, as I began to purge the beer valves.

"Oh really, and what did your intuition tell you when you first met Johnny," I inquired with a scoff.

"Even though I was very young, I still remember what I felt on that fateful day. That day you pointed a shotgun at my mother and then Johnny defended her," Hayley replied.

"Bullshit. I pointed that shotgun at Johnny, not your mother," I said to Hayley in a stern tone.

"Wait Jack, let me finish. Even though it appeared as though Johnny was defending my mother from you, I still felt as if you were the one defending her from him. He was domineering despite his charms, and I perceived a rage underneath the exterior that was his striped suit and fedora that immediately made me uneasy," Hayley said to me.

"You have a real big vocabulary kid. I feel as if I'm talking to a one of the old marms that taught me English when I was your age," I remarked with a snicker.

"I love to read. It's always been an escape for me," Hayley said to me with a smile.

"This right here kid, this is my escape," I said to Hayley and then took a shot of bourbon with a grimace.

"Fernando would drink all the time just like you until—," "Johnny silenced him," I interjected.

"Why didn't you do anything about Fernando abusing my mother?" Hayley inquired in a somber tone.

"I stayed out of your mother's relationships with various men. Until she chose to leave my bar with the very man who nearly killed me," I replied.

"So you only got involved if it was you who was getting hurt. How typical of you," Hayley said to me, as she stood up from the bar and stormed into the kitchen.

"Samson and I just finished doing the inventory on that liquor deal," Chip said to me.

"Good, get the speakeasy looking pretty, we're opening up in ten minutes," I said to Chip, as I tossed him a black vest and tie.

*****

It was 9:34 PM in the speakeasy, as I stared at Chip from across the speakeasy.

The stuttering nervous man wasn't present tonight, as he served drinks to patrons seated at the table in front of the stage. Perhaps Chip was just like any other type of man who loosens up and speaks with confidence once they've been drinking, but just as Hayley, I too had a suspicion about Chip. Maybe I could test him to see who the real Chip Benowitz was, but how? I've never been that good at playing mind games. Maybe I should take a tip from all the broads in this speakeasy who practically have their man wrapped around their fingers from only speaking a few sweet words.

"Chip, come here," I shouted, as I gestured for Chip to join me behind the bar.

"W-We're doing good business tonight," Chip remarked with a grin.

There it was again, but did Chip only stutter and stammer when he was talking to me, or was his split personalities much more complex than that? Maybe if I made him feel comfortable he would speak in a suave and articulate manner like he does with Hayley.

"So Chip … how long have you lived in New York?" I inquired with a grin, as a man dressed in a fine suite with two dames on his shoulders sat down at the bar.

"Around fifteen years now. I couldn't part with this city no matter what economical strife she is going through. In the twenties when I was a stockbroker on Wall Street, I would come home every night to my family feeling like the luckiest man on earth, but then I learned a swift lesson on how fickle money can truly be. The stock market crash of twenty-nine was a severe blow not only to every stockbroker, but to all those gainfully employed on Wall Street. Two of my fellow stockbrokers took their own lives once the market crashed. Police found my pal Artie Fletcher floating in the *East River*. 'He no doubt took a leap off the *Brooklyn Bridge*' is what one police officer told me. My other fellow stockbroker made it on a daily radio news report with how he ended his life. Frank Horowitz dove off the roof of the *New York Stock Exchange*. The radio news report read that Frank wrote a note to his family which he kept in his pocket before he took his own life. I've seen to the fullest extent what money can drive men to do in this city, but I will not be a victim of money. I may be a down and out man just barely providing for his wife and son, but I'll be damned if I abandon them the way my fellow stockbrokers abandoned their families, with shame and cowardice written all over their corpses," Chip replied in a somber tone, and then grabbed the shot of whiskey I was pouring for the fine dressed man sitting at the bar across from me with the dames on his shoulders and gulped it down with a grimace.

"Hey pal, that was my drink. I suggest you buy me another, before I lose my good mood," the man said to Chip in a stern tone.

This was it, a stressful moment that would bring out the stuttering, stammering personality of Chip. I could now gauge how the man reacts in certain situations.

"My apologies, sir, this shot is on me, along with two more glasses of whatever wine these two lovely ladies of yours are drinking," Chip said to the man with a grin, as he quickly poured him and his dames the drinks.

I was wrong once again in trying to predict the mystery that is Chip Benowitz and this made me feel very uneasy when I was around him. Hayley said that she saw in his eyes that the stuttering and stammering man was the real Chip, but I for one just witnessed Chip tell me in full detail about his fellow Wall Street pals ending their life as a result of the market crash of twenty-nine like it was just small talk. A man like Chip whose personality could change at the drop of a hat had me on edge to say the least. Men like him were capable of anything, and that's why I must keep an eye on him at all times when he's working for me at the speakeasy.

*****

It was 2:54 AM in the speakeasy when I noticed Chip talking to a burly man in the corner of the speakeasy with a bruised and battered face.

"Closing time, everybody. We open tomorrow at noon!" I shouted, as I turned off the victrola on the stage.

"Aw but we only just got here," two dames said to me in unison as I walked behind the bar with a sigh.

"All right, one quick drink, then you two dolls need to leave," I said to the dames who sat down at the bar wearing tight black dresses and salacious smiles which only complimented their buxom figures.

"We'll have two shots of Hennessey," one of the dames said to me.

"Coming right up. So … are you two made women?" I inquired, as the two dames were putting on lipstick.

"What does that mean?" one of the dames replied with a wide-eyed stare, as I served them their drinks.

I had to be extra cautious now with every patron that is granted access into the speakeasy. I knew a made woman when I saw one, and the two dames who sat across from me at the bar were without a doubt the wives or girlfriends or just quick forty-eight hour flings of mobster from the Five Points Gang.

"Thanks for the drink *Jackie boy*," one of the dames said to me with a giggle, after she and the other dame gulped down their Hennessey in the manner of a sailor.

"No problem. You two dolls stop by any time," I said to the two dames with a grin, as Chip opened the front door for them. *Jackie boy*, there was only one man who ever called me that, and he was the man trying to kill me. I then noticed one of the dames place her hand upon Chip's cheek, before they both exited the speakeasy.

"Do you know those two dames," I inquired in a stern tone, as Chip walked over to the bar.

"No sir, but they were very flirtatious with me for some odd reason. For a moment there I think they forgot that I was a middle-aged balding man," Chip said to me with a snicker.

"Well goodnight Chip, and be safe. A man like you could easily be preyed upon by either a beautiful dame or a criminal," I said to Chip as I took off my vest.

"W-Well aren't they t-the same thing … g-goodnight Jack," Chip said to me with a snicker and then exited the speakeasy.

"Who are you Chip?" I whispered, as I stared intently at the front door of the speakeasy.

Who was the real Chip? This question remained to be answered, but I feared that when that answer finally reveals itself to me about Chip's true identity, that it will be at a grave cost to me. Whether the man works for the Five Points Gang or not, I was no longer comfortable with him working at the speakeasy, but how else will we do our liquor dealings without Chip?

"Is he gone?" Hayley inquired in a weary tone, as she entered the bar while rubbing her bleary eyes.

"Who, Chip?" Yes he's gone for the night, and I still have yet to find out his true identity. The man is a fucking mystery," I replied with a sigh as I wiped down the bar.

"Oh … I had a bad dream that I was being—,"

"Please spare me kid. I have too much on my mind to listen to your stories," I interjected, as I held out my hand.

"You sound just like Fernando," Hayley said to me in a distressed tone.

"Stop comparing me to that fucking dago, we're nothing alike, you hear me!" I shouted as Hayley stormed into the kitchen.

What more did she want from me? I offered her room and board along with all the amenities a kid her age could ever need. I was once again stuck between a rock and a hard place just as I always seemed to be throughout my life. This I vow, one way or another, I will discover Chip's true identity tomorrow. Whatever game that man was playing, it was a very subtle one. "Get the hell out of my bed," I said to Hayley in a stern tone as I entered the kitchen to the sight of her cozily nestled underneath the covers of my bed, while writing in her book.

"Only if you listen to me for one moment, that's all I ask," Hayley said to me, as she wrapped her arms around her legs and sat upright in bed.

"Goddamn it. Make it quick," I said in a stern tone as I sat down on the bed beside Hayley with a sigh.

"In my dream, I was being …,"

"Well go on, are you going to tell me or not, I need to get some rest," I said to Hayley in a stern tone and then rubbed my bleary eyes.

"Never mind, I can't, I can't tell you," Hayley said to me in a distressed tone, as she stood up from my bed and then collapsed to the blankets on the floor and began to cry.

Now I had to once again sleep no more than three feet away from a kid crying her eyes out all night. I knew that if I told the kid to shut up, it would only make her cry louder and longer throughout the night. So I had to once again let her cry herself to sleep.

*****

It was 7:34 AM in the speakeasy as I awoke to the sound of Hayley laughing at the bar. The kid even had her mother's laugh, and if I closed my eyes for a brief moment I could've swore that it was Dezerae laughing.

"Now what's so funny you two?" I inquired, as I walked up to the bar to the sight of Hayley and Mickey sitting at the bar playing some sort of hand clapping game.

"Don't mind us Jack, we're just killing time before we open up," Mickey replied with a smile, as he continued to clap hands with Hayley.

"I do mind actually. You don't play games when you're working for me," I said to Mickey as I stared intently at his joyful demeanor.

Ever since that boy met Hayley, he has grown more and more of a backbone, but before when Mickey didn't have a backbone, he was easy to mold and unbreakable, like a jellyfish. Now the boy seems intent on getting closer to Hayley at any cost. I remember when I was his age I would swoon over this one girl in particular. Her name was Cassie Perkins and she put a spell on me from the very moment I laid eyes on her. My classmates and I used to call her perky Perkins, because the girl had such high spirits all the time, but recalling those memories of my teen years now always leave me feeling empty inside.

Mickey and Hayley then stared at each other for a brief moment instead of me. I didn't like the influence the two of them had on each other. I felt like I was losing control over the both of them. Is this how it feels to be a parent? How on earth did Dezerae deal with this kid?

"Sorry Jack. When do we open?" Mickey inquired as he walked up to me behind the bar. I then noticed Hayley give me another brooding stare, as Mickey walked away from her to join me behind the bar.

"We open in fifteen minutes. Now clean the bar. I want it looking as shiny as Chip's balding head," I said to Mickey with a grin, as he snickered and began to clean the bar in an expeditious manner.

"Is Mr. Benowitz working today?" Mickey inquired.

"Yes. He should be here at noon. Mickey, what do you make of Chip? What kind of man do you see him as?" I replied. "Well … from my brief interactions with him I can say that he is a hard worker," Mickey replied.

"I agree, but what do you make of the man's personality?" I inquired.

"Well, he always seems deep in thought, like something's weighing heavy on him. He told me once that when he was my age he nearly killed a man with a harmonica," Mickey replied with a snicker.

"A harmonica huh, how on earth did he manage that feat?" I inquired in an incredulous tone.

"He said another boy his age tried to steal the harmonica from him when he then shoved the harmonica into the boy's neck, which caused the boy to gasp for air," Mickey replied, as he gestured Chips retaliation.

"That tall tale of his would have been better if he ended it with the thief dying by the very object he tried to steal," I said to Mickey.

"Have you ever killed a man, Jack?" Mickey inquired, as he stopped cleaning the bar and then stared at me intently.

"What do you think, kid," I replied as I stared back at Mickey for a brief moment before a knock on the front door averted our attention.

"Go see who's at the door," I said to Mickey with a sigh. "Mr. Benowitz is here," Mickey pronounced, as Chip entered the speakeasy.

"You're early. We don't open for another fifteen minutes," I said to Chip, as he sat down at the bar and placed his hand upon his sweaty forehead.

"I know. I just wanted to ensure this place is ready for the lunch hour rush. Take it from me; men are looking for a place to numb their senses in the afternoon in New York City," Chip said to me, as he put on his black vest in a weary manner.

"Might I say, you look disheveled, Chip, like somebody worked you over fiercely in a back alley," I remarked as I stared intently at Chip.

"Sorry boss. I'll try to look as presentable as possible. I don't want to scare away those lovely ladies who frequent this speakeasy," Chip said to me, as he combed what little hair he had left in the mirror at the bar.

There it was again, Chips charming side which continued to puzzle me along with everyone else who worked at the speakeasy. Maybe he's not putting on an act, maybe Chip just has split personalities which present themselves depending on the situation he's in. The mystery that was Chip Benowitz would no longer weigh heavy on my mind, for tonight, I would get all the answers I seek.

*****

It was 7:15 PM in the speakeasy as me, Chip, Samson, and Mickey served drink after drink to various patrons of all shapes and sizes.

"I'm going to find out who Chip really is. Can you and Mickey handle things for an hour?" I inquired as I leaned in close to Samson with a stern look.

"Aye the lad and I have everything covered here Jack, but you know what they say about curiosity killing the cat," Samson said to me.

"Well I assure you Samson that this cat will never become prey for a rat like Chip," I said to Samson, as I took a brief glance at Chip who was serving a group of dames at table 4.

"You don't know if the man is a rat or not. Tread lightly, Jack. Revealing that man's true identity could prove your downfall," Samson said to me.

"I know Samson, but just in case I don't make it back before midnight. I trust you to keep this place up and running with Mickey and Hayley," I said to Samson as I stared intently at him.

"Ah don't talk like that, Jack. You will be back here cursing me out in no time," Samson said to me with a snicker.

"Let's hope so," I said to Samson with a grin, as I patted him on the shoulder and then tucked my pistol between the waist-band of my pants.

"Chip, let's go for a ride," I said to Chip, as I walked over to him as he was talking to the dames at table 4.

"Where are we going, boss?" Chip inquired.

"Somewhere where we can have a moment of clarity away from all these drunks," I replied, as I escorted Chip to the front door with my hand on his shoulder.

"W-Will Samson and t-the boy be all right without us?" Chip inquired in a stuttering manner, as I unlocked the front door of the speakeasy.

"Oh don't worry about those two, they'll be just fine. After you," I replied with a grin as I gestured for Chip to exit the speakeasy first while I followed him to the Pontiac.

"It's a foggy night," Chip remarked, as we entered my Pontiac.

"Yes, a night like this is ideal for us bootleggers," I said to Chip as I started up the car and then began to drive down Minetta Street.

"W-Well I hardly consider myself a bootlegger I-like you and your fellow associates at the speakeasy," Chip said to me in a stuttering manner.

"Then what do you consider yourself as, Chip?" I inquired, as I drove west towards the source of the thick fog, west to Pier 45.

"I'm just trying to keep my head above water and provide for my wife and son," Chip replied, as a horn from a ferry boat sounded, slicing through the thick fog, alerting us that the Pier was still very much alive.

It was Friday night, and according to my sister's will, Johnny and the leader of the Five Points Gang would be doing their business at this Pier. To Samson it may seem like I have a death wish coming to this Pier with Chip and potentially confronting Johnny and the leader of the Five Points Gang all alone, but the way I see it is that I was being hunted by those men and if I was going to die in the near future, then it was going to be on my own terms.

"I wasn't aware that we were doing a liquor deal tonight," Chip said to me, as I parked the car in the back alley across from Pier 45.

"Oh we're not, but our biggest competition is. The Five Points Gang of New York City does their liquor dealings here every Friday night," I said to Chip with a grin, as I lit a cigarette and took a smoke, while another horn from a ferry boat sounded. "H-how do you know this?" Chip inquired in an incredulous and stuttering manner, as I exited the Pontiac and put on my long beige trench coat and newsboy hat.

"You sound surprised that I know this information, Chip," I remarked, as Chip exited the Pontiac.

"I am, boss. This information could get you killed in the swiftest of manners. I remember that news report on the radio a couple weeks ago about that detective who was killed by a member of the Five Points Gang. No offense but if they're so easily killing cops then you're easy prey for them," Chip said to me, as we both sat on the hood of the Pontiac and stared into the fog that concealed Pier 45.

"S-Shouldn't we be getting back to the speakeasy now, Jack?" Chip inquired, as I continued to stare intently into the fog.

"What's your hurry Chip? Let's take a walk down by the Pier," I said to Chip, as I gestured for him to follow me.

"You can take that foggy stroll by yourself if it's all the same to you, boss. I'll take a taxicab back to the speakeasy," Chip said to me.

"I think I prefer a little company for this stroll," I said to Chip as I walked up to him and pulled out my pistol.

"A-Are you going to kill me, is that why you brought me here?" Chip inquired in a stammering tone, as I pointed my Pistol at him.

"Someone will die here tonight, Chip. I don't know who yet," I replied with a grin as Chip and I walked towards the Pier.

It was dead silent as I escorted Chip at gunpoint into the fog of Pier 45. It felt as if I was walking right into a lion's den with nothing but Chip as bait. After a few moments I heard the voices of men speaking Italian very close by.

"Chi c'è, mostrati," a voice shouted through the fog, as I stood behind Chip with one hand on his shoulder and the other holding the pistol against his back.

"Come out, come out wherever you are, or does the Five Points Gang always hide like frightened rats," I pronounced with a snicker.

"Four men then emerged from the fog, as another horn sounded on the Pier, almost as if to trumpet their appearance.

"I told you to lure him here next Friday you bumbling jackass," one of the men said in a stern tone.

I recognized the Rivelli brothers out of the four men, but the other two looked far more intimidating to me, and there was something about that man's tone of voice which I could swear I've heard before.

"I'm sorry, boss. Jack knew everything from the start," Chip said to the burly man in the pinstripe suite and fedora. "St. John's ghost why if it isn't *Jackie boy*," the burly man said with a cackle, as my eyes widened.

"Johnny, it's been awhile. It seems that all your attempts of silencing me and my niece have failed," I said to Johnny, as I held Chip closely against my pistol.

"Failed, look who's here right now you stolto," one of the Rivelli brothers said to me with a snicker.

"Silenzio voi due. Sono affari di Johnny… end this O'Connor," the suave and domineering man in the middle said, as he placed his hand upon Johnny's broad shoulder. The suave and domineering man then whistled and gestured to the Rivelli brothers as the three of them casually entered two cars with nothing but their taillights flickering through the fog as they drove away.

"I had my doubts, but I must say you played the role to a tee, Mr. Benowitz. You should be on Broadway with the rest of those actors," Johnny said to Chip with a snicker as he slowly walked towards us while slowly clapping.

"I knew it. So the whole stuttering and stammering was just an act after all," I pronounced in a stern tone.

"Once again you come so close but fail at the end *Jackie boy*. Chip was stuttering when I first gave him the ultimatum of infiltrating that speakeasy of yours," Johnny said to me

"So the charming and articulate man was the act after all. Bravo Chip, I guess Hayley was right," I said to Chip, as I pulled tightly on his collar.

"I-I did what you wanted. Now please l-leave me and my f-family alone," Chip said to Johnny in a distressed tone.

"Aye you did indeed. Mr. Benowitz. You brought Jack to me. So now you have my word henceforth that the Five Points Gang will let you and your wife and son live out the rest of your lives, but I cannot promise the same for Jack's intentions. Just look at the man now, he wants to kill you for playing him like a fool," Johnny said to Chip with a laugh as he pointed at me.

The way I saw the situation right now was that if I let Chip go then he could either flee from me and Johnny which would be the wise choice, or he could run to Johnny and the two of them could team up and easily silence me.

"I'm sorry Jack, I-I had no choice. He threatened to kill my wife and son if I didn't deliver you to him," Chip said to me. "I'm sorry too … now go back to your wife and son," I said to Chip in a stern tone as I released him.

"T-Thank you Jack. I was wrong about you," Chip said to me, and then ran away from the Pier in a stumbling manner. "A man of your word huh. Will you really leave Chip alone or continue to use him," I inquired, as Johnny pulled out his gun and pointed it at me.

"We know where the man lives, unless he leaves town, I don't doubt the boss will want to use him in any future business deals," Johnny replied.

"That man who left with the Rivelli brothers, he's the don of the Five Points Gang isn't he?" I inquired.

"I would pay more attention to me right now *Jackie boy*. Believe it or not,

I didn't want it to come to this, but that bitch of a sister of yours just wouldn't keep her mouth shut," Johnny said to me.

"She's never been one to keep quiet, but you're going to regret facing me alone, Johnny. Unlike Chip, the Detective and countless others that you've killed and threatened, I know the truth behind that smirk of yours," I said to Johnny in a stern tone.

"The truth, the truth of this city is that men like you are meant to serve men like me. You know I was going to give your niece everything you couldn't give her, but now, I won't shed a tear over choking the life out of her," Johnny said to me.

"You promised my sister the same life. You and your kind are empty men hiding behind expensive suites.

"The reckoning hour is at hand *Jackie boy*," Johnny said to me, as another horn sounded from a ferry boat.

Both Johnny and I then fired at each other as we dove behind stacks of crates on the Pier.

I've never been so grateful for the fog obscuring Johnny's aim, but my aim as well.

"You missed *Jackie boy*, perhaps you need another drink to steady that hand of yours," Johnny said to me with a laugh, as I peered around the stack of crates. My heart was racing and I couldn't see more than five feet in front of me. I would no longer be a victim to Johnny. The way I see it, Johnny was a man who was always the hunter. He was never used to being hunted. I had to face him if I was to ever leave this Pier alive, or as alive as a man like me could ever feel in this day and age. "Aye the bottom of the Hudson will be your final destination *Jackie boy*. Do you still feel the sting from that beating I gave you five years ago?" Johnny inquired with a laugh, but I didn't respond. The man just wanted to distract me with his head games, but I could tell from all his boasting where his location was at the Pier. He was trying to lure me through the fog to him. I had no choice, so I slowly walked towards the docks, as my heart pounded out of my chest with each step I took. I do remember the beating Johnny gave me, and as much as I hate to admit it, it changed my outlook on life. Up until that point I never lost a fight, but my pride was far more scarred than my body. Johnny was far bigger and stronger than me, but this fog would level the playing field between me and him.

"You've never killed a man before *Jackie boy*. I can see the fear in your eyes. Bernadette told me what a coward you are," Johnny shouted with a laugh, as I peered behind another crate and stared out at the docks blanketed in fog.

Would I be just another name on Johnny's kill list, or could I prevail over the bastard and send a clear message to the Five Points Gang to stay out of my business.

"Broken pieces everywhere, I stole my mind and I found I care. Running on the morning tide something you would say to me. We drank the waters of delight we played the games of wrong and right. Did we understand ... they're just footsteps in the sand," Johnny sang in such a joyful manner, an Irish folksong no doubt. I remember this song. Johnny was singing it as he was beating me to within an inch of my life five years ago. "Shut up goddamn it!" I shouted. Just then, I felt a heavy blow to my head knock me to the docks, I then saw Johnny toss my pistol into the river.

"Oh *Jackie boy*, the pipes, the pipes are calling," Johnny sang as he repeatedly kicked me in the stomach.

It felt like five years ago once again, as I was at the mercy of Johnny the Hammer O'Connor, but this time I was far too much of a threat for the man to spare my life.

"From glen to glen and down the mountain side," Johnny sang, as he lifted me up by the collar of my trench coat and repeatedly punched me in the face.

I smirked back at Johnny as he continued to pound my face into a bloody pulp. I would not die with a look of fear and pain as many have died by the hands of that bastard.

"Wipe that smile off your face *Jackie boy*," Johnny said with a snicker as I fell to the docks and began to crawl away from him.

"Time to meet your maker, *Jackie boy*. No guns, I want the satisfaction of killing you myself," Johnny said to me.

I then noticed a splinter of wood beside me as I crawled towards the edge of the dock.

"Come here. I'm not done with you yet. The only reason I shot your sister in the head instead of beating her to death was because I knew hear mouth would alert the other tenants in the apartment," Johnny said to me with a snicker.

I then swiftly grabbed the splinter of wood and stabbed Johnny in the thigh with it. Johnny collapsed for a brief moment, with a cringe, before pulling out the splinter from his leg and limping towards me.

"You son of a bitch," Johnny shouted.

A chain! I spotted another object on the Pier which I could use to incapacitate Johnny!

Johnny then grabbed me by the collar of my trench coat and head-butted me with such a force it felt as if I got hit by a car, but I couldn't blackout, I had to stay conscious. Johnny then pulled me in close to his stern face once more, but I grabbed the chain and wrapped it around his thick neck and held on for dear life as he thrashed. Johnny and I then rolled upon the dock struggling for control over one another, but I managed to gain the upper hand as I tightened the chain around his neck. I then reached for an anchor, but Johnny pulled me away just before I could grasp the potential death weapon.

"You're really looking … to make a name for yourself, huh *Jackie boy*," Johnny said to me in a heaving tone.

I then managed to grab the anchor and swing it towards Johnny, but the man dodged my attack and charged me like a bull, knocking me down once again. Johnny was the anchor of my life, keeping me down, but I knew the anchor which I regained possession of on the docks would be my only salvation in this fight. Johnny swung at me again, but I moved the anchor in front of my face as a shield. I could then hear the bones of Johnny's fingers break as he punched the anchor. I then kicked Johnny right in the spot where I stabbed him in the thigh and he fell to his knees. I was now the one who stood over Johnny holding the twenty pound anchor in my hands as Johnny stared back at me with a painful look on his face.

"Where's that smirk … of yours Johnny. Come on smirk for me!" I shouted as I swung the anchor at Johnny. The first blow sent blood and teeth flying from Johnny's mouth, but I wasn't finished with the bastard. I then struck Johnny in the head with the anchor again, before I tightened the chains around his neck and attached the anchor to the end of the chain dangling around his feet.

"All of this … all for your sister?" Johnny inquired, in a weary tone and scoff, as I pulled him to the edge of the dock.

"No … for me," I replied in a heaving tone as I stared intently into Johnny's bloody face just before I kicked him off the dock of the Pier. I then watched with wide eyes as Johnny O'Connor sunk like a stone into the still black waters of the Hudson.

CHAPTER 6:
DEAR DIARY
- HAYLEY -

Dear Diary,
June 11th, 1:26 AM,

There was a time when writing to you would bring me such comfort, but now I feel as if your pages only reflect my misery, I feel as if you're mocking me. It's been almost seven hours since Jack left the speakeasy with Chip, and I couldn't help but feel unnerved over both of their demeanors before they left. Samson is still here at the speakeasy, he must be waiting for Jack to return before he finally leaves for the night. I wonder why I should even feel worried about Jack right now for if the tables were turned I feel he wouldn't so much as raise an eyebrow over my safety and well being. I still feel that I must continue to write to you, especially when I feel the weight of the world bearing down on me. I couldn't tell Jack about that nightmare I had, but I can always tell you, you won't look at me with harsh judging eyes as Jack did. So I now end this diary entry with that familiar sense of anxiety looming over me.

"Jack, holy fuck, what happened?" Samson inquired in a distressed tone. I then quickly rose from the blankets on the ground with wide eyes and scampered into the bar.

"Jack oh my god!" I remarked in a distressed tone as I placed my hands over my mouth to at the sight of Jack beaten and bloodied with his arm around another man for support.

"Thanks for bringing him back pal," Samson said to the man, as he paid him a couple dollars before draping Jack's arm over his shoulder.

"Jack, goddamn you look like you've been through hell and back," Samson remarked.

"He's ... dead," Jack murmured with a grimace. "What did you say?" Samson inquired.

"He's fucking dead!" Jack pronounced with a snicker and then collapsed heavily into Samson's arms

"Who's dead? Jack … who's dead?" Samson inquired in a distressed tone, but Jack appeared to be unconscious.

"Please tell me he's still breathing" I said to Samson as my eyes began to well up with tears at the sight of Jack laying motionless upon the floor with his bloody head in Samson's lap. "Aye Jack's still with us, but we must care for him throughout the night. He's taken many blows to the head and he has a severe concussion … there's a good chance me may not wake up," Samson said to me in a somber tone.

"What can we do?" I inquired in a distressed tone, as I filled a bucket with warm water at the bar.

"I don't know what hell Jack has just gone through, but you heard that snicker he let out just before blacked out," Samson said to me, as he dragged Jack into the kitchen.

"So what, he looked delirious," I said to Samson, as I entered the kitchen holding a rag and a bucket of warm water.

"We'll find out if he wakes up," Samson said to me with a sigh, as he laid Jack down upon his bed.

"Don't talk like that. He's going to wake up," I said to Samson in a distressed tone, as tears began to stream from my bleary eyes.

Jack was the only blood relative I had left in this cold world, he may not be perfect, but he's all I had. I could feel Jacks faint breathing as I placed my quivering hand upon his bloody chest. I've never seen Jack in this state before, he was always so bold, so brash and defiant, and now I longed for him to utter a single word, any word that would tell me he's still fighting for life.

"Come on, Jack. You've been through worse than this," Samson said with a grin, as he grabbed some bandage wrap from the shelf.

"Maybe we should take him to the hospital," I said to Samson in a distressed tone.

"No, Jack will be better protected at this speakeasy than any hospital in New York," Samson said to me in a stern tone as he ripped a couple feet of bandage wrap.

"We can't treat him as well as a doctor can. What's more important to you, Samson?" I inquired

"Goddamn it Jack. Why do you always have to be so fucking obstinate? I'll try to get some painkillers for Jack's head. In the meantime: check his breathing every hour, clean his head wound, and lightly wrap that bandage around his head," Samson said to me, as he put on his jacket.

"Wait—I thought you were going to help me care for him throughout the night, I'm not a doctor, I'm not a nurse, I'm not even a—,"

"Shut up! I have a life of my own, a life that doesn't revolve around Jack and his damnable pride. You are more than capable of taking care of him throughout the night. I'll return tomorrow before noon. Don't open the front door to anybody who doesn't know the password. There's a shotgun behind the bar just in case," Samson interjected in a stern tone and then exited the kitchen, leaving me alone with Jack as he lay half alive in bed, while I began to cry over him.

*****

It was 4:56 AM in the speakeasy, as I continued to care for Jack throughout this long and grueling night. If Jack was unconscious then perhaps now was the perfect time for me to unburden myself to him without the fear of him harshly judging me, just like how my mother used to talk to my grandmother's gravestone, but Jack wasn't dead and I needed to speak to someone so desperately, rather than continuing to write my emotions upon the stark white pages of my diary.

"Jack ... Jack can you hear me?" I inquired in a somber tone, as I sat down upon the floor beside the bed where Jack lain still, but there was no response from Jack.

"You don't have to respond back, just get well soon. This diary of mine which I have written in for over ten years has seen more than its share of tears than smiles. I just want to talk to someone the way I talked to my mother. I gave you her will, so you read how she still believes that there is good in you. I just wish we lived in a world where we didn't have to struggle in every way, but I suppose that's naïve of me to think that way now. The nightmare I had a couple nights ago terrified me so much it left me shaking for the remainder of the night. In that nightmare I was being ... I was being raped, but I couldn't see the faces of the men who were raping me. I could only hear their aggressive voices and feel their strength overpowering me. It was so horrible and it made me think about Fernando. There were many times when my mother left the apartment to run errands, leaving me alone with that monster. I remember one evening when he laid down beside me in bed after he just finished drinking himself stupid. His hands would then move all over my body and underneath my nightgown, but whenever I moved away or told him to stop, he would just say 'it's all right honey' and continue until he was satisfied with me. I would always fear being alone with Fernando, and then Johnny came along into my mother's life. At first I thought Johnny might be different than Fernando, but perhaps you're right Jack, perhaps my mother only attracted terrible men," I said to Jack in a somber tone, as I laid my head back upon the ground and turned on my side facing Jack.

"When Johnny came into the picture, Fernando disappeared. My mother and I didn't care what happened to him, whether Johnny killed him, or simply threatened him to stay away from me and my mother, we were both just happy that he was out of our lives, until we then realized the monster that Johnny was, I mean is. I would often see Johnny smack my mother whenever she would talk back to him. I saw him smack her once in the kitchen so hard it sent her falling to the ground. I was afraid of Johnny and also confused as to why my mother would continue to suffer his abuse. My mother told me once that Johnny supported us financially and that we must put up with his outbursts if we don't want to live on the street. I lost respect for my mother when she told me that, but looking back on it now I see that she was so controlled and manipulated by all the fear which Johnny put into her, that she believed she had to endure his abuse in order to somehow keep me off the street. Johnny never hit me, because whenever my mother would see that his temper was looking for someone to abuse, she would always step in and take his smacks. It pained me day after day to see him hurt my mother, but I was just a young girl, and he was the biggest man I've ever seen. I'm so sorry this happened to you Jack. Please wake up. You're the only family I have left," I said to Jack in a tearful tone, as I reached out and placed my hand upon his shoulder. After a couple minutes of crying my bleary eyes out I then rolled over on my side away from Jack and tried to get some much needed rest. I just hope to see Jack awake when I awake this morning.

*****

It was 8:15 AM when I awoke to the sight of Jack still lying in bed.

"Oh you're awake, good. I managed to finagle some painkillers for Jack. He's going to need them when he wakes up," Samson said to me as he entered the kitchen.

"Last night you talked as if there was a good chance Jack wouldn't wake up," I said to Samson as I stood up from the ground with a groan and quickly primped my hair in the mirror beside the freezer.

"Last night I was worn to the bone and frustrated, but I have no doubt Jack will pull through. Don't worry we will soon be hearing his scoldings in no time. Samson said to me as he opened the freezer and took out a bucket of ice.

"Thank you. You're a good friend, Samson," I said to Samson as I stared intently at him.

"Ah think nothing of it. I'm merely ensuring my employment at this speakeasy by caring for Jack," Samson said to me with a dismissive wave.

"Samson, I know Jack is not the type of man to ever admit it out loud, but I know deep down he considers you as his friend. You two have been through so much together," I said to Samson.

"Aye, we have. Don't get all sentimental on me now lass. Just tend to Jack while I get the speakeasy ready to open in fifteen minutes. Mickey will be here to help me tonight as well. Oh, I'll bring in the ol victrola and play some Bessie Smith for Jack. He always liked her music," Samson said with a grin and then exited the kitchen with the bucket of ice in hand.

"That's very sweet of you," I said to Samson with a smile, as he placed the glass bottle of painkillers on the nightstand beside Jack and then exited the kitchen with the bucket of ice in hand.

Samson was a good man. Unlike Johnny, Samson's brutish appearance was not a reflection of his heart. He was kind, and Jack should feel grateful to have a man like him by his side, I for one was.

*****

It was 12:35 PM in the speakeasy as I struggled to keep my eyes open.

I wanted to be the first one Jack sees when he wakes up so I stayed by his side in the kitchen as Samson ran the speakeasy. Seeing Jack now in such a vulnerable state really puts everything perspective for me. When I first met Jack he was a man who was completely indifferent when it came to the pain of others. I don't know why Jack grew into such a man, but that will not stop me from caring for him now.

"Samson told me what happened. How's Jack doing?" Mickey inquired as he entered the kitchen and took off his newsboy hat and held it against his chest in the manner in which one would when they pay their respects at a funeral.

"Mickey, I'm glad you're here. Jack is still breathing, but he has yet to wake up," I replied in a somber tone. "You look exhausted," Mickey remarked.

"I've only gotten a couple hours of sleep at the most," I said to Mickey.

"I sure hope Jack wakes up. He could be in a coma, in which case he needs to be cared for in a hospital," Mickey said to me as he stared intently at Jack with somber downcast eyes. "What are you a doctor now? Stop saying things like that. Jack will be awake and ordering us around in no time, you'll see," I said to Mickey in a distressed tone, as my bleary eyes began to well up with tears.

"I'm sorry, here, take this," Mickey said to me in a somber tone, as he handed me a handkerchief from his jacket.

"I then threw my arms around Mickey without so much as gesturing for the handkerchief, for a shoulder has always been better to cry on for me.

"Jack has been through tough times before. He's definitely the toughest man I've ever known," Mickey remarked, as I continued to cry upon his shoulder while my arms wrapped tightly around him.

"Mickey, has Jack ever told you how much he appreciates your work around here," I inquired.

"No, Jack's not that kind of man to give credit where credit is due, but Samson has," Mickey replied, as our embrace ended all too soon for me.

"Well … I appreciate all the work you do around here," I said to Mickey.

"Thank you. I wish we lived in a time where hard work really paid off, but what more could I hope for, I'm just an orphan after all," Mickey said to me with a scoff.

"Stop talking like that. You are more than that life, we are more than that life," I said to Mickey in a stern tone, as I grabbed his hand and stared intently into his downcast eyes.

"Hayley … whenever I'm with you I feel so—,"

"Mickey, get over here, son," Samson interjected in a stern tone, as he popped his head into the doorframe of the kitchen.

"Yes sir," Mickey said to Samson and then exited the kitchen.

I held onto Mickey's hand as hard as I could before he inevitably broke our bond and scampered over to the bar to help Samson.

Dear Diary,
June 12th, 6:45 PM

I thought I'd write to you for now, seeing as how Jack has the music of Bessie Smith to keep him company. Her voice is pleasant and I see why Jack is so fond of her. She sings with such pain, yet she has become a very successful singer as a result of that pain in her heart. If only I could channel all the pain I feel every day into something profitable, but I lack the boldness for such an endeavor. Jack tells me I'm just like my mother, but I always see myself as a timid lamb compared to my mother's bold personality.

I wanted to kiss Mickey again today, but once again, our precious time together was interrupted. The first time we almost kissed was in Jack's Pontiac and now in the kitchen. I felt safe around Mickey, not just in the physical sense of him protecting me, but I felt emotionally safe with him most of all. I could unburden all my sorrows to him without fear of him condemning me in any way.

Now as I continue to stare at Jack lying still as his chest rises and lowers from faint breathing, I can't help but wonder what kind of man he will be when he wakes up. My mother told me that near death experiences give people a clear insight on life. I admit I didn't fully understand what she meant at the time she told me that, but now I understand. I don't expect Jack to be a different man when he wakes up, but I still want him to know that I care for him. I sensed that Jack isn't used to people expression affection towards him, but that is all going to change when he wakes up. I still believe what my mother said in her will about Jack to be true. There is good in him, and it may be very fleeting at times, but I've felt it.

I then turned off the victrola and sat down on the floor beside Jack. I missed Jack's voice already, even when he was scolding me, I yearned to hear his voice.

"Jack I want to sing a song to you my mother used to sing to me. I know I'm no Bessie Smith, but maybe you can find the same comfort in my voice as I did with my mother's voice when she would sing it to me," I said to Jack in a somber tone.

"My dear ... when you awaken
You'll never be forsaken
I'll cherish you through and through
But in your deepest sleep
When dreams enrapture you
I won't let them capture you
So slumber now without a care

Though I still yearn to see your eyes again
Those shinning stars that greet me when
The morning sun begins to rise
But for now in deepest sleep
I'll cherish you through and through

When you return to me
From that tranquil fantasy
Remember how this world awaits you
But now in deepest sleep
Within my heart, I shall keep
Your very spirit through and through

Your light shall never be taken
My dear … when you awaken,"

I sang in a somber tone, as I fought to hold back tears. Singing that lullaby to Jack brought back a rush of emotions to me. Visions of my mother sitting at my bedside singing me that song were some of the most comforting memories I have of her now.

I then began to burst into tears, as I laid my head upon the bed beside Jack's shoulder.

"You sing better than you mother," a familiar voice remarked with a snicker, as I quickly lifted my tear sodden face to the sight of Jack smiling at me.

"Jack you're awake," I remarked as I quickly wrapped my arms around Jack.

"Ah easy, kid, There's not a bone in my body that doesn't hurt right now," Jack said to me with groan and grimace, but I kept my arms tightly wrapped around him, for I was so overcome with emotions of loss and happiness at that moment and I didn't want to let him go.

"I thought I lost you, just like my mother," I said to Jack in a tearful tone, as I slowly released Jack from my tight embrace. "Fear not, kid. Ol Jack Dansby won't leave this world that easily," Jack said to me with a snicker and grimace, as he slowly sat upright in bed with a groan.

"Samson, Mickey. Jack's awake!" I shouted with a smile, as I poked my head out of the kitchen doorframe.

Samson and Mickey then both scampered into the kitchen, as I sat back down upon the floor and held Jack's hand.

"Welcome back Jack. When we found you, you were beaten half to death," Samson remarked with a grin, as he poured a glass of water and took out two painkillers from the bottle upon the nightstand.

"We're happy to see you awake, Jack. This speakeasy wouldn't be the same without you," Mickey said with a warm smile.

"Ah … how long was I out, Samson," Jack inquired with a hissing groan as he clutched the bandages on his head.

"Why are you asking me? I was busy running this place in your absence. Ask your niece, she hasn't left your side since you collapsed in my arms," Samson replied with a snicker.

"Two days," I said to Jack.

"Take these. They will help with the immense pain I'm sure your feeling right now," Samson said to Jack, as he handed him a glass of water and two painkillers.

"What is it?" Jack inquired, as he stared at the pills in his hand.

"I just told you, they're painkillers," Samson replied.

"I'm not taking heroin Samson. I don't care how much pain I'm in right now. I have enough addictions already.

"Suite yourself Jack," Samson said to Jack with a sigh, as he grabbed the bottle from off the nightstand.

"I'll care for you Jack. What do you need?" I inquired.

"A handle of bourbon, some ice, and a hamburger would be heaven right now," Jack replied with a grin.

"I'll get you the burger," Mickey said to Jack.

"I'll get you the bourbon and ice," I said to Jack, as I sprung upright from the floor.

"Whoa, hold your horses you two. Jack, we will care to your every need after you answer this question," Samson said to Jack in a stern tone.

"What is it Samson," Jack inquired with a sigh. "Who's dead," Samson inquired.

"You three are if you don't get me what I asked for," Jack replied in a stern tone.

"No just before you collapsed two days ago you said to me and Hayley that 'he's dead' in a rather maniacal manner," Samson said to Jack in a stern tone.

"Samson's right. You seemed so happy. So who was it, Jack, who is dead.

"The very man who has threatened are lives for the past couple months, Johnny the hammer O'Connor ... I killed him," Jack replied in a stern tone.

"Holy fuck, so you really took him out for good this time. Are you sure?" Samson inquired with a wide-eyed stare, as he knelt down on the floor next to me and placed his hand upon Jack's shoulder.

"I witnessed his death with my own eyes. He sank to the bottom of the Hudson. I then waited five minutes just in case the bastard had some life left in him to surface, but he didn't," Jack replied.

"I can't believe Johnny is really dead," I remarked, with a wide-eyed stare at Jack, Samson and Mickey.

"Ah believe it, kid. I made sure with every breath in my body that he would no longer threaten us," Jack said to me with a grimace.

"So are we safe now that Johnny is gone," Mickey inquired. "For now, but when his associates find out about his death they will surely come to this speakeasy. I saw him, Hayley, for a brief moment I saw the leader of the Five Points Gang at Pier 45 before he took his leave," Jack said to me.

"Then my mother's will was right. Jack, I'm just happy Johnny didn't take you from me like he did my mother," I said to Jack, as I wrapped my arms around his waist.

"You never fail to surprise me Jack," Samson remarked with a snicker.

"I guess I'll take that as a compliment. Now, am I going have to go get that hamburger and bourbon myself?" Jack inquired.

"I'll go to *Sal's Diner* and get you that burger Jack," Mickey said and then scampered out of the kitchen.

"I'll get you that bourbon with plenty of ice," I said to Jack, and then scampered out of the kitchen.

I could tell that Jack enjoyed being waited on hand and foot. He spent a good deal of his life caring for others and risking his life to provide for them all of these comforts which are now outlawed, out of all people he deserves to be waited on. "Not that bourbon. Jack prefers the 'Old Tub' whiskey bourbon," Samson said to me, as he grabbed the half empty bottle behind me.

"Oh all right. I'm sure you know all about Jack's preferences," I said to Samson with a smile as I grabbed the bottle from Samson.

"Aye, painfully so, Jack and I enjoy simple pleasures in life, but there are certain things in which we are quite particular about," Samson said to me with a snicker.

"What about women?" I inquired with a grin.

"Most of the women who are granted entry into this speakeasy are old barflies, but every once in awhile a real dame will grace us," Samson replied, as he wiped down the bar.

"A dame like Ms. Dubois," I said to Samson with a grin. "Aye, I can tell Jack is smitten with that flapper," Samson said to me, as he shook his head.

"Why are you shaking your head, Ms Dubois is a lovely woman," I said to Samson.

"She is indeed. It's just that Jack is always the one to take it one step too far when it comes to a woman like her," Samson said to me.

"What do you mean?" I inquired.

"I mean the last woman Jack was smitten over ended up trying to kidnap you," Samson replied.

"You're talking about Bernadette. Well, I hope Jack learned his lesson with her. She may be beautiful on the outside, but she is vile on the inside," I said to Samson.

"Or Jack made her that way when he smacked her down," Samson said to me.

"Don't blame Jack. Sure he was wrong in hitting a woman, but hopefully she taught him a lesson in how to treat a lady," I said to Samson.

"Bernadette is no lady and Jack is not a man who learns lessons," Samson said to me.

"I don't believe that about Jack. If he didn't learn from his past mistakes then he would surely be dead by now. The decision he made by shunning my mother for leaving with Johnny was all based in his own pain. Jack may be callous and stubborn, but I believe he learns from his past," I said to Samson.

"I hope you're right. For now let us enjoy this moment of calm that Jack has given us by removing Johnny from our lives, however small the moment may be," Samson said to me with a sigh.

"Here's your drink. How are you feeling?" I inquired, as I scooped out a handful of ice from the fridge and dumped it into a rubber pouch Jack was holding out in front of him with two hands.

"Ah I feel like I boxed three rounds with Joe Lois," Jack replied with a grimace, as he placed the sack of ice upon his head.

"Here's your drink," I said to Jack as I knelt down on the floor beside him and placed the tumbler of bourbon on the nightstand.

"Thanks kid. Listen … when I was getting my head pounding in by Johnny I thought of you, and how if I died on that Pier, then there would be nobody left to defend you from that bastard," Jack said to me and then took a sip of bourbon.

"I'm in your debt for risking your life in such a chivalrous manner," I said to Jack in a timid tone.

"What does that word mean Miss Professor?" Jack inquired with a snicker.

"Chivalrous, it means you acted in the manner of a knight to defend me," I replied.

"Oh I'm no such measure of a man, kid. I'm a killer now, just like Samson, but it felt good to end Johnny once and for all," Jack said to me and then took another sip of bourbon with a grimace.

"No Jack. A killer is the wrong term to use. You may have killed Johnny, but you're not a killer by nature. You killed him to defend us. That's an act of chivalry at its purest," I said to Jack as I held his bruised and cut up left hand.

"Comparing me to a knight, are you sure you didn't take a blow to the head, kid," Jack inquired with a snicker. "I've never been surer. Jack … I—,"

"I got your hamburger Jack. The waitress was really rude to me though," Mickey interjected as he entered the kitchen.

"Good I'm starving. Jack said to Mickey as he sat upright in bed with a groan.

"I must say you're the bravest man I know, Jack," Mickey remarked, as he took out the hamburger from the brown paper bag and placed it upon a plate along with a side of fries.

"Yes yes, I'm a knight, I'm the bravest man in the world, but for now could you two just let me eat in peace," Jack pronounced, and then took a large bite out of the hamburger.

"Call me if you need anything," I said to Jack, and then exited the kitchen with Mickey.

"I still can't believe Jack took out Johnny. If all the stories I've heard about that man are true, then Jack must've been fighting for his dear life," Mickey said to me as we sat down at the bar.

"'Believe none of what you hear and half of what you see'," I said to Mickey.

"Oh really why do you say that?" Mickey inquired with a grin.

"It's a saying from one of my favorite writers Edgar Allan Poe. 'Believe none of what you hear and half of what you see,' it means that we must always question everything, because people can deceive us as well as our eyes," I replied.

"Poe … I've heard of him, he's dead right?" Mickey inquired.

"Yes he's long been dead, but his incredible writing will live on forever," I replied.

"Ah Poe was too morbid for my taste, besides Yeats was a more respected writer," Samson said to me as he shook his head.

"Who says Poe yearned for his writing to be respected. All he cared about was telling macabre stories in such a beautiful manner," I said to Samson.

"I should read more. It's just as you said, people in this day and age will fill your head with such lies all for their own personal gain," Mickey said to me.

"Samson … should we feel safer now that Johnny is out of the picture," I inquired.

"Johnny is gone, not the Five Points Gang. Now the way I see it is the Don of the Five Points gang will now have two options regarding the four of us. Option 1, he will back off and leave us be or Option 2, he will retaliate," Samson replied.

"Jack told me you were part of a gang back in Ireland, Samson," Mickey remarked.

"Is this true?" I inquired with wide eyes, as Samson stared back at the both of us with a brooding look on his face.

"Aye it's unfortunately true, but my past life does not dictate the man I am now. Johnny and I may hail from the same homeland, but I'm no killer," Samson pronounced.

"It's all right. I know you're no such man as Johnny," I said to Samson, as he wiped down the bar in an aggressive manner. "So Samson … how does it feel to kill a man?" Mickey inquired.

"Mickey, stop," I said to Mickey in a stern tone, as Samson stared intently at him.

"It's all right. It's a feeling I hope you never have to experience son, a feeling of soul crushing guilt. Even though you may try your best to justify your killing, it won't stop that aching feeling," Samson pronounced.

"Do you think Jack feels that way now over killing Johnny?" I inquired.

"Johnny was an attack dog who needed to be put down sooner or later. As for Jack, I believe there is a shred of guilt that will stay with him from killing Johnny," Samson replied with a sigh.

"He killed my mother, Jack shouldn't—,"

"Feel guilt, because killing always justifies killing. Let me tell you something Ms. Hayley, If we all live by that code, then we are fucking doomed as a race," Samson said to me in a stern tone.

"Let's go," I said to Mickey as I took his hand and stood up from the barstool.

"Where are we going," Mickey inquired, as I walked towards the front door of the speakeasy.

"Some place where death doesn't weigh heavy on my mind," I replied, as I gestured for Samson to open the door. "What place is that," Mickey replied.

"You'll see," I replied with a smile, as Samson unlocked the front door of the speakeasy with a grunt.

"Wait … just because Johnny is dead doesn't mean you two are completely safe. Keep an eye out for each other," Samson said in a stern tone.

"Don't worry. I'll keep two eyes out for her at all times," Mickey said with a grin, as I giggled.

Mickey and I then exited the speakeasy to the sight of something most gruesome.

"What is that?" I inquired, as I pointed down with wide eyes.

"It looks like … a skull, but there's still some skin and hair on it," Mickey remarked.

"Could this be the Five Points Gang sending us a message?" I inquired, as I gripped Mickey's hand tighter.

"Forget about this," Mickey said and then kicked the skull down the alley into Minetta Street.

"Why did you do that?" I inquired in a distressed tone, as Mickey just continued to snicker as the half decomposed head crashed into car after car.

"Come on show me this place where death won't weigh heavy on our minds," Mickey said with a smile, as he lightly pulled my hand.

"It's awfully far away, and it looks like Samson hasn't gotten the Pontiac back from the Pier," I said to Mickey, as we walked down Minetta Street.

"Then we'll take a taxicab there," Mickey said to me as he signaled for a taxicab.

Within a few short moments, a taxicab then stopped immediately in front of Mickey and me.

"Our chariot awaits," Mickey said to me with a grin, as we then entered the taxicab in a zealous manner.

"Mickey, I don't have any money, how are we going to pay the fare?" I inquired, as the taxicab driver turned around and stared at us with a stern look on his grizzled old face.

"Don't worry, I have enough money to pay the fare, as long as you don't want to go to upstate New York," Mickey replied with a grin.

"To *Tompkins Square Park* please," I said to the taxicab driver.

"What's so special about this park?" Mickey inquired with a grin.

"It may be more special to me than others, just because my mother and I used to frequent this park whenever Johnny was away. I remember so many German immigrants in this park living happily with their children. If only the rest of New York was as welcoming as *Tompkins Square Park*," I replied.

"You've got my interest now, so you consider *Tompkins Square Park* to be nicer than *Washington Square Park*?" Mickey inquired.

"Absolutely, did you know that there are thousands of bodies buried under *Washington Square Park*?" I inquired.

"Wow, I had no idea. I'm sure there are many secrets to New York that remain hidden to this day," Mickey replied.

"I'm sure you're right about that. There's no way for a city as large as New York to not have many secrets, but I for one like to divulge them," I said to

Mickey.

"What does divulge mean?" Mickey inquired.

"It means to make a secret known to the public," I replied. I enjoyed talking to Mickey. He looked at me with such kind eyes which always seemed to make me feel comfortable in any situation. He was always a curious boy who was always eager to learn, which I appreciated wholeheartedly. Whenever I was around him I felt as if I could be myself with him in ways I could never do with Samson or even Jack. Mickey remained sweet in a world of bitterness, and he was my best friend, or perhaps more.

"Looks like we're here," Mickey said as the taxicab stopped.

"Your fare is 75 cents," the grizzled old taxicab driver pronounced in a barking tone

"Here you go, sir. Mickey said to the taxicab driver, as he paid him the fare and exited the taxicab.

"Oh thank you," I said to Mickey as I took his hand which was extended towards me in a bashful manner.

"It's so crowded here," Mickey remarked as we entered the Park hand in hand.

"Oh look there's a market," I remarked in a zealous tone as I pointed at the bustling market located at the center of the park with various children were playing with their pet dogs in such a joyous manner.

"This park seems like a safe haven for German immigrants," Mickey remarked, as we walked through the crowed park. "They all deserve a chance at happiness. That's why they came here. I just hope they find it," I said to Mickey.

"How could you not be happy on a beautiful day like this?" Mickey inquired with a smile. Mickey's joy then evoked a warm memory from within me as I stared fondly into his kind eyes.

*****

"You see Hayley. Just look at all the children," Mom said to me, as she lifted me up with a smile.

"They look so happy," I said to my Mom as we walked through the park as kids ran past us.

"Most of these children came here from another country, but we must treat them as if they are New Yorkers," Mom said to me as we sat down on a bench underneath s big maple tree.

"Let's take this god awful bonnet off you, sweetheart," Mom said to me as she took off her bonnet the same time she took off mine with a smile.

"Why do we always put these bonnets on when we go back home?" I asked as mom combed her beautiful blonde hair.

"Johnny prefers us to look that way, but for now we can look however we please, my darling," Mom said to me with a smile, as he jostled my hair with both her hands and then kissed me on the forehead.

"I'm afraid to be happy around him," I said to mom with a frown.

"So am I, sweetheart. Listen … men like Johnny will never understand what makes you beautiful, but you couldn't look more beautiful to me right now with your red hair blowing in the breeze. Remember that, darling," Mom said to me with a smile.

*****

I continued to smile at Mickey, as a warm spring breeze blew through my hair in the same manner as it did when I was at this park with my mother five years ago. Being at *Tompkins Square Park* with Mickey was what my heart yearned for. I didn't want this moment to end, as Mickey and I continued to stroll through the park.

"I sure am hungry let's get something to eat," Mickey said as we walked up to a stand at the market.

"What are these, sir," I inquired, as Mickey and I walked up to a most sumptuous aroma emanating from a food cart.

"Kartoffelpuffer," the burly vendor with a curly mustache replied.

Mickey and I then looked at each other and giggled for we did not speak a word of German and had no idea what the vendor said to us.

"Judging by that smell I don't care what they are. We'll take two," Mickey said to the vendor, as he held up two fingers. "Mickey was adventurous. He had the kind of spirit that brought at smile to my face every time he spoke. The vendor fried the German street food in a quick manner as Mickey and I practically drooled while watching him in the manner of two dogs at a dinner table.

"Two dollars," The vendor said to us, as he wrapped the fried food in paper and handed it to us with a smile.

"Here you go," Mickey said to the vendor as he paid him and then quickly took a large bite out of the steaming food.

"How is it," I inquired with a smile.

"Oh it's hot, but really good. It's a potato cake," Mickey replied.

"It's delicious. Let's sit down on that bench under the maple tree and eat these," I said to Mickey with a mouth full of the fried potato cake.

"Mickey … do you ever think about how your life would be if your parents were still alive," I inquired in a timid tone. "I used to. I used to think that I would be a different man than I am now if my mom and dad were still alive, but as time passed; I found myself no longer thinking about my parents that died when I was only three years old," Mickey replied in a somber tone, as he finished eating the last of his fried potato cake in one large bite.

"I'm sorry. I wish you could've known your parents," I said to Mickey in a somber tone, as I placed my hand upon his.

"A nurse at the foster home told me that my mom died from influenza," Mickey said to me in a somber tone.

"My dad died in the war. He was actually on his way home to meet me for the first time when his platoon was ambushed," Mickey replied.

"I'm sorry Mickey. I wanted to go to a place where death didn't weigh heavy on our minds and now I have you talking about death once again," I said to Mickey.

"It's all right. I guess there's no escaping death in this day and age," Mickey said to me in a somber tone.

"We should go inside. It looks like it's going to rain soon," I said to Mickey.

"So you're afraid of a little rain," Mickey said to me with a grin.

"There are many things in this world that I'm afraid of, but rain isn't one of them," I said to Mickey with a grin as I shoved him in a playful manner.

"Just look at all of these German immigrants. Do you suppose that they're happy right now," Mickey inquired as he played with a toothpick in his mouth.

"Judging by the looks on their faces I would say they're very happy," I replied with a smile.

"I'm happy right now, sitting here with you, Hayley. I didn't think I could ever talk to someone the way I talk to you," Mickey said to me with a smile before quickly averting his gaze with a giggle as I stared intently back at him.

"I feel the same way, Mickey," I said to Mickey, as I scooted closer to him on the bench underneath the maple tree.

Mickey then stared directly into my eyes which sent my heart racing. He almost never looks into my eyes for more than a brief moment, but I felt that he wanted to kiss me, as we both leaned in close to each other. A sudden roar of thunder followed by a downpour of rain stopped Mickey and I from kissing. Were we always fated to come so close, yet never share our first kiss? "Let's get back home. It looks like this storm will rage on throughout the night," Mickey said to me, as we stood up from the park bench and then ran across *Tompkins Square Park* hand in hand to the street.

"Taxi," Mickey shouted, as he whistled and waved his hand at a taxicab driving down the street.

"Were to?" the taxicab driver inquired, as Mickey and I entered the taxicab in a hasty manner.

"Her stop is on Minetta Street," Mickey replied.

"You're not coming in the speakeasy?" I inquired with a wide-eyed stare, as Mickey took off his newsboy hat with a sigh.

"Sorry I have to get back home now," Mickey replied.

The remainder of the taxicab ride back to the speakeasy was spent in what I could only describe as a silent desire, which kept Mickey and I right on the brink of kissing once more, but neither of us was bold enough in that moment to make the first move. In the silence, I thought to myself, what would my mother want me to do in this moment? She would no doubt tell me to not suppress my feelings, for they are beautiful and make me who I am, but I've grown too accustomed to suppressing my feelings over the past couple of months in the speakeasy, and now I feel as if my heart has shied away from what it so desperately needs right now, love.

*****

It was 8:25 PM as the taxicab stopped in the back alley of the speakeasy.

"75 cents," the taxicab driver pronounced in a barking tone, as Mickey nervously searched through a pocket on his jacket for the money as I nervously ran my fingers through my damp hair.

"Well I guess this is your stop. I had a great time today," Mickey said to me in a timid tone and smile, but didn't move in close to try and kiss me.

"So did I," I said to Mickey and then opened the door of the taxicab.

I couldn't stand the tension any longer. I learned over the past couple of months that there was no 'perfect time' to express your affection towards somebody. You simply had to seize the opportunity no matter where or when it presented itself to you, and that's just what I was going to do with Mickey now. I was halfway out of the taxicab when I then stopped and quickly sat back down closely to Mickey, as he stared at me with his kind eyes full of anticipation and fear. I then gently placed my hand upon Mickey's cheek and kissed him.

"Well … good night," I said to Mickey with a smile as our lips parted.

"Good night," Mickey said to me as the beating of my heart seemed to drown out the sound of the pouring rain outside.

I then exited the taxicab and waved good bye to Mickey with a smile, as he waved back at me through the back window of the taxicab as it slowly drove out of sight down the back alley of Minetta Street.

*****

"Ah look whose back. I thought you and that boy would've stayed out till the break of dawn," Samson said to me with a snicker as I entered the speakeasy with a feeling of floating carrying my every step.

"The rain cut our activities short. So how's Jack doing?" I inquired with a smile," as I walked up to the bar.

"Aye but you don't look the slightest bit sad now do you? Jack is sleeping off his medicine of bourbon as usual," Samson replied as he pointed to the kitchen.

It was slow in the speakeasy which was a perfect atmosphere for me to write in my diary before I went to sleep. So I quietly sat down upon the chair in front of the small desk in the kitchen and then began to write.

Dear Diary,
June 13th, 9:00 PM

This must be what heaven feels like. My heart is still racing from my first kiss with Mickey. In that precious moment, I didn't feel the weight of the world bearing down on me. I didn't feel a looming fear from the Five Points Gang. I didn't feel a heavy sadness crushing my heart from my mother's death. I didn't feel insecure over my appearance compared to all the women in New York who were exceedingly more beautiful than me. All I felt at that moment was Mickey's lips gently pressing against mine. It was magical, just like one of Shakespeare's sonnets, and now I finally know firsthand what love feels like.

I didn't think I could ever experience such a day in my life. I thought there was no love in this world for a girl like me, but I've never been so happy to be so wrong. Mickey was my kindred spirit, he possessed not a shred of hatred in his heart, and if he did, he certainly didn't let that hatred consume him, like the other two men I live with do on a daily basis. The feeling I felt in my heart whenever I was around Mickey was pure and gentle and I needed that feeling in my life. Even now as I sit here in this dismal kitchen close to Jack who nearly died in his fight with a man who killed my mother I'm filled with warmth from Mickey's kiss. Mickey was the complete opposite of every man I've ever met. In this day and age, most men looked at me with such coldness in their eyes, as if I wasn't worthy to be loved, but not Mickey, he looks at me as if I was the only girl left in this world who was worthy to be loved.

So now I end this diary entry with a warm sense of joy filling my heart. I hope to dream about Mickey when I go to sleep, so I can see him once more. In this world full of suffering, Mickey was my joy. In this world full of villains, Mickey was my one true hero.

CHAPTER 7:
LUCKY LUCIANO
- JACK -

I was no goddamn hero the way Hayley and Mickey framed me out to be. I was just a desperate man fighting for his life, and just what do I have to show for it now but a throbbing skull as a reminder of the hammer's final blow. I felt strong enough today to start working at the bar, because I sure as hell wasn't about to let Samson take over fully. This was my speakeasy after all and two days is far too long for me to be out of commission.

"Jack you're standing," Hayley remarked, as she scampered over to me and draped my arm over her shoulder, but unlike Samson, I could tell that Hayley's dainty body wouldn't be enough support me if I fell, so I carried most of my weight as I hobbled to the fridge.

"Are you sure you're well enough to be walking so soon? Any other man would be in the hospital right now," Hayley said to me with a wide-eyed stare, as I searched through the fridge for anything that would stop the throbbing pain I felt all over my body.

"I'm not just any other man, kid. I have a business to run. Samson should be here soon to help open up," I said as I pointed to the bar.

"All right, I'm glad to see your strength is returning, Jack," Hayley said to me and then exited the kitchen.

What would we do now? That rat Chip Benowitz was out of the picture so there was no way for us to do any more liquor dealings. I had to come up with a plan once again to keep this speakeasy afloat. To stay afloat in the sea of drunks that was Greenwich Village was my objective and no matter how pitiful it seemed to others, I had to continue bootlegging at any cost.

"Ah good morning sunshine," Samson said with a snicker as he entered the speakeasy and walked up to me behind the bar. "You're early," I remarked as I placed my hand on my forehead with a grimace.

"So how do you feel Jack the bruiser?" Samson inquired with a snicker, as he wiped down the bar.

"I'm no bruiser," I sad to Samson while shaking my head. "I was just trying to come up with a boxing name for you Jack. Seeing as how you can take a punch better than almost any man I've ever seen," Samson said to me with a smile. "How about Jack the Ripper," I said to Samson with a snicker.

"Far too English inspired. Do you really want to be associated with a murderer who was never caught?" Samson inquired with a scoff, as I walked over to the stage.

"Listen, are liquor supply is dwindling, and judging by our low inventory, it looks like we won't make it to the end of this month," I said to Samson with a sigh.

"Aye, I'm all ears if you have any bright ideas," Samson said to me.

"I know what I have to do. It's our last chance effort at keeping this speakeasy afloat," I said to Samson.

"What are you going to do, Jack?" Samson inquired as he stared intently at me, as I put on my Jacket and hat, and tucked my pistol between the waist-band of my pants.

"Just trust me. You got the Pontiac back from the Pier, right?" I inquired.

"Aye, I retrieved your precious Pontiac last night while your niece was out with Mickey doing god knows what," Samson replied.

"Leave her be. The kid actually had some rare time to be a kid for once," I said to Samson with a grin.

"Are you sure you don't need me to drive? You remind me of my uncle Patrick the night he staggered home from the local pub after fighting the meanest bastard in town," Samson inquired, as I stumbled to the front door of the speakeasy.

"No, you need to open the speakeasy in 15 minutes. So did your uncle win that fight?" I inquired.

"Of course he did. He's a Monaghan after all," Samson replied with a snicker.

"I'll be back around happy hour," I said to Samson as I unlocked the door and exited the speakeasy.

*****

It was 11:45 AM as I drove north to *Chelsea*.

I now had to enlist the help of a man who I did business with when I was in my twenties. Are dealings were brief back then and I wonder if he would even recognize me now, but time can be a fickle dame, and right when you least expect it, you're instantly lured back to a life you swore you would never return to, and to a person you never thought you would see again.

"Watch it jackass!" a taxicab driver shouted at me, as I quickly slammed on the breaks of the Pontiac to stop myself from crashing into him.

Samson was right, I was still very much staggered from my fight with Johnny, but I wasn't about to remain bedridden for weeks while the speakeasy fell into financial ruin all around me. I had work to do, and the proprietor of the last remaining speakeasy in Chelsea was the man I needed to see right now. Last I heard from Samson, there were only two speakeasies still running in the lower west side of New York, and soon there would only be one left unless I enlisted the help of *The Sly Troubadour* located in the back alley of Little West 12th Street. Although the Meatpacking District was more hip to the scene of renegade bootleggers such as me, I would still have to keep my guard up every time I walked down a back alley in New York. I remembered the password to my former partner's speakeasy. I just hope he hasn't changed it. I then knocked three times on the front door of the speakeasy and stood quietly with anticipation.

"Password," a voice said to me in a stern tone as the brass window on the door slid open in a swift manner.

"*Absentia*" I said to the eyes staring back at me through the brass window in a stern tone.

"Welcome to *the Sly Troubadour*," the eyes said to me as the front door of the speakeasy opened.

I entered the speakeasy of my former partner to the sight of a flourishing crowd of patrons all of which were dressed to the nines. I then noticed the man I had my eye out for after a couple of moments surveying the scene of his thriving speakeasy that was more successful than mine in every way.

There he was at the stage playing a jaunty piano riff with an upright bass player and saxophonist backing him up. I then lit a cigarette and took a smoke, as I continued to watch the proprietor of this speakeasy charm and dazzle all his patrons in a way which I have failed to do so in the past couple of months. He was pounding on those ivories with all of his heart as if this was the last song he would every play before the police shut down his speakeasy, and it very well may be.

"Thank you folks, enjoy the rest of your afternoon at *the Sly Troubadour*," the man pronounced with a smile through the microphone, as he caught a glimpse of me. He then gestured for me to meet him over at the bar with a nod, as he scampered off the stage with a towel draped over his neck.

"Avery Briggs, you sure haven't missed a step on the ivories," I said to the man with a grin as I walked up to the bar. "Why if it isn't Jack Dansby, my former partner in crime. You look just as disheveled and put through the wringer as you did eight years ago," Avery remarked, as a flapper dame walked up to him and gave him a peck on his flushed cheek with a smile.

I wish I could say the same rude remark towards Avery as he did to me, but the man hasn't aged in the manner which a proprietor of a speakeasy should age. He was slender, tall, with sandy hair and a five o clock shadow to match. Avery's clear blue eyes seemed to glimmer in a way that a child's eyes would glimmer during Christmas morning, and I despised everything about his debonair, movie star good looks.

"It seems that your little joint has become quite the talk of the town in Chelsea," I remarked, as I sat down at the brass gilded bar which put my bar to shame by comparison.

"So why are you here, Jack?" Avery inquired. "You mean I can't just stop by for a visit," I replied

"You're not the kind of man who stops by for visits," Avery said to me with a grin.

"Encore Avery," a crowd of patrons shouted in unison as they sat at the tables in front of the stage.

"Sorry, sorry, I have other pressing matters to attend to, but send all of that love to my band mates on the stage," Avery pronounced with a smile

"I'm taking of now, honey," another flapper girl said to Avery, and then gave him a peck on the cheek.

"Chelsea, I'd like you to meet Jack Dansby, an old former partner of mine," Avery said to the flapper girl, as he gestured to me.

"Oh what happened to your face," Chelsea remarked.

"Chelsea, show some decorum in *the Sly Troubadour* for once," Avery said to Chelsea in a stern tone.

"Of course honey, I'll try to work on that just for you," Chelsea said to Avery and then walked away with a grin.

"Oh what a charming broad," I remarked in a sarcastic tone and scoff.

"Pay her no mind, Jack. She's a bit rough around the edges, but then again all flappers are," Avery said to me with a snicker. "Your speakeasy seems to be very popular with their kind, she's the fourth one I've seen walk in and out of here," I said to Avery.

"It's the location, and also the fact that I make it known that flapper girls can feel free while they're in my speakeasy," Avery said to me.

"I would be lying if I told you I wasn't shocked by how well your speakeasy is doing," I said to Avery.

"So why are you here Jack?" Avery inquired with a sigh. "You're aware of the Five Points Gang, right?" I replied. "Of course, are they the ones responsible for that battered face of yours?" Avery inquired.

I should've never come here. Avery and his speakeasy was my competition when it came to bootlegging, and it seemed that he was succeeding where I was failing. *The Sly Troubadour* was a reflection of everything the *Jack of All Trades* could be, what it should be, but it wasn't. As much as it pained me to look into Avery's smiling mug and ask for help, I didn't see any other option.

"My sister was killed recently at the hands of her boyfriend who was one of the top attack dogs for the Five Points Gang," I said to Avery.

"I'm sorry to hear that Jack. You have my condolences. I'm sure she was a fine woman," Avery said to me.

"Three days ago I killed that man who killed my sister at Pier 45, but the Five Points Gang has posted my face, along with Mickey, Samson, and Hayley up so we can't do any dealings without fear of being caught by them. They have tightened their squeeze over this city over the past 8 years and now they are at the top. They even have influence over the NYPD. So that's why I've come to you," I said to Avery.

"You mean to tell me that you and your crew are wanted by the Five Points Gang and you come to my speakeasy? Once again, you're putting my business in jeopardy, Jack," Avery said to me with a sigh.

"I helped you start up this speakeasy goddamn it. Don't pretend like you don't remember those first couple of weeks where you didn't have a dime to your name and you were panhandling on the street. I taught you how to bootleg successfully in this day and age, and it appears I taught you too well," I said to Avery in a stern tone.

"So what exactly are you asking me for, to split half of my liquor dealings with you just because you and your crew are wanted by the Five Points Gang? I wouldn't survive if I did that Jack," Avery said to me in a stern tone while shaking his head. "No just a quarter of your liquor deals, and only for a couple of weeks. I need to keep my speakeasy running in Greenwich Village, Avery. Not just for my own pride, but for the sake of my niece as well," I said to Avery.

"Jack … you taught me a lot when it comes to this world of bootlegging, and I'm sorry that you and your family are marked by the Five Points Gang, but leave me out of it all. Now you're welcome to stop by here any time and I'll give you a drink or two on the house, but I cannot do business with a marked man," Avery said in a somber tone, as he stared intently at me.

"You know there was a time when I once saw you as a brother. I see now what a little success can do to a man. Good luck Avery. Oh and if that time should ever come when you need my help, just remember my face right now," I said to Avery in a stern tone and scowl and then stormed out of *the Sly Troubadour*.

*****

It was 4:37 PM as I parked the Pontiac in the shady alley beside the speakeasy.

I should turn him in to the police, that smug bastard. That thought continued to race through my head, as I sat in the Pontiac with a sense of overwhelming hopelessness bearing down on me. If I did turn in Avery to the police, then he would turn me in as well, but he has far more profit to lose than me, so for the time being I would have to let *the Sly Troubadour* remain in business.

I then unlocked the front door and entered the speakeasy to a miserable but expected sight. Samson was at the bar, with only two patrons drinking, while Hayley was writing in her book at the corner table.

"Is any one even alive in here?" I inquired in a stern tone. "I take it your business endeavor didn't fall through," Samson said to me, as I walked up to the bar with a sigh.

"Do you remember Avery Briggs?" I inquired, as I poured myself a shot of bourbon.

"Aye, that strapping lad you used to bootleg with when I first met you. What about him?" Samson replied.

"Well that arrogant bastard now runs the most successful speakeasy in Chelsea, maybe even in the entire west side of Manhattan," I said to Samson with a scoff, as I took the shot of bourbon with a grimace.

"So what was it like there? Maybe I should go see if he needs any help," Samson inquired with a snicker.

"*The Sly Troubadour* was everything I wanted the *Jack of All Trades* to be, and more. The patrons, the décor, the entertainment, everything was straight out of a movie set," I replied.

"So I take it the man turned you down when you tried to do business with him," Samson said to me.

"Once he heard I was marked by the Five Points Gang he treated me like an outsider, like he was so much higher up than me when it came to morals. I mean for god sake I taught the man everything he knows about bootlegging," I said to Samson in a stern tone.

"I've been looked down on my entire life by the upperclassman of this city Jack. Just because I'm an Irish immigrant, but now you see how it feels," Samson said to me.

"Are you enjoying this Samson? You know that we are done now. This is the end for this speakeasy. Our liquor supply will dry up within the next two weeks," I said to Samson in a stern tone, as I ripped off my tie and threw it into the kitchen, along with my jacket and hat.

"Perhaps it's time to seek out a new lease in life Jack," Samson said to me, as he placed his hand upon my shoulder. "I'm not the kind of man to up and run when faced with adversity, Samson. You know this about me," I said to Samson in a stern tone as I shrugged off his hand from my shoulder.

"What happened?" Hayley inquired, as she walked up to me and Samson with a wide-eyed stare.

"Go ahead tell her," I said to Samson with a scowl. "Jack's last chance effort at keeping this speakeasy running didn't fall through. We will most likely have to shut down within the next two weeks," Samson replied

"What will happen to us, how will we survive with no income?" Hayley inquired in a distressed tone.

"Ah that's the question, isn't it kid. How does one survive in a city like this? A city where bonds of brotherhood mean nothing compared to that cash in your pocket. If this is the end of this speakeasy, then let's go out with a bang. Either we will have to shut down soon when our liquor dries up, or the police will shut us down," I pronounced.

"What exactly are you proposing Jack," Samson inquired, as the last patron who sat at the bar exited the speakeasy in a staggering manner.

"Avery has won the war of most dominant speakeasy, but we will have a going out of business night where we can throw all caution to the wind. Perhaps are profits on that night will help us seek out a better more comfortable way of life," I replied "I thought you didn't run from adversity," Samson said to me.

"He's not running. He's excepting his fate," Hayley said to Samson.

"Very well, I don't see any other option. When we go down, we go down swinging," Samson said to me with a grin, as he placed his hand on my shoulder.

Hayley then entered the kitchen, as Samson and I cleaned up the bar in the manner of nurses caring for a man on his deathbed.

"So tell me Jack, now that we're alone, I must know something," Samson said to me. "What is it Samson?" I inquired.

"How did you feel at that moment when you killed Johnny?" Samson inquired, as he stared intently at me.

"I felt … liberated and empowered, like an enormous weight was lifted off my shoulders," I replied.

"Well I guess that's where you and I differ then," Samson said to me.

"What are you talking about?" I inquired.

"I just wanted to know if you felt any remorse the way I did when I killed my former gang members, but I see now that no such remorse lies in your heart," Samson said to me as he shook his head.

"Remorse, why on god's green earth would I feel remorse over ending the life of the man who killed my sister?" I inquired in a stern tone as I stared at Samson with bewildered eyes.

"Now you sound just like your niece. When are you two going to learn that killing doesn't justify killing," My former gang members had wives and children, and to this day it tears me up inside knowing that I robbed them of their families," Samson said to me in a stern tone.

"You want me to feel remorse over killing a man whose entire lot in life was to put fear into the hearts of everyone who opposed him and his organization, a man who has killed cops, women, and he would've even killed that kid in there. I did the city of New York a great service on that foggy night I ended Johnny the Hammer O'Connor, and if you cannot see that, then you can get the fuck out of this speakeasy, because it sure as hell sounds like you're valuing the life of that killer," I said to Samson in a stern tone, as I pointed to the front door of the speakeasy.

"You're starting to sound like a killer yourself, Jack. I just hope the hammer hasn't rubbed off on you," Samson remarked. "Think nothing of it. It was either my life or his. The threat on our lives may not be over, but I sure as hell took out the deadliest hitman the Five Points Gang had to offer. This speakeasy is coming to its end. There are no other options now other than to cut our losses and try to find another source of income," I said to Samson with a sigh.

"Where will you and your niece go?" Samson inquired.

"I don't know. Maybe we'll do better off in this world if we go our separate ways," I replied with a sigh.

"That must be, Mickey," I remarked as a knock on the front door echoed throughout the vacant speakeasy.

"Jack, Samson, something bad has happened," Mickey pronounced in a distressed tone, as he entered the speakeasy.

"Mickey what's wrong?" Hayley inquired with a wide- eyed stare, as she scampered out of the kitchen right up to Mickey's side.

"You'll have to be more specific than that," I said with a scoff, as Mickey sat down at the bar and took off his hat.

"I think the Five Points Gang is threatening me," Mickey said to me.

"Why would they even worry about you? You're just—,"

"An orphan, I know what I am Jack, but they know very well that I work for you and that's all that matters to them. I work for the man who took out the hammer, so I might as well be responsible in their eyes," Mickey interjected in a stern tone. "Please tell us what happened," Hayley said to Mickey, as she took his hand.

I just knew Hayley and Mickey have become closer over the past month. I could see a passion in their eyes whenever they were together. They were innocent, naïve, but most of all, they had the rest of their lives ahead of them. The same cannot be said about me and Samson.

"I found this letter with my name on it attached to the front door of the hospital. It reads *'Dear Mickey, we know who you work for and we know where you live. We can offer you protection as long as you offer us that son of a bitch who killed Johnny. You have your whole life ahead of you, so we trust that you will make the right decision. Turn this letter in to any NYPD station by the end of tomorrow with your decision written on it or you will see us soon,"* Mickey read aloud.

"You don't have to worry about these threats any longer. Tomorrow will be our last day in business, after that, you no longer work for me," I said to Mickey.

"It doesn't matter, Jack. They see the boy as your accomplice, the same as me and Hayley," Samson said to me in a stern tone.

"What are you two whispering about?" I inquired in a stern tone, as Mickey and Hayley whispered in each other's ears. "A couple days ago, we found a human head on the doorstep of the speakeasy," Hayley replied in a timid tone.

"A human head, Are you sure?" I inquired with a wide- eyed stare at both Mickey and Hayley who stared back at me with such fear in their young eyes.

"Aye it was Johnny's head no doubt," Samson pronounced, as he locked the front door of the speakeasy.

"What do you know about this, Samson," I inquired.

"It's a fear tactic as old as time when it comes to gangs and organized crime in general. The message the Five Points Gang has sent to you is clear as a bell. They will do to you what you did to Johnny," Samson said to me.

"I'd love to see them try," I pronounced, as I took my pistol out in an aggressive manner.

"Where is Johnny's head, Mickey," Samson inquired.

"Oh ... I kicked it down the alley just before Hayley and I went to *Tompkins Square Park*," Mickey replied.

"I'm starting to like you more and more," I remarked, with a cackle, as I slapped Mickey on the back.

"We have to take this message dead serious Jack, because after this, the Five Points Gang will surely make due on that promise they made to Mickey in that letter," Samson said to me in a stern tone.

"Oh just like Johnny made due on the letter he wrote to me," I said to Samson with a snicker, and then poured myself a shot of bourbon.

"You're going to get us all killed and you're still just as brash as ever. You think that near death experience you had fighting Johnny would make you appreciate life," Samson said to me.

"The way I see it Samson is that the Five Points Gang has continuously underestimated us. You can cower from them all you want just like you cowered from your former gang and up and fled to America, but I'm no such man like you," I said to Samson.

"Why you son of a bitch," Samson said to me in a stern tone.

"Stop it you two. We shouldn't be fighting each other now," Hayley pronounced, as Samson grabbed the collar of my shirt with that familiar Irish fervor burning in his eyes.

"It's just as you said Samson. A man who has been right on the doorstep of death before has no reason to fear a man like you. Now take your damn hand off me," I said to Samson, as I broke the grip he had on the collar of my shirt in a swift motion. "Hayley is right. How could we ever hope to stand against the Five Points Gang if we ourselves can't even stand together? I won't betray you Jack. You've given me a steady paycheck for the past two years, and I'm in debt to you for that," Mickey said to me.

"You should take a page from Mickey. He seems to be more of a man than you are," I said to Samson with a scoff. "Stop Jack, Samson's your friend," Hayley said to me in a distressed tone.

"Friend? This coward wants me to feel remorse for killing Johnny," I said to Hayley with a scoff.

"Let's just all take a few moments to breathe. We've all been through a lot over the past month and our nerves are very sensitive right now," Hayley pronounced, as she held her hands out like a mother trying to calm down her bastard children.

I found it amusing how Hayley was trying to play the role of peacekeeper with everyone. I for one was used to coming to blows with Samson almost on a daily basis, but Hayley seemed really affected by our fighting. I thought the kid would be used to fighting by now considering all the times her mother and Johnny fought right in front of her, or maybe that's why she's trying to keep the peace with me and Samson. The kid was born into a home of violence and now she doesn't want to be subjected to that familiar hell any longer.

It was 9:45 PM in the speakeasy as the remainder of the evening was spent in silence as me, Samson, Hayley, and Mickey cleaned up the speakeasy to get ready for our final night of business tomorrow night. It's been a good run for me, but now I must look for employment for the first time in 8 years. I now couldn't help but think of what Dezerae first told me when I told her I wanted to turn my shut down bar into a speakeasy, she wasn't exactly thrilled to say the least, but she still supported my vision.

*****

"I have to do this Dez. I'm fully aware of the danger and risk of being arrested by the damn police, but I must continue the proud name of the *Jack of All Trades*. During these times where our constitutional rights are being taken away, there needs to be more people who will stand against such a bullshit law,"

I said to Dezerae as she sat down at the bar drinking a glass of chardonnay.

"You could be killed. Listen …I'm not going to tell you how to live your life Jack. You've always been good at adapting during times such as these, but if you feel that this is your path right now, then I urge you to walk it cautiously," Dezerae said to me.

"Now you sound like mom. So how are you and Hayley holding up?" I inquired.

"We're making do week by week, but it seems that no matter how much over time I work at the diner it just never seems to be enough," Dezerae replied in a somber tone.

"You and Hayley will always have a place here, Dez. I don't offer much in means of amenities, but I have electricity and running water," I said to Dezerae with a smirk.

"Thank you Jack, I hope that liquor outlaw will prove profitable to your speakeasy," Dezerae said to me with a smile, as she placed her hand on mine.

"I hope so too, Dez. I will have to compete with many others who I expect to be opening up speakeasies throughout New York, but I'm ready for the challenge," I said to Dezerae with a grin.

"I know you are. You always have been. Perhaps the end of something can prove to be a great beginning of something new," Dezerae said to me with a warm smile.

*****

"Good night," Mickey pronounced, just before Hayley kissed the boy in the manner of a woman kissing her husband who was going off to fight in the war. The kid was growing up fast before my eyes. I just hope she doesn't place all of her hopes and dreams in that boy.

Samson then exited the speakeasy a few moments after Mickey in a silent brooding manner. I really must have offended that Irish brute, because he only becomes silent when he's just about to have an outburst. It was his defense mechanism, and a terrible one at that. The last time Samson went silent, he took out his rage on a drunken German immigrant who wasn't even being rude, but Samson just snapped, and started pummeling him. I didn't fear that Samson would do the same to me, I've already been pummeled to hell and back by Johnny, and I've grown accustomed to that pain that can be numbed by a couple shots of bourbon.

"I'm sorry Jack," Hayley said to me in a somber tone, as she sat down at the bar with a sigh.

"Sorry for what, kid?" I inquired with a grin.

"This speakeasy is your legacy, and it's a shame that there are no other options to keep it alive," Hayley replied.

"Your mother once told me that 'the end of something terrible could prove to be the beginning of something great,'" I said to Hayley, as I wiped down the bar.

"Or vice versa … I didn't think you would ever quote my mother. I believe there are far worse things in this world than alcohol, and taking that away from people caused those terrible things to grow," Hayley said to me as her eyes welled up with tears.

"Well said, and your mother had some good quotes every now and then," I said to Hayley with a grin.

"So what's the plan for us after tomorrow night," Hayley inquired.

"I can't see that far ahead, kid," I replied with a sigh, and then entered the kitchen.

How the hell would I support myself and a 15 year old girl in this day and age? The very thought of it all weighed heavy on me, as I laid my battered head down on the blood stained pillow.

"Jack, do you want to listen to music before you sleep?" Hayley inquired, as she entered the kitchen holding the victrola. "Normally I would, but we have a big day tomorrow, so I need my rest as soon as possible," I replied.

"Oh all right. Good night," Hayley said to me, as she quietly lay down on the floor beside me.

*****

It was 7:24 AM when I awoke with a splitting headache.

"Good morning. I made breakfast," Hayley said to me with a smile, as I walked behind the bar with my hand on my forehead.

Hayley seemed in better spirits for the past week. I wonder if it had anything to do with that boy Mickey

"I'm heading out in ten minutes to run an errand, don't let—,"

"Anybody in the speakeasy who doesn't know the password," I know Jack," Hayley interjected with an eye roll as she brushed her hair.

"If my plan is successful, then the entire west side of New York City will know of this speakeasies going out of business sale," I said to Hayley, as I put on my hat and jacket.

"Why can't I come with you?" Hayley inquired.

"You are my blood relative, kid. It's important in times such as these where we are being targeted by the Five Points Gang to not travel together," I replied.

"You're talking about if one of us dies, then the other one might stand a chance of surviving," Hayley said to me with a somber look on her face.

"It's the cold reality of our lives now, kid. I'm not going to tell you that we're not in danger, hell everyone is in danger in this day and age, but you and I in particular are marked by the most powerful crime organization New York City has ever known," I said to Hayley.

"I'm aware Jack. I just believe that we are stronger if we stick together," Hayley said to me.

"I'll be back in a couple of hours. Be smart, stay safe," I said to Hayley and then exited the speakeasy.

*****

It was 8:05 AM when I decided to take the *Lennox Avenue Line to City Hall*.

I don't normally take the subway, but seeing as my finances will soon be running dry, I would have to save money on gas by taking this steel train full of beggars and immigrants. Subway tokens were relatively cheap, but the trade off was me having to suffer through the stench of this steel train. My plan was to print flyers, 200 of them to be exact. The flyers would read

GOING OUT OF BUSINESS SALE!
ALL LIQUOR HALF PRICED! CELEBRATE THE END OF THE *JACK OF ALL TRADES* STARTING TODAY AT 5PM GREENWICH VILLAGE MINETTA STREET PASSWORD: DELILAH

I know very well of all the consequences of putting the address and password of the speakeasy on a flyer and advertising it all throughout the West Side of Manhattan, but those consequences which used to strike fear into me no longer have any effect over me now. My speakeasy was going to be shutdown one way or another, and I wanted that way to be my way.

An old associate of mine by the name of Louie Stanford runs a printing press on *Beaver Street* near *Battery Park*. I would always call him Louie the loudmouth, because the man always stated his opinion to anybody, anytime, anywhere. The man was so brash he made me look timid by comparison, and now I required his services.

"Back off, do I look like I'm made of money?" I shouted at a homeless man reaching out towards me as I exited the subway. I then walked south down Broadway to *Beaver Street*. The Lower East Side *Financial District* of New York always seemed to be unaffected by this depression. I wonder how all these businessmen feel when they get home after a long day of capitalizing off of everyone who is suffering beneath them. I looked up at all the high-rise financial buildings with a scowl as I passed them by on way to loudmouth Louie's Printing Press. I wanted to make the most out of today, not just financially, but I wanted to build new bridges to replace the many which I've burned down over the past five years.

"Loudmouth Louie, how long has it been?" I shouted, as I entered the printing press to the sight of Louie tinkering with some sort of contraption used to run the press I assume.

"Goddamn is that you Jack. The years have not been kind to your face," Louie remarked with a snicker. The stench of the printing press was so horrible it made the subway smell like a bed of roses by comparison.

"I actually came by to tell you that—,"

"Justin, reset the black ink alignment. I'm getting slanted print!" Louie shouted into a back room like a waitress shouting to a cook in the kitchen of a diner.

"Speak up Jack. I'm very busy now printing for the *New York Times*," Louie said to me in a stern tone.

"I need you to print 200 flyers for me!" I shouted, as I took out the paper which I wrote the message the flyer would read.

"Hold on Jack. Ms, Clemens, get your fucking cat out of my store or I swear to god I will shove him through my printing press," Louie shouted out the front door of the printing press, as I snickered.

"All right Jack let me see," Louie said to me in a stern tone, as he snatched the paper out of my hands and stared intently at it for a brief moment.

"I know you're busy, but I need these flyers as soon as possible," I said to Louie, as I lit a cigarette and took a smoke. "Put that damn thing out. We don't smoke in here. The slightest ember can set this whole store ablaze. I'm sorry to see the final day of your speakeasy, Jack. Seeing as how you helped me start up my business, I will put this request of yours at the top of my list. Twenty-eight words on two-hundred five by seven flyers will not be the cheap, Jack, but I'll try to get you the lowest price I can," Louie sad to me.

"Thanks Louie. You know you haven't changed a bit, and I'm quite happy about that," I said to Louie with a smile as I flicked my cigarette out the front door of his store.

"I could say the same about you, Jack. So what will you do now?" Louie inquired, as he cranked a wheel on the printing press which lowered the rollers.

"I don't know. I thought that keeping my speakeasy running during this liquor outlaw was a noble service to uphold our constitutional rights," I replied.

"Two hundred sheets of white five by seven inch flyers Justin, load them in the printing press so I can print a test batch," Louie shouted into the back room of the printing press. "So how long will this take? I need these flyers as soon as possible," I inquired, as I sat down on a chair by the front door of the printing press with a sigh.

"You don't rush art, Jack. So keep that mug of yours shut while I print out your flyers," Louie replied, as he examined the first flyer which printed out of the press with a buzz, hum, and hiss.

"Looks good to me," I remarked as I looked at the flyer Louie was holding.

"No … you see that right there. That's fading, if I don't address that now then the rest of your flyers will basically look like trash," Louie said to me, and then crumpled up the flyer and threw it away.

"Very well, but I'm not looking for a work of art, just a message that will bring people to my speakeasy," I said to Louie.

"I take my job very seriously Jack. A message, whether it be written, printed, or shouted, must represent the one who is sending the message perfectly. I know your style Jack, and I know what kind of demographics drink at your speakeasy, but if you want to bring in everyone for your final night in business, then trust me with these flyers, I know what I'm doing," Louie said to me in a stern tone, as another flyer came out of the printing press.

"You've never given me a reason not to trust you, Louie," I said to Louie as I looked intently at the flyer he was holding.

"The print is aligned perfectly with no fading," Louie remarked, as he handed me the flyer.

"It looks great," I remarked with a grin.

"Now we can commence with printing two hundred of these flyers. Load two hundred of these flyers into the press, Justin!" Louie shouted into the back room.

"I already did, Jesus Christ, Louie!" a voice who I could only assume to be Justin shouted back from the back room of the printing press.

"All right, that's it Ms. Clemens, this cat of yours is going through my printing press, get ready to hear a loud screech!" Louie shouted out the front door, as a fluffy orange tabby jumped up on the front counter.

"Don't you dare touch my precious Goldie!" a woman shouted, as she ran into the printing press and snatched up her cat from off the front counter.

"If you wanted your cat to be in the *New York Times* so bad you could've just told me. I would be more than willing to print out his obituary," Louie said to Ms. Clemens with a snicker.

"You're an awful man," Ms. Clemens remarked with a gasp and then stormed out of the printing press.

"Don't worry he's only joking!" I shouted with a laugh. "Fifty flyers are printed!" Justin shouted from the back room.

"Good ... so tell me something, Jack. When all is said and done and all the dust has settled in your bar, what's the one memory you will take away from it all?" Louie inquired.

"One memory ... there is no one memory that I can take away from my speakeasy. All the many faces I've met in that bar and all the stories I've heard are all part of one collective memory that represents my speakeasy," I replied in a somber tone.

"One hundred flyers are printed!" Justin shouted from the back room.

"I'm sorry Jack, but for what it's worth, I believe you did provide a service which us fine hardworking New Yorkers deserve," Louie said to me.

"To greener, pastures Louie," I said to Louie with a grin, as I raised my flask of bourbon towards him and then took a swig. "I hope you find those greener pastures, Jack, and remember that no man is an island. My wife tells me that all the time whenever I shut her out," Louie said to me with a snicker. "One hundred and fifty flyers printed," Justin shouted from the back room.

"My island has taken on three new inhabitants now. Some days I want to choke the life out of them. Then other days I'm just glad to have their company," I said to Louie with a snicker.

"Solidarity Jack, we need it now more than ever. If this city ever hopes to rise from this depression then we must all rise together," Louie said to me.

"Now you sound like Charles Coughlin," I remarked with a grin.

"The man is wise. He preaches the truth, that's why he brings in millions of listeners," Louie said to me.

"All two hundred flyers are printed, Louie," Justin shouted from the back room.

"Good work. Take a break, Justin I'll take it from here," Louie shouted into the back room.

Justin then entered the main room of the printing press with the stack of flyers, and placed them down upon the front counter with a sigh before exiting the store.

"The normal price would be $9.95, but seeing as how you have helped me in the past and this is your last day in business, I will only charge you ... $6.95," Louie said to me, as he typed in my total on the cash register.

"That's a good of a price as any, I just hope these flyers pay off," I said to Louie, as I paid him.

"Good luck Jack," Louie said to me with a grin, as we shook hands.

"Thank you Louie. Take care," I said to Louie with a grin and then exited the printing press.

*****

It was 11:27 AM when I arrived at the speakeasy after posting 50 of the flyers all around the *Financial District*. Now it was Hayley, Mickey, and Samson's job to post the rest of them. "I'm back," I pronounced as I entered the speakeasy to the sight of Samson teaching Hayley how to fill a pint of beer from the tap perfectly.

"What are those," Hayley inquired, as I placed the stack of flyers down upon the bar with a sigh and then took off my jacket and hat.

"Those are our final bout, our final cry to this city," I replied as Hayley and Samson intently read the flyer.

"I like it. They're simple, but they send a clear message," Hayley remarked.

"Are you sure this is wise, Jack? Posting the password of the speakeasy for all the eyes of New York to see," Samson inquired.

"What have we got to lose, Samson? I pay no mind to the police anymore. Hell I wouldn't doubt a few cops might even partake considering that this is our last night in business," I said to Samson.

"I'm not talking about the NYPD, Jack," Samson said to me.

"We need one last night of income before we shut down completely. We have to throw caution to the wind. If the Five Points Gang still wants to silence me, then they can give me their best shot," I said to Samson with a scoff.

"You're inviting all of New York to this speakeasy, don't be surprised by who shows up tonight," Samson said to me while shaking his head.

"Mickey should be here at noon. In the meantime, make yourself useful and post fifty of these flyers throughout Chelsea," I said to Samson.

"Chelsea, come on now Jack, that's a bit obvious what you're doing," Samson said to me.

"What are you talking about?" I inquired.

"You're trying to steal all of Avery's business tonight with these flyers, aren't you," Samson said to me with a grin. "You're damn right I am," I said to Samson with a grin. "Aye very well then, Jack. I'll be back in a couple of hours," Samson said to me with a grin, as he grabbed 50 of the flyers off the bar.

"Post the flyers where the most people will see them," I said to Samson, as he put on his jacket.

"Aye Jack," Samson shouted just before he exited the speakeasy.

"Mickey my boy, just in time," I shouted with a grin, as Mickey entered the speakeasy right after Samson exited.

"Good morning," Mickey said to me in a timid tone, as he walked up to Hayley behind the bar.

"What happened?" Hayley inquired in a distressed tone, as she placed her hand upon Mickey's cheek.

I then noticed that Mickey had a shiner on his right eye, but Hayley reacted in such a dramatic way as if the boy was shot full of led and bleeding out.

"You're starting to look more and more like me," I said to Mickey, as I pointed to his battered face and then mine with a snicker.

"It's not funny, Jack," Hayley said to me in a distressed tone.

"It's no big deal really, nothing compared to what Jack went through with Johnny. I just got into a fight with a couple of friends of mine," Mickey said to Hayley.

"With friends like those who needs enemies?" I said to Mickey while shaking my head.

"Please tell me what happened," Hayley said to Mickey, as she grabbed his hand and sat down at the bar.

"Well, they wanted me to help them rob an old couple, then when I refused, they tried to rob me instead," Mickey said to Hayley.

"You did the right thing," Hayley said to Mickey with a wide-eyed stare.

"What lesson did you learn from that scuffle, Mickey?" I inquired.

"I learned not to prey on people who are struggling just as bad as I am," Mickey replied with a sniff.

"Wrong, you should've learned not to trust anybody who tries to give off the impression that they're your friend, because with one drop of the hat you find yourself on the end of their fist wondering why and how they could do that to you," I said to Mickey in a stern tone.

"Perhaps you're right, Jack," Mickey said to me in a somber tone.

"No he's wrong. You can always trust me," Hayley said to Mickey as she stared intently into his battered face.

"Thanks Hayley," Mickey said with a grin.

"I'll go get you some ice to put on those bruises," Hayley said to Mickey.

"She really likes you," I said to Mickey with a grin.

"Hayley means so much to me. Knowing that I have her to talk to makes this world feel a little warmer," Mickey said to me.

I didn't respond back to Mickey's naïve sentiment, I just stared at the boy, and how even though his face was battered like mine, he was smiling. Hayley has really changed Mickey from when I first met him, or perhaps, she brought out something from deep inside of him which he was too timid to show to the world.

"All right, while Samson's posting the flyers in Chelsea, I want you two to post twenty-five flyers all around Greenwich Village," I pronounced.

"Why only twenty-five," Hayley inquired.

"Well because the last seventy-five I want to be posted all around Broadway and *Hell's Kitchen*," I replied.

"I hope these flyers work, Jack. They sure look professionally made," Mickey remarked, as he pressed the ice pack against his battered face.

"That's because they are professional. My old associate Louie who runs a printing press printed these out for me," I said to Mickey.

"I wish I had friends like yours, Jack," Mickey said to me. "Associate, Mickey. Now go ahead you two, only twenty- five flyers shouldn't take you more than thirty minutes to post in the village," I pronounced, as I gestured for Mickey and Hayley to leave the speakeasy with a wave and grin.

Getting my speakeasy ready for its final night in business was heartbreaking for me to say the least. I bet my entire life on the prospect that selling liquor during this prohibition would be profitable and I just know that if Dezerae was alive she would be telling me 'I told you so, Jack.' Be that as it may, I wanted to get this place looking as upscale as possible. Sure I lacked the finances to furnish the speakeasy In the manner that that brash son of a bitch Avery has done with *the Sly Troubadour*, and ever since Samson fired Caroline and her jazz band, the business in my speakeasy has suffered, but now I have to depend on New Yorkers desire to drink, and with all my liquor being half priced, I'm expecting a grand crowd when that clock strikes 5 PM.

Tonight I would go out in a blaze of glory, and every up and coming bootlegger will know my name, for providing such a desired product which should've never been outlawed during such trying times such as these. Hayley was right when she said that there are far worse things in this world than alcohol and those very things will now grow in the absence of alcohol.

Depending on how many patrons enter the speakeasy and how many drinks each patron order will determine how long the speakeasy can stay in business tonight before we shut down. The math was mind boggling, but I figured that with the inventory of alcohol that this speakeasy currently has in stock, we can serve 100 patrons with each patron ordering a maximum of three drinks, but if the turnout for tonight exceeds these expectations, then the speakeasy will run dry and we will have to shut down most likely before midnight.

*****

It was 1:22 PM as Hayley and Mickey entered the speakeasy while laughing and holding hands.

"What took you two so long?" I inquired, as I buffed the bar with turtle wax.

"We stopped at *Sal's Diner* to get milkshakes after we posted all the flyers around Greenwich Village," Hayley replied with a smile.

"Oh where's my milkshake then?" I inquired in a stern tone. "Sorry Jack, we didn't think that—,"

"I liked milkshakes. I drank them nearly every day when I was your age, kid," I interjected with a grin.

"Next time I will buy you one to go then," Hayley said to me with a smile, as she and Mickey sat down at the bar. "Forget it. Some childhood pleasures don't hold the same magic when you grow up, you two will learn that soon enough, but this always makes me feel better," I said to Hayley and then took a quick shot of bourbon with a grimace.

"What more needs to be done for tonight," Mickey inquired. "Much more, Mickey, you remember how this speakeasy used to look when you first started working here, right?" I inquired.

"I sure do," Mickey replied, as he took off his hat and ran his fingers through his sandy blonde hair.

"Well then do your best in recreating that image of this speakeasy in its heyday," I said to Mickey.

"Oh can I help, I love decorating," Hayley inquired with a smile, as she clasped her hands together in front of her chest.

"You damn well better help Mickey. This is a team effort. We need to make enough money tonight that will hold the four of us over until we can find new jobs," I replied.

"Come on, let's go to the kitchen, I know how to recreate the image of the speakeasy that I have in my mind from two years ago," Mickey said to Hayley with a smile as he took her hand.

"Remember you two are both on the clock, so no fooling around in there," I shouted, as Hayley and Mickey scampered hand in hand into the kitchen.

I found myself growing more and more nervous with every minute that drew nearer to 5 PM. What if nobody showed? What if Avery and the Five Points Gang completely shut me out of selling alcohol in New York City? These toxic thoughts weighed heavy on my mind, as I buffed each table in the speakeasy with turtle wax.

*****

It was 2:15 PM when Samson entered the speakeasy with a grin.

"Took you long enough," I said to Samson.

"There's a line of people waiting outside the speakeasy," Samson said to me.

"Well I'll be damned. You told them that we open at 5 PM no exceptions, right?" I inquired with a smile as I took a brief glance through the iron window of the front door.

"Of course what do you take me for? Wow this place looks almost as good as it did when I first started working here," Samson remarked with a grin.

"The kids have been polishing every nook and cranny of this place," I said to Samson with a grin, as Hayley and Mickey walked up to me behind the bar.

"You two did a fine job decorating the stage. Now that Samson is back, you two have two and a half hours to post the last hundred flyers all around Broadway and *Hell's Kitchen*," I pronounced.

"Here you go," Samson said to Mickey as he tossed him the keys to the Pontiac."

"Get back before five PM. There's already a line waiting outside the front door," I shouted, as Hayley and Mickey walked towards the front door.

"We'll be back as soon as we can," Hayley said to me, and then she and Mickey exited the speakeasy.

"How are you feeling, Jack," Samson inquired with a grin. "I'm fine Samson, why do you ask?" I inquired.

"Just curious, that's all. I hope we make a great deal of money tonight," Samson replied.

"I remember your first day working here. You got into three fights with drunks at the bar and nearly got yourself killed in the alley by some mobsters you rubbed the wrong way," I said to Samson with a snicker.

"Aye that day was a learning curve for me. You may not agree, but working with you Jack has actually calmed my nerves compared to the man I used to be, the young angry man I left back in Belfast," Samson said to me.

"No I agree Samson. I know I have an uncanny ability to make even the calmest person snap, but your temperament has leveled out over the past couple of years. I'm really going to miss this place," I said to Samson.

"Why can't you and your niece still live here? Sure you can no longer bootleg alcohol, but that doesn't mean you have to leave this speakeasy which also serves as your home?" Samson inquired.

"No ... I'm going back to *SoHo*, after tonight, Samson," I replied, while shaking my head.

"Isn't that where you lived with your mother and sister when you were a child?" Samson inquired.

"Yes ... the only warm memories I have of this damn city come from *SoHo*," I replied.

"Aye that's understandable; my childhood was nowhere near as nurturing as yours, so I cannot relate to the desire to return to Belfast. There are far too many godforsaken men there who project all their weaknesses on the rest of the innocent people of the town. That's why I left, I couldn't change my homeland, so I had to come here to the so called 'land of opportunities,'" Samson said to me.

"First of all, my childhood in *SoHo* was not nurturing, Samson. Sure my mother tried her best to raise me and my sister, but when your father leaves for the war when you're only twelve years old and never returns, it leaves a mark on you," I said to Samson.

"So why return to *SoHo* then, Jack?" Samson inquired.

"Roots, Samson. First my father died, and then my mother, and then my sister. Sometimes I feel as if I'm losing my identity, like bootlegging has turned me into a man who I don't recognize when I stare into the mirror," I replied.

"Aye you lost your sister, but you gained a niece, don't take her for granted, Jack. I know you say she's so much like her mother, but I see so much of you in her," Samson remarked. "That kid is sharp as a knife, but foolhardy. She has a fire in her, every time I look into her eyes I see a girl who refuses to bend to anybody, especially me," I said to Samson with a snicker.

"She is your fire, Jack. You need each other right now no matter how much you both may deny it," Samson said to me.

"What I need is some dame to come in here and sweep me off my feet," I said to Samson with a snicker, and then took a shot of bourbon.

"Aye we could all us that comfort. Let's hope these flyers bring in all kinds of people to this speakeasy," Samson said to me with a grin.

*****

It was 5:00 PM in the speakeasy when I opened the front door to the first group of patrons who appeared to be upper middle class judging by their modest yet bold attire.

"Welcome to the *Jack of All Trades*," I pronounced, as I let in another group of patrons no more than a minute after the last patrons entered.

"Welcome welcome, all liquor is half priced, take comfort and drink all your cares away," I pronounced.

"Sorry we're late," Hayley said to me, as she and Mickey entered the speakeasy and scampered over to the bar.

"It's going to be a long night, you two, but if we do great business it will be a short night," I pronounced.

"You two take the orders of the two parties sitting at table nine and three," Samson, pronounced, as he pointed to the two groups of people eagerly waiting to be served their drinks.

"Alright Samson, I'll be watching the door for the first hour, then we can switch and I will work behind the bar while you watch the door," I said to Samson, as I turned on the victrola and put on a Cab Calloway record, before scampering to the front door.

"Sounds like a plan," Samson said to me with a grin as another knock on the door resonated throughout the speakeasy. The knocks were becoming more difficult to hear now. This was a good sign, I should never hear the knocks on the front door echo throughout the speakeasy, that means it's dead in here, but tonight I had a feeling that I, along with Samson, Hayley, and Mickey were in for a wild night the likes of which we've never experienced before.

*****

It was 7:25 PM in the speakeasy.

"We're packed like sardines, Jack!" Samson shouted from across the speakeasy, as I frantically served drink after drink at the bar.

"I know, isn't it goddamn glorious. It's just like the good ol days," I said to Samson with a smile.

It was indeed like the good ol days right now in the speakeasy, it was just a shame that in order to relive that time I had to soon after shutdown. I wanted these hours in the speakeasy to last forever, if I could only find a way to prolong them, but the outcome of tonight will end sooner or later and I just had to enjoy the ride.

"Look who it is, Jack," Samson said to me with a grin, as he nudged me with his elbow while pointing to Faye Dubois who was walking towards the bar.

"I had no idea you were going out of business, Jack," Faye said to me with a wide-eyed stare, as she squeezed up front to the bar and sat down.

"I'm afraid so, Faye. Certain powers have rendered me with no choice in the matter. So what can I get you?" I inquired. "Honte à toi. You mean you don't remember my favorite cocktail," Faye said to me with a giggle.

"Give me a hint. I serve so many drinks it's hard to keep track sometimes," I said to Faye.

"What by any other name," Faye said to me, as she leaned over the bar with a smile.

"The Black Rose. I don't know If I have all the ingredients for that particular cocktail, but I'll improvise for you, doll," I said to Faye, as I began to prepare the Black Rose cocktail, while Samson was letting in what appeared to be a group of flapper girls.

"So what will you do after tonight, mon chéri?" Faye inquired.

"Why don't we runaway together, leave this town and live in that countryside you spoke so fondly of," I replied as I put the finishing touches on Faye's cocktail.

"That's not your life Jack. Right now you're, how do you say … wanderlust is beginning to weigh heavy on that heart of yours," Faye said to me, as she pressed her finger against my chest.

"I've been locked up in this speakeasy for years. A little wanderlust isn't so bad," I said to Faye as I handed her the Black Rose cocktail.

"Mmm fantastique, Jack," Faye remarked after she took a sip of the Black Rose cocktail.

"Don't wander too far from this bar," I said to Faye, as two men shouted their drink orders at me.

"There's nowhere else I'd rather be," Faye said to me.

I then pushed myself through the crowd of patrons to the front door of the speakeasy where Samson was diligently watching the door.

"One hundred eighty-five patrons Jack," Samson said to me.

"At this rate we might have to shut down before midnight," said to Samson as I stared through the iron window slot of the front door to the sight of two dames walking towards the front door.

"Password," I said, as the dames knocked on the door. "Delilah," both of the dames said to me in unison. "Welcome to the *Jack of All Trades*," I said to the dames, as I opened the front door.

"Oh Betty this places is too crowded, let's go someplace else," one dame said to the other, as they entered the speakeasy. "I assure you two that there is no place else when it comes to liquor," I said to the dame.

"So I've heard. You speakeasy proprietors are a dying breed," the dame said to me.

"I'm not dead yet doll face. In the meantime, have a seat at the bar and my associate Samson will be with you shortly," I said to the dames with a grin, as I gestured for them to sit at the bar.

"We're bringing in a lot of women tonight," I said to Samson.

"Aye I wonder why that is," Samson said to me.

"Let's stop wondering why and just enjoy it for once," I said to Samson, as I snapped my fingers and pointed to the two dames seated at the bar.

"How are you holding up, Mickey?" I shouted as the noise level in the speakeasy was at its loudest.

"I'm good, Jack. I've never seen so many people in this speakeasy before. It's as if all of New York wants to drink here," Mickey replied.

"Those flyers really did the job. Why don't you go watch the front door, I'll take over your job," I said to Mickey.

"Yes sir," Mickey said to me, and then pushed his way through the crowd of patrons to the front door.

"I don't feel well. I need to rest for a moment," Hayley said to me, as she placed her hand over her stomach.

"Have you been drinking, kid?" I inquired.

"No I just … it's personal. I just need a break," Hayley replied.

"You have five minutes, and not one minute longer," I said to Hayley in a stern tone.

"Jack!" Samson shouted, as he gestured for me to join him behind the bar.

"What now, Samson?" I inquired. "We're all out of rum," Samson replied.

"Oh … well that's not that bad, rum is mainly used in cocktails, so we can still do business with the remaining liquor we have in stock," I said to Samson.

*****

It was 10:27 PM in the speakeasy, as the mass of patrons grew even larger.

"Where is Mademoiselle Hayley?" Faye inquired.

"She's taking a break. Thanks for reminding me," I replied, and then entered the kitchen to the sight of Hayley writing in her book once again.

"What are you doing, kid? This is no time to be writing in that book of yours, we need all hands on deck if we're going make a sizable profit that will keep us off the streets after tonight," I said to Hayley in a stern tone.

"All right I'm coming," Hayley said to me in a sulking tone, as she stood up from the desk and walked up to me.

"We must do everything we can tonight to ensure that the *Jack of All Trades* will live on in the hearts and minds of every New Yorker," I said to Hayley.

"What do you mean by that?" Hayley inquired, as we exited the kitchen to the sight of a wild broad dancing on the bar.

"Hold on, kid," I said to Hayley, as I stared up at the broad who flapped and twirled her dress atop the bar.

"Excuse me .Can you sing, Miss?" I inquired with a grin. "Not according to my ex-husband," the woman replied. "Well I'm not your ex-husband and you don't have to feel inhibited here in the *Jack of All Trades*. Here's five dollars for you to sing on stage for the remainder of the night," I said to the woman.

"Five dollars huh ... you've got yourself a deal, Jack," the woman said to me, as she took my hand and stepped down from atop of the bar.

"Boo boo!" Patrons remarked in unison, as the woman stepped down from atop of the bar.

"Don't worry everyone. She will be performing at the stage now," I shouted, as I pointed to the stage. The booing patrons then began to cheer, as me and the woman walked over to the stage.

"Here I thought this place was just a watering hole for me to burn off some stress, but a gentleman like you has made my night," the woman said to me.

"What's your name?" I inquired, as I quickly unplugged the victrola and then plugged in the microphone.

"Gracie Bishop," the woman replied with a smile, as she quickly primped her hair and dress in preparations before her performance.

"Well Gracie, we need a free spirit like yours on our final night in business, so sing your heart out," I said to Gracie with a grin.

"Any requests?" Gracie inquired with a grin.

"Any song that's relevant, make sure it speaks to the tone of this speakeasy," I replied.

Gracie then began to sing an upbeat jazz song which immediately perked up all the patrons who were seated at the tables in front of the stage.

"Who the hell is she?" Samson inquired, as he pointed at Gracie on the stage.

"That's Gracie Bishop. She's just some random broad wanting to express herself. So I figured that I could use that free spirit of hers to bring back live music to this speakeasy," I replied.

"She sounds pretty good for a random broad. Or I could just be half in the bag already," Samson said to me.

"I assure you that I'm half in the bag right now and I've heard much worse than her. It's a shame that we didn't find her until now," I said to Samson.

"Better late than never, Jack. You got everything you ever wanted right now at this moment, enjoy it," Samson said to me with a grin.

"I'm grateful, but I can't help but worry what tomorrow morning will bring," I said to Samson.

"You and over six million New Yorkers, Jack, at least you're going out in a blaze of glory, and you couldn't ask for better company," Samson said to me, and then patted me on the back.

"What will you do after tonight?" I shouted, as the patrons applauded Miss

Bishop and her rousing jazz performance.

"I suppose I will continue to look for work in the village and if all else fails I could always work at a diner," Samson replied.

"I was expecting more from you Samson. You didn't come all this way from Belfast just to work in a diner did you?" I inquired.

"I came all this way from Belfast to live a peaceful and simple life, but then I met you, Jack," Samson said to me with a grin.

"Ah New York is never peaceful, Samson. It's a wild horse that's always thrashing about. The best you can do is to let that horse run wild and free," I said to Samson, as I served two men at the bar their beers.

"More pearls of wisdom from Jack," Samson said to me with a snicker.

"Go switch jobs with Mickey," I said to Samson. "Another Black Rose mon chéri," Faye said to me, as she walked up to the bar.

"Coming right up," I said to Faye, and then began preparing her cocktail.

"Men like you are a diamond in the rough, Jack," Faye remarked with a grin as she began to reapply her lipstick while looking into a compact mirror.

"I'm nothing of the kind, Miss Dubois. I'm just a bartender," I said to Faye with a snicker.

"No no I mean it. Two few men in this city carry themselves in the manner that you do," Faye remarked. "What manner is that?" I inquired.

"How you say … noble a man of character," Faye remarked.

"You must be drunk six ways to Sunday if you think I'm a man of character," I said to Faye with a snicker.

"Trust me, Jack. I've had the misfortune of being around men with no character and you are not one of those men," Faye remarked with a grin and then took a smoke from her thin ivory cigarette holder.

"You flatter me Faye. You make me feel like more than just a failed speakeasy proprietor," I said to Faye, as I served her the Black Rose cocktail.

"Jack, we're now out of vodka and we only have two kegs left of beer on tap," Samson said to me.

"Once we're all out of beer we're going to have to make an announcement," I said to Samson.

"You should give an announcement anyways, Jack. Everyone needs to hear what's going on in that mind of yours right now," Samson said to me, as he firmly patted me on the shoulder.

"I'm not good at speeches," I said to Samson, while shaking my head.

"Come on, Jack, you've earned it. If you don't give a speech, I will," Samson said to me.

"Ugh very well Samson, I'll give a short announcement, only because I'm worried over what you might say if I don't," I said to Samson and then joined Gracie Bishop on the stage.

"Take a break Gracie," I said to Gracie, as I handed her 5 dollars with a grin.

"Thank you Jack," Gracie said to me with a smile, as she stepped down off the stage and sat down at the bar next to Faye. Faye and Gracie then immediately began exchanging pleasantries as if they were lifelong friends, while I prepared myself for the announcement which I'm sure would make me emotional.

"Attention ... everyone can I have your attention!" I pronounced into the microphone as all the eyes of the speakeasy immediately focused on me.

"Well ... uhm as I was telling my associate over there, I've never been very good at making speeches so I'm going to keep this short and sweet so you all can get back to your drinks. I'm sure you're all aware that tonight is the *Jack of All Trades* last night in business. It has been a long road serving all you New Yorkers alcohol under this prohibition act and I don't regret one moment. This is our constitutional right to drink and be merry, and no matter what the powers at be are, I want you all to remember how you feel in this moment. I now see that the end of something good can very well bring about the beginning of something great," I pronounced, as my quivering face fought to hold back the tears that wanted to come pouring out of my bleary eyes. I then raised my flask with a smile and stared around at all of the smiling faces staring back at me, including Hayley who was crying, as she began to applaud.

"Three cheers for Jack Dansby everybody. This man has spent over five years risking his life all so that you fine people can enjoy a drink during such troubling times," Samson said, as he joined me on the stage.

"To Jack, to Jack, to Jack," every patron in the speakeasy cheered in unison.

"Damn you Samson," I said to Samson with a grin as I quickly wiped a tear from off my cheek.

"Gracie you're back on," I said to Gracie in a stern tone, as I snapped my fingers and pointed to the now empty stage.

"Are you all right Mr. Dansby?" Gracie inquired, as she stood up from the bar with a smile.

"I'm fine doll. Now let's keep entertaining these fine people for as long as we can," I replied with a smile.

The midnight hour was approaching and more patrons continued to enter the speakeasy as if it was the last night to drink alcohol in New York City. I will miss hearing about their days, their problems which they all confided in me about after only one drink. All those moments gave me a sense of importance, as if I was solving all their problems or at least providing them some comfort which we all desperately need.

*****

It was 12:08 AM in the speakeasy.

"How are our sales thus far?" I inquired, as I walked up to Samson behind the bar.

"You won't believe this Jack, but we've already brought in the same amount of money tonight alone as we would normally have brought in over the course of a month," Samson replied in a zealous tone.

"I believe it, and the night is still young," I said to Samson with a grin.

"That was a lovely speech," Hayley said to me with a smile. "Oh well Samson pressured me into it," I said to Hayley with a snicker.

"It showed a lot of class, Jack," Hayley remarked.

"I'm nothing if not a man of class, kid," I said to Hayley with a snicker.

"Can I take a five minutes break? I have a headache from all the noise," Hayley inquired.

"Go ahead, but it's not slowing down one bit, so get back to work in no longer than five minutes all right?" I inquired. "Don't worry I will," Hayley said to me, and then scampered into the kitchen.

"Your niece reminds me of a friend I used to have back when I lived in *Loire Valley*," Faye remarked with a smile, as she walked up to the bar.

"Oh really what was she like?" I inquired, as I served two men at the bar two pints of beer.

"She was very wise, a leader, and every time I talked with her I felt as if I was talking to a woman who was too big to live in such a quaint farm village," Faye replied.

"Where is she now?" I inquired.

"We grew apart as two people tend to do when time gets the best of them. She wanted to come to America with me, but she had to stay and take care of her grandmother in *Loire Valley*. I wonder to this day what she would be accomplishing if she was in America right now, more than I have ... *c'est la vie*," Faye replied in a somber tone, and then took a long smoke from her cigarette.

"Jack we're now out of bourbon and beer," Samson said to me.

"Make the announcement then, Samson. I've never been good at giving bad news," I said to Samson.

"Do you still have the ingredients for my Black Rose, Jack?" Faye inquired with a grin.

"I never had all the ingredients for that complicated cocktail Miss Dubois, but I improvised just for you," I replied.

"Attention, may I have everyone's attention. We are now out of beer and bourbon, I repeat we are now all out of beer and bourbon," Samson pronounced through the microphone on the stage.

Droves of patrons then began to file out of the speakeasy while others remained comfortably seated with their drink of choice still slaking their thirst. This was the beginning of the end and I couldn't help but feel depressed as I watched patrons exit the speakeasy.

"Gracie, keep singing," I said to Gracie, as I turned on the victrola.

"Jack I got only a couple of songs left in me before I retire for the night. I've never sang so much in my life," Gracie said to me with a smile.

"You have a lovely voice Miss Bishop," Hayley remarked with a smile, as she walked up to Gracie while holding a tray of empty glass tumblers.

"Why thank you honey. I had no idea I would run into such kind and supportive people and out of all places, a speakeasy," Gracie said to Hayley with a smile.

"You were in the right place at the right time, Miss Bishop," Samson said to Gracie with a grin.

"Bless you all. I dedicate this next song to all the workers of the *Jack of All Trades* for giving me this opportunity to shine," Gracie pronounced through the microphone on stage, before she began to sing a slow and sentimental song in the manner of Bessie Smith.

Even though the night was no longer young, patrons were still entering the speakeasy, some of course quickly exited after we told them that we're out of bourbon, beer, and vodka and very low on wine, but we were still doing business. I was surprised that word didn't catch the ear of the NYPD considering the business the speakeasy was doing on its final night. It could either be that the NYPD still hasn't found out, or they just simply are too busy with other matters to shut down my speakeasy prematurely. It was getting quieter in the speakeasy. The once blaring sounds of patrons had now lowered itself to the point where I could hear myself think, which I didn't care for one bit.

*****

It was 1:28 AM in the speakeasy when Samson walked up on stage to make another announcement.

"Attention, may I have everyone's attention. We are now out of wine and whiskey," Samson pronounced through the microphone.

"What do you have left?" a patron inquired from the table in front of the stage.

"We still have plenty of gin left," I shouted.

"Ugh I can't drink straight gin, let's go, dear," the woman said as she gestured for her man to stand up and exit the speakeasy with her.

I noticed that Faye still hadn't left the speakeasy. She wanted to keep me company up until that final moment where I make the decision to shut down the speakeasy for good.

"Mickey you watch the front door, while Samson works at the bar. Hayley let's clear these tables," I pronounced.

Just then a resounding three knocks on the front door echoed throughout the speakeasy, but there was something different about the knocks on the front door this time.

"I'm afraid we're out of everything except for gin right now," Mickey said to the group of six finely dressed men and two dames who entered the speakeasy.

"Jack," Samson said to me, as he pointed to the dapper group of patrons with a stern look on his face.

"I know Samson, be ready," I said to Samson, as I stared intently at the group as they slowly sauntered up to the bar.

There was no mistaking it from their appearance, they were mobsters and they had us out numbered.

"Basta guardare questa discarica e i topi che la fanno funzionare," the mobster dressed in a black suite and fedora with a white ribbon who stood in the center of the group with two dames draped on his shoulders pronounced with a scoff.

"What can I get you?" I inquired as the other five mobsters dispersed themselves throughout the speakeasy as they stared daggers at me.

"You can get me a man by the name of Jack Dansby," the mobster replied with a grin, as one of his dames lit the cigar in his mouth.

"I'm Jack Dansby," I said to the mobster, as I grabbed the pistol underneath the bar.

"Ah do you remember me Mr. Dansby?" the mobster inquired.

"I can't say that I do," I replied, as my eyes darted from the mobster at the bar to each of the five mobsters dispersed around the speakeasy.

"Focus, keep your eye on me amico, not my associates," the mobster said to me in a stern tone as he snapped his gold ring-clad fingers in my face.

"Are you all right? You look like you've seen a ghost," Faye inquired with a smile as she walked up to the bar with Gracie.

"Faye, Gracie, you two to need to leave now, it's going to get ugly in here," I said as the mobster at the bar stared at Faye and Gracie with a grin.

"What's wrong—,"

"Mickey, see these two out!" I interjected in a stern tone, as I gestured for Mickey to escort Faye and Gracie out of the speakeasy.

"You're the man who has defied my organization every step of the way for the past year. I'm not surprised you don't recognize me now. Our last encounter was shrouded in fog," the mobster said to me and then took a long smoke from his cigar. "You were there that night, at Pier 45," I said to the mobster with a wide-eyed stare as Faye and Gracie exited the speakeasy before staring back at me with wide eyes.

"I told that bruto O'Connor to never underestimate his enemies, for it may be the last thing he ever does," the mobster at the bar told me while shaking his head.

"What do you want," I inquired in a stern tone and wide- eyed stare at the mobster at the bar whose demeanor was as relaxed as can be.

"You know I respect how you operate Mr. Dansby, despite the fact that you've undercut every one of my dealings in Greenwich Village for over the past year, but I know a man of purpose and drive when I see one," the mobster at the bar remarked

"If you respect me so much, then why do you want me and my niece dead?" I inquired in a stern tone.

"You took out my head dog Mr. Dansby. If I wanted you and your niece dead then both of you wouldn't be staring at me with those wide-eyes of yours right now," the mobster at the bar replied with a snicker and then took a long smoke from his cigar, as the two dames who sat beside him vainly stared into pocket mirrors while reapplying their whorish makeup.

"Johnny killed my sister just because she had information that could very well bring down your entire organization," I said to the mobster at the bar in a stern tone.

"You watch you're fucking tone when you speak to the boss, capisci?" one imposing mobster who had the same bulking build as Johnny said to me in a stern tone and stare as he walked up to the bar.

"Calm down, Leo. I am a civilized man Mr. Dansby, but even a civilized man can be pushed to the point where he no longer decides to live by societies conventions. I know you despise this liquor outlaw with every drop of red blood that pumps through your veins, which is what brings me here to your little watering hole.

"Then why are you here?" I inquired.

"Lucille, Elena, give Mr. Dansby and I some privacy," the mobster at the bar pronounced with a dismissive wave. The two vapid dames then joined the other mobsters who sat at the table near the stage, while I continued to stare daggers with the calm and debonair mobster at the bar.

"One moment, I have to talk to my associates," I said to the mobster at the bar.

"Jack, what are we going to do," Hayley inquired in a distressed tone, as her and Mickey walked up to me from the kitchen.

"Stay calm. It's just as he said, If he wanted us dead then we wouldn't be talking to him right now, so let's not give him a reason to kill us," I replied, as I turned away from the mobster at the bar and placed both of my hands on Mickey and Hayley's trembling shoulders.

"Aye, but how long can you follow your own advice, Jack?" Samson inquired.

"Keep these two close to you, Samson, while I deal with the mobster at the bar," I said to Samson.

"O'Connor killed your sister, a woman. This goes against the code of my organization. When I told O'Connor this he told me he would 'tie up all the loose ends' regarding you and your niece. I thought O'Connor would have no trouble silencing you both, seeing as how his kill count ranges from mother to cop, but I see now how wrong I was in trusting that ignorant Irish fanculo," the mobster at the bar said to me while shaking his head.

"So you claim you live by higher morals than Johnny did. So why are you here exactly? We're out of everything except gin right now," I said to the mobster at the bar.

"I'm not here for a drink Mr. Dansby. I'm here to make you an offer," the mobster at the bar replied. "What kind of offer?" I inquired.

"An offer you so desperately need at this turning point in your life," the mobster at the bar replied with a snicker.

"I'm not as desperate of a man as you may think I am," I said to the mobster at the bar.

"Before I leave this city for good with my vast wealth, I require a new base of operations, and seeing as how Pier 45 is now far too exposed to the eyes people who see fit for me to be behind bars for the rest of my days, that's where you come in Mr. Dansby. Tonight was your going out of business sale, but how does *Jack of All Trades* the most profitable speakeasy in New York City sound to you?" the mobster at the bar inquired, as the five mobsters and two dames walked up to the bar and stood on both sides of him, while Samson, Hayley and Mickey stood beside me.

"It sounds too good to be true," I replied.

"If you allow my associates to use your speakeasy for our base of operations henceforth, then you have my word, you will no longer have to deal in the shadows. You will no longer have to constantly be looking over your shoulder whenever you set foot outside of this bar. You will be a prominent business owner, just like you were before this liquor outlaw act passed. No you will be greater than that, for the business which my organization will bring you will make you the only speakeasy in New York City. What do you say Mr. Dansby?" the mobster at the bar inquired with a grin.

"Jack, no. You know my mother wouldn't want this from you," Hayley said to me in a distressed tone, as she grabbed onto my arm.

"I don't have a choice do I," I inquired.

"All men have a choice Mr. Dansby. There are times when the right choice and the easy choice are one in the same, but I'll ask you once more, do you want to become the only speakeasy in New York City, and have all your financial needs met, or do you want to continue to languish like all the rest of the topi in this city?" the mobster at the bar inquired.

"Before I give you my answer, tell me, what's your name?" I inquired.

"Fair enough mi amico. My name is Charles Luciano, and I am a boss of the Five Points Gang. We are the true law in this city. Now … what do you say Mr. Dansby?" the mobster at the bar replied with a grin.

CHAPTER 8:
ALL THE SCARY FACES
- HAYLEY -

It's been two weeks and I still couldn't believe Jack would do this. They all looked like Johnny, and I couldn't help but tremble each time I walked past one of them in the speakeasy. That man, Mr. Luciano, he manipulated Jack. He knew exactly what to say in order to get Jack to work for him, and now the speakeasy is the central hub for the Five Points Gang, the most powerful crime organization in New York City. It was as if with one choice Jack invited all the monsters of New York City into the speakeasy. Was Jack's reason for doing this solely based on money or was there another ulterior motive which I failed to see in that critical moment?

"Hayley go serve Frankie at table 4 his scotch on the rocks," Samson said to me, as he placed the drink upon my empty tray. "I don't like the way he looks at me," I said to Samson in a timid tone, as I brushed a strand of my hair behind my ear.

"For the first time in over 5 years this speakeasy can now afford the finest of amenities, kid, and that's all thanks to Mr. Luciano. So you will be as pleasant as possible with all of our upscale patrons," Jack said to me in a stern tone, as he aggressively pointed at table 4.

It's true that the speakeasy has undergone many improvements over the past two weeks, such as a new jazz band, a black marble bar with brass lining, and I even have a bed of my own now in the kitchen. The speakeasy was flourishing all because Jack chose to cater to the man who wanted us dead two weeks ago. There was something about Mr. Luciano that frightened me even more than Johnny or even Fernando, could it be because of his suave demeanor, like a wolf in sheep's clothing? Or could it be because he is perhaps the wealthiest man in New York City, and wealth equals power.

"Here's your drink Mr. Angelo," I said to Frankie with a smile, as I walked up to his table and served him the scotch on the rocks. It would always make me more nervous serving Frankie Angelo when he was sitting alone at a table, because the times when he was with his wife he was less likely to flirt with me, and now was not one of those times.

"Whoa, what's the hurry doll? Sit down and rest those pretty feet of yours for a minute," Frankie said to me with a snicker as he gestured for me to sit down in the empty chair across from him.

"S-Sorry but I'm very busy. Is there anything else I can get you?" I inquired as I averted my eyes downward not to look into the eyes of the lecherous Frankie Angelo.

"That will be all for now, but don't stray too far from me, doll," Frankie replied with a snicker and wink.

Were Jack and I now safe from the Five Points Gang now that we were catering to them? Or were we now in even deeper danger? Everywhere I looked in the speakeasy I saw finely dressed mobsters either staring back at me, or feeling up the dames that their currently with. The speakeasy has now become a place inhabited by men who prey off of all the weaknesses of this city. The password of the speakeasy was no longer 'Delilah' Mr. Luciano quickly changed it to 'Lucky Luciano' after Jack took his offer. So now there is no memory of my mother motivating Jack in this speakeasy.

"So then I stomped the fucking mook's head in until he quit asking questions!" a mobster at the bar shouted with a cackle, as I walked up to the bar.

I noticed that Samson was humoring that belligerent mobster at the bar as he shook his head with a grin. Samson may have a past that's similar to the Five Points Gang, but I know he's not a violent man, I can tell by the look in his eyes.

"I'm here Jack," Mickey pronounced, as he walked up to the bar with a sigh.

"Get serving, Mickey. We have to see to it that all of Mr. Luciano's associate's needs are met. That's the purpose of this speakeasy now," Jack said to Mickey in a stern tone, as he tossed him a black vest.

"What a shame," I remarked.

"What was that, kid? Jack inquired in a stern tone, as he grabbed my arm in an aggressive manner.

"Nothing," I replied in a timid tone.

"It's because of these men that you can afford to sleep on a bed now, so I don't want to hear any attitude coming from you, understand?" Jack inquired in a stern tone and stare.

"Yes, I understand, Jack," I replied as Jack let go of my arm with a scoff.

What had happened to Jack? He now treats me the same cruel way he did when I first arrived at this speakeasy three months ago. I wanted the old Jack back, the Jack that smiled at me with such kindness in his eyes moments after he awoke from his near death experience with Johnny.

"Hayley are you all right?" Mickey inquired, as he walked up to me behind the bar.

"What does it matter how I feel anymore," I replied in a somber tone.

"It matters to me," Mickey said to me, as he took my hand.

"I'll talk to you about it some other time when we're not surrounded by these mobsters," I said to Mickey.

"I don't know if that's possible now. I think being surrounded by mobsters is our new life," Mickey said to me.

"No Mr. Luciano said that sometimes 'the easy choice and the right choice are one in the same.' Jack saw no other choice when he chose to cater to these mobsters, but I see a life of mine that doesn't revolve around these terrible men," I said to Mickey in a stern tone, as I pulled my hand away from his grasp.

"Hayley, Mickey, quit holding hands and get back to work!" Jack shouted, as he pointed at the tables.

What would my mother do right now if she was alive? Would she try to talk some sense into Jack by any means possible? I missed her voice so much right now. I needed a breath of fresh air among this sea of scary faces which suffocates me, but where could I go?

"I need a break," I said to Jack as I wiped my flushed forehead with my hand with a sigh and then entered the kitchen.

There's something to be said about a man who would sell his soul to the devil all for the sake of money, but during these times, it sure is understandable. If I were to tell this to Jack he would most likely tell me that he doesn't have a soul. Jack is doing what he believes he must do in order to survive in this world, however, I am not Jack, and no amount of wealth will make me happily cater to men who killed my mother and tried to kill me. Perhaps I should give up on Jack and focus on finding a way out of this speakeasy of monsters. All my basic needs were being met with some nice amenities as well, but I felt more scared now in my comfortable bed surrounded by these mobsters than when I was in the hospital soon after discovering my mother lying dead in our apartment. I felt that any one of these mobsters that surrounded me could use me for any desire they see fit in the moment and I would be too weak and crippled with fear to fight back against them. I then suddenly began breathing at a frantic pace, as I placed my hand upon my heaving chest.

"Hayley are you all right?" Mickey inquired as he entered the kitchen.

"There's no escape from this. We are now bound to the Five Points Gang till death. Was Jack even aware of this when he made that choice?" I replied as my eyes began to well up with tears.

"Why would you want to escape? The Five Points Gang are keeping us from living on the street, which I feared was going to happen to me soon after this speakeasy was going to shut down, but now ... the sky is the limit for us Hayley. We work for the true law of this city. I remember those words that Mr. Luciano said. This means that we are protected by the Five Points Gang as well," Mickey said to me as he sat down beside me on my bed.

"You sound like Jack. So tell me this, if the Five Points Gang is the true law in this city, then who will protect us from them?" I inquired, in a tearful tone, as I stood up from the bed and pointed to the bar.

"Jack is furious. What the hell are you two doing in here?" Samson inquired in a stern tone as he entered the kitchen.

"Sorry Samson," Mickey said to Samson as he scampered out of the kitchen.

"So what are you blubbering about lass?" Samson inquired. "Just leave me alone Samson," I replied in a tearful tone, as I wiped the tears from my face with a handkerchief.

"Listen … I don't enjoy catering to these mobsters, but I do what I must. I know better than most how these men operate, and as long as we show them respect, then all our needs will be met," Samson said to me.

"Is that supposed to cheer me up?" I inquired.

"No I've never been that good at cheering up kids. All I know is that if you work for wolves, then you must not give them a reason to doubt your loyalty, or you will find yourself in their bellies," Samson said to me and then exited the kitchen.

"I had to clear my head, but where in Greenwich Village could I go that would give me peace of mind?

"Where do you think you're going, kid?" Jack inquired as I quickly walked towards the front door of the speakeasy without responding to him.

"Hayley!" Jack shouted as I exited the speakeasy.

I then began running down the alley towards the first taxicab I could see. I didn't know where I was going. All I knew was that I had to get away from all of those mobsters eyes. They all made my skin crawl, especially Frankie Angelo.

"Where to missy," the cab driver inquired, as I entered the cab and slammed the door closed.

"Uhm … take me to Broadway please," I replied. I then looked out the back window of the taxicab with wide eyes to the sight of a mobster staring back at me. I couldn't make out who the mobster was as the taxicab drove down Minetta Street, but I had such an unnerving feeling that he was going to follow me.

I felt more air filling my lungs with every block that the utmost respect even though I was a stand in, he made me feel as if I was on the same acting echelon as him. I wish there were taxicab traveled away from the speakeasy. The skies then began to cloud over as the neon lights of Broadway shined brighter in the distance, as if they were calling to me as I'm sure they've called to many young girls in this city looking to them with wide eyes gleaming with a sense of yearning and hopelessness. Was I destined to cater to mobsters now for the rest of my life, or could I become known to the world for having beauty and grace, just like all the actors on these sparkling billboards?

"You can stop here," I said to the cab driver in a somber tone as I paid him my fair and then exited the taxicab.

I felt so out-of-place as I walked down Broadway Street. Everything was so glamorous, the billboards, the people, the fashion, everything displayed before me was a life I could never achieve as long as I stayed imprisoned in that speakeasy with Jack and all of those mobsters which he so graciously caters to. "I used to be on that billboard. Please support a fallen actress so I may entertain you all once again," a woman dressed in a tattered black dress shouted in such a desperate and heartbreaking tone, as she sat on a mass of blankets upon the ground outside the entrance of a theatre.

"Sure lady and I used to date Katherine Hepburn," a man said to the woman with a cackle and then spit on her.

"Leave her alone!" I shouted, as I scampered over to the poor woman.

"Oh don't fret over me child. I'm used to being treated like garbage," the woman said to me in a somber tone.

"Is it true? Were you really an actress on Broadway?" I inquired, as I sat down on the mass of blankets beside the woman.

"It's all true, but my true claim to fame was standing in as an acting partner for Cary Grant," the woman replied followed by a wrenching cough.

"Oh my mother adored Cary Grant. She would always swoon whenever she watched a film he starred in," I said to the woman with a smile.

"He was a gallant and debonair man who showed me the more men like Cary in this day and age, but as you can see this depression has turned men into pigs," the woman said to me with a scowl and scoff.

"Please can we talk in that diner down the street?" I inquired, as I pointed to the diner down the street from the theatre.

"Of course we can my dear. I am never one to turn down an act of benevolence when it's presented to me," the woman said to me as she stood up from the mass of blankets with a groan.

"I'm Hayley Carmona," I said to the woman with a warm smile.

"It's a pleasure to meet you, Hayley. I'm Nora Lee Bridges," the woman said to me with a smile, as we walked towards the diner.

*****

It was 6:47 PM in the diner as Nora Lee regaled me with stories of her life as an actress of stage and screen.

"How were you able to perform when you were my age?" I inquired with a wide-eyed stare and then took a long sip of my strawberry milkshake, while Nora Lee primped her hair with a sigh.

"At first I was terrified at all of those eyes fixed upon me. When I was fifteen I saw the world and all the people in it as my potential fans. I had such an ego which fueled my performances, but like all young women at that age I inevitably succumb to all those judging eyes, all those scary faces which stripped me bare of my ego," Nora Lee replied, and then took a sip of coffee.

"May I ask ... how did you—,"

"End up like this? The life of an actress is a fickle one. Only the rare few remain and become world renowned. When this depression hit, I could no longer make a living with the few bit parts I managed to get. My mother told me to find a wealthy well off man who could support me during these times, but I told her that I know my talent was genuine and I didn't need a man to support me during these times," Nora Lee interjected, as she lit a cigarette and took a smoke.

"Do you ever regret the life you chose?" I inquired and then took a long sip of my strawberry milkshake, finishing it with a slurp.

"At times, when it gets really cold at night I yearn for a warm bed, but not a man to hold me throughout the night," Nora Lee replied.

"My life is … well … I feel trapped, surrounded by monsters, but I lack the strength to live on my own," I said to Nora Lee in a somber tone.

"You my dear are a competent, intelligent, and most importantly, kind young woman. The only thing trapping you is that fear that you feel. Whoever instilled that fear in your heart is a coward themselves. You must see through all the guises of men. Most of them are cowardly little boys underneath their smug facades," Nora Lee said to me with a snicker, as she placed her hand upon mine on the table.

"Except for Cary Grant, right?" I inquired with a giggle.

"Oh he was a gentleman's gentleman. A prince among thieves," Nora Lee replied with a smile.

Even though Nora Lee was tinted with dirt, and her dress was torn, she was still beautiful. She reminded me of how I looked when I first arrived at the speakeasy. What broke my heart was that Nora Lee was only 32 years old. I believed in her, and I wanted to see her return to her life of stage and screen so much, but perhaps those days are long gone for her. I wanted to help her, but all I could afford was to pay for our drinks at this diner which appeared to be full of finely dressed people enjoying their lavish lives. At least Nora Lee experienced a life of fame. No matter how fleeting it may have been she stood in the limelight and performed with grace.

"If I may ask, when did you lose your mother?" Nora Lee inquired in a somber tone.

"How did you know?" I replied in a somber tone.

"I used to be an actress, sweetheart. I can detect a tone of loss in someone's voice when they speak to me, and you also referred to your mother in the past tense when you told me she was a fan of Cary Grant," Nora Lee replied.

"Well … about three months ago, my mother died. I didn't lose her, she was taken from me by her mobster boyfriend," I said to Nora Lee in a somber tone.

"I'm sorry Hayley. What family do you have left now?" Nora Lee inquired.

"Just my uncle Jack, my mother told me in her will that he has a heart, but most of the time he treats me so cruelly," I replied.

"Your mother knew Jack in a way nobody could. The bond between a brother and sister is unspoken. You can feel what your sibling is feeling with the slightest glance. My older brother Patrick died in the war when I was eighteen years old. That was right around the time when I started getting recognition as an actress on Broadway. When my mother told me the news of my brother's death I was devastated. It was as if at that moment a part of my heart died along with him. Before my brother went off to fight in the war he was always there to support and care for me and my mother. Patrick could read my eyes the way no other person could. Even the acting teachers on Broadway failed to sense my emotions the way Patrick could. I didn't have to act around my brother, because every time I did, he would see right through the ruse. They say actors are the greatest liars. This may be true, but I've always seen actors as storytellers," Nora lee said to me.

"Anything else?" the waitress inquired as she walked up to me and Nora

Lee.

"We're all done," replied after taking a permissive glance at Nora Lee.

"I'm sorry. I wish I could do more for you, but all I can afford is to pay for these drinks," I said to Nora Lee in as somber tone as a rummaged through my purse for money.

"Shhh, don't fret over me honey. My days as an actress are long gone, but you still have a bright future ahead of you. Nobody with a heart as big as yours will remain unseen," Nora Lee said to me with a smile while shaking her head as she placed her hand upon mine.

"I would take you back with me to the speakeasy where I live, but I just know that Jack and the mobsters he caters to will not allow you to live with us, he can barely stand me living with him as it is," I said to Nora Lee in a somber tone.

"Here you are ladies," the waitress pronounced as she placed the check on the table.

"No, I don't want to further impose your life, Hayley," Nora Lee said to me as I counted out the change and placed it on the check.

"I don't want to go back to that place. It's filled with men who answer to nobody, men who kill and instill fear into the hearts of everyone all for the sake of money. I don't feel safe there. Please can I just stay with you?" I inquired in a somber tone, as my eyes welled up with tears.

"Hayley, sweetheart, you're meant for far greater things than panhandling for change outside of a theatre. I understand your fear having to live with those dangerous men, but you must persevere. I know you're strong enough, I can see it in your eyes just as my brother saw in my eyes the passion I had to be an actress," Nora Lee said to me with a warm smile, as her face quivered.

"I feel so alone. No matter what I do it never stops hurting deep down inside of me. She wasn't just my mother, she was my best friend," I said to Nora Lee in a tearful tone.

"My brother was my best friend as well. Remember to keep those memories of your mother whenever those terrible mobsters begin to overwhelm you. Draw from the happy memories of your mother, just as I draw from the happy memories of my brother in times of despair," Nora said to me.

"What will you do now?" I inquired, as I wiped my tear stained cheeks with a black handkerchief.

"I will continue to keep hope in my heart. It's all I can do at this time," Nora Lee replied as she stood up from the chair.

I then quickly stood up from my chair and firmly wrapped my arms around Nora Lee in the manner I used to do with my mother when I was younger.

"Honey … thank you for your act of kindness Now go, this world awaits your beautiful heart," Nora Lee said to me with a warm smile and then exited the diner with a series of coughs.

*****

It was 7: 45 PM as I sat in the taxicab with an overwhelming sense of hopelessness which bared down on me more and more the closer the taxicab driver came to the speakeasy. I don't know why I saw my mother in older women I've met in the past three months, but perhaps it could be because I had no maternal figure to confide in any more.

"Here you go," I said to the taxicab driver in a timid tone as I paid my fare and then exited the taxicab to an ugly sight.

"You nearly gave me the slip there little lady," Frankie said to me with a grin as he flipped a coin.

"Mr. Angelo, why were you following me?" I inquired in a distressed tone, as Frankie quickly stepped in front of the front door of the speakeasy.

"I'm your guardian angel now, doll face," Frankie replied with a grin.

"Guardian angel … what do you mean by that?" I inquired. "You and your uncle work for Mr. Luciano now, therefore   you two will need protection from forces that wish to shut down Mr. Luciano's entire organization. Your uncle Jack appointed me to protect you from such forces," Frankie replied.

"Jack told you to follow me whenever I leave the speakeasy, why?" I inquired in a distressed toned.

"Perhaps your uncle doesn't trust you, but don't worry your pretty little red head over it, Mr. Luciano has appointed his associates to that kid and that Irishman as well," Frankie replied.

"You're talking about Mickey and Samson. Well, neither of them, nor do I, want or need protection from any of you," I said to Frankie in a stern tone.

"It's not up to you sweetheart, or even your uncle Jack. You four work for the most powerful man in New York. Mr. Luciano has paved your way in life where he could have easily written your gravestones so I suggest you show me respect," Frankie said to me in a stern tone as he slowly walked towards me in a menacing manner.

I was terrified. My worst fears have now come true. My mother was dead, and now Jack won't let me breathe fresh air without feeling Frankie breathing down my neck. What could I do now, where could I go, was there any where to go where the Five Points Gang couldn't follow?

"Are you going to let me in my own home?" I inquired in a stern tone and stare.

"By all means … oh and remember, we can either build you and your uncle up or tear you both down in one fell swoop. It all depends on your trustworthiness to our organization," Frankie said to me.

"What's the password?" Samson inquired in a stern tone as he slid open the iron window of the front door.

"Lucky Luciano, It's me Samson, let me in damn it," I replied in a stern tone.

"Hayley, Jack was wondering where you ran off to so hastily," Samson said to me, as I entered the speakeasy to the sight of a very beautiful woman singing on the stage with jazz musicians playing alongside her.

"They're following all of us when we leave the speakeasy," I whispered as

I leaned in close to Samson's face.

"Who's following us?" Samson inquired.

"The Five Points Gang," I replied as the singer on the stage stuck her leg out and pulled up her dress, exposing her legs which were covered in shear black pantyhose.

"I can barely hear you over the hollering, let's go to the kitchen," Samson said to me.

"Wait," I said to Samson as I noticed the beautiful singer walk down to the front table where a mobster stood with his arm draped over Mickey's shoulder.

To my dismay, the mobster then forced Mickey down into a chair and the singer proceeded to dance slowly in front of him, as the mobsters around Mickey hollered like rabid monkeys. I then scampered into the kitchen as my heart raced at the sight of that beautiful singer seducing Mickey.

"Who is that singer?" I inquired, as my eyes welled up with tears.

"Oh that luscious dame goes by the name of Ms. Carmen Valentino. She's supposedly the highest paid female jazz singer in New York," Samson replied.

"If she's so famous, then why is she performing in this speakeasy?" I inquired.

"I guess she's doing Mr. Luciano a favor," Samson replied, and then opened the freezer and took out two bags of ice.

"Why was she trying to seduce Mickey?" I inquired in a distressed tone.

"Think nothing of it. These mobsters want to make that boy a man, but I told them that Mickey is already a man," Samson said to me with a snicker.

"It's not funny. Are you all right with all of this? Every day catering to mobster and then being followed by them as soon as you leave this speakeasy?" I inquired in a distressed tone.

"This doesn't surprise me. This is how crime organizations work," Samson replied with a sigh as he shook his head.

"We have even less freedom now than we did when Johnny was hunting us," I said to Samson in a distressed tone, as the mobsters applauded Miss Valentino's seductive performance.

"These are the cards that were dealt to us. We can play their game and see how these men can enrich our lives, or we can leave the table. I know all too well the consequences of leaving the table, Hayley, and I'm tired of running," Samson said to me.

"Where's Jack?" I inquired.

"He's out finalizing a liquor deal in *East Harlem* with some mobster who goes by the name of Carlo "the Coroner" Bianco," Samson replied.

"I-I need to be alone," I said to Samson in a tearful tone, as I sat down at my desk and opened my diary.

"You have five minutes, Hayley, then—,"

"Just leave me alone!" I shouted, as tears began to stream from my bleary eyes.

They were horrid, every last one of them. I felt their eyes on me in the speakeasy, and now I couldn't escape from them no matter where I ran to.

Perhaps Samson is right. Perhaps I should just accept my life as a servant for mobsters. Frankie's message in the alley struck fear into my heart. I don't want to end up like my mother, but I also don't want to graciously serve the men who took her from me.

"Hayley, Samson said you saw Ms. Valentino performing for me," Mickey said to me as he entered the kitchen.

"I did. You must've really enjoyed it," I remarked in a sulking tone.

"They forced me. Those two mobsters held me down in the chair while Ms. Valentino danced for me.

"Oh please, don't pretend like you didn't like it. I saw that smile on your face," I said to Mickey in a stern tone and stare.

"Hayley, if those mobsters weren't holding me down in the chair I would've never taken a second look at Ms. Valentino," Mickey said to me in a distressed tone.

"You don't have to make excuses for me. I know I could never hold a candle to her beauty," I said to Mickey in a somber tone, as my face quivered in such a manner that could only be evoked from an act of betrayal from someone I care for.

"Hayley I think you're beautiful. Please … I care about you. I worry for your safety in this speakeasy now more than ever, but I'm willing to risk my safety in order to keep you safe in here, or at least try my best," Mickey said to me in a somber tone.

"You couldn't protect me in here no more than you could protect yourself. You're not my hero. You're just a desperate boy looking for a thrill," I said to Mickey in a stern tone as tears streamed from my eyes.

"I am desperate Hayley, desperate to make you happy, and seeing you cry right now hurts me more than those mobsters ever could. I hope you can forgive me," Mickey said to me in a somber tone and then exited the kitchen.

I thought he was special. I thought he was different, but I was mistaken. Mickey almost fooled me into believing that he was loyal to me. Mickey showed me his true colors when Ms. Valentino danced for him. Jack has changed. He's now become another servant for the Five Points Gang who I fear will stop at nothing when it comes to bootlegging liquor. Samson had a history with deadly gangs, so he knew how to stay on their good side. Was I the only one left in this speakeasy who dared to break free from the Five Points Gang?

*****

It was 10:42 PM in the speakeasy as Jack and a ghostly pale man wearing a black trench coat and fedora entered the kitchen with a cackle that made me recoil to the back of my chair.

"Oh you're back. Carlo, this is my niece," Jack said to Carlo, as he sneered at me in such a sinister manner which sent chills up my spine.

"It's a pleasure to meet you Ms. Carmona. Mr. Luciano says that you're braver than most of his associates," Carlo remarked as he tipped his hat.

He resembled a skeleton who someone forgot to bury, a ghoul, a fiend dressed in black. God only know what influence he was having over Jack. This mobster who goes by the name of Carlo "the Coroner" Bianco had the scariest face out of all the mobsters I've seen in the speakeasy.

"Could you give us some privacy, Carlo?" Jack inquired.

"Certainly, I have matters I must attend to in the *Financial District*. Oh and Jack, don't forget to report to me every time you witness such a sight," Carlo said to Jack in a stern tone while pointing his finger at him.

"Yes sir," Jack said to Carlo with a nod.

"Good man," Carlo said to Jack with a grin as he pated he cheek and then exited the speakeasy.

"We need to talk, kid," Jack said to me with a sigh.

"Frankie told me everything. I can't believe you would do this to me. You're becoming one of them, aren't you," I said to Jack in a distressed tone.

"We're all being followed, kid. We have no choice in the matter when we're working for Mr. Luciano," Jack said to me. "Don't speak for me. I'm now a prisoner here!" I shouted, as I jolted up from the chair.

"Mr. Luciano is the most powerful man in New York. If we stay in his good graces then we can have anything we want," Jack said to me in a stern tone.

"You really believe that. Johnny said those same lies just to lure in my mother. They own you, you're just a dog to them," I said to Jack in a stern tone.

"If I'm just a dog then what does that make you, kid? Oh yes, a little bitch whimpering for sympathy," Jack remarked in a stern tone, as he stared at me with such anger burning in his eyes.

What have these horrid mobsters done to Jack? I know my mother wouldn't want this life for me or him, but should I even bother trying to open Jack's eyes to the truth of the matter. Jack's face now resembled one of the countless horrid mobsters in the speakeasy and I no longer see him as my uncle.

"I see family means nothing to you!" I shouted in a tearful tone.

"What family? Mr. Luciano and all of his associates are all the family I need. They can protect me and support me financially in ways I could only imagine before. You're such a goddamn child. Stop speaking for your mother, she's dead and you need to look forward or else you won't these opportunities laid out in front of you," Jack said to me in a stern tone.

"I know you don't mean that. You're just scared," I said to Jack in a distressed tone as I shook my head.

"One of these days, kid, you will look back and thank me for this choice I made, but until then, a word of advice, don't act like your mother towards these mobsters," Jack said to me in a stern tone and then exited the kitchen.

I was beset by forces far stronger than I could ever hope to be, and I see now that those forces have influenced Jack, Mickey, and Samson. I wish I was back at the hospital when I first was rushed away from the crime scene that was my dead mother by the NYPD. Those men that investigated my mother's death didn't feel or give off a demeanor befitting the police. I remember the horrific moment quite clearly. When I called 911 the first men to come to the apartment that night were a bearded man in a trench coat and fedora, and another man dressed in a common policeman's uniform, but then after no more than five minutes, another group of men arrived at the apartment. These men were different than the police. The way they carried themselves, how they dressed, and they're over all demeanor was that of a mobster. I then remember one suave looking man who took the man wearing the trench coat aside to the corner of the living room and spoke to him for a few moments before leaving. The suave man then grinned at me before him and four other men exited the apartment. It was him! The very man who I'm being held prisoner by at this moment, Mr. Luciano was the suave man who visited the apartment with his four associates the night my mother was killed. He was trying to cover up her death, and judging by how everything unfolded up to this point, it appears that extremely wealthy and powerful men like him can get away with murder.

*****

It was 12:56 PM in the speakeasy as I tossed and turned in bed.

I always had trouble falling asleep now just knowing those mobsters where in the next room, and every night the last mobster to leave the speakeasy was Frankie Angelo. That horrid man who calls himself my guardian angel made my skin crawl just thinking about him.

"Take care Samson, and make sure you meet up with Carlo tomorrow," Jack said as he entered the kitchen.

"Are they all gone?" I inquired in a timid tone, as I rolled over in bed, facing Jack who sat down in bed with a sigh as he stripped off his vest and tie.

"It's just me and you now, kid," Jack replied with a sigh.

I then rolled back over facing away from Jack, as my bleary eyes finally began to close from a night full of fear.

*****

"Jack there's been an incident in *Washington Square Park*," a voice shouted in the speakeasy at 8:16 AM, startling me awake as I sprung out of bed and peeked through the open crack of the kitchen door.

"Calm down Mickey, what's happened that's got you in such an uproar?" Jack inquired, as Mickey took off his newsboy hat and sat down at the bar as he heaved in such a concerning manner.

"I was cutting through the park as I always do on my way here when four boys my age started chasing me," Mickey replied, as Jack poured him a glass of water.

"Again, damn son, why does a boy your age have so many enemies?" Jack inquired as he handed Mickey the glass of water.

"No it's not like that. I was minding my own business I swear. That park has changed. Those four boys then caught up to me and threw me down. One of the boys then shouted 'We know you have money. We've seen you enter that speakeasy. Now cough up the cash or you'll be coughing up blood,' one of the boys said to me, as they all started pummeling me," Mickey said to Jack.

"That would explain your battered face. I have to say, you can really take a beating," Jack remarked with a snicker.

Was Jack so cruel and sadistic now that he actually found it amusing every time poor Mickey got pummeled? Jack appeared to humor Mickey every time this happened, but never really showed any concern for his well being. Why was this always happening to Mickey? He didn't deserve pain and it hurt me to see his battered face.

"I then heard four gunshots, and before I knew it, the four boys dropped to the ground beside me," Mickey said to Jack in a distressed tone.

"You're one lucky kid, Mickey," Jack remarked with a snicker.

"It's not luck. I know you know who shot those boys," I said to Jack in a stern tone as I walked up to him behind the bar. "A man wearing a black suite with a black feather sticking out of his fedora then walked up to me and told me to run back to the speakeasy," Mickey said to Jack.

"The man who saved your life from those little rats goes by the name of Donovan "the dead eye" Falcone," Jack said to Mickey.

"So he's the mobster who's following me," Mickey remarked.

"You see Hayley. Just imagine what could've happened to Mickey if Donovan wasn't protecting him," Jack said to me.

"No, they didn't deserve to die. That mobster could've just scared them away. They would've learned their lesson sure enough then," Mickey said to Jack in a somber tone.

"Wake up Mickey. People don't learn lessons in this day and age. The only way to defend your life is to kill," Jack said to Mickey in a stern tone and stare as he pointed at him.

"Did that ghoulish looking man tell you that?" I inquired with a scoff.

"If you're referring to Carlo, then no, I for one always believed in that truth. We work for an iron curtain now. No harm will come to us out there as long as we stay loyal to Mr. Luciano and his associates. I suggest you say thank you to Mr. Falcone next time you see him in the speakeasy. The man gave you a second chance at life after all," Jack said to Mickey.

"What are you becoming?" I inquired while shaking my head.

"Don't start up with me, kid, it's far too early and I'm far too hung over to suffer that self-righteous nagging mouth of yours," Jack said to me in a stern tone.

Four boys were killed just because Mickey took a shortcut through *Washington Square Park* to get here. Although those boys could've killed Mickey if they kept pummeling him, I still agree with Mickey that they didn't deserve to die. I'm sure those four boys had hopes and dreams just like me and Mickey, but this cruel world made them resort to violence and robbery because they saw it to be their only way to survive. Mickey and I were being followed by the most dangerous men in New York, but I for one didn't feel protected. It was as if a hungry lion was protecting me from other hungry lions, and I fear there may soon come a time when that hungry lion chooses to go after the easy prey and devour me. A knock on the door then drew me, Jack, and Mickey's attention, as Jack scampered over to the front door with his hand grabbing his gun tucked between the waist-band of his pants.

"Lucky Luciano, now open the fucking door Dansby, we need to talk," a voice shouted through the iron window of the front door.

"Yes sir," Jack said, and then quickly unlocked the front door in a frantic manner.

"That piccolo bastardo over there has become a liability to our organization," the ghoulish looking man known as Carlo "the Coroner" remarked in a stern tone as he entered the speakeasy with two other mobsters who looked familiar to me. "Ah Ms. Carmona, do you remember us," one of the mobsters inquired with a grin, as the other mobster slowly walked behind me while cracking his knuckles.

"I-uhm I don't know, you look familiar," I replied in a timid tone, as the two mobsters walked closer together, trapping me between them.

"Why don't you refresh her memory, Marco," one of the mobsters said.

"It would be my pleasure," one of the mobsters said and then walked behind the bar and began to fill up a pitcher of water.

"Mickey told me how Donovan intervened when he was getting beaten half to death by the group of boys," Jack said to Carlo.

"You look thirsty. Here have a drink," one of the mobsters said with a snicker, as he tossed the full pitcher of water at me. I then gasped as the entire pitcher of water soaked me to the skin, while the two mobsters began to cackle. My face quivered in fear and embarrassment as the two mobsters cackled at me.

"Why did you do that?" Mickey inquired in a stern tone, as he stood between me and the mobster who tossed the pitcher of water.

"I'm surprised you don't remember us as well bambino," one of the mobsters said with a snicker.

"Well Patricio why don't you refresh his memory," Marco, said to the mobster known as Patricio and then walked over to Mickey and swiftly punched him in the gut, which sent him collapsing to his knees.

"Do you two remember us now," Patricio inquired in a stern tone.

"Yes we met you two at the Pier, That's when I sent you both diving into the river," I replied in a stern tone, as I wiped my soaking strands of hair behind my ears.

"Perché piccola puttana!" Patricio shouted.

"That's enough boys," Carlo shouted, as he grabbed Patricio's hand before it could strike me in my sodden and quivering face.

"Ah, why if it isn't the Rivelli brothers, I didn't think you two would still be employed by Mr. Luciano," Jack remarked with a snicker.

"Keep those delusions of grandeur in check, Jack. Just because you work for Mr. Luciano now doesn't mean we work for you," Patricio said to me in a stern tone.

"He's right Jack. Now back to the matter at hand before this fottuto deficient distracted me with such trivialities," Carlo said in a stern tone.

"What's the problem Carlo?" Jack inquired.

"Four boys are dead, that's the problem, and even though those boys were just pitiful orphans like this one here, four dead bodies are still a great deal to cover up," Carlo replied.

"What do you need of me?" Jack inquired with a sigh.

"We need you to keep your fucking kids out of trouble. My associates who are protecting them will not exercise restraint. They will eliminate the targets that are attacking them," Carlo replied in a stern tone.

"They're not my kids Carlo. If I could put them both on a leash I would," Jack said to Carlo as he made a stern glance towards me and Mickey.

"Don't get me wrong. I can make those four bodies disappear as if they never existed. They don't call me the coroner for nothing, but these two are quickly becoming a liability, and we all know how Mr. Luciano deals with potential liabilities," Carlo said with a snicker.

"Understood sir," Jack said to Carlo in a stern tone and stare.

"Arrivederci Jack," Carlo said and then exited the speakeasy with the Rivelli brothers.

"Goddamn it. We could've used Samson just now," Jack remarked.

"You two heard Carlo. Mr. Luciano doesn't suffer liabilities like me. So stay out of trouble when you leave this speakeasy," Jack pronounced.

"That's impossible. Trouble surrounds us," I said to Jack in a distressed tone.

"Damn it kid!" Jack shouted as he threw a whiskey bottle passed my head into the front door of the speakeasy.

"I-I'm sorry Jack. I'll try my best t-to stay out of trouble from here on out," Mickey said in a timid tone, as Jack rested his head in both his hands upon the black marble of the bar.

"Jack ... I'm scared too," I said to Jack in a somber tone as I placed my hand upon his shoulder.

"Of course you are. You're just a kid. Mickey, clean up that bottle while I take inventory of our liquor," Jack said in a stern tone as he brushed off my hand from his shoulder and then stormed into the kitchen.

Jack put up a tough front as usual whenever he was around all the mobsters. It was his way of showing them that he still runs this speakeasy. No matter how I tried, I was unable to do that. I could never put up a façade to project to the world a false image of me. I don't doubt that acting that way could perhaps help me whenever I'm around these mobsters, but at that moment when Marco Rivelli tossed that bucket of water on me in front of everyone, I felt lower than a drowned rat, and most likely looked like one too.

"How's business, Jack?" Samson inquired as he entered the speakeasy.

"You're late Samson. We could've used your domineering stature five minutes ago," Jack said to Samson in a stern tone as he exited the kitchen.

"What happened now?" Samson inquired with a groan as he put his black vest on.

"Carlo and the Rivelli brothers sent us a message if you know what I mean," Jack replied with a scoff, as he pointed to me and Mickey.

"Aye, I know exactly what you mean. Heed that message Jack. I doubt a man like Mr. Luciano gives people second chances," Samson said to Jack.

"We're still alive. If they wanted us dead they could do so very easily, just like how that mobster killed those four boys who attacked Mickey," I pronounced.

"I need to teach you some basic boxing moves, son," Samson said to Mickey with a grin.

"I just said that four boys were killed. Does anybody even care?" I inquired in a distressed tone.

"Those rats were trying to rob poor Mickey here, as far as I see it, they got what was coming to them," Jack remarked.

"Even though I'm not the one who killed them, I still feel guilty," Mickey remarked in a somber tone.

"Now they won't even get a proper burial. Thanks to Carlo, those four boys will be wiped off the face of this earth," I pronounced in a distressed tone.

"You're always so dramatic, kid. If you really want to prevent others from being killed by the mobsters that follow us, then do what Carlo said and stay out of trouble," Jack said to me in a stern tone.

"Don't you see, we are the trouble now!" I shouted and then scampered into the kitchen.

I sat down on my bed with a sigh, as I wiped the water off my flushed forehead with a towel. That's when I noticed it once again. The dumbwaiter behind the shelves, but Samson had covered it up with a plate of steel. Now if our lives were in danger, which I suspect they could be any day now, there would only be one way out of the speakeasy. I then sat down at my desk and opened up my only friend.

Dear Diary,
July 1st, 9:55 AM,

It seems that now I can only escape into you, or will those horrid mobsters take you from me just as they took my mother? You are so precious to me now. You won't judge me harshly like Jack or betray my affection like Mickey. I've decided that if I'm to die in two days or twenty years from now that I want only you at my funeral. I want you to be buried with me so if there is an afterlife I could then take solace knowing that I have someone who will be there to keep me company.

I could never lie to you. So I will tell you that there is a part of me that still cares for Mickey. Should I give him a second chance, or would he just break my heart again? I believe everyone deserves a second chance, so before you call me a hypocrite, I have chosen to let Mickey back into my heart once again. I now conclude this entry to you with a question which has kept me awake every night for the past two weeks, what must I do to no longer be scared of them all?

"Hayley … I want to tell you something," Mickey said to me as he took off his newsboy hat and sat down on my bed.

"I want to tell you something too," I said to Mickey. "Oh, you go first," Mickey said with a grin.

"No you go first, please," I said with a smile as I sat down on my bed beside Mickey.

"All right … well … when I was getting pummeled by those four boys a thought immediately came to my mind," Mickey said to me in a somber tone.

"What was the thought?" I inquired with a wide-eyed stare, as Mickey made glances at me before staring back down at his hat in his hands.

"I thought I was going to die and then I heard your voice. Hayley, you are the only one that makes my life worth living. Now what did you want to tell me," Mickey replied.

"Just this," I said to Mickey with a quivering smile as my eyes welled up with tears, before I kissed him.

"I know we can overcome these mobsters if we stick together, just like we did with the Rivelli brothers at Pier 45," Mickey said to me with a grin.

"Oh the lovebirds are back. You two start taking drink orders while I prep the bar," Samson pronounced. "Where's Jack," Mickey inquired.

"All he told me was that he's gone to rectify all our follies, whatever that means," Samson replied with a scoff.

"Forget about Jack," I said to Mickey with a grin as I took his hand.

It worried me what Jack was becoming under the influence of these mobsters. It seemed that Jack was adopting more and more of the mobsters' ruthless personalities with each day that past. What would my mother do with Jack right now if she was still alive? Could I ever evoke even half of the courage that my mother had in life to help me no longer be scared of them all? These emotions seemed to fade away as I held Mickey's hand. "Double bourbon on the rocks, and this lady will have a glass of Chardonnay, you have that wine, don't you," a mobster inquired, as I took his drink order. "Yes sir we do," I replied.

"Good, because I don't want you to come back to this table in one minute and tell me that you don't have Chardonnay, because whatever my dame wants, she gets," the mobster said to me in a stern tone.

"Aw you're so good to me baby," woman who hung on the mobsters shoulder who wore far too much deep red lipstick remarked with a giggle.

"I promise you sir that we always have plenty of Chardonnay in stock thanks to Mr. Luciano we do not run out of any type of liquor," I said to the mobster.

"Good girl, now hop to it, we have a Broadway show we're about to attend in twenty minutes," the mobster said as he snapped his fingers and pointed to the bar.

"Oh what play are you going to see?" I inquired in a zealous tone.

"*Mourning Becomes Electra*," the woman replied with a smile.

"It's adapted from some Greek revenge story. So they had me at revenge, but lost me with the Greeks," the mobster said with a scoff, and then took out a cigar from the pocket of his jacket and lit it.

"Oh shut up, a little culture won't kill you," the woman said to the mobster with a playful shove.

"I've never heard of that play, it must be new," I remarked with a smile.

"It is new, honey. My baby here works with Mayor Jimmy Walker and he throws us free tickets to all the new Broadway shows," the woman said to me with a smile.

"That must be nice," I remarked in a timid tone.

She was conceited with a shrill voice and lustrous hair, though I had yet to meet a mobster's dame who didn't fit that description.

"If you two hens keep on clucking we're going to be late for the show," the mobster said in a stern tone as he snapped his fingers at me once more and pointed to the bar.

I envied the woman who was the mobster's eye candy of the month, but only because she had the luxury of seeing all the new plays on Broadway. Why was it that fortune always seemed to favor the criminals in this city? Perhaps that's why Jack has chosen to work for Mr. Luciano. He truly believes that our lives will be better off working for his empire. The speakeasy looked so glamorous, but none of those perks which that mobster's dame told me about were offered to me, and why would they? I'm not eye candy like all of these women in the speakeasy who flaunt their riches at me.

*****

It was 3:16 PM in the speakeasy when a fight broke out right before my eyes.

"Get under the bar," Samson said to me in a stern tone as he gestured for me to hide behind the bar.

"Are you going to do anything?" I inquired, as I crouched down.

"Not a chance. These two mobsters are just waiting for me to take a side. Then I will be a target for them for the remainder of my days in this speakeasy.

"What's happening? Is it almost over?" I inquired in a distressed tone.

"The skinny mobster is holding his own against the fat mobster. I wonder how much longer it will be before these two pull out a weapon and end this bullshit squabble." Samson replied, as he continued to wipe down the bar in a calm manner as if nothing dangerous was happening right in front of him.

"Do you know how the fight started?" I inquired, as I could hear the two mobsters shouting in Italian, as the sound of glasses shattering resonated throughout the speakeasy.

"The skinny mobster was apparently getting too flirtatious with the fat mobster's wife," Samson replied with a snicker.

"Do any of these mobsters know how to resolve their grievances by talking, instead of acting like barbarians dressed in three piece suites?" I inquired in a stern tone while shaking my head.

"Talking is what women do, or at least that's how mobsters see it. These two men are just showing each other who—,"

A gunshot then resonated throughout the speakeasy, as I wrapped my arms around my legs and scooted further underneath the bar.

"Finally, it's over Hayley. You can come out now," Samson said to me while shaking his head.

I then slowly stood up from underneath the bar to the sight of the skinny mobster lying motionless on the floor as a puddle of blood slowly began to form underneath him. My heart was racing and I began to shake as the fat mobster walked towards the bar.

"You, Irishman, you tell Carlo to dispose of this rat, comprendere?" the fat mobster inquired in a heaving tone. "Aye sir," Samson replied in a stern tone and stare.

The fat mobster then exited the speakeasy as he aggressively pulled the arm of his wife who supposedly caused the fight which resulted in the skinny mobster's death.

"Samson, are you now numb to death?" I inquired in a timid tone.

"I wouldn't say I'm numb to it, but I sure am accustom to the sight of a man dying," Samson replied, as we stood over the dead mobster.

I felt sick to my stomach as I stared at the puddle of blood which the mobster lay in.

"Hayley, you look pale as a ghost. Are you all right?" Samson inquired as the speakeasy began to spin around me. The sight of Samson reaching out towards me was the last thing I saw before everything went dark as I collapsed to the floor.

*****

It was 7:56 PM in the speakeasy as I awoke to the sight of Mickey sitting at my desk.

"Oh you're awake," Mickey said to me with a warm smile as he sat down on my bed.

"What happened? The last thing I remember was the sight of that mobster lying in a puddle of his own blood, and then suddenly everything went dark," I said to Mickey in a weary tone as I sat upright in bed.

"Samson said that you fainted. I just got here five minutes ago, but I didn't want to leave until I knew you were all right," Mickey said to me.

"I'm all right, but do you still have to leave so soon?" I inquired in a somber tone.

"I wish I could stay longer, but Nurse Banister said that I'm at the age were if I don't pull my weight around the hospital, then I could very well be kicked out, so I have to get back to helping her clean before she throws a fit," Mickey replied with an eye roll.

"I'll miss you," I said to Mickey as I took his hand.

"No you won't because I got you something that will always keep me close to you, close your eyes," Mickey said to me with a smile.

I then closed my eyes with a smile, as I could hear Mickey rifling through the pocket of his jacket.

"No peaking," Mickey said with a snicker as he attached something I could only assume to be a necklace around my neck. My heart fluttered at that moment, not merely from the necklace around my neck, but from the feel of Mickey's gentle hands on my neck as well.

"All right, open your eyes," Mickey said to me.

"Mickey … It's … beautiful," I remarked with a smile, as my eyes began to well up with tears at the sight of a gold necklace.

"The *M&H* inscribed right here on the pendant stands for Mickey and Hayley," Mickey said to me with a smile as he pointed at the pendent with a shaky finger.

"I love it. It's the most beautiful gift anybody has ever given me," I remarked with a smile, as tears began to stream from my eyes.

"A local Jeweler named Omar who owns a shop down the street from the hospital owed me a favor for all the times I helped him around the shop. He told me he would give me fifty percent off any piece of jewelry I wanted. I then I asked him to create that necklace instead," Mickey said to me with a smile.

"This must've been expensive. I don't know if I'm worth the price of this necklace," I said to Mickey in a somber tone.

"Omar asked me the same thing. He said 'Mickey my boy. Is this girl truly worth all the money you spent just now?'" Mickey said to me with a snicker.

"What did you tell him?" I inquired with a wide-eyed stare. "I told him that it's all worth it just to see you smile," Mickey replied with a smile as he stared up from the hat in his hands to me.

At that moment, I wanted to say those three words to Mickey, those three words which carry so much weight and power in this world, those three words which I've heard in movies spoken by women far more beautiful than me, those three words which I didn't feel worthy of in life, until now, but I was scared over what those three words could mean for our future, so I just firmly wrapped my arms around him. I didn't want that moment to end as I held Mickey more tightly by the second. He made me feel special in a way that even my mother couldn't do.

"I'll be here bright and early tomorrow morning," Mickey said to me with a smile, as we stood up from the bed while holding hands.

"I'll miss you," I said to Mickey with a smile and then kissed him quickly before he could leave without kissing me.

"Welcome back. Just in time for me to get the hell out of here," Samson said to Jack as he entered the speakeasy and walked up to the bar.

"Not before I give you this," Jack said to Samson, as he handed him an envelope.

"What's this?" Samson inquired as he opened the envelope. "Call it incentive from Mr. Luciano. He knows about your past in Belfast and he wants you to do him a favor," Jack replied as he took off his jacket and got dressed in his black vest.

"So you told him about my past, why would you do that?" Samson inquired in a stern tone and stare.

"He pressed me about you Samson. I had to tell him. Mr. Luciano is a man who values knowledge about the associates who work for him.

"Forget it Jack. You can take this 'incentive' or whatever the hell you want to call it back to Mr. Luciano. No amount of money could drag me back to that life of being a hitman," Samson said to Jack in a stern tone as he shoved the envelope full of money back into Jack's chest and then walked away towards the front door of the speakeasy.

"I'll give you a day to mull that choice over!" Jack shouted to Samson just before he exited the speakeasy.

"It's just me and you tonight, kid," Jack said to me with a sigh.

"How could you make Samson chose that life again. This is exactly what Mr. Luciano did to you on that night two weeks ago," I said to Jack.

"Tie your hair up. I don't want any long red hairs in any of the drinks," Jack said to me in a stern tone.

Jack was now ignoring me the way someone would ignore a dog begging for scraps at the kitchen table. Jack wouldn't pay any mind to my opinions, nor would he take me seriously whenever I needed him, but perhaps, I no longer need Jack.

"No, you sound like Johnny. He would always tell me and my mother to tie our hair up, for 'women shouldn't have their hair down in such a way that flouts society,'" I said to Jack in a stern tone.

"You're going to be the death of me one of these days, kid. Have it your way. Let's just start serving our associates in a kind and respectful manner," Jack said to me as he pointed towards the four tables by the stage where groups of mobsters sat smoking their cigars with their dames drinking wine and laughing obnoxiously as they draped themselves over the mobsters.

*****

It was 11:17 PM in the speakeasy when I noticed a horrid sight.

Frankie Angelo entered the speakeasy in a sulking manner and sat down at the corner table near the stage where I used to sit when I wrote in my diary.

"Looks like it slowed down quite a bit after the band left," Jack said to me, as he wiped down the bar.

"I'm not surprised. I bet most of those mobsters just came here to ogle at Ms. Valentino," I said with a scoff.

"Sex sells, kid. I never had a burlesque performer in my speakeasy before. Carlo told me they're all the rage now," Jack said to me with a snicker.

"What would that ghoul know about anything other than disposing of dead bodies? I still prefer jazz," I remarked while shaking my head.

"Redhead ... redhead, come here," Frankie shouted as he gestured for me to come over to him.

"Yes Mr. Angelo," I said to Frankie in a timid tone as I walked up to the table where he sat alone.

"Y-You see this glass of scotch, well I want you to keep your eyes on it and fill it up whenever you see that it's empty," Frankie said to me, as he raised his half empty glass of scotch towards me.

"Yes sir," I said to Frankie with a nod.

"D-Don't you ever get married, sweetheart. You'll soon find yourself bartering with your partner just to get some fresh air," Frankie said to me with a scoff, and then finished the last of his scotch in one gulp.

"Thank you for the advice. I'll be right back with another double scotch on the rocks," I said to Frankie.

"Woah there what's your hurry? This speakeasy doesn't close down till I'm finished drinking, so have a seat," Frankie said to me as he kicked out the chair across from him.

"Uhm I should really be getting back to—,"

"Sit down!" Frankie said to me in a stern tone as he pointed to the empty chair across from him.

"Look what the cat dragged in," Jack said in a facetious tone and snicker as he opened the front door of the speakeasy.

I then noticed a most heartwarming sight as I reluctantly sat down at the table with Frankie. Ms. Dubois had entered the speakeasy with a playful shove and giggle towards Jack

"Bonsoir Hayley," Mr. Dubois said to me with a smile and wave as her and Jack walked to the bar.

"She left me, that ungrateful bitch. After all the years I supported her expenses, she told me I wasn't man enough for her," Frankie told me in a stern tone and scoff, as I stared at Ms. Dubois and Jack talking in such a heartfelt manner.

"Oh, I'm sorry, who left you?" I inquired in a timid tone. "My wife Louis," Frankie replied in a stern tone.

At that moment I wish Jack was and I's positions were switched. I wanted to talk to Ms. Dubois, but I learned that there's nobody who could draw Jack's attention away from her. I would now have to suffer Frankie and all of his misery, but for how long?

"Then s-she told me that if I was a real man I would've fought for her honor when my associate bumped into her and made her drop her glass of wine the other night. She's always busting my balls over such petty bullshit. If I threw fists with every man who dishonored her then I would be long dead by now," Frankie said to me.

"Where did she go," I inquired in a timid tone.

"She told me she's going to live with her sister in Chelsea. I said good fucking riddance to her and her witch of a sister who probably encouraged her to leave me," Frankie replied with a scoff as he raised his empty glass of scotch towards me.

"I'm sorry," I said to Frankie.

"G-Go on and fill this up, doll," Frankie said to me.

"Yes sir, right away," I said to Frankie as I took his empty glass and scampered over to the bar where Jack and Ms. Dubois seemed to be getting very friendly with each other as always.

"How is Frankie doing?" Jack inquired.

"Another double scotch on the rocks, Frankie's wife left him and now he wants to drown his misery," I replied.

"Oh be careful Hayley. A man, how you say, with no rope left will cling to anybody he believes that can soothe his heartbreak," Ms. Dubois said to me and then took a puff from her cigarette.

"You mean a man at the end of his rope," Jack said to Ms.

Dubois with a snicker.

"Mon chéri Jack must you always correct my English?" Ms. Dubois inquired with a grin.

"Not always, Faye. Only when it makes me feel more intelligent than I actually am," Jack replied with a snicker as he prepared Frankie's scotch.

"So always then," Ms. Dubois said to Jack with an eye roll as she giggled and then took a sip of wine.

"Walk slowly when serving drinks. We're in no rush, it's just us four right now," Jack said to me in a stern tone as he placed the scotch on the tray.

Of course Jack was in no hurry when he was talking to the charming, delightful, and beautiful Ms. Dubois, but I want my time spent with Frankie to end as soon as possible. He was even more horrid drunk than when he was sober, on top of all that his wife had left him, so just like Ms. Dubois warned me about, Frankie was now clinging onto me for consolation, but I despised everything about him, and was happy for his wife who made that choice to be rid of him. He never failed to make my skin crawl. I needed a way out of this uncomfortable situation, perhaps Frankie will blackout soon then I can slip away from him to the kitchen.

"W-Women like you, or should I say, girls like you are perfect. Why do women have to age into such cold-hearted witches," Frankie said to me in a slurred tone and then took a sip of scotch with a grimace.

I didn't know what to say anymore to Frankie, so I just sat there quietly at the table across from him as he continued to drink himself further into oblivion. Was there any way out of this situation that wouldn't enrage Frankie anymore than he already is? If there was a way out of this, I failed to see it, as I made brief glances at Jack and Ms. Dubois laughing at the bar.

"I have to go to the restroom," I said to Frankie.

"W-What, oh be back soon. I'm starting to remember my wife's haggard face," Frankie said to me in a stern tone and scoff, as I walked over to the bar.

"Jack, Frankie says we don't close up till he's done drinking. Please I'm so tired," I said to Jack.

"How much has Frankie drunk so far?" Jack inquired.

"He's almost finished with his third glass of scotch," I replied.

"Go to bed kid. Frankie will pass out soon enough," Jack said to me with a dismissive wave towards the kitchen. "Thanks Jack. Goodnight Ms. Dubois,"

I said with a smile. "Bonsoir to you too, Ms. Hayley, and I wish you the sweetest dreams imaginable," Ms. Dubois said to me with a smile.

I was so relieved now that I would no longer have to suffer Frankie's misery for the rest of the night. I then began to get undressed, as Jack and Ms. Dubois continued to enjoy each other's company. I then noticed all the bruises on my legs as I slowly took off my black dress and put on my white nightgown. The cuts I made on my forearm months ago had healed over but left a scar. I then sat down in bed with a sigh as I tied my hair up. The necklace Mickey gave me made me feel as if I could overcome any kind of pain. Just knowing that I will soon see Mickey's beautiful face made me look forward to what tomorrow brings.

"Where's the bathroom?" Frankie inquired in a stern tone from the bar. Oh no, Frankie would now see me again. I now feared how he would react, as I heard his lumbering footsteps draw nearer to me as I sat in bed.

"Oh so this is where you're hiding from me," Frankie said with a scoff as he entered the kitchen.

"I'm going to bed now. Goodnight Mr. Angelo," I said to Frankie in a timid tone, as I held my diary closely against my chest so that Frankie wouldn't see how heavy my heart was beating.

"What's the hurry, doll? I thought we were making a breakthrough," Frankie inquired as he sat down beside me on my bed.

"Please I have to go to bed now," I said to Frankie, as I scooted away from him on my bed.

"Are you really rejecting me too, just like Louis?" Frankie inquired in a stern tone, as he moved closer to me on the bed

"N-No, I'm just really tired," I said replied, as my heart raced faster the closer he moved towards me on the bed. "Good … you are a beautiful girl. I'll bet you don't hear that as often as you should huh, doll," Frankie remarked with a grin as he placed his hand on my exposed thigh.

"You need to get some rest now," I said to Frankie in a stern tone, as I quickly pushed away his hand.

"I need your comfort tonight, doll. D-Don't worry I'll make it quick," Frankie said to me as he took off his belt.

"No, you need to go home and sleep," I said to Frankie in a distressed tone.

"L-Lay down, I'll do all the work," Frankie said to me in a stern tone.

"No get out!" I shouted, hoping that Jack would hear me from the bar.

"I said lay down you little bitch! I 'm the reason you're still alive. So now it's time for you return the favor," Frankie said to me in a stern tone as he lunged towards me pinning me down on the bed beneath him.

Despite Frankie's drunken state, he was still strong enough to quickly hold me down on the bed. This terrifying feeling of a man overpowering me was all too familiar, and it brought back a memory in my mind which I've tried to suppress my entire life.

*****

"What are you doing?" I inquired as Fernando quietly entered my bedroom and lay down beside me.

"Shhh la mia principessa," Fernando replied, as he lay down beside me.

"Where's mom?" I inquired as I could hear Fernando getting undressed.

"She's with your uncle right now," Fernando said as his hand traced up my leg and under my nightgown.

"No stop," I said to Fernando in a whimpering tone but he then quickly held me down and positioned himself between my legs.

I then began to cry as Fernando began to moan. My mom and Uncle Jack were not here to stop Fernando as I cried to nobody in the darkness of my bedroom. The smell of smoke and cologne surrounded me as Fernando continued to play with me in such an uncomfortable manner. I've never felt this feeling before and it hurt me deep down inside.

"Now go back to sleep principessa. I love you," Fernando said to me in a heaving tone, as he got dressed and then left my bedroom, while I shook as tears streamed from my eyes in the darkness of my bedroom wondering why he would do such a thing to me.

*****

No, I wouldn't be a victim to Frankie now as I was with Fernando six years ago. I had to fight against Frankie with every breath. I will no longer be a victim to monsters like him, Fernando, and Johnny.

"Get back here," Frankie said to me in a stern tone, as I broke free from his restraints and reached for the make-shift knife I had stored in the pocket of my dress on the night stand. "Oh no you don't," Frankie said to me in a stern tone, as he grabbed my knife-wielding hand before I could thrust it into him.

"Jack!" I shouted, Frankie then pried the make-shift knife out of my hand and then smacked me down to the floor.

"Y-You are my doll now. Frankie said in a stern tone as he pulled me onto the bed.

"Jack he—," I shouted, but my pleas for help were muffled from Frankie's hand covering my mouth.

In our struggle, Frankie ripped the necklace Mickey gave me from my neck as he tried to pull off my nightgown like a wild animal. I then watched with wide eyes as Mickey's necklace landed in pieces on the floor beneath me.

"I'll show you whose man enough," Frankie said in a stern tone.

Frankie positioned himself between my quivering legs just like Fernando did in the darkness of my bedroom six years ago. Mickey wasn't here to save me, and Jack was too captivated with Ms. Dubois to even hear my screams, I was all alone once again.

"No stop," I said to Frankie in a tearful tone as Frankie pulled off my nightgown.

The cold reality of the moment then began to set in as

CHAPTER 9: BLEEDING HEARTS
- JACK -

"Where's the bathroom?" Frankie inquired with a belch as he walked past me and Faye at the bar.

I then pointed to the kitchen as I stared daggers at Frankie just before averting my gaze back to Faye. The woman sure was a sight for sore eyes after a long day of being ordered around by drunken, mobster dogs like Frankie. Whenever I talked to Faye she made me feel as if we were the only two people in the room, and all the other mobsters in the world paled in comparison to the way she made me feel.

"This place sure is beautiful now, Jack," Faye remarked with a smile as she looked around the bar before taking a sip of wine.

"I would say it's more beautiful now that you've arrived," I said to Faye with a grin.

"Mon chéri Jack … are you now happy here with your niece and those two strapping men who work for you?" Faye inquired with a giggle as she placed her hand upon mine on the bar.

"The choice I made to work for Mr. Luciano has its pros and cons," I replied as I wiped down the bar.

"I understand all too well, Jack. Sometimes not all life choices we make are black and white. Did you believe you could achieve happiness in life from working with Mr. Luciano?" Faye inquired, and then primped her hair while looking into her compact mirror with a pout.

"To be honest … happiness was the last thing on my mind when I made the choice to work for that powerful boss of the Five Points Gang. Financial stability is what fueled my decision," I replied.

"Do you feel stable right now?" Faye inquired, as she snapped her compact mirror shut with a grin.

"I never feel stable when I'm around you," I replied with a snicker.

"What do you mean by that?" Faye inquired.

"I like to call you a good kind of chaos. I feel it whenever I look into those eyes of yours," I said to Faye as we stared intently into each other's eyes.

"Jack!" a voice shouted from the kitchen.

"Was that Hayley?" Faye inquired as her sultry gaze quickly averted from my eyes to the kitchen.

I was far too busy with Faye to humor that kid in the kitchen. She had the impression that the entire world revolved around her and that her little problems were far greater than anything else in this day and age.

"Ah the kid probably saw a spider. Now back to me and you," I said to Faye with a grin.

"Is there a 'you and I' Jack?" Faye inquired with a grin as she leaned in close to me over the bar.

"I'd like there to be," I replied.

"Jack he—," Hayley shouted again from the kitchen, as I scowled in response to the sound of her voice interrupting my precious time with Faye once again, but there was something different about her cry, it sounded like she was struggling with something or someone, then I remembered that Frankie entered the kitchen less than five minutes ago.

"I'll be right back. Don't you leave that barstool," I said to Faye with a grin.

"What is it now kid?" I inquired in a stern tone as I entered the kitchen to a most revolting sight. 'She was just like her mother, fooling around with mobsters,' I thought to myself as I stared at Frankie on the bed with Hayley beneath him. No, wait, I was wrong. The tears and look of fear coming from Hayley's eyes showed me that this wasn't consensual. Frankie Angelo, you son of a bitch! Rage quickly overcame me at that moment and my first instinct was to pull out my pistol and shoot Frankie dead. I then remembered Hayley telling me that Frankie's wife had come to her senses and left him, so killing the bastard would be a merciful act, and I, for one, had no mercy in my heart for the likes of his miserable kind.

"J-Jack h-hold on," Frankie said in a distressed tone as he pulled up his pants. I then swiftly pulled Frankie off of Hayley down to the floor where I then began to kick him repeatedly as Hayley put on her night gown and sat crying on the floor in the corner of the kitchen beside the shelves with her arms wrapped around her legs.

"Get up you son of a bitch. I'm nowhere near done with you," I said to Frankie in a stern tone as I lifted him up from the floor and slammed him against the wall.

"Jack what happened?" Faye inquired in a distressed tone and wide-eyed stare as she entered the kitchen with her hand on her chest.

"Faye, go tend to Hayley," I replied, as I pointed to Hayley in the corner of the kitchen.

"Easy Jack, You know who we both work for. Now get your fucking hands off me," Frankie said to me in a stern tone as I held him firmly against the wall by his collar.

"Your job was to protect her, but after what you just did, nobody will protect you from me right now," I said to Frankie in a stern tone as I stared intently into his eyes now filled with fear, the same fear I saw in Johnny's eyes just before I sent him on a way trip into the Hudson on that foggy night.

I felt more empowered with each punch I threw at Frankie. After weeks of feeling like the Five Points Gang's servant, I was now dealing one of their most disgusting dogs his due justice.

"No guns Frankie, don't you know I killed Johnny with my bare hands," I said to Frankie as I grabbed the pistol from his hand before he could shoot me in the gut and tossed at Faye.

"You're a fucking dog at the end of his ropes just like Faye said. You're too pitiful to be alive among us men, but I have no mercy to put you down," I said to Frankie, as he began to snicker, as blood dripped from his ugly battered face.

"Then w-what will you do now Jack? Do you believe Mr. Luciano or even Carlo will silence me over you?" Frankie inquired with a maniacal laugh.

I then threw a hard right punch square into Frankie's jaw which sent one of his gold teeth flying out of his mouth with a trail of blood.

"Do you know what your ex-wife and I have in common, Frankie?" I inquired with a snicker as I picked up Hayley's make-shift knife on the floor as Faye held Hayley close to her as she cried.

"You're both bitches," Frankie replied with a grin and then spit out blood towards me.

"No, we both leave scars," I said to Frankie as I then stomped down on his chest pinning him down to the ground. I then ripped open Frankie's shirt and pointed the knife against his heaving chest. Death would be mercy for this miserable dog named Frankie. So instead I will mark him in a way he will never forget, just as I'm sure Hayley will never forget what he did to her.

"You're lucky I don't cut your fucking balls off, but a simple J for Jack will suffice," I said to Frankie, as I then began to carve the letter J into his chest.

"That's right, cry you son of a bitch," I said to Frankie as he cried out in pain as I sank the knife about an inch into his chest, ensuring that it will leave a scar. The blood then began to pour out of Frankie's chest as I finished carving the letter J.

"Ah ... you will pay for this, Dansby, you and that little fucking bitch who wouldn't stop flirting with me the entire night. Mark my words; I'll see to it that the both of you spend the rest of your days at the bottom of the Hudson, just like you did to Johnny!" Frankie shouted with a grimace.

I then swiftly kicked Frankie in the head which finally silenced the barking of the miserable dog as he fell over on the blood-stained floor.

"Don't worry I'll dispose of this dog," I pronounced as Faye and Hayley looked at me in dismay while I drug the knocked out Frankie out of the kitchen and towards the front door of the speakeasy.

I knew very well the consequences of beating Frankie half to death, but I couldn't hold back my rage when I saw him raping Hayley. I know her history with Fernando and to then experience that abuse once again with Frankie will surely disturb the kid ol the end of her days. Perhaps my instant guilt overcame me at that moment, the guilt I felt over giving Frankie the job to protect Hayley. Whether it takes me the rest of my life which could very well be one more day, I will make things right for Hayley.

I then exited the speakeasy as I drug Frankie's unconscious body down the back alley.

"Taxi!" I shouted, as I dropped Frankie down upon the sidewalk.

"Keep walking, there's nothing to see here," I said to an elderly woman walking past me with a wide-eyed look of fear in her eyes.

"No fucking way," The taxicab driver said to me in a stern tone while shaking his head, as I pulled up Frankie's bleeding body into the backseat of the taxicab.

"Here … something for your troubles and here's a little extra to keep your mouth shut," I said to the taxicab driver in a stern tone as I pulled out my wallet and then paid him a fare that would no doubt put him on easy street for the rest of the month. "All right. Where should I drop him off?" the taxicab driver inquired as he counted the many bills in his hand with a grin. "Drop this son of a bitch off at Pier 45, on the docks not in the Hudson," I replied in a stern tone, as I shoved the rest of Frankie's bloody body into the backseat of the taxicab and then slammed the door shut.

"You got it," the taxicab driver said to me with a grin.

"Oh and be discreet. Don't take any main streets on your way there, and if the police do stop you, just tell them you're doing business for the Five Points Gang," I said to the taxicab driver.

"Sure thing, I'll have this bleeding bag of bones dropped off at the pier in under ten minutes," the taxicab driver said to me with a grin and then drove off.

Even at night I could still see the trail of blood from Frankie leading me back to the speakeasy. The streetlights cast down on the trail of Frankie's blood served as a reminder of that dog who disrespected me and my family.

"Hayley, Faye, where are you?" I shouted as I entered the speakeasy. I could hear Faye consoling Hayley as she continued to sob in the kitchen. Perhaps I should leave it to Faye I thought to myself as I walked behind the bar and poured myself a shot of bourbon. I've never been good at showing compassion, my compassion for Hayley was in the form of her and Faye watching me beat Frankie half to death. If only Hayley's mother was here right now. In times such as these I would always think of Dezerae and how her judgment would no doubt be sounder than mine.

"Jack … what happened tonight was truly horrific for Hayley. I wish I could console her all night, but I must get back home," Faye said to me in a somber tone, as she sat down at the bar.

"Faye … did I do the right thing?" I inquired with a stern look as my face quivered with tremors of sorrow for Hayley.

"I know you Jack, and at that moment you acted in response to your heart," Faye replied, as she placed her hand upon mine. "I should've acted with my mind. This beating thing in my chest always sends me down the wrong road," I said in a stern tone while shaking my head.

"Hayley told me she was raped before by her father when she was only nine years old. Right now she needs a male figure in her life who doesn't strike fear into her already fragile heart," Faye said to me in a somber tone.

"I don't know if I can be that figure, Faye. I never had a male figure in my life growing up as a boy in *SoHo*," I said to Faye.

"Then you must learn to love, Jack, and If you cannot learn that from Hayley, then I'm afraid there's no hope for you," Faye said to me in a stern tone, and then exited the speakeasy, leaving me alone with nothing but the faint sound of Hayley's sobbing from the kitchen furthering the crushing guilt I felt on this night filled with bourbon, blood, and abuse.

*****

It was 12:26 AM in the speakeasy. I could hear Hayley taking a shower in the kitchen as I scrubbed the blood trail that Frankie left from off the floor. I could still hear Hayley crying over the running water of the shower as I scrubbed harder and harder to erase Frankie's filth from the speakeasy, but if only it were that easy to scrub away such filth, as I'm sure Hayley is trying to do right now in the shower.

"That bastard," I spoke aloud with a grimace, as I stared into the kitchen as steam from the shower began to make its way into the bar. Despite the sound of the running water from the shower, I could still hear Hayley crying. So I then turned on the radio to drown out the misery and keep my mind distracted from the horrible guilt I felt over Hayley's abuse.

"In national news, FDR gave his democratic convention acceptance speech on July 2nd which included new promises to appease the outcries of all Americans stricken by this depression.

'My friends of the democratic national convention of 1932, I know well of the sleepless hours which you and I have had over the past 6 days. You have nominated me and I am here to thank you for that honor. So henceforth, let it be the task of our party to break free from foolish traditions. The 18th amendment is doomed, for I, along with the American people, want repeal. I pledge myself to a new deal for the American people. Lend me your help now to restore America to its own people.'

Democratic presidential nominee FDR will now go on to face Herbert Hoover, which many polls and analysts are already estimating him winning in an overwhelming victory to become the 32nd president of the United States of America."

"Spoken like a typical politician. More promises of hope from a bleeding heart democrat," I spoke aloud with a scoff, and then turned off the radio.

I didn't doubt FDR would most likely become the next president of the United States, but I sure as hell wasn't filled with hope over all of his promises to the American people. Even thought Hoover was a disgrace of a president in my eyes, I didn't care for the empty promises which FDR seemed to weaponize in order to win the democratic nominee for president.

I then heard the shower turn off in the kitchen. *What would I say to Hayley now, or could I just remain silent and leave her be?* I thought to myself. After a few minutes of mulling over my words to the poor kid, I then took a shot of bourbon and entered the kitchen.

"Hayley I … uhm," I said to Hayley in a somber tone as she recoiled from my presence.

"I can still feel him on me. Where were you? Why didn't you stop him sooner?" Hayley inquired in a distressed tone as tears began to stream from her eyes.

"I'm—I'm sorry, Hayley, I'm so sorry," I said to Hayley in a somber tone, as my face began to quiver.

There were only a few times in my life I can recall when　I felt like breaking down in tears. The first time was when my mother told me the devastating news of my father being killed in the war. The second time was when I received the news in the form of a letter from the NYPD, informing me that Dezerae was killed by Johnny, and now the abuse of Hayley at the hands of that dog Frankie has brought me to the brink of tears once again. She was just a kid and she didn't deserve to suffer every day. My attempts to provide and protect her have now resulted in a horrific incident.

"Why, why didn't you stop him sooner, why didn't you stop him sooner?" Hayley said to me in a distressed tone, as she walked up to me and smacked my chest over and over again, as the tears continued to stream down her face.

So I stood there as Hayley struck my chest over and over again until she fell to the floor.

"Hayley … I've been a terrible uncle. I know I can't change what happened tonight, but I promise you in time that I will make things right," I said to Hayley, as I kneeled down on the floor.

"Don't promise me anything. There is no hope for me. I'm just a worthless little girl. That's how all men see me," Hayley said to me in a heaving tone, as she then quickly grabbed the make-shift knife from the nightstand.

"What are you doing?" I inquired with a wide-eyed stare. "Ending the pain," Hayley replied in a somber tone.

"No kid, that's not the way, that's not the way!" I shouted as I swiftly grabbed Hayley's knife-wielding hand as it moved towards her neck.

"Just let me die!" Hayley shouted as we struggled for control over the make-shift knife.

In our struggle, Hayley managed to cut her neck before I took the knife away from her. I saw nothing but misery in Hayley's eyes at that moment. The kind of misery that takes away any reason you had for living.

"Listen to me, kid. I never saw you as worthless. You are a fiercely intelligent young woman and you have far more to live for than I do. I knew that from the very moment I looked into your eyes at the hospital. That fiery passion for life that your mother always had lives in you. You're not going to end your life on my watch, kid, not because of that son of a bitch Frankie," I said to Hayley in a stern tone as I grasped her by her quivering shoulders with both hands. Hayley then firmly wrapped her arms around me, as I tossed the make-shift knife into the bar. The louder Hayley cried, the tighter I held her in my arms, as we slowly rocked back and forth for a few moments on the floor.

"Here, wrap this around the cut on your neck," I said to Hayley, as I grabbed a roll of gauze off the shelf.

"What's the point of covering it up now? I might as well look how I feel," Hayley said to me in a somber tone and dismissive wave.

"Come on, kid, you don't belong on the ground," I said to Hayley, as I gently grasped her shoulders with both hands and raised her to her feet. I then turned off the light with a sigh, as Hayley got into bed in the manner of an elderly woman at the end of her days.

"Leave the light on," Hayley said to me in a distressed tone. "Oh, all right," I said to Hayley, and then turned the light switch back on before getting into bed. There would be consequences I would have to face when I wake up this morning. I know that even despite my best efforts of covering up the beating I gave to Frankie, Carlo would still find out, but the sound of Hayley sobbing in bed a couple feet away from me gave me courage to face him and any other mobster who felt as if they needed to silence me for what I did to Frankie.

*****

It was 11: 18 AM in the speakeasy as I served a quiet mobster sitting at the bar in front of me. *Why can't all mobsters be like him, quiet and non-threatening?* I thought to myself, as the mobster sipped his pint of beer with a quivering hand. I heard the quiet ones are the most disturbed kind of people, like Hayley was when I first met her. Who knows what kind of rage the quiet mobster sitting in front of me at the bar has inside him at this moment, but I sure as hell didn't want to find out.

I had to make sure what happened to Hayley last night never happens again, one time is already too much, but I couldn't trust any mobster to protect her, so I have to rely on myself, Mickey, and Samson to now keep Hayley safe. Those two would be here soon, and I would not leave the speakeasy until they arrive.

"You two are late," I remarked as Samson and Mickey both entered the speakeasy together.

"Ah sorry Jack there was traffic out there, not so much in here I see," Samson said to me, as he walked over to the bar and put on his vest.

"Good let's hope it stays that way," I said to Samson.

"Did I really hear those words come out of your mouth? You really don't want it to be busy in here?" Samson inquired an incredulous tone and grin.

"Where's Hayley?" Mickey inquired, as he put on his vest.

"That's what I need to talk to you both about ... something happened last night, something horrible ...," I pronounced.

*****

It was 12:24 PM in the speakeasy as a couple more mobsters entered with two dames draped over them who didn't look a day over twenty-one.

"I don't know what's more horrible, what Frankie did to Hayley, or what you did to Frankie? I personally would've killed that fucking bastard, but then I would suffer graver consequences than the ones you're in right now," Samson remarked in a stern tone as he looked into the kitchen.

"I simply physically scarred that dog the way he mentally scarred Hayley," I said to Samson in a stern tone.

"By god, how terrible, my heart bleeds for the girl," Samson remarked in a somber tone while shaking his head.

"That's why I need you and your bleeding heart to check up on her every five minutes, there's no telling what these mobsters will do now. That goes for you too Mickey," I pronounced in a stern tone.

"I should've been with her last night, but I won't let Hayley out of my sight from here on out," Mickey said in a stern tone as his face quivered with sorrow the same way mine did last night when Hayley tried to take her own life.

"Carlo, that fiend of a man, he may already know what you did to Frankie," Samson said to me.

"That's only if Frankie's stupid enough to tell Carlo the specifics of the matter. Either way, I expect Carlo will be here within the hour, and I will be ready for him," I said to Samson in a stern tone.

I was ready indeed for that ghost-face son of a bitch who's been calling the shots around here for the past couple of weeks. I didn't care what happened to me, as long as Hayley remained safe, and I trust Samson and Mickey to keep her safe. I doubt even Mr. Luciano has a single associate who he fully trusts, but when you're the boss of the most powerful crime organization in the country, trust can be a liability.

"I'm going to check on Hayley," Mickey said to me.

"Mickey, wait … what happened to her last night is something none of us can fully understand, so—,"

"I understand Jack. I understand you could've prevented all of this from happening sooner," Mickey interjected in a stern tone and stare, as he pushed my hand off his shoulder and then entered the kitchen.

"Aye, judging by what you told us the boy is right," Samson said to me, while shaking his head.

"I know what happened to Hayley was my fault, and if it costs me my life to make things right, then so be it," I said to Samson.

"Let's hope you don't get out of it that easy. I had a friend back in Belfast who used to talk like that to me all the time. 'If it costs me my life I will get that job, if it costs me my life I will kiss that girl.' Don't bet your life whenever things turn grim," Samson said to me.

"I have nothing else to bet, Samson!" I shouted, as the front door of the speakeasy opened and three mobsters entered.

It was him, Carlo, along with his muscle, just as I predicted. At that moment, Samson and I stared daggers at Carlo and his muscle, while he grinned back at us in such a carefree manner. I knew why he was here, and there was nothing carefree about the matter.

"Ah buongiorno, you, Irishman, go do what your people do best and take stock of the liquor, while I talk with Jack," Carlo said to Samson.

"His name is Samson goddamn it," I remarked in a stern tone.

"It's all right Jack," Samson whispered in my ear.

"You and Mickey keep Hayley safe if I don't return," I whispered into Samson's ear.

"Aye you have my word," Samson whispered in my ear and then entered the kitchen.

"Let's go for a drive Jack. Carlo said to me, as the two mobsters beside him walked behind the bar and stood beside me.

"Why can we talk business here?" I inquired.

"It's such a beautiful day out. I thought you would like some fresh air," Carlo replied.

"Very well," I said to Carlo with a stern stare, as the two mobsters then patted me down and confiscated the pistol I had tucked between the waist-band of my pants, before escorting me towards the front door of the speakeasy with Carlo who was whistling an upbeat melody. What a sick and twisted bastard. 'The Coroner' is such a fitting nickname for Carlo. It seemed as if he became joyful, almost giddy, as the prospect of death drew nearer.

"Nice ride. Chevrolet Confederate, if I'm not mistaken?" I inquired, as Carlo and his muscle escorted me to their car parked beside mine.

"Correct, you have an eye for cars," Carlo replied.

"I just respect a fine vehicle when I see it," I said to Carlo. "This car belonged to my father. He bequeathed it to me when he died at the hands of an upstart rat," Carlo said to me. "So I take it your father was also in the business," I said to Carlo as I stared at the gleaming black paint job and black- tinted windows of the Chevrolet Confederate.

"He was indeed. Long before Mr. Luciano rose to power; my father established his organization in the shadow of the war. He learned that during the most desperate of times man can   be swayed in the most drastic of ways. Now Mr. Luciano has carried that torch which burns all those who threaten his power. All right enough reminiscing about the past, time to deal with the matter at hand," Carlo said to me, as he whistled to the two mobsters who stood on either side of me.

The first mobster then opened the door of the car and entered. I didn't want to be sitting in between the two mobsters in the backseat, but that was undoubtedly their intentions so they could easily overpower me. I needed to sit on the side so I could at least have more of a chance of escaping the hearse of a Chevrolet.

"Get in," the mobster said to me, as he pointed a gun against my side.

"After you," I said as I gestured for the mobster who looked like Primo Carnera to enter the car first.

"I insist," the mobster said to me in a stern tone. "No I insist," I said to the mobster.

"Get in the car fottuto sciocco!" the mobster shouted and then grabbed be by the collar and shoved me into the backseat of the car.

"Easy gentleman, as Mr. Luciano says 'we are civilized men' after all," Carlo said as he entered the car and sat beside the driver.

"Where to sir," the driver inquired. "Nowhere," Carlo replied in a stern tone.

"Ah very well sir," the driver said, as the car drove down Minetta Street.

"Nowhere, huh, you know you don't have to use code words when you're around me, Carlo. I know damn well that we're going to Pier 45," I said to Carlo.

"Ah you know what I like about you, Jack? You're smarter than you look," Carlo remarked with a snicker.

"Thanks, I guess. You look exactly how you act," I remarked.

"What's that supposed to mean," Carlo inquired, as the two mobsters sitting beside me grabbed both my arms in reaction to Carlo's irritated tone of voice towards my remark about him.

"It means what you see is what you get," I replied.

"We're here," Carlo pronounced as the car stopped at Pier 45.

"As I said before, you are smarter than you look Jack, so you already know why I brought you here on this sunny day," Carlo said to me, as he and the two mobsters escorted me down past the docks to a warehouse.

"Of course I do. Frankie contacted you, didn't he?" I inquired, as we entered the empty warehouse which has seen better days.

"He sure did. You really sent a clear message to him," Carlo said to me with a snicker.

"He tried to rape my niece. I regret nothing that I did to that fucking dog, so go ahead and do your worst," I said to Carlo in a stern tone.

"Carlo then began to snicker along with the two mobsters holding both my arms. Their snickering then rose to maniacal laughter which echoed throughout the rafters of the empty warehouse.

"Don't worry Jack. You're not going to die on this sunny day. You see, this warehouse used to be Mr. Luciano's base of operations, but now that base is your speakeasy. There's nothing left of this warehouse but memories of death, and soon your speakeasy will share the same fate mi amico. My father died at the hands of a valiant upstart like you. So when I told Mr. Luciano what happened with Frankie, you, and your niece, he told me to simply 'remind him who deals the judgment'. Now of course there are some gray areas in Mr. Luciano's orders, but I've known him long enough to know that he didn't want you silenced for what you did. So gentleman, why don't you quickly remind Jack, so we can get out of here," Carlo said as he pointed to the two mobsters, and then me. Both of the mobsters then simultaneously punched me in the gut which felt like I got rammed by a steel girder on a construction site. The Primo Carnera-looking mobster then took a swing at me but I ducked underneath and retaliated with a punch to his tree-trunk of a stomach.

"Don't fight back Jack, or else we will have to scar you as you scared Frankie," Carlo said to me with a snicker as the mobster I punched in the gut hunched over with a grimace before him and the other mobster unleashed a barrage of punches and kicks which sent me to the ground in a fetal position.

"That's enough gentlemen!" Carlo shouted, as I moaned in pain on the dirty ground of the warehouse.

"Oh Jack, these two associates of mine who gave you this reminder will be at the speakeasy later tonight with their pretty dames, so you better make sure they have a good time," Carlo said to me, as he and the two other mobsters snickered and then exited the warehouse, leaving me writhing in pain on the ground.

*****

It was 1:37 PM as I stood dazed on the corner of West and Barrow Street from the reminder Carlo and his muscle gave me a few minutes ago.

"Taxi!" I shouted and then spit blood out on the street. "Where to?" a taxicab driver inquired as he stopped in front of me.

"Minetta Street," I replied with a hissing groan as I held by bruised ribs and entered the cab.

"Looks like more people are driving nowadays. Maybe this economy is heading in the right direction," the taxicab driver remarked, as I lit a cigarette and took a smoke.

"Don't go judging the economy by the traffic during rush hour," I said to the taxicab driver with a scoff.

"Damn potholes," the cab driver remarked in a stern tone as the taxicab drove over a deep pothole which further battered my bruised ribs.

"Try to drive more smoothly, will you," I said to the cab driver in a stern tone.

"Oh yes your majesty," the cab driver said to me in a sarcastic tone and scoff.

*****

It was 2:02 PM as the taxicab drove down Minetta Street.

"You can stop here," I said in a stern tone.

I then paid the taxicab driver my fare and exited the cab. That son of a bitch Carlo took my pistol, and I doubt he will give me it back if I ask for it. This was all part of my reminder which left the copper taste of blood in my mouth and the sharp pain of bruised ribs every time I moved.

"Jack, can't you ever return to this speakeasy looking halfway decent?" Samson inquired, as I entered the speakeasy and walked up to the bar.

"Carlo and his muscle gave me a reminder," I replied.

"Oh that's what they're calling it now. Well it's a good thing you're still alive and in one piece, for the most part," Samson said to me.

"Where's Hayley?" I inquired as my eyes darted around the speakeasy which was all but empty except for one mobster sitting at the corner table in front of the stage.

"She's safe, she's in the kitchen," Samson replied, as he wiped down the bar.

"Good, that's all I care about right now," I said to Samson as I soaked a rag in warm water and scrubbed the blood off my battered face.

A knock on the front door then averted me attention as I instinctively reached for my pistol.

"Shit, I forgot Carlo took my pistol," I said to Samson. "Did you remember that you took Frankie's," Samson said to me with a grin, as he handed me Frankie's pistol.

"What's the password?" I inquired as I slid open the iron window of the front door.

"Lucky Luciano," an unmistakable feminine voice replied from the outside of the door.

"Faye, you sure are a sight for sore eyes," I remarked as I quickly opened the front door of the speakeasy with a cringe.

"Jack, why do you always look like you've been to hell and back?" Faye inquired with a distressed look in her smoky eyes as she placed her velvet-gloved hand on my battered cheek.

"I asked him the same thing Ms. Dubois," Samson said to Faye as we walked over to the bar.

"I've been to hell before Faye, and every time the devil decided he wants nothing to do with me," I replied with a snicker.

"Don't take your health so lightly Jack. There are those who depend on you," Faye said to me.

"Yes, people depend on me to get them drunk. I know my job Faye," I said to Faye with a scoff.

"I'm talking about Hayley. I came here to see how she's doing," Faye said to me.

"She's in the kitchen, go see for yourself," I said to Faye.

Faye then entered the kitchen, as Samson and I continued to get the speakeasy ready for tonight.

"That flapper is the next best thing to a mother for Hayley," Samson remarked.

"I'm glad Faye's here to console Hayley. I know the kid is very fond of her," I said to Samson in a somber tone as I swept underneath the tables.

"There was a mobster staking out my apartment last night. Do you know who he is?" Samson inquired in a stern tone.

"Yes, his name is Nicolai 'the wolf' Volkov. He's the mobster assigned to protect you," I replied with a sigh.

"A Russian huh, I thought the Five Points Gang only recruited Italians," Samson said to me.

"He's a special case assigned to you. They fear your past history, Samson. So don't tip the hand that could very well pull the trigger," I said to Samson.

"I don't need protection from a goddamn Russian. Just look what that so called protection did to your niece in there," Samson said in a stern tone as he slammed his fist on the bar

"I'm sorry Samson. I wish I had the authority change the current state of affairs," I said to Samson in a somber tone. "Hayley is … weak, she needs to eat," Faye said to me in a somber tone as she sat down at the bar.

"I'll fix her something to eat," Samson said to Faye.

"Just make sure it's not haggis, I wouldn't feed that garbage to a dog," I said to Samson in a stern tone.

"Jack, Hayley is fading. I don't see a will to live in her beautiful eyes," Faye said to me in a somber tone.

"Well then let us hope that boy Mickey can uplift her spirits. He will be here soon," I said to Faye in a somber tone.

"It's this speakeasy. It has such a way of lowering ones spirits," Faye remarked in a somber tone, as she lit a cigarette and took a smoke.

"Then let's get the hell out of here," I said to Faye with a grin.

"What about Hayley?" Faye inquired, as she stared into the kitchen with a somber look in her eyes.

"Don't worry. I trust Samson and Mickey to keep her safe tonight. I trust those two more than I trust myself at times," I replied.

"Are you sure you feel well enough?" Faye inquired.

"I'm taking the day off, Samson. You and Mickey watch over Hayley and don't do anything I wouldn't do," I said to Samson with a grin, as the prospect of spending the rest of the day with Faye breathed new life into my beaten body.

"Very well mon chéri. We can go to my flat, I mean, how you say, my apartment," Faye said to me with a grin, as she stood up from the barstool.

I've never been to Faye's apartment before, although I must admit I've fantasized about it. A day that started out with me being beaten by two mobsters has now taken a turn for the better as I exited the speakeasy with Faye.

Faye always had a way of putting my mind at ease. Her beauty and charm cut through the fog of bourbon and mobsters which danced around in my head on a daily basis.

"Don't tell me this is your car," I said to Faye with a grin as I rubbed my hand across the hood of a rose colored Cadillac La Salle.

"This is indeed my car, is this hard for you to believe?" Faye inquired with a grin.

This was hard for me to believe. The only dames who could afford cars like these hung on the shoulders of mobsters, and I for one have never seen Faye enter or exit the speakeasy with a mobster. Faye was full of surprises, which made me all the more attracted to her as we drove down Minetta Street.

"So do you live in the village?" I inquired as both Faye and I lit a cigarette and took a smoke as traffic gridlocked down 6th Avenue.

"I live in *Magnolia Towers* it's this apartment complex just ahead, right across from the beautiful *Jefferson Market Court*," Faye replied as she pointed at the library's spire which stood boldly in the distance.

"Ah I remember reading about that courthouse in the paper. Many consider it a landmark of the village," I said to Faye.

"I consider it a beacon of knowledge, serenity, and justice," Faye said to me as traffic started moving again.

"Of course, there is also that women's prison right next to it. How do you deal with all those crooked broads every day?" I inquired with a snicker.

"I adore all those women despite what circumstances brought them there. They will often call for me through the bars across the street," Faye replied with a giggle.

"Do those broads try to proposition you for a good time?" I inquired with a snicker.

"Sometimes, but they usually just ask for cigarettes," Faye replied as she parked the Cadillac in front of an apartment complex which looked like its seen better days, but then again, this whole city has seen better days.

*****

"Faites comme chez vous, Jack," Faye said to me with a grin as we entered her apartment.

"English, Faye. Remember I want to know every word that comes out of that mouth," I said to Faye with a grin.

"Uhm … make yourself at home, as they say in America," Faye said to me with a grin.

Faye's apartment reflected her appearance to a tee. The fragrance of sweet perfume and smoke hit my nose as I took a moment to look around the parlor while Faye entered the kitchen.

Faye's apartment was unlike any woman's apartment I've ever been to. It felt as if I was taking a stroll through a garden as I stared at the many potted plants she had decorating nearly every inch of space. I then sat down on the maroon sofa with a sigh as one plant caught my eye in particular.

"One double bourbon on the rocks for you, and one glass of merlot for me. Oh, that plant is called cœur saignant, uhm … how do you say, bleeding heart," Faye said to me as she entered the parlor and handed me a drink I didn't even ask for but sure as hell needed to calm my nerves.

"Why is it called that?" I inquired, as took a sip of bourbon and then stared intently at the plant on the coffee table.

"Don't tell me you cannot see why, Jack. Just look, you see how the blooms are shaped like a heart with blood dripping from it," Faye replied, as she leaned in close to me and pointed to the flower.

"Oh I see it now," I said to Faye with a grin.

"So tell me, Jack, do you have a bleeding heart?" Faye inquired with a grin.

"Only if I'm taking a beating by mobsters," I replied with a grin.

"That's not what I mean and you know it," Faye said to me with a playful shove.

"Then by all means elaborate," I said to Faye with a grin.

"A bleeding heart means that you feel pain when others feel pain. You hurt when you see others hurt," Faye said to me.

"Most everyone in this city is hurting. If I felt pain for every one of them I wouldn't be able to stand," I said to Faye.

"You don't have to bleed for all of them, just the ones who are closest to you. Jack, my heart bleeds for you and Hayley. This life you chose is taking its toll on the both of you," Faye said to me in a somber tone.

"Don't remind me. I came here to get away from that life. I already got one reminder from Carlo, which you can see all over my face," I said to Faye in a stern tone as I pointed to my battered face.

"Hayley cares for you Jack, can you not see that," Faye said to me as she placed her hand on my bruised cheek.

"Ah, easy," I said to Faye with a hissing grimace.

"Oh pardon," Faye said to me as she moved her hand off my cheek, but not before I grabbed it while staring intently into her smoky eyes.

"I care for you, can you not see that," I said to Faye.

Faye then leaned in close and placed her other hand on my cheek as she kissed me on the lips. The touch of Faye's lips was everything I imagined them to be and more. She put a spell on me at that moment, a spell that I didn't want to shake.

"Let's run away together. Leave this city in our dust, what do you say?" I inquired, as I held Faye's smooth and slender body in my arms in the manner that Cary Grant would hold all those beautiful dames in his movies.

"I—I cannot," Faye said to me in a hush tone, as she shook her head and then looked down.

"Why not, when are you going to start taking me seriously, Faye?" I inquired in a stern tone.

"When you start speaking the words of a man who confronts his responsibilities, not a boy who runs from them," Faye replied in a stern tone.

"My responsibilities ... you're talking about Hayley, aren't you?" I inquired.

"Yes, she needs you Jack. Every time she reaches out you slap her hand away," Faye replied.

"That's not true. She tried to kill herself the night Frankie attacked her. We struggled over the knife she was going to use to do the job, but I wouldn't allow it. Did she tell you all about that too?" I inquired in a distressed tone, and then took a swig of bourbon and slammed the glass down on the coffee table.

"Oh my god ... I had no idea. Jack I—,"

"If you want to be a mother to Hayley that's fine by me, but don't shame me as being a terrible uncle," I interjected in a stern tone, as I stood up from the maroon sofa and walked over to the window.

"Mon chéri Jack, I am a strong believer in fate. I believe I was fated to come to America. Just as you and Hayley were fated to strengthen each other," Faye said to me in a somber tone, as she walked up behind me. The smoke from Faye's breath against the back of my neck at that moment sent a chill up my spine. It's true that I wanted to leave this town with Faye and never look back, but did that really make me a boy? Faye held me to a higher moral standard than

I held myself to, and for that, I felt compelled to do right by her.

"That kid would've been better off if I never picked her up at the hospital," I said to Faye in a somber tone, as I stared out the window at the women's prison across the street.

"You don't know that. You're the only family she has left. Without you she would be spending her days in breadlines and her nights shivering on the streets," Faye said to me in a somber tone.

"You don't know that," Maybe that bleeding heart FDR will bring this country out of the gutter it's been in for the past four years," I said to Faye with a scoff.

"Until those powers at be that govern this country make such changes, know that you have the power to help Hayley right now," Faye said to me.

"I have no power, Faye! This was true even before I started working for Mr. Luciano, just look what happened when I tried to exercise power," I said to Faye in a stern tone, as I pointed to my bruised face.

"Jack … just look at those women behind bars across the street," Faye said to me, as she pointed out the window.

"So what?" I inquired with a scoff, as I stared at the women in prison with their arms sticking out through the bars.

"Those women are behind bars, but their will to live is not imprisoned in any way. We all have power to change the lives of the people we love," Faye said to me, as she wrapped her arms around my waist from behind and rested he head against my shoulder.

"What would you have me do Faye? I'm stuck between a rock and a hard place with Hayley," I inquired with a sigh.

"Mon chéri Jack. You've never been the kind of man who lets obstacles stop him, so why stop now?" Faye inquired with a grin, as I turned around and faced her with a stern look which quickly changed to match Faye's charming grin.

"Kiss lovebirds!"

"Go ahead, give us a show!"

The women from the prison across the street shouted, as Faye giggled.

There were two women in my life now. Two women who tested my patience, but strengthened my will. These were the cards I was dealt, and I had to play them for the time being in hopes that more powerful men failed to see through my bluff. No matter how much bourbon I drink to forget them, the constant reminder of Hayley and her mother will always remain in my mind. Faye believes we were fated to meet, I for one, do not share that sentiment. If anybody would've asked me four months ago to risk my life for a kid I would simply laugh in their face, but now I find myself instinctively putting my life on the line for Hayley.

"Sorry ladies!" I shouted out the window with a grin, before I closed the drapes and then kissed Faye.

CHAPTER 10:
PRINCESS OF THE VILLAGE
- HAYLEY -

"Hayley … Hayley wake up," a voice called out to me. "Mom?" I murmured as a familiar feeling of warmth comforted me.

"Hayley … wake up," the voice called out to me once more. "Mom!" I spoke aloud in a distressed tone, as I awoke in bed to the sight of Samson standing over me.

"You were talking in your sleep, lass," Samson said to me. "Leave me alone," I said to Samson in a stern tone, as I scooted away from him on the far side of the bed and wrapped my arms around my legs. Samson's brutish presence scared me more now than ever before. I couldn't even feel safe around Mickey after what Frankie did to me last night.

"Sorry, I was just checking up on you. If you need anything just holler," Samson said to me and then exited the kitchen.

It was obvious that my cries of pain fell on deaf ears in this speakeasy. No matter how much I scrub and claw I can't get the feeling of Frankie off my skin. Now I look at the broken necklace Mickey gave me upon the nightstand as a heartbreaking reminder of how easily a fragile heart can break. *'I'll take this back to the jeweler, he will have it fixed in no time,'* Mickey said to me when he saw what Frankie did to the necklace. Oh Mickey, if it was only that easy. If only that jeweler could fix my heart, but he lacks the tools for that job.

The speakeasy smelled unusually sweet this evening as the fragrance of women's perfume wafted into the kitchen. *There must be more women than usual in the speakeasy* I thought to myself as I sat down at my desk and stared out into the bar. I hated the Italian language, for it reminded me of Fernando. The mobsters would speak Italian all the time in the speakeasy and whenever I heard it I couldn't stop myself from shaking as it took me back to that night when I was alone in the dark with Fernando using me in such a cruel and sadistic manner.

Dear Diary,
July 2nd, 5:16 PM,

It happened again. Are all men inherently evil? Do they all share the same desires that can overpower me in the blink of an eye? I write to you in the very room where it happened, but I also fear leaving this very room of horrors. I wish I could live within your pages, nobody would find me then and I would be truly safe. I dreamt of my mom again, but this time, the sound of her voice calling out to me grew fainter and fainter, almost as if my memory of her was slowly fading away. I know she would tell me to be strong right now, but I just cannot bare another day living. So why don't I end the pain right now? Samson is busy serving the mobsters so I have a small window in which I can do it. Jack stopped me last night from ending it all, but he's gone now, and now he will no longer have to live with the burden of me in his life. Goodbye.

I then took out my make-shift knife from the nightstand drawer and stared at it for a few moments as the dreaded sound of mobsters speaking Italian in the bar thundered in my mind.

"I'll see you soon, mom," I spoke aloud in a somber tone as my eyes welled up with tears. I then opened the door to the shower and turned on the water.

"I'm back, where's Hayley?" Jack shouted. No, I was too late, there would be no ending my pain now, not while Jack is here watching me.

"Hayley, how are you feeling, did you eat?" Jack inquired as I quickly put my make-shift knife in the pocket of my dress. "I had toast earlier," I said to Jack, as he turned off the water running in the shower.

"You need to leave this room, how about we go to *Washington Square Park* and feed bread to some of those obnoxious geese?" Jack inquired with a grin.

"I thought you hated nature," I said to Jack as he opened the fridge and took out a bottle of beer.

"I do, but I remember your mother and I used to go to that park and feed the geese nearly every weekend. This one time I remember a goose bit your mother's hand while she was feeding them, and do you know what your mother did then to that bold son of a bitch?" Jack inquired with a grin.

I then shook my head, as Jack sat down on the bed with a snicker. Jack seemed in a good mood right now, he must've been out with Ms Dubois this afternoon .If only I was talking to her right now instead of Jack.

"Your mother then smacked that goose right in his greedy beak," Jack said to me with a laugh and then took a swig of beer with a sigh.

"That sounds like something she would do," I said to Jack with a smile.

"Is that a smile I see? So all it took was a story of how your mother smacked a goose to finally make you smile" Jack said to me with a snicker.

I see now that Ms. Dubois brings out the best in Jack. I hope her and Jack become closer, because there's nobody else in this world right now other than Faye who I would want as a mother.

"Is Ms. Dubois coming with you?" I inquired in a timid tone as I brushed a strand of hair behind my ear.

"Faye, we may see her tonight, but as for now, she has other engagements," Jack replied.

"Oh I was hoping that she would join us. I know she loves nature," I said to Jack in a somber tone.

"Well don't let that stop us, kid. Come on," Jack said to me with a grin as he spun his car keys around his finger.

"A-Are you sure you're all right to drive," I inquired in a timid tone, as I pointed to the beer bottle in Jack's hand.

"Oh this, you sound like your mother again. Don't worry, kid, I'm not half in the bag just yet," Jack replied with a snicker, and then finished the last of the beer with a swig and tossed the bottle in the trash with a belch.

"How's the weather?" I inquired.

"It's beautiful. Clear blue skies and cool breezes," Jack replied with a grin.

"I suppose I can go with you," I said to Jack. "All right let's go, princess," Jack said to me.

"Don't call me that," I said to Jack in a stern tone.

"Why not, it's a term of respect to a woman your age," Jack inquired.

"I don't care. Just don't call me that," I said to Jack in a distressed tone as my face quivered.

"All right, kid. Let's go," Jack said to me with a grin as he exited the kitchen with a loaf of bread.

"What are you up to Jack?" Samson inquired

"Hayley and I are going out. Mickey will be here soon," Jack replied as Samson and a mobster at the bar seemed to be staring daggers at each other as if they were in a standoff.

"Aye have a good time," Samson proclaimed.

Jack and I then exited the speakeasy as the smell of smoke, liquor and perfume was swiftly blown out of my nose from a cool breeze that blew through the alley of Minetta Street.

It would always bring me to tears every time Jack told me stories about my mother. They were heartfelt stories that left me missing her even more, but it was a good kind of sadness, a sadness that left me feeling better after the tears had ended just from knowing that Jack is helping keep the memory of my mother alive. I would still much rather be spending the day at *Washington Square Park* with Faye right now, but I could tell that Jack was making an effort to be there for me, so I accepted his act of compassion with open arms.

"It sure is a fine day out huh, kid. Almost makes you forget that this country is going through an economic crisis," Jack said to me as we drove down *West 4th Street*.

Jack was right. On beautiful days like these it almost makes you forget about the current state of the world, and the current state of my mind.

"Oh would you look at that. Back to reality," Jack remarked as we arrived at

Washington Square Park to the sight of a long breadline.

"We should feel grateful we don't need to wait in those lines," I said to Jack as he parked the car on the street across from the park.

"You took the words right out of my mouth," Jack said to me. Jack and I then exited the car and walked past the long breadline of sad looking people to the park.

"I guess there's nowhere in this city where we can escape to huh, Jack," I said to Jack in a somber tone as we walked down a trail of the park where the homeless took up residence in make-shift tents.

"You may be right about that kid, but instead of trying to escape all the misery that seems to be around every corner of this city, let's instead try to find what made us happy before this depression and prohibition hit us," Jack said to me.

"Before the depression and prohibition … well I lived most of my life during this prohibition, so I have no memories of what was before this time, or what made me happy," I said to Jack in a somber tone.

"I remember I used to have friends when I was your age in *SoHo* that I would raise hell with in the streets. This was during the war, but they helped me take my mind off things," Jack said to me with a grin and then took a swig from his flask.

"It seems that we were both raised during terrible times," I said to Jack.

"Although it may seem like you were born into hell, remember nobody is born into heaven, kid," Jack said to me, as we sat down on a bench facing the central fountain.

Jack seemed more patient with me today. Could it be because he was drinking, or because Faye put him in a good mood?

"Ah there they are," Jack remarked as a flock of geese slowly waddled up to us.

Jack then tore the loaf of bread and handed me half, as the geese clamored for the bread in my hands like children clamoring for candy on Halloween.

"Oh this one is a glutton, he wants all the bread," Jack remarked with a snicker, as we tossed small morsels of bread at the ground in front of the geese.

"They're gentler than I thought they'd be," I remarked with a smile, as I got one goose to eat out of my hand.

"You're right, I guess your mother and geese don't mix," Jack remarked with a snicker, which brought out a giggle within me.

will give me another reminder," Jack replied as he pointed to his bruised face.

"All right … goodbye," I said to the small lone, white duck as he looked at me with curious eyes before Jack and I exited *Washington Square Park*.

*****

"Oh here you go," I said to a lone white duck which stood behind the flock of geese, but was too small to make his presence known. I related to that white duck as he stood behind a group of larger, stronger, but just as hungry animals as they bullied him around.

"Well I'm all out of bread fellas," Jack proclaimed, as the rest of the clamoring birds focused their hunger towards me.

I then noticed a man sitting on the ground on a mass of blankets by the central fountain, as he held out his hands with a look of despair all over his gray tinted face.

"Where are you going?" Jack inquired.

"I'll be right back," I replied as I walked over to the man at the central fountain.

"Here, take this. You need it more than these geese do," I said to the man as I handed him the bread I had left with a smile. "Bless you child. You are a true princess among thieves," the man said to me, as he took the loaf of bread with a smile. "There was that word again, that word that brought back a horrible memory which flashed in my mind like lightning every time I heard it.

"Did you give the last of your bread to that beggar?" Jack inquired as I walked back to the park bench.

"Yes, everyone was just ignoring him as if he didn't exist," I replied in a somber tone.

"Well you're the one responsible for him is he follows us back to the speakeasy," Jack said with a snicker, as he stood up from the park bench with a groan.

"Are we leaving already?" I inquired.

"I'm afraid so kid. The prime drinking hour is approaching and I have to serve my associates in a gracious manner or Carlo will give me another reminder," Jack replied as he pointed to his bruised face.

"All right ... goodbye," I said to the small lone, white duck as he looked at me with curious eyes before Jack and I exited Washington Square Park.

*****

It was 9:07 PM in the speakeasy, as I awoke from a short nap with the sound of a woman singing echoing throughout the speakeasy.

"Why is he coming here tonight?" Jack inquired as I walked up to him and Samson behind the bar.

"Who's coming here?" I inquired in a weary tone as I rubbed my bleary eyes.

"Mr. Luciano himself. Carlo told me that he wants to talk to you Hayley," Samson replied.

"Why, why would he want to talk to me now? Do you think it has to do with Frankie?" I inquired in a distressed tone as my heart raced with fear at the very thought of being face to face with Mr. Luciano.

"I don't know, kid, but mind your manners when you speak to him. Samson and I are only two men and we can only do so much when it comes to protecting you. Mr. Luciano will most likely arrive here with at least four of his most powerful associates," Jack replied.

"No, no, please don't make me talk to him, please," I pleaded to Jack in a tearful tone, as I pulled on his jacket.

I sat at my desk dreading Mr. Luciano's arrival. Would I be punished for what happened to Frankie, or perhaps just as worse, would Jack be punished? I wasn't ready to face him, not now, not after what Frankie did to me. I have to run away somewhere Mr. Luciano's power won't reach, but does such a place in New York exist?

"I heard Mr. Luciano will be here soon," Mickey said to me as he entered the kitchen.

"That's why I must leave as soon as possible," I said to Mickey, as I gathered my cloths and stuffed them into a sack used to store potatoes.

"You have me, Jack, and Samson to protect you now, isn't that enough?" Mickey inquired

"No, nobody can protect me from him," I replied.

"Then I'm coming with you," Mickey said to me, as he attached something around my neck.

"The necklace, you fixed it," I remarked with a wide-eyed stare at the necklace which once lay in pieces upon the kitchen, but was now restored to its former beauty.

"Omar fixed it right up. I told him I would pay any price but he said to me that whenever it gets broken he would repair it free of charge," Mickey said to me with a smile.

"Thank you. I'll cherish it, but it's not safe for you to be with me now, I can't put your life in danger, I care about you too much … goodbye," I said to Mickey in a tearful tone, and then exited the kitchen.

"Hayley wait," Mickey said to me in a distressed tone, as he placed his hand on my shoulder

"Please Mickey don't make this harder on me than it already is," I said to Mickey, as tears streamed from my eyes. "Hayley I—I love you," Mickey said to me.

Mickey had finally spoken those three words to me, those three words which I was afraid to speak to him, those three words that carried so much weight but at the same time made me feel as if I was floating.

"Mickey … I—,"

A knock on the front door averted my attention away from Mickey's beautiful brown eyes which seemed to glimmer in the low lights of the speakeasy as he stared intently back at me.

I then slowly walked backwards with wide-eyes as Jack scampered up to the front door of the speakeasy.

It was too late now, I had to face him, but I had three noble men protecting me now and that's more than I had four months ago.

"Yes sir," Jack said, as he quickly opened the front door of the speakeasy. I then scampered back to Samson behind the bar, as Mr. Luciano entered with two dangerous looking men standing on either side of him, just like how Jack predicted. The speakeasy then fell silent as everyone stared at Mr. Luciano, as he slowly walked up to the bar with a grin.

"This isn't a funeral home. Keep playing, keep drinking, keep laughing," Mr. Luciano proclaimed, with a twirling gesture of his hand.

Mr. Luciano wore a black three piece suit with a scarlet scarf and neck tie. His suave appearance seemed to strike fear and respect into the hearts of every one he sauntered by at the speakeasy.

"Just stay calm, we'll be by your side," Samson said to me, as I stood behind him.

"Jack, where's that niece of yours?" Mr. Luciano inquired, as he sat down at the bar with his four associates sitting on either side of him.

"I'll go get her sir," Jack replied, and then scampered into the kitchen.

"I'm right here," I said to Mr. Luciano in a timid tone, as I stepped out from behind Samson.

"Ah once I heard the news I've been meaning to talk to you. Let's sit down over here," Mr. Luciano said to me with a grin as he pointed to a table where a young couple was sitting. "Move," Mr. Luciano said to the couple in a stern tone and whistle as he gestured for them leave the table.

"Yes sir," the man and woman said to Mr. Luciano in unison, as they both left the table in a hasty manner.

"Please sit down mio caro," Mr. Luciano said to me.

My heart was racing at that moment, but I then felt Jack, Samson, and Mickey standing behind me which gave me the courage to face Mr. Luciano.

"Now ... it has come to my attention that an associate of mine, well, former associate now by the name of Frankie Angelo attacked you last night. Is this true?" Mr. Luciano inquired, as he played with the many gold rings which adorned his fingers, while one of his associates lit a cigar and placed it in his mouth. Jack, Mickey, and Samson then placed their hands on my shoulder, as I looked up at them with a wide-eyed stare. Jack then nodded at me with a stern look, as I took a deep breath before looking back at Mr. Luciano.

"Y—Yes sir, he did attack me," I replied.

"Quel fottuto bastardo in no way represents my organization. My associates have been searching every dark corner of this city for Frankie, but he continues to elude us. I now ask you this mio caro, to make amends for defiling you; I will see to it personally that Frankie is silenced," Mr. Luciano said to me in a stern tone.

"If you're asking for my permission to kill Frankie then the answer is no. I cannot be responsible for someone dying, no matter how much they've hurt me," I said to Mr. Luciano.

"Well ... I was not expecting that answer. Now normally I would have Carlo and his associates beat that fottuto bastardo half to death, but to my knowledge Jack has already done that," Mr. Luciano said to me with a snicker, as he glanced at Jack.

It was now or never. I now had the chance to make my voice heard to the most powerful man in New York City and I wouldn't pass up that chance.

"I—I just want to be respected," I said to Mr. Luciano in a timid tone, as I brushed a strand of hair behind my ear.

"Ah of course, of course, don't we all mio caro," Mr. Luciano said to me with a snicker as if I said something funny. At that moment, I could tell that Mr. Luciano was patronizing me, but at the same time I felt that he was taking me seriously. I was still afraid of what he would decide to do with me, Jack, Samson, or Mickey. I didn't want to be responsible for anybody getting hurt, so I just made that request hoping that it wouldn't cause anymore violence, but perhaps that was a naïve way of thinking.

Mr. Luciano then whispered in one of his associate's ears for a few moments as I sat in suspense over what his verdict on the matter of my respect will be.

"I've come to a decision mio caro. Your request for respect is a most humble one. When I was your age I had to kill for respect. I remember what it's like, and so …," Mr. Luciano said to me and then whistled with a hand gesture that made everyone in the speakeasy, along with the band fall silent.

"Everyone quiet Mr. Luciano is speaking," one of Mr.

Luciano's associates shouted.

"Grazie Leo. Let it be known that this young lady who goes by the name of …," Mr. Luciano proclaimed as he looked at me with his hand out.

"Hayley Carmona," I said to Mr. Luciano in a timid tone. "Louder mio caro," Mr. Luciano said to me, as he gestured an upward waving motion with his ringed hand.

"Hayley Carmona," I proclaimed, as all the eyes of everyone in the speakeasy were fixed on me. Mr. Luciano then stood up as he gestured for me to stand up.

"Yes let it be known that Ms. Hayley Carmona will be treated with the utmost respect. If it comes to my knowledge that anyone has disrespected her in any way then you will first be reminded, if you then continue to disrespect her, you will then be silenced. Sono stato chiaro," Mr. Luciano proclaimed, as he stared intently at everyone in the speakeasy.

"Yes Mr. Luciano," everyone in the speakeasy said in unison.

"You are now their principessa and will be treated as such," Mr. Luciano said to me. "Don't call me that," ("Don't call her that,")

Jack and I said in unison, as Mr. Luciano stared at us both with a grin.

"What young lady wouldn't want to be called a principessa? Very well then," Mr. Luciano said to me.

"Are you all right?" Jack inquired, as I could finally begin to take a deep breath now that Mr. Luciano and everyone else's eyes in the speakeasy weren't fixed upon me.

"I—I don't know," I replied.

"Andiamo! Leo, we have pressing matters to attend to in Harlem," Mr. Luciano said in a stern tone as him and his associates exited the speakeasy.

*****

It had been two weeks since Mr. Luciano made it known to all of his associates that there would be dire consequences to any one of them who disrespected me, and as a result, my life in the speakeasy was a little less scary, but all the more awkward. Other than a few light pleasantries, the mobsters left me alone. I was still afraid that Frankie was still out there, I didn't want him dead, but I didn't want him alive, because I knew he was plotting vengeance on me and Jack. If he should ever return, I hope that one of these mobsters protects me from him. I don't want to spend the rest of my life looking over my shoulder, but at the same time I couldn't be naïve to the intentions of men. It was those very intentions which left me the way I am now, a broken princess of mobsters.

"Good evening, Ms. Carmona," a mobster said to me as I sat down at the bar.

"Good evening and please call me Hayley," I said to the mobster.

"Yes ma'am," the mobster said to me with a grin and then left the bar.

"Jack, Is that Gracie singing?" I inquired, as I pointed to a woman on the stage, wearing a shear blank dress and gloves.

"It sure is," I told Carlo she has the voice of an angel so he decided to have her work for us," Jack replied with a grin as he dried a glass.

"I prefer Gracie much more over Ms. Valentino," I remarked with a smile.

"What's wrong with Carmen Valentino?" Jack inquired. "She's too tawdry for my taste," I replied.

"Not for me. Carlo has put me in charge of Gracie and Carmen's scheduling, so I have Gracie working the mornings and afternoons, while Carmen works the evenings and nights. These two dames really put this place at ease. I believe these mobsters would eat each other alive if it wasn't for the live entertainment calming them down," Jack said to me as Gracie waved at me from the stage as she sung a most lovely song about how women are saviors and men are oppressors.

"Fill her up, Jack," Gracie said to Jack with a grin as she walked up to the bar holding and empty wine glass.

"What'll you have?" Jack inquired.

"I've been working here for over a week and you still don't remember my drink?" Gracie inquired with a grin.

"Refresh my memory, doll. My mind isn't what it used to be when it comes to remembering women's' signature drinks," Jack said to Gracie.

"You always remember Faye's signature drink," I said to Jack with a grin.

"That's because Faye hammers it into my head much like Gracie is doing right now," Jack said to me with a snicker. "Rose Hibiscus Martini my good man," Gracie said to Jack with a grin.

"You too? What is it with you dames and rose themed cocktails?" Jack inquired with a grin as he prepared Gracie's drink.

"Let me guess, Faye also loves a rose themed cocktail as well," Gracie said as she primped her hair.

"Yes indeed. Her signature cocktail is the Black Rose," Jack said to Gracie.

"You sounded lovely up there, Gracie," I remarked with a smile.

"Thank you, honey. That song always speaks to my heart. I call it an anthem for all women out there in this world who are suffering under the hand of cruel men," Gracie said to me.

"It's nice and you sing it with such emotion," I remarked. "Here's your drink, doll," Jack said to Gracie as he presented the Rose Hibiscus cocktail in front of her on the bar with a grin, and then entered the kitchen.

"I simply love the pink color, not to mention the flavor of the beautiful flowers infused into this drink. A cocktail fit for a princess. What do you think, honey," Gracie inquired, after she took a sip of the Rose Hibiscus cocktail.

"I—I wouldn't know," I replied.

I wish I was more like Faye and Gracie. They're both strong, confident, and beautiful women who write their own destinies instead of having a man write it for them. My encounter with Mr. Luciano was not what I expected it to be. I know how feared the man is throughout New York, but he didn't impose himself on me in a scary manner. He instead made it known to every mobster in the Five Points Gang to treat me with respect. For the good majority of my short life I've been so used to being treated like a dog by everyone except my mother. I wasn't used to being in the limelight, but at the same time, I no longer wanted to live in the shadows of the bright and happy people which surrounded me.

"Mickey will be here soon. How are you feeling?" Jack inquired, as he exited the kitchen holding two wine bottles.

"I'm fine, thanks for asking," I replied in a timid tone, as I brushed a strand of hair behind my ear with a sigh.

The atmosphere in the speakeasy for the past two weeks was more peaceful than usual, and if I closed my eyes I could imagine that I was in just another bar with normal patrons.

"Hayley open your eyes," a familiar voice said to me, as I opened my eyes to the sight of Mickey holding a rose out in front of me.

"For me?" I inquired with a wide-eyed stare as I gazed at the beautiful rose in Mickey's hand.

"No it's for me. Aw you shouldn't have," Samson replied with a snicker, as he walked up to Mickey reached for the rose in his hand.

"Very funny Samson. Yes this is for you." Mickey said with a grin as he moved the rose away from Samson's reach and then handed it to me.

"It's beautiful," I remarked as my eyes welled up with tears and then kissed Mickey on his flushed cheek before wrapping my arms around him.

"You could learn a thing or two from Mickey on how to treat woman," Gracie said to Samson with a grin, as she shoved him in a playful manner.

"Ouch," I said as a thorn from the rose poked my finger. "Are you all right?" Mickey inquired.

"I'm wonderful. I'll go put this in water," I replied with a smile, as I put my bleeding fingertip in my mouth and sucked the blood.

"I just learned more from that rose than I did from Mickey," Samson said to Gracie.

"Oh really, and what exactly did you learn big guy," Gracie inquired, and then took a sip of her pretty pink cocktail.

"I learned that woman are like roses, they're beautiful to look at—, "

"But the closer you get to them the more dangerous they are," Jack interjected as him and Samson laughed in unison. "You two are hopeless," Gracie remarked with a grin and dismissive wave.

What I've always wanted, yet I never thought I would get, a rose from a boy I like. I've written about this in my diary when I lived with my mother. Johnny would never treat her way Mickey treated me, like a princess.

I still hated that word princess for the horrible memory it would bring back to my mind, but perhaps I can create new memories with Mickey, perhaps his love can purge that horrible memory from my mind.

I then entered the kitchen and put the rose in what Jack calls a champagne flute filled with water and placed it on my desk.

"Are you all right?" Mickey inquired as he entered the kitchen and took off his hat.

"Yes it's just … I'm only used to being treated this way by my mother," I replied in a somber tone.

"I wish I could've met your mother," Mickey said to me as he sat down on my bed with a sigh.

"She would've loved you," I said to Mickey as I sat down on the bed beside him.

"You deserve to be treated like a princess more than most women in this world," Mickey remarked.

"Please don't use that word," I said to Mickey as I scooted away from him on the bed.

"Why not?" Mickey inquired

"Every time I here that word, it takes me back to the time … to the time when my father raped me," I replied.

"Oh … I'm so sorry I didn't know, and I'm sorry he ruined that word for you," Mickey said to me in a somber tone.

"Whenever I hear that word I relive that horrible memory of feeling alone in my dark bedroom as he had his way with me," I said to Mickey, as my eyes welled up with tears.

"I'm here for you, you're not alone, and as for that word, there's no girl in this town more deserving of the title than you," Mickey said to me with a grin, as he placed his hand on mine.

"My mother would always call me her little angel. I miss her so much. I see her in all the women who pass through the speakeasy," I said to Mickey in a tearful tone.

"Mickey get over here, son!" Samson shouted from the bar. "I'll be right there!" Mickey shouted back at Samson.

"I'll be back as soon as I can," Mickey said to me and then scampered into the bar.

I should feel happiness right now. I received a rose, a token of love which I never thought I was worthy of, but certain horrible memories of my past always find a way to take me back to that dark and lonely place in my mind. It's a place I've spent a good portion of my life in, and most of all, it's a place that seems to call to me when nobody else will.

"Where are you going?" I inquired as I walked up to the front door of the speakeasy.

"I have to meet Carlo at Pier 45 regarding a pressing matter. I have no idea what that ghoul wants from me, but I can only assume It requires me risking my life, just another typical Tuesday huh, kid," Jack replied with a scoff as he shook his head while putting on his jacket.

"Be careful," I said to Jack, as he tucked Frankie's pistol into his pants.

"Don't worry, kid. You will see my battered face in no time," Jack said to me with a grin, as he placed his hand on my shoulder and then exited the speakeasy.

"Ah there he goes again. Sometimes I think your uncle thrives off danger," Gracie said to me as she walked up beside me holding another cocktail, this one appeared to be the color of a sunset.

"What makes you say that?" I inquired.

"Well you may know him better than me, honey, but from what I gathered from your uncle is that whenever somebody's life is in danger, including his, he seemed to suddenly be filled with such a heroic vigor," Gracie replied.

"Well doesn't everybody act that way during those times?" I inquired, as Gracie and I walked back to the bar.

"No, no, no, most people cower, but Jack is no coward, that much can be said about him," Gracie remarked with a giggle and then took a sip of her cocktail.

"I wish I was as brave as Jack," I said to Gracie as I sat down beside her at the bar.

"Just open your eyes honey. You are a young woman surrounded by dangerous mobsters. You have no doubt inherited your uncle's bravery," Gracie said to me.

"I like to think my mother is more responsible for my bravery. Jack would always tell me inspiring stories of her when he was younger," I said to Gracie with a smile.

"My mother died a few years back. Her dying words to me were simple, but so powerful," Gracie said to me. "What did she say?" I inquired.

"She told me to 'carry myself like a princess'," Gracie replied with a grin as she tossed her hair back.

"Oh ... that word princess, do you feel all women should act that way?" I inquired.

"It's not the same for all women, honey, but I can tell you that I saw a princess in you the first time I saw you," Gracie replied.

Gracie had an uplifting memory regarding that word that causes me to shake with fear. I wish I shared in her memory, but I just cannot seem to wipe the image of Fernando out of my mind whenever I hear that word. Perhaps if I try hard enough, I can imagine Mickey, Gracie, Faye, Jack, and Samson smiling warmly at me whenever I hear that dreaded word. Now all I needed was a test to see if I could combat all the darkness in my mind which Fernando, Frankie, and Johnny created with the love I feel from Mickey, Faye, Gracie, Jack, and Samson. Thanks to Mr. Luciano, all these mobsters see me as a princess, and perhaps I can get one of them to call me by that title.

"Excuse me, can I have that chair?" I inquired as I walked up to a brooding looking mobster sitting across from an empty chair.

"Go ahead and take it, princess," the mobster replied.

That familiar memory of feeling alone in my dark bedroom as Fernando had his way with me flashed in my mind as usual, but I then quickly imagined Mickey's smiling face, as he placed his hand on mine. That familiar feeling of fear was then quickly vanquished from my mind with a feeling of warmth and love.

"I did it," I spoke aloud with a smile as tears of happiness streamed from my eyes.

That word princess would no longer haunt me now whenever I heard it spoken to me, but instead would fill me with strength, a strength I've been searching for and now have finally found.

CHAPTER 11:
HARLEM HEAT
- JACK -

"So why exactly did we have to meet at this abandoned warehouse again, Carlo? I thought the new base of operations was the speakeasy?" I inquired as I entered the warehouse to the sight of Carlo with his arms crossed and his muscle standing on either side of him mimicking his intimidating demeanor.

"This warehouse serves as a decoy, Jack. We cannot tip our hand to all the upstarts plotting to take down our organization. So we meet here to throw off any rat trying to scout out our base of operations, which is the very reason why I had you meet me and my associates here. Our organization is feeling some heat from some upstarts in Harlem. Not a burning heat, a small flame at the most, but we must extinguish that flame before it grows and burns us all," Carlo replied in a stern tone.

"So what exactly do you need from me now," I inquired with a sigh.

"We managed to corner one of those fottuto topi last night who's been bootlegging in Harlem and undercutting our products by a drastic price. Long story short, after we made the ratto cough up blood with every breath he mentioned your name," Carlo said to me with a grin.

"Woah easy now, I have no dealings with any bootleggers other than Mr. Luciano, Carlo. So who is this man you beat half to death?" I inquired in a stern tone.

"His name is inconsequential, but the names he gave up I believe will help us. He mentioned a man you may or may not know who goes by the name of Avery Briggs," Carlo replied.

"Avery … I knew him. We used to bootleg way back in the good old days before the police began to crack down on us like they are now," I said to Carlo.

"Oh so you do know him then. That's perfect. Then you will have no problem silencing him. He's testa del serpente which continues to slither through the grasp of Mr. Luciano," Carlo said to me.

"I already killed Johnny in self-defense. I won't kill my fellow associate all for the sake of liquor sales," I said to Carlo in a stern tone.

"Don't tell me you harbor feelings of compassion for this fottuto serpente. If that's the case, then I will have no choice but to inform Mr. Luciano about your wavering loyalty to him," Carlo said to me.

"I have no compassion for Avery. He brushed me off when I needed his help four months ago, but I'm no killer," I said to Carlo.

"Well it seems we've come to an impasse then. Perhaps you can lure that serpente who goes by the name of Avery with some bait," Carlo said to me with a snicker.

"What do you have in mind?" I inquired, as a flock of pigeons in the rafters of the warehouse cooed as if to answer my pressing question meant for Carlo.

"You claim you're not a killer Jack. I believe that's all cazzate talk from a man who's struggling to keep a powerful force at bay. All men are killers when the prospect of killing can benefit their life at a crucial moment. You will lure that serpente Avery to this point, and then my associates will silence him," Carlo said to me as he handed me an envelope.

"What if I choose not to lure Avery, then what happens to me?" I inquired in a stern tone, as Carlo and his muscle all lit cigars in unison and took a smoke.

"Well then we will have no choice but to see you as a serpente in our midst, and then you will be silenced. Don't worry about your niece Jack. Even if you betray us you can die knowing that we will not harm a hair on that principessa's pretty red head," Carlo replied with a snicker.

"I understand," I said to Carlo in a stern tone.

"Good, I know you'll come through for Mr. Luciano, Jack. He told me how your boldness reminds him of his childhood. He also told me that if you carry out this operation successfully, then you and your niece will be rewarded handsomely," Carlo said to me, as he patted me on the cheek and then exited the warehouse with his muscle in tow.

I hated the man. His condescending nature, his ghoulish appearance, but most of all, I hated the power he had over me and Hayley. Every time I met with Carlo he would give me an ultimatum. I wasn't exactly swooning over that pretty boy Avery, but He didn't deserve to die, even though when I was thirsty for solidarity he hung me out to dry. So what exactly was this reward Mr. Luciano would grant me and Hayley, and would it justify killing another man?

So many thoughts raced through my head as I drove back to the speakeasy. Who could I talk to about this, or would I be putting them in danger just by telling them Carlo's plan to lure Avery and silence him? I'll tell the one man who I believe is tougher than me, a man who has seen his fair share of death and caused it as well, a man who dares not embrace his past in fear that it will consume him, a man named Samson Monaghan.

*****

It was 2:47 PM as I entered the speakeasy to the sight of Gracie singing her heart out on the stage and Samson and Mickey roughhousing behind the bar.

"Samson!" I shouted as I gestured for Samson to meet me by the front door.

"Aye what is it, Jack?" Samson inquired

"We need to talk in private," I replied as Samson and I exited the speakeasy.

"Let's make this quick. I don't like leaving those two kids in the speakeasy without adult supervision for too long. There's no telling what kind of trouble will find them," Samson said to me.

"Don't worry about it. For the past two weeks it seems killed in Belfast," Samson said to me in a stern tone as He pressed the envelope against my chest.

like everyone is giving them breathing room after that decree that Mr. Luciano made for every mobster to treat Hayley like a princess," I said to Samson.

"Very well, so what has that brow of yours so furrowed, Jack?" Samson inquired.

"Carlo gave me an ultimatum once again," I replied, as I began to pace back and forth in front of the entrance to the speakeasy.

"What does he want this time?" Samson inquired.

"He informed me that the Five Points Gang is feeling some heat from a group of upstart bootleggers in Harlem," I replied. "Now how in the hell could the most powerful crime organization in New York, perhaps even this whole country feel challenged by a small group of bootleggers?" Samson inquired in an incredulous tone.

"The very same way that Johnny felt challenged by me and my sister. Use your head Samson. The more desperate a man becomes in this city, the more he is willing to take the odds he would normally cower away from. Carlo told me that those bootleggers in Harlem are undercutting our profits.

"I thought the Five Points Gang dominated the bootlegging market in this city. I had no idea anybody would dare undercut them," Samson said to me.

"You thought wrong. Now that fucking ghoul Carlo wants me to lure the leader of that bootlegging group to this location so they can silence him," I said to Samson in a stern tone as I handed him the envelope Carlo gave me.

"You're in it deep Jack. Mr. Luciano sees you as one of his associates now, and when you work for a man as powerful as him, leaving is out of the question," Samson said to me as he shook his head while reading the letter.

"Bullshit, you fled from your past. If you can do it so can I," I said to Samson in a stern tone.

"So that's why you wanted my advice. Well just look at where I am now. My past didn't let me go and now I'm right back in the thick of it all. This is penance for the two men I

"Wait Samson, there's more I need to tell you. The leader of those bootleggers in Harlem is Avery Briggs," I said to Samson. "Ah your former partner in crime. The plot thickens indeed," Samson said to me.

"Carlo said he would reward me and Hayley handsomely if I carried out this job successfully," I said to Samson.

"So you mean to tell me you're actually considering luring your fellow partner to his death all for the prospect of a reward?" Samson inquired with a scoff.

"Don't you remember, that pretty boy bastard cast me away when I asked for financial aid," I said to Samson in a stern tone. "So now you justify the betrayal you felt from him by killing him. Well aren't you the righteous right hand of god, Jack. Samson said to me while shaking his head.

"What would you have me do Samson?" I inquired.

"It's a soul searching choice. What Carlo is doing to you now is exactly what Macready did to me back in Belfast. They want you to believe that your only chance of success in this world is by working for them. So I will ask you this Jack. Are you the kind of man who sees killing as his only option in life?" Samson inquired as he stared intently at me before entering the speakeasy.

What would I do now? This may be the most difficult decision I've ever had to make in my entire life. When I was a boy in *SoHo*, grueling decisions would never fall just on my shoulders alone. I had Dezerae and my mother who would support me. I wish they were here now. I can only imagine what they would say to me.

*****

"Dezerae go tell your brother it's time for dinner," Mom said to Dezerae, as I sulked in my bed staring at a mold stain on the ceiling.

"Mom says dinner is ready, Jack," Dezerae said to me, as she entered my bedroom with a smile.

"I'm not hungry," I said to Dezerae in a somber tone. "You, not hungry, that's unheard of," Dezerae remarked with a giggle.

"Just leave me alone," I said to Dezerae in a somber tone, as I tossed a baseball up in the air.

"What's wrong?" Dezerae inquired.

"Didn't you two hear me? I said dinner is ready," Mom pronounced as she entered my bedroom.

"Jack won't tell me why he's being so sallow," Dezerae said to mom.

"The boys at school told me they would make my life a living hell if I told the cops about them robbing old man Willard in 7-B last night," I said in a stern tone.

"Oh dear so that's what all that noise was last night. You do what you know in your heart to be right. Your father told me that you will grow up to be your own man soon and you must make these decisions for yourself. Your sister and I will always be here for you if you need advice," Mom said to me as she sat down between me and my sister on the bed.

"Wait, What if the right choice hurts me, or even worse, what if it hurts old man Willard even more?" I inquired, as my mom stood up with a sigh.

"It's never an easy choice to make when someone you care about is depending on you, Jack, but I trust you will make the right choice in the end, and so does your father. Now come on, dinner is getting cold," Mom said to me as she kissed me on the forehead and then exited my room.

"I could've told you everything mom just said if you would just talk to me more," Dezerae said to me with a grin and then exited my bedroom.

*****

Sometimes the most difficult decisions in life simply require another person's perspective. If I only knew how Avery was doing right now. If I only knew what that handsome reward was for successfully luring him to his death. Carlo made it perfectly clear that if I refused to carry out this job of luring Avery to his death then I myself would be silenced. So when it came down to it, it was either my life or Avery's.

"I'm sorry Avery," I spoke aloud with a sigh.

I then entered the speakeasy to the sight of Carmen performing on stage. Normally the sight of that voluptuous dame would raise my spirits among other things, but the thought of Avery being lured to his death by me already weighed heavy on my mind. I had to find him. I had to talk to Avery before I carry out the instructions written in the letter which Carlo handed to me at the Pier.

"I'm going to talk to Avery," I said to Samson as I put on my trench coat.

"Are you going to do it tonight?" Samson inquired.

"I don't know yet. I have to see his eyes and how they stare back at me," I replied and then exited the speakeasy.

My drive to Avery's speakeasy in Chelsea was a drive I never thought I would have to take again, but when you reluctantly work for the wealthiest and most dangerous man in New York, you soon find yourself returning to places that make you feel insignificant and betrayed. Even though that smooth talking pretty boy cast me aside when I needed his financial aid, I was still proud of him for actually making the Five Points Gang feel some heat when it came to his competitive bootlegging strategies. The man was always a sly one. The first time I met Avery he was in the middle of swindling a Wall Street banker. He told the banker 'Your profits will triple within the first month if you invest in my importing business. During hard times such as these, a man of your financial intelligence would be foolish to pass up this opportunity'. Avery took that pompous Wall Street bastard for every penny he was worth which helped us open up the *Jack of All Trades* in the heart of Greenwich Village. Then Avery chose to cut all ties from me when word caught his ear that Hayley and I were wanted by the Five Points Gang. Perhaps Faye was right when she talked about fate. Was I now fated to decide the fate of my former partner?

"What's the password?" a voice inquired; as the bronze window of *the Sly Troubadour* slid open upon my knocking. "*Absentia*," I replied in a stern tone. Whenever I spoke the password to Avery's speakeasy I felt as if I was casting some sort of spell. Perhaps that's what Avery wanted the patrons of *the Sly Troubadour* to feel, like some sort of wizard who had the power to gain access to outlawed liquor with one word.

"Welcome to *the Sly Troubadour*," a voice from behind the brass window said to me, in a somber tone as the door opened. "Where's Avery?" I inquired as I entered the dimly lit speakeasy to the sight of only two patrons sitting at the bar.

"He's busy with his associates now," the woman who let me into the speakeasy replied in a somber tone and then went back to sweeping the floor.

The Sly Troubadour has seen better days. The last time I visited this establishment it looked like a scene from a glamorous movie, but now it appears as if all the life was taken from it. The Five Points Gang was no doubt responsible for the current state of *the Sly Troubadour*. Avery is struggling to keep this place afloat, and perhaps that's why he ventured to Harlem. To place his bets on a new horse, rather than keep beating the dead horse that is *the Sly Troubadour*.

"Avery, we need to talk!" I shouted.

"Jack … goddamn it," Avery said with a wide-eyed stare as he quickly stood up from behind the bar with a gun in his hand. "Easy Avery, I just wanted to see how you're holding up," I said to Avery.

"I almost put a bullet between your eyes because I thought you were another hitman from the Five Points Gang, that's how I'm holding up," Avery replied while shaking his head.

It appeared that Avery didn't know that I worked for the Five Points Gang or that their base of operations was none other than my speakeasy.

"I would ask how's business, but I can see it for myself. What the hell happened to this place?" I inquired as I stared around the once vibrant speakeasy which now resembled a bar in the middle of a warzone. The tables were turned now. My speakeasy was a bustling establishing and Avery's speakeasy was all but abandoned. I thought I would enjoy this sight after Avery refused to help me, but after seeing his red and shifty eyes darting from me to the door, and that somber woman sweeping the floor, my heart instantly bled for the man, because I've been in his shoes.

"The Five Points Gang happened. Over the past few months they have been relentless in their attempts to kill me. I'm actually flattered that the most powerful bootleggers in the country now want me dead. Now we have that in common huh, Jack," Avery replied as he poured me and himself a shot of bourbon with a trembling hand.

"I'm sorry. I know all too well how that feels," I said to Avery in a somber tone as we both took the shot of bourbon in unison.

"I'm actually glad to see you Jack. I've been meaning to contact you, but I have to carefully plan my routes when I leave this speakeasy. Over the past few months I've been building a coalition in Harlem made from some of the finest bootleggers who have all gone into exile after they sensed they're lives would soon come to an end by the Five Points Gang," Avery said to me.

"How is that possible? I can only assume that the Five Points Gang would silence any former associate who they felt would betray them for another competitor such as yourself," I inquired.

"That's the beauty of it all, Jack. They're arrogance has blinded them the point where they don't even realize the mole I have planted in their organization," Avery said to me with a snicker.

I then nearly choked on my second shot of bourbon in reaction to Avery's news of a mole in the Five Points Gang who worked for him. If this was true, then Avery could very well already know everything about my current situation. The Five Points Gang has underestimated Avery and so have I. I had no clue who the mole was, but I knew for sure it wasn't Samson, and it was just me and him in the alley when I told him about Carlo giving me the ultimatum to lure Avery to his death. So that leaves one of Carlo's muscle when we were at Pier 45. If one of those brutes is the mole then Avery knows exactly why I'm here. I had to stay calm. The fact that Avery didn't shoot me dead when he saw me says one of two things. One, he has no knowledge of the job Carlo tasked to me to lure him to his death, or two, he knows everything and is playing the gullible act to lull me into a false sense of security.

"Ah Y-you need live music here again. The sound of silence is a sound of death," I remarked with a series of coughs.

"What's wrong Jack? Don't tell me that bourbon is too strong for you?" Avery inquired with a grin.

"No it just went down the wrong pipe," I replied and then slammed my chest with my fist.

"Drop the charade Jack. I know why you're here," Avery said to me.

"Oh really?" I inquired with a wide-eyed stare as I gripped my pistol underneath my trench coat.

"You wanted to check up on me like you always used to do when we bootlegged in the good old days," Avery replied with a grin.

"Oh … I'm past that Avery, and looking back I suppose those days were less deadly than your current predicament, but I wouldn't call them good days. I just came here because I was in the neighborhood and needed a stiff drink," I said to Avery with a scoff, as I took my hand off my pistol in my trench coat. "So how's business for you in the Village? Are you and your niece still wanted by the Five Points Gang?" Avery Inquired.

What lie could I possibly tell Avery now that would seem believable?

"The hitman who was trying to kill me and my niece met his end in a shoot out with the cops," I replied.

"Good riddance. One less mobster bastard I'll have to cross paths with, but when one dies another rises to fill their position," Avery said to me.

"I wouldn't know I try to distance myself from them as much as possible. To answer your question my speakeasy has seen better days, the Five Points Gang has cornered the market when it comes to bootlegging and I fear we both will be squeezed out completely," I said to Avery.

"Not if we work together Jack. If we join forces we can take out the Five Points Gang and dominate the bootlegging market like we used to. Mr. Luciano has never faced men of our cunning before. He's used to shaking down small time thugs who have no strategy when it comes to the big picture in this day and age," Avery said to me.

"Paint that picture for me Avery. Just what outcome do you see from us joining forces against the Five Points Gang?" I inquired with a grin.

"I've already eluded Mr. Luciano and his attempts at killing me. So I have the momentum. The reason why this place looks so vacant is because this is no longer my base of operations. This speakeasy is now a decoy. My true base of operations is in Harlem. Do you want to see it, Jack?" Avery inquired.

My difficult decision whether or not to lure Avery to his death became even more difficult now. If I joined Avery could our combined forces take down the Five Points Gang once and for all, or would that reward for luring Avery to his death which Carlo told me about at Pier 45 provide me with more financial stability than Avery could ever provide me with?

"Let's go. You've sparked my interest," I said to Avery with a grin as I stood up from the bar.

"Lucille, Jack and I are stepping out, you know the drill," Avery told the woman who swept the floor and then tossed her a sod-off shotgun from behind the bar.

"My kind of gal," I said to Avery with a snicker, as the woman cocked the shotgun with a stern look, as if she was ready to take on every mobster the Five Points Gang had to offer.

"I found her in a brothel the Five Points Gang established in *Hell's Kitchen*. After she told me how a mobster by the name of Frankie Angelo beat her pretty face up real good I propositioned her to work for me. Now vengeance against that bastard fuels her," Avery whispered to me.

"Do you often go to brothels? Those establishments appear to be popping up all over New York just as much as speakeasies lately," I inquired, as Avery ran to a parked Plymouth with his pistol in hand while gesturing for me to follow.

"Brothels are just another indulgence Jack. Ever since the outlaw of alcohol passed people's morals began to slowly diminish. I go to those brothels for an escape into a beautiful dame, but little did I know I would find a fierce companion in Lucille," Avery replied as he started up the Plymouth and drove north down 9th Avenue.

I didn't think it was right how Avery was simply using that woman who was beaten by Frankie Angelo all for her vengeful personality, but as long as he treated her better than a brothel would, I saw no crime in his motives, besides, that dog Frankie Angelo deserves a lifetime of pain after everything he's done.

"What ever happened to the Avery whose biggest worry in life was getting that dame who was making eyes at him from across the bar to go home with him?" I inquired.

"That Avery is still there, but he's currently being hunted like a prized animal," Avery replied in a stern tone.

"Take the Henry Hudson Parkway. It's a straight shot right to Harlem and we can avoid getting gridlocked in the inner city," I said to Avery.

"Good call. So … why are you so calm Jack?" Avery inquired.

"What do you mean? Do you want me to be running around like a frantic chicken with my head cut off?" I replied with a scoff.

"Perhaps you're much more used to being hunted than I am. You always had a steel nerve during all of our bootleg dealings," Avery remarked.

"You always had the silver tongue. We made a good team," I remarked with a smirk.

"Together we can force the Five Points Gang right out of this city," Avery said to me with a smile, as he patted me on the shoulder.

Reminiscing with Avery about our past was making it more difficult for me to eventually lure him down a certain back alley in the Village were for mobsters of the Five Points Gang would be lying in wait to silence him. I had so much at stake now, my life, Avery's life, and the safety and well being of Hayley, Samson and Mickey. I was weighing these difficult decisions in my mind during the drive to Avery's new base of operations. "We're almost there. Jack, I mean it when I say that you would be a fine addition to my coalition of bootleggers. You and I are veterans in this bootlegging war. We've faced dangerous men in the past, and the Five Points Gang is no different," Avery said to me, as he drove down a back alley in Harlem.

"Let's not underestimate their resources, or their reach. Don't forget the Five Points Gang has the NYPD in their pockets, that's a kind of power that can rule an entire city without the fear of being challenged by anybody," I said to Avery as he parked the car in the shady lot which mirrored the shady lot I parked my Pontiac in down the alley of Minetta Street.

"We're not just anybody, Jack," Avery said with a smirk, and then exited the car.

Avery then quickly unlocked the front door of his new base of operations which from the outside appeared to be nothing but an unassuming storefront.

"Down here in the basement Jack. There's nothing up there but broken dreams," Avery said to me, as I paused for a moment while looking down the stairs. I could hear a live band playing a rousing jazz melody, as I followed Avery down the stairs, and then I finally saw it.

"Welcome Jack, to the Fox Den of Harlem," Avery pronounced as he spread his arms out wide.

The speakeasy was bustling. It was as if Avery relocated all of his business to Harlem with great success.

"Please sit down, we have much to discuss," Avery said to me, as he walked behind the bar.

I now see why the Carlo felt challenged by Avery's new speakeasy in Harlem. That glamorous movie scene of his speakeasy in Chelsea was now set in Harlem and it appeared that Avery may be doing even better business here in Harlem than the *Jack of All Trades* is doing in the Village.

What would happen if I relocated Hayley, Samson, and Mickey to work with me and Avery here in Harlem? Would we all be safer from the Five Points Gang here, or would betraying them only fuel their desire to silence us all?

"Jack, this is Bernice Sheffield, Chester Crenshaw, and Arthur Derringer. Gang this wily bastard is Jack Dansby," Avery pronounced as he pointed at two men and a woman who walked up to the bar.

"So this is the man who taught you all you know huh, Avery," Arthur said with a scoff.

"Not everything, but he's taught me a great deal, and with Jack's expertise, the Five Points Gang doesn't stand a chance against us," Avery pronounced.

"Why do we need more help? I thought our profits were the highest they've ever been," Chester said to Avery.

"They are, but what happens if one of us gets a bullet between our eyes when we're out to get the paper? How would you deal with that scenario which could happen like that," Avery said to Chester in a stern tone, as he snapped his fingers in Chester's face.

"We don't need his help, Avery. Besides, I don't trust his face," Bernice said to Avery, as she took a stern glance at me.

"I'm right here, doll. If you want to say something to me then say it to my face," I said to Bernice in a stern tone.

"Fine, I don't trust you, Jack," Bernice, said to me in a stern tone as she leaned in close and pressed her finger against my chest.

"Get your hand off me. You don't even know me or what I've suffered from all by the hands of the Five Points Gang. So I suggest you watch your tone," I said to Bernice in a stern tone as I slapped Bernice's finger off my chest, as I stood up from the bar.

"Shut your yap, Bernice. Jack and I have been through hell and back countless times before and I can assure you that there's no better man to have by your side. I trust Jack with every bone in my body," Avery said to Bernice in a stern tone.

I then stared intently at Avery with a warm smile, as the band on stage began to play one of my favorite songs, Nobody Knows You when You're Down and Out by Bessie Smith.

Avery was so quick to defend my name. How could I ever lure a loyal man such as him to his death? Avery's fellow bootleggers at the speakeasy despised me, and if I were them I would hate me too, but Avery trusted me, and that's all I needed right now.

"I'll be right back, you four get more acquainted," Avery pronounced and then scampered over to a woman at the stage.

"So which one of you three used to be in the Five Points Gang?" I inquired, as I stared at the three bootleggers who stared back at me with stern looks on their faces.

"Well why don't you guess, Jack," Chester said to me. "What do I win if I guess correctly?" I inquired with a grin. "You win the satisfaction of having a keen intuition. If everything Avery told me about you is true, then you should have no problem identifying a former Five Points Gang member among us three," Arthur replied.

"That and a nickel will buy me a lousy cup of coffee," I said with a scoff.

"I told you Jack was green. No matter how much Avery built him up, he still couldn't spot a snake in our den before its fangs are biting down on his neck," Chester remarked with a snicker.

"All right, all right, hmmm let's see here," I spoke aloud, as I stared intently at Chester, Arthur, and Bernice.

"I'm going to go with my gut instincts on this one since I have nothing else to go by … It's you Arthur, you used to be in the Five Points Gang," I said to Arthur with a grin as I pointed at him.

"Oh it appears you're wrong Chester. Jack's intuition is spot on. You're correct Jack, I left the Five Points Gang about a month ago in search of a more stable way of life" Arthur said to me.

"If you want stability in your life then I suggest you quit being a bootlegger. So what drove you away from the Five Points Gang?" I inquired, as Chester and Bernice tended to finely-dressed patrons seated at tables in front of the stage.

"They were breeding me to be a hitman, but I told them I would only kill in self-defense. Then a sinister bastard by the name of Carlo told me 'you either kill for us, or be killed by us'," Arthur replied.

Arthur's past experience with the Five Points Gang was very similar to my current predicament, but he chose to join forces with Avery hoping to find safety and stability in this Fox Den.

"Avery, do you still play the ivories?" I inquired as Avery walked up to the bar.

"Only when the band takes a break," Avery replied with a grin.

"That's good to hear. You have a future as a jazz musician when this bootlegging war ends," I said to Avery.

"I dabble, Jack, but I can't even see that far ahead right now," Avery said to me.

"I see the way the dames swoon over you when you play," I remarked with a grin.

"If I can entertain them for a brief moment in time then I'm doing my job. That's why we're in this business after all, right Jack?" Avery inquired.

"To entertain … well I never saw bootleggers as entertainers. We're more like renegades providing the people a product which they have every right to enjoy, but is now outlawed by a bullshit law," I said to Avery.

"They're one in the same Jack. I ask myself every day why I continue to risk my life all for the sake of alcohol, but I always come to a realization that goes much deeper than that.

"What would that be my friend?" I inquired.

"The very culture of New York is being outlawed by politicians. It's been over ten years since that law was passed, and who knows if it will ever end. I was never one for politics, but I see now how politics have brought this city to its knees. I won't stand for it, not while I'm still breathing," Avery replied in a stern tone.

"Keep that fire burning," I said to Avery with a grin as we toasted our glasses of bourbon. For that brief moment in time I almost forgot about Hayley, Samson and Mickey. It felt like the good old days being with Avery, a kind of feeling which only an old friend could make you feel.

"We need you Jack," You know I would never flatter you, so when I say that your expertise when it comes to bootlegging will give us the upper hand against the Five Points Gang you know I'm telling the truth," Avery said to me.

The choice to join Avery instead of luring him to his death was looking more and more attractive the longer I spent in his speakeasy, but as my mother once said to me 'the choices where people depend on you are never easy to make'. I had only a couple hours left to either lure Avery to his death. Was there another choice I wasn't aware of, another outcome that could both save Avery while also protecting me, Hayley, Samson, and Mickey? The two faces that weighed heavy on my mind now were Avery's smiling face, and Carlo's ghoulish face. Perhaps I will have to make this decision when I'm in the moment. Then I will find out whether my heart or my head is in charge.

*****

It was 9:45 PM in the Fox Den, as I continued to reminisce with Avery.

"Is it always this busy here?" I inquired, as Avery prepared three drinks at once for three patrons sitting beside me at the bar.

"Always Jack. This is why the Five Points Gang is trying to kill me," Avery replied with s grin.

"I have to be getting back now," I said to Avery, as he whistled and pointed to the band on stage with a smile.

"Oh I'll give you a ride back to the Village," Avery said to me.

"No I'll take a taxicab," I said to Avery.

"Nonsense, Jack. The fares of those taxicabs are outrageous for people of our income. Come on let's go," Avery said to me, after nodding at Arthur.

Now was my chance. I could now lure Avery down the alley where four mobsters lie in wait to silence him.

"I don't know about you, Jack, but I find this city to be far more attractive at night," Avery said to me as we drove down the Henry Hudson Parkway.

"I know what you mean. The light only exposes all the filth of this city," I said to Avery with a scoff.

"That's why I always turn the lights off when I'm in bed with a dame," Avery said to me as we both laughed in unison.

This city was indeed a dame that looked better with the lights off, but a dame who needed all her scars to be exposed by the light of day. Only then could that dame begin to heal rather than slowly die in the dark of night.

My heart raced as we approached the ambush point in the alley of Charles Street.

"Your speakeasy is still on Minetta Street right?" Avery inquired.

"Yes but we can bypass some traffic if we cut through this alley," I replied, as I pointed down the pitch black alley to the right of us.

"Are you sure?" Avery inquired in an incredulous tone.

"Yes I'm sure. I know the Village like the back of my hand," I replied.

"Very well, Jack," Avery said, and then took a right into the pitch black alley.

"Ah shit, there's a dumpster blocking our way. So much for your shortcut," Avery said to me. "Now boys" a voice shouted.

I then heard the scraping of a heavy object being moved across the pavement, and when I stared through the rear view mirror I could make out another dumpster being moved behind Avery's car, trapping him in the pitch black alley.

"It's an ambush, Jack?" Avery shouted with a wide-eyed stare, as I stared down with somber eyes as the realization of luring my old friend to his death weighed heavy on me.

"Get out of the car serpente nell'erba!" a voice shouted. As the spark of cigars being lit in the pitch black alley focused my eyes towards two mobsters which stood in front of the car, while two more mobsters stood behind the car.

"I'm sorry Avery," I said to Avery in a somber tone and then exited the car.

Avery didn't respond to me, as he exited the car with his hands up in the air.

"All right you got me, took you all long enough," Avery pronounced with a snicker, and even though I could barely make out Avery's face in the pitch blackness of the alley, I just knew he was grinning from ear to ear, as he's always done whenever he was in life threatening situation.

"Look he has his hands up like we're going to arrest him," one of the mobsters remarked as they both laughed in unison.

This didn't feel right, Avery was my partner, and just like he said at the Fox Den we have indeed gone through hell and back many times before and the very reason we came back from that hell every time is because we looked out for each other.

"Wait, just give him a warning. I assure you he will not defy Mr. Luciano and the Five Points Gang ever again," I pronounced.

"The four mobsters then laughed in unison for a few moments, before I could see them pull out their guns.

"You're right Jack. This serpente nell'erba will no longer slither through our grasp. So are you with us or him?" one mobster inquired in a stern tone.

Wait, I've encountered this dire situation once before in my youth, if I could only remember what I did back then it would aide me right now in this pitch black alley surrounded by mobsters.

*****

"Well Jack, are you with us, or are you with that miserable old bastard Willard?"

Chase Dunham, the leader of the small gang which were about to rob old man Willard inquired as they cornered me in the alley beside my apartment in *SoHo*.

I then pulled out a silver dollar from my pocket and stared at it as a smile began to form on my face.

"While we're young, Jack!" Chase shouted, as he shoved me in the shoulder.

"All right, heads I help you rob the old man for all he's worth," I said to Chase.

"What about tails?" Chase inquired in a stern tone as I flipped the silver dollar high in the air.

"At that brief but crucial moment in time, I then swiftly took my chance to escape; as I swiftly punched Chase in the gut as he and the three other gang members' eyes were fixed on the silver dollar as it flipped through the air.

"Get him!" Chase shouted as I ran down the alley to the closest police department I could find. My silver dollar diversion saved me for now, but I wasn't out of the woods just yet.

*****

"All right fellas. Heads I'm with you," I pronounced, as I took out my silver dollar with a grin.

"What? Shine a light on them for god sake," one of the mobsters said in a stern tone. Another mobster then turned on a spotlight which he already had set up in the alley.

"I said heads I help you four kill this snake who's been undercutting your boss for the past month," I pronounced.

I could then see Avery continuing to grin out of the corner of my eye while the four mobsters gathered in front of me and Avery, as I flipped the silver dollar high into the air. Just like Chase Dunham and his gang, the four mobsters' eyes were fixed on the silver dollar as it flipped through the air.

Avery and I then pulled out our pistols and shot two mobsters square in the chest before the silver dollar landed on the pavement

"Shoot the light," I said to Avery as I entered his car. "Better luck next time boys," Avery pronounced, and then shot the spotlight which sent the once lit back alley back to pitch blackness.

"There are two of them left, I said in a distressed tone as I pointed forward towards two dark figures which became briefly lit as they open fired on Avery's car.

"This is the last time I give you a ride home. Hold on," Avery said to me in a stern tone as he started up his car, while the two mobsters shot at the windshield, which instantly shattered.

"We're trapped!" I shouted in a distressed tone.

"Like hell we are," Avery said to me in a stern tone, as he backed up the car into the two mobsters who rolled over the top of the car and landed on the pavement in front of us.

"These two won't stay down," I remarked, as the two mobsters stood up from the ground as they slowly aimed their guns towards us.

"No witnesses Jack, or else these two will report back to their superiors," Avery said to me, and then rammed the car into the two mobsters, pinning them both between the dumpster and the front of the car.

Avery was right. We had to silence them, or else they would immediately report back to Carlo. So I pointed my pistol at one of the mobsters pinned between the car and the dumpster, while Avery pointed at the other and then we fired twice in unison.

"You have some talking to do Jack, but first I need a drink, we'll discuss everything at your speakeasy," Avery said to me in a stern tone, as he backed out between the dumpster and the wall of the back-alley.

*****

It was 10:27 PM in the speakeasy as Avery and I entered to the sight of nobody but Samson wiping down the bar.

"You both have blood splattered on your faces; just what kind of hell have you gone through this time Jack?" Samson inquired.

"Are there any mobsters in the speakeasy right now?" I inquired, as I stared with wide-eyes all around the speakeasy.

"Answer my question first and then I'll answer yours, Jack," Avery replied in a stern tone.

"Damn it Samson … Avery and I just killed four mobsters of the Five Points Gang," I said to Samson in a stern tone and then began to pour two shots of bourbon in the shakiest manner my hand has ever shook before.

"Jesus Christ," Samson remarked as he shook his head. "It's nice to see you too, Samson, how long has it been," Avery inquired and then took the shot of bourbon with a cough and grimace.

"Not long enough. There are no mobsters of the Five Points Gang in the speakeasy, Jack," Avery replied.

"Good. I don't know how long it will be before Carlo finds out what just transpired. Where's Hayley?" I inquired, as I locked the front door of the speakeasy.

"I suppose she's trying to sleep right now, and as for Carlo, I'd say he should be here within the hour to check up on you, and when I say check up I mean to silence you both," Samson replied.

"You were going to kill me, weren't you, Jack. So what reward did Carlo promise you if you took me out?" Avery inquired in a stern tone, as he stood up from the bar and walked over to me.

"If I wanted you dead you wouldn't be talking to me right now," I replied.

"I could say the same thing to you," Avery said to me with a grin and scoff.

"Let's just focus on getting you back to your speakeasy in one piece," I said to Avery.

"No Jack, you're going to tell me everything that Carlo told you about me right now," Avery said to me in a stern tone as he pointed his pistol at me.

"Do you really want to make me your enemy after my cunning got us out of that alley alive," I inquired in a stern tone, as I looked away from Avery for a brief moment before swiftly pulling out my pistol and pointing it towards Avery.

"Easy gentleman, both your nerves are frayed beyond high heaven, why don't you both just sit down and have another drink," Samson pronounced.

"I don't want another fucking drink, Samson. It's all I do now to stop the shaking, but I suppose that's all part of being a bootlegger during these times!" Avery shouted, as he stared intently at me.

"I can relate to the shaking, but just to let you know if you kill me now then you will not make it out of here alive," I said to Avery in a stern tone.

"Just as those mobsters underestimated you in the alley, you underestimate me at this very moment," Avery said to me with a snicker.

"Put the gun down Jack," a feminine voice said to me.

"Well, well, Gracie Bishop. I'd be lying if I said I wasn't surprised, but this day has been full of surprises. So you're the mole working for Avery," I said to Gracie, as she pointed a gun at me.

"I work for myself Jack. Avery Simply gave me a chance to put an end to the tyranny that is the Five Points Gang. Nobody would every suspect a woman who's easy on the eyes to be a mole. Avery was right when he told me that," Gracie said to me in a stern tone.

"Looks like you thought of everything once again old friend. Carlo was right when he called you a snake in the grass," I said to Avery with a scoff.

"I'm staying out of this. If you all want to kill each other then I'll be happy to mop up the blood you all spill," Samson pronounced, and then began to whistle a jaunty tune, as the stand-off between me, Avery, and Gracie intensified.

"Gracie was watching you closely Jack, but I never told her to take you out. She told me that you began to care more and more for that niece of yours almost like a father. I then said to Gracie Jack, a father, quit making jokes, doll, but she swore to me that you were a good man," Avery said to me.

"You should know that good men just don't make it in this day and age," I said to Avery in a stern tone, as I kept staring at Gracie out of the corner of my eye.

"Jack what's happening?" Hayley inquired as she exited the kitchen while rubbing her eyes.

"Stay in the kitchen," I said to Hayley in a stern tone, as I glanced at her out of the corner of my eye while still keeping my eyes on Avery and Gracie.

"Why are you all pointing guns at—,"

"Just stay in the kitchen kid. It's not safe out here," I interjected in a stern tone. Hayley then scampered back into the kitchen, as I continued my standoff with Avery and Gracie. "Put the gun down Jack, for your niece's sake," Avery said to me

"Don't you use her you son of a bitch. She never asked for this life," I said to Avery in a stern tone.

"Jack please. We're not your enemy. I know you had no choice in the matter when it came to following Carlo's orders. You gave me a job here no questions asked, and I am grateful for your act of kindness," Gracie said to me in a distressed tone and wide-eyed stare, as the pistol she pointed at me began to shake in her hand.

"If I knew you were a just a mobster in doll's clothing then I would've never let you work here," I said to Gracie in a stern tone.

"Gracie is far from a mobster, Jack. That's why I trust her more than Arthur. None of us ask for the lives that we're thrown into, we just have to adapt and make do," Avery said to me.

"I'm in it too deep now. All because of you and your need to be the best has once again pulled me back in," I said to Avery in a stern tone.

Was there a way out of this standoff between me, Avery, and Gracie? If I shot either one of them then the other one would no doubt shoot me. That whistling Irish fool Samson over at the bar said he is staying out of the standoff and I believe him. So I was outnumbered, but I was always used to being outnumber my entire life.

*****

"Don't let him escape!" Chase Dunham shouted as him and the three other gang members chased me through the alleys of *SoHo*. Where the hell is a cop when you need one I thought to myself, as I nearly tripped over a few trash cans, while knocking some over to try and slow down Chase and his gang. I then spotted a most welcome sight, a police officer standing on the corner of Prince and West Broadway.

"Help, officer, help!" I shouted, as I stumbled out of the alley while waving my hand at the cop who appeared to be talking with a business man.

"Easy now, what's the problem son?" the cop inquired, as I ran up to him in a heaving manner while pointing behind me. "There's a gang chasing me. They're planning on robbing my neighbor and they said if I don't help them then they will make my life a living hell, please help, my life isn't the only life in danger," I replied in a distressed tone, as Chase and his gang stared at me for a brief moment and then ran back down the alley after noticing I was with a cop.

"Well then that is quite a bind you're in. So I presume by the looks of it all that you chose not to help that gang," the cop said to me.

"Yes but they know where I live. Please help I cannot avoid them for the rest of my life," I said to the cop in a distressed tone.

"Yes street gangs are abundant in this city. Calm down son. Tell me where you live," the cop said, as he gestured for me to get in his squad car parked across the street.

"You mean you're going to actually help me?" I inquired in an incredulous tone.

"To protect and serve, son. It's a motto I live by," the cop replied with a warm smile which made me smile just knowing that I could now protect Mr. Willard and myself from Chase and his gang.

*****

That cop helped put the fear of the law into Chase Dunham and his gang planning on robbing Mr. Willard, whereas now the police and the Five Points Gang are partners who work together to put the fear into basically all New

Yorkers. Now the police serve the Five Points Gang while at the same time enforcing an unjust alcohol outlaw. There was no way out of this standoff between me, Avery, and Gracie, unless I once again did something drastic.

"Don't even think about trying that silver dollar distraction on us, Jack. We're not slow like those dead mobsters in the alley," Avery said to me with a scoff.

"I wasn't planning on it, and don't try to read my mind," I said to Avery.

Just then, a knock on the front door averted the attention of me, Avery and Gracie for a brief moment.

"That's probably Carlo," Samson pronounced.

"Perfect, I can finish the job and take out that ghoul just like I took out his muscle," Avery said with a snicker.

The enemy of my enemy was my friend at this moment, but was Avery and Gracie truly my enemies at this moment?

"Samson, answer the door," I said to Samson in a stern tone.

"Very well, why don't you three take a deep breath before I open this door," Samson pronounced, as he walked up to the front door.

"Yes sir," Samson said as he stared through the iron window of the front door for a brief moment.

"Avery, has Carlo ever seen your face?" I inquired in a distressed tone, as I composed myself before Carlo entered the speakeasy.

"No he hasn't, but my face will be the last face he will ever see," Avery replied as he put on my trench coat and hat and then sat down at the bar, as Gracie sat beside him.

"Four of my men were just found dead by the NYPD at the ambush point. What exactly happened Jack?" Carlo inquired in a stern tone as he walked up to me.

"First tell me the award you promised me for luring that snake to his death," I replied.

Carlo then swiftly slapped me in the face with one of his black gloved hands which echoed throughout the quiet speakeasy.

"You don't give me orders Jack. You're nothing but a fottuto servitore!" Carlo shouted.

"Did you come here alone?" I inquired, as I made a brief glance at Avery at the bar, as he then stood up and walked towards the front door, almost as if he could feel the rage I felt towards Carlo which was swelling up inside of me right now.

"My four associates were just found dead, of course I came here alone. Now ask another moronic question Jack!" Carlo shouted and then slapped me in the face once again.

"That will be the last mistake you make tonight," Avery said to Carlo and then locked the front door.

"Who the hell are you?" Carlo inquired in a stern tone.

"I'm none other than the man you and your associates have been trying to kill over the past couple months," Avery replied as he took off my hat and trench coat.

"Well well so we finally meet face to face serpente. I must admit you even surprised Mr. Luciano. Perhaps you do have what it takes to join us," Carlo said to Avery with a snicker, as Avery pointed his gun at Carlo with a grin.

So now Carlo was trying to proposition Avery to join the Five Points Gang. This was no doubt a desperate plea to save his life. Even though Carlo appeared calm and collective, he knew that there was a good chance that he would be silenced by Avery tonight.

"Serpente huh, Jack told me that's the name the Five Points Gang has given me and quite frankly I kind of like it. If you can't beat 'em join 'em ... well I've already beaten you and your associates so that's not going to happen tonight. Jack, take his weapons, all of them. I want this man vulnerable with no hope just before he dies, just like the many fine people he and his associates have killed," Avery said to me as I disarmed Carlo of two pistols and a knife.

"So you mean to silence me tonight, serpente. Well let me tell you what your future entails if you do such a cosa sciocca. First you, and all who are in league with you will be silenced. Then your bloodline will be silenced. We will erase you from history, not that history will ever remember a smug serpente like you," Carlo said to Avery in a stern tone.

"You call me a snake, yet you say history won't remember me. I think you're forgetting about a certain snake history remembers quite well," Avery said to Carlo.

"Are you really comparing yourself to the devil Avery?" I inquired.

"Jack I'm trying to monologue here if you don't mind," Avery replied in a stern tone.

"It's not too late Jack. Put a bullet in this serpent's head and you and your niece will live a comfortable life full of riches only a handful of men in New York have," Carlo said to me.

"No more of your empty promises. That's what lured my sister into dating that bastard Johnny. Well I've learned from her mistake," I said to Carlo in a stern tone.

"You heard the man. Now sit down, I want you to be looking up at me before you die," Avery said in a stern tone as he pointed to a chair.

"So you both have chosen death I see. I thought you two men would be wiser, but Mr. Luciano was right as always when he said that 'upstarts are fueled by their hearts not their heads'," Carlo pronounced with a snicker as he sat down in the chair.

"Don't worry, Gracie. You can lower your gun now. Carlo is all mine," Avery said to Gracie as he gestured for her to lower her gun.

"Be careful. He's not acting like a man who's about to die," Gracie said to Avery.

"It's all part of his façade. They call you the coroner, am I right?" Avery inquired.

"Indeed, it's a name which was passed down to me from my father. A name that has struck fear into the hearts of little upstarts like you," Carlo replied in a stern tone as he glared at Avery with such maliciousness burning in his eyes.

Avery was savoring this moment, savoring the fact that he has the upper hand. It was always in his nature to gloat, but I feared that Carlo was the last man you would ever want to gloat over.

"So if your job is to dispose of all the dead bodies the Five Points Gang are responsible for, then who will dispose of your dead body?" Avery inquired with a grin.

Carlo then began to snicker, as did Avery. Their snickering then rose to a sinister laughter which created such a tension throughout the speakeasy as I walked backwards slowly towards the bar, while my eyes were fixed on Carlo's every move.

I then noticed Carlo pull out something from underneath the table, as he and Avery continued to laugh.

"He has a gun, Avery!" I shouted in dismay and a wide- eyed stare as I pointed at Carlo. I was positive that I disarmed Carlo of every weapon he had, but it appeared that the coroner had a pistol hidden in a compartment underneath the table.

Avery then fired before Carlo and the coroner was finally silenced.

"Good riddance coroner," Avery said, and then spit on Carlo's vacant ghoulish face as the bullet hole between his eyes bled onto the floor.

"Don't worry Jack. To answer this bastards question, Gracie and I will dispose of his body in the Hudson," Avery said to me as he wiped the splatter of Carlo's blood off his face with a handkerchief.

"There's no sweeping this under the rug, Avery. Mr. Luciano will interrogate me over the five deaths that just occurred tonight," I said to Avery in a stern tone as I walked up to the corpse of the man once known as the coroner.

"Then join us Jack. You, your niece, and your entire work staff, we can protect you all from the Five Points Gang. This is our time now, Jack We have the momentum and we must continue this heat we're applying to them until they all burn," Avery said to me in a distressed tone.

"This is no kind of place to raise Hayley, Jack," Gracie said to me in a somber tone.

"No I'm tired of fleeing from tyrants, fleeing from men who believe that they are the law. I built this speakeasy with the dream of giving comfort to the very people who feel oppressed. I'm not going anywhere ... take care, Avery," I said to Avery.

"So long, Jack. I hope you and your niece find some semblance of happiness in this world," Avery said to me, as he and Gracie lifted Carlo's dead body off the chair and proceeded to carry it towards the front door.

"Goodbye Jack. I hope we meet again under more pleasant circumstances," Gracie said to me in a somber tone.

"I wouldn't bet on it ... wait, you're going to have to shoot me Avery," I said to Avery, as I scampered to the front door. "Why? What are you talking about?" Avery inquired in a bewildered tone, as he dropped Carlo's dead body on the floor.

"It will look too suspicious that I don't have a scratch on me after five mobsters of the Five Points Gang were killed tonight," I said to Avery.

"I see, you want it to look like you tried to kill me tonight so Mr. Luciano won't suspect you had anything to do with killing five of his associates," Avery said to me.

"Yes, it just might keep me unnoticed from his prying eyes," I said to Avery.

"I—I can't, you'll hold it against me for the rest of your life if I shoot you," Avery said to me while shaking his head.

"I'll hold it against you if you don't. Please do me this favor," I said to Avery.

"As you wish Jack, where do you want it?" Avery inquired with a sigh.

"Jack what happened?" Hayley inquired with a wide-eyed stare as she exited the kitchen.

"Everything's fine," I replied in a stern tone as I gestured for Hayley to stay back, for what is about to happen will most likely traumatize her even more than she already is.

"Right here, do it," I said to Avery in a stern tone, as I pointed to my shoulder.

"Jack, but your niece is—,"

"Just do it Avery, now!" I interjected with a grimace, as I tapped my shoulder in an aggressive manner.

Hayley then stared at me with wide-eyes as Avery aimed his pistol at my shoulder and then pulled the trigger.

CHAPTER 12:
THE FLAPPER GIRL
- HAYLEY -

My heart would always skip a beat whenever I heard gunfire ring out throughout the speakeasy. Two nights ago I witnessed Jack do something insane even for him. I witnessed him willingly getting himself shot by some unknown man, and I couldn't help but wonder why on earth he would ever do such a thing. I've asked him three times since that night filled with blood and gunfire, but he always gives me the same cryptic response 'it was necessary for us to stay in Mr. Luciano's good graces'. What does that mean? Has Jack lost his mind, or was the act of him willingly getting himself shot part of something which is beyond a girl like me could ever comprehend?

It was 2:27 PM in the speakeasy as Ms. Valentino took the stage and began to sing a song which would've been better suited for a singer like Gracie for I believe she has a more pleasant singing voice.

"How's the shoulder?" Samson inquired as he prepared a drink for a patron while I sat at the bar drawing a picture of a woman in my dairy who I saw on a billboard displayed in bright lights on Broadway.

"It burns like hell, but I'll live," Jack replied with a hiss and grimace every time he made the slightest movement with his right arm.

Samson then whispered in Jack's ear, as I stared at both of them before going back to my drawing of the glamorous woman who prominently graced the billboard on Broadway.

"Why are you drawing Faye?" Jack inquired, as he pointed at my diary.

"What, oh … this isn't Ms. Dubois," I replied in a timid tone, as I brushed a strand of hair behind my ear.

"It sure looks like Faye," Jack remarked with a grin.

"I saw this woman on a billboard in Broadway," I said to Jack as I drew the short wavy, black hair of the woman.

"She looks like she could be Faye's twin sister," Jack remarked with a grin.

"She does, do you know when Faye will be here?" I inquired, as Jack grimaced in pain from his shoulder wound.

"I wish I had tabs on that dame, but she has always been a free spirit," Jack replied.

"Could you tell me where she lives? I would love to visit her sometime," I inquired.

"I don't know how Faye would feel about you showing up unannounced on her doorstep kid," Jack replied.

"Please, I—I just want to talk to her," I said to Jack with a wide-eyed stare, as he grinned at me.

"All right kid, anything to get you out of my hair," Jack said to me, and then wrote something down on a slip of paper.

"Thanks you," I said to Jack with a smile as the very prospect of spending the day with Faye warmed my heart. "Here's her address. I can't guarantee you that she will even be home at this hour, so don't be disappointed if nobody answers the door," Jack said to me, as he handed me the slip of paper with Faye's address written on it.

"It's all right. I'm not going now," I said to Jack with a smile, as I tucked Faye's address into the pocket of my dress.

"Have you seen Mickey lately?" Jack inquired.

"The last time I saw him was last Wednesday. He told me he would be doing more work at the hospital lately," I replied.

"Oh, that's too bad. I could always count on him to be here rain or shine. I sure as hell need him more now than ever," Jack said to me.

"Ever since you ordered that man to shoot you in the shoulder," I said to Jack.

"I told you before it was—,"

"I know what you're going to say Jack, but I don't understand," I interjected.

"Where are you going?" Jack inquired, as I walked towards the front door of the speakeasy.

"To visit Ms. Dubois," I replied.

"I thought you said you weren't going now," Jack said to me, as I unlocked the front door of the speakeasy.

"I changed my mind," I said to Jack and then exited the speakeasy.

*****

"Where to?" the cab driver inquired in a raspy tone as I entered the taxicab.

"To *Magnolia Towers* on 6th Avenue please," I replied to the cab driver as I read Faye's address from the slip of paper Jack gave to me.

The days were getting shorter, as a slight chill in the air began to grow, but that didn't bother me one bit, for autumn was my favorite season. Greenwich Village never shined with such beauty as it did in the autumn months. I loved to go hiking with my mother upstate during those autumn months. It was an escape from the loud and overwhelming noise that was Greenwich Village. Now I feel I've grown numb to all of those loud noises, but my heart still yearns for the beauty that is autumn.

I missed Mickey. I hope he's thinking about me just as much as I'm thinking about him now. I could visit him at the hospital, but there's something about Ms. Dubois that always warms my heart when I'm around her. I suppose Jack feels the same way I do even though he would never admit it out loud, but Ms. Dubois always has a way of easing all my worries with the mere sound of her voice. On that horrific night Frankie attacked me; Ms. Dubois sat on the floor and held me tight in her arms as I cried my eyes out. I used to think of her as the mother I used to have, but now I think of her as an older sister, or aunt that I never had, but so desperately need.

For such a pretty name, the *Magnolia Towers* apartment complex appeared gray and derelict, as I exited the taxicab and stared up at the apartment complex. According to the slip of paper Jack gave to me, Ms. Dubois lived in F-17 on the fifth floor of *Magnolia Towers*. I sure hope she is home, or else this trip would be very disappointing. I wanted to talk to Faye about many things, many things only a woman like her would have a keen perspective on. I then pressed the intercom button for F-17 at the entrance of *Magnolia Towers* and waited nervously to here Faye's sweet voice.

"Qu'est-ce, uhm, who is it?" a voice inquired from the intercom.

"Um Ms. Dubois, its Hayley, Hayley Carmona from the speakeasy. Can I please come in?" I replied in a timid tone. "Oh Hayley, oui viens ma chérie. Come in, come in," Ms.

Dubois replied and then buzzed me in to the *Magnolia towers*.

I then entered *Magnolia Towers* with a smile and scampered over to the elevator.

"Oh did you also come to see Ms. Dubois?" I inquired with a smile, as I entered the elevator in the lobby to the sight of a black cat with piercing green eyes sitting in the corner grooming itself.

The black cat then meowed as the elevator door close, almost as if to tell me to press the fifth floor button. So I then pressed the fifth floor button and the elevator made a loud creaking noise which startled me at first, but the black cat remained calm as he continued to groom himself. The light in the elevator began to flicker as well, and it felt as if at any moment it would break down and I would be trapped in the elevator with the black cat, but I've had much worse company before, I thought to myself as I kneeled down and petted the black cat to help calm my nerves. The elevator bell then rang as me and my feline companion reached the fifth floor of *Magnolia Towers*.

"Well we're here," I said to the black, as I exited the elevator to the sights and sounds of babies crying, men shouting, and water dripping from the ceiling of the fifth floor.

"Foutez le camp, you pig!" a feminine voice shouted as the door to F-17 opened in front of me just before I was about to knock.

"I thought French whores like you would be more open- minded," a man said with a scoff, as he walked past me while buttoning up his shirt.

"Oh Hayley I—I'm sorry you had to see that," Ms. Dubois said to me as she held red sheets closely against her chest.

"I can leave if this is a bad time," I said to Ms, Dubois in a timid tone, as I averted my eyes from her half exposed body. "Nonsense, mon chéri," Please come in, you and Sable," Ms. Dubois, said to me with a smile as she gestured for me to enter her apartment.

"So is he your cat?" I inquired as the black cat known as Sable rubbed against my leg as he entered Ms. Dubois' apartment.

"I would like to think so, but he's a very independent boy," Ms. Dubois replied with a giggle.

"He's very pretty," I remarked with a smile.

"Indeed he is. Make yourself at home, while I get dressed," Ms, Dubois said to me with a smile, and then scampered into her bedroom.

Ms, Dubois' apartment was filled with all sorts of plants I've never seen before. It was as if I was in a park or garden, a park or garden with the thick fragrance of smoke and sweet perfume wafting all around me. I wonder who that man was who Ms, Dubois kicked out of her apartment? Whoever he was, his attitude towards Ms, Dubois was very disrespectful. He reminded me of the mobsters in the speakeasy, which is where I wanted to escape from.

"I'm so sorry Hayley. I tried to kick that pig out of my apartment before you arrived, but he was too persistent for my taste," Ms. Dubois said to me, as she walked into the kitchen wearing a silk, black robe with beautiful lavender sash and trim. She then poured some milk into a small tin saucer and placed it on the coffee table. Sable then jumped up on the coffee table and began to lap up the milk, as Ms. Dubois lit a cigarette and then sat down beside me on the sofa with a sigh.

"I'm glad you're hear Hayley. I've been meaning to check up on you and Jack, but my work at the library across the street keeps my head buried in books," Ms. Dubois said to me, as she took a smoke.

"Oh are you a librarian?" I inquired in a zealous tine and wide-eyed stare, as Sable stared at me for a brief moment before going back to lapping up the pool of milk in the tin saucer.

"Qui, I work as a bibliothécaire, a librarian at the library in the women's prison next to the Jefferson Court Market. Oh where are my manners, mon chéri. Let me fix you something, you must be famished from the trip over here," Ms. Dubois said to me as she walked over to the kitchen.

"Thank you. I like your apartment. My mother used to care for plants too but they never looked as healthy as yours do," I remarked, as I walked around the apartment while looking at all of Ms. Dubois plants displayed in such a way that seemed to mirror Ms. Dubois beauty and class.

"I wish I met her, but judging by what you told me about your mother. I'm sure we would've have been bons amis," Ms. Dubois said to me.

"What does that word mean?" I inquired with a smile. "Bons amis means good friends," Ms. Dubois said to me with a smile, as she poured a bottle of red wine into two glasses. "I love the French language, it's so ... pretty, like every word no matter what it means in English sounds so nice," I remarked.

"Perhaps I can teach you some French phrases," Faye said to me with a smile as she placed a tray filled with various meats and cheeses on the coffee table and then the wine bottle with the two full glasses of wine.

"Oh I would love that," I said to Faye in a zealous tone and smile, as I grabbed the glass of wine from off the tray. I wanted to be like Faye in every way, everything about her was the epitome of beauty and class, which was sadly everything I wasn't at the moment.

"All right repeat after me. Excusez-moi monsieur," Faye said to me with a smile.

"Excusez-moi monsieur," I repeated back to Faye.

"Très bien. You just said excuse me sir, but relax your throat and mouth more when you pronounce the 'm'," Faye said to me and then stood up from the sofa and walked over to a beautiful victrola which stood on an end table by the window. "If you don't mind me asking, why do you continue to visit the speakeasy now?" I inquired as Faye rifled through her collection of records on the book shelf beside the window.

"What do you mean mon chéri?" Faye inquired.

"Well, It's not exactly the safest of places to be for a woman like you," I replied, and then took a bite of cheese and salami from the tray on the coffee table.

"Just what kind of woman am I then?" Faye inquired with a grin as she placed a record on the victrola.

"A Flapper, or at least that's what Jack and Samson call you," I replied, and then took a sip of wine with a slight grimace. "A Flapper, a clapet, I hear that word thrown at me where ever I go. If being a Flapper mean to be a free woman who lives life to the fullest and doesn't bend to the will of any man, a woman who sets her own path in life, rather than following a man's path, then perhaps qui, oui je suis un clapet in every sense of the word," Faye said to me with a grin, as she raised her up her glass of wine as the victrola began to play a pretty French song sung by a woman with such an angelic voice.

"I think it's wonderful. I want my hair to look like yours," I said to Faye, as I pulled out a strand of my wavy red hair with a frown.

"Nonsense Hayley. Your hair is magnifique," Faye remarked, as she quickly sat down beside me with a smile.

"What does that mean," I inquired in a timid tone and then took a sip of wine.

"It means magnificent. Your hair is very unique mon chéri, and trust me when I say that men are very attracted to your hair," Faye said to me with a smile, as she gently moved a strand of my hair behind my ear.

"Thank you. I saw a woman on a billboard on Broadway last week who looks just like you," I said to Faye.

"Oh do you have a photo of the billboard?" Faye inquired. "No sorry, but I drew the woman in my diary," I replied as I opened my diary and turned to the page of the drawing.

"Oh … we do have similar facial features, but this woman is most likely a how do you say … celebrity," Faye said to me with a smile, as she stared at my drawing of the woman on the billboard.

"If you bear such a resemblance to her, then you could easily be a celebrity as well," I said to Faye with a smile.

"That life is too bright for me, Hayley. I couldn't bear always living in the how do you say … limelight. That light tends to change the hearts of many a woman," Faye said to me, as she lit a cigarette and took a smoke.

"Faye, you're the most beautiful woman I've ever met, and not just on the outside," I remarked.

"Merci, I echo your sentiment mon chéri," Faye said to me with a smile, as she placed her hand on my flushed cheek.

"I hope Mickey feels the same way about me," I said to Faye.

"Ah I've seen the way he looks at you," Faye said to me with a smile.

"How does he look at me," I inquired in a timid tone. "Like you're the only woman in the room," Faye replied with a smile.

"Do you really think so?" I inquired.

"Absolutely. Mickey is a sweet boy and his eyes often speak the words his mouth is too shy to utter," Faye replied with a smile.

"He told me he loved me right in front of all the mobsters in the speakeasy," I said to Faye.

"When I was your age living with my mother in my homeland of *Loire Valley*, I became, how you say … captivated by a boy named Julien. He always had a way of uplifting my spirits no matter how distraught I was, but when the war began, Julien and his family fled *Loire Valley* in fear of the death which was imminent. Before he bid me adieu Julien kissed me so passionately. To this day Julien's farewell kiss still lingers on my lips," Faye said to me in a somber tone.

"I'm sorry, Mickey also has a way of uplifting my spirits whenever the mobsters are bearing down on me," I said to Faye, as I placed my hand on hers.

"Then you must fight to keep him in your life mon chéri. One of my biggest regrets in life is not fighting hard enough to keep Julien's love," Faye said to me.

"I will … what about you and Jack?" I inquired with a grin. "What about us?" Faye replied with a grin, as she refilled her empty wine glass.

"You two are always engaged in such intimate conversations whenever I look at you both," I replied with a grin.

"I'm waiting for Jack to show me more," Faye said to me with a sigh.

"When I first met Jack at the hospital he treated me as if I was a random child on the street begging for money," I said to Faye.

"How does he treat you now?" Faye inquired, and then took a smoke.

"He has grown so much since then, as have I," I replied.

"Hayley, I told Jack if you couldn't teach him how to love, then there's no hope for him," Faye said to me with a grin while shaking her head.

"I know Jack regards you in a much deeper way than any other woman who enters the speakeasy," I said to Faye and then took a sip of wine.

"I know there is more to Jack than he would like to show me or the rest of the world for that matter. If Jack should ever choose to bare his soul to me, then I will begin to take him seriously," Faye said to me.

"Is Jack the only reason you visit the speakeasy?" I inquired. "Jack and you, mon chéri. Also the renovations to that speakeasy have now turned it into such a glamorous establishment," Faye replied.

"That's all because we work for the leader of the Five Points Gang now. I didn't tell you, two days ago I witnessed Jack willingly get himself shot in the shoulder by a man who didn't appear to be a mobster," I said to Faye.

"Sacrebleu, I would ask why on earth Jack would do such a thing, but how you say … that ship has sailed," Faye said to me in a stern tone as she shook her head, while taping her cigarette in the black marble ashtray on the coffee table.

"He told me that getting himself shot in the shoulder was necessary for us to stay in Mr. Luciano's good graces," I said to Faye.

"I wonder, what if Jack did that as an act of penance," Faye said to me.

"Do you really think he feels that much guilt over everything?" I inquired, as I refilled my glass of wine.

"Jack is one of those men who would rather die than owe anybody anything. You say that he's grown since you first met him. That is wonderful to hear mon chéri, but he still has much more growing to do, and only women like us can help him blossom into the loving man I believe he's hesitant to reveal to the world," Faye said to me.

Was Faye right? Was it solely up to me and her to help Jack? God knows Jack had no other compassionate women in his life. The longer I spent drinking wine with Faye in her apartment the more clearly I began to understand the intentions of not just Jack, but all men. I loved talking to Faye, no matter what the subject was, her view would always put my heart and mind at ease.

"I-I would love to work at the library with you," I said to Faye in a slurred tone and grin, as she placed another record on the victrola.

"I would love that as well mon chéri, but that library is not open to the general public. It is a library for the women inmates at the prison," Faye said to me.

"Well if you ever need any help just let me know. I love being around books," I said to Faye with a smile.

"Oui literature is magique. Have you ever heard of Jules Verne?" Faye inquired.

"I have, but I haven't read any of his books yet," I replied. "Oh mon chéri now that is a crime, follow me," Faye said to me with a grin as she stood up from the sofa and gestured for me to follow her.

I then stood up from the sofa with a slight stagger as the wine had taken its full effect on me, but I felt happy at this moment, warm and happy, as if I was with my mother. I then followed Faye down the hallway to her bedroom where her collection of books was displayed.

"Oh you must read a lot. Your collection is very impressive," I remarked, as I stared with wide-eyes at the two book cases against the wall of Faye's bedroom which were filled with books of all shapes, sizes, and colors.

"Oui I find it calms my mind. Now where is Monsieur Verne … ah here he is 20,000 Leagues Under the Sea," Faye said to me, as she took out a book from the book shelf and handed it to me with a smile.

"A-Are you giving me this copy?" I inquired in an incredulous tone, as I sat down on Faye's bed.

"Of course mon chéri. Books are meant to be shared," Faye replied with a smile as she sat down beside me on the bed.

"Thank you, have you ever read Edgar Allan Poe?" I inquired, as I opened 20,000 Thousand Leagues Under the Sea. "Oui Monsieur Poe is very renowned in France," Faye replied with a smile.

"His writing speaks to me in a way no other author has," I said to Faye.

"Oh it's getting late. Shouldn't you be heading back to the speakeasy, god only knows what Jack is up to in your absence," Faye said to me with a giggle.

"Oh please can I just stay a little longer," I inquired with a wide-eyed stare as Faye grinned at me.

"Of course mon chéri," Faye said to me with a smile, as she placed her hand on my knee.

I felt more at home with Faye in her apartment than I've ever felt in the speakeasy with Jack, or even Mickey. Faye was beautiful in every way and I wanted to emulate her as much as I could.

"Faye uhm … could you help me dye my hair your hair color?" I inquired in a slurred tone, as we entered the living room.

"Hayley you're hair is like a warm fire on a cold winter's night. Why on earth would you want to change that beautiful color?" Faye replied with a wide–eyed stare.

"Nobody has ever said that about my hair before," I said to Faye in a timid tone and grin, as I stroked my hair.

"You should always embrace your features mon chéri, they're what make you beautiful," Faye said to me.

"Not according to all the billboards and movies I see of women who look like you, it's as if my hair color is almost banned," I said to Faye in a somber tone.

"There is no definition of beauty. Beauty is how you say … in the beholder's eye," Faye said to me.

"Sometimes I'm tired of looking at the same ol me in the mirror. I just wish I was someone else, someone who looked glamorous," I said to Faye as I stared into the bevel mirror which stood in the corner by the window.

"Is it all because you live in that speakeasy with those pigs?" Faye inquired with a giggle.

"I often feel suffocated in the speakeasy, like all the mobsters are breathing all the air I so desperately need for myself, and that's when I begin to feel the walls close in around me. I don't feel that with you though. I feel safe here," I said to Faye as I sat down on the sofa and then took a sip of wine.

Is this what having an older sister felt like? Faye didn't attack me or make me feel insignificant whenever I would open up to her like Jack would still do.

Faye would always support me and nurture all the pain that pours out of me. I now wished I lived here with Faye in her apartment, but I feel as though I would be imposing on her life. There is a sense of comfort which I feel when I'm around Faye that rivals my mother. I believe I could confide in Faye as I did with my mother.

"It's raining. Tell me Hayley, what do you wish to be by the time you're my age?" Faye inquired, as she stared out the window with a pensive look on her face as she took a smoke.

"I … I want to be like you," I replied.

"Nonsense, I am no perfect portrait mon chéri," Faye said to me with a grin.

"Nobody is perfect, but you're perfect to me," I said to Faye with a grin.

"Oh if only Jack would speak to me the way you speak to me then I may very well give him a chance," Faye said to me with a giggle.

"J—Jack's entire mood lights up when he's around you. I can see the sparkle in his eyes whenever you enter the speakeasy and sit down at the bar in front of him," I said to Faye with a smile, as I walked up beside her and stared out the window, as the rain continued to pour.

"Oui that's the reaction I seem to evoke out of most men mon chéri, but with Jack, I know it's more genuine than the others. You and Jack have been through so much loss, and trust me when I say that you two are perfect for each other," Faye said to me.

"No y—you and I are perfect for each other. Why would you say that Jack and I are perfect for each other?" I inquired

"You both share a mutual loss, being your mother and his sister. That loss can form a strong bond between you and Jack," Faye said to me.

"I always break down crying whenever Jack tells me stories of my mother, but the stories are often happy stories," I said to Faye.

"Jack is keeping the memory of your mother alive by telling you those stories," Faye said to me with a smile.

"I like the rain, it always has a way of slowing down this city to the point where it's almost peaceful," I remarked, as I stared out the window.

"Oui I always find the rain to be cleansing, but no matter how much it rains, this city remains just as filthy as ever," Faye said to me as she shook her head and then took a smoke.

"Now you're starting to sound like Jack," I remarked with a grin.

"Oh we wouldn't want that now would we. I think we both have drunk enough wine for the evening," Faye said to me with a giggle.

"My head is spinning," I said to Faye, as I sat down on the sofa.

"Mon chéri you can stay here until you have your wits back. I wouldn't dare send a young drunken woman out into the rain," Faye said to me with a smile.

"Thank you, I just need to lie down for a moment," I said to Faye as I laid my head against the armrest of the sofa with a sigh.

"Damn these blackouts," Faye said in a stern tone, as the lights in her apartment flickered for a few moments.

"Oh maybe I should turn off the musique," Faye said to me. "No it's nice. Could you leave the music on please?" I inquired in a weary tone, as the combination of the wine, rain, and the music began to lull me into a state of warmth and comfort.

"Oh course mon chéri," Faye said to me, and just before my eyes closed I noticed tears streaming down Faye's smoky eyes and down her flushed cheeks as she walked passed me and entered her bedroom.

*****

It was 9:32 AM as I awoke on the sofa in Faye's apartment. My head was still spinning from the wine, but I felt more clear- minded than I did last night.

"Faye … Faye," I spoke aloud, as I slowly stood up from the sofa with a slight stumble, but quickly managed to regain my composure. I then walked into Faye's bedroom but all that remained was the scent of smoke and sweet perfume.

"Was last night a dream?" I spoke aloud as I walked back into the living room and sat down on the sofa with a sigh.

I then noticed a slip of paper tucked underneath one of the potted plants which stood on the coffee table.

Mon Cheri Hayley,

I didn't want to wake you. I have to go to work at the library across the street now, but I will be back at 6PM. You may stay in my apartment to sober up if you wish, but if you choose to go back home please lock the door when you leave. Our time last night reminded me of the time I spent with my best friend when I was your age growing up in *Loire Valley*. Please be kind to yourself. I see a beautiful flame burning from within you, and though it may flicker and dim, don't you dare keep it hidden from the world.
Love Faye
P.S.: Help yourself to croissants and coffee I left in the kitchen

I then tucked Faye's lovely note into my dress pocket and walked into the kitchen with a smile. The part of me that wanted to live with Faye was beginning to grow the more time I spent in her apartment. I didn't shake in fear when I was around Faye, unlike in the speakeasy where I would constantly begin to shake in the presence of all the mobsters and even Jack, Mickey and Samson. Men always had that effect on me, but being around Faye was always a feeling of warmth, love, and acceptance.

It was 12:21 PM as I sat in a violet armchair in Faye's bedroom while still drinking coffee and eating croissants.

I then opened the doors of the closet in Faye's bedroom and stared with wide-eyes at the wonder that was Faye's clothing. Faye is only a couple inches taller than me, I wonder if I could fit into most of her glamorous dresses. I thought to myself as I held Faye's glamorous dresses dress against my drab and dusty black dress. This black dress with sequins was beautiful. Would Faye notice if I took her dress? I then quickly took off my worn ugly dress and put on Faye's glamorous black sequin dress and stared at myself in the mirror which hung on the wall beside the bookcases. I didn't look like me anymore I thought to myself as I smiled while staring at my transformation in the mirror. I looked like a real woman, a woman men would lust after, a woman who would be truly seen. I then noticed a short black wig on a mannequin head sitting on the shelf of the closet. Did Faye wear a wig? If so, then what does her real hair look like? I needed to look like Faye, for I couldn't bare looking at myself in the mirror any longer, all it did was remind me of the woman who was raped, but now I could become a stronger woman, and everything in Faye's closet would help me achieve that strength. I then snatched the short black wig off the mannequin head, along with the black sequin dress, lipstick, and rouge. I then placed everything I took from Faye's closet into a brown paper bag from the kitchen. I felt so guilty at that moment, but the overwhelming urge to look like Faye took over all of me. She wouldn't miss anything I took, I thought to myself as I took a deep breath and then exited Faye's apartment and locked the door.

"To Minetta Street please," I said to the cabdriver as I entered the taxicab.

"You got it miss," the cabdriver said to me.

I wonder how Jack, Samson, and Mickey were doing at the speakeasy. I was always nervous to enter the speakeasy after being away for hours, for that place is so tumultuous.

"Thank you," I said to the cabdriver as I paid my fare and exited the taxicab.

"Hayley, where have you been?" Jack inquired in a stern tone as I entered the speakeasy to the sight of him and Samson behind the bar serving mobsters.

"I was at Ms. Dubois apartment," I replied in a timid tone. "Oh, you must've really enjoyed it there. How is Faye doing?" Jack inquired with a grin, as Samson whispered in his ear and then pointed to a man sitting by himself at a table near the stage.

"She's doing fine. I'll be in the kitchen" I replied and then scampered into the kitchen.

What occasion should I wear the dress, wig, and makeup I took from Faye's closet? Faye always looked that way every time I saw her, so why shouldn't I? I then tied my hair up into a small tight bun the way my teachers used to tie their hair, but nobody would see my raggedy, ugly red hair any longer. I then placed Faye's short black wig over my head and tucked in any strands of red hair that remained visible underneath the black wig. I then smiled and pouted as I stared into the mirror in the manner which I saw many leading actresses do on the silver screen. I then applied the wine colored lipstick to my lips in a delicate manner, as the sound of mobsters barking in the speakeasy grated in my mind, but my transformation would give me more strength now, I would no longer have the appearance of a street orphan, I would now be a flapper girl who flouts societies conventions and does as she pleases in the face of any man!

It was 5:42 PM in the speakeasy as I served drinks to a table of mobsters who wouldn't stop making eyes at me in such a lecherous manner. I suppose I can attribute that to my new appearance as a flapper. It had been a couple days since I left Faye's apartment and I haven't seen her here in the speakeasy since. I was happy hour in the speakeasy, though I never understood that term, for all the mobsters in the speakeasy still appeared angry even when they were drunk.

"So you're still going with that flapper look, huh Hayley," Samson said to me with a smirk as I walked up to the bar. "What's it to you? Table three wants another pitcher of beer," I said to Samson.

"Oh so this Hayley has more of an attitude I see. Well be careful, you act that way towards the wrong mobster in here and he won't care that you're a dolled up young woman when he silences you," Samson said to me as he filled up the empty pitcher with beer from the sputtering tap.

"Worry about yourself. I don't need to be lectured by you," I said with a scoff as I brushed a strand of my straight black hair behind my ears and pinned it with a silver broach I always keep with me that used to belong to my mother.

"Oh now you sound like your uncle, talking to me in such a condescending tone. I'm just looking out for your safety," Samson said to me as he placed the full pitcher of beer on the tray.

"My days of running to you or Jack, or even Mickey for protection are over. That was the old Hayley," I said to Samson. "Well what does the new Hayley run to then?" Samson inquired with a grin as he wiped down the bar.

I didn't answer Samson's question at that moment, not because I found the question to be irritating, but because I had no answer.

"Here you go gentleman. Is there anything else I can get you?" I inquired with a grin and my hand on my hip.

"Yes princess, how about you make me forget that I have a wife for one night if you catch my drift," one mobster replied, as the table of mobsters then began to laugh in unison.

"In your dreams," I said to the mobster in stern tone and then scampered into the kitchen and sat down at my desk with a sigh.

Is this what it felt like to be a flapper girl? To be constantly disrespected all because of your appearance. Old Hayley was disrespected by these mobsters and now new Hayley is also being disrespected, but in a different manner. Now these mobsters objectify me, as they would do to Faye, Gracie, and Carmen the burlesque performer.

"Hayley Mickey is here!" Samson shouted, as he stuck his head into the doorframe of the kitchen.

I haven't seen Mickey in weeks. The very thought of looking into his warm brown eyes sent my heart racing, but how would he react to my new look?

"Hayley … is that really you?" Mickey replied in an incredulous tone, as he took his hat off and slowly walked towards me.

"It sure is me. What do you think?" I inquired with a smile, as I stood up and posed in the manner of which all those glamorous actresses posed on the billboards on Broadway.

"I … uhm, I'm surprised to say the least," Mickey replied.

"That's all you have to say? You don't like it, do you? I can tell by the look in your eyes," I said to Mickey in a distressed tone. It was at vulnerable times such as these where the old Hayley would begin to cry, but I wouldn't let that part of me to take over any longer. I was a flapper girl who didn't need a man's approval!

"I just miss your red hair, please tell me that's a wig," Mickey said to me as he leaned in close and stared intently at my short black hair.

"It is a wig, but that doesn't matter, because I don't need your approval, honey," I said to Mickey with a scoff and then stared into the mirror as I applied more lipstick on my lips which had faded over the past couple hours.

"I thought you would be happy to see me. I—I've missed you," Mickey said to me as he walked up behind me as I continued to apply more makeup in the mirror.

"I thought you would support me, but once again Faye was right when she told me that 'Men only care about what makes them feel good,'" I said to Mickey with a scoff.

"You know that's not true when it comes to me Hayley," Mickey said to me in a stern tone, as his reflection in the mirror stared at mine with wide-eyes.

"So when do you get off work today? I was wondering if you wanted to go to *Tompkins Square Park*," Mickey inquired. "I'll pass, parks are too dirty for my liking," I replied with a dismissive wave.

"Since when … I don't care much for this new Hayley," Mickey remarked in a stern tone.

"Why not, because for the first time in her life she's not bending to the will of another man?" I inquired in a distressed tone.

"Why are you being so aggressive towards me? I'm not a mobster," Mickey said to me in a distressed tone.

"You're right at least a mobster would be confident enough to handle a woman like me," I said to Mickey with a scoff.

"Oh … all right. I see now that you've become someone else. You're not the Hayley I used to love … goodbye," Mickey said to me in a somber tone and then exited the kitchen with his head hung low.

If Mickey didn't support the new me, then I no longer needed him in my life. Still a few tears streamed from my smoky eyes down my rosy cheeks, as I continued to apply more makeup on in the mirror after Mickey left. Why must men always feel the need to have control over every aspect of a woman's life? If Mickey did truly love me then he would've accepted me for who I am now, not for who he wanted me to remain as.

"Where's Jack?" I inquired as I walked up to Samson behind the bar.

"It's Sunday, where do you think he is missy?" Samson replied, as he prepared a drink for a woman at the bar who had the appearance of Faye, mixed with Bernadette and Gracie all in one. This speakeasy sure attracts so many beautiful women, and now I saw myself as one of them.

"Oh so he's doing a liquor deal then. I forgot Jack still needed to put himself in danger. Why doesn't Mr. Luciano have the liquor delivered straight to the speakeasy?" I inquired.

"To hell if I know, why don't you ask him that yourself. He and Jack will be back soon," Samson replied with a scoff, as I stared at the glamorous woman seated at the bar who drunk her cocktail in such a delicate manner.

"Oh well maybe I'll tell him what I really think of him and the Five Points Gang," I said to Samson as I stroked my hair in the same manner which the glamorous woman seated at the bar stroked her hair.

"Oh you go right ahead and do that, and then save him the trouble and throw yourself in the Hudson," Samson said to me with a snicker.

Samson's warnings didn't scare me. I knew all too well the power Mr. Luciano had, but I would no longer be intimidated by men like him, the new Hayley flouted all men who try to control her.

"So I told my nephew here to keep his mouth shut until the dame opened hers," Mr. Luciano said to Jack with a laugh as he, Jack and a younger man who appeared to be around Mickey's age entered the speakeasy.

"I'm sure your uncle has taught you a great deal of wisdom huh Stefano?" Jack inquired as the three of them walked up to the bar.

"He has. Uncle Charles is the wisest man in New York," the young man known as Stefano replied with a grin. My heart fluttered from the sight of him, he looked like a mirror image of Mr. Luciano only much younger. He was dressed in the same dapper attire Mr. Luciano was dressed in and carried himself with such confidence, as if he could do anything he wanted and suffer no consequences.

"Don't forget that nipote. Oh, where are my manners, this is my nephew Stefano. You will be seeing more of him in the speakeasy. I told his mother not to worry about what his bambino eyes would witness here because he has the family business in his blood and I know he won't cower in the face of danger, right nipote?" Mr. Luciano inquired as he patted the cheeks of the handsome young man with a smile.

"Yes uncle," Stefano replied with a grin.

"You see, he's so obedient. He gets that from his father who used to be a brick layer until that last brick ended up laying him out," Mr. Luciano said with a snicker and then lit a cigar and took a smoke.

"What do you mean by that?" I inquired.

"Let Stefano tell the story. Jack, remember what I told you, at any cost, comprendere?" Mr. Luciano said to Jack in a stern tone and then exited the speakeasy after gesturing towards a couple of mobsters to follow him.

"My father died from a twenty pound brick landing on his head from four stories up. He only took his helmet off for a brief moment," Stefano said to me.

"I'm sorry," I said to Stefano.

"Ah it's more embarrassing than tragic. Uncle Charles always busts my balls by telling me to tell people that story. He says it's a lesson of how blue-collar workers will always finish last in this day and age.

"I would say it's a lesson to never take your helmet off if you work in construction," Jack said to Stefano as he walked behind the bar and then whispered into Samson's ear.

"That's so cruel of him to say that about your father," I said to Stefano in a somber tone, as he took off his fedora and combed his hair back in a swift manner

"He died seven years ago, but Uncle Charles has been there for me ever since," Stefano said to me.

"Oh I—I'm Hayley, Hayley Carmona," I said to Stefano in a timid tone as my entire flapper girl attitude melted as I stared into Stefano's piercing blue eyes, but I couldn't shy away as I did before in the presence of another man, for that was the old Hayley.

"It's a pleasure to meet you, doll. I'm Stefano Moretti," Stefano said with a grin, as we shook hands. Stefano then quickly pulled my hand in and kissed it, before I could even pull it away.

"Hold your horses. I don't care who your uncle Is. I'm not just some doll for you to tug at," I said to Stefano in a stern tone as I pulled my hand away with a scoff.

"Uncle Charles said that's how I should greet all beautiful women," Stefano said to me with a grin, as the jazz band began to play on the stage.

"Well, thank you for the compliment, but I'm not your typical woman," I said to Stefano with a grin.

"Oh I know. Uncle Charles told me all about you," Stefano said to me with a grin as he leaned in closer.

"Oh really, did he tell you that I'm not a woman who hangs on the arm of any man who flatters her," I said to Stefano with a scoff and grin as I looked at myself in my compact mirror while primping my hair.

I knew right from the start by Stefano's handsome looks and social status of being the nephew of Mr. Luciano that he was used to getting anything he wanted, but I still enjoyed flirting with him nonetheless. I felt like one of those glamorous actresses in movies who play hard to get with the leading man. I would be lying if I said I wasn't attracted to Stefano, but my heart was still bleeding out from ending it with Mickey. Perhaps I'll give Stefano a chance and see what kind of man he truly is. "Are you free tonight Ms. Carmona? I would love to take you for a night out on the town," Stefano inquired with a grin.

"Please call me Hayley, and just what do you have in mind, honey?" I inquired with a grin.

All I can tell you now is that it will be a night that is worthy of a woman like you," Stefano replied with a grin.

"So do you always move this fast with women, or did your uncle teach you that as well?" I inquired with a grin.

"The way I figured, if I didn't move this fast then some other man might beat me to the punch," Stefano replied.

"Why do all of you men live as if you're in an ongoing competition with each other?" I inquired.

"If the prize is you, Hayley, then I will compete against any man," Stefano replied with a grin.

"I'm not merely a man's prize, get that through your head honey," I said to Stefano with a scoff, as I spun around in the barstool and watched the jazz band perform with a sigh.

"Then let me get to know you better tonight," Stefano said to me with a smile and wide-eyed stare as he stood up from the barstool and stood in front of me, blocking my view of the jazz band performing on stage.

"Before I even consider your proposal, I first need to know what exactly you have planned for tonight," I inquired.

"All right, I wanted it to be a surprise, but … I was planning on taking you out to see a show on Broadway with me," Stefano replied.

My entire mood lit up at that moment. Seeing a Broadway show was a dream of mine, and if Stefano had those kinds of resources to make that happen, then I would gladly go on a date with him tonight!

"Oh what play will we be seeing?" I inquired in a zealous tone, as the old Hayley in me came to the surface for a brief moment.

"Uhm … you strike me as a woman who likes fantasy. We can see A Midsummer Night's Dream. I think it's based off of a play written by a poet named Shakespeare," Stefano replied.

"I adore Shakespeare, how did you know?" I inquired in a zealous tone.

"Call it a man's intuition, so what do you say Hayley, would you do me the honor of joining me tonight?" Stefano inquired with a grin.

I just couldn't say no to Stefano's proposal of taking me out to the Broadway show of A Midsummer Night's Dream tonight, it all sounded far too wonderful to turn down.

"I accept your proposal," I replied with a grin.

"Fantastic. You've made my day, Hayley. I'll pick you up at eight," Stefano said to me with a smile, and then exited the speakeasy in a jaunty manner.

"It looks like Mr. Luciano's nephew sure has you smitten," Samson remarked with a snicker as he wiped down the bar.

"He's taking me to a Broadway show tonight," I said to Samson.

"I take it you and Mickey are old news then?" Samson inquired.

"Old news for the old me, I have to get ready for tonight," I said to Samson.

"Be careful with that boy. He comes from a different world than Mickey, a world of privilege and crime," Samson said to me.

"I can handle myself," I said to Samson in a stern tone before I entered the kitchen.

To think that six months ago I was lying in the hospital with not a hope in this world after I found my mother's dead body, and now I'm going to see a Broadway show tonight with a handsome and charming man. My heart was already racing and it was seven hours before Stefano would be here to pick me up. What would I where tonight? I wanted to keep my appearance as a confident, beautiful, and strong flapper girl, just as Faye imbued into me when I was in her apartment.

*****

It was 7:38 PM in the speakeasy as I applied makeup on in the mirror in the kitchen.

For the first time in my life I didn't feel invisible. I felt like one of those women displayed in neon lights on Broadway. I felt like someone else, but because of that, I felt happy. I then noticed that I was still wearing the necklace which Mickey gave to me as a heartfelt give. So I took off the necklace without looking at it and quickly stuffed it underneath my undergarments in the bottom drawer of my dresser. I modified one of my mother's burgundy dresses to fit my slender figure by cinching the waist. This glamorous dress is what I would be wearing tonight.

"Is that you Hayley? You look like Faye's little sister," Jack remarked as I walked up to the bar with a grin.

"I wanted to look my best," I said to Jack.

"Oh there's Faye," Jack said with a grin as he whistled and gestured for Faye to join him at the bar.

Oh my god, this was the first time I saw Faye since I left her apartment with her black wig, black dress, and makeup. She would know from a mere glance at me that I took her accessories from her closet, would she be furious with me? I couldn't live with myself if Faye hated me now for taking her belongings.

"Hayley is that you?" Faye inquired in an incredulous tone and grin as she walked up to the bar while fanning herself with a fan ornately decorated with black feather.

"U—Uhm hello Ms. Dubois," I said to Faye in a timid tone as my entire flapper girl demeanor crumbled at the sight of Faye, I was now just a little girl who took her possessions without asking.

"I see you've put my wig and dress to good use mon chéri," Faye said to me with a grin as she sat down at the bar.

"I'm sorry. I just needed to be someone who wasn't me, I just—I just needed to escape from my own life. Here I'll give you your wig and dress back," I said to Faye as tears began to well up in my eyes which made my mascara run down my flushed cheeks.

"Hayley, what kind of friend would I be If I didn't let a fellow clapet borrow my belongings," Faye inquired.

"I just took them, I didn't even ask you. I don't know what came over me at that moment. I just wanted to wear your beauty and confidence," I said to Faye.

"Beauty comes from within mon chéri, but I hope my belongings can help you realize how beautiful you truly are," Faye said to me.

"I'm going on a date with the nephew of Mr. Luciano tonight, he should be here soon to pick me up," I said to Faye as I carefully wiped the mascara with a handkerchief which ran down my cheeks.

"Oh that's wonderful. How are you two going to spend the night?" Faye inquired, as Jack served her a cocktail with a grin. "We're going to see a show on Broadway. I've always dreamt of someday witnessing one of those plays and the wonderful actors who perform with such passion on the stage. They all inspire me to—,"

"Hayley," Stefano pronounced with a smile as he waved at me from across the speakeasy.

"That's him oh my god," I said to Faye in a distressed tone as I quickly primped my hair and touched up my makeup in my pocket mirror.

"Oh he sure is an Adonis, if only he was ten years older. So what show will you two be seeing tonight?" Faye inquired with a grin.

"A Midsummer Night's Dream," I replied to Faye, as I stared at Stefano talking to one of his uncle's associates in a cordial manner.

"Wonderful. In that case I will say to you a quote from Hamlet, one of Monsieur Shakespeare's greatest plays. 'To thine own self be true,' mon chéri," Faye said to me with a warm smile as she placed her hand on my cheek.

"Thank you Faye," I said to Faye with a smile.

"If my belongings can help you discover who you truly are then I would be more than happy to let you borrow them," Faye said to me with a smile as she gently grabbed both of my shoulders.

"He's coming," I said to Faye with a smile as I gestured towards Stefano with a nod as he made his way to me after exchanging pleasantries with all the mobsters who I'm sure where ingratiating themselves onto him just because he's the boss's nephew.

"You look beautiful," Stefano said to me with a grin, as he took my hand and kissed it in such a quick manner which sent my heart a flutter.

"I now bid you two adieu. Remember Shakespeare's quote mon chéri," Faye said to me, as she stood up from the bar and then began to mingle with a couple of mobster's dames who stood by the stage as the jazz band was tuning their instruments. "Who's she," Stefano inquired with a whistle and grin as he stared at Faye.

"That's Faye Dubois and she's my dearest friend," I replied with a smile.

"Well what am I chopped liver?" Stefano inquired in a facetious tone.

"Oh stop it," I said to Stefano with a smile and playful shove.

"Well, shall we?" Stefano inquired with a grin as he held his hand out towards me.

"We shall," I replied after I took a deep breath and then took Stefano's hand with a smile as we exited the speakeasy.

It was 8:02 PM as Stefano and I exited his midnight blue Plymouth convertible and walked up to the line of dapperly dressed attendees waiting to see A Midsummer Night's Dream.

It was a warm night in *Midtown* New York. The kind of night where the summer breeze lingered as it blew softly through your hair. I noticed that Stefano was growing impatient as he stood in line with the rest of the attendees.

"What's wrong?" I inquired.

"We shouldn't be waiting in a line like the rest of these commoners. Follow me," Stefano replied with a whistle and gesture towards me, as If I was already his pet.

"Don't you whistle at me," I said to Stefano in a stern tone as I scampered towards the ticket counter.

"What are you going to do?" I inquired.

"Something I saw my uncle do many times before," Stefano replied with a grin, as we walked up to the ticket counter.

"Oh get back in line kid"

"Do you know where you are?"

"The audacity!" the attendees shouted at Stefano and me as we stood at the ticket counter.

"Cool your jets goddamn it!" Stefano shouted at the attendees, and then leaned in close to the man behind the ticket counter.

Stefano then whispered something into the ear of the man who stood behind the ticket counter as a stern look began to form on his face.

"Yes of course r—right this way sir and madam," the man said in a stammering tone as he gestured for us to enter the theatre.

"What did you say to him?" I inquired, as I took Stefano's arm.

"I simply told him who my uncle is," Stefano replied with a grin, as we entered the theatre.

The reception as Stefano and I entered the Belasco Theatre was grand to say the least. I felt as if I was living another young woman's life when I was with Stefano, a young woman who threw caution to the wind and didn't shy away from anything or anybody. Stefano and I were then handed playbills by a smiling woman who stood in the center isle of all the seats. Stefano then whispered in the woman's ear just like he did with the man at the ticket counter with a stern look on his face.

"Uhm right this way … here are your seats. Row B seat 9 and 10. Is there anything else I can get you two before the play begins?" the woman inquired, as Stefano and I sat down in our seats.

"We're fine for now," Stefano replied in a stern tone. "Thank you," I said to the woman as she scampered away in a frightened manner.

"You see doll, we don't have to pay a dime for anything in this city. My uncle is so revered even all these blue-collared commoners know of his stature," Stefano said to me as he laid his arm down upon my shoulders with a grin.

"It must be nice getting anything your heart desires all because your uncle is the leader of a crime organization. I just want you to know that you have fulfilled one of my dreams tonight," I said to Stefano with a warm smile, as I stared wide- eyed at the stage which was being set up with various backdrops and spotlights.

"Any time doll. My uncle says that when I turn eighteen I will be fully initiated into the Five Points Gang. Then I will have real influence," Stefano said to me.

"What are you planning on doing?" I inquired.

"I'm not sure yet, but Paul Kelly will no longer be in the picture," Stefano replied.

"Who's Paul Kelly?" I inquired, as I stared at a flamboyantly dressed man scamper across the stage.

"You mean to tell me you don't know our founder Paul Kelly? Well I shouldn't be surprised. That bastard pretends like he pulls all the strings, but my uncle is the true leader of the Five Points Gang," Stefano said to me.

"I had no idea. I thought Mr. Luciano was the leader of your organization," I said to Stefano.

"Everybody answers to somebody toots, it's just a shame that my uncle still answers to that man," Stefano said to me in a stern tone.

"Perhaps it's a good thing that I've never met him before," I said to Stefano, as a few actors scampered across the stage.

"Did you know that Italians and the Irish have been clashing over power in New York for the past ten years? My father was even half Irish on his mother's side which sickens me to say that Irish blood is in me too," Stefano said to me with a scoff while shaking his head.

"You shouldn't speak that way about your father. It sounds to me that your uncle has distorted your image of him, before he died," I said to Stefano, as the scarlet curtains closed on the stage.

"My old man never honored me in life so why should I honor him in death?" Stefano inquired in a stern tone. "I'm sorry, but your uncle is—,"

"It's starting," Stefano interjected as he pointed to the rising scarlet curtain.

"Ladies and gentleman, I present to you, A Midsummer Night's Dream, Act I," a man dressed in a plum and amber striped suit with a frilled collar pronounced and then exited left off the stage.

The actress who played Hippolyta captivated me right from the start of act I. She was beautiful, strong, and didn't bend to the will of Theseus until her heart was fully committed to him. "Go, Philostrate, stir up the Athenian youth to merriments; awake the pert and nimble spirit of mirth," the actor who played Theseus pronounced, as Philostrate scampered away in a childlike manner.

It was all so magical. The last time I remember reading this play was when I was eight years old in my bedroom as my mother was fighting with Johnny, but Shakespeare's magical imagery and dialog transported me away from the misery I felt for my mother at that time.

"Are you all right," Stefano inquired, as tears began to well up in my eyes, as I stared at the beautiful Hippolyta and Theseus professing their love to each other for all the creatures of the woods to witness.

"I'm fine," I replied with a warm smile as I carefully wiped the tears forming in my eyes before they could run my mascara. I then felt Stefano's warm breath upon my neck as he leaned in close to me.

"Not now please, I don't want to miss a moment of this play," I said to Stefano as I leaned forward on the edge of my seat.

"If not now then when?" Stefano inquired in a stern tone," as the curtain closed on act 1 of A Midsummer Night's Dream. I then clapped along with the rest of the attendees, but Stefano was nowhere near impressed with the play.

"It's all so beautiful, don't you agree?" I inquired, and then quickly checked my makeup in my pocket mirror.

"Oh sure I'm enchanted," Stefano replied in a sarcastic tone and scoff. It became clearer to me now that Stefano only took me out tonight so he could have his way with me, but I was in no way that kind of girl.

Stefano then leaned in close to me once more, but the scarlet curtain began to rise as I leaned forward to the edge of my seat inadvertently evading his advances once more. I could see out of the corner of my eye that Stefano was growing impatient, but I wasn't going to relent to his desires which were selfishly based as he treated me like a doll he could play with at anytime. If Stefano wanted to kiss me or go even further, then he first must respect and acknowledge how I feel at this moment.

"How now, spirit! Wither wander you?" the actor who played Puck inquired, as a fairy approached his from the opposite end of the stage.

I remember this line in particular. The character Puck filled me with such a sense of joy when I first read this play.

"He looks so stupid," Stefano remarked with a snicker, as he pointed at Puck.

"Shhh," I said to Stefano with a stern glance.

"Don't you shush me," Stefano said to me in a stern tone.

Why couldn't all men in this day and age speak in the beautiful manner in which Shakespeare writes? Why must I be surrounded by barbarians who curse, shout, and disrespect each other with every breath? My heartfelt at peace here at   the theatre listening to the beautiful versus spoken by talented actors upon the stage. The irony that the one who made this moment possible was also the very one I wish wasn't part of it. Stefano had different intentions tonight, which was obvious by his incessant advances towards me as if we were parked in his car right now. Judging by the sulking look on Stefano's face, he may never take me to see a play on Broadway ever again, so I had to cherish this moment

"How long is this play?" Stefano inquired.

"I think its five acts long," I replied with a glance towards Stefano who was slouching in his seat as if he was being tortured by this beautiful play.

Samson was right when he told me that Stefano and I come from different worlds, but there was no bond between Stefano and I which was strong enough to merge our worlds together as the bond of love does to young couples from different worlds.

"Tempt not too much the hatred of my spirit; for I am sick when I do look on thee," the actor who played Demetrius said in such a heartfelt yet scornful tone.

"The wildest hath not such a heart as you," the actress who played Helena said to Demetrius, as they're eyes burned with such a passion for each other, a passion I could only hope one day another will feel for me.

The characters Demetrius and Helena reminded me so much of Jack and Faye, for their emotions towards each other were complicated, but passionate. They both were attracted to each other for the very reasons why they couldn't fully commit to each other. Jack was often stubborn and cruel with Faye who effortlessly casts a spell over him just as Helena did with Demetrius. It amazes me how Shakespeare's plays can transcend hundreds of years, for love is a language that will never change.

"I have to go to the bathroom," Stefano said to me with a groan, as he stood up from his seat and then scampered down the aisle.

Part of me wondered if Stefano would come back from the men's room, while another part of me wishes he wouldn't. If I could share this moment with anybody right now it would be Faye. She would no doubt be just as captivated by A Midsummer Night's Dream as I am. I still feel bad over the possessions I took from her, but as she reassured me at the speakeasy, she wanted me to keep what I took from her as long as it took for me to discover who I truly am. I loved looking and talking like Faye, it gave me confidence around men who would normally make me feel so small. Stefano saw me for who I truly was as my attention was focused on the play rather than him and that meant that my personality was unattractive to him. He wanted me for my appearance, not my heart or mind, but I wouldn't let this truth ruin the experience of a lifetime. My dream in life ever since I was eight years old was to see a play on Broadway. I have now achieved that dream, but there's still a feeling of emptiness inside of me. Perhaps I shouldn't be searching outward for someone to make me feel whole rather than inward at the very core of why I constantly feel this way.

"I'm back, is that goat man still talking?" Stefano inquired as he sat down in his seat with a sigh.

"You mean Puck, no, just watch," I replied to Stefano as I pointed to the stage at the actors who played Lysander and Demetrius engaged in a fight regarding their love for Helena.

"Finally something I can relate to," Stefano remarked.

Was Stefano used to fighting other men for woman that he liked or even loved? If so, would he act this way towards another man who showed an attraction towards me? I wasn't used to any man fighting for my attention until I became a flapper. Faye must be used to having men fight over her everywhere she goes, but it would just make me feel so guilty over the pain I'm causing them both. Hermia and Helena were just as conniving in love as Lysander and Demetrius.

Did love bring this deceitful nature out in everyone's heart or was it only those who felt the weight of love too heavy to bear and resorted to drastic measures in order to keep that love? I never saw myself as a woman who could put a spell on any man like Faye or Helena could. Which is why being a flapper is very much like playing a character in a Shakespeare play. I can escape into the character that is a flapper whenever I feel my old fears and insecurities begin to overwhelm me. I loved the character Puck. He was so whimsical and mischievous, but also very wise, and every time he entered the stage I would bounce in my seat and lightly clap. "Here she comes, curst and sad: cupid is a knavish lad, thus to make poor females mad," the actor who played Puck pronounced as Hermia entered the stage.

"I'm starting to like him," Stefano remarked with a snicker as he pointed at the actor who played Puck.

I was glad Stefano was beginning to warm up to A Midsummer Night's Dream. There was only one act left of the play and I wasn't going to let him ruin the experience for me. It was quite remarkable how I could find similarities in my life and Shakespeare's writing. The flamboyantly dressed actors performing on stage were no longer strangers to me now, for I felt as if they mirrored me, Jack, Faye, Mickey, and Samson. My mother would've loved to see a play on Broadway even if she had to see it with Johnny, she would've still found happiness in that moment as I am right now. It then occurred to me, am I destined to follow in my mother's footsteps? I'm already on a date with a mobster, even if he's only 17 years old, Stefano has shown me his hatred towards an entire race of people. Whether his hatred for the Irish stems from his relationship with his father or perhaps his uncle Mr. Luciano is poisoning his mind, I still felt that I needed to get through to him before his uncle turns him into another cold-hearted killer like Johnny who has no regard for human life.

"I'm hungry, we should've brought snacks with us," Stefano whispered to me.

"Me too, could we stop at a diner after the play and get something quick?" I inquired.

"Absolutely, I'm starving," Stefano replied.

The actors who played all the fairies of A Midsummer Night's Dreams were positively magical in every sense of the word. The way they spoke, dressed, and moved, transported me out of New York and into the woods near Athens.

"Come my lord, and in our flight, tell me how it came this night that I sleeping here was found, with these mortals upon the ground?" the actress who played Titania inquired in a stern tone.

Even though Titania, the fairy queen, was one of the strongest female characters in the play, I didn't resonate with her as much as I did with Hippolyta or Helena. It could be because Titania was wedded to Oberon the fairy King and she was used to fairies waiting on her hand and foot. I've never been the kind of woman who felt comfortable giving orders to people, but perhaps I should be now. Perhaps I need to embody more of Titania, for she very much has that flapper girl spirit which I have adopted.

I then began to see more of Jack's personality in Theseus rather than Demetrius as he comprehended the true intentions of the fairies whether they are truly good or evil. There was that side of Jack which to me felt more responsible when I was around him. Then there was the side of him who willingly gets himself shot in the arm. Perhaps I should stop trying to find similarities with the characters of A Midsummer Night's Dream to the characters in my life and just enjoy this play for what it is, fantasy.

I was now watching a play in which the characters were watching a play. A troupe was performing a play for Theseus, Hippolyta, Lysander, and Demetrius.

"For, by the gracious, golden, glittering gleams, I trust to take of truest Thisby sight. But stay O spite! But Mark, poor knight," the actor who played Pyramus pronounced.

I could tell A Midsummer Night's Dream was almost over as the play Theseus and Hippolyta were watching ended in a most tragic fashion, but the words tragedy and Shakespeare   go hand in hand after all. I doubt there's a writer in the world of literature who writes more about tragedy than Shakespeare does. Even Edgar Allan Poe would have to take the backseat to Shakespeare when it comes to tales of tragedy. Sure Edgar Allan Poe's writings are generally darker and more morbid than Shakespeare's writings, but Shakespeare has such a contrast of heart-fluttering joy and heartbreaking despair in his writings which always struck and chord in me whenever I would read them to escape from my own despair.

"So, goodnight unto you all. Give me your hands, if we be friends, and Robin shall restore amends," the actor who played Puck pronounced and then bowed before the curtain lowered.

The curtain then rose as all the actors and actresses of A Midsummer Night's Dream stood lined up on the stage and bowed, as the attendees of the Belasco Theatre gave them a rousing standing ovation. I then jolted up out of my seat, while tugging at Stefano who appeared to revert back to his sulking behavior.

"Is it over?" Stefano inquired.

"Yes it's over," I replied, as I applauded and cheered in such a zealous manner. This night was truly a dream come true for me. I felt as if my peace of mind was soothed by watching A Midsummer Night's Dream. The attendees then began to toss beautiful flowers upon the stage for the actors and actresses. This in turn made me feel a little guilty that I didn't bring anything to give to them.

"Ladies and gentlemen the play has now concluded. Would all attendees please file out of the theatre in a civil fashion, goodnight," a man dressed in a black suite pronounced with a smile, as Stefano and I walked down the aisle.

*****

It was 10:27 PM as Stefano drove down Broadway as the lime lights continued to shine as if to beckon us not to leave.

"It was all just so beautiful ... thank you," I said to Stefano as I leaned in and kissed him on the cheek.

"No problem, doll. I'm starving, if you spot a diner let me know," Stefano said to me.

"All right," I said to Stefano as downtown traffic halted us.

"I'm glad that goat man what's his name ... Puck got the last line of the play," Stefano said to me, as traffic began to move again.

"Oh me too. I love his character and how he is an observer like us, but also a very wise fairy who affected the other characters in such a profound way," I said to Stefano in a zealous tone and smile.

"You sure know a lot of big words. I've never met a girl like you before," Stefano remarked with a grin.

"I'll take that as a compliment. I know most girls my age are either working in factories or not working at all, I guess I should feel grateful that I'm neither of those kinds of girls," I said to Stefano.

"You work for my uncle, so you are above all those other girls who work for pennies on the hour," Stefano said to me. "Oh there's a diner right over there called ... Jezebels," I said to Stefano as I pointed to the diner's rose-colored neon sign which shone brightly through the dark, smoke-filled streets.

"Jezebels huh, sounds more like a gentlemen's club than a diner. Either way I'm starving after that play," Stefano said to me.

"Stefano Moretti!" a man shouted from the car in the next lane as the window rolled down.

"That's me," Stefano said.

"Avery Briggs sends his regards," the man said to Stefano in a stern tone as he pulled out a gun and fired.

"Get down!" Stefano said to me, as he pushed me down below the window while he managed to weave in between traffic to evade the unknown man who was shooting at him.

"Oh my god who is that?" I inquired in a distressed tone. "A rival of the Five Points Gang, hold on," Stefano replied in a stern tone.

"Drive to the speakeasy, we'll be safer there," I said to Stefano in a distressed tone.

"I know where to go toots, just shut up. Goddamnit I really wanted a burger at that diner," Stefano said in a stern tone as he drove down Minetta Street and peeled into the alley.

"My uncle was right, I always need to carry a gun with me even if I'm going to the bathroom," Stefano said to me in a distressed tone, as we exited the car, and banged at the front door of the speakeasy in a frantic manner.

"Look!" I shouted in dismay as I pointed to the man that was following us who was parked at the end of the back alley with its lights on and engine revving.

"Open the fucking door!" Stefano shouted, as the car began to speed down the alley straight towards us.

"What's the password!" a familiar voice inquired, as the car drew nearer to Stefano and me.

"Lucky Luciano," I said in a distressed tone. The front door then opened as Stefano and I dove into the speakeasy just narrowly dodging the unknown, rival mobster driver who was hellbent on killing us.

"For fuck sake! Jack, get in here now!" Samson shouted. "We were shot at," I said to Samson as I stood up and dusted off my dress which I noticed a rip form at the bottom. "What happened?" Jack inquired in a stern tone and wide-

eyed stare as he scampered up to Stefano and me who were still breathing heavily from our near death experience.

"Grill me a burger, Samson," Stefano said to Samson in a stern tone, as he snapped his fingers and pointed to the bar.

"Don't you snap your goddamn fingers at me lad. I don't fucking care who your uncle is," Samson said to Stefano in a stern tone, as Stefano walked past him in a flouting manner and then sat down at the bar.

"Samson, just make the kid some food. Maybe it will calm his nerves a bit," Jack said to Samson, as he placed his hand on his chest.

"Tell me what happened this time, kid. It appears that new look of yours has only gotten you into more trouble," Jack said to me as he stared out the iron window of the front door, and then sat down at the table with a sigh.

"I'm all in one piece, thanks for asking, Jack, and no my looks have nothing to do with Stefano and I being targeted. Before the man shot at us at the stop light, he said 'Avery Briggs sends his regards,'" I said to Jack.

"Goddamn it … has he really resorted to this," Jack said in a stern tone while shaking his head.

"Jack, do you know Avery Briggs?" I inquired.

"I know him all too well. He was the man you saw shoot me in the shoulder," Jack replied as he pointed to his shoulder, but don't tell Stefano I know him," Jack replied as he leaned in close to me and glanced at Stefano.

"That was Avery Briggs, but why are his associates trying to kill me?" I inquired in a distressed tone.

"Come on doll, I know you're smarter than that. I was the target, not you," Stefano said to me as he walked up to the table. "Of course he was the target. Killing the nephew of Mr. Luciano would no doubt send a severe message to the Five Points Gang.

"Wouldn't it make more sense for that rival gang to kidnap Stefano rather than kill him," I said as my eyes darted from Jack to Stefano in a nervous manner.

"Is something funny Jack?" Stefano inquired in a stern tone as Jack began to laugh as if I told a joke.

"No, not so much funny as in sad. This kids intellect is far greater than most of the mobsters that surround us, including your uncle," Jack replied as he pointed at me.

"Take that back" Stefano said in a stern tone, as he stood over Jack.

"Or what, kid. Do you really want to brawl with me?" Jack inquired with a grin as he stood up from the chair and stood face-to-face with Stefano.

"You're burger is ready!" Samson shouted from the bar. "You're lucky I'm starving," Stefano said to Jack in a stern tone and then walked over to the bar and starting eating his burger.

"I would stop seeing him, unless you want more nights of rival mobsters trying to kill you both," Jack said to me in a stern tone.

"I can take care of myself, Jack. Stefano made my dreams come true tonight by taking me to that Broadway play," I said to Jack.

"So that's the reason huh, take it from me, kid, your mother was attracted to Johnny for the same reason, don't follow in her footsteps," Jack said to me.

"Listen to me. Just because that boy is not legally an adult doesn't mean he's not dangerous. His uncle is breeding him to be a prominent member of the Five Points Gang. So you ask yourself this, do you really want to follow in the footsteps of your mother and get close to a potential mobster who could end up killing you in a fit of rage?" Jack inquired in a stern tone as he leaned in close to me.

"He's not ruthless like the others," I said to Jack.

"Oh so you think you can change him?" Jack inquired with a snicker as he shook his head.

"I don't know … I just see a heart underneath his brash exterior," I replied.

Whenever Jack tried to be a father figure to me it would always end with us shouting at each other. Stefano and I both had stern uncles who impose their will onto us. We have something in common in that regard.

"I'm going home," Stefano pronounced with a sigh, as he put on his jacket and fedora.

"Be careful. Do you want Jack or Samson to escort you back home?" I inquired in a distressed tone, as Stefano walked up to me and Jack at the table.

"No need. Besides, the last thing Jack and Samson want to do is give me a ride home," Stefano replied with a scoff.

"Are you sure? If you get plugged by some Harlem mobster it will be on my head. Then your uncle will silence me," Jack inquired.

"Well then you better pray I make it back to Chelsea in one piece then, Jack," Stefano said to Jack with a grin.

"I don't pray, kid. Good luck," Jack said to Stefano as he walked to the bar.

"I hope I can see you again. This night was almost perfect," Stefano said to me.

"I would like that very much. Don't go getting yourself killed out there," I said to Stefano with a smile.

Stefano then quickly leaned in and kissed me. A kiss I could feel he wanted to give me many times tonight but I kept rejecting all of his advances so I wouldn't miss a precious moment of A Midsummer Night's Dream. Unlike Mickey, Stefano's lips were passionate and strong which made my legs tremble slightly.

"Goodnight," Stefano said to me with a grin.

"G-Goodnight," I said to Stefano in a stammering tone and smile, as my face became flush with a heat which Stefano so effortlessly stoked from within me.

Stefano then looked back at me with a grin before exiting the speakeasy. I then noticed as I turned around that Samson and Jack were both staring at me with stern looks and their arms crossed, as if I committed a crime.

"What are you two staring at?" I inquired.

"I hope that kiss was worth it, kid," Jack said to me.

"It's none of your business," I said to Jack in a stern tone.

"That kid literally is my business and yours too. Don't roll your eyes at me," Jack said to me in a stern tone as I walked past him in a flouting manner and entered the kitchen.

I still felt like I was floating from Stefano's passionate kiss. He may be the privileged nephew of the most power mob boss of New York, but the way he makes me feel is indescribable even for my literary mind. Jack warns me to not follow in my mother's footsteps, as if I was oblivious to the danger I was in every time I was with Stefano, but that danger also made being with him more thrilling.

I then looked into the mirror as I slowly got undressed. I was now growing so used to the sight of my black wig, which I quickly tucked a strand of my red hair underneath the wig whenever I saw a strand peeking out. So I decided to leave my wig on as I put on my white bath robe before sitting down at my desk and opening my diary.

Dear Diary,
September 23rd, 11:35 PM,

My life is full of passion and excitement, and I attribute all of this to my new flapper girl look. If this is the true me then I'm sorry it took me this long to find her. You know better than anybody all the misery I have endured over the past six months. Now I feel as if I'm a flower that's suffered a long cold night to finally bloom to the dawn's first light. Could Stefano be the one who awakens the true me? Faye's words still echo in my mind about that Shakespeare quote. 'To thine own self be true' well I now feel more comfortable and less nervous and scared around men than I ever have before. I sometimes shudder to think of how my life would be if I didn't have you to talk to. Could I talk to Jack, Samson, or Stefano the same way I talk to you now? They all seem too brash and insensitive, even Mickey, but he rejected the new me, or should I say the true me. Right now I feel fulfilled in this moment as I write to you. Writing to you has always given me that sense of fulfillment where nothing and nobody else could compare. Is writing to you the true me, or perhaps

... is being a writer the true me?

"Please keep it down I'm trying to sleep," I said to Samson in a weary tone, as I sat down on my bed with a sigh.

"Oh aye princess, you won't hear a peep from us," Samson said to me in a sarcastic tone, as he took a bag of ice out of the freezer.

I could still feel Stefano's kiss linger on my lips as I began to doze off in bed. My future in this speakeasy was tumultuous, but now full of purpose, a purpose in life which I never thought I could ever find again, a purpose that made me look forward to waking up tomorrow morning.

*****

"Why are you putting your bonnet on, honey?" my mother inquired as she put on gold earrings in front of the mirror in her bedroom.

"I don't know, I'm just tired of always having to comb my hair," I replied.

"Or is it because I told you that Johnny prefers our hair covered in bonnets?" my mother inquired.

"Well … I don't want to upset Johnny, but it's just easier this way for me," I replied.

"Angel listen to me, your voice, your smile, your hair is what makes you special. Just look at all of those glamorous actresses you see in movies, none of them are covered up one bit," my mother said to me with a smile as she kneeled down in front of me.

"But Johnny said to me once that if I ever want to become an actress then I would have to start by doing anything a man tells me to do," I said to my mother.

"Don't ever share your dreams with that ape, darling. He comes from an old world of crime and privilege. I for one believe you would make a most beautiful actress," my mother said to me with a warm smile as she placed her hand on my cheek.

"What if I don't want to be an actress?" I inquired.

"Anything it may be, anything that makes you feel truly happy, that is what you must pursue in your life, my angel. My mother replied with a smile as she looked back into the mirror and continued to primp her hair.

"I know what I want to be," I said to my mother, as I took off my bonnet and shook my hair around with a smile.

*****

"Hayley …,"

"Hayley, did you hear me? I said take the drink order of the party at table 7," Samson said to me in a stern tone, as he pointed to the mobster couple who sat at table 7,

"On my way," I said to Samson, as I stared pensively at a strand of my red hair which I pulled out from underneath my black wig and wrapped around my finger.

It had been a week since my tumultuous date with Stefano. I wonder how his life is faring living with his mother in Chelsea. We never officially planned our second date, but my heart felt as if the time we spent apart was far longer than a week. Whenever I felt myself missing Stefano to the point where I couldn't bare it, I would write in my diary about him and I then felt some solace in the moment.

"May I take your order," I inquired with a smile, as I walked up to the mobster couple at table 7.

"What do you want?" the mobster inquired as he nudged his dame who was draped all over the mobster as if she was just another article of clothing for him.

"Uhm ... I'll have a Manhattan," the mobster's dame replied.

"That's my kind of girl. I'll have a pitcher of your finest lager and a double whiskey on the rocks," the mobster said to me.

"All right so ... uhm two whiskeys, one Manhattan, and a pitcher of lager," I said to the mobster as I read him and his dame's order from my notepad.

"No, no, goddamn it, can't you take a simple order, or am I going to have to talk to that lug head of an Irishman who appears to be the one in charge at this joint?" the mobster inquired in a stern tone as he pointed to Samson at the bar.

"I'm sorry sir, could you just clarify your order for me one more time, I said to the mobster in a timid tone.

"Wow why on earth does Mr. Luciano have such feeble- minded kids working at this joint, he must've lost his goddamn mind," the mobster remarked in a stern tone, as his dame giggled into his neck.

"You can insult Samson all you want, but when you start insulting this doll and my uncle, well that's when I get mad," a familiar voice said in a stern tone.

"Stefano I didn't see you come in," I said with a wide-eyed stare and smile, as Stefano walked up to the mobster at the table with as stern look on his face.

"I slipped in when you were sitting at the bar, I wanted to surprise you," Stefano said to me with a grin.

"Oh uhm s-sorry Mr. Moretti, but she's a lousy waitress you must admit," the mobster said to Stefano in a stammering tone.

"Come here ... now what kind of waitress is she, and what kind of man is my uncle?" Stefano inquired in a stern tone after swiftly smacking the mobster in the face.

"She's a great waitress sir, and your uncle is the wisest and most powerful man in New York. Please forgive me," the mobster said to Stefano in a pleading manner as if his life hung in the balance of Stefano's forgiveness.

"That's more like it. Now it would be in your best interest to apologize to her now," Stefano said to the mobster in a stern tone who was now practically squirming in his seat along with his dame.

"I-I'm sorry for treating you that way miss, I was out of line," the mobster said to me in a stammering tone.

"You're forgiven," I said to the mobster, as I glanced at Stefano with a smile.

"Thank you. How have you been this past week?" I inquired after I quickly kissed Stefano on his cheek.

"Ah my uncle has been showing me the ins and outs of his business. I'm turning 18 in three days so he wants to make sure I'm ready to work for him," Stefano replied as we sat down at the bar.

"Oh we should celebrate your birthday," I said to Stefano with a smile.

"Why not tonight, my uncle and ma just want family to be there when I celebrate my birthday," Stefano said to me.

"Do you have anything in mind?" I inquired with a grin as I leaned in close to Stefano.

"I know just the place where we could go tonight. You just keep looking beautiful and I'll pick you up around 8," Stefano replied with a grin.

"I can't wait," I said to Stefano with a smile. I then noticed Mickey enter the speakeasy as he glanced back at me with somber eyes.

I didn't know Mickey was still working here. Jack must still need his help around the speakeasy. Things will be very uncomfortable between Mickey and me henceforth, but I wouldn't let that stop me from having a good time with Stefano. Mickey rejected me when I needed his support, he tried to keep the image of me which he loved, but that very image wasn't the image I wanted for myself any longer.

I then quickly kissed Stefano at that moment Mickey glanced at me. I wanted him to see that I wasn't a miserable little girl who was crying over him, for that was the old Hayley. "That was nice, who are you looking at?" Stefano inquired, as Mickey entered the kitchen.

"Nobody important," I replied. "Carmen you're on!" Samson shouted.

"Burlesque in the afternoon, that seems unnatural," I remarked as I rolled my eyes at the sight of Carmen disrobing as all the mobsters began to hoot and holler like monkeys at a zoo at the sight of Carmen's exposed body.

"That dame is one of the best things to happen to this speakeasy, well second best to my uncle of course, he turned this rat hole into a thriving and sophisticated joint where the most prominent men of New York can come to soothe their pain," Stefano said to me, as he gazed at Carmen who began to dance slowly with two black-feather clad fans covering the most desired areas of her body.

It seemed that all men, no matter what age were attracted to Carmen and Stefano was no different. She had such a lustful allure that instantly made all the men around her swoon like a pack of wolves staring at a virile deer. I wonder how she deals with all of these mobsters. I for one wouldn't have the heart to do anything that bold especially in front of an audience of men who could very well kill me if I so much as looked at one of them in a disrespectful manner.

"Well I would love to stay her and watch Carmen all day but I have matters I must attend to. My ma is sick and she only trusts me to take care of her," Stefano said to me.

"Oh I'm sorry. I hope she gets better," I said to Stefano in a somber tone.

"She'll be fine, the doc who visited our apartment diagnosed her with the common cold and gave her a bottle of antihistamines, whatever those are," Stefano said to me.

"Those are drugs that help treat many illnesses," I said to Stefano.

"You're so smart, I like that. You should really be a teacher, doll," Stefano said to me with a grin as he stood up from the bar and put on his fedora.

"Do you really think so?" I inquired with a grin, as the mobsters became louder at the sight of Carmen pulling off her red sequin skirt.

"Absolutely, If you were my teacher I may not have dropped out of school when I was twelve," Stefano replied with a snicker.

"I can still teach you a thing or two," I said to Stefano with a grin. I then noticed Mickey exit the kitchen with an envelope in his hand. He then exited the speakeasy without so much as even glancing at me this time.

"Well … I'll see you tonight," Stefano said to me with a grin and then exited the speakeasy.

"I didn't know Mickey still worked here," I said to Samson.

"Aye, that boy needs work and Jack wouldn't reject him after all the loyal services he's provided for us," Samson said to me.

"Why not he rejected me," I said to Samson as I pulled out a strand of my red hair and wrapped it around my finger.

"Ah now I see, just because you and Mickey were close, you no longer want him to work here just to avoid all the uncomfortable moments," Samson said to me with a snicker.

"Why was he here anyway?" I inquired.

"He was here to collect his paycheck, or does he need your permission for that," Samson replied, as he wiped down the bar. "No he doesn't, and I'm not still hurt over him, so don't even assume that," I said to Samson in a stern tone.

"Oh aye, then tell me this, why have you only been talking about Mickey right after that suave lad Stefano just paid you a visit?" Samson inquired with a snicker, but I didn't reply to Samson, as I entered the kitchen in a stern manner.

'You're not the Hayley I used to love … goodbye.' Those were the last words Mickey said to me before we stopped seeing each other. If this was true, then is the new me even worthy of being loved? I thought to myself as I held the necklace Mickey gave me in my hands while staring into the mirror at the new me.

*****

It was 8:27 PM in the speakeasy as I got myself ready for my date with Mickey.

I'm glad he was running late, because I still wasn't used to putting on my black wig and all this makeup. At times it felt unnatural to me, as if I was another actress performing on stage like those talented actresses in A Midsummer Night's Dream did so wonderfully. The confidence I used to feel from this entire flapper girl look was now beginning to fade, but I couldn't go back to the old Hayley.

"Stefano is here," Jack said to me as he grabbed a bag of ice from the freezer.

"Oh uhm all right, tell him I'll be right out in five minutes," I said to Jack and then frantically applied rouge and lipstick in the mirror.

"Go easy on the makeup kid," Jack said to me. "I have to look my best," I said to Jack.

"Let me tell you something, kid. I've seen Faye with no makeup on and she looks just as fine, and furthermore, I'm sure she feels more natural without all of that makeup on her face," Jack said to me.

"All I care about is what Stefano thinks, not you," I said to Jack in a stern tone as I applied mascara to my eyes.

"That kid is being bred to be the new leader of the Five Points Gang if and when his uncle gets silenced. So I don't need to warn you what you're getting yourself into," Jack said to me. "I know he told me all about it. He also told me that his uncle isn't the true leader of the Five Points Gang," I said to Jack.

"Woah hold on one minute, kid. You mean to tell me that Mr. Luciano isn't at the top of the Five Points Gang?" Jack inquired in an incredulous tone.

"No he isn't, he answers to a man who Stefano told me is the true founder of the Five Points Gang," I replied as I grabbed my purse and primped my black hair one last time.

"What's his name, this founder of the Five Points Gang who I have yet to meet?" Jack inquired.

"I have to go now. I can't keep Stefano waiting," I replied and then exited the kitchen.

"Stefano!" I shouted, as I waved at Stefano who was talking up Carmen on the stage.

"Hayley!" Stefano shouted with a smile as he jumped off the stage and scampered towards me in the manner of a soldier returning from the war to embrace the woman he loves.

"You look perfect," Stefano remarked, as he stared at me from head to toe.

"Thank you. You don't look too bad yourself," I said to Stefano with a giggle.

"I wanted to look my best for you so I wore my favorite suit. We are going to be the talk of the club tonight, doll," Stefano said to me with a grin.

"Oh we're going to a club," I inquired.

"Not just any club toots, The Stork Club on East 51st Street," Stefano replied as we exited the speakeasy. "I've never heard of that club," I said to Stefano.

"I wouldn't expect you would. That club entertains celebrities," Stefano said to me.

"Oh wow, are you sure they will let us in?" I inquired as I entered Stefano's Plymouth.

"I'm positive we will be allowed in that club. My uncle knows the owner. His name is Sherman Billingsley and he used to be a former bootlegger. Now he runs the Stork Club which caters to the most elite people of the world," Stefano replied, as we drove north through *Gramercy Park* to East 51st Street.

Never in my life would I imagine that I would be going to such a place. Stefano had connections in this city all thanks to his uncle, but a small part of me also worried for him, for Stefano would now become a target for rival gangs, just like the danger we ran into after we saw A Midsummer Night's Dream. Would we also run into more danger at this glamorous club?

"Will we be safe at this club?" I inquired.

"Don't you worry your pretty head over our safety, doll. My friend here will see that no rival mobster will get the jump on us tonight. My uncle also sent two of his associates to the club to watch over us," Stefano replied as he pulled out his hand gun with a grin.

Whenever I saw a handgun my heart would begin to race. No matter what the circumstance was, I always expected death when I saw a gun.

"I hope it doesn't come to that. Judging by how you described this club, it sounds more formal and upscale than the typical speakeasy," I said to Stefano.

"Oh it's a world's difference from that speakeasy you live in. Don't be surprised if you see Cary Grant with his arm candy of the week at this club tonight," Stefano said to me with a snicker.

"It all sounds so glamorous. So how is your mother doing?"

I inquired

"Oh she's cleared the hump. She's doing well enough now to the point where she's strong enough to discipline me when I speak out of tone to her," Stefano replied with a scoff.

"I'm glad to hear she's feeling better. You should listen to her more than your uncle," I said to Stefano. "Why do you say that?" Stefano inquired.

"Just take it from me, don't ever take your relationship with your mother for granted," I replied.

"She wants to meet you. She says that your reputation precedes you, whatever that means," Stefano said to me.

"Oh that's so flattering of her to that about me, but I don't have much of a reputation," I said to Stefano.

"To my ma you do. She calls you a spitfire of a girl," Stefano said to me with a snicker.

"Oh really? What does your uncle say about me?" I inquired.

"My uncle told me to be careful around you. He said you're not a typical orphan," Stefano replied.

"Oh that's all he sees me as, an orphan," I said to Stefano in a stern tone.

"It's nothing personal, my uncle sees everyone except for Paul Kelly as inferior to him and his social standings," Stefano said to me.

"He's the founder of the Five Points Gang right?" I inquired. "Yes but not for long," Stefano replied in a stern tone as he parked the car on the street outside of which I could only presume was the entrance of the Stork Club.

"What do you mean by that?" I inquired. "We're here," Stefano said to me.

Stefano's words always had such sinister undertones, but I felt that he didn't fully want to confide in me over such matters that involved the power hierarchy of the Five Points Gang. Did Stefano also see me as 'not a typical orphan' just like his uncle does, or am I more special to him than that.

"Your hair, why is it red?" Stefano inquired as he pointed at the strand of red hair I had wrapped around my finger.

"Oh uhm that's just this one strand," I said to Stefano as I brushed the strand of my red hair behind my ear.

"That's odd. You could always cut off that strand so it doesn't clash with that pretty black hair of yours," Stefano said to me as we walked towards the entrance of the building I presumed was the Stork Club which there was already a line of finely dressed people waiting outside.

"I don't think we'll be able to cut to the front of the line with these people like we did for that Broadway play," Stefano said to me as we waited in line outside the entrance of the Stork Club.

"That's all right, I'm in no hurry," I said to Stefano with a smile as I took his hand.

Stefano wasn't a very easy going man, and especially now that rival gang members were trying to silence him. I tried my best to calm him down whenever I sensed he was losing his nerve, because I know all too well how scary of a feeling that can be.

"Finally," Stefano remarked with a scoff as we stepped up to the entrance of the Stork Club.

"Woah no kids allowed in the Stork Club. This establishment caters to the most prominent people in the world so run along now," a smug man in a tuxedo pronounced in a stern tone and dismissive wave as he stood in front of the scarlet velvet rope which separated us from entering.

"I'll have you know my uncle is Charles Luciano who's friends with Mr. Billingsley, and he told me I would be granted entry with my girlfriend tonight to celebrate my birthday," Stefano said to the smug man in a stern tone who continued to stare at us as if we were just street urchins. The smug man then whispered to another smug man dressed in a tuxedo who then scampered into the club.

"We will sort this all out, for now step aside," the smug man said to Stefano as he gestured for us to move to the side. A couple then entered the Stork Club who appeared as if they were leading actors, but I didn't recognize them. The other smug man who ran into the Stork Club then returned and whispered into the other smug man's ear as he stared at us with a furrowed brow.

"You have my apologies sir and madam. You two will be treated to all the finest luxuries the Stork Club has to offer, right this way," the smug man said to Stefano as he lifted the scarlet velvet rope.

"That's more like it," Stefano said to the smug man in a stern tone and scoff as we entered the Stork Club.

"Oh my, this must be what heaven is like," I remarked with a smile and wide-eyed stare as Stefano and I stood for a moment at the entrance to the main Ballroom and took in the luxury. Even though Stefano did come from a privileged family, I could tell by the sense of awe in his eyes that even he was overwhelmed by the sheer luxury of the Stork Club.

I felt more out of place in this club than I ever have anywhere in my entire life, but yet somehow I was granted entry into such a luxurious establishment.

"Don't worry doll, just stick with me and we will have one hell of a night," Stefano said to me with a grin.

"Who says I'm worried?" I inquired with a scoff as Stefano and I walked throughout the Ballroom looking for a table or booth that was empty.

"Over there," Stefano said to me as he pointed to a booth at the far side of the Ballroom as the band began to play a melody which made me feel as if I was a background actress in a Katharine Hepburn movie. The emerald velvet booth and dining chairs paired with the gold drapes and carpet were breathtaking to say the least. Everyone in the Stork Club appeared happy with not a care in the world, which was a stark comparison to the speakeasy.

"You mind if we sit down?" Stefano inquired to a couple sitting at one end of the crescent booth.

"Uhm who let you in here son," the man inquired with a snicker and then took a puff from his cigar.

"I let myself in here," Stefano replied in a stern tone as we sat down in the booth.

"I'm Hayley and this is Stefano. He's celebrating his birthday here tonight," I pronounced, as the couple stared at us in such a condescending manner as if we were dogs trying to speak English.

"We'll have whatever entrées the chef recommends, along with a bottle of your finest Champagne and a double Brandy on the rocks," Stefano said to the waiter.

"I wanted to order for myself. You didn't even let me look at the menu," I said to Stefano.

"It's all right toots. I know what's best for you," Stefano said to me with a grin as he laid his arm over my shoulders and pulled me in close to him.

"You know you have to pay for all of that, don't you son?"

the man sitting in our booth said to Stefano with a grin. "Perhaps you didn't hear my doll. This is my birthday celebration. Nobody pays for anything on their birthday," Stefano said to the man in a stern tone.

"Stop calling me your doll when we're in public. I have a name," I whispered to Stefano with a stern look, as he then shushed me with a dismissive wave.

"I'm sorry I didn't get your names," I said to the couple sitting in our booth with a smile.

"Well I'm Pat DiCicco and this is my wife," the suave looking man with the slick black hair and three piece suite said to me with a grin as he dismissively but playfully gestured to the woman sitting beside him.

"I'm Thelma Todd. Forgive my husband he can be a bit of a philistine on occasion," the beautiful blonde woman wearing a shear gold dress who I could only assume was an actress remarked with a playful shove to her husband.

"Excuse me, I got you work didn't I," Pat inquired with a grin and scoff and then took a puff from his cigar.

"You most certainly did my dear, but it wasn't one-hundred percent attributed to you. My last audition was my best performance yet," Thelma said to Pat with a smile.

"You two make a nice couple," I remarked with a smile.

"I'm going to go mingle before they serve us our food and drinks," Stefano said to me, and then stood up from the booth and walked towards the center of the ballroom and quickly vanished amidst the sea of celebrities.

Stefano was acting very cold and distant towards me ever since I told him not to call me his doll in public, but I stand   by my actions and refuse to be treated like a man's property. I could tell that unlike the speakeasy, the Stork Club was filled with renowned women who respected their husbands but didn't feel beholden to them.

"Here you are madam, one bottle of Rose Dom Perignon and one double brandy on the rocks. For your entrées Fillet Mignon with a balsamic reduction with sautéed spinach and garlic roasted white truffle potatoes," the waiter said to me, as him and another waiter served me the most exquisite meal I had ever laid eyes on.

"Do you want some of our champagne?" I inquired with a smile as I handed Thelma the bottle of Dom Perignon.

"What do you think you're doing? I'm not sharing with the likes of them, not after how they treated me," Stefano said in a stern tone as he snatched the bottle of champagne out of my hand before Thelma could grab it.

"What happened, why are you mad?" I inquired, as Stefano popped the bottle of champagne in an aggressive manner and quickly poured him and myself a glass before cutting into the Fillet Mignon.

"So tell me, who may I ask is paying for this lavish meal you two kids are devouring" Pat inquired with a snicker.

"My uncle, you may have heard of him. His name is Mr. Charles Luciano and he has the true power in this city while you showbiz celebrities dance around for pennies," Stefano replied with a scoff and then took a sip of brandy.

"Don't be rude," I said to Stefano with a gasp, as I tried to keep a refined etiquette while eating the lavish meal that was in front of us.

"Charles Luciano ... can't say that I've heard of that man. Is he in showbiz?" Pat inquired, as I then stared at Stefano with wide eyes and shook my head, urging him not to tell the showbiz couple sitting across from us that his uncle is a powerful mob boss for a criminal organization that has deep roots all throughout New York City. I then remembered that the Five Points Gang have most if not all of the NYPD in their pockets, so there would most likely be no consequences for Stefano bragging about his uncles criminal influence over New York.

"He's the boss of the Five Points Gang. He's the reason you're drinking that cocktail right now," Stefano said with a grin as he continued to eat his lavish meal in the unrefined manner of a prison inmate.

"You don't say. Well, well, Thelma, that's why this boy is so devil may care, his uncle is a multi-millionaire," Pat remarked with a snicker.

"So you have heard of him," Stefano said to me.

"Slow down," I said to Stefano as he already finished his double branded with a gulp.

"Shut up, don't tell me how much to drink," Stefano said to me in a stern tone and stare as he poured himself another glass of champagne.

"No, but I am fully aware of that bootlegging organization which provides a great majority of the alcohol to New York," Pat replied.

"All right ladies and gentleman. I implore you all to now take to the dance floor for the jazz melodies of the divine Calypso 7," a man dressed in a tuxedo pronounced, as I stared into the mirror which boarded the perimeter of the club.

"Let's go babe," Stefano said to me, after he finished another glass of champagne with a gulp.

"No I'm uhm, I just need to rest for one moment," I said to Stefano as I wrapped my red hair around my finger.

"What is with you tonight? First you take the side of that pompous showbiz couple sitting at our booth and now you don't want to dance with me. You're ruining my birthday celebration toots," Stefano said to me in a stern tone.

"Don't order me around. I don't feel like dancing," I said to Stefano in a stern tone.

"I didn't ruin the time you spent watching that stupid play on Broadway, so do me this favor and dance with me," Stefano said to me in a stern tone, as he grabbed my hand.

"Don't pull on me like I'm a toy, and you most certainly did try to ruin that beautiful experience for me during A Midsummer Night's Dream," I said to Stefano in a stern tone as I pulled my hand out of his grasp.

"Fine, you just sit here while I hob knob with these actresses, all of which are more fun than you right now," Stefano said to me with a scoff and then walked towards the dance floor, as I finished my second glass of champagne.

"Excuse me, where's the ladies room," I inquired, as a waiter walked towards the booth where I now sat alone.

"It's just to the left of the main bar," the waiter replied as he pointed to the bar where a group of men dressed in tuxedos were gathered around a woman dressed in a pink dress, like a group of snarling boars gathered around a flamingo.

Even the ladies room of the Stork Club appeared to be more luxurious than most people's apartments in New York City. I felt that I was beginning to see the real Stefano tonight as his insecurities were only fueled by the amount of alcohol he was drinking. I felt nervous around him now, but not nervous in a passionate way, nervous in a fearful way, nervous in the way that Fernando and Johnny would always make me feel.

I then began to cry as I stared into the gilded mirror of the ladies room, while a couple of beautiful actresses entered while giggle among each other. So I then entered the stall for more privacy, as I wiped the trail of mascara which ran down my left cheek. I always wondered what this luxurious life would feel like, and now I see it's not what I imagined it to be. I didn't belong with all of these celebrities. It's obvious Stefano invited me with him tonight just to hang on his arm like those mobster's dames do at the speakeasy, but that's not who I am, and this flapper girl look which I have adopted over the past three weeks no longer empowered me as a young woman.

"Oh I'm sorry," I said as I bumped into a woman in a sparkly, emerald leotard who was carrying a large tray which was strapped over her shoulders.

"You're fine honey. Let's not go crying over spilt milk," the woman said to me, as I helped her pick up cigarettes, candy and small bottles of liquor which fell out of her tray.

"No it's just I'm—,"

"Not having a good time here, join the club," the woman interjected with a grin and sigh as I sat down in my booth.

"How did you know?" I inquired in a somber tone.

"It's written all over your face, honey, oh and I see your beautiful red hair underneath that black wig by the way," the woman said to me with a grin.

"Oh uhm, nobody is supposed to see that," I said as I tucked the strand of red hair underneath the black wig.

"Why not? Take it from me, honey, you'll get far in this town playing a ditz, but you'll get even farther playing yourself," the woman said to me with a smile.

"You really think so?" I inquired in a somber tone. "Absolutely, here, it's on me," the woman said to me with a smile, as she gave me a couple of candy bars.

"Thank you. I'm Hayley, Hayley Carmona," I said to the woman with a smile.

"Pleased to make your acquaintance Hayley, I'm Lucille Ball, but my friends call me Lucy, well, the few ones I have left that is," the woman said to me with a smile as she shook my hand.

"All right I coming, keep your skirt on Carnegie!" Lucy shouted and then walked away towards the main bar.

"I'm back," Stefano said to me with a grin and then sat down in our booth.

"I met the nicest woman who gave me free candy," I said to Stefano as I showed him the candy I received from Lucy.

"What was her name?" Stefano inquired. "Lucille Ball," I replied.

"Hmmm I never heard of her, she must be a nobody. You know my uncle always said that dames who—,"

"'My uncle said this, my uncle said that.' that's all I ever hear from you. Why don't you speak for yourself for once," I interjected in a stern tone.

"All right, do you want to know what I think?" Stefano inquired in a stern tone.

"Yes I do," I replied with nod.

"I think that my uncle was right about you. You're not the typical orphan. You act just like your ungrateful uncle," Stefano replied in a stern tone.

"I'm not ungrateful, but I'm also not an accessory for men like you to use to build up your ego one moment and then abuse the next moment. Your uncle is right. I'm not your typical orphan, and I'm not a flapper girl either. I'm Hayley Carmona, a writer, who is so much more than you could ever understand," I said to Stefano in a stern tone as I stood up from the booth, pulled off my black wig, and then threw it at him.

"Goddamn, so your hair is red after all, what a shame. Well you had me fooled toots, are you done with your little outburst now?" Stefano inquired while shaking his head as I fluffed out my hair in a majestic manner.

"I am done, with you," I replied in a stern tone.

"Go crawl back to that speakeasy toots. I'll be running it in due time, and my first order of business will be to send you and your uncle out on the streets where your kind belongs!" Stefano shouted as I walked towards the elevator of the Stork Club with a grin.

CHAPTER 13:
THE BOLD IRISHMAN
- JACK -

It was 11:24 PM in the speakeasy as I served Marty Brennan one last shot of bourbon. Marty was a mobster, but he didn't talk to me in the manner of the typical mobster. Marty had a wife and son, so he was in some sense of the word a family man, but a family man who was always down on his luck, which goes to show you that the Five Points Gang let their fellow members fall by the wayside, while kids like Stefano are being bred to run this crime organization. I hope Hayley doesn't swoon too hard over that boy. I see a fear in his eyes which could make him very dangerous, a fear that if his uncle continues to fuel will burn inside of him and turn the boy into a killer, or perhaps, that's just what Mr. Luciano wants.

"You've had enough. Go home and sleep off your stupor," I said to Marty as his head hung low after one too many shots of bourbon.

"You're right. I know I've had one too many when even you are starting to look good to me," Marty said to me with a laugh, and then staggered towards the entrance of the speakeasy.

"Get out of here, and give Beth and Lincoln my regards," I said to Marty with a grin as I smacked him with a rag in a playful manner.

"I'll be right there!" I shouted, as a knock on the front door alerted me to another potential mobster looking to blow off more steam on this slow and quiet night.

"What's the password?" I inquired as I slid open the iron window on the front door.

"Jack it's me," a familiar voice replied.

"Hayley … goodnight Marty," I said to Marty as I opened the front door of the speakeasy.

"I'm so tired," Hayley said to me as she entered the speakeasy and sat down at the bar with a sigh.

"So I heard you were at the Stork Club," I said to Hayley, as I walked behind the bar.

"Who told you?" Hayley inquired.

"Mr. Luciano. He was in here a few hours ago talking about how much

Stefano drools over you," I replied with a snicker.

"Well he can drool over somebody else, because I never want to see his smug face ever again," Hayley said to me in a stern tone

"So I take it things didn't go well in paradise. So tell me, how was it being in the most renowned nightclub in the world?" I inquired with a grin as I leaned in close to Hayley.

"The food, drinks, and decor were all exquisite, but Stefano was horrid, along with most of the people in that club. So I wouldn't call it paradise," Hayley replied in a somber tone.

"Where's your black wig," I inquired, as Hayley stroked her red hair which I must admit was a sight for sore eyes.

"I'm done with that whole look. It started feeling like I was imprisoning my true self in the body of some other woman. Oh damn it, I threw it at Stefano before I left the Stork Club. Do you think Faye will be mad?" Hayley inquired with a wide- eyed stare.

"Faye probably has several wigs, so I wouldn't worry about it," I replied.

"How have you been?" Hayley inquired with a warm smile as she placed her hand on mine.

"Well my shoulder still burns like hell, but Mr. Luciano is none the wiser," I replied.

"I missed you while I was at that club," Hayley said to me. "Stop lying kid. You were dining with the most elite celebrities in the world at that club," I said to Hayley with a scoff, as I wiped down the bar.

"I mean it. That whole world isn't for me, but I'm glad I got to experience it," Hayley said to me. "How did Stefano react?" I inquired.

"He threatened you and me. He said he was going to be running this speakeasy very soon and his first order will be to fire us both," Hayley replied with an eye roll.

"That boy has delusions of grandeur, but if Mr. Luciano does make that decision, then we should be prepared," I said to Hayley while shaking my head.

"He's spiteful. I regret ever going out with him," Hayley said to me, as she stood up from the bar with a sigh.

"I'm proud of you kid," I said to Hayley.

"Why?" Hayley inquired with a smile as she brushed a strand of hair away from her face.

"You learned from your mother's mistake," I replied.

"She is my greatest teacher, along with you, Faye, and Samson. Goodnight," Hayley said to me with a smile. "Goodnight. I'll be closing up in fifteen minutes," I said to Hayley with a smile.

I must admit I was worried at first that Hayley would follow in her mother's footsteps when it came to getting involved with mobsters, but it's clear to me now that she's far wiser than her mother ever was at such a young age. Still there is the issue of that boy Stefano. I don't know what the consequences will be from Hayley ending her fling with Stefano, but I must be prepared for anything.

I then locked the front door and turned off the lights of the speakeasy before entering the kitchen. Hayley was writing in her diary at her desk which surprised me at first, but I soon came to realize that whenever she went through hell you would always find her pouring her heart out into the pages of that diary. It was her way of coping with everything. My way was the bottle and music, a way which has comforted me for as long as I can remember.

*****

It was 7:45 AM in the speakeasy when I awoke to the sight of Samson riffling through the fridge like a homeless man searching through a dumpster.

"Ah you're here early," I said to Samson with a groan as I sat upright in bed and took a swig of water.

"Aye, the heat in my apartment stopped working and I couldn't stop shivering," Samson said to me.

"Did you tell your landlord?" I inquired as I stood out of bed and stared into the mirror, a sight that's continued to worsen over the past couple of years, but I've never been one to try to reverse the effects of time, I merely hold on for dear life hoping that I will make it to the end of this ride called life in one piece. "I told that bastard yesterday and do you know what that lazy hole said to me?" Samson inquired.

"Let me guess, he said something that would normally get your blood boiling to the point where he would no longer be standing upright," I said to Samson as I got dressed.

"He told me 'You Irish are used to the cold so deal with it for now. I have many other problems in this building,'" Samson said to me in a stern tone.

"Many other problems, what is more important than heat? I swear you find me a decent landlord in this town and I'll find you the holy grail," I said to Samson with a scoff, as I adjusted my bowtie and vest before exiting the kitchen.

"It's a shame isn't it? How I left one depression in Belfast just to arrive in another depression here in America," Samson said to me.

"Yes but that's not why you fled to America," I said to Samson.

"There are many Irish mobsters in this town who hold their allegiance to Mr. Luciano. Not a day goes by where I don't feel the pressure to be another one of his hired guns," Samson said to me.

"Mr. Luciano may be a boss of the Five Points Gang, but he's not the founder. Hayley told me that Stefano said that an Italian man by the name of Paul Kelly is the founder of the Five Points Gang," I said to Samson.

"Paul Kelly huh, well let's hope he never pays us a visit," Samson said to me.

"Why do you say that?" I inquired, as a knock on the front door pounding into my head.

"Just look what happened when Mr. Luciano paid us a visit. This is how gangs work Jack. If you're visited by the top brass of one of these gangs then it usually means you're about to meet your maker," Samson said to me.

"We're still alive and kicking Samson. So that theory of yours is wrong," I said to Samson, as I slid open the iron window of the front door.

"Lucky Luciano," a mobster said to me in a stern tone, as I then opened the front door to the sight of a wall of a man standing beside another man who stood as tall as Hayley.

They were an odd looking couple of mobsters who I've never seen in this speakeasy before, but they seemed too focused on each other to pay me any mind as they sat down at a table in front of the stage.

"Samson, take their orders," I said to Samson in a stern tone as I walked behind the bar.

"I've never seen them before," Samson said to me.

"Me neither, so keep your guard up," I said to Samson, as I patted him on the back.

"Of course Jack. My guard never drops from the moment I enter this establishment," Samson said to me, as he patted me on the back and then walked over to the table where the tall and short mobsters were seated to take their orders.

"Oh there you are. I didn't notice you," I said to Hayley, as I walked up to the corner table where she was seated writing in her leather book in such a studious manner.

"I suppose I have that affect now that I no longer look like Faye," Hayley said to me with a grin as she brushed a strand of her hair behind her ear and then took a sip of coffee.

"What do you mean?" I inquired as I sat down across from her at the table with a sigh.

"Being invisible," Hayley replied.

"Trust me kid, you're far from invisible. You may be the boldest fifteen year old girl I've ever known," I remarked with a snicker as I lit a cigarette and took a smoke, while Hayley continued to write in here leather book with a grin.

"Thank you, Jack. A girl like me must be bold in a city like this if she ever hopes to survive," Hayley said to me.

"I'm glad to see the real Hayley's back. Always be yourself kid. Your mother wouldn't want you to be anyone else," I said to Hayley with a grin as I stood up from the table and walked over to the bar where Samson was preparing the drink orders for the tall and short mobsters.

"What's the matter, Samson? You look like you've seen a ghost," I inquired.

"That tall mobster, he called me a name … a name I haven't gone by in over six years," Samson replied, as he stared intently at the tall mobster.

"What did he call you? Some racial slur I assume?" I inquired, as I stared at the tall mobster who was engaged in a stern conversation with the short mobster, a conversation that could very well lead to someone being silenced.

"No no, it was nothing like that. It was a name from my past," Samson replied.

"Oh now you have to tell me, or else I'll never drop the subject," I said to Samson with a snicker.

"Very well, Jack. If it will shut your mouth then so be it. The tall mobster called me 'Samson the Bold,'" Samson said to me.

"Ah so what, I mean you are bold, but not as bold as you were when I first met you," I remarked.

"You don't understand Jack. This was my nickname back in Belfast when I was working for Macready's gang," Samson said to me.

"Oh, so the sorted plot of Samson thickens," I said to Samson.

"If they know my past name, then do they also know Marcus Macready? If that ruthless bastard still draws breathe, then I can only assume he still wants me silenced after all these years," Samson said to me.

"Take it from me Samson. When you're dealing with a mad Irishman like Johnny O'Conner or your former mob boss, it's best to get to the root of the issue," I said to Samson.

"You want me to further investigate, don't you? Just like you did with that stammering bald fellow," Samson inquired.

"Better to die by my own terms than by someone else's design. What I did with Chip was merely greeting my fate instead of delaying it. I saw through his act, but I welcomed Johnny because I was tired of running from him. It seems that you must now do the same," I said to Samson.

"Our pasts are nothing alike Jack. I've told you this before," Samson said to me in a stern tone as he shook his head.

"Our pasts may be different, but they seem to be taking the same road right now. I said to Samson.

"Aye, but I swore to never be that man again. I buried him along with my soul when I killed those two men in Belfast," Samson said to me as he placed the drinks on a tray and walked over to the table where the tall and short mobsters were seated. Samson was a brute ever since the first day I met him, but a brute that feared his own rage. When I killed Johnny I immediately felt a sense of freedom wash over me as I watched the black Hudson wash over him. Perhaps I should be called 'Jack the Bold.' I am half Irish on my father's side after all. I have no idea who the tall and short mobsters are, and how they know about Samson's past, but something tells me by the worried tone in Samson's voice and the sinister sneer's on the tall and short mobster's faces that the story of my associate Samson is about to reach its climax.

"I asked them their names and the short mobster told me 'our names are of no concern to you now mi amico,'" Samson whispered to me.

"Goddamn it … why must mobsters always play head games?" I inquired.

"It keeps them alive. Honesty will send you on a one way trip to your maker when you're a mobster," Samson replied. "Mickey's here," Samson remarked, as Mickey entered the speakeasy, and scampered up to the bar.

"Let's take a drive Samson," I said to Samson, as Mickey quickly got dressed in his black vest and bowtie.

"We can't leave the kids alone," Samson said to me. "They'll be fine. Mickey and Hayley have been through it all in the past couple of months, besides I need some fresh air," I said to Samson.

"All right, where to Jack?" Samson inquired, as he put on his leather jacket.

"Let's go to your place. I haven't seen that rat hole in quite some time," I replied with a grin as I put on my trench coat.

"This is New York, Jack. The whole city is a rat hole," Samson said to me with a scoff, as I tucked my pistol between the waist-band of my pants.

"Hayley, Mickey, Samson and I are stepping out, so look out for each other and don't do anything stupid. We'll be back in a few hours," I pronounced, as Hayley and Mickey stared at me with wide-eyes as Samson and I exited the speakeasy.

*****

It was 10:09 AM as Samson and I drove to his apartment in *SoHo*.

"Where did it all go wrong for this country? When I first arrived here from Belfast I was a bright-eyed lad who was filled with all the opportunities I read that America has to offer people like me. Then the swift reality of the matter hit me like a swift right hook to the gut," Samson said to me.

"Speaking of right hooks, do you remember when we first crossed paths?" I inquired as I drove down Greene Street.

"Aye I was wound tighter than an Englishman's watch back then," Samson replied with a grin.

Samson was incredibly bold when I first met him, but do I prefer the more calm and calculated Samson who sits beside me, or would the bold Samson from five years ago prove more helpful to me now during these trying times?

*****

It was 5:47 PM as I walked back to my car after visiting mom in *SoHo*.

I hope mom and Dezerae have a change of heart, because I sure as hell am not going to change my mind on this. I didn't expect them to support my decision of continuing to sell liquor after the alcohol outlaw was passed, but maybe in time they will realize that I'm not doing this just for me.

"Then pay up now Monaghan, or do we have to send your limey ass back to England?" one man inquired in a stern tone as he and another man stood in front of a man sitting on the curb smoking a corn-cob pipe.

"What did you just call me," the man seated on the curb inquired in a stern tone as his eyes widened with rage as if the other man cursed his mother's name.

I didn't want to get drawn into this fight, so I kept my head down as I walked towards the three men who now stood face to face with each other.

"You heard me, now where's are money you fucking—,"

"No man uses that English slur to describe the likes of me you son of a bitch. I be from Belfast Ireland!" the man smoking the corn-cob pipe shouted as he swiftly punched one of the men, knocking him down to the pavement before he could finish his sentence.

"You there, help us take this bastard down and we'll pay you a pretty penny," one of the men said to me as I walked past them.

"How pretty of a penny are we talking about? Three against one hardly seem fair, but judging by your friend's glass jaw it looks like you both should leave this man alone," I replied to the man

"I was hoping it wouldn't come to this. Now pay up Monaghan, and you too pal. You walked down the wrong alley," the man said in a stern tone as he pulled out a handgun and pointed it at the Irishman with the corn-cob pipe, while the man on the pavement pulled out a handgun and pointed it at me as he slowly rose to his feet with a grimace.

"Wait, how about this. Heads I pay you, tails you let us go," I said with a grin as I took out a silver dollar from my pocket.

"How about you pay us right now or we fill you both with led," one man pronounced in a stern tone.

"Wait," the man who was knocked to the ground by a swift right hook to the jaw a few moments ago said and then whispered into the other man's ear.

"Fine we'll take that bet pal," one man said to me with a grin.

I then flipped the silver dollar high up into the air as both of the men averted their stares from me and the Irishman smoking the corn-cob pipe to the silver dollar, which was exactly what I intended for them to do.

The Irishman smoking the corn-cob pipe then grabbed one man by the collar and head-butted him as I connected a combination jab to the other man's face and body blow which disarmed him and sent him to the ground.

"Get their guns!" the Irishman smoking the corn cob pipe shouted surprisingly with the pipe still in his mouth during the entire fight. The Irishman and I then quickly grabbed the two men's hand guns off the pavement, but the enraged Irishman wasn't finished inflicting pain on them by any means.

"Remember this feeling boys every, time, you, slur, my people!" the Irishman shouted as he kicked each man in the stomach over and over again until they cried out in pain, as I lit a cigarette and took a smoke.

"Now get the hell out of here!" the Irishman shouted and then spit on the ground as the two men stumbled out of the alley.

"Crafty move, oh look, it was tails after all," the Irishman said to me in a heaving tone and grin as he pointed to my silver dollar on the pavement.

"You have a brutal right hook my friend. I could use a man of your caliber," I said to the Irishman with a grin as I put the silver dollar in my pocket.

"Use me for what?" the Irishman inquired in a stern tone as he wiped his mouth and then cracked his neck.

"To sell liquor at my bar in Greenwich Village," I replied. "Haven't you heard this whole country is now dry," the Irishman said to me with a laugh.

"Oh I've heard, and I'm fully aware of the consequences of this endeavor. That's why I'm going to start bootlegging alcohol by any means possible. So that this unjust law will not suppress fine people like you and I who deserve the right to drink. I said to the Irishman.

"Fine people, you don't even know me," the Irishman said to me with a scoff and then began to walk away down the alley. "I know you're an Irish immigrant who's looking to make a living here in this so called land of opportunity. I can't afford to pay you a great deal, but something is better than nothing!" I shouted, as the Irishman turned around and walked back towards me.

"Very well … when can I start?" the Irishman inquired. "Let's start right now. I'm Jack, Jack Dansby," I said to the Irishman with a grin as I extended my hand towards him.

"I'm Samson Monaghan," the Irishman said to me with a grin as he shook my hand.

*****

"Ah I remember these gray and restless mornings in *SoHo* all too well," I said to Samson as we exited my Pontiac and walked towards his apartment.

"Aye every morning is gray when you live in *SoHo*," Samson remarked as we walked up the stairs were a rat scurried past me.

"Now why exactly did you want to drop by my humble lodgings Jack? You always have an ulterior motive," Samson inquired as we entered his apartment which appeared as a back- alley only slightly homier.

"Jesus Christ Samson, would it kill you to clean up this place every once in awhile," I inquired as I slowly walked around the sad looking living room.

"This isn't your speakeasy Jack, so don't fucking order me around," Samson replied in a stern tone.

"I then looked out the torn blinds to see a familiar car parked outside of Samson's apartment. A car of the man who was supposed to protect Samson, a car of a Russian hitman

"What are you staring at down there?" Samson inquired, as he walked over to the window and handed me a bottle of beer. "Nikolai … how often do you see him staked outside your apartment?" I replied as I pointed out the window towards the menacing Russian mobster known as Nikolai 'the wolf' Volkov who was seated in his car smoking a cigarette.

I see that bastard at least three times a week. Whatever deal Luciano has formed with him now, I fear one day it will wear thin, and he will then be the man who attempts to silence me," Samson replied as we stared intently out the window at the nonchalant Russian hitman.

"The wolf vs. the bold huh, I'd pay to see that fight," I said to Samson with a snicker.

"It's all a big laugh to you isn't it," Samson remarked with a scoff, as he turned on the radio to a station that was playing some god awful Irish music.

"I laugh at it all because showing fear is how these mobsters gain power. You know this better than anybody, and that fucking music on the radio takes me back to Pier 45 when Johnny was singing an Irish folk song as he bashed my head in," I said to Samson in a stern tone.

"Oh I didn't know Johnny did that to his victims. Well that bastard's reign of killing is now over thanks to you," Samson said to me as he changed the station on the radio to a most pleasant sound.

"Now that's more like it, Louie Armstrong. This is the kind of music you should be listening to," I said to Samson with a grin as I swigged the last of my beer and placed the bottle down on the tarnished end table.

"My people's folk songs are precious to me. Whenever my heart yearns to return to Belfast I listen to that radio station," Samson remarked.

"So your heart yearns for what it previously rejected huh. Well to answer your question I wanted to visit your place because I heard Mr. Luciano talking about you yesterday," I said to Samson as I lit a cigarette and took a smoke.

"What did the boss man say?" Samson inquired as the sound of Louie Armstrong's trumpet blared throughout Samson's apartment which caused me to snap my fingers as I paced back and forth.

"He said 'my nephew has a brilliant plan. We can us the Irishman to bait him. If we force his hand in such a manner then I will be at the top,'" I replied.

"Ah so that smug little bastard Stefano is already pulling the strings of his uncle's organization, but who exactly do they want me to bait?" Samson inquired while shaking his head.

"I don't know, but I have a feeling we're about to find out soon enough," I replied.

The truth of the matter was that I could protect Samson about as well as I could protect myself, but Mr. Luciano has now chosen to use him in some sort of plan. Samson is a good man who helped me out of countless scrapes over the past ten years. He was bullheaded but remained loyal to me, and loyalty, especially in this town is worth its weight in gold.

"Then we shouldn't linger here. We may have already tipped their hand," Samson said to me.

"Whose this? She's pretty," I remarked with a grin as I picked up a picture frame of a woman with long wavy hair and a sweet smile wearing a white dress as she sat posing on a bench. "Don't touch that," Samson said to me in a stern tone as he snatched the picture of the woman out of my hand.

"Oh did I strike another nerve. I take it from your reaction she must be some old flame from Belfast," I said to Samson. "If you must know … that's my little sister Siobhan," Samson said to me as he stared intently at the picture.

"You never told me you had a sister. Well I see where you don't get your good looks from," I said to Samson with a snicker.

"Don't start with me Jack," Samson said to me in a stern tone as he pointed aggressively at me.

The more I found out about Samson, the more I had in common with him. Samson hated it when I pried into his personal life, as did I when he pried into mine, but him and I have now reached a point in our lives where I believe confiding in each other will help us stay alive.

"So where is she now?" I inquired.

"Goddamn it!" Samson shouted as he threw the beer bottle at the wall.

There was pain written all over Samson's brooding face at that moment, a pain I can relate to when it comes to a sibling.

"Fine, you can take that pain with you to the grave then," I said to Samson with a scoff.

"I wanted her to come with me. I pleaded for her to come with me. I told them there was nothing but fear and death for them if they chose to stay in Belfast. My dearest Siobhan and me mother, but they both told me that we must face our fears, not run from them. This was the night when I killed my two associates who worked for Marcus Macready," Samson said to me in a somber tone.

"I see ... so what was she like, your little sister?" I inquired, as I stared at the shards of broken glass scattered on the floor.

"Don't talk like that, don't you talk about her as if she's met her maker. Siobhan is still alive damn it!" Samson replied in a stern tone.

"Calm down Samson. Up until this moment I had no idea you even had a little sister, but I see the wound from leaving her still hasn't healed," I said to Samson in a somber tone.

"She had a heart twice as big as her dainty body ... and funny. She always put a smile on my face when the rest of the world had given me a fat lip and black eye," Samson replied, as he stared at the picture of his sister on the table.

"She sounds like Dezerae," I said to Samson with a grin.

"I took her for granted. Looking back on all those nights when I would come home after Macready and his muscle were done teaching me a lesson, Siobhan would always tend to me as if I was a child. She didn't question the choice I made, she just accepted me as her older brother who was a mobster," Samson said to me in a somber tone.

"Well that's where your sister and mine are drastically different; Dezerae would always make it known to me whenever she disapproved of my decisions in life. I hope now that she would be proud of the decisions I made with Hayley," I said to Samson.

"Enough reminiscing, I can't change the past anymore than I can change myself," Samson said to me.

"You're looking at it all wrong. The past may be written in stone, but we can always ...," I said with a pause as I stared out the window with wide eyes.

"What is it?" Samson inquired.

"The Russian, he left his car," I replied just as Louie Armstrong on the radio wailed heavily on the trumpet as if to announce Nikolai 'the wolf' Volkov's move.

Three bangs on the front door of Samson's apartment then cut through Louie Armstrong's trumpet playing as Samson and I simultaneously drew our handguns and walked slowly towards the front door.

"What on earth is that?" Samson inquired as he stared at a sharp object sticking out of the door.

"It looks like a nail. Are you ready?" I inquired in a stern tone and stare as I grabbed the doorknob while Louie Armstrong's trumpet playing on the radio began to fade out.

"Aye," Samson replied in a stern tone, as he pointed his handgun at the door.

I then swiftly opened the door to the sight of nobody, as Samson and I stood back to back pointing our guns down each end of the hallway.

"Look, it looks like 'The wolf' left a decoration on your door," I remarked as I pointed to what appeared to be a letter nailed into the front door of Samson's apartment.

"Did he ever hear of knocking goddamn," Samson inquired in a stern tone, as I gently pulled the letter off the nail.

"Men like him operate very theatrically, or maybe even the big bad wolf realized he couldn't take on both of us," I remarked with a scoff.

"You do the honors. I was never one for theatre Jack. No matter how many times Siobhan would talk to me about it," Samson remarked as he pushed the letter away from him.

"Fine, but something tells me you and I are going to be the lead roles in this play whether we like it or not," I said to Samson as I opened the letter and began to read it out loud.

GENTLEMEN,

MR. LUCIANO REQUESTS BOTH OF YOUR PRESENCE AT THE SPEAKEASY POST HASTE. HE AND HIS NEPHEW ARE CURRENTLY WAITING FOR YOU

BOTH AND IT WOULD BE IN THE BEST INTEREST OF NOT ONLY YOU TWO, BUT ALSO YOUR NEICE AND THE BOY KNOWN AS MICKEY TO MEET WITH HIM NOW. IF YOU BOTH SHOULD CHOOSE NOT TO COMPLY, THEN YOUR NEICE AND THE BOY WILL BE USED AS AN INSURANCE MEASURE FOR MR. LUCIANO.

THE WOLF

"Son of a bitch," I said in a stern tone as I crumpled up the letter in my hands.

"I told you we shouldn't have left those two alone," Samson said to me as he shut the door to his apartment.

Samson and I then ran down the stairs of his apartment and entered my Pontiac. I have no idea what Mr. Luciano wants of me and Samson, but I sure as hell hope that he leaves Hayley and Mickey out of it, but judging by that threatening letter from the wolf, it sounds like Mr. Luciano means business.

"Let's not provoke Mr. Luciano when we enter the speakeasy," I said to

Samson as I tucked my pistol between the waist-band of my pants, while speeding back to Greenwich Village as fast as my Pontiac will get me there.

"Aye, but once again I'm going to tell you to take your own advice, seeing as how you rarely seem to do it in these situations," Samson said to me.

*****

It was 10:53 AM as Samson and I exited my Pontiac, took a deep breath, and then entered the speakeasy.

"Ah Jack, Samson, have a seat. I was beginning to think you gentleman wouldn't show, but your niece here reassured me that you both would comply. Mr. Luciano pronounced, as Samson and I entered the speakeasy to the sight of Mr. Luciano, Stefano, Hayley, Mickey, and three of Mr. Luciano's muscle seated at the center table of the speakeasy.

Mr. Luciano was always to suave and calculated when it came to confronting anybody who could potentially pose a threat to him. This is why he always made sure that he and his muscle outnumber me during our meetings.

"Are you all right kid?" I inquired, as I sat beside Hayley with a stern look on my face.

"I'm fine, but Mr. Luciano hasn't told me or Mickey what this meeting is about," Hayley replied.

"Don't worry, we're about to find out," I said to Hayley. "Can I get you all anything," Samson inquired.

"Not this time Samson. This time Leo will be serving us all," Mr. Luciano replied, as he snapped his fingers and pointed to the bar, which prompted the strapping mobster known as Leo to quickly stand up and scurry over to the bar in an obedient manner.

"So why are we all here?" Hayley inquired to break the silence as everyone stared sternly at each other.

"Shhh, don't speak unless you're spoken to," I said to Hayley with a nudge, as Mr. Luciano grinned at me while playing with his rings.

"Excuse me," Hayley said to me in a stern tone and stare. "To answer your question principessa, we're here because my big mouth nephew has told you all about our founder Paolo Antonio Vaccarelli," Mr. Luciano replied as his muscle put a cigar in his mouth and lit it.

"Are you talking about Paul Kelly?" I inquired, as Leo placed a tray full of a bucket of ice, two bottles of bourbon, eight tumblers, two wine glasses, and a bottle of Pinot Noir on the table.

"Don't speak unless you're spoken to," Hayley said to me in a mocking tone, as Leo began to serve me a double bourbon on the rocks.

"Yes one in the same, Jack. You see Paolo is how you say obsolete in my eyes, and I don't believe he has what it takes to run this organization which he founded. However he still has influence over many of our members," Mr. Luciano replied.

"So let's just silence him Uncle Charles," Stefano said to Mr. Luciano.

"Don't speak unless you're spoken to nipote!" Mr. Luciano shouted as he backhanded Stefano which I must admit gave me much pleasure seeing that boy get disciplined.

"If I were to do such a thing then it would result in a civil war within our organization, a war of the old members who are loyal to Paolo vs. the new members whose loyalties lie with me. Therefore we must play into Paolo's ways and lure him into a challenge which he would never refuse," Mr. Luciano said.

"What kind of challenge?" Samson inquired, as I took a sip of bourbon.

"That's where you two gentleman come in. You see Paolo was a former boxer, and not a half bad one at that. Before my time, Paolo and this organization was at war with the Eastman Gang. Back then boxing matches were the way we settled our fights over territories. So Paolo challenged Munk Eastman's right hand man Jack Shimsky to a boxing match over control of the Lower East Side territory of New York. Paolo won that fight against Shimsky in the third round ensuring our control over the Lower East Side. Now since there's still a part of me that respects that relic, instead of shooting him in his sleep like my nipote so ignorantly suggests I wanted to end him with one last bout," Mr. Luciano said.

"A boxing match huh," I said with a scoff as I took another sip of bourbon.

"Corretta, Jack. You have two days to train Samson, because he will be the one who fights Paolo right here in this speakeasy," Mr. Luciano said as he pointed at Samson.

"What, why me? Why not Jack? He did kill Johnny after all," Samson inquired with a wide-eyed stare at Mr. Luciano.

"When I gave Paolo the choice he chose you over Jack because of your past. You see Paolo represents the past, and I'm tired of reporting to him on every move I make with this organization," Mr. Luciano replied in a stern tone.

"What are the stakes to this boxing match?" I inquired. "Samson is my champion, therefore if he wins the fight then Paolo will relinquish the supreme authority of founder of our organization to me and depart New York to live a life he so chooses," Mr. Luciano replied, as the mobster sitting next to him whispered in his ear.

"Aye, but what if I lose the fight?" Samson inquired.

"If you should happen to lose the fight, then Paolo will remain founder until the end of his days and you, along with Jack, principessa, and that boy will be cast out of this establishment. You can thank Stefano for this outcome, for I wanted to silence you all, but he told me that you would all die on the streets without my generous financial support," Mr. Luciano replied as he and Stefano snickered, while Hayley stared daggers at the young mobster in training.

"I built this establishment," I pronounced in a stern tone.

"Then you better train Samson here to the best of your abilities. Jack. Do you know why they call me Lucky?" Mr. Luciano inquired.

"No but I've always wondered why," I inquired.

"Three years ago during the Castellammarese War I was the number one target for Joe Masseria, my former boss and now dead man. Therefore I incurred beatings stabbings, and a slash to the throat. Do you see this scar mi amico? I call this a decoration of power which I proudly wear upon my face," Mr. Luciano inquired as he pointed to the jagged scar on his cheek which I always wondered about, but never had the courage to ask the man.

"So that's your origin story," Samson said with a grin. "I'm also quite fortunate when it comes to playing cards. So now with my champion Samson the Bold along with Lucky Luciano, Paolo won't stand a chance in this fight," Mr. Luciano pronounced with a laugh, as all the rest of the mobsters laughed simultaneously.

"So two days, that's all the time we have to train?" Samson inquired.

"Corretta, Samson, and consider yourself grateful for that amount of time Paolo granted you, oh and Samson … do not underestimate Paolo," Mr. Luciano said to Samson in a stern tone as him and his entourage exited the speakeasy.

"What now?" Samson inquired.

"We get you in as best fighting condition as we can in two days, that's what now," I replied in a stern tone, as I placed my hand on Samson's shoulder.

*****

It was 6:25 PM and the days were getting shorter, along with Samson's patience as we trained in a gym in *SoHo* which has seen far better days.

"Come one Samson you have to keep your right hand up when you punch with your left or else Paul will see that opening and knock you right on your ass," I said to Samson in a stern tone as he punched the pads I wore on both my hands.

"Oh really, and how on god's green earth do you know that. This whole arrangement is ridiculous. Two days to train for what? To fight a man I've never seen before. I have no idea what kind of fighter Paul Kelly is," Samson said to me in a stern tone.

"That's exactly why you must be prepared for anything," I said to Samson as he took a few quick jabs at the pads.

In all honesty, Samson didn't fight like the Samson I first met five years ago. That Irish fervor inside of him had grown dim over the past five years, but I, Hayley and Mickey's future depend on Samson finding that fire within him once more. Or perhaps I had to be the one to stoke that dim flame within him until it burns hot enough to win in the fight against Paul Kelly. "You're enjoying this aren't you, Jack," Samson said to me in a heaving tone.

"I'd be lying if I said no, but considering how much is at stake I'm taking this dead serious," I said to Samson, as I turned on the radio.

"I have no personal quarrel with this man Paul Kelly. So how the hell am I going to beat him senseless?" Samson inquired in a stern tone, and then took a swig of water.

"Let me try something … all right square up to me. Now pretend I'm Paul Kelly," I said to Samson as I put the pads on both of my hands.

"Very well, so Mr. Kelly are you ready to start seeing stars by the likes of me fists?" Samson inquired in a stern tone. "What was that 'start seeing stars by the likes of me fists?'"

I inquired.

"I'm just trying to intimidate the man," Samson replied.

"Hayley wouldn't be intimidated by that statement you just made. In fact, I'm starting to think she would've been a better choice to fight Paul Kelly than you," I said to Samson.

"Shut up Jack. You should be the one boxing Kelly, not I," Samson said to me in a stern tone as he lightly jabbed the pads in the manner of a frail old man doing his weekly exercises just to keep from keeling over.

"Paul Kelly chose you because of your past, but I see now that past of yours is dead in your heart and mind. Everything that drove you to flee to America, all those memories of Macready and Siobhan might as well be nothing but fearful thoughts to a cowering Irishman," I said to Samson in a stern tone.

"I've never backed down from a fight in my entire life. So watch your tone Jack, or else I might have to show you why Macready first called me Samson the Bold," Samson said to me in a stern tone, as I walked over to the radio with a grin and raised the volume. It was working. I could see the passion in Samson's eyes begin to burn brighter the more I taunted him, so I continued with my taunts.

"Show me then. If this is all you can muster, then it's no wonder why you abandoned Siobhan and your mother just because you felt the heat from Macready you limey bastard," I said to Samson in a stern tone.

"How dare you!" Samson shouted.

Samson's eyes widened with rage at that moment and it was the exact same look I remember he gave to those two men in the alley five years ago before his swift left, right combination knocked one of them down to the pavement. Samson then delivered a swift combination of punches which I managed to block the first two thrown at me, but it was clear that Samson was no longer training with me at that moment, he wanted to inflict pain on me, and that rage was exactly what I wanted to awaken within him..

Samson's third and fourth punch connected hitting me in the gut then swiftly to the side of the head and then all went black.

*****

"Jack, wake up," a voice said to me as I felt water splash over my face.

I then opened my eyes to the sight of Samson standing over me heaving in such a primal manner as I sat in the corner of the ring.

"Ugh damn now that's more like it Samson," I remarked with a grimace, as I pulled myself up from the ropes of the ring while holding the side of my head.

"I know what you're trying to do," Samson said to me.

"I'm trying to bring out your boldness. I know you may be afraid of losing control, but there are many good people depending on you, pal," I said to Samson.

"I hope I didn't hit you too hard, but you know how that word gets me seeing red," Samson said with a snicker as he sat down on the stool in the corner of the ring.

"Let me put it this way. Even in my fight against Johnny he never hit me as hard as you just did," I said to Samson with a grin.

"Well Johnny was a sadistic bastard, he wanted to savor your pain, I just wanted to shut your mouth," Samson said to me with a snicker.

"So why did Macready give you the name Samson the Bold?" I inquired.

"Well … I was a younger and hungrier man back then, a man who would do anything to prove himself, and Macready used that against me. On one balmy August night I was blowing off some steam at the Fox & Boar which was the local watering hole much like the speakeasy only with even more old drunkards at the end of their ropes," Samson said to me as he took a swig of water then practiced his body blows on the heavy bag.

"Well don't leave me in suspense Samson. So far your origin story sounds like the typical Irishman's week night," I said to Samson with a grin.

"I am the typical Irishman, but the name Samson the Bold was a name that made me into someone I never thought I'd be, someone that could protect others, but to protect was not part of Macready's mentality. So the night grew old as I found myself south to the gills and in a shouting match with Jackson Mulroney, the owner and barkeep at the time who had enough of my drunken fervor," Samson said to me as he continued to punch the heavy bag while I paced back and forth in front of him as the music of Cab Calloway played on the radio.

"I take it your tolerance for the drink was weaker back then?" I inquired with a grin.

"No I just drank more. Back then drinking was more than just a hobby for me; it was a way for me to calm that constant rage I felt boiling up within me veins. So Mulroney then pulled out his trusty shillelagh and kicked me out of the Fox & Boar. I then found me self shirtless and staggering down an alley I've staggered down many nights before, but three men suddenly blocked my path," Samson replied.

"Finally some excitement," I remarked with a grin.

"Despite my drunken fervor I was in no mood for a brawl, I just wanted to get home, but the three men quickly surrounded me, as if they had a plan from the very moment they saw me. I told the men to leave me be, but they had no intention of letting me escape that alley unscathed," Samson said to me.

"Three against one again huh, you always seem to get outnumbered Samson. This fight against Paul Kelly should be pleasantly fair than what you're used to," I remarked with a snicker.

"There's no such thing as a fair fight Jack. One fighter will always be stronger or faster than the other, but these three men first attacked me one at a time, which was their first mistake. My skills as a fighter were at their prime in those days, and I countered each of the men's punches, knocking them into the walls of the alley, but they were far from finished. One of the men locked me up, while the other man landed a swift left hook to me jaw, but I head-butted the man who had me in a tight embrace from behind and then delivered my signature left, left, then right hook to the man in front of me, knocking him down to the pavement," Samson said to me as he demonstrated the fight he was in with the three men against the heavy bag.

"You're an animal. Did those men get the best of you," I inquired.

"Shut up and let me finish. The third man struck me in   the back of the head with a studded shillelagh which sent me toppling over to the pavement. Back then pain was just a four letter word which I didn't fear slightest bit. I was wondering why the men hadn't taken the little money I had in me pockets as they began to kick me, but by that moment I was impervious to that four letter word called pain, as I rose to my feet and knocked out one man with a rising uppercut. At that moment I couldn't help but think of the threat these three men could pose to me mother and sister. A hidden strength deep within me was then awakened as I overpowered all of the men's attempts to take me down. In my final bout I threw a wild series of punches which connected to all three of the men.

"So that's how Samson the Bold came to be," I said to Samson with a grin.

"I'm not finished damn it. You're just like Siobhan whenever I told her a story. The three men then stumbled away from me down the alley, as I cursed at them with such a rage I've never felt before. I remember the taste of blood lingered in me mouth that entire night as I stumbled back to my flat. Everything was hazy, as me mother and Siobhan took care of me. The next day, I was then given the news by Macready himself that he hired the three men to attack me in the alley as part of an initiation into his gang which I passed. Macready then told me I was the boldest son of a bitch he's ever laid eyes on, and that's how the name Samson the Bold came to be," Samson said to me with a sigh as he stopped punching the heavy bad and sat down on the bench against the wall.

"Samson … your sister and mother were the ones who gave you the strength in that fight. They were the ones who made you bold, not Macready," I said to Samson.

"Think nothing of it Jack. It was my pride that resulted in me being Macready's right hand man. Me mother always said I had too much of me father's pride in me, for pride cometh before the fall … and I've fallen hard. America was supposed to be an uplifting country, but I find myself just reliving my past here," Samson said to me in a somber tone.

"I don't believe that, Samson. You're a protector, and tomorrow night Paul Kelly will be the one who falls in the fight. You've done nothing but protect me, Hayley, and Mickey, and I know I've shown you far less gratitude that you deserve," I said to Samson in a stern tone and stare as I placed my hand on his shoulder.

"Ah look at you getting all sentimental on me. You act as if I won't come back from the fight against Kelly tomorrow night," Samson said to me.

"No I have faith in you," I said to Samson with a smile.

"That's good to hear Jack. Well … we should be getting back. I don't trust Leo to run the speakeasy while we're here training," Samson said to me with a groan as he cracked his neck.

"Mr. Luciano assured us Leo would protect the kids, but I'm worried that that Italian tower of a man is going to be my replacement," I said to Leo.

"Aye he may very well be your replacement Jack. It doesn't exactly take a rocket scientist to serve alcohol," Samson said to me with a snicker.

"Oh I know you're proof of that. The kids will be fine. We've been training for six hours, come on, I'll buy you a burger," I said to Samson with a grin.

*****

It was 6:24 PM as Samson and I entered the speakeasy to the sight of Leo serving a mobster and his dame drinks at the bar, while Hayley and Mickey were taking drink orders at the tables by the stage.

"You see everything is still running smoothly," I remarked. "All thanks to Leo. He's more of a barkeep than you could ever hope to be, Jack," a familiar bratty voice remarked, as I turned around to see Stefano staring at me with a smirk in the same manner his uncle does.

"Yes he appears to be more of a competent barkeep than I expected. So what brings you by Stefano?" I inquired, as Samson and I walked over to the bar and put on our black vests and bowties just as Carmen took the stage with her jazz backup band.

"I don't need a reason to check up on my investments. I'm eighteen now, which means I legally have a stake in this business," Stefano replied.

"Thanks for your help. Samson and I will take it from here," I said to Leo.

"Very well Mr. Dansby. Good luck in the fight tomorrow mi amico," Leo said to Samson as he patted him on the shoulder with a snicker, before exiting the speakeasy.

"Samson how was your training?" Mickey inquired with a smile as he walked up to the bar.

"I knocked out Jack, but other than that the entire concept of training two days for a fight against a man I've never met is eejit anyway you look at it," Samson replied with a scoff.

"Leo told me that every mobster in New York will be betting on your fight with Paul Kelly," Mickey said to Samson. "Oh perfect, nothing like having the weight of every criminal in New York on my shoulders, as if there wasn't enough at stake in this goddamn fight," Samson said to Mickey in a stern tone as he slammed his fist down on the bar.

"Oh save that rage for tomorrow night, you'll need it," I said to Samson.

"Samson, how are you feeling?" Hayley inquired as she walked up to the bar holding a tray full of empty glasses.

"Sore, but ready to prove me worth tomorrow night," Samson replied.

"I believe in you Samson, and even though I've never seen Paul Kelly, I just know you're going to win," Hayley remarked with a warm smile.

"Oh really, and what makes you say that young lady," Samson inquired with a smile.

"I know this because I feel it in my heart," Hayley replied.

"You heard her Samson, that's all the inspiration you need to win against Kelly," I said to Samson with a laugh.

"I mean it. Samson is a good man, and good men will always prevail in the end," Hayley pronounced with a stern look on her flush face.

"What fairytale did you read that bullshit line from?"

Stefano inquired with a laugh as he walked up to the bar. "You're betting against Samson aren't you," Hayley said to Stefano with a wide-eyed stare.

"You got that right toots. Paul Kelly has never lost a fight, and even though he's in his mid fifties. I still have no doubt he will lay out this limey Irish bottom feeder," Stefano pronounced with a smirk as he pointed to Samson.

"What did you just call me boy?" Samson shouted, as he hurdled over the bar and lunged towards Stefano.

"Ignore the kid. Save your rage for Kelly!" I shouted as I tried my best to restrain Samson from knocking that little bastard Stefano's head right off.

"Mark my words. A day will come when death looks you in the eyes, boy. Then we shall see who blinks first," Samson said to Stefano in such a venomous tone while pointing to him as if he just placed a curse on the young mobster's life.

"There's no way your uncle is betting against Samson, if Paul Kelly wins the fight then he remains the founder and top boss of the Five Points Gang," Hayley said to Stefano.

"I know, but I figured if I bet against that ape Irishman over there then it's a win win for me. Either way my uncle and I will be making changes to this speakeasy no matter what the results of the fight may be," Stefano said to Hayley

"I was at the meeting yesterday in case you forgot, so don't try to make up delusions of grandeur in your head," Hayley said to Stefano in a stern tone.

"Oh I did forget actually. Why on earth my uncle let a woman attend that meeting is beyond me, but I guess he pities you in the way that someone would pity a stray dog," Stefano said to Hayley with a snicker and then exited the speakeasy.

I couldn't stand the boy's arrogance. It was all nepotism at its worst when it came to Stefano and his uncle. Every time the boy spoke I had to hold back every fiber of my being from doing what Samson was about to do a few moments ago. Was the boy bitter now because Hayley sent him his walking papers, or was it his uncle who was responsible for his growing ruthlessness? "That was pretty sinister what you said to Stefano. It sent a chill down my spine," I said to Samson with a grin.

"Aye that's what Macready said to me on the night of my initiation," Samson said to me in a stern tone.

"Death has looked me in the eyes many times over the past six months," I said to Samson as I wiped down the bar.

"Aye but you never coward from death. I've always respected that about you," Samson said to me with a grin.

"Tomorrow night death may look you in the eyes once more," I said to Samson.

"Aye then I'll throw me signature left, left, right hook combo to death's face and then we shall see who blinks first," Samson said to me with a grin.

*****

It was 7:37 PM in the speakeasy as droves of mobsters began to pour in to watch the fight. A small construction crew even built a boxing ring for Samson and Paul, so this match would be no ordinary street brawl like Samson was used to.

"Any sign of Mr. Kelly or Mr. Luciano?" Mickey inquired as he walked up to the bar.

"Well I have no idea what Mr. Kelly looks like so we will find out the very moment that man disrobes and steps into the ring. As for Mr. Luciano, I predict he will be arriving shortly," I replied.

"I used to bet on boxing matches, but I never thought that the fate of this speakeasy would now be in the hands of Samson," Mickey said to me.

"I hope you bet on Samson to win tonight," I said to Mickey with a grin.

"I sure did. I bet all the money I have on Samson winning in the 3rd round," Mickey said to me with a grin.

"Let me go check on him," I said to Mickey and then entered the kitchen to the sight of Samson sitting on my bed with a towel hanging over his head.

"How are you feeling?" I inquired.

"Anxious, the calm before the storm is always a bigger fear for me than the actual storm," Samson replied.

"I'm sure when that bell rings all your nerves will begin to fade away. You're just not used to a fight in front of an audience this big," I said to Samson.

"Have Paul Kelly or Mr. Luciano arrived yet?" Samson inquired as he shadow boxed in front of me.

"Not yet, but I'm sure they're arrival will be announced in a grand fashion," I replied.

"Jack, no matter what the outcome of this fight may be, I just want you to know I will give it me all against Kelly," Samson said as he stared intently at me.

"I expect nothing less from you. Now come on let's show these mobsters who the champ will be," I said to Samson with a grin, as I patted him on the shoulder. Samson and I then exited the speakeasy to an array of applause and boos as we walked towards the ring in the center of the speakeasy.

"It appears that many mobsters are rooting for Kelly in this fight," Samson remarked.

"Many are also rooting for you, but drown out all of that noise and try to stay focused," I said to Samson.

"Samson, wait!" Hayley shouted as she scampered over to Samson.

"Aye what is it lass?" Samson inquired with a grin.

"Good luck in the fight. I just know you will prevail, but remember, you're not just fighting for us and the speakeasy. You're also fighting for your own fate," Hayley said to Samson and then kissed him on the cheek.

"Aye I'll keep that in mind. Thank you Hayley," Samson said to Hayley with a warm smile, as Samson and I then entered the ring.

"Look there's Mr. Luciano," I remarked as I pointed to Mr. Luciano who had just entered the speakeasy with Stefano and four other mobsters.

"Ah il mio campione," Mr. Luciano said as he entered the ring and walked up to me and Samson.

"So where's Mr. Kelly?" Samson inquired.

"He shall be arriving very shortly. He and his right hand man will be greeted like kings in this speakeasy, but you mi amico will be the one to end his reign," Mr. Luciano replied with a grin as he began to pace back and forth in the ring.

"So what does Paul Kelly look like, what's his fighting style?" I inquired.

"I will tell you that Paolo is a man that—,"

An uproarious applause then arose from the audience as they gathered towards the front door of the speakeasy, but I couldn't see who had just entered.

"I take it that's Kelly who just arrived," Samson remarked as he punched his fists together.

"He is here. Where's the goddamn referee?" Mr. Luciano inquired in a stern tone.

Mr. Luciano then whistled to the referee who was talking to Stefano for some reason.

"Sorry Mr. Luciano," The referee said to Mr. Luciano as he entered the ring, but my eyes, along with Samson's were fixed on the crowd of mobsters near the front door, waiting for Paul Kelly to emerge and enter the ring.

At this point it was the loudest the speakeasy had ever been and I couldn't so much as hear myself think as two mobsters entered the ring.

"Those two, I remember them. The tall one was the first mobster to call me Samson the Bold, but which one is Kelly?" Samson inquired as he pointed to the burly mobster standing beside a mobster who stood only as tall as Hayley, while Mr. Luciano greeted them both as if they were good friends who had no ill-will against each other.

"The burly one must be Kelly," I said to Samson as Mr. Luciano and the two mobsters continued to talk. Now the three of them all had stern looks on their once smiling faces.

"We're all counting on you Samson, but most importantly of all I'm counting on you mi amico, do not disappoint me," Mr. Luciano said to Samson in a stern tone as he placed his hand on Samson's shoulder and cheek, and then exited the ring. "Ladies and gentleman. This boxing match this evening will determine whether Paul Kelly will remain our founder and top boss. If his challenger Mr. Samson Monaghan wins, than Mr. Luciano will become the new top boss of the Five Points organization," the referee announced, as Samson stared daggers across the ring at the two mobsters, not knowing which of them was about to be his opponent.

"All right gentleman, would you both please join me at the center of the ring," the referee announced.

This was it, the moment we would finally find out who Paul Kelly was. I patted Samson on the back as he walked up to the center of the ring while the tall and short mobsters locked arms on each others' shoulders for a moment.

"Oh you've got to be fucking kidding me," I remarked in a bewildered tone as the short mobster then quickly disrobed and walked to the center of the ring. Paul Kelly was the short mobster all along, but then I remembered Mr. Luciano telling us two days ago not to underestimate him.

I then noticed the expression on Samson's face go from confused to smiling, but I was more confused and intrigued as to how the child-sized founder of the Five Points Gang Mr. Paul Kelly had never lost a fight.

"Don't underestimate him Samson!" I shouted, as Samson and Paul Kelly touched gloves.

"Mr. Kelly, Mr. Monaghan, you're both civilized gentleman so I want a clean fight. This isn't a street brawl, this is an official boxing match that has rules and regulations, and I trust you gentleman will abide by those rules and regulations, understood?" the referee inquired.

Samson and Kelly then confirmed to the referee that they would abide by the rules with a nod.

"Mr. Kelly isn't what I expected," Hayley remarked.

"You got that right kid. That's exactly why Samson must not underestimate him," I said to Hayley.

"All right gentleman go to your corners," the referee announced.

"He's short Samson which means he's going to go for your body, remember to keep your left up when you give your right hook!"I said to Samson in a stern tone.

The bell then rang and the boxing match between Samson and the founder of the Five Points gang had now begun, as the mobster who filled the speakeasy cheered, hollered, and shouted racial slurs at both Kelly and Samson as they squared up and sized each other up.

Samson then threw the first punch, two left jabs which were blocked by Kelly. Those punches were not so much punches as they were to test Kelly's reflexes. This was a ridiculous looking fight. Samson was nearly a foot taller than Kelly, but Kelly seemed to not be intimidated by the size difference one bit as he moved in close to Samson and threw a combination of body blows just as I predicted he would. Samson managed to block the first two body punches, but dropped his left which Kelly capitalized on with a swift rising uppercut which didn't fully connect to Samson's chin, but still shook him up quite a bit.

"Keep your left up Samson. Bring him in close, but don't drop your left no matter what!" I shouted, as Samson threw a strong combination of punches which would lay out any man, but Kelly wasn't just any man, he was an experienced boxer, one who had fought a man of Samson's size before judging by how he blocked and dodged all of Samson's punches.

Kelly was surprisingly nimble for a man in his mid fifties, and I feared that Samson's patience in this fight could be his downfall. Kelly was sizing up Samson, but Samson kept throwing the same combination of punches at Kelly. The bell then rang signaling the end of round one, as Kelly and Samson retired to their opposite corners of the ring.

"Kelly told me he wanted to fight me because of my name. He wants to rewrite history by taking me down, something about Samson and the philistines," Samson said to me as he sat down on the stool I placed in the corner of the ring.

"Oh so the man is cultured. Well good for him. You on the other hand keep dropping your left as if your fist is made of led," I said to Samson in a stern tone, as I wiped his forehead with a wet rag and handed him a bottle of water.

"He fights like a young man, but with the wisdom of a seasoned boxer," Samson remarked in a heaving tone.

"He fights like an old man trying to hold on to power. Remember bring him in and then wait for an opening," I said to Samson in a stern tone as I massaged his shoulders as he took a swig of water and then spit it out in the bucket.

The bell then rang as Samson and Kelly both sprung from their stools and immediately went on the offense. Something was wrong, Samson didn't have that passion in his eyes like he did the moment he knocked me out yesterday, could it be that Paul Kelly had gotten into his head or was Samson's strength already beginning to fade? I now feared that if that flame within him wasn't stoked soon then it would die.

Kelly continued his body blows to Samson, as he continued to block them.

"Keep it up Samson, tire him out!" I shouted.

Then Samson made a huge mistake, Samson threw a sweeping right hook at Kelly which left his body open. Kelly then threw three body blows along with a right hook which sent Samson staggering over to his corner.

The mobsters rooting for Kelly were ecstatic at that moment, as the mobsters rooting for Samson shouted in fear and bewilderment. Samson couldn't land a punch on Kelly. The old man was too damn nimble. I then began to imagine what Hayley and I's life would soon be if Samson lost this fight and it hit me like a ton of bricks.

"Samson, I believe in you, don't give up!" Hayley shouted in a distressed tone as she ran up to the edge of the boxing ring. Samson then grinned, spit out blood, and slammed his fists together before facing Kelly. I had no doubt Samson could take more punches than Kelly, but could he land any punches on the nimble old man? Samson then threw a combination of jabs and body blows at Kelly one of which connected to the old man which sent him staggering slightly back as the second bell rang signaling the end of round two.

"He's so calculated, like no man I've ever fought before," Samson remarked in a heaving tone, as I wiped wet rag over his battered face.

"Samson I want you to imagine, Kelly as Macready. You're no longer fighting Kelly right now. You're fighting the man who made you fear for the safety of your mother and little sister, the man who used you when you were at your hungriest. That's the man you're fighting now!" I shouted as I massaged Samson's shoulders. The bell then rang signaling the start of round three, as Samson shouted a primal yell before springing from his stool and facing Kelly. It was now or never. I just hope I motivated Samson enough to awaken that rage within him.

Samson and Kelly started the round on the offensive with a barrage of jabs and hooks, both of which connected. This was good, now we shall see how well Kelly takes a punch.

"Keep at him Samson, don't let up. Give him all your rage!" I shouted.

Samson then threw his signature left, left, right hook combo, but Kelly blocked all three punches and connected with three body blows which sent Samson staggering and hunched over.

"Is that all you got you bastard!" Samson shouted as he faced Kelly, but Kelly just grinned and moved in close to Samson once again. Kelly then threw a couple of body blows but Samson has experienced this tactic in the last two rounds and I hope he's learned how to counter Kelly's punches or this might be the final bout of Samson the Bold. After blocking Kelly's body blows, Samson then threw a right hook which again left him open for an uppercut from Kelly, which connected square into Samson's jaw, but Samson then threw a punch I wasn't expecting and neither was Kelly. A sweeping left hook from Samson then connected into Kelly's face, as Kelly's uppercut sent Samson falling to the ring in unison with Kelly as all the mobsters in the speakeasy roared at such a climactic bout, but I for one was horrified at the sight.

"What happens in a double knockout?" one mobster inquired.

"There won't be a double knockout. Get up Samson!" I shouted, as I slammed my hands on the edge of the ring.

The referee then stood between Samson and Kelly who both lay motionless in the ring and began to count.

"1...2...3—,"

CHAPTER 14:
SAINTS AND JEZEBELS
- HAYLEY -

"Please get up, Samson. We believe in you," I shouted in a distressed tone as the referee continued the counts while all the mobsters in the speakeasy were shouting for their respected fighter, or should I say the fighter they bet their entire life savings on.

"4...5...6," The referee pronounced as my eyes widened at the sight of Samson's arm grabbing the rope of the ring, while Paul Kelly remained motionless.

It was so loud in the speakeasy, I wonder how or even if Samson could hear me or Jack's voices among all these money hungry mobsters who wish to only capitalize off his pain?

"Where are you going, kid?" Jack inquired as I scampered over to the edge of the ring so I could be closer to Samson's ear than anybody in the speakeasy.

"You can do it, you're almost there!" I shouted, as Samson began to pull himself up from the ropes of the ring as the referee continued to count.

"7...8...9...10," the referee pronounced, as half the entire speakeasy erupted with joy at the sight of Samson standing as Paul Kelly was on all fours holding his head with a grimace.

"The winner of this match by knockout is Samson Monaghan," The referee announced as he grabbed Samson's arm and raised it high above his head.

"You did it you son of a bitch," Jack shouted with a laugh as he quickly entered the ring and hugged Samson which made my eyes begin to well up with tears.

"Incredible. Paul Kelly's never lost a fight. Samson's the toughest man in New York!" one mobster beside me shouted, as I saw Samson gesturing for me to join him in the ring

"Hayley get up here, you too Mickey!" Jack shouted with a smile as he gestured for me and Mickey to join him and Samson in the ring. Mr. Luciano then entered right at that moment and aggressively grabbed the microphone from the referee with a smile.

"Sistemarsi, Sistemarsi, quiet!" Mr. Luciano shouted, as the entire speakeasy quickly fell silent.

"I'm so proud of you Samson," I said to Samson with a warm smile, as I wrapped my arms around his waist.

"My fellow associates ... Samson the Bold!" Mr. Luciano shouted triumphantly as he gestured to Samson who remained silent if you don't count his heaving breaths which were amplified from the microphone Mr. Luciano held so close to his poor battered face.

"Il mio campione, I never doubted you for a moment. So what do you have to say for yourself Samson," Mr. Luciano inquired with a smile.

"I want to say ... that we Irishmen ... are a proud people ... who should never be counted out, and as long as I have someone or something to fight for in this world, then I will fight with all me heart," Samson replied in a heaving tone into the microphone.

"Well said mi amico. Such valiance displayed by this man right here. Thanks to him my authority over this organization now reigns supreme," Mr. Luciano pronounced with a grin, as once again half of the speakeasy cheered in response to Mr. Luciano's proclamation of victory over his only boss.

What would this mean for me, Jack, and Mickey? Would it mean that we three are safe for now and can continue to live in the speakeasy as was the deal? I then noticed Mr. Luciano whisper something into Samson's ear as they both exited the ring.

"Samson, wait!" I shouted as Mr. Luciano placed his arm on Samson's shoulders as they walked towards the front door, but two mobsters suddenly blocked me from getting any closer to Samson as I watched him exit the speakeasy with Mr. Luciano.

*****

"It was 3:47 PM in the speakeasy as I wrote in my diary at the bar. It had been two weeks since Samson's victory over Paul Kelly, but I have yet to see him since. God only knows what Mr. Luciano promised Samson as they left the speakeasy together, but I had a terrible feeling in my heart that Samson may have agreed to Mr. Luciano's duplicitous offers. Everything was back to normal in the speakeasy now, well as normal as things could be in a speakeasy that caters to mobsters.

"Have you heard from Samson lately?" I inquired as Mickey walked up to the bar with a sigh.

"No, but I sure miss him," Mickey replied as Jack exited the kitchen and walked up to the bar.

"Jack where's Samson. Is he all right?" I inquired in a stern tone.

"You ask me this every day, kid. Last I heard from Leo, Samson was working closely with Mr. Luciano," Jack replied, as he wiped down the bar.

"I thought Samson swore to never return to that life," I said in a somber tone.

"It's not that simple, kid. You do what you have to in this day and age in order to survive. That life returned to him, despite him fleeing his past, that past still managed to catch up with him. Perhaps now that stubborn Irishman has finally begun to embrace his past," Jack said to me.

"Hayley, mon chéri, it's good to see you back to your true self," Faye remarked with a warm smile as she walked up to the bar.

"Faye, I missed you," I said to Faye with a smile as I hugged her.

"I heard there was a boxing match here," Faye pronounced with a grin as she sat down next to me at the bar.

"There sure was, and just what rock have you been hiding under these past three weeks?" Jack inquired with a grin.

"That rock mon chéri, as you so crassly put it is my work at the library," Faye replied with a scoff as she lit a cigarette and took a smoke.

"This was no ordinary boxing match, Faye. Samson fought against Paul Kelly, the founder of the Five Points Gang, and he won," I said to Faye.

"Oh my, then why do you not look happy?" Faye inquired, and then tapped her long violet-painted nails upon the bar. "Well, we haven't seen Samson since, I fear Mr. Luciano has propositioned him," I replied in a somber tone.

"Samson is a brute, but I sense his heart makes the final decisions," Faye said to me with a sigh which grew into a smile as Jack served her favorite cocktail.

"He's more than a mobster, and it would break my heart to see him return to that life," I said to Faye in a somber tone.

"Hayley, you have such an encompassing heart. You know that's the trait of a saint," Faye remarked with a warm smile. "I would never use that word to describe me," I said in a timid tone, as I brushed a strand of hair behind my ear.

"Shhh quiet you two," Jack pronounced in a stern tone as he turned up the volume on the radio.

"Public enemies, Bonnie Elizabeth Parker and Clyde Chestnut Barrow have struck again! Reports from Sherman Texas have stated that the duo robbed a store owner at gunpoint and once again ended up evading the police. As Sherman county police arrived on the scene of the robbery, the store owner was found dead from two gunshot wounds to the chest. The store owner was later identified as Howard Hall and if further investigation indicates that Bonnie Parker and or Clyde Barrow were responsible for the shop owner's death, then this would bring the kill count of the criminal duo up to nine. If anybody has any information on these deadly fugitives please contact your local authorities so that the hand of justice can stop their crime spree," the radio sounded.

"It seems like those two are only robbing small town shops. They're cunning, but you can only run for so long before the law finds you," Jack pronounced.

"Well in your case Jack Mr. Luciano has the entire NYPD in his pocket. So you don't have to worry about breaking the law," Faye said to Jack with a scoff, and then took a sip of her Black Rose cocktail.

"Why would she stay with him?" I inquired.

"Who, Bonnie Parker? I heard those two are around twenty years old. So they must be thinking with their hearts, not their heads," Jack replied while shaking his head.

"It's not always bad to let your heart make the decisions," I said to Jack.

"In this case it is, kid. You see the heart is irrational. The heart doesn't live in reality," Jack said to me.

"Those two must be in love. Or what they feel is love for each other, is most likely how do you say … infatuation, as Jack stated they are fairly young after all," Faye said to me with a sigh.

Bonnie and Clyde were only five years older than me, and yet they've killed nine people. Jack knows what it feels like to end someone's life and so does Samson, but even though I'm surrounded by men who kill with no hesitation, I could never bring myself to end the life of another. Was Bonnie Parker following Clyde Barrow because she loves him? Does love make you blind to everything and everyone around you to the point where you can kill with no remorse all for the sake of love? I didn't fully agree with Jack when he said that the heart doesn't live in reality, but I do understand what he means. If the heart can indeed bring someone to kill when the head would most likely consider all the consequences, then perhaps love can be a dangerous double-edged sword.

"Speaking of jezebels, how's your life, Faye?" Jack inquired with a grin.

"Pardon, I don't claim to be perfect Jack, but I'm no jezebel," Faye replied in a stern tone as he smacked Jack on the shoulder.

"Don't call her that," I said to Jack in a stern tone.

"Don't fret mon chéri Hayley. Jack has called me far worse in the past," Faye said to me with a grin, and then lit a cigarette and took a smoke, as Carmen took the stage.

"Do you think Carmen likes working here?" I inquired as I stared at Carmen on stage who wore a gold sequin dress which hugged her curvaceous body in such a way I could never wear a dress.

"She told me that Mr. Luciano pays her handsomely, but she doesn't want to be tied down to this speakeasy for the rest of her life," Faye replied.

"Neither do I," I said to Faye with a sigh.

"Well then let us depart, mon chéri," Faye said to me with a smile, as she stood up from the bar and put on her black trench coat.

"Where are we going?" I inquired in a zealous tone.

"We shall see what the day has in store for us, but first let's drop by my flat," Faye replied, and then finished drinking her cocktail with one last swig.

"Jack, Faye and I are stepping out, are you going to be all right by yourself?' I inquired as I put on my gray wool jacket. "I'll be fine. Mickey will be here soon. You two stay out of trouble though," Jack shouted from the kitchen.

"Au revoir Jack," Faye pronounced, as we then exited the speakeasy.

*****

It was 4:15 PM as Faye parked her rose Cadillac at the entrance of *Magnolia Towers*.

"This chill in the air reminds me when I was your age growing up in *Loire*

Valley," Faye said to me as we exited her Cadillac and walked up to the entrance of *Magnolia Towers* where a couple of homeless people were camped out.

"Was it cold in the Valley?" I inquired.

"Un instant ma chérie, uhm one moment," Faye replied as she held out her hand towards me and then scampered up to one of the homeless people at the entrance of *Magnolia Towers*. "I felt guilty that I was so accustomed to the sight of homeless people where I didn't so much as to even bat an eye at them, whereas Faye addressed them in such a compassionate manner, the manner in which all people suffering through this depression should be treated.

"It's cold outside. Do you two have somewhere to sleep tonight?" Faye inquired with a wide-eyed stare as she kneeled down in front of the old man and woman huddled together under layers of tattered blankets.

"You're looking at it ma'am," the homeless man replied in a somber tone.

"I can take you both to the Church of the Ascension on *5th Avenue*. The clergy there will help you in ways I sadly cannot," Faye said to the homeless man.

"Margret ... Margret, wake up. This kind woman is going to take us to a church where we can sleep for the night," the homeless man said, as he nudged the old woman beside him who was resting her head on his shoulder.

"Oh bless your heart. You're the first person to acknowledge us here. You are a saint my dear," the old woman said to Faye with a smile as her gray tinted face quivered.

"I am no saint, mon ami, but the clergy at the Church of the Ascension are in my opinion the closest to sainthood as anyone could be. Shall we?" Faye inquired with a warm smile as she stood up and extended her hand towards the homeless man.

"I'm Bernard and this is my wife Margaret," the old man said to Faye with a smile, as he grabbed her hand and pulled himself off the ground.

"It's a pleasure to meet you both. It was no mere coincidence that our paths crossed. I believe we were fated to meet each other this afternoon," Faye pronounced, as she helped Margaret off the ground.

"We're ready," Bernard said to Faye.

"Merveilleuse, Hayley do you want to accompany us to the church or wait in my flat for me to return?" Faye inquired, as Margaret and Bernard entered Faye's Cadillac.

"I—uhm, I'll wait in your apartment," I replied.

"I won't be long. Make yourself at home. Flat F-17 mon chéri," Faye said to me with a warm smile as she handed me the key to her apartment and then entered her Cadillac and drove east to the church.

Why didn't I go with Faye and the homeless couple to the church? Perhaps it could've been because I didn't want to be reminded even more of how miserable everyone's lives are right now including mine, I thought to myself during the slow elevator ride to Faye's apartment.

"Meow," a sound called out to me as I unlocked the door and entered Faye's apartment.

"Hello there," I said with a smile at the sight of Faye's black cat Sable walking up to me in a curious manner.

"Faye will be back soon, but is there anything I can get you?" I inquired as Sable meowed again and then rubbed up against my leg.

"Oh you're hungry aren't you? Well let's see if Faye has any milk left for you," I said to Sable with a smile and then opened the fridge.

"All right, this should hold you over till Faye gets back," I said to Sable with a smile, as I poured the milk into an ivory saucer and then placed it on the coffee table next to one of the many beautiful plants that decorated her apartment.

*****

It was 5:07 PM in Faye's apartment as the sound of a man shouting at a woman in the hallway in such an aggressive manner startled me to the point where I put a record on the victrola just to drown out the sound. That sound of a man and woman shouting at each other would always bring me back to the times when my mother would fight with Johnny. It's a memory that continues to stay with me to this day, a memory that makes me shake with a nervous fear.

I then poured myself a glass of merlot as the sound of a woman singing in French playing on the victrola began to soothe my nerves. I then began to wonder if I would've turned into a woman like Bonnie Parker if I stayed with Stefano. At first I was so attracted to him, but as Faye said, that was all just infatuation. The way Stefano made me feel was small and I will never give my heart to anyone who makes me feel that way. I wonder if Mickey still cares for me. It would be selfish and conceited of me to think that he does, although a part of me still hopes for it.

"Come here, Sable," I said to Sable as I gestured for him to join me on the sofa.

Sable then jumped up onto the sofa and sat down on my lap. Whether it is from the wine, the music, or Sable, I felt at peace at that moment as my eyes weighed heavy and I began to slowly drift off on the sofa.

*****

"Hayley I'm back," a voice called out to me.

"Mom, mom, why were you gone so long?" I inquired in a murmuring tone as I rolled over on the sofa and opened my eyes to the sight of Faye in the kitchen putting away a bag of groceries.

"Thank you for feeding Sable. He gets so restless on an empty stomach," Faye said to me with a warm smile as she sat down on the sofa and petted Sable, who was sleeping above me on the back of the sofa.

"He's wonderful company. How did everything go at the church?" I inquired in a yawning tone, as I sat upright on the sofa.

"The Church of The Ascension was already full of people with no place to sleep for the night, but the priest allowed Bernard and Margret to stay. He told me he would 'never close the doors to one of god's children who are in desperate need of help,'" Faye replied as she lit a cigarette and took a smoke.

I always found the smell of smoke to be repulsive no matter where I was, except when I was with Faye in her apartment. The smell of the smoke combined with Faye's sweet perfumes was actually pleasant to me. Besides, a woman like Faye couldn't be repulsive if she tried. I'm glad Faye was able to help that sweet old homeless couple. I always tend to freeze up when I'm around strangers, but Faye immediately took action because she believed it was fate that she crossed paths with them at the entrance to her apartment.

"Oh where are my manners, you must be hungry mon chéri," Faye said with a sigh as she stood up from the sofa and walked over to the kitchen.

"I am a little hungry," I remarked with a grin as a stroked Sable who continued to sleep on the back of the sofa in such a peaceful manner.

"When I was your age, my mother always told me that 'a real woman never starves herself of food or love, for they are both essential to the heart and soul,'" Faye said to me with a smile.

"What are you making?" I inquired with a smile as I stood up from the sofa and walked over to Faye who appeared to be mixing flour, egg, and cheese together in a bowl.

"I'm cooking Gougères. They are a wonderful cheese puff that my mother used to cook for me all the time," Faye replied with a warm smile.

"Can I help?" I inquired in a timid tone.

"Of course mon chéri, I was just about to ask," Faye replied with a smile as she gestured for me to join her at the counter.

"What can I do?" I inquired with a smile.

"Could you shred the Gruyère cheese with that grater s'il vous plaît?" Faye replied with a smile.

"Oh all right," I said to Faye with a smile, and then began grating the wedge of cheese upon the grater.

"This meal may not be luxurious like you're used to at the speakeasy, but it has always fed me and my mother when we were at are coldest and hungriest in the valley," Faye said to me. "Faye ... Jack and I may work for an incredibly powerful man, but that doesn't mean I live luxuriously. My life right now at this moment being with you in your apartment feels more luxurious than all my days spent with Jack at the speakeasy," I said to Faye.

"That's so sweet of you to say mon chéri. I'm sorry if I offended you. I know you, Jack, Samson, and Mickey are doing the best they can to survive. It must be, how you say ... wrecking your nerves being surrounded by those mobsters all day and night," Faye said to me, as she placed her hand gently on my cheek.

"Nerve-wrecking indeed, but It has made me stronger. Those mobsters, as terrible as most of them are, have taught me how to not let anybody make me feel small. I learned that from the mistake my mother made," I said to Faye in a somber tone, as my eyes began to well up with tears.

"Did you ever cook with your mother?" Faye inquired.

"Yes, but all I remember when I was cooking with her was Johnny storming into the apartment and ruining our precious moment together with his rage," I replied in a somber tone as a tear began to stream down my cheek.

"I'm sorry … your mother sounds like she tried with all her heart to keep you safe and happy," Faye said to me.

"I feel safe and happy now," I said to Faye with a smile and sniff as I continued to help Faye cook the Gougères.

"You will be even happier once the Gougères are done baking," Faye said to me with a warm smile.

*****

It was 6:26 PM in Faye's apartment as the savory aroma of the Gougères filled her apartment.

"What are you doing in here, mon chéri? The Gougères are done baking," Faye inquired with a smile as she entered her bedroom.

"Oh wonderful, I'm starving. I was just looking at your collection of literature," I replied in a timid tone. I wonder if Faye doesn't fully trust me to be alone in her apartment ever since I took her wig, dress, and make up without asking. I thought to myself as Faye walked over to her bookcase.

"Oh have you read 20,000 Leagues Under The Sea yet?" Faye inquired with a smile.

"Oh um … I haven't started reading it yet, sorry," I replied. "Do not fret. Monsieur Verne will always be there for you whenever you need to escape into his stories, but for now let us eat," Faye said to me with a smile as she gestured for me to follow her into the kitchen.

"It smells so good." I remarked as I entered the kitchen to the sound of Faye singing along to a French song playing on the victrola.

"After dinner I have to stop by the prison to drop off some literature to my friends," Faye said to me as we sat down at the table.

"Do your friends work at the prison?" I inquired, as I grabbed three steaming Gougères out of the basket and placed them on my plate as Faye poured me and herself a glass of wine.

"No they're serving time at the prison," Faye replied.

"Oh you're friends with criminals," I remarked as I took a bite of the Gougères.

"You sound surprised mon chéri," Faye said to me with a grin.

"Well uhm … I guess I didn't expect someone like you to be friends with criminals. I mean I'm not friends with any mobsters at the speakeasy," I said to Faye as the delicious flavors of the Gougères brought a smile to my face.

"Someone like me will be friends with anyone with a good heart. Those women in that prison across the street have made bad decisions, but that doesn't mean they're bad people Tout le monde mérite une seconde chance, everyone deserves a second chance mon chéri," Faye said to me, and then took a bite of a

Gougères.

"Do you think I should give Mickey a second chance?" I inquired.

"That's for your heart to decide mon chéri. Why did you stop seeing him in the first place?" Faye inquired.

The reason why I stopped seeing Mickey and then started seeing Stefano seemed so childish to me now. I did miss Mickey's kindness and the way he looked at me as if he was looking straight into my heart, not just my hair, makeup or what I'm wearing.

"He uhm, he didn't accept my flapper look," I replied

"That's the reason why? Oh mon chéri. I understand what you felt at that moment, but that sweet boy was speaking from his heart. He didn't want to hurt you," Faye said to me.

"It's too late now. I wouldn't blame Mickey if he never even wanted to hold my hand again," I said to Faye, as I took a bite of another savory Gougères.

"Hayley, you are very young. It's never too late for you to pursue whomever your heart beats for. Are you done eating now?" Faye inquired with a smile, as she reached over the dinner table and placed her hand upon mine.

"Now I'm done," I replied with a smile as I popped another Gougères into my mouth

"Splendid, I could just drive you back to the speakeasy after we're done washing the dishes, or do you want to accompany me to the prison?" Faye inquired, as she began to clean the table.

"I would very much like to come with you to the prison," I replied with a sigh as I stood up from the kitchen table and stared out the window at one of the women who had her arms sticking out through the bars of her cell.

What did Faye see in these women who were serving time in prison to consider them her friends? I thought to myself as I stared intently at the woman whose face remained shrouded by the darkness of her cell.

"I'm ready when you are mon chéri," Faye said to me with a smile.

"I'm ready," I said to Faye with a smile.

"Could you carry these books s'il vous plaît?" Faye inquired as she pointed to a stack of books on the kitchen counter. "Sure, are these for the prisoners oh I mean your friends at the prison," I inquired as I lifted the stack of books with a slight grunt.

"Qui, they were requested by a few of the women, one of which is an avid reader of English literature," Faye replied, as she put on her black trench coat.

"Goodbye Sable," I said to Sable with a smile, as Faye and I exited her apartment.

*****

It was 7:02 PM as Faye and I entered the prison/library/ courthouse known as *Jefferson Market Court*.

"Who is this, Ms. Dubois?" one of the prison guards inquired in a stern tone as he pointed at me with his club.

"This is my guest Ms, Hayley Carmona," Faye replied with a smile.

"Does she have any identification," the guard inquired inn a stern tone as he looked at me as if I was trying to break out one of the women in the prison.

"Oh uhm I don't have any identification with me now," I replied in a timid tone.

"Either way we will have to search her and all of these books. You can hollow out a book and store anything from a knife to a gun, especially these thick books," the guard said to Faye, as another guard searched my body.

"Oh come now William, you know I would never destroy these books I hold so dear," Faye said to the guard.

"I'm afraid your word means nothing in the eyes of the law Ms. Dubois. Justice is blind and deaf. I cannot take your word just because you work for the courthouse or else I would be held liable if one of these women were to break free," the guard said to Faye as another guard searched through each of the five books.

"I understand you're just doing your job, but you need to treat these women more like people and not animals," Faye said to William.

"You don't tell me how to do my job and I won't tell you how to do yours. You're all clear," William said to Faye with a smile.

"Wonderful, Lets go Hayley," Faye said to me, as she gestured for me to pick up the books and follow her and an armed guard down a narrow hallway were the sound of women shouting echoed as if we were in a cave.

"Where's Louise Claudette? I have her copy of Pride and Prejudice," Faye inquired.

"Oh she's in here cell right now," the guard replied.

"Can we arrange a visit so I can give her the literature she requested?" Faye inquired.

"Yes we can arrange that," the guard replied, as we walked to a room where I could only assume was where all the women prisoners met with their visitors.

"Wait right here," the guard pronounced, as he gestured for Faye and I to sit down at a table and then exited the room.

"Louise will be pleased to see us both," Faye said to me with a smile.

"So why is she serving time here?" I inquired as I sat down beside Faye.

"You can ask her that yourself mon chéri. She should be the one to tell you her story, not I," Faye replied as she primped her hair while looking into her pocket mirror.

I've never talked to a prisoner before and I must admit I was a little nervous waiting for this woman named Louise Claudette. I didn't know what crime she committed, so my mind began to race while Faye sat beside me smiling as if she was about to meet a lifelong friend.

"Louise …,"

"Faye … Cela fût bien trop long," Louis said to Faye as an armed guard escorted her to the table were Faye and I sat.

"You have ten minutes," the armed guard said in a stern tone, and then walked away, as Louise sat down at the table with a sigh.

"Tu as l'air bien mon chéri. Comment la vie à l'extérieur vous traite-t-elle?" Louise inquired. Louise had the face of a woman who once had a passion for life, but now the flame in her eyes and heart has now grown dim. She reminded me of my mother the way she smiled and because of that I wasn't nervous as she walked up to me and Faye. Now I was even more curious as to why she was serving time in this prison.

"Pas beaucoup mieux que ta vie ici, j'en ai peur. Parlons en anglais pour que mon invité Hayley puisse nous comprendre," Faye replied as she gestured to me with a smile.

"Very well my dear. So I hope you brought the literature I requested," Louise said to Faye.

"Oh yes right here," I said to Louise and then handed her the weather hardcover copy of Pride and Prejudice. "Wonderful ... I remember reading this when I was your age. Now I long to feel that sense of wonder while my life languishes in here," Louise said to me in a somber tone as her face quivered with sorrow.

"How much longer is your sentence?" Faye inquired in a somber tone as she placed her hand on Louis' hand.

"No touching. You get this one warning then your visitation is over!" one of the armed guards shouted from across the room in an aggressive tone as he pointed a club at Faye.

"A year, eight months with good behavior," Louise replied in a somber tone.

"Remember mon chéri, I'm right next door from you. So you're never alone," Faye said to Louise.

"Faye ... you might as well be in another state. I cannot leave my cell without these brutish men breathing down my neck with every step. I won't survive another eight months in here," Louise said to Faye in a somber tone.

"If I may ask ... why are you serving time in this prison?" I inquired in a timid tone.

"I walked in on my husband with another woman. Cette pute then quickly ran out of the bedroom where I used to lie with my husband, but not before telling me that he no longer loved me. Are marriage was now tainted as was my heart. The heart-wrenching betrayal I felt at that moment of my husband's infidelity culminated with me quickly grabbing a knife from our kitchen and stabbing him three times in the chest," Louise replied.

"Did you kill him, your husband?" I inquired. "Unfortunately no. he survived," Louise replied with a scoff.

"So you wanted him to die?" I inquired.

"At the moment I did, but now as I look back at that afternoon, I cannot help but regret what I did. Philippe's unfaithfulness wasn't worth me serving two years in this god forsaken place," Louise replied in a somber tone.

"I—I'm sorry," I said to Louise in a somber tone.

"Let my story be a lesson to you. Men are never worth the trouble," Louise said to me in a stern tone.

"Ah don't try to scare Hayley, Louise. She has been through more than most women our age," Faye said to Louise.

"Is that so mon chéri. Well you continue to live with that fire inside of you that obviously hasn't dimmed," Louise said to me.

"It has dimmed, many times, but I never let it go out. You deserve a second chance in life, and I hope this literature will keep your fire burning for the time being," I said to Louise with a smile.

"Times up!" the armed guard shouted at Louise. "Dépêchez-vous il ne regarde pas," Louise said to Faye with a wide eyed stare.

"Stay strong mon chéri," Faye said to Louise as they quickly kissed and embraced each other. I then noticed Faye take out a small envelope and slip it into the pocket of Louis' prison uniform.

The armed guard then escorted Louise out of the visitation room as she waved one last goodbye before the door slammed shut behind her.

"She wasn't what I expected," I remarked.

"Cast aside all those preconceived notions when you're in here Hayley. Only until you meet with these women do you know their hearts true intent. Now come on, we have two other women to visit," Faye said to me.

*****

It was 7:47 PM as Faye and I were visiting the last woman prisoner. She was a colored woman by the name of Harriet Struthers. This woman was far more vulgar and aggressive than Louise Claudette, but Faye always had a way of bringing out the sweet side of anybody she talked to, and Harriet was no exception.

"If I may ask, why are you serving time in this prison?" I inquired.

"Theft, can you believe that bullshit, honey? They will lock up a proud woman who has the rest of her life ahead of her all because of theft. Money can be replaced, but not people's lives," Harriet replied in a stern tone.

"What did you steal?" I inquired.

"A few grand from a liquor store in Brooklyn, but I needed that money to keep my grandmother off the street. This economy turns good people into robbers, but I don't regret what I did for my grandmother. People turn a blind eye in this day and age far too often, it makes me sick," Harriet replied.

"How is your grandmother doing now?" I inquired.

"She's surviving. The money I took from that liquor store helped pay for her medical needs, but she's in no way living the life she deserves to live. I fear by the time I get out of here she will be dead," Harriet replied in a somber tone.

"How much longer do you have in here mon chéri?" Faye inquired in a somber tone.

"Another year. You know when I was your age child I never thought about the consequences of living life to its fullest. Now I suppose all those choices finally caught up with me," Harriet said to me in a somber tone.

"This isn't the end of your life Harriet. You will see your grandmother again. I know she longs to hold you in her arms. You must keep that love alive within your heart, because without love, we're all doomed," Faye said to Harriet as she stared intently at her.

"We have your copy of Not Without Laughter by Langston Hughes," I said to Harriet with a smile, as I handed her the novel.

"Oh I suppose now's as good a time as any to read this book. Faye is an angel in a world of demons. You do your best to listen to her if you know what's good for you," Harriet said to me.

"I always do," I said to Harriet with a warm smile.

"Hurry he's not looking," Faye said to Harriet and then quickly embraced her with a kiss before slipping another small envelope into the pocket of her prison uniform just like she did with the last two women.

"Times up!" the armed guard shouted and then walked over to us in a stern manner.

"Godspeed mon chéri. I know we will meet again outside of this prison," Faye said to Harriet as the armed guard escorted her out of the visitation room.

I couldn't help but wonder what it was that Faye slipped into the pockets of the three women prisoners as we exited the prison in a somber manner.

*****

It was 8:25 PM as Faye and I entered her apartment.

"You gluttonous little boy, are you hungry again?" Faye inquired with a smile, as Sable walked up to her with a meow.

"It's raining," I remarked with a sigh as I stared out the living room window to the sight of a light rainfall washing over the city.

"I'm too tired to drive you back to the speakeasy mon chéri, but you can stay here for the night if you want," Faye said to me as she poured milk into a saucer for Sable.

"Uhm I don't know If I should stay here for the night. Jack might need my help at the speakeasy," I said to Faye as I took off my gray wool jacket and sat down on the sofa.

"It's your choice. If you do decide to leave remember to lock the door on your way out s'il vous plaît," Faye said to me as she took off her blouse and skirt in a slow and weary manner.

"Faye … uhm,"

"Yes Hayley?" Faye interjected as she now stood in front of me wearing only her black undergarments.

"What was in those small envelopes you slipped into those three woman's pockets at the prison?" I inquired.

"Oh … I didn't know you saw that. Can I trust you Hayley?" Faye replied as she sat down beside me on the sofa with a sigh, while still wearing nothing but her black undergarments which made me move slightly away from her on the sofa.

"Of course. I trust you with all my heart Faye and I want you to feel the same trust with me," I said to Faye as I stared intently at her bleary eyes.

"You have such an old soul mon chéri. That's what I adore about you. What I slipped into those three beautiful woman's pockets at the prison was three copies of a key," Faye said to me.

"A key? What does the key open?" I inquired.

"Those three women do not deserve to languish what could be the most fulfilling years of their lives in that prison. They did commit crimes, but they are still good people. I know you agree with me after meeting with them," Faye replied.

"I do believe they are good women, but you still didn't answer my question. What do those keys open?" I inquired as I became more nervous as to what Faye's answer would be.

"Those keys are copies of the master key that opens all the doors in the prison. I managed to, how you say … seduce one of the guards to a point where came home with me. Then I snuck out of my flat early in the morning and made three copies of the master key before he awoke from his drunken stupor," Faye replied.

I was left speechless at that moment. Faye was trying to break those three women out of prison, but would her plan be successful, or could it result in something terrible? I had no idea Faye's scheme this entire time was to commit a crime herself. In some ways this changed my opinion of her, but Faye's motives for helping those three women break out of prison were selfless, but that didn't matter in the eyes of the law.

"Faye … what if you get in trouble for this? What if those women try and escape with the key but fail? Aren't you worried that they will tell the guards about how you helped them? I don't want to see you locked up behind bars like those three women. Why would you do this?" I inquired in a distressed tone.

"Hayley … I did this because I felt the outcry of those three women resonate in my heart every day. I wouldn't be able to live with myself If I didn't do something to help them. Just as Harriet said, 'too many people turn a blind eye in this day and age.' They say justice is blind in America, but I am not. I may work for the prison, but I will not stand by while good women languish behind bars," Faye replied in a stern tone.

Faye was like a mother, older sister, and aunt to me and I would never turn her over to the police no matter what crime she committed, but I still felt disappointed in her actions. I won't go so far as to say that Jack was right when he called Faye a jezebel, but now I won't say that his comment was completely false.

"I just—I just couldn't bear losing you just as I lost my mother," I said to Faye in a somber tone as my face quivered.

"Mon chéri, the heart may not lead you down the safest path, but it's always a path worth taking. I'm aware of the consequences of helping those three women break out of those wretched confinements, but I must be the one who can give them a second chance in life as they so rightfully deserve," Faye said to me as she stood up from the sofa with a sigh and stared out the window at the prison across the street as the rainfall grew heavy to almost reflect the fear and sadness I felt over Faye's actions. Faye then lit a cigarette and took a smoke as many thoughts raced through my head, thoughts of Faye being arrested and serving time, or even worse.

"Faye … Do you see me and Jack as criminals just because we work for the leader of a very powerful crime organization?" I inquired in a timid tone, as Sable jumped upon the sofa and rubbed his head against my arm.

"In the eyes of the law, you and Jack would be seen as just another member of that notorious gang, but that's not who you two are to me. You and Jack do not have criminal intent in your hearts. It is a shame that we live in such a time where you're either a criminal, or you only have a few cents to your name," Faye said to me while shaking her head.

"Or both, Jack turned to bootlegging because he believed he could profit on the desire many people have to drink, but so did many other men like hi," I said to Faye who then gestured out the window towards the prison where a woman was gesturing back to her.

"Oh she wants another cigarette. I'm far too tired and the rain is far too heavy for me to grant her wish this evening," Faye said with a sigh and then walked over to the kitchen.

"Do you often do favors for those women?" I inquired, as I stared out the window at the woman who was then gesturing to me as if one cigarette would uplift her spirits so dramatically. "It's been a long day, I'm going to sleep. I hope you don't think any less of me after tonight, mon chéri. I also hope to see you in the morning, but I understand if you want nothing to do with me now well … bonsoir," Faye said to me in a somber tone and then exited the living room leaving me alone with Sable, who was staring up at me with curious emerald eyes glimmering with anticipation of what my decision was going to be.

I then took a couple of cigarettes from the pack off the kitchen table and put them in my bag, as I put on my wool jacket and shoes.

"You must love living with Faye. I hope you continue to have her in your life," I said to Sable as I stroked him with a warm smile. I then exited Faye's apartment in a stealthy manner. I then crossed the street and stood under the barred window where the woman prisoner was gesturing for Faye to give her a cigarette.

"Little girl, have you got a cigarette for me? Please a need a smoke so bad. I promise I'll make it worth your while?" the woman prisoner shouted as she stuck her pale bruised arms through the bars with a smile.

"All right I suppose I won't get in trouble with the police by giving you a cigarette or two, but I'm not very good at throwing," I shouted, as I stared up at the woman prisoner, while the rain began to drench my face and hair.

"Oh fuck those cops, what they don't know won't us. Here, just tie the cigarettes to this string," the woman shouted, and then tossed a string which appeared to be made out of her prison uniform through the barred window.

"All right … done," I shouted, as I finished tying the two cigarettes to the string tight enough to where they wouldn't slip out, but not too tight to where they would break.

"Ah beautiful!" the woman prisoner remarked, as she pulled up the two cigarettes in a hasty manner.

"All right now what do you have for me?" I shouted, as the woman lit the cigarette and took a long smoke.

"Huh what are you talking about?" the woman prisoner inquired in a bewildered tone.

"You said you would make it worth my while if I gave you cigarettes," I replied.

"Oh let this be a lesson for you sweetheart. Never trust a criminal. I'm behind these bars because I trusted a criminal just like you trusted me to keep my word," the woman prisoner said to me with a laugh and then left the barred window, leaving me standing in the rain wondering if Faye would ever use me in such a cold-hearted manner.

CHAPTER 15:
GREENER PASTURES
- JACK -

"She still hasn't returned, that kid. I wonder what kind of trouble she and Faye are getting themselves into. Every time Hayley leaves the speakeasy, the part of me that misses her struggles with the part of me that hopes she never returns. Still I believe the kid is too smart for her own damn good, and her and Faye will either invite trouble or go looking for it, and in a town like this they won't have to look too far. I also haven't seen Samson since his fight with Paul Kelly, and I can only assume what Mr. Luciano has persuaded him into doing. Right now it was me Leo and Mickey running the speakeasy. Leo was an adept barkeep, but that's what worried me. It was just as Samson said; Mr. Luciano is trying to replace me with this towering man who can mix a cocktail in under five minutes.

"Carmen chop chop, Mr. Luciano has some new associates which will be arriving soon and he wants to show them a good time here," Leo said to Carmen in a stern tone as he snapped his fingers and pointed to the stage in the same manner as Mr. Luciano.

"Hold your horses Leo. I'm not a machine that can be automatically turned on at your beck and call," Carmen said to Leo as she quickly primped her hair.

"What a pity that is, am I right Jack?" Leo said to me with a snicker, as I snickered back while filling up a pitcher of lager.

"So Leo … what kind of man were you before you started working for Mr. Luciano?" I inquired.

"I was a man who had no idea how strong I truly was. Then Mr. Luciano helped me realize the strength I had. If I wasn't working for that man right now then I would be on the streets most likely robbing Wall Street business men," Leo replied with a smirk.

"Now those Wall Street business men are seeking you out to kill their bosses, right?" I inquired with a scoff.

"I'm not a hitman like Nikolai or your former associate Samson. I'm simply an enforcer," Leo said to me.

"So you've never killed anyone at the orders of Mr. Luciano? I must say I'm surprised to hear that," I said to Leo, as I noticed a mobster at the table in front of the stage was giving Mickey attitude to the point where the boy began to cower in his domineering presence.

"Killing, believe it or not, doesn't send as powerful of a message as other forms Mr. Luciano taught me to inflict on his enemies," Leo said to me.

"What forms are those, if I may ask?" I inquired, as I saw that mobster smack Mickey in the face, but it was really more of a tap.

"Psychological, mi amico. You simply need to fuel your enemies' fears and then you have them cowering like that boy over there," Leo replied with a snicker as he pointed at Mickey. "That boy over there is Mickey and he's a hard worker. Is he still being protected by Falcone?" I inquired in a stern tone.

"Last I heard Falcone is still protecting that runt, but not for much longer," Leo replied.

"Oh really. Why's that?" I inquired.

"I've already answered too many of your questions, Jack. "Right now you know all you need to know, comprendere?" Leo inquired in a stern tone, as Mickey slowly walked up to the bar with a somber look on his face.

"Inteso," I replied with a stern look as Leo walked over to the stage.

"What happened Mickey?" I inquired.

"T—That mobster told me 'kids like me were born to serve men like him' then he smacked me in the face, all because I asked him twice what his drink order was," Mickey replied in a stammering tone.

"What a conceited son of a bitch, and just what makes him so special? You know Carlo said the same thing to me, then he met his end soon after. They don't want us to tow the line, kid. For the time being we must serve them," I said to Mickey while shaking my head, as I stared at Leo who appeared to be flirting with Carmen at the stage as she was getting ready to perform.

"I—I wish Hayley was here, she's fearless," Mickey remarked in a stammering tone, as he placed a tray of empty glasses on the bar.

"She sure is. She gets that fearlessness from her mother," I said to Mickey with a grin, as Leo scampered over to the bar. "Mickey, I have a new job for you. You will now be Carmen's new errand boy. You can thank me later," Leo said to Mickey with a smirk.

"Oh uhm all right," Mickey said to Leo in a timid tone.

I must say if Leo told me my new job was to attend to that buxom dame Carmen I would be much more enthusiastic, but it appeared that the boy wasn't the least bit happier over the news.

"Well go. I believe she has some odd jobs for you. If you're lucky she might have you act as her foot rest," Leo said to Mickey with a laugh as he nudged me with his elbow, but I could only smirk at the callous comment Leo made to Mickey.

"Was that suppose to be an act of kindness?" I inquired, as Mickey scampered over to Carmen on the stage.

"You don't see it as one?" Leo replied.

"I don't know yet. What does Carmen need so badly?" I inquired, as I stared at Carmen who was talking to Mickey who didn't look her in the eyes for more than a moment before staring downward towards her shiny red heels.

"She's what I call a high maintenance dame, but she brings in the business, and you and I both know how a dame like her can persuade a man to empty his wallet just like that," Leo said to me with a grin and snap of his fingers.

Leo Cordero wasn't what I expected a man of his appearance to be. He no doubt swore his allegiance to Mr. Luciano, but he has never even killed a man like Samson and I have. This doesn't mean I didn't worry over the strong possibility of him replacing me. I still sensed a shred of compassion in him, but that wasn't enough to make me trust him. Working with Leo was in no way like working with Samson. Samson and I have watched out for each other for years from men like Leo. Even though Leo told me he had never killed a man, I still had no doubt that he would be able to if Mr. Luciano gave him enough incentive. Men of immense wealth like Mr. Luciano can persuade a man to do almost anything that goes against his morals, and by the time that task is over the man no longer remembers who he was before the incentive of money was placed onto the table.

"Well well looks like you're missing two of your associates Jack," Stefano remarked with a grin as he walked up to the bar. "Was that your plan all along, to get rid of Hayley and Samson?" I inquired with a scoff and stern stare at the arrogant young bastard who now carried himself with an air as if he ran the speakeasy.

"You're still here, so I still have one last rat to smoke out of this establishment," Stefano said to me with a snicker. "Hayley didn't leave because of you, kid," I said to Stefano. "I'm sure she left because of you. Who would want to live with a failed bootlegger as an uncle," Stefano inquired with a snicker.

Stefano was doing to me what he succeeded in doing with Samson, but my temper wasn't as easily triggered as the bold Irishman's was. Stefano wouldn't lure me into ringing his scrawny little neck, because I knew there would be mobsters in this speakeasy that would rise up and fill me full of lead at that very moment.

"Calm down kid, here, this shot's on me, or do you have to ask your uncle for permission to drink," I inquired with a snicker as I poured Stefano a shot of bourbon.

"Soon you'll be asking me for permission Jack, and when that day comes … you'll see who holds all the cards," Stefano said to me after he took the shot of bourbon and slammed the glass on the bar with a grin.

Stefano was beginning to talk in the same rhetoric as his uncle, but I wasn't intimidated by him one bit. Every time the boy spoke to me I just remember when his uncle smacked him in front of everyone during the meeting. That act of discipline showed me that Stefano was in no way giving orders to any mobster.

"Leo what's that kid doing with Carmen?" Stefano inquired as he stared at Mickey who was talking to Carmen on the stage. "I appointed him to be her new errand boy. Hopefully now she won't be such a drama queen and perform when we tell her too," Leo replied.

"That orphan rat has no business being around her, he's not good enough to even lick her heels," Stefano remarked with a scoff as he continued to stare at Mickey with such resentment burning in his eyes.

I now realized that Stefano's fascination with Mickey was entirely based in jealousy. First Stefano was jealous that Hayley used to be close with Mickey, now Stefano is jealous that Mickey is working for Carmen. The boy projects all of his anger and insecurities on Mickey because he thinks Mickey is beneath him and too weak and timid to fight back. I have noticed a change in Mickey's demeanor now that Hayley is gone. The boy has reverted back to his timid self that wouldn't so much as look you in the eye for more than a moment before hanging his head low and mumbling under his breath. Mickey was a good kid, but I couldn't fight his battles for him, it's all part of becoming a man, and Mickey will have to learn one way or another how to stand tall around all of these mobsters.

"He's lousy at taking drink orders, just like Jack's niece. So I thought he might do better serving Carmen. Do you have a better idea?" Leo inquired.

"No ... not yet at least," Stefano replied

"Shhh quiet!" I shouted as I turned up the volume on the radio.

"In national news, Franklin Delano Roosevelt has won the presidential election becoming the 32nd president of the United States of America, thoroughly beating his Republican incumbent Herbert Hoover in a landslide democratic victory!" The radio sounded triumphantly as absolutely nobody in the speakeasy cheered or expressed any happiness over that bleeding heart democrat's victory.

"None of that news matters to you Jack. My uncle is your president now, and he has far more influence over the state of New York than Frankie," Stefano said to me with a snicker.

I was in no way optimistic over FDR's victory, but I don't see how he could possibly do any worse running this country than that travesty Hoover has done. I wanted results, not talk. Only until I no longer see breadlines three blocks long and bums begging for money in every park will I then be happy with FDR, but that may just be wishful thinking on my end. I've been searching my entire life for this so called "Easy Street" and I have yet to find it. Do these mobsters who surround me believe that their lives are on easy street, or perhaps they chose to join the Five Points Gang because they believed that Mr. Luciano would take them there, as I so foolishly believed him on the night he first arrived at the speakeasy? I've now come to the conclusion that easy street doesn't exist. Every street in this town will lead you to the same rotten place where the only dreams are the ones you have when you're blacked out drunk.

"Tell me Leo, Is Hayley still being watched?" I inquired as I stared intently at Leo.

"Mr. Luciano knows all too well not to underestimate a dame, as for your niece, she has proved to be quite unpredictable, and unpredictable elements tend to become hazardous if not monitored," Leo replied.

"You should go into politics," I remarked.

"Why do you say that," Leo inquired with a scoff.

"I say that because you answered my question without answering my question," I replied with a scoff.

"So I will tell you this, if the wolf harms Hayley in any way, then I won't do to him what I did to Frankie. I'll silence that Cossack just as I did with Johnny," I said to Leo in a stern tone.

"So that's the line you're going to draw in the sand huh Jack? Well Mr. Luciano will not bend to your will, so do you really want me to relay that threat to him?" Leo inquired with a grin, as we stared at each other with such intensity burning in our eyes.

"Jack I need to borrow the Pontiac," Mickey said to me as he scampered up to bar.

"What the hell for?" I inquired in a stern tone.

"Ms. Valentino needs these products from the store," Mickey replied.

"Carmen!" I shouted as I whistled and gestured for her to come over to the bar.

"What is it Jack? I'm getting ready to perform," Carmen inquired, as she cupped her ample bosom with her hands and pushed them up and together so even more of her cleavage would be exposed.

"Is this going to be a normal thing, ordering Mickey to buy your unmentionables? I inquired in a stern tone as I waved the list in front of Carmen's green eyes which rolled in disdain.

"Leo told me that Mickey is my new errand boy. Isn't that right honey?" Carmen inquired with a smile as she grabbed Mickey's cheek.

"Fine, but you better knock the socks off all of us tonight. Now that we're pampering you like a princess," I said to Carmen with a scoff as I handed Mickey Carmen's list.

"Thank you Jack, I'll be right back Ms. Valentino," Mickey said before he exited the speakeasy.

"It's slowing down in here, why don't you take the rest of the evening off. You don't want to work yourself to death," Leo said to me.

"Very well, I could us some fresh air," I said to Leo, as I loosened my tied and put on my trench coat.

I then exited the speakeasy with a realization that Leo was now running things, and that realization made me worry over my future at the speakeasy.

The crisp Fall air felt refreshing against my flushed and flustered face, as I walked down Minetta Street to the sight of three cops restraining a flailing man holding a sign that read: "GIVE ME LIQUOR OR GIVE ME DEATH!"

"Why not both?" I spoke aloud with a grin as I walked past the man who now laid face down into the pavement while the three cops apprehended him.

"Take it easy pal"

"Maybe a night behind bars will give you some time to reflect on assaulting that poor woman," the cops said to the man in a stern tone, and then shoved him into the car.

Was there a way out of this town? Was there a way out of the Five Points Gang? I thought to myself as I walked east down a street that I've walked down many times with Samson, but now I walk it alone. Was there a way for me to escape all of this, or like Samson, would my past inevitably find me no matter where I fled to? It then occurred to me, If the wolf is following my Pontiac which Mickey is using to pamper that conceited dame Carmen. Then perhaps I could visit Faye and Hayley without that Cossack knowing where they live.

"Taxi!" I shouted with a whistle as I tried to hail for a taxicab while standing on the street corner. After a few moments of smoking a taxicab then slowed down in front of me with a sputter and pop of the muffler.

"You should get that muffler checked out," I remarked with a grin.

"Oh are you going to pay for it Rockefeller?" the taxicab driver inquired with a scoff.

"To *Magnolia Towers*," I replied as I flicked my cigarette into the gutter as I entered the taxicab.

*****

It was 4:27 PM as the taxicab parked in front of *Magnolia Towers*.

"Keep the change, spend it on fixing that muffler," I said to the taxicab driver as I paid my fair and then exited the taxicab. "Oh you're too kind," the taxicab driver remarked in a sarcastic tone and then drove off with a pop and sputter from his muffler.

Before entering *Magnolia Towers*, I crossed the street and I stared up at the window of Faye's apartment for a brief moment before two familiar faces came into frame. It was Faye and Hayley in the window smiling as they primped each other's hair in the manner that Dezerae would primp Hayley's hair when she was younger. They looked right, they looked happy together.

"Hayley," I spoke aloud in a somber tone, as I came to the conclusion that Faye could give Hayley everything I couldn't. It pained me to admit it, but Stefano was right. Hayley's life living with Faye was all for the better, and a failed bootlegger uncle would only bring more pain into her already painful life. My smile as I stared up at Faye and Hayley then slowly diminished along with my head as it lowered in the shadow of Faye and Hayley's happiness.

"Good luck kid," I spoke aloud in a somber tone and then walked away from *Magnolia Towers*.

It's just as well anyways. I couldn't be tied down to a kid for the rest of my life. I thought to myself as a woman from the prison across the street from *Magnolia Towers* was waving down to me through the barred window.

"Hey handsome spare me a cigarette and I'll make it worth your while," the woman prisoner shouted.

"Oh really, and just how exactly are you going to do that from all the way up there?" I inquired with a grin, as I lit a cigarette and took a smoke.

"Come on baby, give a tired gal like me a break," the woman prisoner replied in a pleading tone.

So these are the women which Faye deals with every day. Well I wasn't about to trust or even humor these kinds of women. I know all too well if you give them an inch they'll take a mile.

"Take it from me, don't ever try to con a con man," I said to the woman prisoner as I walked away from the prison.

"It's just one cigarette you cheap son of a bitch show some charity," the woman shouted at me.

I had no room in my heart for charity. My life was under the oppression of one of the most powerful men in New York, and I felt powerless this time without Samson and Hayley by my side. Whatever pretty penny Mr. Luciano offered Samson in order to get him to work for him as his muscle would cost that Irishman his soul. Would the next time I see Samson involve him pointing a gun at me as per Mr. Luciano's orders to silence me for good this time? Forming bonds that stood the test of time was nearly impossible in this day and age, but it has always been that way for me even when I was just a kid living with my mother and sister in *SoHo*.

*****

"So is your dad fighting in the war too?" I asked Matthew as we tossed balls against the side of the school.

"No he runs a deli a couple blocks from here" Matthew replied.

"You're lucky," I said to Matthew in a somber tone, as we continued to bounce balls against the wall, while other boys and girls played their games in the schoolyard.

"Why do you say that?" Matthew asked.

"You know where your dad is every day," I replied in a somber tone.

I was jealous of Matthew. Not for his nice clothes or the way he seems to make all the girls smile whenever he talks to them, but because he had a dad to see every day when he came home from school. I couldn't bring myself to listen to him talk about his dad knowing that I won't have those times with my dad any time soon. So I pushed him away, because he could never understand my life with my mom and sister.

"So when is your dad coming back from the war anyways?"
Matthew asked me.

"I don't know and don't ever ask me that again!" I shouted. I then shoved Matthew aside as I ran into the school with tears welling up in my eyes.

*****

"Jack … Jack anybody home in there?" Leo inquired, as he snapped his fingers in front of my face.

"Yes what is it Leo?" I inquired, as I rubbed my bleary eyes.

"Stefano said that his uncle wants this place to cater more to rival gangs. He said that we must first try to strike a deal before pulling the trigger," Leo replied.

"Or strike a deal and then pull the trigger. If Mr. Luciano wants to tell me something then he can tell me to my face. I won't take orders from a wet behind the ears kid with delusions of grandeur," I said to Leo in a stern tone, as Carmen began to sing a rousing song which made all the mobsters holler and whistle the very moment she opened that pretty mouth of hers. "Are you talking about Stefano? Let me inform you Jack that if Mr. Luciano is assassinated then that kid will become the new leader of the Five Points Gang," Leo said to me in stern tone.

"I'm well aware of how your organization works, but for the time being let's just do our jobs. If you try too hard to predict the future you won't see the present coming as it punches you square in the jaw," I said to Leo.

"That dame is really something else huh, Jack. I say she's worth every penny Mr. Luciano spent on her," Leo remarked as he stared at Carmen on the stage.

"She's decoration, nothing more. Women like her have come and gone through these doors so often I've lost count, while men like you swoon over them like hungry dogs," I remarked with a snicker, as Carmen pulled her skirt up as she sat down on a chair and stuck her shapely stocking-clad legs out with a smile.

"Men like me. I think you meant to say 'men like us' mi amico. Mr. Luciano told me all about how you struck out with that dame Bernadette, then you struck her and tossed her out of this speakeasy. You're a spiteful man, Jack" Leo remarked.

"Bernadette was dating the man who killed my sister. The way I see it, I should've done far more than just smack her," I said to Leo with a scoff and then took a shot of bourbon with a grimace.

"Ah yes and just look at all the course of events that simple smack set into play," Leo said to me.

"Yes and if I hadn't gotten my nose broken when I was thirteen I would've been much more popular with the girl as well doctor," I said to Leo in a sarcastic tone and scoff.

"You're a wild man Jack, a man who has laughed in the face of death many times. Mr. Luciano respects men like that because he is a man like that," Leo remarked with a laugh.

Carmen's raunchy show had then concluded which was met with applause from all the drunken mobsters throughout the speakeasy. I first became a bootlegger to provide liquor to all the hardworking blue-collar men who deserved a drink, but all I see now in the speakeasy is mobsters who believe they're all above the law, and above men like me. I'm no longer catering to my own people, and that very thought made me sick every day. "Sex and liquor fuel this town, Jack, and if you can corner both those markets then you will become a very wealthy man," Leo said to me with a grin as he draped his arm on my shoulder with snicker.

"Did Mr. Luciano tell you that?" I inquired.

"No that's a life lesson I've come to learn over time. I call it an unshakeable truth of this world," Leo replied.

"Another unshakeable truth is that men will kill for both of those creature comforts," I said to Leo, as I noticed a man talking to Carmen on the stage which appeared to make her upset.

"That man said I can take a break now," Mickey said to Leo instead of me, as he scampered up to the bar.

"What's wrong with Carmen?" I inquired, as I pointed to Carmen who was now crying on the stage, as the man who was talking to her then walked away in a stoic manner.

"That man told me that Carmen's father died," Mickey replied in a somber tone.

"Ah yes I recognize the devastation written all over her face. I've seen that pain in a woman's eyes before," I remarked, as I stared intently at Carmen, who then stormed off the stage and into the kitchen.

"Poor gal, well she's an adult, she'll get over it soon enough," Leo said to Mickey.

"At least she had a dad," Mickey said to Leo in a somber tone.

"You want a shot, Mickey? Leo inquired with a grin. "Uhm sure I can take a shot," Mickey replied with a grin. "Wait, can you hold your liquor? If not then I might as well make you a glass of lemonade," Leo said to Mickey with a snicker, as Carmen scampered out of the kitchen with tears in her eyes and then exited the speakeasy.

"Lemonade," I whispered as I stared intently at an empty glass on the bar.

*****

"Watch where you're going," Dezerae said to me, as I entered our apartment and then stormed into my bedroom.

"Are you in one of your moods again?" Dezerae asked me as she entered the bedroom.

"Just leave me alone. Go play hopscotch with that boy you like from across the street," I replied in a stern tone.

"I don't like him. I just … don't mind being around him," Dezerae said to me in a stern tone as she smacked me on the shoulder as I laid face down in bed with my pillow absorbing all my tears.

"I made lemonade and peanut butter cookies," Mom pronounced as she entered the bedroom with a smile.

I never understood how mom stayed so happy day after day when dad was fighting in the war. Even Dez appeared happier than me every day. Every day I was reminded at school or in the streets that my dad was gone it was as if someone grabbed the knife that was in my chest and kept twisting it back and forth. Mom still always knew how to make my life a little less painful, and Lemonade and cookies always did the job.

"You better hurry. I'm not saving any cookies for you," Dez said to me with a giggle and then scampered out of the bedroom.

"Wait I'm coming," I said to Dez with a smile as I wiped the tears from my cheeks and then scampered out of the bedroom to the kitchen table.

"Mind your manners you two," Mom said to us as Dez and I quickly scarfed down our first peanut butter cookie with a smile as the doorbell rang.

"Oh I'll get it," Mom said to us as she walked over to the front door while holding a glass of lemonade.

"Oh my god," mom said as she opened the door and dropped her glass of lemonade on the hardwood floor. The shattering of the glass drew my attention towards mom who stood frozen staring at someone on the other side of the door.

*****

"Lemonade is for babies," Mickey remarked, and then slammed an empty shot glass on the bar, as I stared at him with a scowl.

"I need some fresh air," I pronounced, as I put on my trench coat as Mickey grimaced after taking his shot of bourbon.

"Don't take too long Jack!" Leo shouted as I exited the speakeasy.

Greenwich Village had never felt as cold as it felt to me now. Not because it was early November and the chill in the air was enough to make every muscle in your body contract, but because I was now left to serve mobsters like an obedient dog. A dog I sensed would soon be put down and replaced. That day could very well come in two minutes or two weeks, but when it does, I no longer felt a desire to laugh in the face of death, as Leo so boldly put it.

A small group of protestors at the end of the alley then chanted "Freedom to drink, freedom to live!"

What choice did those desperate people have now? When you outlaw something so many people take comfort in and then strip them of all the recourses they need just to live in a town without that comfort, they will then become wild and toss all their once precious morals aside. My childhood in *SoHo* was sad but comforting, but right now my life in Greenwich Village is nerve-racking and oppressed. I then lit a cigarette and took a smoke as it began to snow.

"The first snowfall of the year," a voice remarked from the alley, as I grabbed my pistol to the sight of a dame walking towards me wearing a beige trench coat and matching fedora. I could tell by the way she walked this was no ordinary dame, and I was right.

"Gracie Bishop, I didn't think I'd ever see you back in the village," I said to the dame with a grin, as she walked up to me.

"As a kid I used to love it when it snowed in New York, but that was before—,"

"They outlawed what keeps us warm when it's cold," I interjected with a scoff.

"Believe it or not Jack, but there are other ways to keep warm that don't involve downing half a bottle of bourbon," Gracie said to me with a grin.

"Not for me ... so why are you here Gracie. I doubt you just wanted to talk about the weather with me," I inquired.

"Oh It's nice to see you too Jack. Always straight to business," Gracie said to me as she rolled her eyes.

"I never said it was nice to see you. I know who you work for, and I know what weight this visit carries," I said to Gracie, as she began to pace back and forth in front of me.

"I'm here on behalf of Avery. You could say he feels terrible of the manner in which you two parted ways. He still wants you to join us in Harlem," Gracie said to me.

"Go home Gracie, wherever that may be for you. I'm not some pawn to be used in this battle for the soul of New York," I said to Gracie in a stern tone, as a flicked my cigarette to the ground and pointed aggressively at her.

"You have a soul too Jack. Or do you want to continue to work for the devil?" Gracie inquired.

"Are you referring to Mr. Luciano?" I inquired.

"The one and only, that man and his organization must be taken down before his stranglehold chokes the last breaths out of all the people who have nowhere else to turn but to him," Gracie replied in a stern tone.

"I'm still breathing Gracie, and the devil is in the details. So don't you stand there with a straight face and tell me that Avery comes off as an angel after everything he's done," I said to Gracie.

"Compared to Mr. Luciano he does," Gracie said to me. "Yes and compared to a warthog I come off looking like Cary Grant. So let's not make stupid little comparisons that mean nothing when you're looking at the big picture," I said to Gracie in a stern tone.

"Avery saved your life, Jack! Do you—,"

"And I saved his, so now we're even!" I interjected in a stern tone.

"Where's Hayley? I want to say goodbye" Gracie inquired. "She lives with Faye now," I replied.

"Oh good for her, so Hayley found the courage that you lack to break free from the devil. You're not a terrible uncle to her Jack, but she will live a far happier life with Faye. A life that doesn't make the poor girl shutter every time a man walks past her," Gracie remarked.

"I don't see why Avery could've tried to recruit me to his gang himself. Or did he think that I those smoky eyes of yours would persuade me in a way that nothing else could?" I inquired with a scoff.

"Avery is the most wanted man by the Five Points Gang. He needs at least four of our members to accompany him whenever he leaves the Fox Den," Gracie replied.

"Oh so he sends you of course, because who would ever suspect a smoky-eyed dame like you would be a spy," I said to Gracie with a scoff.

"This is your way out Jack. The offer still stands. I'll tell Avery you need time to think about it," Gracie said to me.

"You're cunning Gracie, but still naïve. There is no way out. The sooner you realize this, the sooner you can give up trying to take down Mr. Luciano.

"I hope you realize that you're a good man Jack, and it would be a shame to see you die by the hands of that devil, as so many other good men have died." Gracie said to me in a somber tone, as her smoky eyes stared intently into mine, trying to work their magic on me, but there was no offer Avery or Gracie could make that I would take. This speakeasy is my home, and if I die here, then so be it.

"So long Gracie. Oh and word to the wise, don't try to infiltrate this speakeasy ever again. Those men in there won't hesitate to shoot a dame no matter how smoky her eyes may be," I said to Gracie and then entered the speakeasy.

*****

It was 11:24 PM in the speakeasy as Leo and I cleaned up the bar while serving the last couple remaining mobsters who seemed to be wide awake as if they took a large amount of amphetamines and needed to blow off steam.

"I don't care much for that jukebox. Call me old fashion but victrolas have a much more rich sound," Leo remarked, as I turned the Jukebox on and played Bessie Smith.

"I bought this jukebox when my jazz band quit. I guess you can say it was my way of trying to forget the past and move on," I said to Leo.

"Mr. Luciano says that strong men learn from the past while weak men live in it, so which man are you, Jack?" Leo inquired. "I'm a man who's far too tired to humor you, that's the man I am," I replied, and then took a shot of bourbon with a cough and grimace.

"Very well mi amico. Those kinds of men will always learn lessons the hard way," Leo said to me while shaking his head. "Now you're sounding more like Samson," I remarked with a scoff.

"Samson has embraced his past. That bold Irishman no longer runs from who he truly is," Leo said to me.

"Another one," one of the mobsters said to me in a stern tone as he tapped the bar and gestured to his empty tumbler. "Why don't you two call it a night, we're about to close up soon," I pronounced to the mobsters seated at the bar.

"We close up when I say so Jack and these two gentlemen want to continue to drink, so I suggest you serve them," Leo said to me in a stern tone.

"The night is young Jack. Why do you want to kick us out so soon?" a mobster inquired with a grin.

"Then you serve them. I'm going to bed," I said to Leo in a stern tone and then entered the kitchen with a sigh.

I then sat down on Hayley's bed and grabbed her pillow which still smelled sweet like flowers, or perhaps Faye's strong perfume rubbed off onto Hayley and now the fragrance lingers on her pillow. Those two sure are made for each other, but as for me and Leo, I couldn't bring myself to stomach him any longer. I knew all too well that the time in which Mr. Luciano phased me out of this speakeasy completely was drawing nearer, and I had two options when that time came.

I could give in to that smoky-eyed dame Gracie, and join Avery in Harlem, or I could remain here and wait to be silenced by any of the countless mobsters gunning for my position. The choice wasn't easy, but then again, no choice in my life has ever been easy.

My mother once told me that my father's choice to leave her, me and Dezerae to fight in the war was the hardest choice he's ever made. Did my father think at the time that he had to protect us from those foreign powers across the sea, or was he simply a man who felt duty bound to that call of action? Either way the apple has fallen far from the tree. I now had nothing to prove to anybody other than that hung-over face I see in the mirror when I wake up every morning. Samson always said to me that 'you can measure the dignity of a man by how others regard him.' If what Leo said about Samson is true and he's now fully embraced his past, then Samson is no better than Mr. Luciano now. I had a naïve feeling that Samson was fighting Paul Kelly for the future of me, Hayley and the speakeasy, but I see now that Samson was fighting for Mr. Luciano all along. If I dwelled any longer on these thoughts then I wouldn't be able to get any sleep tonight, so I took one last shot of bourbon with a grimace before I laid my head down on the pillow with a groan as the sound of Leo and the two mobsters laughing at the bar pounded in my head.

*****

"Jack we have a problem" a familiar voice said to me in a distressed tone, as I awoke in bed to the sight of Mickey standing over me.

"Goddamn it … what is it now Mickey," inquired in a stern tone and groan, as I sat upright in bed.

"I overheard Leo talking to another mobster. He said your time at the speakeasy is up," Mickey said to me, as I stared at myself in the mirror.

"Oh really, and just what the fuck is that supposed to mean?" I inquired in a stern tone as I stared daggers at Mickey who recoiled like a timid dog.

"I think we both know very well what it means Jack, but the question is what are we going to do about it?" Mickey inquired. "There is no 'we' kid. You go tend to that buxom dame Carmen and stay out of my affairs if you know what's good for you," I replied as I put on my vest and tie.

"Jack … you built this speakeasy from the ground up. You gave a poor orphan like me a living wage every week. I will never turn my back on you. Hayley taught me a great deal and I'm grateful to her and you," Mickey said to me.

"You've got a good heart kid, but a time will come when you will be forced to make a choice that goes against every beat of that heart, and when that time comes, what will you do then?" I inquired as I placed my hand on Mickey's shoulder.

"I—I don't want to kill anybody Jack," Mickey said to me in a timid tone as his light brown eyes averted from my intense stare.

"That's why you need to stay away from me when it all goes down," I said to Mickey as I adjusted my bowtie in the mirror.

"You could leave this all behind, Jack. Just drive west and don't stop till you see the coastline," Mickey said to me. "What's so special about the west coast?" I inquired.

"I heard life is better there. I've heard people can live out their dreams on the west coast," Mickey replied.

"Oh really, well you heard wrong, kid. This depression is happening all over the country, even all over the world. Sure the weather out west may be more pleasant, but that's not a good enough reason for me to abandoned all that I've worked so hard for here in this city," I said to Mickey in a stern tone.

"It doesn't have to be out west Jack. Just go to wherever you feel warm inside.

"Now you sound like Hayley," I remarked with a scoff as I shook my head.

"I hope she's happy living with Faye," Mickey said to me.

"It was her call. I don't doubt living with Faye would have its rewards, especially if you're a man, but for Hayley, Faye is just what the doctor ordered," I said to Mickey.

"I miss her. Do you think that it would be alright for me to visit her?" Mickey inquired in a timid tone. "Why are you asking me kid?" I inquired.

"Oh well, I thought that you and Hayley had an arrangement with Faye when it came to visiting her apartment," Mickey replied.

"No this is a free city kid. Well not as free as it used to be, but you go wherever you want to. I'm not even technically your boss anymore," I said to Mickey.

"Leo's hasn't threatened me, but I fear what's in store for you Jack," Mickey said to me, as he stared at the stage as Carmen was getting ready to perform with her band.

It then occurred to me like a bolt of lightning striking through the fog that was my hung-over brain, if Mickey did visit Hayley at *Magnolia Towers* then there's no doubt he would lead that Cossack hitman Nicolai right to where they live. I had to keep their location as secret as possible so the Five Points Gang couldn't use them to gain leverage over me. So for now, there would be no visiting *Magnolia Towers*.

"Wait Mickey, you can't visit Hayley at *Magnolia Towers* or anywhere for the time being," I said to Mickey as I grabbed his arm before he exited the kitchen to go tend to Carmen's every demand.

"Why not," Mickey inquired.

"Falcone and Nicolai are most likely following you the very moment you leave the speakeasy. If any of them found out where Hayley and Faye live, then they would have leverage over us. Now I know all too well that Hayley and Faye are two tough women, but not tough enough to handle a hitman. Now you have to promise me that you will not give those hit men any lead into the location of Faye and Hayley. Their lives could depend on it," I said to Mickey in a stern tone as I stared intently into his downcast eyes.

"So I either never see Hayley again or I potentially risk her life by visiting her?" Mickey inquired in a somber tone.

"I'm sorry kid, but you know what the responsible choice is. Being a stranger to Hayley and Faye will keep them safe. We have to distance ourselves from them as much as possible so they can live their lives," I replied with a sigh and then exited the kitchen. It pained me to tell Mickey not to visit Hayley. She gave that boy a new lust for life. I was used to distancing myself from people who I used to be close with. For me it was as easy as playing another record on the victrola, sure the last record held some sentimental value, but there's always another song I could play to drown out past remorse.

*****

It was 6:18 PM in the speakeasy as Leo and four other mobsters walked up to the bar.

"Jack, my fellow associates request you take a ride with them. I'll take over here," Leo said to me as he walked behind the bar.

"Oh really, and what does this ride entail fellas?" I inquired.

"Just come with us willingly Dansby, or else we will escort you," one mobster replied as he cracked his knuckles.

"Sure, I could use some fresh air," I said to the mobster as I put on my trench coat.

There were four of them this time. Have they now taken the necessary precautions to silence me for good? One way or another, they wouldn't silence me without a fight.

"Get in," one mobster said to me in a stern tone, as he opened the door of a polished black, Chevrolet Confederate. It always surprised me how I saw no bullet holes in any of these mobsters cars. How did they keep their cars looking so pristine while still engaging in shootouts on a frequent basis?

I then entered the back seat of the Chevrolet to the sight of man with a black bag over his head. I had no idea who this man could be, but I knew he had to be connected to me in some way. "So who's he?" I inquired as the rest of the mobsters piled into the crammed Chevrolet and then began to drive east. "That's why you're here Dansby. You're going to identify this man for us," one mobster replied with a snicker, and then lit a cigar and took a smoke.

I knew where we were going. Either these four mobsters forgot to put a bag over my head too or they felt that is wasn't necessary because our destination was one I was all too familiar with.

"Ah Pier 45. You know you fellas should really spruce up this place if you're going to continue to do your business here. A few decorative rugs would really—,"

"Enough with the fucking small talk Dansby. We have information we need from you and from this man here. Now andiamo," a mobster interjected in a stern tone and whistle as he shoved me out of the Chevrolet.

"Remove his hood," one mobster said in a stern tone. The hooded man was then revealed to me as I stared intently into his battered and bewildered face.

"Do you know this man Dansby?" one mobster inquired in a stern tone as he pointed to the man.

After a closer look I did recognize the man. It was Arthur Derringer, and he worked for Avery's gang in Harlem, but I couldn't tell the mobsters that, or they would brand me as a member of Avery's gang.

"Nope, never seen him before in my life. Is he important?" I inquired as I shook my head.

"Possibly, Mr. Luciano has good reason to believe that you are a mole for Avery's gang. This man goes by the name of Arthur Derringer and after we beat him to within an inch of his life he told us that you have history with Avery," a mobster said to me in a stern tone.

"You beat any man to within an inch of his life and he will tell you what you want to hear, but that doesn't make it true," I said to the mobster with a scoff.

How did they capture Arthur? Was it during a shootout or did they just take him off the streets? Either way I knew he didn't have much longer to live.

"We understand it's your word against his. So Mr. Luciano has given you a choice Dansby. If you're not affiliated with this rat's boss Avery Briggs, then you will have no problem silencing him right now," one mobster said to me as he pointed to Arthur who stared at me with wide-eyes.

"I'm not a killer. I serve drinks," I said to the mobster in a stern tone.

"Says the man who killed the Hammer. Mr. Luciano says that all men are killers. They just need to be motivated to the point that brings out that killer inside of them. Don't worry Dansby, this man's fate was sealed long before we picked you up," one mobster said to me.

"What if I refuse?" I inquired.

"Then that will tell us all we need to know. So make your choice Dansby. It's getting cold out and I don't want to be standing here beside this rat all evening," one mobster said to me in a stern tone.

"I won't do it," I pronounced in a stern tone. "Very well," one mobster said to me.

"Thanks Ja—," Arthur's timid voice was then swiftly cut short as a mobster pulled out a pistol and shot him in the head.

Even though Arthur sold me out, I couldn't bring myself to kill him. Mr. Luciano wanted undying loyalty from all of his associates. This is why I failed his test, because loyalty is not something I feel towards anybody in this city. I then wiped off some of Arthurs blood which splattered on my cheek, as two mobsters lifted him up off the ground where a puddle of blood formed underneath him.

"You know Jack's right. A few decorative rugs would really spruce up this warehouse," one mobster remarked with a snicker.

"So what are you now an interior decorator?" one mobster inquired as he helped the other mobster drag Arthur's body to the Chevrolet.

"No I just have an eye for what looks good. Speaking of which, how are things with you and that stacked dame from Queens," one mobster inquired.

They were cold bastards. These mobsters killed men as if it was a mundane action. I saw no remorse in their eyes as they dragged Arthur's body to the Chevrolet and prepared him for a one way trip to the bottom of the Hudson.

"Mind if I smoke? It calms my nerves whenever I see someone killed," I inquired as my shaky hand lit the cigarette in my quivering mouth and then took a smoke.

"Get out of here Dansby. By not killing that man you've told us all we need to know," the mobster standing beside me said in a stern tone and scoff.

"What does that mean ... what does that mean?" I shouted in a distressed tone as the mobster walked away with a snicker, leaving me cold and alone in the warehouse where I felt an overwhelming sense of fear consume me

*****

It was 7:05 PM as I entered the speakeasy with my hand on my pistol to the sight of Leo staring intently at me with a grin as he wiped down the bar.

"Jack, you look like you've seen a ghost," Leo remarked with a grin as I walked up behind the bar.

"Don't play coy with me Leo. You know damn well what I've just seen," I said to Leo in a stern tone.

"It's nothing personal Jack. This is all business, and when an associate of Mr. Luciano's helps his biggest competitors, then that associate must be ... handled properly," Leo said to me, as Carmen began to sing a somber melody on the stage.

Why was I still alive? When was it coming? I thought to myself as my heart began to race with all the possibilities of my imminent death. Over the past year I've grown far too accustomed to constantly looking over my shoulder for a mobster plotting to silence me. I'm so tired of it all. When I first set out to bootleg liquor for all the hardworking people of New York I never would've thought that I would become a target for mobsters. I just wanted to serve drinks to good people. People who deserved the right to drink. People who didn't kill over liquor, but reveled in it. Those are the kinds of people I wanted to be around. Have I lost sight of my vision along the way? Or have I just made bad choices that could never be made right?

"What a lovely voice. That dame could sing professionally if she wanted to," a mobster seated at the bar remarked with a grin as I served him his martini.

"That's Carmen Valentino. She has all the bells and whistles to be a recording artist, but does she have the bravery?" I inquired as I stared intently at Carmen who appeared as if she was about to break down crying as she continued to sing her somber love song.

"The bravery to sing your heart out? It sure looks like she does to me," the mobster replied, as he stared at Carmen.

"No, the bravery to venture out of these slums to find greener pastures," I said to the mobster in a somber tone as Carmen finished singing her love song to a small applause from the mobsters seated at the tables in front of the stage. No doubt she would've gotten a bigger applause if she performed one of her scandalous burlesque numbers, but I could see in her tearful eyes that she was in no mood to throw these hungry mobsters a bone.

"Take it from me Jack. I've been all over this world and no such place exists," the mobster said to me with a scoff and then took a sip of his martini.

"Then maybe you're looking in all the wrong places," I said to the mobster.

The rest of the evening dragged on as I worked in a quiet tension with Leo. He was now calling all the shots when it came to serving drinks in the speakeasy. The feeling of no longer being needed in a place that I built was devastating. I knew what was coming next, but I didn't know when it was coming. So what could I do now? Flee now Jack. You still have time to get a head start. I thought to myself as Leo served the last drunken mobster at the bar.

"Buona note Ricardo," Leo said to the last mobster as he exited the speakeasy in a staggering manner.

"I'll take it from here Leo. Good night," I said to Leo as I wiped down the bar.

"Very well Jack. Take pride in this speakeasy. It has served the Five Points Gang well," Leo said to me as he put on his jacket.

"This speakeasy is the only thing I take pride in," I said to Leo. Leo then placed both his hands on my shoulders and kissed me on the cheek before he exited the speakeasy, leaving me alone with a sense of still dread as the heavy beating of my heart was the only sound to be heard in the speakeasy.

I then sat down in my bed with a sigh and put on the record "Nobody Know You When You're Down and Out" by Bessie Smith on the victrola before I laid my head down on the pillow. "Come and get me you bastards," I whispered before my heavy eyelids slowly closed.

*****

"Grab 'em," a voice pronounced in a stern tone as I awoke to the sight of two mobsters who quickly pulled me out of bed and restrained both of my arms.

"Oh are you the wakeup service?" I inquired with a groan. "Shut up Dansby, turn that garbage off," one mobster said to the other mobster in a stern tone after throwing a combination of punches to my gut and face which sent me to my knees before the other mobster pulled out his gun and shot my victrola.

"Andiamo Dansby," one mobster said in a stern tone as both mobsters dragged me into the bar.

I then heard slow clapping echoing throughout the speakeasy from a man sitting at the corner table in front of the stage.

"On your knees Dansby," one of the mobsters said to me in a stern tone as he kicked the back of my knee and pushed down on my shoulders sending me to my knees like many men who I've witnessed being silenced, only I was now in their position. "Oh Jack, I would say I'm going to miss your sense of humor, but we both know that's a lie," the man seated at the corner table said to me as he stood up from the table and walked up to me.

"Stefano isn't it past your bedtime kid," I said to Stefano with a snicker as I grinned at the would-be leader of the Five Points Gang.

Stefano then began to snicker along with the two mobsters who held me down to my knees before gesturing to the mobsters, which unleashed a fury of punches and kicks from the two mobsters that rattled my skull for a few long and agonizing moments.

"Come on fellas enough with the foreplay," I said with a grin and then spit out blood and a loose tooth at Stefano's feet.

"You know what my uncle calls you Jack?" Stefano inquired with a grin.

"Oh I've got to hear this," I replied with a scoff.

"Jack "Wild Card" Dansby, but now you're about to be dealt with so Uncle Charles no longer has to worry," Stefano said to me as he kneeled down in front of me.

"Wild card huh, I like it," I remarked with a snicker.

"You're scum, and after you're out of the picture the wolf will find Hayley and silence her as well. We cannot have any loose ends threatening the future of my uncle's organization," Stefano said to me.

"My god ... who was the one responsible for fucking up your mind kid? Was it your uncle or your father?" I inquired as I shook my head.

"I'm my own man!" Stefano shouted and then punched me in the face, which felt like a slap compared to the blows the other burly mobsters were inflicting on me.

"I thought Mr. Luciano would want to witness my death himself considering everything I've put him through," I said to Stefano and then spit out more blood on the floor.

"My uncle is busy right now smoking out the rest of the Avery Gang in Harlem. They will all be scattered to the winds before the end of the year," Stefano said to me.

"Just tell us when boss," one of the mobsters said.

"Do it. I've humored Jack long enough," Stefano said in a stern tone.

This was the end. It was only fitting that my life would end in this speakeasy. I then closed my eyes as I heard one mobster pull out his gun and then, two gunshots rang out in the speakeasy, but why two?

"How did you get in here!?" Stefano inquired in dismay as I opened my eyes to the sight of the two mobsters lying dead on the floor beside me with led lodged between both of their eyes and Samson pointing his gun at Stefano with a grin as the boy frantically struggled to open the front door of the speakeasy before he fled.

"Samson ... I—how?" I inquired as I stared in bewilderment at the very man who I believed to be Mr. Luciano's new hitman.

"On your feet Jack. We don't have much time," Samson said to me with a grin as he extended his hand to me.

I then grabbed Samson's hand and pulled myself up off the floor with a groan as my heart and mind raced with an array of emotions.

"Samson, why? You will be hunted now along with me. You had a way out, to embrace your past, but now you'll have to go back to running from it," I said to Samson in a distressed tone.

"It's just as you said Jack. I am a killer. I kill to protect the ones I care about, and it's just as I said after my fight with Kelly 'as long as I have someone or something to fight for in this world, then I will fight with all me heart.'" Samson said to me as he placed his hand on my shoulder.

"How did you get in here anyway?" I inquired.

"I knew Stefano and his muscle were planning to silence you tonight, but their biggest mistake was trusting me with that information. So I entered the speakeasy through the dumbwaiter. Hayley gave me that idea," Samson replied with a snicker.

"Thank you. I—I was wrong about you Samson. You're a man of loyalty and I'm honored to have you by my side," I said to Samson.

"You gave me a second chance in life Jack, that moment you hired me off the streets. I knew I had to repay the favor, but now we must leave this speakeasy and never look back," Samson said to me as he opened the cash register and quickly divided the money into two stacks.

"So why didn't you take the shot. I knew you could've killed Stefano as he was struggling to open the front door?" I inquired as I quickly put on my trench coat.

"No matter how twisted that boy's mind is, he's still just a boy, and I saw fear in his eyes at that moment," Samson replied. "I take it you don't kill children," I inquired, as I shoved a few changes of clothes into my suitcase along with a couple of records.

"No. I wouldn't dare. Jack, where will you go now?" Samson inquired.

"To greener pastures Samson. I hope you find them as well," I replied.

Samson and I then exited the speakeasy.

"Aye if such a place exists I know your heart will lead you to it Jack .The Five Points Gang knows your Pontiac all too well. Take one of their cars. It will make it harder for them to track you." Samson said to me.

"Right … I guess this is goodbye," I said to Samson as I tossed my suitcase in the backseat of the black Chevrolet.

"I now say to you what my cousin Killian said to me before he left Belfast in search for those greener pastures. 'We will see each other again in this life or the next,'" Samson said to me as his face quivered.

"You're damn right we will," I said to Samson as my eyes began to well up with tears. I then hugged Samson and entered the Chevrolet and drove slowly out of Minetta Street as I stared at Samson in the rearview mirror as he grinned with a pipe in his mouth.

*****

"I'm so sorry Jack. Your dad … he won't be … he won't be coming home from the war," My mother said to me as she continued to cry her eyes out while sitting between me and Dezerae on my bed.

"Why, he promised me he would come back," I said to my mother as my eyes began to well up with tears.

"Your dad was shot last night. The captain of his regiment said he held on to life for so long throughout the night, but his wound was too severe. He died early this morning," my mother said as her face quivered in a manner I've never seen before.

"No I don't believe it. Dad would never break his promise to me," I said to my mother as tears began to stream down my cheeks.

"Your dad went to greener pastures now honey," my mother said to me as she wrapped her arms around me and Dezerae.

"I want to go with dad." I said to my mother as I buried my face into her shoulder.

"Honey … you can't. Those greener pastures are not meant for you now," my mother said to me.

CHAPTER 16:
TALES FROM SOHO:
WOMANHOOD
- HAYLEY -

Dear Diary,
November 20th, 9:16 AM,

    They're fighting again, Faye and her new man of the week. They woke me up early so I thought I would write to you now. It's been two weeks since I made the choice to live with Faye and never look back at that speakeasy. I was so happy that Faye allowed me to live with her. I thought she would for sure tell me I should be living with Jack the only family I have left, but I reassured her that I'm a woman who can make her own life choices and living with her would be the best thing for me. At first I loved the peacefulness of Faye's apartment compared to the terribly loud speakeasy, but now the fighting I've been hearing from Faye and her gentlemen callers brings back terrible memories of the countless fighting I had to suffer through when I lived with my mother and Johnny in *SoHo*. So now I write to you as Faye and the man she slept with last night scream their lungs out at each other. I feared for Faye's safety whenever a man would lose his temper with her just as I feared for my mother's safety whenever Johnny would come home, but Johnny is dead now, and that little girl who shuttered at all the times voices were raised in that cramped apartment in *SoHo* has now grown up a great deal. I can attribute my emotional growth to living with Jack in the speakeasy. I wonder how Jack is fairing in the speakeasy right now. I miss his smile and the way he would always seem to lighten the mood with his sense of humor. So I now conclude this diary entry with a sense of longing for the ones I left behind, but at the same time a sense of hope in becoming the independent woman my mother always wanted me to be.

*****

"Sors d'ici!" Faye shouted as the man stormed out of her bedroom with not so much as a glance towards me sitting on the sofa with my diary in my lap.

"And speak English goddamn it. You're in America now toots!" the man shouted back at Faye as he put on his jacket and then exited the apartment with a swift slam of the door which startled Sable who was peacefully lying on the coffee table.

"I—I'm sorry you had to hear that Hayley. That man changed his entire personality as the sun began to rise this morning," Faye said to me in a somber tone as she lit a cigarette with a shaky hand and then took a smoke.

"He was just like the last man who came over here last week. It's clear they only want one thing from you," I said to Faye in a somber tone.

"Have I become that transparent mon chéri?" Faye inquired as she put a record on the victrola and then walked over to the window.

"I just worry for your safety. I don't want any of those men to hurt you," I replied in a somber tone.

"That man? Hurt me? That man was a how do you say … lamb in the streets and in the sheets," Faye said to me with a giggle which made me giggle along with her.

I just wanted to see Faye smile. The nights when I would hear her sobbing in her bedroom broke my heart. In some ways, I wanted to prevent what happened to my mother by being braver and protecting Faye from these men she so carelessly invites into her apartment. I owe that to Faye, for she has given me a chance at a life that's no longer under the rule of a powerful mobster and his delusional nephew. Faye was my sister, my mother, my aunt, and my best friend, and I will always be there for her, as she has always been there for me.

"So what shall we do today mon chéri?" Faye inquired with a smile as she sat down next to me on the sofa and draped her arm over my shoulders.

"Uhm I don't know. Do you have anything in mind?" I replied.

"I have the day off from work at the library so I 'm open for anything," Faye replied with a smile.

"I would be happy just spending the day with you talking about literature," I said to Faye with a smile.

The truth of the matter was that whenever Faye and I left the apartment I felt an instant sense of despair at the current state of the world. It seemed as if more and more people where either waiting in breadlines or living on the streets in makeshift tents. I was so close to becoming like one of those people, but now my life with Faye was as blessed as it ever was.

"How about we discuss literature at this lovely café I used to frequent in Washington Commons Village," Faye inquired, as she picked up Sable with a smile and stroked him until he began to purr with delight.

"Oh I would love that," I remarked with a smile. "Then it is settled," Faye said to me with a smile.

*****

It was 11:24 AM as Faye and I drove down Jane Street to the sight of protestors which lined both sides of the street.

"I adore the Village Hayley. Living here reminds me of the time my mother and I visited my uncle in Paris when I was a little younger than you. It left such an impression on me that I longed for such a place where I would be able to live life to the fullest of my heart's content, but it breaks my heart when I see other good people suffering from these controversial laws," Faye said to me.

I could tell that Faye was the kind of woman who couldn't bear witnessing the suffering of others. Where everyone else in this city would turn a blind eye to others in pain, Faye would look directly at their pain and try with all her heart to heal them as she has done with me. Faye's warm smile began to slowly fade as her and I drove down the streets of Greenwich Village. There were breadlines and homeless people lining the streets, so many that it felt as if only darker days were ahead. They all wore tattered clothing which matched their gray and somber faces that stared downward as they waited in line for a means to survive the cold night. Renowned writers like Edgar Allan Poe could find beauty in such despair, but I for one wasn't able to do such a thing.

"Where will they go now? What will they do?" I inquired in a somber tone as I stared at all the people waiting in breadlines as it began to lightly snow.

"They will do what they must now in order to survive. This city continues to bleed and bleed from these laws, but nobody is making an attempt to heal the wound," Faye replied while shaking her head.

"What about that new president elect, I think his name is Franklin Delano Roosevelt. I heard him talking on the radio about something he calls the 'New Deal'. I hope he can bring about the healing which we all so desperately need right now," I said to Faye.

"I hope so as well mon chéri, but he is a politician after all. We're here, wait …," Faye said to me with a wide-eyed stare as she parked the car in a vacant lot in Washington Commons.

I saw nothing but closed down shops as I stared down the street of Washington Commons. I was hoping to talk about literature over coffee with Faye this afternoon, but once again, life had other plans.

"This was the café. The owner was a lovely man. Just last month this café was opened for business, what happened here?" Faye inquired in a somber tone as she placed her hand upon the boarded up front door.

"Life happened," I replied in a somber tone, as I tried to imagine the lovely café when it was full of happy patrons.

"I hope Bernard is all right, wherever he may be. Come on let's go home," Faye said to me in a somber tone and then kissed her hand and placed it on the front door of the closed down café.

*****

It was 10:24 PM at Faye's apartment as Faye sat across from me on the maroon chair smoking a cigarette with a half empty bottle of wine in her hand.

"H—Hayley do you ever feel like a rose?" Faye inquired in a slurred tone.

"I … I don't know. What do you mean?" I replied.

"I feel like a rose every day in this city. A rose t—that languishes in the cold of the approaching winter, as I long for the warm sunlight. Sure men are attracted to me but then once they feel my thorns the morning after they loosen their grasp and abandon me," Faye said to me in a tearful tone as she stood up and walked over to the window with the half empty bottle of wine and cigarette in hand.

"I suppose that all beautiful things need some sort of protection, but I find your thorns to be beautiful," I remarked with a warm smile.

"Mon chéri I'm glad you're here with me, lord knows what I might do if I didn't have you in my life," Faye said to me with a quivering smile, as she lay down upon the sofa with a sigh with her black silken robe fully opened.

This vulnerable moment with Faye brought back a memory of when I lived with my mother in *SoHo*, a memory that gave me warmth as I stared at Faye sleeping peacefully on the sofa.

*****

"M—Mom, are you all right?" I asked my mother as I slowly entered the kitchen after hearing the scary fight which she and Johnny just had.

I then saw my mom crying as she held her cheek at the kitchen table. Did Johnny hit her again? There was a part of me that wanted to try and stop Johnny every time he fought with my mother, but she always told me to stay in my bedroom whenever I heard shouting, so I did just that.

"Honey ... I'm sorry if we woke you up. Johnny is gone now. He went to go meet with his boss," my mother said to me, as she stood up from the kitchen table and took my hand.

"I heard Johnny say he would silence you if you kept talking. What does he mean?" I asked my mom as she and I walked back to my bedroom.

"Pay no mind to him angel. Just know that I would rather give my life for you than live in a world without you. I don't know what I would do if I didn't have you in my life," My mother said to me as I laid my head down on the pillow.

"He hit you again, didn't he," I said to my mother with a frown as she tucked me into bed.

"Honey, Johnny will have to do far more than a slap to keep me from protecting you," My mother said to me with a warm smile.

"I—I don't want you to get hurt anymore," I said to my mother, as my eyes began to well up with tears.

"Angel … you are a far stronger woman than me. I see it in your eyes, and I will ensure that men like Johnny, well, dogs like Johnny never hurt you. I love you," My mother said to me and then kissed me on the cheek before she left my bedroom.

*****

Back then in our apartment in *SoHo*, my mother was the thorns to my rose. She saw me as a strong woman at the age of twelve. Whenever Johnny tried to get close to me, my mother would always protect me from his grasp. She was the bravest woman I've ever known and I see so much of her personality in Faye, which is why I now must take care of Faye, just as she and my mother have taken care of me in the darkest of times.

I then grabbed the scarlet blanket from off the chair and draped it over Faye with a warm smile, as I curled up on the end of the sofa next to her.

"Goodnight," I said to Faye as Sable then curled up next to me on the armrest of the sofa with a purr.

*****

It was 7:27 AM as I awoke on the sofa to Faye's slender, pale foot pressed gently against my face.

So I gently grabbed Faye's slender, pale ankle and moved her foot away from my face, as Sable jumped up onto the back of the sofa with a meow. Faye drunk that entire bottle of wine last night so I can only imagine the hangover she will have when she wakes up.

"Good morning sir, and how did you sleep?" I inquired with a smile as I stroked Sable.

"Faye's apartment was colder in the morning than I was used to, but it was just another change in my life I would have to adapt to. Faye seemed so depressed last night, so I wanted to do something nice for her this morning, something that would make her smile as she wakes up. So I quietly stood up from the sofa and walked over to the kitchen. I decided to attempt to cook Faye breakfast, but not just any breakfast, a French breakfast. So I stood on my tiptoes to reach the cookbook that was in the cabinet above the stove and began to skim through it in search of a traditional French breakfast recipe. As I skimmed through the stained pages of the cookbook all I found was croissants which Faye and I have eaten countless times for breakfast, so I kept looking for a recipe that would impress Faye. I then came to the breakfast dish I was searching for, it was called crepe suzettes, but my smile then quickly faded as I realized that the entire cookbook was written in French. Wait I can still make Faye French Toast. I remember watching my mother make it one morning. I thought to myself as I then cracked three eggs into a bowl, added a dash of milk, vanilla extract, cinnamon and nutmeg and then mixed it all up as Faye rolled over on the sofa with a faint moan.

"Go keep Faye company," I said to Sable as he jumped up onto the counter and stared at me with curious eyes, but Sable seemed far too interested in me cooking breakfast than curling up beside Faye on the sofa.

Cooking was a very calming activity. I see now why my mother always had a smile on her face when she was cooking for me or even Johnny. The French toast was coming out wonderfully, as I finished cooking the last slice and placed it on a white, chipped dish. I then topped off the French toast with a sliced up banana and maple syrup before placing the dish on the kitchen table.

"Oh I forgot about the coffee," I spoke aloud.

I then put three tablespoons of coffee into the French Press coffee maker which I've seen Faye use many mornings so I figured If Faye could operate that sophisticated coffee maker with ease than so could I. I then noticed Faye slowly sit upright from the sofa with a yawn as she rubbed her bleary eyes.

"Bonjour Faye," I said to Faye with a smile, as she stood up from the sofa and closed her robe as she walked over to me. "Bonjour mon chéri ... what is all of this?" Faye inquired with a smile.

"I made French Toast and coffee. I wanted to make crepe suzettes, but your cookbook is written all in French," I replied. "This is all so wonderful, Hayley," Faye remarked with a warm smile as she wrapped her arm around me in the same manner my mother used to.

"Oh no," I spoke aloud with a wide-eyed stare as I noticed the French Press coffee maker erupted and spattered coffee all over the stove.

"I'm sorry. I thought I used the right amount of water and coffee," I said to Faye in a timid tone.

"Aw do not fret mon chéri. There's still enough coffee left for the both of us," Faye said to me with a giggle which quickly turned my frown into a smile.

"I thought you might not be feeling well considering you drunk that entire bottle of wine last night," I said to Faye as she turned on the radio and then sat down at the kitchen table with a sigh.

"Oh one bottle of merlot isn't enough to get the best of me mon chéri," Faye said to me with a smile, as I poured a cup of coffee for each of us.

"I'm glad you had bananas and maple syrup to top the French toast with," I said to Faye with a smile.

"Oh this is magnifique mon chéri. Who taught you how to cook French Toast like this?" Faye inquired with a kissing gesture to her hand and a mouthful of French Toast.

"I remember the recipe from my mother. She always seemed so happy when she was cooking," I replied, and then took a bite of French Toast.

"My mother always told me that the kitchen is her, how do you say ... sanctuary. She found peace in the kitchen cooking for me even when are village in *Loire Valley* was experiencing gunfire and explosions," Faye said to me.

"I wasn't born during the time of the war, but the time I'm living in now feels like a war for me," I said to Faye.

"The way we endure such terrible times is by staying together, you and me, mon chéri. No matter how much they deny it, no one person can make it solely on their own in this day and age," Faye said to me with a mouthful of French Toast, as she reached out across the kitchen table and placed her hand upon mine.

"Are you going to work at the library today?" I inquired and then took a sip of the strong but smooth French roast coffee. "I am, but with a breakfast like this, I can conquer anything the world throws at me," Faye replied with a smile.

A sense of boredom and loneliness overcame me every time Faye would leave the apartment to go to work at the library across the street. Sure I still had Sable to keep me company, but there's only so much comfort a cat can provide to a girl like me. Faye was my best friend, and If I could I would come along with her to the library, but I had a feeling I would just get in her way. So my afternoons were mainly spent cleaning up the apartment, writing, reading, and listening to the radio. It was a more peaceful life than the one I had with Jack in the speakeasy and I no longer found myself shaking, but there was still a part of me that missed Jack.

"All right I have to get ready for work now," Faye said to me, as she stood up from the kitchen table and gathered the dishes.

"Oh I'll take care of this. You go get ready," I said to Faye with a smile, as I gathered the dishes.

"You're an angel," Faye remarked with a warm smile and then scampered into her bedroom.

"In international news, the Soviet Union and France signed a non-aggression pact today marked by the rapprochement of the Danube Federation." The radio sounded.

"At least some people are trying to find common ground," I spoke aloud as I washed the dishes in the sink.

The news on the radio would always depress me. I remember back in *SoHo* whenever Johnny would enter the kitchen he would immediately demand my mother to turn the radio station from the joyful music she had playing to a doom and gloom news station. I've now grown into a woman who likes to stay well informed as a result of hearing more news than music in my life.

"Oh Hayley why must you listen to such reports of the world, that's all just scared men signing pacts which they believe will help them keep their power," Faye said to me as she entered the living room while putting on an earring, wearing a beige dress and black jacket, a look that did not suit Faye one bit if you ask me, but she still looked beautiful as always.

"I just want to hear how the rest of the world is doing," I said to Faye, as I finished washing the dishes.

"America is far from perfect mon chéri, but I wouldn't dare live anywhere else in the world right now," Faye said to me as she put on a more modest shade of lipstick compared to the wine-colored shade of lipstick she wears when she's not working at the library. Faye's appearance as she got ready for work at the library was like a different person, even though she still spoke like the Faye I know and love, she appeared as a modestly dressed stern librarian. Is this what jobs do to adults? Do jobs force you to cover up your true identity all for the sake of income? If this was the case then I could only imagine how suppressed Faye must feel every day at work. Sure Faye has a passion for literature which is why she works at the library, but our passions can only take us so far when the need for income becomes such a loud voice that drowns out all the rest.

"Is that uniform comfortable?" I inquired as I entered Faye's bedroom to the sight of her pining and tying her hair back as she looked in her dresser mirror.

"Not as comfortable as wearing my silk robe if that's what you're wondering," Faye replied with a smile as she put on a spray of perfume and then scampered into the living room.

"Are you late?" I inquired as Faye opened the living room window.

"No I just scheduled a talk at this time with one of my friends in cell 18," Faye replied, as she stuck her head out the window and waved to the same woman who tricked me into giving her a cigarette a couple weeks ago.

"Bonjour Sidney!" Faye shouted with a smile.

"Oh she's your friend," I said to Faye with a frown and eye roll as I stared at the woman waving back at Faye through the barred window of the prison.

"Is there anything I can get you mon chéri?" Faye shouted. "Surprise me!" the prisoner known as Sidney replied.

"I'll be down in ten minutes!" Faye shouted.

"I don't like her. She took advantage of my kindness," I said to Faye.

"Whatever do you mean mon chéri?" Faye inquired as she wrapped up a slice of French toast along with four cigarettes and stuffed it into her purse.

"She told me she would make it worth my while if I gave her a couple cigarettes, so I did just that, but then all she did in return for my generosity was laugh at me," I replied.

"Hayley … if you gave Sidney a couple of cigarettes in hopes of a reward then that wasn't true generosity. You do not show love in hopes of rewards, you show it unconditionally. I will be back between 5 to 6 PM. Remember to lock the door if you leave the apartment, have a wonderful day," Faye said to me as she placed her hands upon my shoulders and kissed me on the lips.

"You too," I said to Faye as she exited the apartment leaving me with Sable who wanted to follow Faye to the library but knew very well that all the food was here.

"So what shall we do now curious boy," I inquired with a sigh as I picked up Sable and walked over to the window.

*****

It was 11:23 AM as I stepped out of the shower to the blaring sound of an ambulance driving down the street. Compared to the alley of Minetta Street, *Magnolia Towers* was a very loud place to live, but still far less stressful than the speakeasy.

I then began to water all of Faye's many plants that decorated her apartment, as Sable followed me as if he wanted to help, but I knew he really just wanted to be fed.

"I'll feed you after I'm done feeding the plants," I said to Sable, as I finished watering all the plants in Faye's bedroom.

I then noticed a small box underneath the dresser. This box couldn't have jewelry in it, which made me wonder why it was hidden. Part of me wanted to open the box while another part of me respected Faye's privacy, but my curiosity got the better of me at that moment as it usually does. Faye was such an open person, which is why I was so curious over the box underneath the dresser. So I then opened the box to the sight of several folded up letters which were worn and ripped as if Faye reads them over and over again.

Reading through all of these letters would take the whole afternoon, and I still had to do more chores around the apartment. So I took one letter from the box and then began to get dressed. I then entered the living room and put on a French record that Faye plays whenever she needs to relax after a hard day's work.

"All right I'm getting your milk," I said to Sable as I placed the folded up letter on the kitchen counter and then grabbed a pint of milk out of the fridge.

"You're always such a curious boy," I remarked with a smile as I Sable jumped onto the counter and lightly pawed at the folded up letter.

"Here you go," I said to Sable as I placed the saucer of milk down on the floor and then grabbed the folded up letter and sat down on the sofa with a sigh. What information could this letter contain that would make Faye hide it. I thought to myself as I began to read the letter with wide eyes.

Dear Faye,

I cannot remain in New York any longer. The Ellis Island ferry departs tomorrow morning at 9 AM. This will be my final letter urging you to come back to France with me. I felt a deep sense of sorrow for you last night when you told me that going back to the Valley would only wither your heart even more. You may feel as if your heart belongs here in America, but I know your roots reside in the Valley. My time spent here in New York with you was a wonderful experience, but unlike you, I cannot find it in my heart to abandoned my family. If your life is truly better here in America then you will never hear from me again, but if there is still a part of you that wants to make amends for the way you parted ways with your mother, then please come back to the Valley. Every day we long for the sunshine that is your smile and the beautiful song that is your voice.

Sincerely, Jérôme

Who was this man named Jerome, and why was he urging Faye to return back to the town where she was born? I thought Faye departed her family in *Loire Valley* on good terms, or, perhaps, that's just what she wanted me to believe. This short but emotional letter created so many questions I never had about Faye while answering none of them. I now wanted to read the rest of the folded up letters in the box underneath the dresser in Faye's bedroom in hopes that the other letters would answer the questions I had about her that are now racing through my mind, but I felt that one letter was enough for today.

A sudden knock on the door startled me as I folded back up the letter and put it back into the box underneath the dresser with care as to not call attention to it whenever Faye should decide to read it again.

"Coming!" I shouted, as I scampered to the door as Sable followed me with a meow.

"Good afternoon Miss …,"

"Oh I'm Hayley, Hayley Carmona," I said to a man who shockingly resembled Fernando right down to his tall height, olive-skinned complexion and thin mustache, which made me recoil and close the door slightly.

"Is Ms. Dubois there?" the man inquired.

"No she went to work at the library across the street, but she'll be back around six," I replied in a timid tone, as I tightly gripped the doorknob.

"Oh yes of course. Just tell her that her rent is due this Friday," the man said to me in a stern tone as he stared behind me for any sight of Faye.

"I will, thank you," I said to the man

"Wait … who are you," the man inquired as he quickly held out his arm, preventing me from closing the door on him.

"I'm uhm, Faye's niece," I replied.

"Oh really. I thought Faye had no family here in America," the man said to me.

"Faye is my godmother. My mother died seven months ago so now I live with Faye," I said to the man in a somber tone.

The more questions the domineering man asked me the larger web of lies I had to weave, but within that ever growing web of lies was a truth to which I could tell the man with conviction, my mother was dead, and Faye was my godmother. "All right, since you're family I will allow you to live here with Ms. Dubois. Have a good day miss," the man said to me with a smile.

"Thank you, you as well, sir," I said to the man in a timid tone and then closed the door.

"That was close," I said to Sable with a wide-eyed stare as I picked him up and held him close to my heart which was beating out of my chest at the possibility of being evicted from Faye's apartment.

*****

It was 6:22 PM when I heard the apartment door open.

"Hayley I'm home," Faye pronounced as I averted my gaze at a portrait of her and her mother on the nightstand to the front door.

"How was work?" I inquired as I entered the living room.

"It was monotonous as usual. Only time I ever feel any excitement is when a prisoner is allowed time in the library to read," Faye replied to me as she quickly stripped down to her undergarments and then put on her silk black robe.

"Oh well. If you ever need help feel free to ask. I don't mind alphabetizing books," I said to Faye with a warm smile.

"Oh is it that boring for you here. Didn't Sable keep you entertained?" Faye inquired as she picked up Sable from off the kitchen counter and kissed him firmly on the forehead, which made him close his eyes in an irritated manner.

"No it's not that. I would just love to work at the library with you, for free of course," I replied, as Faye poured Sable a saucer of milk and herself a full glass of wine.

"Perhaps mon chéri, it looks like you cleaned up a bit around here. I appreciate that," Faye remarked with a sigh as she sat down on the maroon chair with her glass of wine and lit a cigarette.

"I did, I didn't want you to have to clean up when you got home from work," I said to Faye as she rested her head back on the chair and took a long smoke from her cigarette.

"Merci, you're a godsend mon chéri. Did anything else happen when I was at work? Faye inquired as she put a record on the victrola.

"Uhm well, a man stopped by. He said the rent is due—,"

"This Friday I know. That's our landlord Giovanni. He's nothing if not persistent when he needs money, but when I tell him about how long it takes for the shower to get hot water he disregards me, bastard," Faye interjected in a stern tone.

"There's more uhm, he was interrogating me, so I told him I was your niece. Sorry I'm not very good at lying under pressure," I said to Faye in a timid tone.

"It's quite all right, mon chéri. I would've told Giovanni the same thing. You know my mother always used to tell me 'you lose a feather from your angel wings with every lie you tell,'" Faye said to me with a smile as she sat back down on the maroon chair with a sigh.

"I've never heard that saying before," I said to Faye.

"It's bête I know, but whenever I lie I think of that phrase. I suppose I have no wings left now huh," Faye said to me with a scoff and then took a sip of wine.

Faye seemed so exhausted, not just physically, but her spirit seemed as if it was fading away. When I first saw Faye in the speakeasy, she appeared before me as such a beautiful, charming, and lively woman, a woman who infused others with life, but now I see that all may have been a façade which women were taught to paint over their faces to cover up their true despair, a façade I was never good at painting on my own face. I'm now beginning to see Faye without that rosy veil that was the speakeasy clouding my view of her, for she is just as human as me. I still wanted to know how exactly Faye and her mother parted ways. So I felt that now would be the best time for me to get Faye to talk about that sensitive subject.

"How often do you think of her?" I inquired as the French music playing on the victrola seemed to match my somber tone. "You know ... back in *Loire Valley*, there were days where my mother's voice was the last voice I would want to hear at the end of the day, but now I cannot help but hear her voice constantly racing through my head. 'Faye you must do this, Faye you must do that, remember Faye,'" Faye replied in a distressed tone as she stood up from the chair with her empty glass of wine in hand and pointed to her head with a circular motion as she began to pace back and forth in front of me.

"Do you remember the day you left the Valley?" I inquired in a timid tone as Faye quickly filled her empty glass with more wine.

"I do ... the last thing I said to my mother the day I departed *Loire Valley* was that I didn't want her voice to haunt me as   an old woman. She would constantly compare me to my older cousin Jerome. 'You should go live with Jerome in Paris Faye. America is full of ignorant philistines,' my mother told me. I told my mother that she was wrong about America for it's the land of dreams. Jerome and his father had a very comfortable life in Paris, a life I knew I could have here in America. My mother was more scared than I was at the prospect of a woman living on her own without a man to support her, and yet that's exactly how she raised me," Faye replied.

"You're father … where is he now?" I inquired.

"I never knew the man. My mother told me he fled *Loire Valley* the morning after he slept with her. Now you see why I have resentment towards most of the men in this world. My mother was then branded a whore and I was branded a bastard child by most of the villagers of *Loire Valley*. Now I feel as If I've taken on the reputation of a whore and bastard child. I thought America was the land where one could go to start anew, but now I've come to realize that who we are deep down will always remain and traveling to a new place will not change that, but I was too young and naïve to realize what my mother most likely already knew," Faye replied.

I was glad Faye was confiding in me. It made me feel as if she really was my godmother, and that we could tell each other anything that troubled us. At the same time I was also sad that Faye's relationship with her mother wasn't what I pictured it to be, but then again, nobody's relationship with their mother is based solely in happiness and nurturing times. The painful memories linger in our hearts just as strongly as the joyful memories, and Faye was now reliving those memories that made her pace back and forth by telling them to me. Faye was giving me a clear view into the world of a French American immigrant. All the immigrants who lived in New York had stories of what led them to America and Faye's story of following her dream to live in a country where you can thrive no matter who you are or where you're from was pure and virtuous in my book.

"Hayley … I was only able to depart *Loire Valley* because of a lie I told my mother," Faye said to me in a somber tone and then took a smoke as she continued to pace back and forth in front of me.

"W-What do you mean?" I inquired as Sable sat next to me on the sofa while intently watching Faye pace back and forth. "My mother wanted me to live with Jerome in Paris. She believed Paris was the best place for a young woman like me. She completely, how do you say … disregarded my dream to live in America. She told me that she would pay for my train ticket to Paris if I was ever interested, but would not financially support my dreams that involved America. So I then lied to her and told her that I was wanted to live with Jerome in Paris. My mother then paid me nearly half of her life saving which I then used to pay for the boat trip to America and this apartment," Faye said to me.

"Oh … I'm sorry your mother didn't support your dream. That must've been heartbreaking," I said to Faye in a somber tone as I stroked Sable.

"You can say that I lied my way to America, but I knew with all my heart that I wouldn't find such happiness living with my pompous cousin in Paris,"

Faye said to me.

"Faye, if you could go back and change that choice you made, would you?" I inquired.

"I've often thought about that mon chéri, but whenever I do, I think about all of the wonderful people I've met in America, people like you who I wouldn't have known if I chose to live in Paris," Faye replied as she sat down beside me.

"Are you happy here in America?" I Inquired.

"No matter how difficult my life may be here in America, I do not regret it one bit. I am at peace here in the Village with you and Sable and I wouldn't want to be anywhere else in the world," Faye replied with a warm smile as she draped her arm over my shoulders.

"I think we're kindred spirits, Faye," I remarked with a smile.

"Absolument mon chéri, I believe we share the same soul," Faye said to me.

"I'm glad I'm living here with you Faye. I no longer feel afraid or nervous as I did when I was with Jack in the speakeasy. You make me feel like home," I said to Faye with a warm smile. "I echo that sentiment mon chéri. Now I must retire for the night. I don't work tomorrow, perhaps we can go shopping in the Village," Faye said to me with a smile.

"Do you have enough money for that? Remember Giovanni told me—,"

"Shhh, you let me worry about that," Faye interjected. "Do you want Sable to sleep with you or me?" I inquired? "Let's let him decide. He's a big boy after all, aren't you," Faye replied with a smile as she kissed Sable on his forehead.

"Goodnight Faye," I said to Faye as I laid down on the sofa and draped a blanket over me, as Sable sat on the armrest.

"Goodnight mon chéri. May you have the sweetest dreams," Faye said to me with a smile and then entered her bedroom with a slight stumble.

"So do you want to sleep with me or Faye?" I inquired as I stared at Sable who meowed and then stretched before laying back down on the armrest of the sofa.

"Oh, all right. Goodnight," I said to Sable with a smile, as I closed my eyes to the soothing sight and sound of Sable purring at my feet.

*****

It was 8:15 AM in Faye's apartment as I awoke to the sound of Faye taking a shower.

I then sat upright from the sofa with a yawn and walked over to the window. It was a clear and sunny day in Greenwich Village, the kind of day that seemed to almost make one forget about the current economic strife that was responsible for more and more people living on the streets, but all I had to do to remind myself of that was to look down from the beautiful blue sky to the gray people waiting in breadlines below.

I then caught eyes with the woman prisoner across the street named Sidney who tricked me for a couple of cigarettes three weeks ago. She had her pale arms hanging through the barred window of the prison as she smiled while smoking a cigarette. "Good morning honey!" Sidney shouted, as she waved at me, but I didn't reply back to her as I quickly closed the drapes of the window and walked over to the kitchen.

"All right I'm getting your milk," I said to Sable in a yawning tone as he meowed at my feet. I then poured milk into a saucer and placed it on the floor as Faye entered the living room with a towel wrapped around her hair and body.

"You are such a spoiled boy. You should be thanking mon chéri Hayley for how sweetly she cares for you," Faye said to Sable with a giggle.

"There's no need for that. He thanks me by keeping me company," I said to Faye with a smile.

"En effet, Sable is better company than most men I've been with and far less finicky," Faye said to me with a laugh and then dried her hair with the towel.

"I'm going to take a shower now," I said to Faye.

"Very well mon chéri, when your done we can go shopping," Faye said to me in a zealous tone as she played a joyful French record on the victrola.

I then entered the bathroom and slowly took off my nightgown to the sound of Faye singing in the living room. I've lost weight. I thought to myself as I stared at my bare body in the mirror. My mother told me that I would start 'losing baby fat' around the age of 16, so did this mean I was now beginning to grow into a woman? I certainly felt better about my physical appearance living in this apartment with Faye than I did in the speakeasy with those predatory eyes of all the mobsters judging my every move. The water was still hot as I stepped into the shower and began to wash my hair. Living in this apartment with Faye was an experience that made me feel more like a woman than I've ever felt before. In the speakeasy, Jack, Samson, and Mickey treated me like a child and didn't regard me in the same manner which Faye regards me. I still missed Jack and wondered how he was fairing in the speakeasy, but had no desire to ever go back. I then noticed as I began to wash my arms and legs that all the cuts and bruises I always seem to have on me have healed and my ivory skin no longer bared the appearance of an orphan girl who lived on the street.

"Hayley I have to go to the library to drop off a couple of books. I'll be back in fifteen minutes then we can go shopping," Faye shouted.

I then heard the front door of the apartment close as I turned off the water. Back in *SoHo*, my mother would never leave me alone in the apartment on account of Johnny. She learned from her mistake with Fernando, but she was too late to undo the damage that he did to me. I then put on my black dress and dried my hair in a vigorous manner as Sable jumped upon the nightstand by the living room window where the victrola was playing a most soothing French song.

"You don't like that song?" I inquired with a smile as Sable meowed and pawed at the victrola.

"Well what's your favorite kind of music then?" I inquired with a smile as Sable continued to stare intently at the spinning record playing on the victrola as if it was a mouse running in circles.

My curiosity to read more of Faye's letters hidden in the box underneath her dresser in her bedroom began to grow as 15 minutes had passed and Faye still hadn't returned from the library. Faye was such a fascinating woman. Her life was full of plot twists like a protagonist of a great novel. So I then entered Faye's bedroom and grabbed the box of letters underneath the dresser. Which one should I read now? I thought to myself as Sable jumped up upon the bed beside me.

"Oh you think I should read that one?" I inquired as Sable pawed at one of the letters as I was riffling through them all.

"Very well, I trust your judgment curious boy," I said to Sable with a smile as I chose the letter he pawed at to read and then quickly put the box back underneath the dresser before exiting the bedroom. I then sat down upon the sofa and began to read the letter.

Dear Faye,

I heard cannon fire last night which made me fall out of bed. I then began to think of your smile and voice and before I knew it, no such sounds of war echoed in my ear. I told my mother that you are my sole purpose in this world and a life lived without you is not a life I want. I can think of no better day than walking hand in hand with you through the golden field of wheat by your house as you tell me about all of your beautiful dreams and aspirations.

I know the war is approaching the Valley, but the love I feel for you will keep my resolve steadfast and resolute. You make me feel like so much more than the simple son of a tailor, and when I'm holding you in my arms I feel as if I can brave all the evils the world lays before me. I never thought my future would be anything more than working in my father's footsteps, but now I've cast aside all the plans I had for a life without you. We can leave the Valley together. Please meet me tomorrow morning by the birch tree that's begun to bloom. I want to give you something as a token of my unwavering love for you.

Love, Julien

I then held the letter against my chest as my eyes began to well up with tears. I remember Faye telling me about this boy. I see now why Faye kept this letter. Julien's letter was written so beautifully I felt as if he was writing to me. He spoke with a passion and eloquence that rivaled any famous poet. Julien was the boy that lingered on Faye's lips. I wonder what the gift was that he gave her by the blooming birch tree.

I then kissed the letter before folding it up and putting it back in the box underneath the dresser in her bedroom.

"Hayley I'm back," Faye shouted as the door opened, but another voice also caught my attention, the voice of a man.

"So this is where you live," the man's voice remarked, as I slowly peeked my head out the bedroom door into the living room.

*****

Dear Diary
December 4th, 7:43 PM

It had been two weeks since Faye returned to the apartment with that man. His name was Reece Callahan, and my first impression of him was that he seemed respectable and sweet with Faye. He also had a charming sense of humor which reminded me of Jack. He was a clean cut man in his forties who worked for the mayor of New York, or at least that's what Faye told me about him. He was nice to me for the most part, making small talk and exchanging pleasantries whenever he was waiting for Faye to get ready. He had a welcoming smile and a warm attitude when he talked to Faye, but yesterday evening worried me when I heard them fighting. I just hope Reece is not putting up a prince façade as most men in this day and age do just to get closer to beautiful women like Faye.

Was Reece Callahan a true prince or just another monster in prince clothing? Only time will tell, but I will be watching him carefully, I care far too much about Faye to see her get hurt by another man.

"You look beautiful. Are you going out with Reece tonight?" I inquired as Faye primped her hair in the mirror in a frantic manner and then put on a dark shade of red lipstick, the kind of shade that would make any man fall head over heels for her.

"Oui, Reece is taking me to a Broadway show," Faye replied with a smile.

"Oh what show are you seeing?" I inquired in a zealous tone as I sprung up from the sofa and scampered over to Faye. "It's a musical called Take a Chance. I wanted to see Alice in Wonderland, but Reese was quite adamant on this musical so I—,"

"Took a chance," I interjected with a giggle.

"En effet mon chéri. I do not want to grow into an old woman set in her ways," Faye said to me as she adjusted her scarlet belt around her black, lacy dress which matched her smoky eyes and feathered hat.

A knock on the front door then sparked Faye's attention as she scampered into her bedroom.

"Oh let Reece in and tell him I'll be ready in five minutes," Faye shouted from her bedroom.

"All right!" I shouted as I walked up to the front door with Sable at my feet.

"Good evening Hayley. Is Faye ready?" Reece inquired with a smile as I opened the door.

"She said she'll be ready in five minutes," I replied with a smile as I gestured for Reece to enter the apartment.

"I'm sure you look beautiful Faye, but we have to go now or we're going to be late," Reece shouted and then looked at his watch with a sigh.

"Uhm do you often attend Broadway shows?" I inquired, as Reece and I sat down on the sofa.

"Only when I want to show off a beautiful woman like Faye. I'm amazed her face isn't gracing billboards on Broadway," Reece replied with a grin.

"Faye told me she doesn't have the temperament to be an actress, but I agree, she is more beautiful than most of the leading actresses I've seen on the silver screen," I said to Reece. "She most certainly is. Whenever I'm with her I feel as if I'm in the presence of royalty, but I know Faye would laugh at that sentiment," Reece remarked with a smile.

"That's sweet of you to say. She really likes you as well, I can see it in her eyes," I said to Reece.

"Women like your godmother are a rare kind in this day and age," Reece said to me.

"Do you mean French Immigrants or flapper girls?" I inquired.

"Well … both I guess, which makes her all the more rare," Reece replied.

"Sorry to keep you waiting mon chéri," Faye said to Reece with a smile as she entered the living room.

"Oh you know I could never get mad at you when you speak French to me," Reece said to Faye with a snicker.

"Oh then I shall only speak in French to you from now on," Faye said to Reece with a giggle as she took his arm.

"Have a good time," I pronounced.

"Oh Hayley, here's some money in case of an emergency," Faye said to me as she handed me five dollars.

"Oh thank you," I said to Faye.

"You can go down to the bodega around the corner and buy whatever your heart or stomach desires if you like," Faye said to me and then kissed me on the cheek before taking Reece's arm again.

Faye and Reece then exited the apartment leaving me with the curious face of Sable staring up at me.

"What shall we do tonight, curious boy?" I inquired as I picked up Sable.

Sable then meowed and pointed at the front door, as if to tell me he wanted to follow Faye on her date with Reece.

"No no, those two are on a date. We would only inhibit their fun," I said to Sable.

I hope he treats her right. I thought to myself as I stared intently at the front door of the apartment. Faye deserved a man who treated her no less than Julien did. If I felt heartbreak over reading Julien's letter then I can only imagine the heartbreak Faye still must feel. I wanted to ask Faye about Julien's letter just as I asked her about her cousin Jerome's letter, but now Faye is with a new man and I felt it wasn't the right time to bring up such heartbreak of the past.

"Shall we read another one of Faye's letters, Sable?" I inquired as I entered Faye's bedroom while holding Sable who meowed at my idea.

"You're just as curious about Faye as I am, aren't you?" I remarked with a smile and then kissed Sable on the head before putting him down on the bed.

"How about this one?" I inquired as I picked out a letter from the box and showed it to Sable. Sable then meowed and sniffed the letter, which I took as an indication of approval from the curious boy. I then entered the living room and sat down on the sofa with a sigh as Sable jumped up on the back of the Sofa and curled up in a comfortable position for hearing another story about Faye.

Would be upset with me if she finds out that I've been reading her letters? I thought to myself, as I pensively stared at the letter. Hopefully right now Faye is having a good time with Reece attending that Broadway show. I then opened the letter with a wide-eyed stare and began to read with Sable peering over my shoulder.

Dear Faye,

This may very well be the last letter I write to you as a free woman. My hands are still shaking from what I just did. I just stabbed my husband three times after walking in on him in bed with another woman. He then fled our apartment and right now I hope he bleeds to death, but on the slim chance that he does survive, I expect the police will arrive shortly. I could run from them all, but I've never been that good at running like you. I will face the consequences of the crime I committed. I write you this letter in hopes that you will visit me in whatever prison I am most likely sent to. You're the strongest woman I know Faye and if I had a mere shred of your strength I wouldn't lose my mind and try to commit murder, but I suppose that's what love does to sane women, it makes them crazy. I came to this country a couple years after you hoping that Philippe would stand by my side, but this once naïve young woman from Minerve has now learned a great deal of how cruel the world can be. I hope with all my heart to see you again mon chéri, whether it be from prison or the next life, for those are the only two paths I have left now.

Love, Louise

I remember visiting this woman in prison with Faye a month ago. She tried to kill her husband after she caught him in bed with another woman. Was Louise right? Did love really turn sane women crazy, or was that just her personal experience with love? Unlike Faye, Louise didn't come to America alone. Her husband Philippe came with her, but then betrayed her love. Faye gave this heartbroken and imprisoned woman a copy of a key which she managed to charm from one of the guards. Faye didn't care about the consequences that she would face for helping a prisoner escape. Faye just felt that her relationship with Louise was far more important than the law.

"That's enough for tonight," I said to Sable with a sigh, and then entered Faye's bedroom and put the letter back in the box underneath the dresser. I was getting hungry, so I thought I would use the money Faye gave me to buy some food at the bodega around the corner if it's still open.

"Do you want to come with me," I inquired with a smile as I put on my jacket and scarf, while Sable meowed at my feet.

"All right then let's go, or as Faye would say, allons-y," I said to Sable with a smile as I grabbed my purse. I then exited the apartment with Sable in tow as a light snowfall dusted Greenwich Village like powdered sugar upon a sweet pastry.

*****

It was 8:45 PM as I wandered the street corners near *Magnolia Towers* in search of the bodega Faye spoke of.

"Uhm Faye didn't say what corner the bodega was on," I said to Sable as we walked left towards a street corner where a taxicab driver was fighting with his passenger in the back seat. The taxicab driver then exited the taxi in an aggressive manner, opened the door and pulled out the man, as he kicked and shouted obscenities at him.

"Cough it up, you old bastard. This is no charity. Pay me my damn fair!" the taxicab driver shouted as he repeatedly kicked and punched the poor old man who appeared to be drunk. The taxicab driver then took money out of the old man's walled before spitting on him and entering the taxicab.

I wanted to help the old man, but I feared for my safety if I did. I know what Faye would do in this situation, but I just couldn't bring myself to get involved.

"Come on Sable," I said to Sable, while gripping the make- shift knife in my purse as we walked past the old man who groaned in pain upon the sidewalk.

"Oh there's the bodega. It looks like it's still open," I remarked, and then scampered over to the dimly lit bodega.

"So what shall we buy?" I inquired as Sable and I entered the bodega to the sound of a bell ringing overhead.

"Candy was something I very rarely got to enjoy in life, and that's just what I wanted to buy now.

"Wait … no I'm not going to waste this money Faye gave me," I said to Sable as I averted my eyes from the enticing candy at the front counter and then grabbed a basket and walked down the canned foods aisle. I then loaded the basket with two cans of soup, a loaf of bread, a pint of milk, and half a dozen eggs.

"That'll be four dollars and seventy-five cents, miss," the man behind the counter said to me.

"Oh we still have money left, Sable. Also one of these please," I said to the man behind the counter as I grabbed a candy bar and placed it upon the counter with a smile.

"Anything else, miss?" the man behind the counter inquired with a sigh.

"That will be all, right Sable?" I replied as I glanced at Sable with a smile.

"Four dollars and eighty-five cents," the man behind the counter said to me.

I then paid the man behind the counter and exited the bodega with the bag full of groceries.

*****

It was 9:47 PM as Sable and I entered *Magnolia Towers* to the sight of more homeless people camping out in the lobby. I've grown too used to seeing this dismal sight every time I enter and exit *Magnolia Towers* but it still fills me with sorrow nonetheless.

"Are you hungry Sable?" I inquired as I unlocked the front door and entered the apartment. I then put down the bag of groceries on the kitchen counter, poured a saucer of milk for Sable, and then started heating up a can of soup on the stove.

Faye must get lonely in this apartment with nobody to talk to but Sable. I don't know if I could ever live alone in an apartment. Despite certain people causing me to shake with fear, I still prefer being around them than being alone. The speakeasy was like another world compared to Faye's apartment. I could actually hear myself think, and write in my diary without a mobster interrupting my thought process with a callous remark. In Faye's apartment all I had to deal with was the occasional meow from Sable, which was a most pleasant sound to my ears. Perhaps that's why Faye allowed me to live with her, so she wouldn't feel so alone.

"Let's eat together shall we," I said to Sable with a smile as I pour myself a glass of wine and then poured the pot of soup into a bowl and then sliced a thick piece of bread from the loaf. I then took Sable's saucer of milk along with my meal to the coffee table. I've now listened to Faye's French music on the victrola so often to the point where I'm beginning to know the words to the songs. It was soothing music that made me imagine what it must feel like to live in Paris, a beautiful city where Faye refused to live with her cousin and uncle.

Faye was attracted to America in the same manner which I was attracted to Paris. We both believe that we can find happiness and fulfillment in those places. I do admit that my fascination with Paris is attributed to Faye, but If all Parisians act like Faye, then that city is a truly a lovely place.

"Are you done eating already?" I inquired with a mouthful of chicken soup, as Sable lapped up the last of the milk in the saucer upon the coffee table.

"No no, you can't eat the bleeding heart. It will make you sick," I said to Sable as he sniffed the bleeding heart plant on the coffee table.

"Who knows when Faye will be back, but until then, you just keep out of trouble, curious boy," I said to Sable with a smile, as I finished eating my soup. I then washed and put away the pot and bowl before sitting down on the sofa with a sigh as Sable jumped up upon the nightstand and curled up beside the victrola.

"Do you like this music, Sable?" I inquired with a smile, as I grabbed my diary and began randomly flipping through all of my entries over the past 6 months.

Sable already appeared soundly asleep beside the victrola upon the nightstand. It was such a peaceful tableau as Faye would call it, the image of Sable sleeping beside the victrola upon the nightstand in front of the window as it snowed outside. I then got undressed and put on my nightgown before lying down on the sofa. I felt warm and sleepy from the wine as Sable's purring acted as a lullaby for me, and within moments, my eyes began to close.

*****

I awoke at 8:05 AM to the sound of the front door opening.

"Faye, what's wrong?" I inquired with a wide-eyed stare as Faye scampered into her bedroom with tears in her eyes and then slammed the door shut.

"Faye … can I come in?" I inquired in a timid tone as I stood by the door of her bedroom listening to her sobbing.

"Oui, you may," Faye replied in a sobbing tone.

I then entered Faye's bedroom to the sight of her sobbing on her bed with her mascara running down her cheeks.

"Please tell me what happened," I said to Faye in somber tone, as I sat down beside her on the bed.

"I'm just weary mon chéri. Last night was quite the, how do you say … ordeal," Faye replied, and then walked over to the dresser mirror and primped her hair.

"Why was it an ordeal? What happened with you and Reece?" I inquired.

"I have to get ready for work now. I'll indulge you when I come home," Faye replied with a dismissive wave. "Did—did you sleep with him?" I inquired.

"Hayley s'il te plaît. This isn't the time. Merde I'm going to be late for work," Faye said to me in a stern tone as she got undressed.

"All right I'm sorry," I said to Faye in a somber tone and then exited her bedroom as she entered the bathroom and turned on the shower.

It was unlike Faye not to confide in me whenever she was upset, but I wouldn't pry any further. I understood all too well what it feels like to have someone try to make you talk to them when all you want to do is be alone with your sorrows.

Now I could only speculate what happened with Faye and Reece last night, but I wanted to know the truth. There was that time when I heard Faye and Reece fighting in the bedroom of the apartment. Hearing them fight brought back so many horrible memories for me in *SoHo*, memories that never fail to make me feel like a weak little girl.

I was getting tired of listening to French music so I turned off the victrola and then turned on the radio to a news station.

"In international news, the French government built by radical socialist

Édouard Herriot has fallen, as a result of Herriot's Chamber of Deputies refusing to pay their war debt to the United States," the radio sounded as Faye entered the living room with a towel wrapped around her hair and body.

"What more do we owe you greedy Americans? Vous agissez tous comme si vous étiez les maîtres de ce putain de monde. When will you all learn that we are one heart?" Faye inquired in a stern tone as she turned off the radio.

I noticed Faye would always speak in French whenever she was upset and wanted to blow off steam without me fully understanding her, but from my intimate time living with Faye I have begun to understand more key words when she speaks only in French and what she just said was most likely a negative remark about America.

"I—I just wanted to hear the news of the world," I replied in a timid tone, as she frantically dried her hair.

"Let me spare you the trouble. Right now the world is run by cowardly men who posture as bold leaders," Faye said to me in a stern tone.

"Maybe the new president elect FDR will be different," I said to Faye.

"Maybe or maybe history will just repeat itself as it's done for thousands of years," Faye said to me with a scoff and then scampered into her bedroom.

I could tell by Faye's pessimistic mood that what happened with her and Reece last night was still fresh in her mind this morning. Faye was the most positive and happiest woman I've ever known and seeing her upset like this was devastating to me. I could always depend on Faye to uplift my spirits with the mere sound of her sweet voice, but she didn't speak to me in such a tone this morning. Faye was hurting, and all I could do at the moment was be there for her any way I could.

"Do you want me to make coffee?" I shouted, as Sable jumped up onto the kitchen counter with a meow.

"No, no, you'll just make a mess," Faye shouted back to me from her bedroom.

"Oh … all right," I said to Faye in a somber tone.

"I fear that if I'm late again I will be fired from the Library and then I will have to fully depend on … never mind. I'll be back around 6 PM," Faye said to me in a frantic tone as she adjusted her tan skirt and jacket and then sprayed some perfume on her chest and neck.

"No stay here!" Faye shouted at Sable as she exited the apartment which made the curious boy recoil.

"Have a good day," I said to Faye as she slammed the door shut. Sable then meowed has he gently pawed my leg.

"I know, I know, I'm worried about her too," I said to Sable as I picked him up and kissed him on his forehead. I then stared out the window to the sight of Sidney waving through the barred window of the prison to Faye who was crossing the street, but Faye paid her no attention as she entered the Library. "Hey honey, your name's Hayley right!" Sidney shouted as I opened the window and stuck my head out as far as I could.

"Yes what do you want?" I replied with a shout.

"You live with Faye, right? Maybe you can tell me what's got her panties in such a knot," Sidney shouted.

"I don't know for sure. It might have something to do with a new man she's been seeing!" I shouted.

"Ah of course it's about a man. Men are the root of all the evils in this world!" Sidney shouted.

"I wish she would talk to me about it!" I shouted.

"Give her time honey. Faye will come through. Oh wait, can you give me some food, I swear I'll make it worth your while," Sidney inquired with a shout.

"Oh so you can trick me again!" I shouted.

"What are you talking about?" Sidney inquired with a shout.

"You don't remember me do you?" I inquired with a shout.

I then thought of what Faye said to me about how true acts of love do not hope for rewards, they're unconditional. I then quickly put on my jacket and boots and grabbed the candy bar I bought from the bodega last night before exiting the apartment. "Sidney … Sidney are you there?" I shouted as I stared up at the bared window of the prison.

"I'm here honey," Sidney replied with a smile as she poked her head and arms out the barred window.

"I have something for you!" I shouted as passersby stared at me with stern looks.

"Oh what do you have honey?" Sidney inquired with a smile.

"It's a surprise," I replied with a shout.

"Very well," Sidney shouted as she lowered a cup attached to a string down to me.

"All right raise it up!" I shouted. After I placed the candy bar in the cup.

Sidney then quickly pulled up the cup to her and her face instantly lit up with joy when she saw the candy bar.

"Three Musketeers huh. I've never seen this candy bar before," Sidney remarked with a smile as she stared at the candy bar with wide eyes as if it was a bar of gold.

"Neither have I. I think it's new. Well, I hope you like it!"
I shouted.

"Honey wait!" Sidney shouted, as she reached out her pale slender arm through the barred window.

"What is it?" I inquired.

"You have a good heart honey. Don't let anyone tell you differently," Sidney shouted as she lowered the cup attached to the string once again.

I then noticed that Sidney left half of the candy bar in the cup for me.

"Thank you!" I shouted with a mouthful of the candy bar as Sidney shouted back with a warm smile.

*****

It was 6:47 PM as Sable and I finished eating dinner together on the living room coffee table to the sound of the radio's local news reports.

"Breaking News in Greenwich Village, an inmate from the *Jefferson Market Court* Woman's Prison has escaped today. The inmate's name is Louise Claudette and she is considered to be extremely dangerous. Ms. Claudette was sentenced to two years in *Jefferson Market Court* Woman's Prison for stabbing her husband. Investigator Jake Ledowski believes the woman is still in Greenwich Village tying up loose ends with an accomplice who may have helped her escape before she flees the city entirely. Current whereabouts of escaped inmate Ms. Claudette are unknown at this time, but if anyone knows of any information regarding Ms. Claudette please report to the NYPD," the radio sounded.

Oh my god will Faye be implicated in helping Louise escape? Is that why she still hasn't returned home? I thought to myself as my heart began to race. That guard that Faye slept with just so she could make copies of his keys to give to Louise, would he turn in Faye? Or would he stay silent from the risk of losing his job? Faye was all too comfortable when it came to playing with fire. I loved and hated that about her. That woman Louise Claudette nearly killed her husband in an act of rage when she walked in on him with another woman. Faye believed she deserved a second chance in life, but does she now have that chance? Will Louise come here to Faye's apartment? Or has Faye already met with Louise in a secret location to bid her farewell on her second chance in life? All of these thoughts raced in my head as the radio blared the local news reports.

"That's enough of that," I spoke allowed as I turned off the radio and then put on a soothing record of a random French singer on the victrola.

Perhaps Faye was right, when she said 'listening to the news all the time will make you crazy' but now I was so worried about Faye.

I then picked up Sable in a hasty manner and held him tightly as I swayed back and forth with my face buried in his lustrous black fur. Suddenly, the sound of the door opening caused me to drop Sable as I scampered over to the door to the sight of Faye, but she was with Reece.

"Faye, you're back, I was so worried," I said in a distressed tone as I tightly wrapped my arms around Faye.

"Aw mon chéri, here, these are for you. Could you please put them in water while Reece and I talk," Faye inquired with a smile as she handed me a bouquet of flowers.

"They're beautiful, but why are these for me?" I inquired, and then took a deep inhale of the sweet fragrance the vibrant bouquet emitted into the air.

"Sidney told me what you did for her. You also deserve these flowers for having to deal with me," Faye replied with a smile and then kissed me on the cheek before entering the bedroom with Reece and closing the door behind her.

I then went to the kitchen to find a vase or any container that I could fill with water and put the bouquet of flowers in as I could hear Faye and Reece begin to argue again in the bedroom. I then found a silver pitcher atop the fridge which I filled with water and then placed the bouquet of flowers in.

"That wasn't part of our arrangement!" I heard Faye shout from the bedroom in a distressed tone.

"You're so goddamn ungrateful!" I heard Reece shout from the bedroom.

"I'm so sorry for dropping you," I said to Sable as I kneeled down and stroked him while staring at the bedroom door in fear as I did back in *SoHo* when Johnny and my mother would constantly fight behind the closed door of their bedroom. Back then my mother tried her best to protect me from Johnny, as I sense Faye is trying to do with me now. It seems that Reece is just another wolf in sheep's clothing, but what arrangement do Faye and Reece have exactly?

"Or else you'll be on the streets toots, with the rest of those beggars camped outside the entrance of this apartment!" Reece shouted as he exited the bedroom and stormed past me as we both stared daggers at each other for a brief moment before Reece exited the apartment.

Reece called Faye toots just like Stefano used to call me. Such a condescending word is only used by men who don't respect women in any way. I'm now beginning to see Reece for who he truly is, a kind of man who I've suffered my entire life, "Putain de connard!" Faye shouted in a stern tone as she scampered up to the front door of the apartment.

"Faye … are you all right?" I inquired in a somber tone as Faye quickly poured a glass of wine.

"I am now mon chéri. I'm so sorry for the callous way I treated you this morning. It was eating me up inside the entire day," Faye said to me in a somber tone as she sat down next to me on the sofa with a sigh.

"Oh I don't care about any of that now. I was just so worried about, you know, well I'm sure you were informed," I said to Faye.

"Spit it out mon chéri," Faye said to me.

"The breaking news. Louise Claudette, one of the women prisoners you gave the key to escaped from the prison," I said to Faye with a wide-eyed stare.

"Qui, but do not fret mon chéri. The guard I seduced in order to retrieve the key to copy and then in turn give to the three women prisoners might as well throw his job away if he turns me in," Faye said to me in a weary tone as she arched her back with a faint groan.

"Oh right, he might as well turn himself in if he turns you in," I said to Faye.

"Exactly mon chéri. I thought of this exact scenario when I seduced that truie," Faye said to me with a grin and then took a sip of wine.

"I hope she finds a better life … Louise," I said to Faye.

"She will. I have faith in her. A wise woman never makes the same mistake twice. Louise is a good woman who was betrayed by a terrible man, but in this day and age society looks upon those women as terrible people. This is a, how do you say … travesty," Faye said to me as she shook her head and then lit a cigarette and took a smoke.

"So what arrangement do you have with Reece?" I inquired in a timid tone.

"Oh I'm sorry you heard that," Faye replied with a dismissive wave and then took a sip of wine.

"You don't want to tell me?" I inquired.

"It's complicated mon chéri. He helps me pay rent," Faye said to me with a sigh.

"In exchange for what?" I inquired, as Faye then stood up from the sofa and raised the volume on the victrola and began to sing and dance in front of me.

"Faye, Faye, what does he get in return?" I shouted.

"Hayley, you're still a child, you wouldn't understand our arrangement," Faye said to me, as she continued to dance and sing with a glass of wine in her hand.

I then quickly stood up from the sofa and turned off the victrola.

"I am not a child!" I shouted with a stern look as Faye's dancing and singing continued for a moment of silence before stopping.

"Hayley," Faye said to me with a smile and then took another sip of wine.

"I have suffered more loss than most adults four times my age! The moment my mother died I stopped feeling like a child because I didn't have her there to nurture me. I had nobody to make me feel like a child when that's all I wanted to feel like. I feel as if I missed out on a part of my life that I could never get back until I started living here with you. You make me feel like an adult when I'm around you, but you still comfort me in the same ways my mother used to in *SoHo*. So don't tell me I wouldn't understand anything you're going through because you know that's not true!" I shouted in a distressed tone as I pointed aggressively at Faye who stared silently back at me with wide eyes. Faye then quickly wrapped her arms around me as I began to sob.

"I'm so sorry mon chéri. For a moment I forgot about your past. I've been so insensitive with you lately, so wrapped up in my own torment that I've failed to see just how much you've helped me in my life," Faye said to me with a smile.

"H—How have I helped you?" I inquired in a tearful tone.

"Hayley, you're the best thing to ever happen to my life and I mean that with all my heart," Faye replied with a warm smile as she placed her hand on her chest.

"What about Reece?" I inquired, as I wiped the tears from my flushed cheeks.

"What about him? I give him what he wants in the bedroom and he pays for half our rent. That's our arrangement. Some nights it sickens me to lay with him, but I do what I must in order remain off the streets.

"I could try to find a job to help pay for rent," I said to Faye. "No no no I couldn't ask that of you mon chéri. It's just as you said. I do not want you to miss out on such an important part of your life all because you're working in some god awful factory assembly line. If I was half as intelligent as you are at your age then I would've planned ahead more before I departed the Valley in such a hasty manner, but all I cared about was proving my mother wrong, and even now, I still try to prove her wrong," Faye said to me in a somber tone.

"How else could I help you then? I'll do anything to help you," I said to

Faye in a distressed tone, as she turned back on the victrola.

"You already have mon chéri. God knows what I might have done to myself every night coming home from work if I didn't have you to greet me. Just be yourself and nothing less," Faye said to me with a smile as she grabbed both my hands.

"What are you doing?" I inquired with a grin and sniff, as Faye pulled me in close to her with a smile.

"Showing you how do dance a simple waltz, mon chéri," Faye replied with a smile.

"But women don't dance with each other," I said to Faye.

"Says who? Forget about those silly conventions, now un, deux, trios un, deux, trois" Faye said to me with a giggle as she guided each of my clumsy steps to match her graceful ones.

"I guess it's not as complicated of a dance as I thought it was," I remarked as I began to match the steps and dance in sync with Faye.

"There you go mon chéri. You see, anybody can learn this dance. My mother taught me it when I was around your age. She said 'Faye you must learn the waltz if you're to ever court a decent man.' Little did my mother know that nobody in America even dances the waltz anymore," Faye said to me with a giggle as we continued to dance the waltz.

"Then why do you continue to dance?" I inquired with a smile.

"To keep her spirit alive, besides, I find it to be such a beautiful dance fit for royalty," Faye replied with a smile.

Dancing the waltz with Faye was such a beautiful moment, a moment that will keep me warm on the coldest of nights. Faye and I now fully understood and respected each other as women. All I ever wanted in life was to be loved and respected by those around me. I now had that relationship with Faye and it gave me a new sense of hope.

After Faye and I finished eating a light dinner of pasta called Crozets de Savoie, I spent the remainder of the night writing in my diary as Faye pampered Sable with affection while drinking wine and listening to music on the victrola.

"I'm going to sleep," I said to Faye in a yawning tone as I lay down on the sofa.

"I have tomorrow off from work. Let's spend the day together," Faye said to me with a smile, as Sable meowed in response.

"I would like that very much," I said to Faye with a warm smile, as she turned off the victrola.

"Then it is settled. I love you mon chéri, goodnight," Faye said to me.

"I love you too, Faye," I said to Faye with a smile and yawn as my heavy eyelids closed to the beautiful sight of Faye smiling back at me from the bedroom doorway.

*****

It was 9:18 AM as I awoke to the dulcet melody of Faye singing in the kitchen as she made breakfast.

"Bonjour, mon chéri," Faye said to me as I sat upright on the sofa while rubbing my bleary eyes.

"Good morning," I said to Faye in a yawning tone as I walked over to her.

"I am making my favorite breakfast crepe suzettes," Faye said to me with a smile, as she prepared what looked like simple pancake batter in a bowl, but I know that it must be much more refined and complicated than that, because it's a French breakfast after all. This was the breakfast I attempted to make for Faye, but couldn't read the cookbook because it was all in French so I decided to make French toast instead which still pleased Faye. Mornings spent with Faye were such a lovely and warm experience for me. When Faye was in a good mood she was the type of woman who made it impossible for you to feel sad when you were around her, but if she was in a bad mood, then you felt devastated that such a beautiful person like Faye was going through such pain. Unlike Jack, Faye wasn't afraid to wear her heart on her sleeve. She always displayed such a wide range of emotions from the very first moment I met her in the speakeasy. I have yet to meet a man or even a boy who wasn't afraid to delve the depths of his heart when he was with me. Even Mickey became quiet and stoic whenever something was troubling him. I wonder how he's doing now.

"I would've made a mess if I tried to make those. I don't have your magic touch," I said to Faye with a giggle as I watched her fill the crepe suzettes with diced up bananas and strawberries which she prepared in a bowl prior to this final stage.

"Nonsense mon chéri, you possess so much magic within you. Perhaps you just need that special moment to evoke such magic," Faye said to me with a warm smile as she stroked my hair and then delicately rolled up the fourth crepe suzette on the pan with diced up strawberries.

"Did your mother used to make you this breakfast?" I inquired with a smile as I sat down at the kitchen table, while Faye poured me a cup of coffee.

"Oh heavens no. This dish is far too elegant for my mother's liking and patience. She would often prepare simple stews, casseroles, and baked goods for me," Faye replied with a smile. "So what attracted you to make this breakfast?" I inquired as I took a bite of the banana-filled crepe.

"Hayley, I will be honest with you. I vowed to only cook such refined dishes like this for the ones I love, and so far you and I are the only ones I've made this dish for," Faye replied with a grin and then took a bite of a strawberry-filled crepe.

I was surprised and flattered that Faye only made this refined breakfast dish for me. I then thought of Julien, the boy who expressed his love for Faye in such a beautifully poetic manner. Would Faye have cooked the breakfast I'm eating now for Julien back then?

"My mother once told me 'the way to a man's heart is through his stomach' back then I didn't know what that meant, but now I see that men value a woman that can cook above woman with their own dreams that don't involve cooking,"

I said to Faye, and then took a sip of coffee.

"Most men are gluttons. They seek out a woman who can satisfy all their desires to the point where we have nothing left to give them, and then they continue to ask, beg, and demand more from us," Faye said to me as her voice rose to a stern tone. "Faye open up we need to talk!" a voice shouted along with three hard knocks at the front door which averted me and Faye's attention from each other to the front door. "Oh speak of the devil," Faye said to me. "Who is it?" I inquired with a wide-eyed stare.

"It's Reece most likely," Faye replied with a sigh as she stood up from the kitchen table, and then walked over to the front door.

"But you said we would spend the day together," I said to Faye in a somber tone.

"I'm sorry Hayley. Some other time perhaps," Faye said to me in a somber tone and then opened the front door.

Reece and I then glanced at each other for a brief moment before he whispered something in Faye's ear.

"Just give me a couple of minutes to get ready," Faye said to Reece.

"Well hurry up I don't have all goddamn day, toots," Reece said to Faye and then checked his watch while shaking his head. "You can wait in the lobby. I'll be right down," Faye said to Reece as she pointed out the door.

"Why can't I wait here in the kitchen? Whatever you two are eating smells pretty good," Reece inquired, as he walked towards the kitchen table.

"I said wait in the lobby!" Faye shouted.

"All right Jesus Christ. So much for French hospitality," Reece said to Faye in a stern tone and scoff and then muttered what I could only assume to be offensive remarks about Faye under his breath as he exited the apartment.

"He always shows up at the worst time," Faye said to me while shaking her head.

"What did he whisper to you?" I inquired.

"Something a desperate man would whisper. A man who couldn't understand the heart of a woman even if his life depended on it," Faye replied in a stern tone and then entered her bedroom.

I hated Reece. The more I heard him speak, the more he resembled Johnny. Faye would always choose Reece over me when it came to her undivided attention. Reece seemed to have a power over her, which was solely based on money. Is that what money does to people in this day and age? Does it make them deaf to the outcry of their own hearts?

"I'm so sorry Hayley. I swear I didn't plan for Reece to interrupt our day together," Faye said to me in a somber tone as she primped her hair and adjusted her black sequin dress in a hasty manner.

"He's done this twice now. Where are you going with him anyways?" I inquired in a sulking tone.

"We're going out to a gathering. That's all I can tell you mon chéri," Faye replied and then began to frantically apply a cherry shade of lipstick to her lips in the living room mirror.

"Secrets cause cancer Faye. That's what my mother used to tell me," I said to Faye.

"Then may god have mercy on my soul. I have to go now mon chéri I cannot keep Reece waiting. I love you, do not forget that," Faye said to me and then kissed me on the cheek before exiting the apartment.

"Well she left us again for that man, Sable, and all because he pays for half the rent of this apartment," I said to Sable with a sigh as I picked him up and walked over to the window.

Whenever I was left alone in the apartment back in *SoHo* I would always use those moments to reflect on not only my life but my mother's life and what I could possibly do to help her during her fights with Johnny, but whenever those fights arose I would always react the same. My mother would cry out for me to stay away or to close the door of my bedroom as Johnny was hitting her, and that's what I did every time, for I didn't possess the courage to help my mother back then in *SoHo*.

*****

Dear Diary
December 18th, 9:46 PM

I've been thinking about it for quite some time now. Why should it only be reserved for people much older than me? Young woman like me also have fantastic stories to share with the world. I believe my life, as fraught with pain and loss as it may be also is blessed by beauty, and the measure of any brilliant writer is finding the beauty in misery. My life living with Faye has given me a new perspective, but has also picked open at a wound which I've been trying so hard to heal. So I now conclude this diary entry because Sable is meowing for me to feed him. I hope that I will be a braver and wiser woman the next time I write to you.

"Then why did you parade me around the room like your fucking trophy eh?" Faye inquired in a stern tone and scoff as she and Reece entered the apartment in such an aggressive manner which made me spill Sable's saucer of milk as I placed it down on the floor.

Faye and Reece then immediately stormed into the bedroom and slammed the door shut and I just knew what was coming next.

"Don't act so damn prideful toots. It's not like you have a squeaky clean reputation to uphold," I heard Reece shout from the bedroom, as I stared at the closed door with wide-eyes.

"It's all right Sable, it's all right, they're just talking," I said to Sable as I picked him up and then sat down on the sofa as my heart began to race at the sound of Faye and Reece' aggressive voices shouting at each other behind the closed bedroom door. I then began to hold Sable closer and stroke him faster the louder Faye and Reece fought to the point where Sable meowed aggressively at me and wriggled from my embrace.

"I do not jump to attention at your every beck and call!"

Faye shouted in a distressed tone from the bedroom.

"If you want me to continue to pay for half the rent of this rat-hole apartment you will, sweetheart. You may be beautiful, but you're not as smart as you make yourself out to be," Reece said to Faye in a stern tone as the bedroom door opened.

"Then maybe I'll tell your wife about our arrangement," Faye said to Reece in a stern tone.

What happened next was a sight I never wanted to see ever again, but it happened right in front of my very eyes nonetheless. Reece then stood still for a brief moment before he swiftly smacked Faye in the face so hard which sent her falling to the floor.

"You ungrateful bitch, how dare you try to blackmail me!" Reece shouted as he stood over Faye who lay on the floor crying with her hand pressed against her face.

"Faye!" I shouted in dismay as I sprung up from the sofa. "Hayley please stay back," Faye said to me in a pleading tone which evoked a most terrible memory of my life back in *SoHo*.

*****

"Mom!" I shouted as I shuddered at the sight of Johnny smacking her to the floor.

"Hayley, please go to your room," my mother said to me as she fought back tears.

"You're so goddamn ungrateful Dezerae. After everything I've provided for you and Hayley you continue to defy me at every turn," Johnny said to my mother in a stern tone as he pulled off his belt.

"The part of me that wanted to protect my mother at that moment was quickly overpowered by the fear Johnny put into me with a single stare, that single stare sent me running to my bedroom with tears in my eyes as I could hear my mother crying from Johnny whipping her with his belt.

*****

That little girl in *SoHo* who was frozen by fear no longer lived within me now. I no longer cared about my well being as I stared in rage at Reece standing over Faye crying on the floor. All I cared about was protecting Faye.

"No, get away from her!" I shouted as I took out my make-

shift knife from my purse and then lunged towards Reece.

"Ah ... you little bitch you stabbed me," Reece remarked with a grimace as he held his side and staggered back from me and Faye with wide eyes.

"Hayley!" Faye shouted in a gasping tone as I stood between her and Reece while pointing the bloody knife at Reece in an aggressive manner.

"I—I swear, I—I'll kill you if you hurt her again," I said to Reece in a stern tone, as I put my arm in front of Faye while pointing the knife at Reece.

"Ah goddamn it. Make your choice Faye. You either kick that kid out of this apartment or you can say goodbye to my money," Reece said to Faye in a stern tone and cringe as Sable hissed at him from upon the kitchen counter.

Faye then stood up from the floor and placed her hand on my shoulder, but that didn't calm me down, I wouldn't feel calm nor would I lower my knife until Reece was gone.

"Get out, you're bleeding on my floor," Faye said to Reece in a stern tone.

"You two will rue this, day mark my words," Reece pronounced in a stern tone and grimace as he held his side before staggering out of the apartment.

"Hayley what's gotten into you?" Faye inquired in a distressed tone. As she poured herself a glass of wine.

"I couldn't let it happen to you just like it happened to my mother. I won't see you hurt by men like Johnny knowing that I had the courage my entire life to protect you," I replied as I dropped the knife and tears began to pour from my eyes.

"You should've never been subjected to this part of my life. I see now it's too painful for you," Faye said to me in a somber tone as she dropped to her knees and gently grabbed me by the shoulders.

"No, you're wrong. I believe we were meant to be together. You deserve so much better than men like Reece," I said to Faye as I shook my head.

"Hayley stop. No such man exists in this world!" Faye said to me in a stern tone as she shook me within her grasp.

"That's not true. What about Julien? He treated you the way you deserve to be treated with love and respect. Tell me, what was the token of his unwavering love that he gave to you by the birch tree?" I inquired in a distressed tone.

"Quoi … you've been reading my letters haven't you?" Faye inquired with a wide-eyed stare as she stood up from the floor and scampered into her bedroom.

"Please tell me Faye. What did Julien give you by the birch tree?" I inquired in a distressed tone, as I entered Faye's bedroom to the sight of her crying in bed.

"He gave me nothing but this pain I still feel in my heart. I waited there underneath that beautiful birch tree that afternoon, but Julien never showed up. I then found out by his neighbors that his parents had forcibly taken him with them when they fled the Valley in fear of the approaching war to live in Marseille. So there you have it Hayley. No such fairytales of princes exist in this world we live in," Faye said to me as tears streamed from her eyes.

"Then why did you keep his letter?" I inquired in a somber tone, as I place my hand on her shoulder.

"You're far too wise for your age mon chéri. I received this letter in the mail today, but I'm too distraught to read it," Faye said to me in a sobbing tone and smile as she handed me a letter.

My eyes then widened as I recognized the rough handwriting of the letter.
"Oh my god," I remarked with a wide-eyed stare.
"Well, who is it from?" Faye inquired as she leaned in close to me.

CHAPTER 17:
TALES FROM SOHO:
BOYHOOD
- JACK -

Dear Troublemakers,

I would say a dead man is writing you this letter from beyond the grave, but once again, Samson saved my life. It's all over, my vision of the speakeasy. That little bastard Stefano attempted to silence me in the middle of the night and he would've succeeded if it wasn't for Samson sneaking in through the dumbwaiter and shooting two of the mobsters in the head who were about to do me the same service. Samson and I then parted ways after taking our fair share of all the money in the registers. Every hitman working for the Five Points Gang is most likely looking for me. The information I know about Mr. Luciano could bring his entire organization to its knees, but only if he continues to try and silence me.

I saw you both a couple weeks ago in the window. I wanted to come up and say hello, but I wouldn't doubt I would be leading a hitman of the Five Points Gang right to your apartment. I couldn't put you both through that. You girls both looked happy together and that's how you two should stay. I've already put you through so much kid. I know I'm a lousy excuse for an uncle, but you possess an intelligence that's so fierce it makes me wonder how we're even related. I cannot tell you where I'm living right now because I'm the Five Points Gang number one target. I will get by in my life as I always have. Do not look for me kid. You and Faye are a good fit in this screwed up puzzle called life. Faye can give you everything I never could. So now I have finally come to peace with what I've battled with in my head throughout my entire childhood and now adulthood. I'm just a lowlife rat who feeds off people far greater than me and now I find myself cornered like said rat, but not you two, no matter what happens, I feel it my gut that you two troublemakers will be just fine

Jack

Why was I living here in this apartment complex that I out paid a family of three for? Was it just because I didn't want to live on the streets? Was it for sentimental reasons or was it simply because *SoHo* was the only place in Manhattan where I had roots? I thought by coming back here to the very apartment complex where I used to live with my mother and sister that I would find some sense of what those enlightened people of the world call a semblance of happiness, but all I've found is a mangy rat which scurries its way between the walls of my apartment at night when I'm trying to sleep, not to mention all the Hispanic children who cry bloody murder all throughout the early morning. This apartment complex is not how I remembered it, but back then I had my mother and Dez to keep me company, now all I have is that rat.

"Rent Dansby, you're a day late!" a voice shouted with three bangs on the door.

Oh yes, I also have the landlord Mr. Rosenberg. Long story short, he's the kind of man who would see you bleeding in the gutter and wonder how he could make a profit from it. I guess he and I aren't so different after all.

"Yes, I have your rent," I said to Mr. Rosenberg with a groan as I opened the front door to the sight of the man holding a bat in one hand and a check book in the other hand.

"Where you planning to beat me to death if I didn't pay up?" I inquired, as I counted out the money.

"I'm not a violent man Mr. Dansby. I respect my tenants as long as they respect me. I know very well how cut throat of a man you are though. Most people would've let that family take this apartment, but not you, huh, son," Mr. Rosenberg remarked with a smirk.

"I'm not most people. Besides, since when does being selfless get you anywhere in this day and age?" I inquired with a scoff as I slapped the rent payment down into Rosenberg's wrinkled grimy hand.

"Fair enough, is there anything that needs addressing in your apartment before I go?" Mr. Rosenberg inquired.

"Yes get a damn exterminator over here. I swear I'm sharing this apartment with a whole family of rats," I replied in a stern tone.

"This is New York City Mr. Dansby, if you don't like rats then go west," Mr. Rosenberg said to me with a snicker and dismissive wave and then walked away as I slammed the door with a scowl.

"Leave it to a Jew to get blood from a stone," I spoke aloud with a scoff, while shaking my head.

Living here in *SoHo* sure as hell didn't feel like greener pastures for me. Should I have taken the advice of the many starry-eyed people and gone west to California? I don't know why I felt that *SoHo* was my greener pastures when I bid farewell to Samson and departed the speakeasy three weeks ago, but it's the first place that came to mind. To this day I still can't help but associate greener pastures with *SoHo* and the death of my father.

*****

It was 6:17 PM as I put the letter I wrote for Hayley and Faye in the mailbox at the entrance of the apartment.

"Jack I knew I'd find you here!" a boy said to me in a gasping tone. My eyes then widened as I looked closer at the boy who I at first brushed off as a common orphan.

"Mickey ... what the hell ... how did you find me?" I inquired in a stern tone as I grabbed Mickey's arm and pulled him in close to me.

"I remember you talking to Samson about how you used to live in *SoHo* when you where my age. So I figured I might as well see if you're still in the city. I thought you left this town for good. Why are you still here, Jack?" Mickey inquired.

"Forget you ever saw me Mickey. There could be hit men of the Five Points Gang staked out on each street corner." I replied in a stern tone as I scampered into the lobby of the apartment.

"I'm not a kid Jack. I've had my brushes with death too," Mickey said to me.

"You think you're not a kid just because you don't fear death? That just makes you a stupid kid," I said to Mickey with a scoff.

"Then what does that make you, Jack?" Mickey inquired in a stern tone.

"A stupid babysitter," I replied in a stern tone as I lit a cigarette and took a smoke.

It then occurred to me as I was starring at the still starry- eyed orphan Mickey. This couldn't have been a coincidence that he found where I now live. Was the boy still working for Mr. Luciano at the speakeasy after all this time? Have they promised the gullible kid a pretty penny to lure me in to a trap where a hitman from the Five Points Gang fills me with led in a back alley before I have the chance to blink? It would only be fitting seeing as how I tried to do the very same thing to Avery, but ultimately decided I couldn't lure my former partner to his death. I wanted out of it all, but sometimes in order to escape hell, you must keep going deeper and deeper until you find yourself face to face with the devil himself. I needed to know who Mickey worked for and I'll stop at nothing to get my answers from him.

"Mickey, come up with me. We have matters to discuss," I said to Mickey as I flicked my cigarette into the gutter.

"Uhm sure Jack. So this is where you used to live when you were my age huh?" Mickey inquired as we entered the apartment.

"Yes this was my childhood. Only back then I was much more like you," I replied, as we entered the elevator.

"How so? I mean other than the fact that you were my age. How else were you like me?" Mickey inquired as the creaky elevator dinged and the doors opened to the sight of my next door neighbor Mrs. Böhm talking to her husband who appeared as a bag of bones propped up by a cane.

"Guten Tag, Mr. Dansby, wer ist das?" Mr. Böhm inquired. "English damn it. I don't understand any of that Führer language of yours," I said to Mr. Böhm in a stern tone as I tried to unlock the door which always sticks.

"You're a terrible man," Mrs. Böhm remarked with a gasp and then entered her apartment with her husband.

"There was that so hard!" I shouted at the closed door. I then rammed the door of my apartment until it finally opened and I stumbled in.

"I thought you liked it when Faye spoke other languages to you at the speakeasy," Mickey said to me.

"That was Faye and she was speaking French. You just saw that old broad and heard that ugly language that came from her even uglier mouth," I said to Mickey.

"I don't know, it didn't sound ugly to me," Mickey remarked.

"To answer your question, I was like you because I didn't have a father at your age and because of that ... I had nobody to place boundaries in my life," I said to Mickey as I slammed the door shut. Every time I slammed the door of my apartment shut I could hear the rats scurry in the walls, as if I disturbed them from a slumber.

"Are you happy here?" Mickey inquired, as I turned on the radio and peered through the stained olive curtains covering the living room window.

"Oh sure I'm as happy as a rat in a wall," I replied with a scoff.

"I wonder how Hayley and Faye are doing," Mickey inquired.

"You wonder many things don't you. Tell me Mickey, are you still working at the speakeasy?" I inquired as I walked slowly towards Mickey who appeared nervous, but that boy was always nervous, from the first moment I met him, and this may very well be the last.

"N—No they kicked me out a day after they tried to kill you," Mickey replied in a stammering tone as I stood face to face with him.

"You're lying. They brought you here to kill me. To tie up loose ends. You're still working for them aren't you, you little rat bastard," I shouted as I grabbed Mickey by his collar and slammed him against the living room wall which caused the rats to scurry once more.

"No Jack I swear, please you have to believe me! They made me no offer. They didn't even see me as a threat or they would've killed me like they've done to so many other more important men. I'm just an orphan Jack. That's all I'll ever be," Mickey said to me in a distressed tone.

"Don't play the innocent card with me kid. I know all the games all too well. Sit down now!" I shouted as I took out my pistol and pointed it at Mickey.

"Is everything all right in there Jack," Mrs. Böhm inquired from across the hall.

"Everything's fine. Now mind your own goddamn business!" I shouted back.

"Are you really going to kill me Jack? After all we've been through?" Mickey inquired with a wide-eyed stare as he sat down on the sofa.

"Why not, nobody would miss you, and I would be tying up loose ends myself. You would no longer be a liability on my life when it comes to the Five Points Gang using you to get to me," I replied.

"You're right, the police probably wouldn't even report my death if they saw me face down in the gutter," Mickey said to me in a somber tone.

"Don't worry you won't feel a thing … aren't you going to run, fight for your life?" I inquired as I pulled back the hammer of the pistol.

"No … all I've ever done is run from predators. All I've ever done is live among rats. I'm tired of fighting," Mickey replied as tears began to stream from his eyes.

"So be it. I'm sure where I'm sending you will be a far better place than this one. Say hello to my father for me," I said to Mickey as I pointed the gun at his head. A sudden memory then began to flash in my mind as I stared intently at Mickey.

*****

"Please Mr. Dansby I'll work for your lowest rate. I just need to get a steady paycheck no matter what the amount may be," Mickey said to me in a somber tone as a belligerent Italian kept shouting his drink order at me as if his life depended on it. "You're drink is coming right up, sir. You, son, I already told you that I can't hire another worker right now, besides; I doubt you have what it takes to work here judging by those soft hands of yours. Now get out. I don't know how the hell you got in here in the first place," I said to the boy named Mickey who appeared to be an orphan.

"Fanculo questo! I'd rather drink from the gutter than stay one moment longer in this rats nest," the belligerent Italian said to me in a stern tone as he slammed his fist on the bar.

"Then go right ahead. The gutter is more suitable for your kind you ignorant fucking guido," I said to the Italian with a scoff and dismissive wave, as he sat upright from his stool.

"I'll teach you to respect my people!" The Italian shouted. "Watch   out!" Mickey shouted, as gunfire rang out throughout the speakeasy.

"You son of a bitch!" Samson shouted as he tackled the Italian to the ground.

"What happened?" I inquired in a bewildered tone, as Samson gave the Italian his one-two jab, right hook combination which knocked the Italian out cold on the floor.

"If that boy hadn't of wrestled for control of this man's gun, then you would be pushing up daisies right now Jack," Samson replied in a heaving tone, as he stared at the gun, and then began to drag the Italian out the front door.

I hate to admit it, but that orphan just saved my life, and even after I just turned him down. That kind of selflessness and dignity is a rare gem in this day and age, and I would be a fool to not let Mickey Sullivan work for me.

"Mickey wait … you can start working here tomorrow—,"

"Oh thank you Mr. Dansby. You won't regret this. I swear," Mickey interjected with a smile as his face lit up at my decision. "It won't be easy work, but as long as you listen to me and Samson, then you will learn all the ins and outs of working in this speakeasy," I said to Mickey in a stern tone as we shook hands.

"Thank you. You're a generous man Mr. Dansby. No matter what people in this town say about you I know this to be true," Mickey said to me with a smile and then exited the speakeasy just as Samson entered and walked up to the bar.

"Why was the boy smiling? Oh you aired him, didn't you? Samson inquired with a smile as he walked behind the bar and smacked me on the back.

"I figured we could use a little more help around here," I said to Samson as I wiped down the bar.

"I thought you said we had no room in the budget to take on another worker," Samson said to me.

"We don't, but as you said, that kid saved my life a moment ago, and I owe him a life debt," I said to Samson as I stared intently at the front door of the speakeasy.

*****

My eyes then widened as I aimed and fired my pistol. "W—what are you doing?" Mickey inquired.

"Shooting the rat," I replied, as I then reached behind the sofa where Mickey was still quivering and grabbed the rat by the tail. I then opened the living room window and tossed the dead rat right onto a passing taxicab, but I'm sure the cab driver was used to seeing rats, as Mr. Rosenberg said to me 'this is New York City after all.'

I can't believe the idea even crossed my mind to kill Mickey. Have I really become such a heartless bastard that I've forgotten that the boy saved my life when I first met him?

"Thank you Jack," Mickey said to me in a somber tone. "We're now even. You saved my life the first time we met.

I almost forgot that," I said to Mickey with a sigh.

"I'm glad you remembered. So where do we go from here?"

Mickey inquired.

"Have there been any attempts at silences you by the Five Points Gang in the past couple weeks?" I inquired with a stern stare.

"There was a fire at the hospital, but this was no ordinary fire," Mickey replied.

"What do you mean by that?" I inquired as I peered out the living room window to the sight of the cabdriver cursing upwards at me before he kicked the dead rat off the hood of his taxicab.

"Well, the fire started on the ward where I sleep, but after it was put out and all the other orphans returned to the hospital, all my belongings appeared to be ransacked while all the other belongings of the hospital remained untouched.

"Ah so you're saying that a hitman from the Five Points Gang started a fire in the hospital just to ransack your belongings in hopes to acquire information about me? That sure sound like something a powerful crime organization would do, or should I say a desperate crime organization. Was anybody hurt?" I inquired in a somber tone, as I lit a cigarette and took a smoke.

"Luckily no. Jack I—,"

"You're staying here now. No questions asked. I won't be held accountable for orphans in a hospital being killed. I already have enough blood on my hands," I interjected in a stern tone.

"Are you sure about that Jack? Just a moment ago you wanted to kill me," Mickey said to me.

"All right Mickey. If you want to go back to the hospital be my guest, but get used to more attempts of the Five Points Gang using you to get to me," I said to Mickey with a scoff.

"I don't want to put any of my fellow orphan's lives in danger either Jack, and if that means I have to live here in *SoHo* with you, then so be it," Mickey said to me.

Mickey's personality seemed changed. From what I last recalled the boy always had a glimmer in his eye that no matter how many beatings he would take those eyes of his would continue to glimmer. Now the glimmer in Mickey's eyes was gone and he no longer talked with a sense of wonder and excitement as he used to do when I first met him. Had the world finally broke the poor boy, or perhaps, had Mickey just grown up and let that that boyhood flame of his die as I did when I was his age.

I wasn't thrilled over sharing my rat infested apartment with Mickey, but perhaps the boy could prove himself useful and take some led for me when the moment comes.

"Jack I could go looking for work. I'm sure we will need the income soon," Mickey said to me.

"Just let me worry about that. We're still fine for now. The fair share Samson and I took from the register at the speakeasy will keep us breathing for at least another month. If you really want a job, how about you start by cleaning up this place," I said to Mickey.

"All right," Mickey said to me in a somber tone.

I then entered my bedroom and shut the door with a sigh. Ambulance and police sirens were constantly blaring in *SoHo*. I don't know why I hear them more now than I did when I was Mickey's age. Back then I was ignorant, but fearless, until I got the news that my father died, and then fear hit me out of nowhere like a swift right hook. Is that why I came back here to *SoHo*, to make amends with my past, or perhaps the boy inside me who died long ago? I had to pay someone a visit, someone who I haven't sat down and talked with in many years.

*****

It was 7:46 PM as I walked through the black, wrought iron gates covered in frost. The streetlights then turned on as I walked up to a sight I haven't seen in nearly ten years.

"Hi ma, uhm … I know it's been years, but I need to unburden to someone. I could always tell you anything no matter how bad I screwed up and you would simply smile and drape your arm over me," I spoke aloud in a somber tone as I sat down on the bench in front of my mother's gravestone at the New York City Marble Cemetery.

"Ever since Dezerae was murdered, I kept asking myself what I must do to gain the upper-hand over the kind of men who killed her. Now the man who killed Dezerae is dead by my hands, but more remain. Your granddaughter Hayley sure has opened my eyes. At first I thought she was a curse, a burden on my life at the worst possible time. Now I see her mother in her eyes whenever she stares at me. I almost had a family, sure at first I saw them as nothing more than my employees, but now I see how much blood, sweat, and tears they all shed for me. The cookies were delicious ma, but the lemonade still leaves a sour taste in my mouth, a taste that has now mixed with blood. I'm not ready to talk to him yet, so tell dad I said hi," I spoke aloud in a somber tone, as I tossed my cigarette on the ground before stomping on it and then exited the cemetery. I never cared much for the winter. Christmas time in *SoHo* for me, Dezerae and my mother was always the same. My mother would do her best to corral my sister in for dinner, while I was in some seedy back alley trying to bet all the money in my pocket for a better life. Even at that young age I knew how the world worked, but I just thought I had enough courage to make it bend to my will.

I really shouldn't be leaving Mickey alone in the apartment, I thought to myself as I drove north down Houston Street. Sure the boy has been through hell and back, at the hospital and working for me at the speakeasy, but if the time should ever come, will he cower in the face of a hitman, like he cowered before my pistol, or will that glimmer in Mickey's eyes return and burn with an intensity that no mobster could extinguish? I couldn't help but see a reflection of me whenever I stared at Mickey. Staring at the boys somber eyes that once glimmered, was like reliving my childhood.

*****

It was 8:27 PM as I walked down the hallway of the apartment to the grating sounds of my neighbors shouting and stench of stark soups boiling.

"I'm back, Mickey!" I shouted as I entered the apartment. "Bang! You're dead Jack. Mickey said to me with a grin as he pointed his finger at me in the shape of a gun from the hallway.

"That's not funny," I said to Mickey in a stern tone as I took off my trench coat with a sigh, and then took out a bottle of bourbon and a tumbler from the freezer.

"Samson taught me to always mind the corners first when you enter a room where men could be waiting to kill you," Mickey said to me.

"Wise words from a man who has literally laughed in the face of death more times than even me. I won this bottle from shooting dice with a man looking to double his luck. Do You want a shot?" I inquired with a grin as I poured myself a shot of bourbon.

"Sure, anything to calm my nerves," Mickey replied.

"Do you have any memories of your parents," I inquired, and then took a shot with a grimace.

"There is one memory, but it's ... hazy at best," Mickey replied and then took a shot with a cough and grimace.

"Tell me," I said to Mickey in a somber tone, as I lit cigarette and took a smoke.

"Well ... all I remember was a stern man holding my hand as he pulled me along the cold hallways of the hospital. He didn't even look down at me as he handed me off to the nurses," Mickey said to me in a somber tone.

"How do you know that was your father?" I inquired as I stared out the living room window to the sight of two policemen arresting a protestor as if he was more dangerous than Mr. Luciano.

"The hospital has his name on record. He was my biological father," Mickey replied in a somber tone.

"Maybe you could hire a private eye to find him, wherever he may be," I said to Mickey with a scoff as I shook my head at the sight of the policemen beating the protestor with their clubs before shoving him into the back of their car.

"I don't have the money for that. Besides, I don't want to ever meet him," Mickey said to me in a somber tone as he walked over to the kitchen and grabbed the bottle.

"What are you doing?" I inquired with a grin as I grabbed Mickey's wrist before he could grab the bottle of bourbon on the kitchen counter.

"Having another shot," Mickey replied.

"You've had enough kid," I said to Mickey as I grabbed the bottle of bourbon.

"What about you Jack? Do you have any memories of your father that stand out in your mind?" Mickey inquired.

Before I answered Mickey's questioned I thought about it for a brief moment. The only memory I had of my father was the news of his death in the war. Anything before that was as if he never existed.

"No I don't look back to the past kid," I replied with a scoff. "Because it hurts to remember, doesn't it," Mickey said to me in a somber tone.

"Now you're sounding like Hayley. I'm going to sleep," I said to Mickey with a scoff and then entered the bedroom.

Goddamn wherever I go in this city I'm bound to babysit kids. I thought to myself as I got undressed with a groan and then lay down on my bed which had all the comfort of an army cot. The boy was right, it did hurt to remember, and I wasn't about to delve deeper into my mind just to pull out a sentimental moment between me and my father. It wasn't worth it. I now felt this city bearing down on me more than it ever has been, but I wasn't about to run or cower from all the men who wish me dead. I was born right here in this now rat-infested apartment complex in *SoHo*, but back then I had a family.

"What do you think of your little boy now ma?" I spoke aloud as I raised the half-empty bottle of bourbon up in the air with a scoff before my heavy dizzy head fell into the pillow and all faded to black.

*****

"Jack … Jack get up, it's time to open presents. A familiar voice said to me as I rolled over in bed with a groan.

"Dad said he has a feeling you'll love the gift Santa got you." The voice said to me with a giggle.

"Jack get up, the police are here!" a familiar voice said to me in a distressed tone as I awoke to the site of Mickey shaking me by the shoulder with that familiar look of fear in his eyes.

"Get the hell off me! What do they want?" I inquired with a wide-eyed stare. As I stood up and grabbed my pistol.

"What are you doing?" You're not really thinking of shooting at them are you?' Mickey whispered as we both stared out the bedroom door down the hallway where the voices of at least two policemen caught my ear.

"Those two policemen could be in the pocket of Mr. Luciano," I whispered to Mickey as I pointed out the bedroom door.

"If that was true wouldn't we both be dead by now?" Mickey inquired.

"Hmmm, you may be right, but I have to find out what they want, keep this somewhere safe," I said to Mickey as I handed him my pistol and then tried to compose myself in the cracked mirror above the dresser before exiting the bedroom

"Good morning Mr. Dansby," one officer said to me as I walked up to three policemen who stood in the middle of the living room scoping every inch of the apartment for god knows what.

"Good morning officers, and what do I owe this visit?" I inquired.

"Is it just you and the boy living here?" one policeman inquired as he gestured for another policeman to go to the bedroom and keep an eye on Mickey.

"Yes, unless you also count the rats in the walls," I replied with a scoff.

"We've gotten reports from other tenants in the building that you may be a disturber of the peace," One police officer said to me.

"Disturber of the peace huh, what the hell does that mean?" I inquired.

"Just keep the noise down, or next time our visit here won't be so pleasant. Rats may live here as well, but that doesn't mean you have to behave like them. We are civil people after all," one policeman said to me.

"Are we really … very well officer, me and the boy will keep the noise down," I said to the policeman with a grin.

"Thank you Mr. Dansby. You know a decorative rug would really spruce this place up," one policeman said to me with a snicker, which made the other two policemen snicker as my eyes widened.

The three policemen then exited the apartment, leaving me stunned by that comment of the decorative rugs. This was the same comment one of the mobsters made after he shot Arthur Derringer in the head. Were those three men really mobsters just disguised as policemen, or was I simply losing my mind over the slightest comment? Mickey was right, If those three men were mobsters or policemen who were in Mr. Luciano's pocket then they would've had no trouble filling Mickey and I with led before we had the chance to blink.

"What did he say to you?" I inquired as Mickey walked up to me.

"He just asked me how long I've been living here. He seemed like a genuine police officer, but I can't trust my eyes any more, not after what I've seen over the past year," Mickey replied.

"I feel the walls closing in around us. We need to get the hell out of here now," I said to Mickey in a stern tone as I put on my trench coat.

"Where are we going?" Mickey inquired.

"Somewhere where we can be at peace with our thoughts and away from all those prying ears of our neighbors," I replied. Mickey and I then exited the apartment to the sight of Mrs.

Böhm peeking through the crack of the door which she then quickly shut at the sight of us.

"If that old bat reported us to the police then she has a death wish," I said to Mickey as we entered the elevator.

"We weren't even being loud. Compared to the speakeasy it's dead quiet here," Mickey remarked.

"Exactly kid. That's why we're going somewhere that plays music. Somewhere where the constant sound of rats scurrying in the walls and that old bat Mrs. Böhm arguing with her half- dead husband in that Führer language won't echo in my head," I said to Mickey in a stern tone as we entered the car.

"What happened to your Pontiac?" Mickey inquired as we entered the black Chevrolet previously owned by mobsters.

"I ditched it. I couldn't very well be driving around in a car which the Five Points Gang are familiar with," I replied.

I missed that old Pontiac. That war horse has served me well through many deals that have gone south. It used to belong to my father, until he passed it down to me in his will. I remember Dezerae was angry that I got dad's car, but she soon got over it when she started dating men who would lure her in with many shiny objects. It's weird that I never really associated my trusty Pontiac with my father. Perhaps it's because my Pontiac was always there for me when I was in danger. The same cannot be said about my old man.

"Mercer Street huh, how did this street look when you were a kid?" Mickey inquired as I parked the Chevrolet on Mercer Street.

"I remember there being more families living on this street when my pals and I used to play stick ball," I replied as I stared down Mercer Street hoping to hear or see any signs of happiness.

"All the apartments look abandoned," Mickey remarked.

"This entire city is abandoned kid, I don't know why I came back," I said to Mickey as I shook my head and then lit a cigarette and took a smoke.

"Was that your favorite sport?" Mickey inquired with a grin as we slowly walked down a back alley of Mercer Street in search for any signs of hope.

"What? What are you talking about?" I inquired.

"Baseball, did you play it often with your friend in this street?" Mickey inquired which made me recall an amusing memory from my youth in Mercer Street.

*****

"Two strikes Jackie-boy. I'm betting fifty cents you will strike out," Tommy said to me with a grin as I stood ready to swing at anything he pitched.

"Shut up and pitch!" I shouted.

It was the bottom of the ninth inning and the score was five to four with Tommy's team in the lead, but Ben was on second and ready to bolt as soon as I swung the stick. I couldn't lose to Tommy and his team again or I would never hear the end of it at school tomorrow. Tommy then winded up and pitched the ball straight down the middle which I predicted him to do. The crack of the ball hitting the stick was like music to my ears as Tommy and his two outfielders shouted 'I got it' in a panic as I ran to first while Ben rounded third.

"Oh shit," Tommy shouted as the sound of shattering glass echoing throughout Mercer Street

"Keep going Ben!" I shouted as Ben slowed down his sprinting towards home plate. Ben then made it to home plate as I followed closely behind him.

"That's out of bounds Jack!" Tommy shouted as he pointed to the broken window on the third floor of an apartment building a block away.

"Ah bullshit we clearly stated before the game that windows are out of the park homeruns," I said to Tommy as I pointed to the broken window.

"You little bastards, you will all pay for this!" a man shouted as he stuck his head out the window.

"Don't look at us. Jack was the one who broke your window. Come on let's get out of here!" Tommy said to his pals as they then ran down Mercer Street.

"Don't move you two!" The man shouted.

"Sorry gramps but I think I hear my mother calling me for diner!" I shouted with a grin and then laughed along with Ben. "He's got a gun Jack!" Ben shouted as he pointed to the man who pointed a gun at us.

"Run!" I shouted as Ben and I then ran into the closest back alley.

"You could've gotten us killed," Ben said to me in a heaving tone.

"We won the game didn't we," I said to Ben with a laugh. "We sure did," Ben said to me with a smile and then laughed along with me as he draped his arm over my shoulder.

*****

"Where are you now Ben?" I spoke aloud with a smile as I stared at the broken window which was now boarded up.

"What did you say, Jack?" Mickey inquired.

"Nothing … just pitch me a rock will you, kid," I said to Mickey as I grabbed a pipe from the trash with a grin.

"Oh uhm all right," Mickey said as he searched for a rock. "Give me all you got kid," I said to Mickey with a grin as I tossed my cigarette on the street and then stood ready for Mickey's pitch.

"This one's for you Ben!" I shouted with a grin as I pointed the pipe at a window About a block away.

Mickey then pitched me the rock straight down the middle just like Tommy did twenty-five years ago. I then made connection with the rock as the sharp ting of the pipe echoed throughout Mercer Street.

"Ha ha!" I shouted with a warm smile as the rock shattered the very window I pointed at in tribute to my best pal Ben.

"Let's get out of here!" Mickey said in a distressed tone as he stared up at the broken window with wide eyes.

"Why? That apartment is long abandoned just as you said. I said to Mickey with a scoff and then slowly walked back to the Chevrolet as homeless people stared at me with stern looks on their gray faces, but I couldn't help but snicker at that moment. "Look what I found in the gutter," Mickey said to me in a zealous tone and smile, as he showed me a tan baseball glove.

"Well well and it's not even in terrible condition either," I remarked with a grin.

"Why would someone throw away a perfectly good glove?' Mickey inquired as he put on the glove and punched it twice with a smile.

"Maybe it's someone who abandoned their dreams of playing for the major leagues," I replied with a snicker.

"Well it's mine now," Mickey said with a smile, as we entered the Chevrolet.

It was nice to see the kid so happy over something I wouldn't much less glance at. I suppose it's in Mickey's nature to now appreciate the little things in life rather than take them for granted. When I was his age my mother began her descent into a depression which took its toll on me and Dezerae in many ways we weren't prepared for. My teenage years were spent painting the town of *SoHo* red with Ben while spending the least amount of time I could at home where my mother lived life less and less with each passing day. To me it felt as if my father's death took the light from her bright eyes. Before we knew it, it was now up to Dezerae and me to take care of her, but neither of us wanted that for our lives. I no longer saw my mother as a loving woman who would comfort me whenever I got into a scrap with a gang, but as a miserable woman who couldn't lift herself out of bed to even greet us when we would visit her. She gave up on life when we needed her the most. Now I can't help but think how me and Dezerae's lives would've turned out if my mother hadn't of lost her will to live.

"Jack … Jack," Mickey said to me, as I sat in the Chevrolet staring down at the steering wheel.

"What do you want?" I inquired and then exited the Chevrolet.

"I was just wondering, was that boy Ben your best friend? Mickey inquired, as we entered the apartment complex as it began to snow.

"He was ... but that's another story of my life that goes nowhere," I replied, as Mickey and I entered the elevator.

"Jack, you and Samson are the closest thing I've had to a father—,"

"Stop, don't get sentimental with me now kid. Hayley is better off living with Faye, just as you're better off living far away from me," I said to Mickey in a stern tone as the elevator door screeched open to the sight of something quite alarming.

"I know Jack and the orphan boy are here. It would be in the best interest of Mr. Luciano and your husband over there fighting for breath to assist me," a man wearing a black trench coat and fedora said to Mrs. Böhm in a Russian accent which was even more offensive to my ears than Mrs. Böhm speaking in German.

"Shit," I said with a wide-eyed stare as I put my finger over my mouth and pulled Mickey along with me in an aggressive manner to the right hallway.

"I—I swear to you sir, I don't know of any man named Jack or boy named Mickey who live in this apartment.

"Akh, zhenshchiny takiye ubeditel'nyye lzhetsy dlya obychnogo cheloveka, no ya ne obychnyy chelovek," the man said to Mrs. Böhm as he took out a knife and held it against her wrinkled neck.

"Who is that man? Why does—,"

"Shhh shut up," I interjected as I put my hand over Mickey's mouth.

"Please I don't understand that language," Mrs. Böhm said to the man in a distressed tone as a grin began to form on his face at the sight fear filling Mrs. Böhm's eyes.

"Are you willing to swear on your husband's life? It won't give me the rush I normally feel when I end someone's life seeing as how your husband's current state wouldn't be described by any means as 'full of life' but I will end him nonetheless if I find out you're lying to me grandma," the man said to Mrs. Böhm with a snicker.

"We have to help them, Jack," Mickey said in the same selfless tone as Hayley would if she were by my side at this very moment.

"Goddamn it!" I said to Mickey in a stern tone and then quickly reached out and pulled the fire alarm on the wall beside me.

The alarm then went off as tenants of the apartment complex ran out of their apartment in a frantic manner towards the elevator, as if there was nothing valuable left in their apartment for them to take with them.

The man then was pushed away from Mrs. Böhm by groups of tenants who believed they had to flee the apartment because of a fire.

"Now let's go," I said to Mickey as I ran towards Mrs. Böhm while the man was distracted by all the chaos that was occurring.

I then pushed Mrs. Böhm into her apartment and swiftly shut the door.

"You haven't seen the last of me grandma!" the man shouted.

"I thought you hated me. Why did you protect me and the boy?" I inquired.

"Unlike you I'm not a spiteful person. I don't know what business you have with that man who threatened my husband's life or who he is exactly, but you should keep that boy away from you," Mrs. Böhm said to me as she pointed aggressively at me.

"That man is the Five Points Gang most dangerous hitman named Nikolai 'the wolf' Volkov and he doesn't make threats, he makes promises," I said to Mrs. Böhm and then peered through the peephole of the door at the sight of more tenants fleeing for their lives.

"Don't worry ma'am, there's no fire. Jack just pulled the alarm to distract that man," Mickey said to Mrs. Böhm.

I knew he was still searching for me, hunting me. I could feel it with every day that passed. That son of a bitch Cusack will not stop until he has silenced me, and now Mickey.

After the fire department showed up and all the tenants returned to their apartments like rats returning to the sewers after a heavy rain forced them to the surface Mickey and I continued to stay in Mrs. Böhm's apartment for a little while for good measure just in case Nicolai was still lurking around the complex.

"All right we've waited long enough," I said to Mickey as I stared out the peephole to the sight of nothing but the front door of my apartment.

"Thank you for not telling that hitman where we live," Mickey said to Mrs. Böhm in a timid tone as I opened the door with my hand on my pistol.

"It doesn't matter what she said don't you get it kid. We all heard Nicolai, he will be back, but I will be ready for that son of a bitch," I said to Mickey as I gestured for him to follow me to our apartment.

"You're a kind young man, why on earth are you living with that man?" Mrs. Böhm inquired

"Because I have no place else to go," Mickey replied in a somber tone.

"Let's go," I said to Mickey in a stern tone as I held my pistol up to my face.

"Auf Wiedersehen und viel Glück ihr zwei," Mrs. Böhm pronounced as I scoffed and shut the door of our apartment.

*****

"Like rats waiting to be killed. Why did I ever come back to this place?" I inquired in a stern tone as I paced back and forth in front of Mickey while holding a bottle of bourbon which kept me from losing my head completely and taking out all of my frustration on the boy.

"Do you think that hitman wouldn't of found you if you gone west," Mickey inquired.

"Where did you find that baseball?" I inquired.

"Same place I found the glove. You would be amazed at what people in this city throw away," Mickey replied as he tossed the baseball up in the air and caught it with his gloved hand.

How did Mickey appear so calm? It both intrigued and angered me that the boy's whole demeanor was that of a kid waiting for his dad to play catch with him. Was Mickey not afraid of Nicolai or just simply ignorant over the possibility of either one of us being filled with led by Nicolai when we least expect it?

"Toss that over here," I said to Mickey with a grin as I put down the bottle of bourbon on the kitchen counter.

Mickey then smiled and tossed the baseball to me with no hesitation, but I missed catching the baseball as it nearly hit the bottle of bourbon on the counter.

"Sorry was that too fast for you," Mickey inquired with a snicker as I picked up the baseball and stared intently at it for a moment. I remember this feeling, the feeling of holding a baseball while I played catch with someone, but this someone wasn't Ben, no his voice was more authoritative, but still comforting to me.

"If only we were at the park I would show you my curve that left all the kids on Mercer Street swinging for the fences but hitting nothing but air," I said to Mickey with a snicker as I lightly tossed the baseball back to him.

"Give me your best shot," Mickey said to me with a grin as he stood up from the sofa and squatted in a catcher position on the far end of the living room.

My eyes then widened as I stared intently at Mickey, but it wasn't from the sight of another rat crawling out of the wall, it was from a memory of someone I thought I had no memories of, but I was wrong.

*****

"Come on, give me your best shot Jackie," my dad said to me with a smile as he squatted in the pitcher position.

I loved playing catch with my dad in the courtyard, but I felt as if this time there was something in the way he looked at me that made me feel as if this was our last game of catch. He had a sad look in his eyes the past couple of days whenever he talked to my mom. I never talked to my dad about his feelings, the only time we would really talk was either about sports or my school work. I really wanted to show my dad that I've been practicing my fast ball so I winded up and then threw the ball to him as hard as I could.

"Ooh grounded it," my dad remarked with a snicker as the ball bounced off the ground into his glove.

"Yeah but that's the hardest I can pitch the ball," I said to my dad.

"Power without control is dangerous, Jackie. Try again, but this time ease off on the speed and focus hitting me right here," my dad said as he tossed me the ball and pointed to his glove.

"All right, but I want to pitch the ball like Cy Young. How am I going to impress the others if I throw the ball like Dezerae?" I inquired.

"Cy Young had strength and control. If you go through life trying to impress others then you will be left with nothing but an empty feeling inside of you, son.

Now come on," my dad said to me as he punched his glove with a grin.

I then tried to focus more on hitting my dad's glove rather than throwing the ball as hard as I could, and I did just that.

"There you go Jackie! You see strength without control is pointless in this world," My dad said to me with a smile as he ran over to me and patted me on the shoulder.

"So did I impress you?" I inquired.

"You most certainly did, son," my dad replied with a smile as he kneeled down in front of me.

"All I ever want to do is impress you," I said to my dad.

"Jackie, you're an incredible boy who's as tough and sharp as nails. Not a day goes by where you don't impress me. I love you Jackie remember that. Listen … this may be our last game of catch for awhile," my dad said to me as his face turned serious which made me turn serious as he placed his hands on my shoulders.

"W—Why," I inquired as my eyes widened at the thought of not playing a game of catch with my dad for a long time.

"I'm going away to fight for freedom, but I promise you I will be back," my dad said to me with a warm smile, but I could tell my dad's smile wasn't real, because for the first time in my life I saw tear begin to well up in his eyes.

*****

"I was expecting more heat than that. Come on, give me your best shot," Mickey remarked with a snicker as he caught the ball I pitched right down the middle to him.

"It was a strike, that's all that matters," I said in a somber tone and sigh as I lowered my head and then grabbed the nearly empty bottle of bourbon and some ice from the freezer.

"Jack … what will we do if that hitman comes back?" Mickey inquired in a timid tone as he walked over to the kitchen counter.

"Not if, when, when he returns. Men of Nicolai's cold- blooded caliber do not make threats, they make promises," I replied and then took a sip of bourbon with a slight grimace.

"Well you out-smarted him once, you can do it again," Mickey said to me.

"You don't understand do you, kid. Even if I do manage to outsmart Nicolai or even manage to kill him, then he will just be replaced by another hitman. Mr. Luciano himself wants me silenced for the precious information I have on him, and his unlimited resources will stop at nothing to accomplish that," I said to Mickey in a stern tone.

"What information do you have on him?" Mickey inquired in a timid tone.

"Why do you want to know?" I replied with a scoff.

"I heard him tell Mrs. Böhm that he's looking for me as well. If you tell me the information, t—then maybe—,"

"You'll have the upper hand on him. No, I'm not telling anybody what I know about Mrs. Luciano. The less you know about him, the longer you'll live," I interjected in a stern tone as I walked over to the window, closed the drapes and then turned on the radio.

Will my fate be the same as Dezerae's? Am I to die by the hands of a killer all for the sake of keeping an incredibly wealthy and powerful man in power for however much longer this liquor outlaw will last? Dezerae died in vain, the information she entrusted to Hayley and then Hayley entrusted to me was no threat at all to Mrs. Luciano now.

*****

"So do you think Mr. Luciano knows that his power-hungry nephew plans to assassinate him on his thirty-sixth birthday?" I heard a mobster inquire as I pretended to be asleep.

"Shut your goddamn mouth Lorenzo. Stefano promised us that we would be his right hand men if we helped silence his uncle, so mum's the word until the job is done," the mobster replied in a stern tone.

"First we have to handle 'Wild Card" Dansby here sleeping soundly," one mobster said with a snicker.

"His former associate, you know that bold Irishman who knocked out Paul Kelly has provided us with all the leverage we need in order to silence him," one mobster said with a snicker. "All right enough talk it's getting late and I'm starving," one mobster said as I could hear heavy footsteps getting louder before they stopped right in front of my bed in the kitchen.

"All right grab 'em!" a mobster pronounced in a stern tone.

*****

Not even Mrs. Luciano would expect his own family to silence him, but I doubt he would believe me over his own blood. No matter how ruthless Stefano may be, he's still just a kid who had been taught by a man who knows better than anybody how to capitalize off the vices of everyone in this miserable town.

"Turn that up," I said to Mickey as I pointed to the radio which began its international evening news reports. In international news the Marxist theorist Eduard Bernstein has died at the age of eighty-two years old. Bernstein lived a life full of tumult and radicalization. The socialist who once worked with Karl Marx was banned from his home country of Germany in 1887 for challenging the socialist policies, but then returned in 1901 after the ban was lifted. Before Bernstein's retirement in 1928 he joined the anti-war socialist party known as USPD and was one of only a few members to condemn Germany for the spread of the World War. The radio sounded.

"Good riddance. Another socialist scab ripped off the face of this earth," I said with a scoff, as I wiped down the kitchen counter in the same manner as I used to wipe down the speakeasy bar.

"Are you pro war?" Mickey inquired.

"Of course not, but I know the effects that socialism has had on this country. I'm not a capitalist by any means, but I sure as hell am not a socialist either.

"I don't care what laws are written up by all those men, as long as they get good people off the street," Mickey said to me. "It's not that simple kid. It never is with politicians," I said to Mickey with a sigh as I walked over to the window and peered through the drapes.

"Nurse Sumner at the hospital told me that politicians are fueled by a passion that doesn't go beyond their careers," Mickey said to me.

"Smart broad," I remarked as I stared intently at all the parked cars outside of the apartment complex.

"Are you going to stare out that window all night?" Mickey inquired.

"No, but I'd rather die standing than in bed asleep," I replied.

"I would rather die with music playing rather than these dull news reports," Mickey said to me.

I then turned the dial on the radio to the Jazz station as the soothing sounds of "Lullaby of The Leaves". "What's this music?" Mickey inquired.

"Some Broadway tune," I'm sure Hayley would love it," I replied with a grin.

"I sure hope Hayley and Faye are doing all right," Mickey said to me.

"Last I saw they were smiling in the window while primping each other's hair," I said to Mickey with a grin.

"Faye is a kind woman. She told me that I was a prince among vagrants. At the time I wasn't quite sure what she meant, but now I understand," Mickey said to me with a warms smile.

"Oh really well she never praised me in such high regards. Faye's a woman who will instantly charm you to the point where you're willing to run away with her after only one conversation, but I don't think she's looking for anything permanent when it comes to a man," I said to Mickey with a sigh.

"What makes you think that?" Mickey inquired.

"In case you haven't noticed kid, Faye is a flapper, and a loose one at that. She would frequent the speakeasy nearly every week trying to entice some poor down on his luck bastards for a good time," I said to Mickey as I opened up the fridge and made a sandwich with the few scraps of ham and Swiss I had left. I then sat down on the end table by the window and continued to stare out the window for any signs of Nicolai lurking in the shadows.

"Goddamn it!" I shouted as the lights in the apartment flickered before going out completely.

"I can't see anything," Mickey remarked.

A sudden pounding on the front door of the apartment caused me to instinctively grab my pistol. The pounding then continued as if a wild animal was ramming the door.

"Who's there?" I shouted, as I slowly walked towards the front door, but the pounding continued with its aggressiveness. "Stay by the window," I said to Mickey in a stern tone.

It now sounded like someone was trying to break into the apartment under the cover of the blackout as brief as it may be, but to the mind of a desperate man, a few moments of darkness is all you need to turn the tables in your favor.

"Is that you Nicolai?" I shouted with a grin as I grasped the doorknob.

"Jack don't open the door please just stay here by the window," Mickey said to me in a pleading manner. This pounding at the door, it's not how a hitman would operate. Nicolai would either pick the lock of the door or shoot it open. From what I gathered, the man is methodical when it comes to details. It was still pitch black and I needed any source of light before I started shooting into the dark. So I quickly lit a match and then swiftly opened the front door. The electricity then turned on as I stared intently down the empty hallway of the apartment.

"Ah shit," I spoke aloud as the match burned my fingertips before I tossed it on the ground and stomped on it. I then tucked my pistol between the waistband of my pants and closed the front door.

"There was nobody there," I said to Mickey with a sigh. "That's a relief," Mickey said to me.

"What the hell are you doing?" I inquired in a stern tone as Mickey was stuffing his face with my sandwich, as if I made it for him.

"Oh sorry, I'm just so hungry," Mickey replied with a mouthful of my sandwich.

"Give me that," I said to Mickey in a stern tone, as I grabbed the plate from his hands and stuffed the rest of the sandwich in my mouth.

"Do we have any more food?" Mickey inquired.

"We're all out of food now. Here … go get the necessary staples at Julio's Bodega across the street, and no candy," I said to Mickey in a stern tone as I handed him twenty dollars. "A—Are you sure we should separate. W—What if that hitman is waiting for this chance to use me to get to you?" Mickey inquired in a stammering manner.

"You're a grown man. Start acting like it," I said to Mickey in a stern tone as I handed him my pistol.

"Uhm all right, I won't let you down," Mickey said as he grabbed the pistol, as his skinny arm lowered slightly under the weight of the gun.

"Oh Mickey," I shouted as Mickey opened the front door of the apartment, as the lights flickered again.

"Yes Jack?" Mickey inquired.

"You can treat yourself to some candy if you like," I said to Mickey as I tossed a quarter to him.

"T—Thanks Jack," Mickey said to me in a timid tone and then exited the apartment.

Did I just send Mickey to his death? If Nicolai was using Mickey to get to me, then he would most likely be watching his every move and waiting for this opportunity like the sadistic drooling wolf he is. When I was Mickey's age, *SoHo* was my playground and I feared nobody as I roamed the streets with Ben, but the times have now changed and that fearless nature which burned so brightly in me has now faded. It was only across the street, I'm sure Mickey could make it back to the apartment safely I thought to myself as I lit a cigarette and took a smoke. The longer he lived with me, the more he reminded me of Ben. Mickey had loyalty to me, the kind of loyalty which a stray dog would have if you fed him a scrap of meat. Throughout my life growing up in *SoHo* I've lost that sense of loyalty as the world around me has lost its sense of humanity.

"Come back safe. I can't take another death on my conscience, or at least what's left of it," I spoke aloud in a somber tone, as I stared pensively out the window at the yellow neon sign of Julio's Bodega across the street.

*****

It was 10:56 PM in the apartment as I watched the mold on the ceiling grow while listening to Charles Coughlin on the radio. What's taking him so long, I thought to myself as police sirens sparked my attention. What poor bastard has broken the law this time? Was an old man caught drunk on a street corner, or perhaps the police have shut down another speakeasy, to eliminate the competition for Mr. Luciano. Either way, I trusted the NYPD about as much as I trusted FDR and all of his empty promises. What good am I if I can't be a barkeep in a world that yearns for liquor? I remember Dezerae would always use the word 'catalyst' when describing me. I didn't quite know what she meant by that, if she was insulting, or praising me. Now I see that Dezerae simply saw me as a man who will either fuel good or evil depending on which one benefits him in the moment. Was there any way out this? Was there any way to stop Nicolai and ultimately Mr. Luciano that didn't involve me killing some poor soul?

"Jack I'm back open up," a familiar voice shouted while knocking on the door.

I then stood up from the couch and grabbed my pistol as I stared through the peephole of the door to the sight of Mickey holding two bags of groceries while his eyes darted nervously from side to side.

"Quick, get in. Did you notice anybody following you?" I inquired in a stern tone as I quickly slammed the door shut.

"I was only across the street, but I didn't see any man who looked like that hitman following me," Mickey replied as I rifled through the bags of groceries.

"What the hell is this?" I inquired as I pointed at a glass bottle.

"You mean to tell me you've never seen lemonade before?" Mickey inquired with a snicker, as he opened the bottle and poured himself a glass of lemonade.

"I have, I just never wanted to see it again," I replied, as I lit a cigarette and took a smoke.

"Lemonade reminds me of summer, when I used to have friends at the hospital who I would play baseball with. So why don't you like lemonade?" Mickey inquired with a grin and then took a gulp of lemonade as visions of a pitcher of lemonade shattering on the door step and my mother dropping to her knees flashed in my mind.

"I just don't like it," I replied in a stern tone.

"Come on try some it's refreshing," Mickey said to me as he poured me a glass. I could down half a bottle of bourbon in five minutes with no more than a belch, but the sight of that lemonade in the glass struck a fear in me, as if I was looking down the barrel of a mobster's gun.

"Come on are you afraid? It's just lemonade," Mickey inquired with a snicker, as he moved the glass of lemonade closer to me, which brought forth a memory of me and Ben in *SoHo*.

*****

"Come on, are you afraid?" Ben inquired with a snicker, as he shoved a candy bar down his pants in a stealthy manner when the shopkeeper was busy talking up my mother in a way that always made me feel uncomfortable.

"I'm not afraid," I whispered to Ben with a wide-eyed stare as he smirked back at me.

"Well knows your chance. That old bastard moved in quick on your ma no more than a week after your dad died. Are you going to defend your dad's honor or what?" Ben inquired as he nudged me with his elbow.

"Watch this," I said to Ben as I quickly grabbed a bottle from the cooler without looking and shoved it down my pants. "Ma me and Ben are going to play ball in the courtyard," I said to my mother.

"All right boys. You two be safe and look out for each other," my mother said with a warm smile, as the shopkeep stared at her cleavage like a hungry dog. I then stared daggers at the shopkeep before Ben and I exited the store with our stolen goods.

"Nice, did you get a bottle of beer?" Ben inquired as we giggled in the back-alley beside the general store.

"I don't know let's find out," I replied as I pulled the bottle out of my pants.

"If it's a beer we should share it," Ben said to me with a snicker.

"All right … No," I spoke aloud as my smile quickly faded at the sight of a bottle of lemonade in my hand.

*****

No longer will I associate lemonade with the death of my father. I was a grown man for god sake, but the mere mention of that drink made me feel like a little boy and not in a good way. "I'll show you who's afraid, kid," I said to Mickey with a scoff as I aggressively grabbed the glass of lemonade from his hand and began to gulp it down. The sourness of the lemonade then hit me harder than a shot of fifty proof whiskey. I then felt myself taken back to the kitchen with Dezerae as my mother received the news of my father's death, but I continued to drink the lemonade as that memory bared down hard on me. I then finished drinking the lemonade and threw the glass out of the window.

"That one's for you, pop," I spoke aloud in a somber tone. "Why did you do that for?" Mickey inquired with a wide-

eyed stare.

"Just clearing my head of bad memories," I replied as I began to put away all the groceries.

"Are all the memories you have of *SoHo* bad?" Mickey inquired.

"Not all of them, just the ones I haven't made peace with yet. My times spent with Ben are memories that never fail to bring a smile to my face, whether we're playing stickball or stealing drinks from a shopkeeper on a hot summer day," I replied with a grin.

"What about all the memories of your family?" Mickey inquired as I began to grill up a ham and cheese melt on the pan. "All those memories are scabs I'm not going to pick at," I replied as the sandwich sizzled on the pan.

"Oh can you make me one too, please," Mickey inquired in a zealous tone.

"You just ate my sandwich an hour ago and now you want me to make you another one?" I said to Mickey with a scoff. "Here, you can have half of my Heath Bar," Mickey said to me with a smile as he broke his candy bar in half.

"Ah fine, just to stop you from acting a like a dog begging for table scraps," I said to Mickey with a snicker as I cut the ham and cheese melt in half and slid the plate over to him in the manner I used to when I worked at the speakeasy.

"Thanks Jack. Mickey said to me with a smile and then took a big bite out of the ham and cheese.

"I'm turning in for the night hopefully the sounds of the rats in the wall won't drive me mad and I'll be able to at least catch a couple of winks. Do me a favor and clean up the kitchen a little bit before you doze off," I said to Mickey as I checked all the locks on the door

"Jack we should have a code word just in case we don't end up killing each other," Mickey said to me.

"Oh right so we don't mistake each other for Nicolai. All right, how about this when I call out 'lemonade' you call out …," I said to Mickey as I gestured to him to give me his code word.

"Uhm … oh how about 'summer'," Mickey said to me,"

"Summer, lemonade, lemonade, summer, those words go well together. I hope these code words keep us from killing each other by accident," I said to Mickey.

"I hope so too," Mickey said to me in a somber tone.

"Keep the lights and radio low. The last thing we need is that old bat Mrs. Böhm getting her panties in a knot over us again, hell maybe Nicolai will take her off our hands," I said to Mickey with a snicker.

"That's not funny," Mickey said to me while shaking his head.

"I wasn't trying to be," I said to Mickey as I grabbed my half of the ham and cheese melt and then entered the bedroom. I swear that kid's sympathy will be the death of me.

Sympathy is just the kind of weakness a cold-blooded hitman like Nicolai feeds off of. When the day comes I hope Mickey doesn't bend to the will of that killer by showing him his orphan heart. I for one will show that Cossack the meaning of the word regret. He will regret his attempt to silence me and Mickey. I won't be treated like a rat any longer by men like Mr. Luciano. I once served drinks to good people, but now the world has changed my narrative.

"I may see you soon ma and pop, but until then … lemonade!" I shouted.

"Summer," Mickey shouted back.

"Not tonight, not tonight," I spoke aloud with a grin as I held my pistol up against my chest before my bloodshot eyes closed to the faint sound of rats squeaking in the walls.

*****

A week had passed since Mickey and I developed the code words 'lemonade' and 'summer' in attempts to keep us safe from each other and Nicolai. Christmas had also passed for me and Mickey as if it was just another day. There was no decorations, no pretty lights, no ol Saint Nick, just the cold and snow bearing down on all New Yorkers who didn't have enough warmth in their hearts to keep warm. Mickey had gotten a job for Julio at his bodega across the street even though I told the boy I still had enough cash to pay for another month's rent in this rat hole of an apartment, but he and all of his moxie took the job regardless. Mickey said he needed to work to keep his mind from dwelling on bad thoughts, but all I could think about was what if Nicolai ends up capturing the starry-eyed kid and beats him in the manner which Johnny first did to me? I know the boy is loyal, but a professional hitman like Nicolai knew how to make people give up information no matter who they were. I was the Cossack's main target and I knew he would use Mickey to get to me, but what would I do when that time comes, would I watch the poor boy die right in front of me like I did with Arthur, or would I try to save him at the cost of my own life?

Driving down Mercer Street gave me perspective into how much my life has changed over the past twenty years. *SoHo* now seemed smaller, sadder, and quieter, compared to Greenwich Village. This city was a melting pot of week old fermented stew which not even the rats cared to eat. Everyone tells me 'go west Jack' as if traveling to those sunshine states will cure all my problems. I've lived in this city my entire life and things are worse than ever right now. If I did make the choice to go west and abandon Mickey and Hayley their lives may be better off without me, but would my life be better off without them?

"Watch where you're going jackass!" a disheveled looking man shouted as he scampered in front of my Chevrolet just as the traffic light turned green.

"You watch where you're going pal. The lights green, or are you so drunk that all the colors have blurred together?" I inquired in a stern tone and then honked my horn twice which only enraged the drunken bastard to the point where he began slamming his fist on the hood of the Chevrolet.

"Walk away pal," I said to the drunken man in a stern tone as I pulled out my pistol and pointed it at him.

The drunken man then raised his hands up with a snicker and staggered away across the street. Why was a bullet the ultimate form of motivation in this city? Have we all lost our sense of reason to the point where we would rather take a bullet to the knee over perpetual sobriety? I was already beginning to feel withdrawal from not a drop of liquor in two days, and it made me shake more than I usually do. I was no longer in the bootlegging game, therefore I didn't know of any speakeasies other than the one I used to run that haven't been put out of business by Mr. Luciano. Just keep driving west Jack and don't stop until you no longer smell or hear the wails of homeless people, I thought to myself as I drove west down Spring Street to the sight of a bread line four blocks long. So what is keeping me here in this miserable city I once called home? Mickey has a job working at Julio's Bodega across the street and Hayley is living happily with Faye. Mickey was right, I should go west, and I was a damn fool to think that *SoHo* was my greener pastures. I'm leaving this city and I'm never looking back.

I then pulled into the parking lot of the apartment complex but something caught my eye as I was parking.

"I knew you'd be back?" I shouted as I pulled out my pistol and pointed it at a man dressed in a black trench coat and fedora as he quickly climbed out of the window of my apartment and down the fire escape. It had to be Nicolai. Nobody else would climb that rusty ice-covered fire escape just to reach my apartment. It was 8:03 PM, which meant that Mickey would still be working at the bodega for another hour before his shift ends.

"You're mine Nicolai!" I shouted and then fired twice at Nicolai from behind my Chevrolet, but hit nothing but the fire escape he crouched behind.

Nicolai then fired down at me, and hit the roof of my Chevrolet, as homeless people began to flee from their make- shift tents to avoid being hit by the barrage of led me and Nicolai were firing all over the apartment complex. I then ran up to the bottom of the fire escape as Nicolai dropped down to the ground, but fired at me once more, which sent me diving behind a beat up car in the parking lot.

I then fired at Nicolai as I chased him down the back-alley of the apartment complex. I had the Cossack on the run and I couldn't let him get away, for he now knows where Mickey and I live.

"You're a lucky man Jack, but your luck has run out!" Nicolai shouted with a cackle, but was nowhere to be seen in the back-alley. I knew his game, Nicolai was luring me deeper into the shadows of the back-alley, but I wouldn't take his bait.

I then ran into the apartment and entered the elevator as my heart and mind raced with thoughts of what Nicolai's cold- blooded mind could be capable of. I then entered the apartment with my pistol held up to my face to an ugly sound coming from the radio.

"Lemonade ... lemonade ... lemonade!" I shouted with a wide-eyed stare.

"That son of a bitch changed my radio station," I spoke aloud in a stern tone, as the sound of a god awful Russian singer on the radio assaulted my ears. I couldn't leave this city now, if I did, then Mickey and perhaps Hayley and Faye will surely die by the hands of Nicolai.

*****

It was 9:16 PM as the sound of the front door of the apartment opening jolted me upright from the couch.

"Summer!" Mickey shouted.

"Lemonade!" I shouted back, with my hand firmly grasping my pistol.

"I'm so tired. Julio left me alone at the bodega for four hours," Mickey said to me with a sigh and then popped open a bottle of root beer and sat down on the couch beside me.

"Nicolai was here," I said to Mickey in a stern tone and stare which made him nearly choke on the root beer he was gulping down.

"A—Are you hurt. H—He knows where we live, w—what do we do now Jack?" Mickey inquired in a distressed and tone and wide-eyed stare.

"We stay vigilant. I almost had the son of a bitch but he was playing a cat and mouse game with me in the back alley which I wouldn't fall for," I replied while shaking my head and then lit a cigarette and took a smoke.

"We can't stay here. He will kill us in our sleep no doubt. We have to get out of here, Jack, we have to get out of here now," Mickey said to me in a distressed tone as he paced back and for in front of me with his fearful eyes darting all over the place.

"Mickey, Mickey, damn it get a hold of yourself," I said to Mickey in a stern tone as I grabbed him firmly by his shoulders and then swiftly slapped him in the face.

"I don't want to die Jack, not yet," Mickey said to me in a somber tone as his eyes began to well up with tears.

"Your attitude right now is exactly what Nicolai wants. That sadistic Cossack wants you groveling before he silences you. When you were with Hayley you were a different kid, or should I say man, but now you're pitiful," I remarked with a scoff as I shoved Mickey away from me.

"I miss her and Samson. Why do good people have to part ways with each other in this world? Why can't we all just stay together? We're already divided now more than ever. It's not fair!" Mickey shouted in a distressed tone.

I knew exactly what Mickey was feeling at that moment, but I had to toughen up his heart, I had to prepare him for the ruthlessness that was Nicolai 'the Wolf' Volkov. Mickey is a tough kid, but he often lets his heart do the driving while his mind is locked up in the trunk. I know Hayley and Faye would argue that I'm the same way, but I know if I was to nurture Mickey then he would only end up cowering in the face of death. Only death can go face to face with death, love will only turn you into a soft cowering fool, but Mickey was much more bold and courageous of a kid when he was around Hayley, but she's not her now, so he had to learn how to be a man in the face of death. I taught myself this lesson when I was Mickey's age right around the time when my ma's mind began to go off the deep end, So many people were bearing down on me back then in *SoHo*. The only difference now is I have no family left, but I still have a teenage boy to go to hell and back with.

*****

"Chase and his gang will be here soon. How the hell are we going to get out of this one?" I inquired in a distressed tone, as I stared at Ben and then around the back-alley for any possible exits, but Ben and I were trapped like rats.

"Don't worry Jack, I have a plan, follow my lead," Ben said to me with a grin as Chase and his gang ran towards us into the back-alley.

"You two rats are going to pay this time. Say your prayers, because you won't see a lick of mercy from us," Chase pronounced in a stern tone as he pointed at me and Ben.

I didn't know what Ben had in mind, but I trusted him, he's never let me down before and I know he will get us out of this scrape.

"Well well, it took you long enough. Go ahead and do your worst," Ben said to Chase with a grin.

"Oh I'm going to enjoy this," Chase said with a grin as he cracked his knuckles.

"Not yet boys, wait till you have them surrounded," Ben shouted as he looked up at the blacked-out windows of the back-alley.

"Who the hell are you talking to?" Chase inquired with a bewildered stare.

"Nobody, it's just me and Jack here in this back-alley," Ben replied with a snicker, as I snickered along with him.

"He's bluffing Chase. Knock his lights out," Donnie said to Chase in a stern tone

"So long boys, maybe next time," Ben pronounced and then ran over to the closest door in the back-alley and then pulled the fire alarm on the wall beside it, unlocking all the doors in the back alley which gave me and Ben a way to escape another hopeless situation.

*****

From Ben to Avery and then Samson, I've had my fair share of con-artist companions over the years. I guess you can say those clever bastards have all rubbed off on me, or perhaps I've rubbed off on them as well. If only those three were with me now, then I wouldn't fear the likes of Nicolai one bit. Piece after piece I feel as if all the strengths I once had have been stripped from me. I had one eye on Nicolai, while the other eye still searched for those greener pastures wherever they may be.

*****

It was Wednesday, 2:56 PM. A couple days had passed since my encounter with Nicolai, but my nerves were on high alert especially now that I haven't had a drop of liquor in two weeks.

"Summer!" Mickey shouted.

"Lemonade!" I shouted back as I stared out the living room window to the sight of nothing but snow-covered streets and cars.

"Do you work today?" I inquired.

"No, but I'd much rather be at the bodega with Julio than in this apartment," Mickey replied as he opened the fridge with a sigh.

"And I would much rather be at my speakeasy plying up some buxom dame with a stiff drink, but this is our reality now, kid," I said to Mickey with a scoff.

"We're out of milk," Mickey said to me.

"I'll go get some at the bodega, along with a pack of cigarettes. At least the government hasn't outlawed those," I said to Mickey as I put on my trench coat.

"I'll be back in ten minutes, you know the drill," I said to Mickey in a stern tone as I put on my hat and then quickly checked my pistol.

"Right," Mickey said to me with a nod. I then exited the apartment with my hand firmly grasping my pistol underneath my trench coat, as I stared wide-eyed down the hall way to the sight of a rat scurrying into a hole in the wall.

"I need milk and cigarettes. Please tell me you have at least one of those two in stock," I said to Julio as I entered the bodega.

"I have both in stock, mi amigo," Julio said to me with a smile.

"Fantastic," I remarked as I grabbed two quarts of milk out of the cooler in front of the counter.

"You're Jack huh? I've seen you around *SoHo* with Mickey. He's told me all about you," Julio said to me.

"Hopefully not everything, give me a carton of Lucky Strikes. That should last me for at least another two weeks," I said to Julio, as I pointed to the cigarettes on the shelf behind him.

"Mickey is a hard working young man. I wish I found him years ago when I was setting up shop here in *SoHo*," Julio said to me with a smile as he grabbed a carton of Lucky Strikes and put them in a bag along with the two cartons of milk.

"Why are you telling me for tell it to him," I inquired as I my eyes darted around the bodega for any signs of Nicolai. "Well I thought since you're the boy's father you would feel proud of his work ethic," Julia replied.

"Ha ha I'm not the boy's father. He's an orphan who's living with me for the time being," I said to Julio, as I tossed a couple dollars on the counter.

"Ah very well señor, I wish you both the best of luck," Julio said to me, as I quickly grasped my pistol in response to somebody entering the bodega, but it was just an old woman. I then quickly grabbed the bag of milk and cigarettes and exited Julio's bodega.

*****

Did Mickey tell Julio I was his father? Or did he just come to that naïve conclusion just because we live together? I thought to myself as I lit a cigarette and took a smoke.

It then began to snow just as I crossed the street to the apartment. Every time it snowed *SoHo* felt like a mother whose children had all moved far away from her. So now all *SoHo* did was cry her eyes out, much like my ma did right up to the very end. That's what *SoHo* felt like to me now, nothing but a mother mourning for all the people who wanted nothing to do with her. Goddamn, since when did I become so poetic? Perhaps Hayley has rubbed off on me after all.

"Lemonade!" I shouted as I entered the apartment, but what I saw made me drop the quarts of milk in the same manner as my ma did when she dropped the pitcher of lemonade on that horrible afternoon she was informed of my father's death. So there I stood frozen staring at Nicolai standing beside Mickey who sat tied up to a chair in the living room.

"I never much cared for that drink. Too sour for my taste," Nicolai said to me with a sneer, as Mickey tried to speak despite his mouth being gagged.

"I guess you and I have that in common then," I said to Nicolai in a stern tone as I grasped my pistol.

"Ah ah, drop the gun or I'll splatter this boy's brains all over your precious radio," Nicolai said to me with a grin as he pointed his gun at Mickey's head.

I then dropped my pistol while staring intently at Mickey who shook his head at me. Mickey didn't deserve any of this. His only crime was being loyal to me over the years, a crime which has put many lives in danger. If there was an outcome to where Mickey and I would come out of this alive I failed to see it. Somebody will die this afternoon, but I would do everything to make sure Mickey and I weren't added to Nicolai's long list of silenced people.

"Khoroshiy, now kick the gun over to me," Nicolai said to me as my eyes darted around the apartment for anything I could use to gain the upper-hand over him.

I then kicked my pistol over to Nicolai, as the milk spread underneath my feet.

"Chloroform is how I subdued this boy. It's always been my preferred method before I silence somebody. Don't cry over spilt milk Jack. I know now that you're a man who can easily take a life and sleep soundly the following night. The first time I took a life was when I was only a little younger than this boy, and the life I took was none other than my brother's," Nicolai said to me.

"Either kill me and Mickey now, or shut your fucking mouth, because we would rather die than hear you monologuing," I said to Nicolai in a stern tone.

"Have a seat Jack," Nicolai said to me with a snicker, as he slowly picked up my pistol from off the floor while still pointing his gun at Mickey's head.

"I'd prefer to die standing," I said to Nicolai with a grin. Nicolai then quickly took aim at me and fired. I then collapsed to the floor as Mickey screamed through his gag once more. Nicolai wanted me to hear his origin story, that's why he shot me in the ankle, but I stand by what I said, I would rather die than hear the origin story of a killer.

"That's better. Now where was I … oh yes my younger brother Sergei was the first life I took, it was either him or me, so as any good older brother I spared him a life of being tortured by the bratva that ruled over our defenseless town of Uglich. Throughout our lives we like to think that we are not killers, but civilized creatures. I then found out at a very young age how those naïve moralities can weaken a man's resolve, not strengthen it," Nicolai pronounced in a somber tone, as I as I hissed and groaned on the floor while clutching my right ankle. The blood from my ankle then mixed with the milk as they both spread throughout the floor moving closer to Nicolai and Mickey.

"Ah … I—I see why Mr. Luciano recruits killers like you. He has a real eye for psychopaths," I said with a grimace.

"You interrupt me again Jack and this boy will have a jagged scar across his cheek," Nicolai said to me as he pulled out a switchblade knife and pointed it against Mickey's cheek. I didn't want Mickey to suffer any longer for being in league with me. He had his whole life ahead of him, but Nicolai had us both incapacitated.

"I've learned that fear can accomplish a great deal in life, so much more than love. My younger brother wouldn't kill me at the behest of the bratva, but I knew they would kill us both regardless. So I shot my brother in his sleep, may he forever dream of a world better than the one we live in now. After the bratva had disbanded and left Uglich, I stared out at the Volga River and felt a sense of emptiness that crushed me. My brother and I used to skip stones on that river and I would always skip my stone further than him, he admired me for that," Nicolai said to me in a somber tone.

Think Jack, think goddamn it. You've been in life and death situations like this before and come out on top. I thought to myself, as my ankle continued to bleed all over the floor.

"Mr. Luciano is yet another tyrant which I've cast my stone to. I do his bidding because I am not bound by naïve moralities. I see why he wants you dead. A man like you who I must admit, has much cunning, but still naïve when it comes to sentimentalities, could be a threat to his organization. Now stand up and speak Jack. I will now grant your wish of dying on your feet," Nicolai said to me with a snicker.

I then slowly pulled myself up from the kitchen counter with a groan.

Would these be my final words? If so, then I knew exactly what I was going to say to Nicolai as I stared at Mickey who nodded back at me.

"Fuck you and your mother Russia," I said to Nicolai in a stern tone as I stood on one leg while leaning against the kitchen counter.

"Spokoynoy nochi Jack," Nicolai said to me as he pointed his gun at me.

"No," Mickey shouted as he broke free from the ropes that bound him to the chair and grabbed Nicolai's gun before he could silence me.

I then hopped towards Nicolai as he quickly kneed Mickey to the gut and then back handed him into the radio on the nightstand.

"No!" I shouted with a wide-eyed stare as Nicolai pointed his gun at

Mickey.

I then tackled Nicolai into the living room window before he could shoot Mickey.

I then managed to knock Nicolai's gun out of his hand and out the shattered window, leaving only my pistol left on the floor.

"Mickey, get the gun!" I shouted as I pointed at my pistol on the floor now in a puddle of milk and blood. Nicolai then head-butted me as we fought halfway out the broken living room window.

Mickey then grabbed my pistol as Nicolai's headbutt sent me crashing to the floor. He was a skilled fighter, swift and precise, unlike the previous mobsters I've dealt with, but I knew Mickey and I could overwhelm him. That son of a bitch has never faced the likes of us before.

"Accept your fate, boy" Nicolai said to Mickey with a grimace as he struggled to take my pistol away from him. Mickey then fired off two shots, but neither of them hit Nicolai as he held both of Mickey's arms and then headbutted him down to the floor. I then sprung up from the floor as if there was no led lodged deep into my right ankle. I then clutched Nicolai's arm before he could shoot Mickey who appeared to be knocked unconscious from Nicolai's powerful headbutt. I then managed to gain control over my pistol and tossed it into the kitchen, before Nicolai swiftly kicked my wounded right ankle sending me collapsing to the floor once again.

"I wish I was fighting your former partner Samson right now. I know he would've put up a better fight than you," Nicolai said to me with a snicker as he wiped his bloody nose and then took out his switch blade knife.

"Jack!" Mickey shouted as he threw his baseball glove over to me.

Nicolai then snickered as I put on Mickey's glove as I prepared to block all of Nicolai's knife strikes.

Nicolai then lunged towards me with his knife, but my first block was successful as his knife went through the stitched fingers, while just barely missing my finger. I then twisted my glove and punched Nicolai's hand which made him drop the knife. Nicolai then made a brief glance at my pistol on the kitchen floor before he ran to the gun.

"Jack!" Mickey shouted, as I picked up Nicolai's knife just as he picked up my pistol.

Then before I knew it Mickey stood in between me and Nicolai.

Nicolai then fired at me with the pistol as I thrusted towards him with the knife. I stabbed Nicolai in the chest, but I also felt such a pain at that moment, a heart-wrenching pain of witnessing Mickey taking a bullet for me.

"No!" I shouted with a wide-eyed stare as Mickey fell to the floor in front of me. Nicolai then shot at me before he slowly fell to the ground, but missed as I grabbed my pistol from his hand.

"J—Jack ... d—don't kill him. He will just be replaced by ... another hitman," Mickey said to me as he coughed up blood. "Ah you should listen to boy. He knows how this cruel world works," Nicolai said to me with a snicker as he clutched his chest and coughed up blood.

"His name is Mickey Sullivan," I said to Nicolai in a stern tone as I pointed my pistol at his head and then pulled the trigger.

"J—Jack it hurts, it hurts so bad," Mickey said to me with a grimace, as I held him in my arms.

"Come on kid you've been through worse than this," I said to Mickey with a quivering smile.

"Jack … I've always … I've always thought of you as the f—father I never had," Mickey said to me.

"No, shut up. Don't you dare talk like that. I won't hear it. You're the bravest kid I've ever known. Take my hand and imagine you're holding Hayley's hand. Don't let go of it you hear me … Mickey!" I shouted, as tears began to pour from my eyes. Mickey then grasped my hand tightly, as I lifted him up in my arms.

"Don't let go kid, don't you dare put that weight on me. We'll have you patched up in no time," I said to Mickey in a distressed tone and then quickly hobbled out of the apartment with Mickey in my arms who continued to hold firmly onto my hand.

CHAPTER 18:
BELLEVUE
- HAYLEY -

"Don't let go of my hand Faye," I said to Faye as we sat in the backseat of a taxicab.

"H—Hayley … I'm so weak," Faye said to me in such a faint tone.

"Please hurry," I said to the cabdriver in a distressed tone.

"I'm driving as fast as I can doll. Which hospital was it again?" the cabdriver inquired.

"Bellevue Hospital on First Avenue!" I replied in a distressed tone as the sight of Faye's pale face sent my heart racing.

This was the third time Faye's body had begun to fall apart in the past two weeks, but this time it appeared all her lovely spirit had all but left her. I remember my Aunt Doreen going through a similar health crisis when I was around ten years old. My mother took my Aunt to Bellevue Hospital because no other hospital seemed to show any compassion to her illness. Aunt Doreen died in Bellevue a year later, but Faye would not share her fate. This city needed Faye during such bleak times and I needed Faye in my life all the time.

"We're almost there Faye," I said to Faye as I continued to hold her hand tightly, but Faye's clammy grip on my hand began to loosen.

"All right we're here," the cabdriver pronounced as he parked the taxicab in front of the emergency room entrance of Bellevue Hospital.

I couldn't leave the car and let go of Faye's hand, so I tried to get the attention of the nurses inside.

"Help, please help!" I shouted as I stuck my arm out the taxicab window and waved at the nurses behind the desk of the emergency room entrance.

The nurses then noticed my pleas and scampered out towards the taxicab.

"Please help her," I said to one of the nurses as my eyes welled up with tears at the feel of Faye's grip on my hand going limp and the sight of her warm eyes now closing.

"We need a stretcher!" one of the nurses shouted back at the entrance to the emergency room.

"Don't worry we will treat her right away. Please tell us what happened," the other nurse said to me as two other nurses quickly pushed a stretcher towards the taxicab.

"Excuse me, I believe you owe me my fare, doll," the cabdriver said to me in a stern tone as the two nurses gently lifted Faye from the taxicab and onto the stretcher.

"Here," I said to the cabdriver in a stern tone as I threw all the change I had left in the pocket of my dress at him while still holding on to Faye's limp hand.

The cabdriver then sped off away from Bellevue as I scampered alongside Faye who lay pale and motionless on the stretcher.

"Don't worry. We never turn away the sick at Bellevue. I assure you she will receive our best care," one of the nurses said to me as we entered the emergency room, but the nurse's words failed to comfort me at that moment, for all I wanted was to see Faye's beautiful face smiling back at me.

*****

It was 11:26 PM as I sat beside Faye who lay in bed with tubes attached to needles injected into her pale arms. Every memory I've ever had of a hospital has been a cold memory, especially now since Faye's warmth had all but left her body. It pained me to say that she resembled a corpse in an open casket, but that was the first image that came to my mind as I sat in this white, cold hospital where cries of agony echoed throughout the halls.

"Please I've been waiting here for over an hour. What's happened to my friend?" I inquired in a distressed tone as I clutched the arm of a nurse walking by.

"We've managed to stabilize her condition, but she will need to remain her for the time being, or at least until we can diagnose her ailment," the nurse replied.

"I won't leave her. Can I sleep here?" I inquired with a wide-eyed stare.

"You may stay here, my dear. I'll need you to fill out information on your friend right now if you wouldn't mind," the nurse replied as she handed me a clipboard with a sheet of paper and pencil attached to it.

"Oh, all right. I'll fill out as much information as I can about her. When will she see a doctor again," I inquired.

"Doctor Schuster will be in at five AM," the nurse replied. "M—My Aunt Doreen died at this hospital when I was ten years old. Please I can't lose Faye, she's everything to me," I said to the nurse in a somber tone.

"I assure you our doctors will give her the most advance treatment. When you're done filling out the information leave it on the desk please," the nurse said to me with a warm smile and then walked away.

I didn't know Faye's private health information. We never really talked about such matters during all those lovely nights in her apartment as we drunk wine and confided in each other. Was Faye hiding this ailment of hers from me? The only patient information I could fill out for Faye was her age, name, date of birth, height and weight, as for medication and sexual partner history I would have to leave those questions blank for now. I then walked over to the front desk of the emergency room and handed the nurse Faye's information.

"That's all I could answer," I said to the nurse in a somber tone.

"Thank you. Your friend can fill out the rest when she wakes up," the nurse said to me with a smile.

"She is going to wake up right?" I inquired in a somber tone, as two nurses ran past me while pushing an elderly man on a stretcher who was coughing up blood.

"I know Doctor Schuster will do everything in his power to treat your friend. Please try to get some rest," the nurse replied. "Thank you," I said to the nurse and then walked slowly back to Faye.

"Please ... don't leave me. You taught me what it means to be a woman in this day and age and I need you now more than ever," I said to Faye as tears began to stream from my eyes.

"I then gently rested my head on Faye's chest and the feel of her faint breathing gave me some hope, but not enough hope to last me through the night.

*****

I awoke from Faye's soft chest to a gentle nudging as the chaotic sounds of Bellevue began to echo throughout the halls. "Oh let her sleep," a familiar voice said as I felt a hand stroke my hair.

"We need to take your vitals Ms. Dubois," a voice said in a stern tone.

"Faye, thank god you're awake," I remarked as I wrapped my arms around Faye.

"No thank you mon chéri. You saved my life last night," Faye said to me with a warm smile, the very smile I longed to see for many cold and lonely hours, the smile that felt like medicine for my soul.

"Good morning. I'm Doctor Schuster," the doctor said to me as I sat upright from the chair and rubbed my bleary eyes. "Good morning. So what happened to Faye?" I inquired. "From your initial blood work and vitals all signs indicate that you have hypoplastic anemia, Ms. Dubois," Dr. Schuster replied.

"What must we do now Doctor?" Faye inquired with a sigh as she primped her hair in the small round mirror on the nightstand as if she was about to go out on a date.

"Your diagnosis remains inconclusive considering that your white blood cell count is dangerously low and has not risen despite our efforts. This leads me to believe that your anemia is not simply caused by a deficiency. Your case is rare Ms. Dubois but you're not the first. I can initially diagnose you with contracting an M group virus. Cases of this virus have rampantly spread throughout the United States over the past ten years. I have treated your case before and the one common denominator in all the cases has been ... well, Mr. Carmona can you give us a moment to talk in private," Dr. Schuster said to me with a sigh as he took off his glasses and rubbed his eyes.

"No anything you can say to me you can say in front of Hayley," Faye said to Doctor Schuster.

"Very well Ms. Dubois. How many sexual partners have you had in the past three months?" Dr. Schuster inquired.

"Oh … well … I've slept with around eight men who have all been forgettable," Faye replied with a scoff.

"That sounds about right," I remarked, Faye then playfully slapped me on the shoulder.

"I've read from similar cases in Africa of this virus which has spread from unsterilized needles. However this new M group strain of virus shows all the characteristics of a sexually transmitted disease as well. This virus is known as H.I.V.-1 and I, along with all of my staff here at Bellevue have been studying around the clock for a cure or even treatment to the fatal effects of this virus," Doctor Schuster said to Faye.

"I see … what now doctor? How much life do I have left to live?" Faye inquired in a somber tone.

"Don't talk that way. There must be some treatment that will help you," I said to Faye in a distressed tone.

"Ms. Dubois, Ms. Carmona, I will be honest with you both. This virus has been fatal to all those who have contracted it," Dr. Schuster pronounced with a sigh and then took off his glasses and cleaned the lenses with a handkerchief.

"No, there has to be something we can do," I said to Dr.

Schuster as tears began to well up in my eyes.

"Hayley it's all right. This is my punishment for being such a loose woman. My mother always told me 'Ouvre ton coeur à un homme avant d'ouvrir tes jambs'" Faye said to me.

"What does that mean?" I inquired in a sobbing tone, as Dr. Schuster read through Faye's information on the clipboard. "'Open your heart to a man before you open your legs.' I don't know which man I contracted this virus from, but I assure you I didn't open my heart to him. So this is now my penance and I will accept it with all the grace I have left in my frail body," Faye pronounced with a warm smile, as she placed her hand on my cheek.

"You may stay her at Bellevue as long as you want Ms, Dubois. However, the only treatment we can provide for you is vitamin supplements, a bed, and daily meals. I'm not a doctor who gives people a life expectancy Ms. Dubois, but my advice to you would be to live your life to the fullest," Dr. Schuster said to Faye.

"I always have doctor and this diagnosis won't change anything, merci," Faye said to Dr. Schuster with a warm smile. "Nurse Rose will be with you shortly," Dr. Schuster said to Faye and then stood up from her bedside with a groan and walked down the hall of patients moaning in their beds.

"I won't leave your side," I said to Faye, in a somber tone as I took her clammy hand.

"Hayley … I want you to take my job at the library. I know you're more than capable and possess more passion when it comes to literature than any woman I've ever met. I will vouch for you to ensure the warden at least gives you work at the library," Faye said to me.

"No, I won't replace you. Nobody can do that job better than you. Stop talking like this. You're alive damn it, you're alive!" I said to Faye in a distressed tone as my voice rose to   a level which quickly awoke the patients who were sleeping in their beds beside Faye.

*****

Dear Diary,
January 8th, 10:25 AM,

    It was a new year, but I felt no sense of hope as I watched Faye live out her languishing days in Bellevue. It was unlike Faye to take the word of a man even if he was a doctor, but it seemed as though all of Faye's charm and wit had succumb to the doctors devastating diagnosis. Why did this have to happen to her? Faye is a good person I know this with all my heart. Of course she has made choices in her life which have resulted in people getting hurt, but I see now that love just isn't enough to make it in this day and age. Jack has told me this before, but I just disregarded his callous remarks. If someone as beautiful as Faye can be dealt such a cruel fate, then what hope do I have in this day and age?

    Virginia Rose was the name of the nurse who cared for Faye. She was only five years older than me, but a wonderful nurse nonetheless. She had a sweet southern accent and manner of speaking which was similar to Faye's in that her tone of voice could brighten your day for a brief moment. Whenever Faye's health would turn for the worst and my heart break once again at the sight of her, Virginia would do everything in her power to make Faye smile, which then made me smile behind the tears that continued to pour day after day.

    Bellevue was a haven for forlorn people, but I refuse to think of Faye as one of them. Being a writer, I can imagine a great deal, but I can't imagine a world where Faye loses her lust for life.

"Virginia, when did you first want to be a nurse," I inquired, while Faye slept soundly in bed as Virginia gently took her vitals.

"When I was your age, I watched my father die from polio. Ever since then I made a pledge to him and my mother that I would devote my life to caring for the sick. That's when I began studying to be a nurse. Your friend Ms. Dubois is the sweetest woman I've ever met and it's my privilege to care for her," Virginia replied with a warm smile.

"I don't want to lose her. Whenever I think about it I feel this crushing pressure on my chest, as if the whole world is bearing down on me from the mere thought of Faye's absence. I—I just don't feel like I'm strong enough to make it without Faye," I said to Virginia in a somber tone.

"I can't speak for Ms Dubois, but my mother always told me that when my father died he passed all of his strength and wisdom onto me.

"When my mom died last year, I never thought anyone could ever fill the void she left, until I met Faye, and now ...," "Oh mon chéri please stop crying. I don't want to be responsible for your mascara constantly running down your cheeks," Faye said to me with a smile as she sat upright in bed. "You know I don't wear eye makeup anymore," I said to Faye in a sobbing tone.

"Do you want to touch up my countenance then? I assume I look quite ghastly?" Faye inquired with a smile.

"You look beautiful Ms. Dubois. How are you feeling?" Virginia inquired with a smile.

"I feel like a flickering flame. Some days I have enough strength to face the day, then other days I feel like I'm about to be extinguished," Faye replied.

"Nurse!" an elderly man shouted with a groan from across the hall.

"I'll be right with you Geoffrey," Virginia said to the elderly man.

"Faye is there anything I can get you?" I inquired, as Virginia walked over to the elderly man in pain known as Geoffrey.

"Hayley, I would absolutely adore a cigarette and glass of wine right now. This hospital doesn't allow all the things I took pleasure in after a hard day's work," Faye replied.

"Oh, uhm I can go back to the apartment and get those for you," I said to Faye as I put on my jacket.

"You're an angel, mon chéri. This hospital is not my natural environment," Faye said to me with a sigh.

"I'll be back as soon as I can," I said to Faye as I grabbed my purse.

"Oh one more thing mon chéri. Did the warden at the prison allow you to pick up my shifts at the library?" Faye inquired.

"Oh no, Even though I told him you vouched for me he said he wouldn't allow some random child off the street to work at the library," I replied.

"Ce bâtard!" Faye shouted.

"I'm sorry Faye. I wish I—"

"You have nothing to apologize for mon chéri. That man has always harbored ill will against me ever since I contradicted him while he was detaining a poor woman whose only crime was stealing bread and milk for her child," Faye said to me in a stern tone.

"I'll be back soon. Try to eat and get some more rest," I said to Faye and then walked away, and just as I looked back at Faye before I exited Bellevue I noticed her crying.

*****

January had never felt so cold as it does now. I would do anything to keep Faye in good spirits, but I knew she was putting on a brave front for me. Just like a parent would do anything for their children to prevent them from worrying, but I wasn't a child and I knew the truth of Faye's diagnosis which sent a chill through me more frigid than any January wind could blow as I thought about it. Faye was dying, I knew it, she knew it, but she wouldn't accept it, and neither would I. The way I lost my mother was so sudden, but with Faye I have to witness the light in her grow dimmer and dimmer each day which is too painful for me to bear.

"Take care," the cabdriver said to me in a raspy tone as I paid him the fare and then exited the taxicab with the cigarettes and a bottle of wine in hand.

I then entered Bellevue to the sight of rows upon rows of beds lined up in the hallways. It felt as if this city was at war judging from all the sick patients at Bellevue.

"Please h—help me," a woman said to me as she struggled for each breath while grabbing my hand as I walked past her.

"Help somebody please, she can't breathe," I shouted hoping my pleas would be heard over the moans and wails of all the sick people that overcrowded Bellevue.

"Stay with us Marie," a doctor said to the woman as he and two other nurses tended to her in a hasty manner.

"Will she be all right?" I inquired, as the two nurses lifted the out-of-breath woman known as Marie onto a stretcher and wheeled her away, but the doctor didn't respond back to me as he tended to Marie.

"Nurse where's Faye Dubois?" I inquired as a nurse walked past me.

"We moved her. She's now in room fifteen on the second floor," the nurse replied and then scampered away.

Was it a good or bad sign that Faye was moved to her own room? I thought to myself as I ran up the steps to the second floor of the hospital. It was quieter on the second floor of Bellevue, but the sounds of moans still echoed throughout the cold hallways.

"Faye. Why did they move you here?" I inquired as I entered room 15 to the sight of Faye sitting on a chair with her legs crossed as she stared out the window with a look of sorrow on her pale face.

"I suppose they deemed my case important enough to study me like a lab rat," Faye replied with a scoff.

"I have your wine and cigarettes," I said to Faye as I placed the bottle of wine and cigarettes down on the tray table beside her bed.

"Merci mon chéri. I—I need help standing," Faye said to me.

"Oh here," I said to Faye as I handed her the bottle of wine and cigarettes.

"Where's Nurse Rose?" I inquired as I took off my jacket. "She will be here soon to ... ah yes, check on my condition along with Dr. Schuster," Faye replied with an eye roll and then popped open the bottle of wine and took a swig.

"I also brought your make-up," I said to Faye as I took her makeup out of my purse.

"Not now mon chéri. Now I just want to drink this wine and pretend I'm somewhere that doesn't lead to the grave. Somewhere warm, somewhere with people laughing, like your uncles speakeasy," Faye said to me in a somber tone and then took another swig of wine

"I miss the speakeasy too, and Jack. I hope he's doing all right," I said to Faye as I took off my jacket and sat down on the bed.

"My entire life, I lived so carefree, like a child. Now I see that way of life has its price. Don't make the same mistakes as me Hayley," Faye said to me in a somber tone and then took a swig of wine as her pale, skinny arm shook as it struggled to lift the bottle to her pursed chapped lips.

"Faye … there is no woman I would want to grow up to be more than you. You have always been—,"

"Then you are a fool. There's a good reason why I'm not a mother, just look at me. This is why no man stays with me for more than a couple of weeks. This is why my mother always forbade me to go to America. This is why I will die alone with a cigarette in my mouth and a bottle of wine in my hand," Faye said to me in a distressed tone, as her bloodshot eyes began to well up with tears.

"Now you sound like Jack. Well you know the one thing you and Jack have in common?" I inquired as my face quivered at the sight of Faye's mental and physical anguish.

"We're both stubborn eh?" Faye replied with a scoff and grin and then took a smoke.

"No you both have such big hearts. Hearts that often get you into trouble," I replied to Faye with a warm smile.

"I don't want to be a burden to you mon chéri. You deserve better than me. I am a mess, I was a mess even before I came to America. I thought by leaving *Loire Valley* that all of that, how do you say …. emotional luggage would be left there as well. If you're to learn anything from me mon chéri then please learn this, no matter where you travel in this world the problems in here and in here will always remain with you," Faye said to me as she pointed to her head and chest.

"You mean emotional baggage, and I have more than most women three times my age. So what does that say about me?" I inquired, as I took the bottle of wine from Faye with a grin and took a swig.

"It says you're on course to being more fucked up than me," Faye said to me with a giggle followed by a series of dry coughs which made Faye's entire frail body shudder.

"Ah Ms. Dubois, how are you feeling?" Dr. Schuster inquired as he entered the room with Nurse Rose.

"A little better now that mon chéri brought me my real medicine," Faye replied with a grin and then took a swig of wine.

"You really shouldn't be drinking or smocking Ms. Dubois, it will only inflame your virus," Dr. Schuster said to Faye while shaking his head, as Nurse Rose waved and smiled at me in such a sweet manner.

"First you tell me to live life to the fullest, now you tell me not to drink or smoke. So which is it then doctor?" Faye inquired in a stern tone.

"My staff here at Bellevue are on the verge of a breakthrough when it comes to this M group virus known as H.I.V.-1, but in order for us to do so we need your help Ms. Dubois. Please work with us, if not for yourself, then for future generations who find themselves stricken with this virus.

"Are you asking me to be a martyr doctor?" Faye inquired.

"No, I'm merely asking you to cooperate with us. You're not a lab rat Ms. Dubois, you're a woman who we don't want to give up on. Bellevue Hospital has recently been labeled a mortuary more so than a hospital all because of the rising death rates in all of the patients who are treated here," Dr. Schuster said to Faye as he put on his stethoscope and took her vitals.

"That's not very uplifting news doctor," I said to Dr. Schuster.

"At least he's honest eh," Faye remarked with a scoff, as Nurse Rose sat down on the bed beside me.

"Can you walk Ms. Dubois?" Dr. Schuster inquired. "Let's see ... oh," Faye replied as she slowly stood up from the chair but then quickly collapsed to the floor.

"Faye," I said as I quickly sprung from the bed and reached out to Faye who lay on the floor.

"We're here for you Faye," I said to Faye as I took her skinny, pale arm and draped it over my shoulder, while Nurse Rose did the same with Faye's other arm.

"My body is failing me. How did it ever come to this," Faye inquired in a sobbing tone as we lifted her to her feet.

"We'll take it from here Ms. Carmona," Dr. Schuster said to me as he draped Faye's arm over his shoulder

"Oh all right," I said to Dr. Schuster in a timid tone as I slowly sat down on the bed, while watching the heartbreaking sight of Faye struggling to walk when only a couple of weeks ago we were dancing in her apartment.

*****

A week had passed and Faye's condition seemed to be getting better some days then worse the other days. She was fighting with all the strength she had. I wish I could do more to help Faye, but sadly I'm not smart enough when it comes to medicine. I will never save a life with my writing, but perhaps I can one day write a story which will give people hope, and I know exactly which woman I will base the main character off of. I never had a chance to say goodbye to my mother but somehow that made her death not hurt as much. Now with Faye I feel as though each day may be her last, but the same could be said to any one of us in this dangerous city that sheds no tears for women like me or Faye.

"Good morning Hayley," Nurse Rose said to me as she and Faye entered the room.

"Faye you're walking," I remarked with a smile.

"Qui the medicine Dr. Schuster has me on has given me more energy," Faye said to me with a smile.

"You have also gained some weight back which is another good sign," Nurse Rose said to Faye with a smile.

It was a wonderful sight to see Faye walking again. The color in her cheeks has also returned which warmed my heart. Whatever the medicine was that Dr. Schuster had Faye taking it was working wonders. I personally have never had much faith in doctors. All of those stern men dressed in white have never given me good news so now whenever I find myself around one of them I wrap my arms around my stomach so they don't notice my heavy breathing. This was a habit of mine that brings me some comfort in times of grief, but pales in comparison to someone I love wrapping their arms around me.

"Mon chéri Virginia when was the last time you went for a night out on the town?" Faye inquired with a grin.

"Oh I don't remember, but when you're feeling strong enough perhaps you can show me a night on the town," Virginia replied with a giggle.

"Absolutely, I will show you a night you will never forget," Faye said to Virginia with a grin as she combed her hair while looking in the small round mirror on the cart beside her bed.

"I want to come too," I said in a zealous tone and smile.

"Of course mon chéri, the three of us will paint the town red," Faye pronounced with a laugh.

"Take it easy sugar. You're not ready to party yet, but when Dr. Schuster diagnosis your condition as greatly improved, then perhaps you will be released from Bellevue," Nurse Rose said to Faye with a grin.

"Until then. I feel my strength returning every moment," Faye said to Nurse Rose.

"Dr. Schuster will be back to check on you later around 6 PM. Stay out of trouble in the meantime," Nurse Rose said to Faye with a grin and then exited room 15.

Faye and Nurse Rose seemed to be kindred spirits, but then again, Faye could be a kindred spirit with any class of woman, for her personality was all encompassing, I knew this to be true the first moment I spoke to her at the speakeasy. Those times with Jack, Samson, Faye, Mickey, and Gracie feel like a lifetime ago whenever they cross my mind, but I feel like I've grown so much since then and I owe it to all those people who have looked out for that frightened little girl that was once me. "Mon chéri, I could use a touch up now if you're still willing," Faye said to me with a warm smile.

"Of course, but you already look beautiful so I won't have to apply much makeup," I said to Faye as I took her makeup out of my purse and placed it on the cart beside her bed.

"It pains me to see all the patients in this hospice. When I was your age I was ill with pneumonia and my mother and I had to take a train to the closest hospice. On the train ride all I remember was my mother wrapping me up in a blanket and holding me in her arms as I shivered from a fever. If I didn't have you here with me Hayley I might start shivering again," Faye said to me as her face quivered, while I applied a light foundation of powder to her nose, cheeks, and forehead.

"No matter how cold this winter becomes, I'll always feel warm when I'm with you," I said to Faye with a smile.

"I love you Hayley. No matter what fate befalls me, remember that," Faye said to me with a smile as her eyes began to well up with tears.

"Please don't talk like that," I said to Faye in a somber tone as I stopped applying blush to her cheeks.

"I know, I know, mon chéri. If I was you I wouldn't want to hear those words either, but life is so fleeting, and you must know that I love you with all my heart," Faye said to me with a warm smile.

"I love you too Faye … now stay still while I apply your mascara. I've only done this a few times with my mother so I hope I don't make you look like a clown," I said to Faye as I giggled to mask the tears which were welling up in my eyes as well.

"I trust you mon chéri. I cannot even say that about my relatives in Paris, they envisioned a different life for me, one that involved being an obedient housewife of a wealthy pompous ass I'm sure," Faye said to me.

"Is that really such a bad life?" I inquired, as I stared intently into Faye's eyes while delicately applying the mascara to her eyelids.

"Well you know I'm not obedient for any man, no matter how deep his pockets may be," Faye said to me with a scoff.

"I know and that's what I admire most about you. Someday women will run the world, I believe this," I said to Faye with a smile.

"What do you mean someday? Women already run the world mon chéri. You just have to look behind that façade that all men put in front of us to see the truth. Without a loving woman those so called 'powerful men' would fall apart." Faye said to me with a grin as I grabbed the plum colored lipstick off the cart.

"Is this shade all right," I inquired, as I showed Faye the plum lipstick.

"Ah you know me too well mon chéri," Faye said to me as she pouted her lips.

"I never looked good in this shade. I don't have full lips like you," I said to Faye.

"Men don't care about the size of your lips only what comes out of them and what goes into them," Faye said to me with a giggle.

It brought me such joy to see that Faye's sense of humor had returned. I never want to see Faye in the manner she was in when I rushed her to Bellevue in the taxicab two weeks ago. "All right finished, I hope you like the job I did," I said to Faye in a timid tone.

"Oh now I look like I'm ready to turn down a man at a bar," Faye said to me with a smile as she stared into the small mirror on the cart beside the bed.

"You will be soon, I know it," I said to Faye with a smile.

"It's getting late mon chéri. You don't have to sleep here again," Faye said to me.

"The landlord Mr. Giovanni told me that the rent is due by the end of the month the last time I visited the apartment to feed Sable. I then told him about your condition but he showed no compassion and just slammed the door in my face," I said to Faye in a somber tone.

"What do you expect? Landlords in this city are strictly business and nothing else. They all would sooner see you die in a gutter than not pay them," Faye said to me in a somber tone as she began to cough and clutch her stomach with a grimace.

"Here drink some water," I said to Faye as I poured her a glass of water.

"Merci, Hayley please go check on Sable. He's not an alley cat. You know he's used to us pampering him so he won't survive out in the cold," Faye said to me in a raspy tone, and then took a swig of water.

"What about you?" I inquired with a wide-eyed stare.

"Shhh I'll be all right mon chéri. Dr. Schuster will be checking on me soon," Faye replied with a dismissive wave.

It was always in Faye's nature to put the well being of others before her own. Even now She can't help but worry about Sable. I must admit I too was worried if Sable was eating enough during our absence from the apartment. If I left Faye now to go check on Sable at the apartment and something terrible then happened to her while I was away I would never forgive myself.

"We're stronger together Faye," I said to Faye in a somber tone.

"Qui I concur mon chéri, but there will come a time when our hearts will have to learn how to beat on their own," Faye said to me.

"I—I hope that day never comes," I said to Faye in a somber tone.

"You know … you would make a wonderful mother mon chéri," Faye remarked with a warm smile.

"So would you. I will be back as soon as I feed Sable," I said to Faye as I leaned over and hugged her. I then grabbed my purse and exited room 15.

*****

"Sable … Sable where are you?" I inquired as I entered the apartment and began searching for Sable.

If only Bellevue allowed pets then Sable would be able to comfort Faye as he's always done before she came down with this terrible condition. I then began to worry as I searched Faye's cold and empty bedroom and still didn't find Sable. Did he find someone else to feed him in the apartment complex, perhaps a nurturing neighbor who could use his company during this cold and unforgiving winter? I then turned on the lights and sat down on the sofa in the living room. I noticed most of Faye's once beautiful plants were now dying. So I then quickly filled up the ornate silver watering can and began to carefully water each withered plant. It appears that all withers in the absence of Faye's love. It pained me to see Faye's plants dying just as she was struggling at Bellevue. After I finished watering all of Faye's plants I then poured myself a small glass of wine and sat down on the sofa with a sigh. I felt more at home in Faye's apartment than anywhere else in the world, even without Faye sitting beside me on the sofa I could still smell the smoky and sweet fragrance that is her which made me remember the time my aunt Doreen died at Bellevue and how difficult it was for me to accept she was gone.

*****

"Sweetheart … you're aunt Doreen, has died," my mom said to me as she placed her hands on my shoulders.

"W—Where is she now?" I asked my mom as two nurses exited the room where aunt Doreen was resting as they pushed a bed with a white sheet draped over a still body down the hall of the hospital.

"Your grandmother always used to tell me that we go to greener pastures when we die. Doreen suffered for months, but now she is at peace," my mom replied as tears began to stream from her eyes.

"H—How can she be gone? I can still smell her perfume," I asked my mom.

"Me too … I just wish I was there for her when she needed me the most," my mom said to me as she began to cry, but I still didn't understand why my mom was crying because I still felt aunt Doreen from all the goodness she left behind.

*****

I then began to feel the effects of the wine as I laid my head back against the armrest of the sofa. Drinking wine will always be associated with happy times in my mind as my heavy eyelids began to close in the haze of that warm and comforting feeling which I can only describe as Faye.

*****

I awoke to the weight of something resting on my chest as I slowly sat upright from the sofa while rubbing my bleary eyes. "Sable! Where have you been curious boy?" I inquired in a zealous tone and smile as I picked up Sable and held him close to my chest.

"You must be hungry. Let's see if Faye has any cans of tuna left for you. Oh my god Faye. I fell asleep, I need to get back to Bellevue," I said to Sable as I quickly opened a can of tuna and plopped it on to a dish along with a saucer of milk.

Sable then meowed and pawed at my ankle as I quickly put on my jacket and shoes. He was lonely and knew I was leaving him once again. I wish I could bring him along with me to Bellevue, but pets are not allowed in the hospital.

"I'm sorry Sable, but I have to get back to your mother, she's sick and needs me to be there for her. Now you be good all right curious boy," I said to Sable as I kneeled down and kissed him on his forehead and then exited the apartment as Sable's somber meows echoed throughout the hallways.

*****

"Taxi … taxi," I shouted as I crossed the street to a light snowfall which seemed almost pleasant as the cool snowflakes lightly graced my flushed cheeks.

"Long time no see, redhead," a voice shouted down at me. I then looked up at the second floor of the women's prison to the sight of a familiar face grinning down at me.

"Oh hello Sidney, I can't talk right now I have to get back to Faye," I shouted.

"What's your rush honey? I'm sure Faye will understand you catching up with her favorite inmate," Sidney shouted. "Faye is sick she's being treated at Bellevue as we speak!"

I shouted.

"Ah knowing Faye I'll bet she's trying her best not to let it get the best of her," Sidney said to me and then lit a cigarette and took a smoke.

"She is … it's just not fair that someone as loving as Faye could come down with this illness," I said to Sidney.

"Hayley, Faye is not a perfect woman. She has committed crimes which even you don't know about. Yes her heart always does the talking, but life often catches up to women like her," Sidney said to me.

A taxicab then stopped in front of me as Sidney continued to smoke in such a relaxed and carefree manner. It seemed as if Sidney wasn't even concerned for Faye's condition which upset me, but I didn't have time to defend Faye as much as I was tempted to. I had to get back to Faye's bedside at Bellevue. I cannot let her shiver alone as she feared she would in my absence.

"Faye isn't perfect none of us are, but she is good!" I shouted up at Sidney in a stern tone and then entered the taxicab. "Where to?" the cabdriver inquired with a raspy voice and cough.

"To Bellevue Hospital please," I replied.

*****

It was 9:47 AM as the taxicab parked in front of the main entrance of Bellevue Hospital.

"Thank you," I said to the cabdriver as I paid him his fair and then exited the taxicab.

'Please be all right Faye' I thought to myself as I entered Bellevue Hospital to the sight of many pale bodies lying on stretchers which lined the halls of the hospital. The great Mr. Edgar Allan Poe would most definitely write a beautiful poem about Bellevue, but sorrow and grief evoked no such sense of eloquence within me like it did with Mr. Poe. The very sight of all these sickly people lying motionless and reaching out to the nearest person dressed in white was a sight that made me hopeless. Do I have to use sorrow and grief as an inspiration for my writing? Is that what it truly means to be a brilliant writer? "Faye …" I said in a distressed tone as I entered room 15 to the sight of a large man with a cast on his leg.

"Virginia, where's Faye?" I inquired in a distressed tone as I grabbed Nurse Rose by her arm as she scampered by me in a hasty manner.

"Oh Hayley, we had to move Faye to the ICU. Follow me," Nurse Rose replied.

My heart then raced at the very possibility of losing Faye, about not ever seeing her warm smile or hearing her sweet voice ever again. I then wrapped my arms tightly around my stomach to keep my heart from beating out of my chest as I followed Nurse Rose to the ICU where Faye was being treated. "What happened to her?" I inquired in a distressed tone. "Faye came down with pneumonia last night, as we rushed her to the ICU all she kept telling me was to inform you were she was. She even made a joke about her paleness makes her eye shadow pop even more. Dr. Schuster has managed to stabilize her fever but this virus is so resilient that the Doctor's formulated treatment for Faye has now become ineffective," Nurse Rose replied.

"I—I thought she was feeling better. W—What happens next?" I inquired as my eyes began to well up with tears.

"Be with her Hayley. That's all you can do now," Nurse Rose replied in a somber tone as she opened the door to room 34 of the ICU.

"Faye … F—Faye," I spoke allowed in a somber tone as I entered room 34 to the very sight which I never wanted to see again, the sight of Faye as pale as a ghost lying motionless in bed, as two needles attached to tubes stuck into her arms.

"Faye … I'm so sorry I wasn't there for you last night," I said to Faye as tears began to stream from my eyes. I then dropped to my knees and gently grabbed Faye's cold hand, but she didn't grab my hand back as she did in the taxicab when I rushed her to Bellevue.

"Mon chéri, I—I had a dream about you. Faye said to me in a faint tone.

"I fell asleep at the apartment I'm so sorry I should—,"

"Shhh you felt at home in the apartment. That's all I ever wanted for you, to feel at home," Faye said to me with a cough. "You are my home," I said to Faye in a somber tone as she began to squeeze my hand with all the strength she had in her body.

Faye had taken another turn for the worst, but despite her condition she continued to smile whenever I was at her bedside. I felt so helpless once again. If only I could do more to help Faye, but this virus that plagues her is even beyond Dr. Schuster's control. Perhaps I could take Faye's mind off of all the pain she's going through. Anything is worth a try.

"How is Sable?" Faye inquired with a cough.

"I just fed him. He wanted to come with me, but I know Bellevue wouldn't allow pets," I replied in a somber tone as I handed Faye a glass of water.

"You could bring him here and see how they react. I'm sure the staff won't mind accommodating a dying woman," Faye said to me with a snicker and then took a sip of water.

"We're all dying Faye, but the moment you start accepting death is the moment you stop living," I said to Faye.

"No … the moment you accept death is the moment you've made peace with your life and all the decisions you've made," Faye said to me as she shook her head and sat upright with a faint moan.

"Where do you think he is now?" I inquired. "Who mon chéri?" Faye inquired.

"Julien, I know you still think about him," I replied.

"I don't know. I hope he's living a happy life wherever he is," Faye said to me.

"Do you ever dream of the Valley, of your life when you were my age living with your mother?" I inquired in a somber tone as I walked over to the window and stared down at the gray streets blanketed by white snow. The blanket of snow seemed to cover up all the filth on the streets and add a sense of beauty which this city never had in the summer, but I suppose that's all nothing more than what I did when I put makeup on Faye to cover up any signs of sickliness on her face.

"Qui … but my last dream was about you Hayley; don't you want to hear it?" Faye inquired with a grin.

"Yes please?" I replied with a smile as I quickly sat back down at Faye's bedside.

"I saw you … looking in the mirror at me, and you were my age and so beautiful," Faye said to me with a smile. "H—How did you know it was me?" I inquired.

"I felt it in my heart. Besides, your hair is the most beautiful hair I've ever seen and in my dream you were slowly combing it in the mirror with such a somber look on your face," Faye replied.

"Maybe my hair was all tangled. I often look sad when I'm combing knots out of my tangled hair," I said to Faye with a smile.

"No I don't believe it had anything to do with your hair mon chéri. I saw a longing in your eyes when you were combing your hair, but then I reached out to you and you smiled at me. You then grabbed my hand and then began to write and that's when I woke up," Faye said to me with a smile, as the door of the ICU room opened.

"How are you feeling Ms. Dubois?" Dr. Schuster inquired as he entered the room and sat down on the other side of Faye with a sigh.

"I feel like, how do you say … a faint flame flickering in the dark," Faye replied.

"You must keep burning Ms. Dubois. I know we are close to a breakthrough of how this virus works and potentially how it can be treated. Your white blood cell level is dangerously low right now and we must keep those I.V's in your arms if we're to ever keep you from slipping into a coma. I'm going to strengthen the dosages of the medication your on right now to see if it can effectively combat the virus and raise your white blood cell count," Dr. Schuster said to Faye in a somber tone.

"You do what you feel is right for me doctor, as I will do the same," Faye said to Dr. Schuster.

"Nurse Rose will be just outside the door. If you need anything feel free to call for her," Dr. Schuster said and then exited the room.

"I cannot stay her Hayley. If I'm to die soon, then I want to go surrounded by all the things I love," Faye said to me. "Could you at least try the stronger dosage of medication?"

I inquired.

"What good would it do for me now mon chéri? You saw that look in the doctor's eyes, that's a look of hopelessness. He may be a kind and gentle man, but Dr. Schuster has seen so much death on a daily basis, and because of that I feel he is now lost in the dark," Faye said to me with a cough.

"What do you mean?" I inquired.

"The doctor is now experimenting on me with no sense of direction. He says he's on the verge of a breakthrough, but I know that's just wishful thinking. Hayley ... will you help me leave this place or will you leave me here to continue these hopeless experiments?" Faye inquired in a somber tone. "Please don't make me chose for you," I said to Faye in a somber tone as my mind raced with the possible outcomes that each choice would have on Faye and me.

"You brought me here mon chéri, and thus saved my life that night over two weeks ago, I trust you to make this choice for me now," Faye said to me.

"I—I need some time to think about this," I said to Faye in a somber tone as my face quivered at the very thought of such a life-determining decision.

"Hayley," Faye said to me in a faint tone as she reached out her hand as I stood up from her bedside and scampered out of the ICU room with my hands on my face.

I never had the chance to say goodbye to my mother before she was killed by Johnny, nor did I ever think I had any authority over her life, but with Faye everything was different. Whatever decision Faye made I would wholeheartedly support so why was she leaving her life in my hands? I thought to myself as I sat on a chair in the waiting room of the ICU beside an elderly man with a blanket covering him as he shivered.

"Why are hospitals always so cold?" the elderly man inquired as he turned to me.

"It would be nice if they raised the heat. I'm sure it would make a lot of patients more comfortable," I replied.

"No no, I mean emotionally. This hospital is supposedly renowned for not turning away anybody, yet these doctors and nurses still treat us with such a sense of emotional detachment. I see no warmth in their eyes or the tone of their voices as they care for my wife," the elderly man said to me.

"Why is your wife here?" I inquired in a timid tone.

"My wife Marge has influenza. She's been battling it for the past couple of weeks now, but I fear her strength is waning," the elderly man replied in a somber tone.

"I'm Hayley," I said to the elderly man.

"I'm Leonard. Pleased to meet you," the elderly man said to me in a somber tone and cough.

"D—Do you feel she can still pull through, your wife?" I inquired in a timid tone, as I tightly wrapped my arms around my waist.

"I ... I don't know. All I know is that I want to be there when she passes, whenever that may be. I've loved her from the first moment I laid eyes on her when we first met in high school. She's my best friend," Leonard replied in a somber tone.

"I hope she pulls through," I said to Leonard in a somber tone and then stood up from the chair and walked away.

Faye wants to die surrounded by everything she loves. Most people aren't that lucky in death. I could either side with the doctors and keep Faye here at Bellevue where her life would slowly fade away like a beautiful sunset you wish could last forever, but your wishful thinking is naïve for we all know the nightfall is inevitable. Or I could side with Faye and take her back to her apartment where she might die faster, but she will be happier nonetheless. I wanted to see Faye smile, but I wanted her to live as long as possible as well. Dr. Schuster says he's on the verge of a breakthrough when it comes to treating the virus Faye has, but is that just wishful thinking?

*****

It was 12:47 PM as I entered the apartment to the sight of Sable sleeping on the kitchen counter in such a peaceful manner.

"I'm back Sable," I said to Sable as he slowly sat upright from the kitchen counter with a meow.

"Let's see if we have some food left for you," I said to Sable as I searched through the kitchen cupboards.

"It looks like all we have is milk," I said to Sable in a somber tone, as I poured milk into a saucer. Sable then quickly began to lap up the milk as I stared intently at him.

"Do you want to see Faye before the end curious boy? I'm sure you would put a smile on her face," I said to Sable as I slowly petted him.

Faye, Sable, and I needed each other, we were stronger together, but we could survive alone. Faye trusted me to make the right decision regarding whether or not she stays at Bellevue or returns to the apartment. What would my mother want in this situation? I thought to myself as I turned on the radio and then stared out the living room window to the sight of Sidney shouting down at a passerby on the street.

"Hello Sidney!" I shouted, as I opened the window and waved.

"Hayley. Do you have any more candy for me?" Sidney inquired.

"No I'm sorry," I replied.

"Is Faye still in hospice?" Sidney inquired. "Yes, but … she may not be," I replied.

"I don't know what that means honey, but I want to apologize for how I reacted a couple days ago. Faye has repeatedly broken the law in order to make me feel comfortable in this prison. I was just too blind to see that she was my only friend," Sidney shouted.

"I'm your friend Sidney. No matter what happens to you!"
I shouted.

"Now I have two friends. When I get out of here I promise you we will paint the town red together," Sidney said to me.

"Faye said the same thing to me and the nurse who is treating her at

Bellevue," I shouted.

"Great minds think alike honey. I would rather live one day as a free woman than two more years behind these bars," Sidney shouted.

"I have to take a shower, but I'll be back in a couple of hours with some candy!" I shouted.

"Wonderful. I'm not going anywhere!" Sidney shouted as we both waved goodbye.

Was Sidney right? Was a life lived to its fullest only for a day worth more than years of suffering behind bars? I didn't want to be the one to make this choice for Faye, but she trusted me more than anybody to make it. I just want Faye to be happy if that's still possible considering her dismal condition.

"Uhm ... two Three Musketeers bars please," I said to the shopkeep in a timid tone as he took a quick glance at me.

"Anything else?" the shopkeep inquired.

"That will be all," I replied, and then handed the shopkeep the money for the candy and then exited the bodega.

"FDR is a communist spy!" I man shouted as he held a sign saying NEW DEAL SAME SUFFERING. I then continued to walk past the angry man, without so much as a glance his way. I didn't know that much about Franklin Delano Roosevelt, but I hope he can bring about change that will help all the people who are suffering in this city. To put all of your hope on one man may seem foolish to a lot of people, but hope is hope in my opinion. I don't believe in false hope. Hope is hope and anything that can keep you breathing in this world is worth holding onto.

"Sidney ... Sidney are you there?" I shouted up at the barred window of the prison.

"Redhead ... you know I had a dream about you yesterday," Sidney shouted with a grin as she stuck her pale arms out the bars of the window.

"Oh you too? I don't know why anybody would every dream about me, but it's quite flattering," I shouted with a grin. "So I'm not the first to dream about you huh honey?"

Sidney inquired as she lit a cigarette and took a smoke.

"Yes Faye just recently had a dream about me, but let's talk about your dream first over candy," I replied as I took out the two candy bars and waved them in the air with a smile.

"Oh my favorite," Sidney shouted with a smile and then slowly lowered the little cup attached to a string down to me.

I then gently placed one of the candy bars in the cup as Sidney waited in the manner of a little girl waiting for her mother to serve her a treat after a hard day at school, but I suppose that's what prison does to people, it makes them appreciate the simple pleasures of life much more than they used to.

"So in my dream I had last night you and I were—"

"What are you two doing?" a man inquired in a stern tone as he walked up to me.

"You're interrupting a conversation I was having with my friend you old bastard!" Sidney shouted at the man and then took a bite of the candy bar.

"Ah go rot behind those bars you filthy broad!" the man shouted. Sidney then spit down at the elderly man, but missed hitting him as walked away with a scoff.

"Sorry honey. As I was saying, in my dream you were helping me break out of this prison, but just as I was about to take my first steps as a free woman my legs broke and I collapsed to the floor. You then tried to drag me, but I then urged you to leave me behind and live your young life to its fullest," Sidney shouted.

"I wonder what that means!" I shouted and then took a small bite of the candy bar, as a couple of stray cats walked up to me.

"It means I will never be free from these bars, but you have brought me happiness, honey!" Sidney shouted.

I could imagine it all now, my life with Sidney as a free woman. In many ways it would probably be similar to my life with Faye, but the cold reality of this world seemed to not allow the dreams of beautiful woman to come true.

"So who else has dreamt about you, honey?" Sidney inquired.

"Oh yesterday Faye told me she had a dream of me where she was staring at me in a mirror as I was brushing my hair. I then took Faye's hand with a smile and began to write in my diary," I replied.

"You're a special girl, honey. Take it from me. I see all sorts of people come and go down this street, but you have a glow about you," Sidney remarked.

"W-What do you mean I have a glow?" I inquired.

"Do I have to spell it out for you honey? I mean you bring light to people's lives. I can't make it much clearer than that," Sidney replied with a snicker and then took a smoke.

What Sidney said about me was so beautiful, yet I was still confused by its sentiments. How could a girl like me with such a dark life bring light to anybodies life? Perhaps through my writing I could continue to bring light to the darkness which many people are going through right now, perhaps my choice could bring light to Faye's darkness, but I was still afraid to make that choice for her.

"Thank you Sidney. I have to be getting back to Bellevue now!" I shouted.

"Thank you honey, and send Faye all of my love!" Sidney shouted and then blew me a smoky kiss with a smile.

*****

It was 6:24 PM as I exited the taxicab and entered Bellevue to the sight of four nurses caring for a man lying on a stretcher who was threshing in pain. After a day of searching my soul and talking with Sidney, I now know the choice I was going to make for Faye.

"Faye … I'm back," I said in a timid tone as I entered the ICU room to the sight of Faye sitting in a chair, staring longingly out the window.

"Mon chéri … how is Sable?" Faye inquired in a faint tone and sigh.

"I've been feeding him every time I go to the apartment," I replied as I took off my jacket and sat on the bed.

"All I hear are sounds of agony in this hospital, poor people screaming out in pain," Faye said to me in a somber tone. "How are you feeling today?" I inquired.

"Worse than yesterday, but better than tomorrow I presume," Faye replied.

"Did Dr. Schuster give you any good news?" I inquired.

"He told me that he's still on the verge of a breakthrough when it comes to treating this virus that's ravaging my body, but I know that's all connerie. I've grown quite skilled at telling when men are trying to paint a Renoir over a Dali," Faye said to me with a grin.

"What do you mean?" I inquired.

"I mean no matter how many words of hope the doctor uses to appease me, it will not change the way the way I feel inside. My body is a Dali painting now, filled with surreal expressions of darkness, which the Doctor is trying to paint over with the beautiful and innocent expressions that are a Renoir painting," Faye said to me with a scoff.

"I've never even been to an art museum, so I'll take your word for it," I said to Faye with a giggle.

"You would love it mon chéri. There are so many places in this world that you deserve to lay your beautiful eyes upon and bask in the beauty," Faye said to me with a warm smile before a series of wrenching coughs sent her hunched over in her chair. "Can I get you anything?" I inquired with a wide-eyed stare as Faye continued to cough in such an aggressive manner.

Ever since I've known Faye she has smoked at least three times a day and yet I have never heard her so much as utter a cough, but ever since Faye came down with this virus, wrenching coughs have become so frequent.

"I wish I had Sable in my arms right now. He would always calm me down whenever I would fret over some bâtarde who treated me like less than a woman," Faye replied.

"Faye … let's go home," I said to Faye with a warm smile, as I took both of her cold shaking hands.

*****

It had been two weeks since Faye and I left Bellevue and returned to the warmth and comfort of her apartment. Dr. Schuster gave her medication to take in hopes that it would stabilize her condition for those critical times where all hope seemed lost. Faye's mood immediately brightened at the sight of Sable when she entered the apartment. That's the Faye I want to see. I feel deep down in my heart that I made the right decision in helping Faye get released from Bellevue, but I learned a great lesson about the human spirit in that hospital, a lesson that you could only learn when someone you love is depending on you.

"What time is your shift?" Faye inquired, as she made coffee quite effortlessly in the French press which was always difficult for me to manage, but Faye always had that special touch.

"10 AM I'm just grateful that Marla quit or else they wouldn't have been so desperate to hire me," I replied.

"I've worked with Marla for almost a year and I could tell she was on her way out of that library, but you mon chéri, I have no doubt you will do much better work than she ever did. You are a writer after all," Faye said to me with a warm smile, as she poured me a cup of coffee. My soul inspiration for working at the prison library across the street were Faye used to work was to pay the monthly rent. Sure staying at Bellevue was free, but at the cost of Faye's happiness, and that's all I cared about. Faye has smiled more this morning than she had in her entire two week stay at Bellevue. Neither Faye nor I know how long she has left, but all we can do now is live our lives to the fullest. "All right I'll be home at 8 PM," I said to Faye with a mouthful of croissant.

"I will cook something special for you mon chéri." Faye said to me with a warm smile.

"There's no need for that. You need to rest," I said to Faye as I put on my jacket.

"Cooking is healing for me mon chéri, and I will continue to cook to the grave," Faye said to me.

"All right, If you insist. Goodbye," I said to Faye.

"Have a wonderful day," Faye said to me with a smile and wave, but more wrenching coughs suddenly took over her body as I exited the apartment to the sight of Faye grasping onto the kitchen counter with a painful grimace.

I always felt so worried about leaving Faye to go to work at the library, but she assured me that I must stay focused and not let my thoughts dwell on her condition. Work at the prison library was not what I expected it to be. The majority of my days working were spent cleaning and barely anything to do with books. Some days I would deliver books to women inmates like I did with Faye except I wouldn't get to visit the inmates. I would just deliver the requested literature to the prison guard and they would then inspect it. After their inspection they would then give the book to the women inmates. I wanted to get to know the inmates, but I had no authority when it came to that option. The only inmate who I could talk to now was still Sidney. When I told her that I'm now working at the library she was thrilled to say the least. Faye had made such an impression on the women inmates in this prison, apart from helping them break out of the prison, but also to their hearts. Faye treated them all as they deserve to be treated, like humans.

*****

"Hayley ... Hayley!"

"Yes Mrs. Bronson," I replied, as I scampered over to Mrs. Bronson at the front desk of the library.

"Collate the historical fiction section and then sweep the entrance and you may retire for the night," Mrs. Bronson said to me in a stern tone as she pointed to each section of the library with her pen.

"Yes Mrs. Bronson," I said to Mrs. Bronson in a timid tone and bow. Mrs. Margaret Bronson was the head librarian for the prison, the occupation that Faye used to have before she went on an indefinite medical leave due to the virus she's been living with for the past month now. She was a prude and stern old lady who I have yet to see smile, the total opposite of how Faye managed the library, but there can only be one Faye in this world and right now she needs me more than ever to help pay the rent.

As I was collating the historical fiction section of the library I noticed a woman reading a book with such a zealous expression on her face. Judging by her clothes she appeared to be an inmate who didn't look much older than me. Why was she here? I thought to myself as I took glances at her while working on making historical fiction look as presentable as possible to readers.

"Time's up," a guard shouted as he walked over to the young inmate.

"Oh please just five more minutes. I have to know what Heathcliff does next," the young inmate pleaded to the guard.

"Tomorrow, reading hours have ended for you," the guard said in a stern tone as he aggressively pulled the young inmate up by her arm and escorted her out of the library.

"Mrs. Bronson, why is she here?" I inquired as I pointed to the young inmate as she was escorted past the main desk.

"Oh that's Molly Cradleton. She ... murdered her father," Mrs. Bronson replied with a sigh as she took a glance at the young inmate known as Molly.

"Why? I mean how was she found guilty of murder?" I inquired with a wide-eyed stare as Mrs. Bronson rifled through a file cabinet.

"Hayley her case is over. Now do you want to be a detective, or do you want to work at this library?" Mrs. Bronson inquired in a stern tone.

"Both," I replied in a muttering tone.

"Excuse me?" Mrs. Bronson inquired.

"Nothing, I'll get back to work now," I said to Mrs. Bronson in a timid tone, as I noticed a guard whisper into her ear.

Why do adults always seem to be secretive around me? Except for Faye, every adult felt the need to keep me out of the conversation which sparked my curiosity even more on the matter of Molly Cradleton and the murder of her father. I would be lying if I said I never thought about killing Fernando, but Johnny killed him before the very thought could consume me. I hope to see Molly Cradleton in the library tomorrow so I can get to the bottom of why she is an inmate at this prison, but until then, I must follow Mrs. Bronson's orders.

"Are you finished yet, Hayley?" Mrs. Bronson inquired in a stern tone.

"Almost," I replied as I gazed at the cover of Personal Recollections of Joan of Arc by Mark Twain before placing it back on the shelf. I remember Ms. Joan of Arc. The word heroine has always been associated with her, a title which any woman in this day and age could only dream of achieving.

I then scampered over to the entrance of the library and grabbed the broom.

"Remind me Ms. Carmona. Where was your past work?" Mrs. Bronson inquired as I quickly swept the entrance of the library.

"I—um worked at a …,"

"At a what? Spit it out," Mrs. Bronson inquired in a stern tone.

I couldn't tell Mrs. Bronson I worked for my uncle at a speakeasy, or I might be fired, so I decided to tell a half truth. "I worked for my uncle at a diner," I replied in a timid tone, as I could feel Mrs. Bronson's stern stare through her thick bifocals pierce through me as I continued to sweep in a nervous manner.

"That explains your abundance of energy, but your work ethic lacks diligence," Mrs. Bronson remarked.

"My uncle would always tell me that I'm a lousy waitress, among other things," I said to Mrs. Bronson in a somber tone. "Well we are short staffed here so just do the work I assign to you and we won't have any trouble. Oh and as for the inmates in the library, you are strictly prohibited to interact with them, understood?" Mrs. Bronson inquired in a stern tone.

"Yes Mrs. Bronson," I replied with a bow.

"Good, a young girl like you should pay no mind to hopeless courses like Molly Cradleton. Don't forget to punch out when you're finished sweeping," Mrs. Bronson said to me with a sigh.

*****

"Faye I'm home," I said as I entered the apartment to the sight of Faye sprawled out on the sofa with her chiffon, plum robe half open as she held a half empty bottle of wine in her hand.

"Oh bienvenue à la maison mon chéri. How was your day?" Faye inquired in a weary tone as she slowly sat upright on the sofa.

"The usual. Mrs. Bronson was stern as ever with me. She said I was prohibited to interact with any inmate at the library," I replied with a sigh as I took off my jacket.

"Nonsense, nowhere in the librarian handbook does it say you are prohibited to speak with the women of the prison," Faye said to me.

"There was this one inmate, she didn't look much older than me," I said to Faye in a somber tone.

"*C'est la vie* mon chéri. Did you think only women my age are imprisoned?" Faye inquired as she stumbled towards the kitchen.

"Let me help you," I said to Faye as I put her arm over my shoulder.

"Merci, you must eat now mon chéri. You need the energy more than I do," Faye said to me with a cough, as her body shuddered like a windowpane during a storm.

"We both need to eat. How did you get the wine?" I inquired as Faye served me a plate of roasted chicken and potatoes au gratin.

"I have my ways of procuring that which is precious to me," Faye replied with a grin, as she placed my plate upon the kitchen table.

"As long as those ways don't involve sleeping with any more men," I said to Faye with a sigh as I sat down at the kitchen table.

"Oh what do you take me for mon chéri? I would never do such a thing just for a bottle of cheap wine like this. I merely charmed that sweet old widower Mr. Prichard down the hall. His wife was born in Cannes so we had plenty to talk about," Faye replied, as I took a hearty bite of the roasted chicken.

"At least you spent time with him. I'm sure he's lonely," I said to Faye, as Sable rubbed against my leg beneath the table. "He is, he told me that he would provide the wine if I provide my lovely wit," Faye said to me with a mouthful of chicken.

"That's good that you're keeping him company, even if your soul motivation is wine," I said to Faye with a grin and then took a bite of the potatoes au gratin.

"My soul motivation is to live mon chéri. It always has been. Just as that Doctor at Bellevue said, I am living life to the fullest," Faye said to me.

"You're my inspiration Faye. I—I would've never grown so much over the past year if It hadn't been for you, thank you," I said to Faye as I reached over the kitchen table and placed my hand on Faye's hand with a warm smile.

"That is flattering mon chéri, but you are who you are from the moment you're born into this world, and who you are is most magnifique," Faye said to me with a warm smile as she placed her hand on my cheek.

"Everything is delicious Faye. Don't worry I'll clean the dishes, you go rest," I said to Faye as I gestured for her to lie down on the sofa in the living room. Faye then turned on the victrola and put on a record before sitting down on the sofa with a sigh.

I could tell Faye to not drink wine and not to smoke as well, because Dr. Schuster said that drinking and smoking will only inflame the virus, but I might as well tell Faye not to live either. I chose to help Faye be released from Bellevue, now I will have to live with all of those consequences. Faye's condition was always up and down throughout the week. She continued to take the medication which Dr. Schuster prescribed for her, but her frailty seemed to always persist. Faye was fighting every day against such a devastating virus which no doctors can seem to cure or even treat. Some nights I often think about coming home after work at the library to see Faye lying on the sofa, but I fear one of those nights were Faye doesn't wake up. It makes my heart race whenever those thoughts become more of a reality. Right now as I clean the dishes while watching Faye hold Sable so dearly against her chest I can't help but smile, because all I want to see is Faye happy.

"Do you remember what you said to Virginia?" I inquired as I stared out the window of the living room to the sight of a light snowfall.

Qui of course mon chéri. I told her the three of us would go out and paint this town red when I recover from this virus," Faye replied with a smile.

"Do you feel recovered?" I inquired.

"My spirit does, but my body is struggling every day," Faye replied in a somber tone and then took a sip of wine before she slowly stood up from the sofa.

"What are you doing?" I inquired, as Faye took my hand and then placed her arm on my shoulder with a smile. "Dancing mon chéri. When was the last time we danced in front of this window?" Faye inquired with a smile.

"I don't remember. Are you sure you feel strong enough to dance?" I inquired as Faye and I slowly danced to the French ballad which was playing on the victrola.

"My mother always used to tell me 'Si tu es assez fort pour danser alors tu es assez fort pour vivre' If you're strong enough to dance then you're strong enough to live," Faye said to me with a smile.

Even in Faye's weak condition she didn't miss a step of the waltz. I on the other hand stumbled like such an ungraceful child as I tried to match her steps.

"Ah ah look into my eyes," Faye said to me with a giggle. "Sorry it's just hard to remember the steps," I said to Faye as I stared into her bleary yet beautiful eyes.

"Then let us forget about such formalities," Faye said to me with a giggle as she began to dance in more of a swing style. Swing was more of my style of dancing. It was free and passionate with no strict steps involved.

"Faye are you all right?" I inquired with a wide-eyed stare as Faye legs buckled and she used me to support her.

"I'm fine mon chéri now let's keep dancing," Faye replied as she tried to keep up with the fast-paced swing dance, but I wouldn't dance with her for I knew Faye was in no condition to continue.

"You need to rest now," I said to Faye as she pulled on my arms.

"No I can dance all night mon chéri," Faye said to me with a smile.

"Faye please you have to—,"

"I said no. I'm strong enough to dance. You hear that mother," Faye said in a distressed tone as her face quivered while looking up.

"Faye then collapsed to the floor and began to cry as Sable and I gathered around her.

*****

"Get some rest," I said to Faye as I exited the apartment to the sight of her staring somberly out the living room window while smoking.

Faye had fallen once again last night and I couldn't help but cry along with her every heartbreaking time it happened. Should I have been strong for Faye during those moments and remained stoic in the manner of any typical man? No, I wouldn't react that way, I love Faye and when she hurts I hurt as well. I just wish I could do more for her, but even the staff at Bellevue didn't have the end all be all cure or treatment to the virus that plagues her.

Every day Faye was beating the odds, just as she always did in life. Now my life working at the library has me wanting to do some sleuthing in the manner of this new female detective I've read about named Nancy Drew. I know the case is already closed regarding Molly Cradleton which explains the sentence of her serving time at the women's prison, but I must know more about her, and last I recall she wanted to continue reading Wuthering Heights, so I should expect to see her in the library tonight.

"Hayley, dust the top shelves of the non-fiction section," Mrs. Bronson said to me in a stern tone.

"Yes Mrs. Bronson," I said to Mrs. Bronson as I grabbed the feather duster and ladder as two guards were escorting a prisoner into the library.

"Hayley!" the inmate shouted as the guards ordered her to quiet down.

"Sidney!" I shouted back with a smile and wave forgetting for a moment that I was in a library.

It was Sidney. This was the first time I've seen her face-to- face, well almost. Mrs. Bronson said I was prohibited to interact with any of the women inmates at the prison, but Faye says that's not true. If I wanted visiting hours with Sidney or Molly I would have to arrange that with the warden and I doubt they would grant a girl like me those privileges like they did with Faye. So now I will seize this opportunity to talk to Sidney, but now instead of shouting to each other like we're used to, we must whisper in secrecy.

I noticed the guards remained within an arm's reach of Sidney, as if she was really that dangerous, but I was used to seeing the kind, sweeter side of Sidney, not the side which got her sentenced to serving time at this prison.

"Pssst Redhead," Sidney said, as I dusted the top shelves. "I never thought I'd see you face-to-face," I said to Sidney without turning around to face her, in fear that the guards would most definitely reprimand me.

"Do you work here now?" Sidney inquired. "Yes I started last week," I replied.

"Do you have any candy for me?" Sidney inquired. "Sorry I don't have any," I replied.

"How is Faye doing?" Sidney inquired.

"I said quiet down. I won't warn you again," the guard said to Sidney in a stern tone.

"I'm just reading aloud. It helps me immerse myself into the story," Sidney said to the guard. "She's taking it day by day," I replied.

"Give her all my love, honey," Sidney said to me.

"What are you reading?" I inquired, as I half turned my head towards Sidney while the guards were looking away from her.

"A book Faye recommended to me the first day we met called Pride and Prejudice. At first I thought it was just some snobby tale of privileged Brits, but then I really began to relate to the main broad of the story.

"I adore Jane Austen. That's a wonderful story," I remarked with a warm smile, and then quickly turned around and continued dusting the top shelves, as the guards turned back around to face Sidney.

"Times up," one guard proclaimed in a stern tone.

"Come on let's go," the other guard said to Sidney in a stern tone as he nudged her with his club.

"Just give me a minute you screw," Sidney said to the guard in a stern tone.

"All right grab her!" one guard said in a stern tone, as the other guard helped him grab Sidney by one of her arms as they both then aggressively escorted her out of the library.

"Bye redhead. It was great to see you," Sidney said to me with a smile, as I smiled back at her before she was escorted out of the library.

"Ms. Carmona!" Mrs. Bronson shouted.

"Yes Mrs. Bronson?" I inquired and then quickly climbed down the ladder and scampered over to Mrs. Bronson at the desk.

Did Mrs. Bronson know that Sidney and I are friends? I thought to myself as I stood at the front desk of the library as Mrs. Bronson rifled through papers.

"It has come to my attention by the warden that you have a prior history with Ms. Seville," Mrs. Bronson said to me in a stern tone.

"Uhm … I don't know who that is Mrs. Bronson," I said to Mrs. Bronson in a timid tone, as she stared sternly at me. "That inmate who was just dragged out of my library is Sidney Seville. She is sentenced to two more years at this prison for racketeering," Mrs. Bronson said to me in a stern tone.

"Oh well I can assure you I have no history with that woman. She's only ever cursed down at me from her jail cell as I was walking down the street to get back home," I said to Mrs. Bronson in a stammering tone.

"Yes sadly we cannot prevent her from doing that, but if you don't want to end up like her then it would be in your best interest not to indulge her taunts. Do you understand Ms. Carmona?" Mrs. Bronson inquired in a stern tone.

I hated it when adults would call me 'Ms. Carmona'. It was because I felt a connection to Fernando every time I heard his last name, a name I never want to be associated with, a name of a monster.

"Yes Mrs. Bronson," I said to Mrs. Bronson with a slight bow.

The evening hour seemed to lull at the library. I thought that being surrounded by literature would be a dream come true for me, but I seemed to only be excited whenever an inmate would enter the library.

*****

It was 8:03 PM at the library.

I was slowly skimming through the collective works of Mark Twain in the fiction section when in walked Molly Cradleton looking disheveled and wide-eyed, as one guard escorted her by her bruised, pale arm.

How would I ask her without the guard noticing and furthermore without upsetting her? I thought to myself as I took a brief glance at Molly before turning back around and dusting the shelves of the fictional section. Molly Cradleton murdered her father yet she only has one guard to watch her, while Sidney serves time at this prison for racketeering and she had two guards watch her. I didn't understand why this was so. Was it because Sidney was older and had a history of not cooperating with the guards? Judging by Molly's frail and timid appearance one guard would be enough, but you should never judge a book by its cover.

She had pretty brown eyes. I thought to myself as I took another brief glance at Molly as Mrs. Bronson handed her a book with a stern look on her face. Mrs. Bronson projected no such passion and whimsy for literature in the manner that Faye does. It's almost as if she detests working here at the library.

"I love Emily Bronte," I said to Molly with a warm smile as I pointed at the book in her hand.

"Yes her writing is lovely," Molly said to me in a timid tone.

"What did you say" the guard inquired in a stern tone as I quickly turned around facing towards a dusty copy of The Great Gatsby and away from Molly to arouse no suspicion from the guard.

"Nothing," Molly replied.

"Keep quiet or the warden says you will lose your reading privileges for the rest of the month," the guard said to Molly in a stern tone as he nudged molly with his club.

How could a girl like her ever be capable of murdering her father? I thought to myself as I noticed the guard stroll over to the front desk of the library. Now was my chance. I had to know why, and there was no more time to talk about literature with Molly.

"Pssst Pssst. I could lose my job for this, but I must know … why did you do it?" I whispered as I walked up to Molly with a wide-eyed stare as my eyes darted from her to the guard and Mrs. Bronson at the front desk.

"Do what?" Molly replied. "Kill your father" I whispered.

"Leave me alone," Molly replied as her face quivered with grief, the kind of grief which could make any girl no matter how frail and sweet she may look capable of taking another life, the kind of grief that always remains and continues to eat away at you.

"Please tell me, what did he do to you?" I inquired in a distressed tone as I sat down at the table across from Molly.

"Mind your own business," Molly said to me in a stern tone and wide-eyed stare.

"You're right. I'm sorry," I said to Molly.

Molly then muttered something under her breath but I couldn't make out what she said exactly, as I quickly turned back around to face her.

"What did you say?" I inquired with a wide-eyed stare.

"I said he killed her! He killed my sister!" Molly shouted as she stood up from the table and slammed her book down which the guard noticed as he ran over to us.

"All right Molly your reading time is up," the guard said to Molly in a stern tone, as he grabbed her arm.

"I regret nothing. He was a drunken monster. He threw her down the stairs and my mother did nothing but watch in horror!" Molly shouted in a distressed tone. The guard then wrapped his arms around Molly's narrow waist as she flailed and screamed while tears poured from her still pretty brown eyes.

"Oh my god I'm so—"

"So I then stabbed him the next night after he blacked-out. He was a monster, I enjoyed killing him. He took her from me, my sister, she was my best friend and he took her from me!" Molly interjected in an aggressive tone as the guard continued to pull her down the hall as her cries of grief and malice echoed throughout the quiet library.

"Ms. Carmona I warned you not to interact with any of the women inmates. You're now a liability to this prison just like that French woman before you was. Leave this library, your employment here is terminated," Mrs. Bronson said to me in a stern tone as I stood frozen from Molly's heartbreaking outburst.

*****

"Mon chéri what happened?" Faye inquired in a weary tone as I entered the apartment at 10:14 PM.

"I'm so sorry Faye," I replied in a tearful tone, as Faye and Sable greeted me.

"Sorry for what mon chéri?" Faye inquired with a somber look in her bloodshot eyes, as she wrapped her arm around me. "I was fired from the library," I replied as Faye and I sat down on the sofa. Sable then gentle jumped into my lap with a sympathetic meow, as I continued to cry.

"Ah this is a travesty. Why on earth would they ever fire such a brilliant literary mind like yours from the library?" Faye inquired as she stroked my hair in the same manner my mother used to do when I was upset.

"I talked to an inmate. I had to know why she killed her father. It's all my fault my damn curiosity got the best of me again and now how are we going to pay rent? How are we going to buy groceries or—,"

"Shhh I would've done the same thing if I was you. Don't you ever apologize for—," Faye interjected as a series of coughs cut her voice short.

"Faye, are you all right?" I inquired in a tearful tone, as Sable meowed once again at the sight of Faye's wrenching coughs.

"Don't … you ever apologize for being curious. More women need to be as curious as you in this day and age," Faye said to me in a raspy tone as she held my head against her shuddering chest.

"What will we do now for money?" I inquired as my warm tears poured onto Faye's chest.

"Look at me mon chéri. The three of us have each other, and that's all we need," Faye said to me as she stared intently into my eyes.

CHAPTER 19:
DUST BOWL DREAMS
- JACK -

I couldn't save him. They couldn't save him. That so called 'crack staff' at Bellevue in their fancy white coats took care of the bullet lodged in my ankle but gave up as soon as Mickey flat lined. He sure saved me though. Mickey Sullivan was a good-hearted man, who showed me loyalty to the very end, which men like me don't even deserve. I remember Dezerae saying to me 'You never know your true worth in life until you see yourself through someone else's eyes'. What I saw through Mickey's eyes just before he died was pain, a lifetime of pain and suffering experienced by a sixteen year old boy, and he didn't hesitate to experience more pain just to protect me from that son of a bitch Cossack who now lies with led between his eyes. I was the only one other than the priest who attended Mickey's funeral. It was almost as if the world chose not to see him. Mickey was a far better boy than I was at his age and he was on his way to grow into a far better man than I am now. Mickey's only mistake in life was getting involved with a lowlife like me. The Five Points Gang has now taken my family and friends. Perhaps its best that I—

"Pal, are you daydreaming or shooting dice?" the desperate man I was gambling with in some filthy back-alley in Queens inquired in a stern tone as his nervous eyes darted in every direction.

"Seven, pay up pal," I said to the man with a grin. "Goddamn it!" the man remarked as he reached into his pocket and handed me five dollars.

"Pleasure doing business with you," I said to the unknown man with a grin, for all I needed to know about him was that he had money.

"You're a lucky man, but you know what they say about luck huh," the unknown man said to me.

"Let me guess, it's an illusion," I said to the unknown man with a scoff.

"No it's a vice, just like a drug. You see men like us become addicted to the effects of luck and we start to have well delusions of grandeur," the unknown man said to me.

"I'm no man like you, I'm five dollars richer," I shouted as the unknown man walked away down the back-alley.

I was nothing but a gambling drifter now living out of his car. This is what the world has in store for me. When I rushed Mickey to Bellevue three weeks ago I never returned to the apartment in *SoHo*. I knew the Five Points Gang would be checking up on their top hitman, so I could no longer remain there. How many more of them have to die before I can feel safe in this city? I thought to myself as I walked down a street in Long Island bordering the *East River*. 'The smugglers dream for bootleggers' that's what Long Island is called. I wonder if that title is still true to this day. I saw no signs of bootleggers getting ready for a potential jackpot of a deal which would arrive by boat, but then again, bootleggers are like rats, they only scurry about when there is something to feed off of AKA liquor deals. I was once one of them. I was once a proud owner of one of the most flourishing speakeasies in New York City. I was once an uncle, a brother, a son, and even a friend, but now I'm no better than those rats I see peeking out of every sewer.

"Please spare change for a beggar sir," a boy Mickey's age inquired in a somber tone as he walked up to me and held out his hands.

"Don't spend it all in one place, kid," I said to the poor boy with a grin as I reached into my pocket and handed him the five dollars I won from the unknown man in the back alley and then ruffled his hair as my face quivered by how much he resembled Mickey.

"Oh boy thank you sir," the poor boy said to me with a wide-eyed stare as if I handed him a hundred dollar bill.

There was no way I could make things right, I was too deep in the belly of the beast known as the Five Points Gang. I wonder how Hayley and Faye are doing. With their brains and beauty they're probably in the lap of luxury right now.

"It's arriving in Montauk, you moron. Now get ready," a man said to another man as they both stared nervously in the manner of a typical bootlegger.

I was almost positive those two men were bootleggers, and I had to tail them. I then ran to my car as fast as I could and parked on the side of the street across from where the two men were loading up before their big deal. I must admit it warmed my heart to see bootleggers getting deals to this day. I thought Mr. Luciano had scattered them all to the winds except for my former associate Avery Briggs of course, his kind cannot be driven out so easily. I've done business in Montauk once before with Samson. Back in those days that bold Irishman and I were the top dogs, but then the Italians came along and changed everything. Whatever deal these two rookie bootleggers were trying to seal in Montauk, I would be the one to take it from them on this frigid, February afternoon.

So I tailed the two rookie bootleggers as they drove east to Montauk. It would be a long trip and quite frankly I didn't know if I had enough gas to make it all the way to Montauk. Was this potential liquor deal worth it? I thought to myself as I'm sure the two rookie bootleggers were thinking to themselves as I tailed them closely for the next 25 miles down the Sunrise Highway.

An hour had past as I continued to tail the two rookie bootleggers east down the Sunrise Highway. I didn't know what my plan would be to take their liquor deal, or if there even is a liquor deal arriving by boat in Montauk, but a strange calm began to take over me.

*****

It was a clear and beautiful day. The waves crashed gently as I walked along the shore while swinging a stick in my hands as I pretended to be a swashbuckling pirate.

"Dezerae, I found something!" I shouted as I found something washed up on the shore of Montauk Point

"What is it?" Dezerae inquired as mom braided her hair. "It's just a bottle … oh wait there's something inside it," I replied with a wide-eyed stare.

I always loved going to Montauk Point with my mom and sister. It felt like another world separate from *SoHo*. Everything was calm and peaceful there and I didn't feel an overwhelming sense of fear or stress take over me like I did every time I stepped out of our apartment. If only I could feel this way all the time, but I know my mother couldn't afford to live here in these fancy beach houses, we're barely getting by as it is in *SoHo* after dad died in the war.

"Oh my, looks like you found a message in a bottle," my mother remarked with a smile, as I walked up to her and Dezerae while holding the bottle.

"How do I get the message out?" I inquired as I pulled out the cork and first tried to grab the paper with my fingers and then a stick, but the message was at the bottom of the bottle.

"Are you really that dumb, Jack? Just break the bottle," Dezerae said to me.

"Don't call your brother dumb," my mother said to Dezerae. "Fine," I said to Dezerae as I threw the bottle down onto a rock, smashing it into pieces.

"Be careful my little explorer," my mother said to me. "Well what does the message say?" Dezerae inquired as I stared intently at the smudged writing on the damp paper. "It says … 'SEND HELP' I replied.

"Someone needs help from across the Atlantic," my mother said to me.

"Who needs help?" I inquired.

"I don't know honey. Whoever wrote this message didn't leave their name, are you going to help them?" my mother inquired with a warm smile as we stared intently at the message.

"How could Jack help? He didn't even know how to get the message out of the bottle," Dezerae said to mom. "Shut up," I said to Dezerae.

"Oh stop it Dezerae. I have faith in your brother. I know if someone needs help then Jack will do his best to help them," my mother said to me with a warm smile as she wrapped her arm around me.

*****

I can't believe I almost forgot about these beaches. Some of my fondest childhood memories were not the ones I spent living in *SoHo*, but here on the shores of Montauk Point. Here on these shores is where my sense of hope and wonder in life were reignited once again. Ever since my old man died in the war, I lost my passion for life, while all the other boys my age were happy as can be. The beaches of Montauk felt like a magical place to me ever since I found that message in a bottle. I never knew who wrote that message calling for help or what kind of help they even needed, but I felt as if I was destined to find it, just I as was destined to intercept this liquor deal from these rookie bootleggers.

Two hours had now past and the rookie bootleggers still hadn't noticed me tailing them for the last 100 miles. They were too focused on the shoreline of Montauk Point to pay attention to me.

I should've thought this through more carefully. How was I going to steal this liquor deal from these bootleggers and make it out of Montauk Point alive? I needed a plan that wouldn't involve a shoot out between me and those two rookie bootleggers, but no such plan came to mind as the bootleggers parked their car at the lighthouse.

I couldn't let them see me. I thought to myself as I parked my Chevrolet as close as I could by the shore. I then exited the Chevrolet with my pistol in hand as I kneeled down behind the bushes that bordered the path leading to the lighthouse. If there was a liquor deal arriving by boat, then it should be here any minute now. I could see the glow of the two rookie bootleggers' cigarettes in the distance as they smoked by the entrance of the lighthouse before taking out two shotguns from the trunk of their car. I underestimated these two bootleggers, they were no rookies, but who did they work for, Mr. Luciano or Avery Briggs? Either way, the two bootleggers were heavily armed and I would be filled with led within the blink of an eye if I was to engage in a shoot out with them.

"The shipment should be here any minute, Tony. Stay on guard, just because we're at a beach doesn't mean we should be calm," one bootlegger said in a stern tone.

"You're never calm Frankie. You should take my advice and do some of that meditation those Chinamen invented," the bootlegger known as Tony said with a scoff.

Oh my god, it was him. I never thought I would see him again, but there's no mistaking it now. One of the bootleggers was Frankie Angelo; the man who I carved my initials into with a knife when I caught him raping Hayley in the kitchen of the speakeasy was now bootlegging.

"We have to check out this lighthouse. There could very well be some fucking mook up there watching our every move and I won't have anybody foil this deal for us," Frankie said to Tony in a stern tone as he scratched his chest with a grimace. Frankie and Tony then entered the lighthouse with their shotguns in hand, as I remained crouched behind a bush on the beach contemplating my next move. The pains from all of my injuries over the past year then began to inflame as I scampered over to the entrance of the lighthouse. Why was it that during crucial moments such as these my injuries would always flare up, as if God was telling me 'Turn back Jack. You're not strong enough for what lies ahead.' Well I've never been the kind of man who pays heed to God's warnings, and where ever he is, he sure as hell isn't in New York.

So I as I began to enter the lighthouse I noticed something at sea. This was it, the boat transporting the liquor deal which Frankie and Tony traveled to Montauk for, and I just happened to be in the right place at the right time. I then heard a scream coming from the lighthouse as the boat docked at shore. What was happening up there in the lighthouse? I thought to myself as my eyes darted from the boat to the top of the lighthouse.

"Goddamn it," I spoke aloud while shaking my head and then entered the lighthouse with my pistol held up to my face.

The screams became clearer as I slowly walked up the spiral staircase of the lighthouse and that's when I heard a third voice.

"Send help, I repeat, send help. This is an S.O.S calling out. Please send help to the lighthouse on Montauk Point. I don't have—,"

"I told you not to let that old bastard out of your sight Tony. Now tie him up," Frankie said to tony.

"Send help," I whispered as I stared intently up at the lighthouse while visions of my childhood on the beach at Montauk Point reading that message in a bottle with a wide- eyed gaze flashed in my mind. 25 years later, I was still the one to help all along. I thought to myself as sounds of Frankie and Tony beating the old man echoed throughout the lighthouse.

"No witnesses. This old man has seen too much," Frankie said in a stern tone as I slowly walked up to the room at the top of the lighthouse and stood beside the open door as my heart raced and ankle burned.

"Do we really have to kill him, Frankie? I mean who's he going to tell anyway?" Tony inquired.

"I said no witnesses Tony, or have you learned nothing from working with Mr. Luciano. All it takes is for one pair of eyes to land you behind bars or six feet under," Frankie shouted.

"Frankie look, it's here!" Tony shouted.

"Finally. Well, what are you looking at me for? Get your ass down there and complete the deal. Don't worry, I'll silence this old bastard," Frankie said to Tony. Tony then ran out of the room and down the staircase without even noticing me standing beside the doorway, but that's what money does to a man, it clouds his thought process. I for one was no longer motivated by that liquor deal. This old man, whoever he may be, didn't deserve to die by the filthy hands of the miserable dog known as Frankie Angelo, and now I knew that I was the only one who could help him.

"Long time no see Frankie," I said with a grin as I entered the room to the sight of Frankie standing over the old man who sat tied to a chair and beaten to within an inch of his life.

"Who are you?" Frankie inquired in a stern tone and wide-

eyed gaze as he pointed his shotgun at the old man.

"Oh I'm surprised you don't remember me, but all you need to do is look at your chest to know who I am," I replied.

"Dansby … well this really is my lucky day. I score a huge liquor deal and I get to kill the man who scared me for life," Frankie said to me with a wide-eyed stare and snicker

"Let the old man go Frankie. Or are you too afraid to face me man to man?" I said to Frankie in a stern tone.

"I don't know how you found out about our liquor deal here in Montauk, Jack, but you and this old man will be dead before daybreak, and then I'll finish what I started with that pretty little niece of yours," Frankie said to me with a snicker.

I couldn't let Frankie get inside my head. I had to stay focused or this old man and I may very well be drawing our final breaths on this frigid February afternoon, but I had an idea that could stir a sense of doubt in Frankie's desperate mind.

"It sounds like someone's driving away," I remarked with a grin.

"He would never. Hurry it up you moron. We have a visitor," Frankie said to me and then shouted out the window down at Tony.

"I always had fond memories of these beaches," I said to Frankie with a grin, as his nervous eyes darted from the window and me. I could've shot the dumb dog Frankie when his attention was first drawn towards the window, but I didn't want this old man to be collateral. My timing had to me precise. "That's one of your many flaws Dansby. You let your heart do the talking," Frankie said to me with a scoff as the old man tried to speak through his gagged mouth.

How could I save this old man who was bound and gagged by Frankie? I thought to myself as Frankie and I stared intently at each other, and just then to break the intense silence, a most fortunate sound arose.

"What's that noise … that son of a bitch!" Frankie shouted, as he pulled the old man bound to the chair along with him and stared out the window.

"It looks like your associate has learned a thing or two from working with Mr. Luciano," I said to Frankie with a snicker.

This evened the odds for me and Frankie. His partner had not only abandoned him, but took the entire liquor shipment for himself as well.

"You're all alone Frankie. Now let the old man go and I promise I'll let you out of Montauk with nothing but a reminder of how terrible you are at bootlegging," I said to Frankie with a grin.

"Oh no, Jack. You're my consolation prize now. Tony may have double-crossed me, but the satisfaction I will get from killing you will make up for it. Every fucking day this scar on my chest burns. Every day it serves as a reminder of one last job I have to finish," Frankie said to me in a stern tone and grimace as he scratched the scar on his chest.

What was Frankie's plan if the miserable dog even had one? Frankie was cornered and desperate and I've learned throughout my life to always take a desperate man dead serious. I had to distract Frankie from the old man so I could take my shot, but how?

"Now drop your gun and slide it over to me or this old man never walks again without the reminder of how terrible you are at being a hero," Frankie said to me with a snicker, as he pointed his shotgun at the old man's kneecap.

"I'm not a hero. I followed you two here on a whim, but now I have a chance to finally put down a miserable dog that I spared awhile back," I said to Frankie in a stern tone.

"Look who's talking Jack. I heard you're no longer working for Mr. Luciano. I heard he has every one of his associates searching every borough of New York for you," Frankie said to me with a grin.

"All of his attempts at silencing me have failed. Mr. Luciano is nothing but a tyrant who fears losing his power. I've spent my entire life dealing with bullies like him," I said to Frankie with a scoff.

I was stalling for time. I didn't want to see this old man become a gimp just because I didn't comply with Frankie, but I know Frankie will shoot me dead the very moment I slide my gun over to him.

"I'll give you till the count of three to slide your gun over to me Jack, then I will blow this old man's knee to pieces," Frankie said to me in a stern tone.

Frankie may have the old man as a bargaining chip for my life, but I still saw fear in his shifty eyes as they darted from me to the old man.

"So how's your ex-wife Frankie? Or are you still married to that broad who bust your balls on a daily basis?" I inquired with a grin.

"Shut your damn mouth Dansby!" Frankie shouted.

If there's one thing I knew it was how to provoke a desperate, miserable dog into acting irrational, I've been doing that my entire life, and that's just what I was going to do with Frankie.

"One ...," Frankie said in a stern tone, as my heart raced, but I continued with getting inside Frankie's head and knocking more screws loose.

"Maybe I'll look up your wife in Chelsea. After you I'm sure I'll come off as an Adonis to her," I said to Frankie with a snicker.

I knew Frankie wanted to kill me more than he wanted to hurt the old man, and that's exactly what I was betting on. Once again I was betting my life on someone else's rage.

"Two ...," Frankie said in a stern tone, as the old man tried to scream through his gagged mouth.

"After you I'm sure I would come off as huge. Now what's her number—,"

"You're a dead man Dansby!" Frankie interjected in such an aggressive tone, as he raised his shotgun towards me, the old man then pushed back on his chair knocking into Frankie as we both fired our guns.

Thanks to the old man Frankie missed me and blew a hole through the wall of the lighthouse, but I hit Frankie in the shoulder.

"Using a shotgun in close quarters, you really are a dumb dog," I remarked as I grabbed Frankie's shotgun from off the floor, as he clutched his shoulder with a grimace.

"Go on Dansby. Finish me off," Frankie said to me with a grin and grimace as he stood up from the floor.

"No," I said to Frankie, as I lowered my pistol.

"What do you mean no? I know you're a killer, so do it Goddamn it!" Frankie shouted, with a grimace.

"At first I thought by following you two that it would be a huge pay off for me. I would take your liquor deal and be back in the bootlegging business, but now I realize I didn't come here for the money, liquor, or even revenge," I said to Frankie in a stern tone.

"Then I'll see you in hell Jack," Frankie said to me in a stern tone, and then opened the window of the lighthouse and jumped out.

My eyes then widened at the sight of Frankie lying motionless on the shore.

"Are you all right old man?" I inquired as I untied the old man from the chair and removed the gag from his mouth. "I've been better, but I'm still alive and kicking thanks to you stranger," the old man replied as we stared out the window at Frankie's motionless body, as the waves washed over him. "Let the sea take him. Men like him don't deserve a gravestone," the old man remarked with a stern look as he shook his head.

I first drove to Montauk in search of a means to survive. I wanted to get back into the bootlegging game so badly. Over the past five years liquor has been by life, but I found something here in Montauk that will keep me going.

"I'm Jack Dansby," I said to the old man.

"Thomas A. Buckridge. You're a good man Mr. Dansby. I have no doubt in my mind that man down there would've killed me if you hadn't of intervened. I owe you my life," the old man said to me with a warm smile.

"Ah you owe me nothing. Well … take care of yourself Tom," I said to Thomas, as I walked away.

"Wait Mr. Dansby," Tom said to me with a groan. "Call me Jack," I said to Tom.

"Why did you come here then?" Thomas inquired.

"What do you mean?" I replied.

"It's just as you said. If not for money, liquor, or revenge, then why did you come here to Montauk Point, what did you find my friend?" Thomas inquired.

I then smiled as visions of me as a child playing on the beach and reading that message in a bottle then flashed in my mind.

"I found peace of mind," I said to Thomas with a warm smile and then exited the lighthouse.

"Well what do you know," I remarked with a smile at the sight of one bottle of bourbon on the ground. Frankie's associate must have overlooked this bottle in all of his rush to double cross Frankie. I then looked up at the lighthouse to the sight of Tom waving at me.

"Cheers," I spoke aloud with a smile as I raised the bottle of bourbon and then took a swig.

*****

It was February 27 and I had only 20 dollars in my pocket. Gambling in back alleys could not sustain me any longer. I needed a steady paycheck fast or I will end up waiting in breadlines like the rest of those miserable people.

"Are you all right honey?" the waitress inquired as I sat with my head in my hands at *Sal's Diner* in Greenwich Village. "I'm as all right as any man can be in this day and age," I replied with a sigh.

"So what'll you have?" the waitress inquired.

"Start me off with a cup of coffee and ... a Monte Cristo," I replied.

"Coming right up," the waitress said to me with a smile.

She was young for a waitress and not bad to look at either, but all I've done my entire life was look at women. I've never wanted to spend the rest of my life with one of them. I used to visit this diner awhile back when I needed a break from the speakeasy, now I would give anything to serve liquor there once again. Or you could say that I've already given everything and now I'm left with nothing and nobody.

I then lit a cigarette and took a smoke as a sharp dressed man wearing a proper business suit and fedora sat down next to me at the bar.

"Here you go hun, enjoy," the waitress said to me as she placed the Monte Cristo sandwich and cup of coffee on the bar. "A Monte Cristo huh, I didn't know this diner served such an upscale sandwich," the businessman said to me with a smile. "I wouldn't consider the Monte Cristo an upscale sandwich," I said to the businessman and then took a big bite of the sandwich.

"So have you heard of the story of Monte Cristo?" the business man inquired as the waitress served him a cup of coffee.

"Never heard of it pal. This is just my favorite sandwich because of the ingredients," I replied with a mouth full of the sandwich.

"Well The Count of Monte Cristo is a story about a man who loses everything and devotes the rest of his life to seek revenge on the man responsible for it," the businessman said to me.

"You remind me of my niece. She was fascinated with all those kinds of stories," I remarked with a scoff.

I had no idea I was eating a revenge sandwich, but it sure tasted good. I could see how a man could be fueled by revenge, but I have no intention on hunting the man who continues to hunt me. I know the deeper I go, the harder it will be for me to escape

"Well I best be off now. It was nice to make your acquaintance," the business man said to me as he extended his hand towards me.

"Oh Jack Dansby," I said to the business man with a mouthful of Monte Cristo.

"Dashiell Hammett," the business man said to me with a grin, as we shook hands. He then exited *Sal's Diner* with a series of gut-wrenching coughs as if he was about to keel over and die at that very moment, but I thought nothing of it, as I turned back around on the barstool and buried my face back into the revenge sandwich.

"Turn up the radio would you doll," I said to the waitress as I pointed at the radio which played a song that brought back memories of a time when I believed the sky was the limit for me.

"Oh my mother loves this song," the waitress remarked. "Of course she does. Way to make me feel old," I said to the waitress with a grin and then took a smoke.

"My mother always said I had the looks to become an actress on the silver screen, but I've been turned away from five auditions in the last three months, so it hasn't been a dream come true for me here in New York.

"Oh that's rough doll … so when do you get off?" I inquired with a grin.

*****

Two weeks had passed since I last met that pretty young waitress at *Sal's Diner* and you could say that spring was in the air.

Her name was Dottie Lee Harper. She was a 26 year old waitress with an unshakable dream of becoming an actress. There was a part of me that wanted to give that girl a bitter dose of the truth, but I've always had difficulty telling young girls who were easy on the eyes how this city works, so I was a sap when it came to supporting her dreams. I told Dottie my entire back story of how I used to run the most popular speakeasy in New York and she just smiled and chewed her gum. Either the doll wasn't aware of how dangerous it was be to be around me, or she just didn't care. Dottie still had starry eyes, the kind of eyes which continued to sparkle despite the strife of this city. Dottie was a breath of fresh air in the smoke-filled streets of Greenwich Village. She often spoke like a teenager, but had the body of a mature woman. I would be lying if I said I wasn't attracted to her, maybe if she came into my speakeasy when I was a somebody things would be different, but I suspected I was just an old man down on his luck in her pretty eyes, one of many that she sees come in and out of the diner. I still enjoyed being around Dottie. I now found myself going to *Sal's Diner* just to talk to her. She would then ask me after five minutes of small talk what I wanted and I was always tempted to tell her 'you doll face'. Was I really that lonely, or was Dottie really that charming and beautiful?

"I moved out here to Manhattan from Savannah Georgia two years ago. I now live with my aunt Norma. Did you know she stared as a background role alongside Thelma Todd and Cary Grant," Dottie said to me as she poured my cup of coffee. "Impressive. What was the movie?" I inquired as I lit a cigarette and took a smoke.

"'This Is the Night'. The movie wasn't very successful, but my aunt continued to try to get roles alongside big stars like Cary and Thelma," Dottie replied.

"So you have acting in your blood huh," I remarked with a grin.

"You can say that. What about you Jackie, what makes your blood boil?" Dottie inquired with a grin as she put her hand on her hip.

"Well I always wanted to open up my own bar and serve good hardworking people drinks and all the creature comforts in this day and age, but that dream is now over. I've now turned back to gambling which I've always had a knack for,"

I replied. "Oh gee Jackie don't you know that lifestyle will get you killed," Dottie said to me.

"I could get killed just by walking down the wrong back- alley in this town, but if it serves as a shortcut then I will take it," I said with a scoff.

Dottie then leaned over the counter with her face resting in her hand as she smiled at me.

"You know something Jackie, you really make me feel—,"

Two police officers then barged into the diner, as Dottie's flirtatious grin quickly turned to a wide-eyed stare of concern.

"We're looking for the owner of this diner, Sal McCormick," One police officer pronounced in a stern tone as he walked up to the bar while the other police officer walked into the kitchen.

"Oh gee officers what's the problem?" Dottie inquired. "I got him!" a voice shouted from the kitchen.

I had a bad feeling in my gut. I knew why these two boys in blue wanted Sal, but I was still thinking about how I make Dottie feel exactly.

"Sal McCormick you are under arrest for serving alcohol per the liquor outlaw act," one police officer said to Sal in a stern tone as he handcuffed him.

"I swear I did no such thing officers. You won't find a drop of liquor at my diner," Sal said in a distressed tone.

"Sal what's going on?" Dottie inquired as she held both of her hands together in front of her chest as I shook my head with a grin.

"It may be true that we haven't found any alcohol in this establishment, however one of your associates and countless other patrons of this diner have seen you doing dealing down by Pier 45," one police officer said to Sal.

"So long baby," Dottie said to Sal with a grin as she blew him a kiss and then waved goodbye.

"Dottie … you sold me out. After everything I've done for you!" Sal said to Dottie in a distressed tone and wide-eyed stare as one police officer escorted him out of the dinner.

"A girl has to look out for number one, Sal," Dottie shouted. Well, well, it appears there was more to Dottie Lee Harper than just a sweet voice and pretty face. She played the clueless doll role to a tee with her boss Sal. He had no idea she made a deal with the police to shut down his bootlegging, but was this deal really worth betraying a man who gave her a job when she needed it the most?

"You little bi—," Sal shouted as the as the diner doors shut behind him.

"We had a deal officer," Dottie said to one of the police officers as she twirled her curly blonde hair around her finger.

"Yes Ms. Harper. You will be compensated in the amount we agreed on," The police officer said to Dottie as he jotted down information on a small note pad.

"What will happen to this diner?" I inquired.

"Seeing as how this diner no longer has an owner and that owner is now arrested for breaking the liquor outlaw act. We have no choice but to shut down this establishment," the police officer replied.

"No. what will I do for work now?" Dottie inquired in a distressed tone.

It looks like Dottie's plan had backfired on her. Sure she was going to get paid by the police for selling out her boss, but now she was out of work, unless I stepped in at this crucial moment.

"I have experience managing establishments. I can take the job as the owner of this diner," I said to the police officer in a stern tone as I stood up from the barstool.

"That's out of the question. How do we know you're not a bootlegger waiting for his opportunity to get back in the game under the guise of this diner?" the police officer inquired in a stern tone while shaking his head. Usually the police in this town were pretty slow on the uptake, that's why they needed help from girls like Dottie, but this police officer was sharp, he immediately detected my motives.

"I can vouch for him officer. I swear to you he's on the up and up, and if you detect any foul play from him then I will help you put him behind bars like Sal," Dottie said to the police officer with a grin and wink towards me.

"Very well Ms. Harper. We will be inspecting this diner weekly and if we do find anything that leads us to believe that there's alcohol being served here or laundered here then not just this man will be behind bars, but you along with him," the police officer said to Dottie in a stern tone, as he pointed to me and then her.

"Launder, oh gee officer I don't even know what that word means, but you can count on my man Jackie here to keep this diner clean," Dottie said to the officer with a wide eyed stare.

"I hope so for both of your sake, good day," the police officer said to Dottie and then exited the dinner.

"Looks like we're in this together," I said to Dottie with a grin.

"We sure are Jackie, but if you scratch my back I'll scratch yours," Dottie said to me with a grin.

"How long have you known about Sal?" I inquired.

"For about a couple of months now, but I always had a feeling Sal was dirty and I'm not going to let anybody stand between me and my dream of becoming an actress," Dottie replied.

"No regrets huh?" I inquired.

"You of all people should know you can't stay clean if you want to make it in this city," Dottie replied.

"That's true, and the ones who remain clean are quickly covered by the filth of the ones who made it. So where do we go from here?" I inquired.

"Well I suppose you do some of that managing you told the officer about," Dottie replied with a grin.

Dottie and I were in this new business venture of running *Sal's Diner* together or should I now rebrand it as Jack & Dottie's Diner, or better yet, Jack's Diner. I believed the police officer who told us there would be weekly inspections of the diner so for the time being I had no desires to even stick one of my feet back in the bootlegging business. If I was to go down then Dottie would go with me and vice versa. I must admit the girl was very street smart, which surprised me since she's from Georgia. It's funny how life tends to pair you up with people, sure I wanted to be around Dottie, but now she holds nearly all the cards, except for the Jack of course.

*****

Two weeks had passed since Dottie and I became business partners together and she has been showing me the ropes of running a diner every day. It turns out that running a diner is not that similar to running a bar as I first expected it to be. Dottie informed me that I have to order various meets and produce from the distributors every week. Without those food distributors this diner would quickly go bankrupt just as the speakeasy did without any liquor deals. I decided to keep all of the three cooks and wait staff. I wasn't about to fire them and go looking for new competent people to work at the diner, besides, Dottie informed me that they were honest hard working people who were in no way affiliated with Sal's bootlegging. It still felt good to have a purpose of managing an establishment once again, even if it's not a bar.

*****

It was 12:27AM at the diner. Business was slow and me, Dottie and Gloria were closing up for the night. Gloria was a Hispanic woman who had a great work ethic, but in my experience working with Hispanics I would say they work circles around most other classes of people.

"All right ladies, let's call it a night," I pronounced. "Thank you Mr. Dansby. Have a lovely night," Gloria said to me with a smile and slight bow before exiting the diner with four bags slung over her shoulders.

"Jackie, do you want to meet my aunt Norma?" Dottie inquired with a smile as she wiped her glistening forehead.

"What's the occasion?" I inquired, as I wiped down the bar as visions of the speakeasy and finely dressed patrons sitting at the bar flashed in my mind.

"No occasion. I just want you to meet her," Dottie replied. "Some other time Dottie. I have a lot of numbers to go over, but if you're ever free my place is always open for a night cap," I replied with a grin.

"Oh gee Jackie and what does a nightcap include," Dottie inquired with a grin, as she put her hand on her hip.

"Drinks, music, I can't promise you the world, but I can promise you a good time.

"Some other time Jackie," Dottie said to me with a smile as she patted me on the shoulder.

"All right, but my offer still stands if you ever change your mind," I shouted as Dottie walked towards the front door of the diner.

"So does mine!" Dottie shouted back as she exited the diner.

I just wanted one night with Dottie in my arms. Just one night would be enough for me, but she wanted me to meet her aunt and I wasn't about to give her the wrong idea of my desires, no matter how physical they may be.

Dottie may be willing to give me a chance, but am I willing to go the full nine yards for her? I don't know why I was always reluctant to make that commitment when it came to women, but I wasn't getting any younger, and Dottie was the kind of girl who's charm and beauty had men lined up down the block just to be around her. I had nothing to offer Dottie, nothing a younger more successful man could offer her in a much greater amount. At least now I had an apartment to sleep in rather than sleeping in my Chevrolet for the past month. Working as the owner of the diner didn't pay much, but it paid enough for me to rent an apartment two blocks away from the diner on the lower east side of the Village. It wasn't a penthouse in the *Financial District*, but at least the walls of the apartment weren't filled with rats.

"Home sweet home," I spoke aloud with a sigh as I entered the apartment. I was almost back on my feet, but this emptiness I've felt has only grown stronger ever since Samson and I parted ways, and then Hayley went to go live with Faye, and then the cherry on top, Mickey killed by that Cossack Nicolai. They were all my family and no matter how much danger it put them in they always supported my dream of the speakeasy. I can't even say that about my sister and mother.

The yellow neon sign from the bodega across the street lit up my entire bedroom in the apartment at night. There were some sleepless nights where I was tempted to tell the owner of the bodega to turn the damn thing off, but decided to leave him be with his obnoxious advertising.

I miss drinking myself to sleep after hard night of working at the speakeasy. Now liquor was so scarce I had to tail the likes of Frankie all the way to Montauk Point just for one bottle of bourbon which lasted me two days. I had nothing but the bare necessities in my apartment, which I suppose is all a man like me deserves.

I then took off my diner uniform and laid my head down on the pillow with a groan.

The yellow neon light then began to flicker as my eyelids weighed heavier and heavier with each lonely moment.

"Finally," I spoke aloud as the flickering yellow neon light went out, leaving my apartment bedroom in darkness.

*****

It was 7:26 PM at the diner as Dottie, Gloria and I were working an unusual rush of customers for this evening hour.

"Oh come on Dottie. Do you really believe that bleeding heart FDR is going to change this country for the better?" I inquired in an incredulous as I grilled a burger for a customer seated at the bar.

"Give him a chance Jackie. The bar is set pretty low. Maybe he'll surprise you," Dottie replied.

"He's just another democrat playing into people's fears, but if by some slim chance FDR does change this country for the better then I will be the first one to admit I was wrong," I said to Dottie with a snicker.

"Jack Dansby admitting he's wrong. Now I would love to see that," Dottie said to me with a smile.

"Order up!" I shouted as I dinged the bell and placed the medium well burger with a side of fries on the counter.

Sure I wasn't the best short order cook, serving drinks has always been my specialty, but when it came to grilling food I wasn't half bad. I left the more complicated dishes to the other more experienced cooks.

"Alfonse!" Dottie shouted as she scampered over to the bar and wrapped her arms around the neck of a sharp dressed young man. Unless they greet their relatives in such a affectionate way back in Georgia, the young man Dottie was draped all over at first sight had to have been her boyfriend. I knew it, there was no way a girl like Dottie could stay single for too long. Did I miss my chance with her? Or did I never really have a chance to begin with? I thought to myself as I watched Dottie hop up on the bar and kiss the man known as Alfonse like he just came back from war. I was filled with nothing but resentment at that moment as I stared daggers at the young man who Dottie continues to shower with affection.

"So when do you get off?" Alfonse inquired with a grin. "That's my line you little bastard," I spoke aloud with a scowl as I continued to stare daggers at Alfonse from the bar.

"One moment let me ask Jackie," Dottie replied with a smile.

"My shift is over in five, do you need any more help around here?" Dottie inquired with a sigh as she took off her apron.

"What's the hurry?" I inquired.

"I have plans tonight," Dottie replied.

"Oh well that's too bad, I need you to mop the floors and clean the tables. Then make sure all the grease traps are cleaned," I said to Dottie in a stern tone.

"How could you Jackie? These past couple of weeks have been brutal on all of us," Dottie said to me in a distressed tone. "I can do those jobs for you Mr. Dansby. Go have a good time Ms. Harper," Gloria said to me and Dottie. "You're an angel Gloria. I won't forget—," "No, Gloria you can go home now. Dottie you're still on the clock until you do as I say," I said to Dottie as her eyes followed mine as I glanced at Alfonse at the bar.

"Oh I know what this is about. Are you really that petty of a man Jack?" Dottie inquired, as I aggressively cleaned the grill. "I don't know what you're talking about, but this diner would be shut down and you would be out of work if it wasn't for me intervening with the police. Now be grateful you have a job," I said to Dottie in a stern tone.

"Prick," Dottie remarked as she walked away towards Alfonse.

"What was that?" I inquired in a stern tone.

"Nothing," Dottie replied in a high pitched voice she uses to get more tips.

I then watched Dottie explain in an aggressive manner to Alfonse at the bar why she had to cancel her plans with him tonight.

It did give me satisfaction knowing that I had control over Dottie's schedule, but I knew I couldn't keep every eligible man in New York away from her. Dottie and I then spent the next two hours cleaning the diner in silence. Dottie was acting like a sulking teenage girl with me and in many ways that's just what she was. I took the job as owner of this diner to hopefully get back into the bootlegging business, but I know the police won't let that happen. The prospect of working with a girl like Dottie made me feel like a school boy at first, but after I saw her showering Alfonse with affection at the bar, I was immediately brought back to the cruel reality of this world. I was just an old man down on his luck, watching more beautiful and successful people pass me by from the sidelines, but if I could help Dottie accomplish her dreams of becoming an actress then maybe she will only have eyes for me.

*****

Six days in a row working at that diner had really worn me down to the bone. Today was Sunday, my day off, and I was going to use it to try to get Dottie an acting deal of any kind. I knew as much about acting as Dottie knows about bootlegging, but I know the one place to go to in this town if you want to be a star of the silver screen. So after a quick smoke, I entered my Chevrolet and drove east to Broadway.

The only acting I've seen by Dottie was when she pretended to be clueless when the police barged in and arrested her former boss Sal for bootlegging. I must admit she fooled me, but could she charm those Hollywood big wigs at auditions? So far the poor girl had been turned away from five auditions in the past couple of months, so I don't know what I could possible find here on Broadway which isn't already on Dottie's radar.

All I could see as I walked down Broadway were signs reading SHOW CANCELLED or PRODUCTION SHUT DOWN. It appeared that Broadway was struggling just like every other part of New York, but that's not what all the bright neon signs and billboards of glamorous celebrities would have you believe. I then continued to walk further down Broadway, but every marquee read the same discouraging sign.

"You got your work cut out for you Dottie and so do I," I spoke aloud with a sigh as I shook my head and then lit a cigarette and took a smoke. To my surprise I then came across a show which wasn't cancelled that Dottie may have a chance of scoring a role in. It was an off Broadway Burlesque show. The call sheet read—

BARFLIES
A MUSICAL

MY MUSICAL IS A LUSTY AND HEARTFELT ROMP OF A TALE

WHICH FOLLOWS THREE SISTERS WHO MUST NAVIGATE THE PREJUDICES OF THIS WORLD.

WE ARE LOOKING FOR THREE BEAUTIFUL GIRLS WITH CLASS AND SASS.

AUDITIONS BEGIN TODAY AT 8AM THROUGH MARCH 14th. MY MUSICAL DOESN'T CATER TO CELEBTRITY ELITES. I WANT TO SEE REAL GIRLS AT THE AUDITIONS WHO KNOW HOW IT FEELS TO BE SLAPPED IN THE FACE, BUT HAVE ALSO SLAPPED BACK.I NEED YOU GIRLS AND TOGETHER I KNOW WE CAN MAKE BOTH OF OUR DREAMS COME TRUE AND BRING A BREATH OF FRESH AIR INTO THE WEEZING LUNGS THAT IS BROADWAY!

"Well this show has Dottie written all over it," I spoke aloud with a grin and then pulled a tab off the call sheet which had the address of the theatre along with the date and time which the auditions are being held. This show was playing at the Cherry Lane Theatre in Greenwich Village and it was   only a couple blocks away from the speakeasy. I would be getting dangerously close to the speakeasy where every mobster is no doubt trying to silence me just to stay in the good graces of Mr. Luciano, but I had to check out this theatre, for Dottie's sake.

I put on my hat and trench coat before I exited the Chevrolet which I parked in a back-alley across from *Washington   Square Park*. Parks were good settings to stay one step ahead of anybody trying to kill you. The wide open spaces of *Washington Square Park* were good for me because I could see someone coming hundreds of feet away, whereas in a dark back alley I would be dead before I could turn my head. I still had my hand clutching my pistol as I walked through *Washington Square Park* to the sight of a mass group of Hispanics living in tents. I could say it was a shame that the Hispanics were sullying the natural beauty of the park, but *Washington   Square   Park* has been sullied long before the Hispanics arrived in New York.

I then arrived at the Cherry Lane Theatre and was quickly disappointed by the appearance of the theatre which wasn't much bigger than the apartment complex in *SoHo* where I used to live as a child, but everybody has to start somewhere if they want to accomplish their dreams.

"Hello I work with a girl who would be absolutely perfect for this musical. She's an aspiring young actress whose beauty and charm will knock your socks off," I said to a woman sitting in one of those pompous chairs you see directors sitting in on movie sets.

"My good man I'm not the playwright of this musical. He's over there with the girls," the woman said to me with an eye roll.

"Girls, wait a minute," I said to the woman with a wide- eyed stare as it appeared that the three girls this playwright needed for his musical were already standing right in front of him.

"Are you the boss around here?" I inquired as I walked up to a stout man wearing a black scarf, glasses and one of those French hats I've seen Faye wear before.

"Indeed I am, Lorenzo Calderon," the playwright replied.

"I'm Jack Dansby, but who I am isn't important. Please tell me you didn't already cast these three girls as the leading roles of your musical," I said to Lorenzo in an incredulous tone as I pointed at the three girls.

"Take five ladies. Mr. ... Jack is it. If you're a manager of some sort, then save your breath. I have already cast the three leading roles for my musical Barflies," Lorenzo said to me as he held his hand out to keep me from talking.

"Damn it ... that's a shame. I thought you wanted a real star, not these clueless dames who couldn't tell you the time of day if they were staring at a clock," I said with a scoff as I stared at the three girls.

"I'm going to be honest with you," Lorenzo said to me as he gestured for me to lean in close to him.

"I'm listening," I said to Lorenzo.

"One of them is abysmal. She is one dimensional at best and lacks the certain spark I need to play the role of Isabelle," Lorenzo whispered to me.

"Then say no more Mr. Playwright," I said to Lorenzo with a grin.

"Whoever you have in mind my good man for the role of Isabelle tell her to be here and ready to bare her soul," Lorenzo said to me.

"I guarantee you won't be disappointed with her," I said to Lorenzo with a grin.

"I should hope not. I first came to this country from Barcelona with a vision to bring a tale that would illuminate Broadway, but so far all I've seen are girls who want nothing than to have their fifteen minutes of fame and nothing else. Nobody sees the big picture in this day and age. Oh which reminds me ... Dorothy, Dorothy," Lorenzo shouted as he snapped his fingers at one of the girls who were giggling which each other at a table full of refreshments.

"Yes Mr. Calderón?" Dorothy inquired with a wide-eyed stare.

"You're out my dear. I cannot in good conscious continue to lead you on when you've given me nothing but a prissy entitled attitude," Lorenzo said to the girl named Dorothy with a dismissive wave.

"Wait please Mr. Calderón. I can do better I swear, I swear I can be what you want me to be," Dorothy pleaded as her eyes began to well up with tears.

"The stage is no place for you Dorothy. You are pretty, but just pretty isn't enough to make it in this day and age," Lorenzo said to Dorothy.

"Please it's my dream to make it on stage and then on the silver screen. I will do anything," Dorothy pleaded with Lorenzo as tears began to pour from her warm doe eyes.

"Ah my dear if only you could've showed me this emotion over the past day then I might reconsider my decision. This dream isn't for you Dorothy, goodbye," Lorenzo said to Dorothy with a dismissive wave as he read over the screenplay. Dorothy then scampered out of the theatre with her hands over her face. I felt responsible for Dorothy being fired from the musical, but sometimes you have to crush other people's dreams in this town in order to make your dreams come true.

*****

It was 9:07 AM at the diner as Dottie entered without so much as even glancing at me as she took off her trench coat and hung it up on the hook in the kitchen.

I couldn't wait to tell Dottie I managed to get her an audition. I know she wants nothing more than to slap me in the face after I ruined her date night with that young Casanova she was swooning over, but if there's one thing I've learned about women is that they'll always give you a second chance. Sure there are many scumbags out there who don't deserve a second chance, but I believe what I'm doing for Dottie is pretty damn selfless.

"Dottie," I said with a whistle as I gestured for her from the far end of the bar.

"Don't whistle Jack. I'm not some show dog," Dottie said to me with an eye roll as she walked over to me.

"Not yet you're not," I said to Dottie with a grin, as Gloria entered the diner.

"Good morning Dottie, Good morning Mr. Dansby," Gloria said with a warm smile.

"Good morning Gloria, Dottie and I said in unison.

"What do you mean by that show dog comment Jack," Dottie inquired.

"Well Dottie I just happened to score you an audition for a role in an off Broadway musical," I replied to Dottie with a smile as I handed her the literature of the musical Barflies.

"You're kidding. Now don't you go playing with a young gal's dreams Jackie," Dottie said to me with a smile as her eyes lit up while reading the literature.

"I wouldn't dare," I said with a snicker.

"Oh my god Jackie this is wonderful. How did you find this musical? Last I recall all Broadway shows were shut down," Dottie inquired with a smile.

"They still are, so I went off Broadway to find this musical. I think the role is perfect for you," I said to Dottie.

"Jackie ... why are you doing all this for me?" Dottie inquired as her blue eyes began to glisten with tears as she stared fondly at me.

"Well, uhm I was in the neighborhood and I remembered how much you want to be an actress. So I thought why not help out Dottie while I'm—,"

Dottie then quickly wrapped her arms around my neck and kissed me firmly on my stammering mouth. She tasted just as I imagine, like cherries with a hint of smoke. It was my intention to win Dottie back, but I was still speechless over her sudden display of affection towards me.

"Now get out of here and go to that audition," I said to Dottie with a grin as I pointed to the door of the diner.

"Time for the weekly inspection of your diner Mr. Dansby," a police officer pronounced as he entered the diner.

"Go Dottie. Gloria and I will be fine. Go act your heart out," I said to

Dottie.

"Thank you Jackie," Dottie said with a smile along with a giddy scream as she scampered out of the diner.

"Inspect away officers. I'm an open book," I pronounced, as the officers began to go over every inch of the dinner as if they were detectives investigating a murder scene. Unlike Sal, I wasn't about to risk my relationship with Dottie over a liquor deal, no matter how profitable it was. It gave me peace of mind knowing that I've now abandoned my dreams of being a bootlegger and running a speakeasy. Dottie and this diner was all I needed now.

*****

It was 8:06 PM as Gloria and I were eagerly waiting for Dottie to return with good news about her audition. I even promised that snob playwright Lorenzo a bottle of bourbon if he cast Dottie for the role of Isabelle in his musical Barflies, but I doubt that will have any effect on Dottie getting the part. Dottie would be judged by Lorenzo by her acting talent alone, but I had faith she would get the part.

"I hope Ms. Dottie gets the part in that musical," Gloria said to me.

"Me too, Gloria, that role was made for her," I said to Gloria.

"You're a very generous man Mr. Dansby," Gloria remarked with a warm smile.

"If you're trying to butter me up so that you can leave early then forget about it," I said to Gloria with a snicker.

Dottie then entered the diner, but my smile from seeing her quickly turned to a scowl when I saw that she was with Alfonse. "This is the man who made it all happen. Alfonse this is Jack Dansby. He got me the audition for the musical. Jack this is my boyfriend Alfonse," Dottie said to me with a smile.

"So don't leave me in suspense. Did Lorenzo give you the part," I inquired as I stared intently at Dottie, with not so much as even a glance towards Alfonse.

"He did! Mr. Calderon said that I had that spark he was looking for. Now the rehearsals begin. This is all happening so fast," Dottie replied with a smile and a slight bounce up and down.

"Congratulations, Ms. Dottie. Gloria said to Dottie as they hugged each other.

"Thank you Gloria. I hope to see your smiling face front row center on opening night," Dottie said to Gloria.

"I wouldn't miss it for the world," Gloria said to Dottie with a warm smile.

"You're a generous man, Jack," Alfonse said to me with a grin as he draped his arm around Dottie's shoulders.

"Just call me Saint Jack," I said to Alfonse with a scoff and then entered the kitchen as the sound of Dottie and Alfonse talking amorously echoed in my ear.

I was the furthest from a saint any man could be. I was a fool, a fool to think that Dottie would ever go for a man like me. Even a young beautiful girl like Dottie didn't even take me seriously when I wanted to be more than friends. Faye was the same way. Even after I greased the hinges of the rusty doors to Broadway to open up a crack for her she still only has eyes for Alfonse. It was the story of my life, a story I was tired of watching each times it happened. I never measured up to younger, more attractive and successful men.

"Damn it!" I shouted as I entered the walk-in freezer of the kitchen and punched a hanging leg of lamb as hard as I could.

"Are you all right Mr. Jack?" Gloria inquired.

"I'm fine Gloria. I'm just prepping the frozen meats. Now go make sure we're ready for tomorrow," I replied in a stern tone, as I stared at my raw knuckles bleeding from the icy lamb leg.

"I'm looking for Mr. Dansby. I know he works here," A voice pronounced.

"Who might you gentlemen be?" Dottie inquired.

"You can call us his former associates. Ones that have come to settle a grievance he caused in his past life.

"Oh gee, well Jack just left ten minutes ago, but I'll be sure to pass the message to him," Dottie said.

No, those voices, it can't be. Two members of the Five Points Gang have tracked me down to this diner. I knew this lingering feeling in my gut was justified, but I couldn't put Dottie and Gloria in any danger. My pistol was under the bar, but I doubt I could get to it unnoticed.

"No need doll face. Just give Jack this message," one mobster said to Dottie.

"Of course, is there anything else I can get you two gentleman?" Dottie inquired as I slowly peeked my head through the kitchen doorframe to see Leo and another mobster standing in front of Dottie in their typical domineering manner. "Yes come over to the speakeasy on Minetta Street for a taste of the good life. Nice diner, it would be a shame if anything happened to it," Leo replied to Dottie with a snicker as him and the other mobster exited the diner.

I then quickly grabbed my pistol underneath the bar and held it up to my face as my eyes darted in every direction. I heard the threat Leo made, but I didn't know when or how he would exact such a threat.

"Who were those men Jackie," Dottie inquired in a distressed tone.

"They're mobsters," I replied.

"What have you gotten yourself into Jack?" Alfonse said to me in a stern tone.

"Get out. This doesn't concern you!" I shouted at Alfonse as I pointed at the front door of the diner.

"It's all right Alfonse. We'll talk tomorrow," Dottie said to Alfonse with a kiss to his cheek. Alfonse then exited the diner as my mind raced with all the possible ways Leo would try to smoke me out.

"Jackie, those men wanted me to give you this," Dottie said to me as she placed a letter on the bar.

It was another letter from a member of the Five Points Gang. Whenever I read these letters whether they're from Johnny or Nicolai, I wonder just how they decide what will make me bend to their will. Mr. Luciano believes he knows me, but if that was true then I would've been dead a long time ago. "Those two men made me feel uneasy," Gloria remarked with her hand on her chest.

"Me too honey," Dottie said to Gloria as she wrapped her arm around her while I began to read the letter from Leo.

Jack Dansby,

I will spare you the pretenses seeing as how I know you know who writes you this letter. You have continued to enrage Mr. Luciano to the point where he now has raised the price of your head to $100,000 dead or alive. We thought for sure Nicolai would've silenced you, but we should've never sent a Cossack to do an Italian's job. No matter how many men he has killed, I told Nicolai not to underestimate you. I told him you are the wild card who could very well find himself on top within the blink of an eye. Now I see you have a new familia. If you care for their safety then you will return to the speakeasy next Saturday at 8 PM for a talk with Mr. Luciano. If you choose not to talk with the man whom you stole from and killed many of his associates, then your precious familia will be silenced and your diner will be burned to the ground.

*****

The Monday that followed Leo's letter left me in a daze for the entire afternoon. Sure I've been threatened by the Five Points Gang in the past, but this time it felt different. I cared for Dottie, and even though she still may only have eyes for Alfonse, I couldn't be responsible for her death, but if I returned to the speakeasy this Saturday night, then I would surely be silenced by either Leo or any other upstart mobster son of a bitch looking to make a name for himself. I was no hero as Hayley painted me out to be. I was no martyr who would suffer or die for someone or something he believed was greater than himself. I was just a diner owner trying to get by.

"Gloria, can you hand me the spatula," I inquired as I gestured for the spatula hanging on a hook over the grill. Gloria then handed me the steel spatula with a smile as a memory of my mother hit me like a ton of bricks.

*****

"Ma can you hand me the spatula?" I inquired, as my mother smoked a cigarette while staring out the living room window.

"Oh my god," my mother said with a gasp, as I slapped the three burgers onto the sizzling pan.

"What is it Ma, what happened?" I inquired as my mother walked into the kitchen with her hand on her chest and a wide- eyed stare at me.

"I just saw your father sitting on the sofa," my mother said as she pointed to the sofa in the living room while the burgers on the grill continued to sizzle.

"Dad died ten years ago Ma, now hand me the spatula," I said to my mother as she continued to stare at the empty sofa.

"I know what I saw Jack. He was sitting right there," my mother said to me in a stern tone as she pointed at the sofa. "Dad is gone. I've accepted it, Dezerae has accepted it. You need to see a doctor," I said to my mother as I shook my head. "Don't take that tone with me. You have no idea what I sacrificed in order to raise you and your loose sister. Now look at you two, big shots huh. She can't hold down a job without sleeping with her boss, and just look at you," my mother said to me in a stern tone and scoff.

"Well at least I'm not spending my life feeling sorry for myself. You're pathetic," I said to my mother in a stern tone.

"Oh I forgot your dream is to open up a bar. Way to aim low Jack," my mother said to me with a scoff.

"Shut up!" I said to my mother in a stern tone as my face quivered at the sight of what she had become, a cruel woman whose mind has taken a turn for the worst.

"You want to be a bartender, you can't even cook a burger without burning it," My mother said to me with a laugh as she entered her bedroom and slammed the door. I then quickly grabbed the spatula and flipped the three burnt burgers with scowl.

*****

"Mr. Jack … Mr. Jack," Gloria said to me. "Yes what is it," I inquired.

"The burger is burning," Gloria remarked.

"Ah shit!" I shouted as I flipped the burnt burger, and then threw the spatula at the wall as the sound of my mother laughing at me echoed in my mind.

"Are you all right Mr. Jack?" Gloria inquired with a wide eyed stare.

"I'm fine Gloria. I'll grill up another burger for that gentleman at the bar. Just tell him it will be another five minutes," I replied in a somber tone.

"Yes sir," Gloria said to me and then exited the kitchen.

She didn't know, neither did Dottie, or anybody who worked for me at this diner. If I told them what Leo's letter read, then they would just be living in fear for the next week wondering if I would chose my life over theirs.

Dottie had today off, which meant she would either be spending it with Alfonse or rehearsing for her role in Barflies. I still wanted to be there for Dottie. I'm sure her aunt is supporting here every waking moment when it comes to rehearsing for Barflies, but I want to be there for her as well. Musicals were never my scene, but I'll be damned if I pass up an opportunity to get closer to Dottie.

"Turn up the radio," I said to Gloria as the name FDR caught my ear.

"In national news, President Franklin Delano Roosevelt has declared a nationwide bank holiday. Known as the Emergency Banking Act, this declaration was brought to fruition in hopes to reestablish public confidence within all Americans.

In entertainment news playwright Maxwell Anderson debuts his play 'Both Your Houses' in New York to a grand premiere on Broadway," the radio sounded as I served the gentleman at the bar his medium-well burger with a side of coleslaw.

"Thank you," the gentleman at the bar said to me with a smile.

"Looks like FDR has declared another national holiday," I said with a scoff.

"I think he's a good man," Gloria remarked.

"Really what makes you say that Gloria?" I inquired. "He has kept all his promises," Gloria replied.

"He may have already done more for this country than Hoover, but FDR hasn't won me over yet. I'm waiting for something incredible to come from him, or else he's just another bleeding heart democrat," I said to Gloria.

"It's good to hear about that playwright. Maybe shows will now be returning to Broadway," Gloria said to me.

"I hope so. Wouldn't that be perfect for Dottie," I said to Gloria with a grin.

"Ms. Dottie really likes you. I see it in her eyes. She lights up when she sees you," Gloria remarked with a smile.

"She lights up more when she sees Alfonse," I said to Gloria with a scoff.

"Dottie is a very beautiful and talented young woman, but she's also very fragile. She needs your support," Gloria said to me.

"Inspection Mr. Dansby, I'm Officer Baker. So how's business?" a police officer inquired in a stern tone as he entered the diner and walked up to the bar while flashing his badge.

"Business has been steady enough to get us by. Didn't we just have an inspection a few days ago officer," I replied to the police officer.

"Well now we're having another one. The NYPD has been accused of being too lenient when it comes to the liquor outlaw act, and lenient is the last word we want to be associated with," the police officer said to me in a stern tone.

"Well Inspect away then officer. We're on the up and up," I said to Officer Baker. I had no other options left when it came to Leo's letter, unless I turned to the police for protection, but not protection for me, for Dottie, Gloria, and the diner. If Officer Baker was one of the too few cops in this city that weren't in the pocket of Mr. Luciano then I had to take that chance and tell him my dire situation, but something tells me that Officer Baker doesn't do Mr. Luciano's bidding, or else I would be dead by now, so I had to take this chance and enlist his protection.

"You're all clear Mr. Dansby," Officer Baker said to me. "Wait!" I shouted as Officer Baker walked towards the door of the diner.

"Yes what is it?" Officer Baker inquired. "I ... I need your help," I replied.

*****

So I confided my entire life story to Officer Baker. Something I may regret down the road, but I had nowhere and nobody else to turn to for protection. I was just one man, and I was tired of constantly looking over my shoulder. Tired of grasping my pistol under my pillow every time a loud noise wakes me up at night, but most of all, I was tired of putting good people in danger.

"My precinct is not actively trying to shut down Charles Luciano's enterprise, but we do not in any way work for him," Officer Baker said to me as we both stood in the kitchen while Gloria served the only two patrons in the diner.

"What does that mean, Officer," I inquired.

"It means that word has caught our ears of a man which Mr. Luciano has put a reward of $100,000 dead or alive, but now I know that man is you Mr. Dansby," Officer Baker said to me in a stern tone.

"So what are my options Officer?" I inquired in a somber tone.

"I'm going to tell you something you will never hear from another police officer. Leave this town Dansby. Spare that doll and everyone else the pain of knowing you and I'll spare them a bullet from the Five Points Gang," Officer Baker said to me in a stern tone.

"No, no I cannot let them win, not again," I said to Officer Baker in a stern tone.

"Have it your way Mr. Dansby, but just to let you know, Mr. Luciano will stop at nothing when it comes to eliminating a threat to his enterprise, and he has deemed you a great threat," Officer Baker said to me.

"If I leave town before Saturday, Do you promise to protect this diner along with everyone who works here?" I inquired.

"You have my word. Mr. Dansby that this diner along with all the employees will remain safe," Officer Baker replied. "All right Officer, I know what I have to do," I said to Officer Baker.

*****

"You seem quiet. Are you all right Jackie?" Dottie inquired. "I'm just tired," I replied with a sigh as I stared intently at the clock.

"Mr. Calderon says I have the potential to be the next Marilyn Miller. I told him I had no idea who that was and I just wanted to be me," Dottie said to me with a smile.

"So how are rehearsals going?" I inquired as I wiped down the bar.

"Exhausting, between rehearsals and working here at the diner a girl has no energy left," Dottie replied.

"Do you think you could run this diner if I wasn't around?" I inquired in a somber tone as Dottie primped her hair.

"Heavens no Jackie, I told you rehearsals are draining me," Dottie replied.

"I'll ask Gloria then," I said to Dottie in a somber tone as I continued to stare intently at the clock.

"Are you going somewhere, Jackie?" Dottie inquired.

"No I'm not going anywhere in life. You're the one that's going places," I replied.

"Thanks to you Jackie, I better see you front row opening night," Dottie said to me with a smile.

"When is opening night?" I inquired with a grin.

"Oh uhm, Mr. Calderon said April 22," Dottie replied.

April 22. I had no idea if I would still be in Manhattan during that time, or furthermore, if I would still be alive and kicking. I wanted to see Dottie on stage acting her heart out, but I fear that the Five Points Gang already know all about Dottie and her dreams of becoming an actress. I helped make Dottie's dream come true and I'll be damned if I'm going to be the one who's responsible for ending it. I had to see somebody's dreams come true in this day and age, and even if they weren't my dreams, it would still give me hope.

"It's time Jack," Officer Baker said in a stern tone as he entered the diner.

"I'm ready," I said to Officer Baker in a somber tone and sigh.

"What is he talking about Jackie?" Dottie inquired with a wide-eyed stared.

"I have to leave Dottie. I've worn out my welcome here at this diner and it would be selfish of me to put you and Gloria in danger. There is a program which the FBI has started which will relocate me and provide me protection along with you and Gloria from the Five Points Gang," I said to Dottie as my face began to quiver.

"No, no please don't take him officer," Dottie said in a distressed tone as she walked up to Officer Baker.

"This was Jack's choice Ms. Harper. He knows all too well the vast recourses the Five Points Gang and Mr. Luciano posses in order to silence him for good. We will continue to monitor this diner weekly in Jacks relocation. Jack is just one man so he employed our services," Officer Baker said as I put on my trench coat and grabbed my suitcase from behind the bar.

"Jackie … I need you in my life please, please stay," Dottie said to me as she grabbed my arm while her eyes began to well up with tears.

"Don't worry, you still have Alfonse," I said to Dottie.

"Not anymore. I didn't tell you, once he found out that you have history with the Five Points Gang, he wanted nothing to do with me, he up and split out of my life, just as you're about to do," Dottie said to me as tears began to stream from her eyes. "I'm sorry, but this is all for the best. Let's go," I said to Officer Baker.

Officer Baker and I then exited the diner to a light spring rain as we walked up to his squad car.

"This choice is irrevocable Jack. I'm going to ask you one last time, are you ready to leave this all behind?" Officer Baker inquired as I stared at Dottie crying her eyes out through the diner window.

Well look at what I've become now. The very thing I swore I wasn't, a martyr. If I could go back in time and reject Mr. Luciano's deal that night in the speakeasy I would, but I can't change what I've done.

"Where will my new life begin officer?" I inquired as I entered the back seat of the squad car.

"The FBI has three locations in mind for you Jack. These locations will keep you out of the reach of the Five Points Gang," Officer Baker replied, as we drove northeast past the speakeasy and my first apartment in Greenwich Village.

"What are these locations?" I inquired in a somber tone as memories of all the good times spent with Samson, Hayley, and Mickey god rest his soul flashed in my mind.

"The locations are, Anchorage Alaska, Rollins Montana, or Bakersfield California. Make your choice Jack," Officer Baker said to me in a stern tone.

"You're putting me on the spot Officer," I said to Officer Baker as my heart raced at the three options.

"Time is of the essence Jack. We need to create your new identity in one of the locations of your choosing," Officer Baker said to me in a stern tone.

"Hold on, what do you mean my new identity?" I inquired.

"You're no longer Jack Dansby. You're no longer a former bar owner, turned bootlegger, turned speakeasy owner, turned mobster, turned diner owner. You no longer have a niece, nor do you have any friends. You were not born in New York. You have no affiliation with this city whatsoever. The FBI is creating your new identity as we speak, now chose a damn location," Officer Baker said to me in a stern tone.

They were taking away my identity. Sure there are many times in my life where I can't stand to live with myself, but I would rather be Jack Dansby any day rain or shine than a solitary man living a lie for the rest of his life. I couldn't do this, the family I now have in this miserable yet beautiful city are the reason why I'm still alive. Sure I may put them in danger, but they're the only family I have, and for better or worse, we're all in this together.

"I … I can't do this," I said to Officer Baker as we stopped at a red light.

"What do you mean you can't do this?" Officer Baker inquired in a stern tone.

"I can't do this!" I shouted and then exited the squad car. "They will find you, Jack. No matter where you go without our protection they will find you!" Officer Baker shouted as I ran down a back-alley in east Greenwich Village.

"That's not what I paid you for!" a man shouted as he aggressively grabbed the arm of a young girl cowering on the street corner.

"Take it easy pal," I said to the man in a stern tone as I shoved him away from the young girl who appeared to be crying.

"Wait, Hayley?" I inquired with a wide eyed stare.

CHAPTER 20:
JACK OF HEARTS
- HAYLEY -

"Jack, is it really you?" I inquired with a wide-eyed stare as the tears wouldn't stop streaming from my bleary eyes.

"It's really me kid," Jack said to me with a warm smile.

"Wait a minute. Don't tell me you know this little hooker pal?" the man inquired with a scoff.

Jack then swung at the man in such an abrupt manner, as if he was just waiting to unleash all of his anger on the next person he lays eyes on.

"I hope that answers your question pal," Jack said to the man who was lying on the pavement groaning.

"I never thought I would see you again," I said to Jack in a sobbing tone as I wrapped my arms around him.

"Don't worry, I'm here now kid, and I'm not going anywhere. No matter what happens from here on out, we're in this together," Jack said to me as he held my head against his shoulder.

I couldn't believe Jack was back in my life. At my lowest most degrading moment Jack saved me from continuing with what I would be regretting for the rest of my life. The way which Jack hugged me back felt different, as if he actually missed me over these past grueling months, or perhaps I've just been longing for his comfort now more than ever. Staring into Jack's handsome grizzled face brought back as sense of comfort I never had with Faye, but she is the very reason why I almost sold my body to that pig.

"Where are you living now?" I inquired as Jack took my hand and led me down the street in a nervous manner.

"I will tell you all about it later when we're off the street," Jack replied, as his eyes darted from side to side.

Was Jack in danger at this moment? He sure acted like someone was following him, but who?

"Can we go to your apartment?" I inquired with a sniffle as a taxicab drove over a puddle which splashed all over my burgundy dress.

"Asshole!" Jack shouted as he shook his fist in the air towards the passing taxicab. Jack hadn't changed one bit, and I wouldn't have it any other way.

"I'm afraid not. I can never go back there again," Jack said to me as he shook his head.

"Then we can go back to my apartment," I said to Jack. Whatever trouble Jack was in we would face it together, just as he said.

"Say it isn't so, kid. Tell me that son of a bitch I knocked out a few moments ago was spouting nonsense when he called you a hooker," Jack said to me.

"I'll tell you all about it when we get off the street," I said to Jack, as we crossed the street and scampered through the parking lot of *Magnolia Towers* where Faye awaits for my return.

*****

It was 9:18 AM as Jack and I entered the elevator of *Magnolia Towers*.

I was sad, but also excited for Jack and Faye to finally reunite after all this time. I know their relationship was never set in stone, but I always felt warmth between the two of them. Part of me always wanted Jack and Faye to fully commit to each other. I believe they are meant for each other. They're not perfect people, but their outgoing personalities seem to motivate each other in a good direction.

"Faye … Faye are you awake, we have a special visitor," I pronounced as Jack and I entered the apartment.

"Oh mon dieu. Is that really you mon chéri Jack?" Faye inquired in a faint tone as she sat on the sofa with a sable on her lap and a maroon throw blanket draped over her.

"It's me Faye," Jack replied with a smile, but the joy on Jack's face from seeing Faye quickly turned to sorrow after he saw her condition.

"Faye thought you would be dead by now, but I told her Jack is too stubborn to die," I said to Jack with a giggle which quickly turned to sobbing.

"Not yet … what happened to you Faye? You look like you've aged ten years since we last met," Jack inquired as he took off his trench coat and sat down on the chair across from Faye and Sable.

"Life happened mon chéri," Faye replied with a series of coughs as she lit a cigarette and took a smoke.

"Faye has a virus … but the doctor at Bellevue said there is no cure," I said to Jack in a somber tone.

"I never did trust doctors," Jack said with a scoff as he shook his head.

"You don't trust anybody mon chéri, but the virus I have is not something which I can overcome. I'm happy to see you Jack and I hope you found some semblance of happiness in your life these past couple of months," Faye said to Jack with a warm smile.

"Semblance … not quite sure what that word means, but where I am right now with you two is exactly where I want to be.

"This isn't the Jack I know," Faye remarked with a grin.

"This is the Jack I've been too blind to see. Do you two ladies have room for one more in this apartment?" Jack inquired. "Jack … we've been struggling to pay rent. The landlord might not let you stay here," I said to Jack as I sat down on the sofa next to Faye.

"Oh putain Giovanni. If he was going to evict us he would have done it a month ago," Faye said with a dismissive wave.

"Well then say no more ladies. This is all the money I've made running that diner on the corner of Minetta Street," Jack pronounced as he took out a thick stack of cash from his wallet and smacked it on the coffee table.

"Jack what about—,"

"Stop. We're in this together now. We suffer together, we die together, we live together," Jack interjected and then opened up the fridge and poured himself a glass of lemonade.

"Thank you mon chéri," Faye said to Jack with a warm smile as she slowly walked over to him.

"You look like you've been through a war," Jack remarked in a somber tone.

"So do you mon chéri," Faye remarked with a warm smile and then placed her hand on Jack's cheek.

"I didn't think the three of us would ever be together again," I pronounced and then wrapped my arms around Faye and Jack. "Hayley why are you wearing my dress?" Faye inquired. "Yes kid, why are you wearing her dress," Jack inquired. "I didn't think we were going to make rent this month so I—,"

"No don't tell me you resorted to that," Faye inquired in a stern tone.

"I didn't go through with it. Jack intervened right when a man showed me interest," I replied.

"I'll always be there to intervene when a man shows interest in you, kid," Jack said with a snicker and then finished drinking his glass of lemonade.

"I'm so sorry mon chéri. Listen to me … I do not want that thought to ever cross your mind again. No matter how terrible things may seem, selling your body is something a young intelligent woman like you should never do," Faye said to me as she stared intently at me while placing her hands on my shoulders.

"You did it and you were much older than me," I said to Faye. Jack then laughed in response to Faye as he walked over to the window with a sigh.

"I cannot undo the bad choices I've made in life, and now you see what penance god has in store for me, but you mon chéri, you must be better than me," Faye said to me in a somber tone as her face began to quiver. Ever since Faye contracted the virus know as the most aggressive and deadly form of H.I.V every word she spoke to me seemed like it could be her last, and I held on to her every word because I still feared the day would come when I would no longer hear her beautiful words reassuring me whenever I lost all hope in life.

"What Faye is trying to say is that you should learn from us kid," Jack said to me as he lit a cigarette and took a smoke while staring out the living room window.

"Jack, you're limping, what's wrong," Faye inquired.

I noticed Jack's limp as well right when we met on the street corner, but I didn't mention it to him. I'm sure if Jack wanted to tell me he would've, but he rarely opens up to me.

"I got shot in the ankle by a fucking Cossack working for the Five Points Gang," Jack pronounced.

"Oh my god, does it hurt every day?" I inquired in a wide-eyed stare.

"Only when I think about the pain, then it burns like the fires of hell," Jack replied.

"How many more bullets can you take mon chéri?" Faye inquired in a somber tone.

"Just one, just one more bullet than Mr. Luciano can take," Jack replied.

"You plan on killing him. That is suicide. The times I've spent batting my eyes with Mr. Luciano I've learned a great deal of the measure of his will. If you become him, then you lose," Faye said to Jack as she slowly walked over to the window and placed her hand on his shoulder.

"There's no way out for me Faye. You and Hayley are my life. I won't bend to his will, not now, not ever," Jack said as he shook his head.

"He won't stop will he," I said to Jack. "I'm afraid not kid," Jack replied.

"Then let's leave this town. The three of us can go west far beyond Mr. Luciano's reach," I said to Jack.

"I had that choice given to me by the FBI kid and I chose to be here with you and Faye. I'm not going to flee," Jack said to me in a stern tone.

"Then it's just as you said, we're in this together," I said to Jack.

"I wouldn't have it any other way mon chéri," Faye said to me with a warm smile.

"Mr. Luciano may have all of his of mobsters at his beck and call, but I have two of the toughest ladies in New York," Jack pronounced with a grin.

*****

Dear Diary,
April 3rd, 3:47 PM,

It had been two weeks since Jack stumbled back into me and Faye's life, and the three of us were inseparable ever since. These precious moments of hearing Jack and Faye bicker in a lighthearted and flirtatious manner were reminiscent of the times I spent back at the speakeasy. Hearing them flirt with each other warmed my heart. It was almost as if I had a mother and father.

Jack made it clear to me and Faye that a waitress he used to work with would be staring in a Broadway musical this month and he couldn't miss the show. So Jack would regularly drive through Broadway just to see if the show was advertized on billboards. Faye seemed in good spirits ever since Jack returned, almost as if a missing piece of her personality was now whole from Jack's return.

*****

"What's her name again," I inquired.

"Dottie Lee Harper," Jack replied, as we drove down Broadway.

"What's the name of the play she's in?" Faye inquired. "Barflies," Jack replied.

"I do not see it mon chéri," Faye remarked.

"Oh I forgot Barflies is off Broadway. I know where we need to go now ladies, but we can't linger there. You never know who could be following us," Jack pronounced.

I was worried that mobsters could be following us, but with Jack and Faye with me I felt as safe as a girl my age could feel in this town.

"Is she pretty?" I inquired. "Is who pretty?" Jack replied.

"That actress you worked with at the diner?" I replied with a grin as I leaned my head forward between Jack and Faye.

"She's not bad to look at," Jack remarked.

"That means Jack is smitten with her," Faye said with a giggle.

"Dottie is a fine young woman and I—,"

"Oh is that it, look," I interjected as I pointed at a small marquee reading: Barflies the musical opening April 22nd.

"That's it," Jack pronounced.

"What a quaint little theatre," Faye remarked as Jack slowly drove past the small theatre on Cherry Lane.

"So you're not going to go inside," I inquired as I stared intently at the front door of the theatre, but couldn't see any actors behind the rose-tinted glass.

"I can't, I can't put Dottie in danger, not when she's about to fulfill her dreams," Jack replied in a somber tone as he continued to drive slowly past the theatre.

"Oh pour l'amour de Dieu," Faye pronounced and then stomped down on the brake pedal sending Jack's Chevrolet halting in front of the theatre.

"Hayley go. Jack is too busy feeling sorry for himself to be supportive to the ones he claims he cares about," Faye said to me In a stern tone as she gestured for me to exit the car.

"Don't worry Jack. I won't draw attention to myself, I'll be quick," I said to Jack with a smile as I exited the car. "Goddamn it," Jack shouted as I scampered to the front door of the theatre.

I was so excited to see her, but I had to be quick, I didn't want to bring any danger to Ms. Harper either, and I know the Five points Gang know what I look like just as much as Jack even if I'm not their number one target like Jack is.

"Uhm is Ms. Harper here?" I inquired.

"It depends, who might you be?" a man wearing glasses and a white scarf wrapped around his neck inquired with a stern look.

"I'm Jack Dansby's niece Hayley Carmona," I replied in a timid tone, as two scantily- dressed women scampered past me with a giggle.

"Well well so you're Jack's niece. I'm Lorenzo Calderon the playwright of this musical. So why do you need to see one of my leading actresses?" the man inquired.

"I just want to pass a message from Jack to Ms. Harper.

"Why couldn't Jack pass that message himself?" Mr. Calderon inquired.

"It's a long story I'm sure you don't have the time for," I replied.

"You're right about that my dear. Dottie, Dottie, you have a visitor," Mr. Calderon shouted as he snapped his fingers and pointed at me.

"Who is it Mr. Calderon," a woman dressed in a sparkly red and gold sequin bra with matching bottoms inquired with a wide-eyed stare as she scampered over to me.

She was more beautiful than I even imagined, Ms, Dottie Lee Harper with her short curly blonde hair, big blue eyes which seemed to reflect all of the stage lighting in almost a magical way, and not to mention her curvaceous body. Woman like her were meant for the stage and screen, and I found myself nervous just being around a woman of her upper echelon.

"Oh my god your hair is a triumph to all women honey," Dottie remarked with a smile.

"Oh t—thank you. You must be Ms. Harper. You don't know me but I'm Jack Dansby's niece and I—,"

"Oh my god where is Jack now. Is he all right," Ms, Harper interjected in a distressed tone as she kneeled down and grabbed me by the shoulders.

"He's all right. We're together now. Jack wanted me to tell you that he will be there opening night to see your show," I said to Ms. Harper.

"I owe your uncle a great deal sweetheart, but he up and left me. I could never repay him for how he helped me get cast in this musical, but this is a start, here honey," Ms. Harper said to me as she handed me two tickets.

"Thank you. I see now why Jack helped you. He wants to see your dreams come true despite his dreams being only memories now," I said to Ms. Harper with a warm smile. "He's a loving man. I hope I see him again," Ms. Harper said in a somber tone as her eyes began to well up with tears. "Dottie while you're still young!" Mr. Calderon shouted. "I'll be right there Mr. Calderon!" Ms. Harper shouted. "He wants to see you again too, but, you know all about—," "I know, I know. In the meantime, give Jack this for me," Ms. Harper said to me and then kissed me firmly on the lips as the taste of cherries and smoke was imbued onto my lips.

"Oh uhm … all right. Thank you so much for the tickets to your show," I said to Ms. Harper in a flustered tone and flushed face.

I then exited the theatre and walked around the corner to where I presumed Jack was parked.

"Get in kid!" Jack shouted as I saw him slowly drive by past the theatre.

"She's wonderful Jack," I remarked with a smile as I entered the car.

"She sure is," Jack said to me.

"She gave me two tickets to her show," I said to Jack as I handed him the tickets.

"Is that all she gave you mon chéri?" Faye inquired with a smile as she pointed to her lips.

"Oh uhm there was something else she wanted me to give Jack but uhm …," I said with a smile as Faye stared back at me with a grin.

I felt uncomfortable kissing Jack on the lips, but maybe Faye could help me.

I then whispered into Faye's ear what Ms. Harper wanted me to give to Jack.

"Oh say no more mon chéri," Faye said to me with a smile. "Jack this is from Ms. Harper," Faye said to Jack and then kissed him firmly on the mouth in the exact same manner which Ms. Harper kissed me.

"All right then let's go home ladies," Jack pronounced with a smile as Faye and I giggled.

*****

It was 5:07 PM as Faye, Jack, and I entered the apartment.

"Oh no," I spoke aloud as Faye and Jack stared intently at me.

"What's wrong kid," Jack inquired.

"Ms. Harper only gave me two tickets to her show," I replied as I held out the tickets in my hand.

"What's wrong with that, mon chéri?" Faye inquired.

"That means we won't all be together," I replied.

"Ah don't worry, mon chéri. I can handle myself for two hours. Besides I have Sable to keep me company," Faye said to me with a sigh as she sat down on the sofa and picked up Sable.

"Two hours is more than enough time for a mobster from the Five Points Gang to break into this apartment and silence you, just like they did …," Jack said to Faye in a somber tone as his voice trailed off before walking over to the kitchen and pouring himself another glass of lemonade.

"Don't try to scare me, mon chéri. If those brutes believe that a sickly French woman and her cat are a threat to their organization then they can go ahead and silence me," Faye said to Jack as she lit a cigarette and took a smoke.

"I should've asked Ms. Harper for three tickets. Then we wouldn't be fighting now," I said to Jack in a somber tone.

"You have nothing to apologize for kid. So Faye … do you have a death wish?" Jack inquired as he sat down on the chair across from Faye.

"Why would you think that?" Faye inquired in a stern tone.

"First you demanded Hayley take you out of Bellevue, now you want to be in this apartment alone for two hours knowing all too well that a mobster is just waiting for that opportunity," Jack replied.

I could see it in Jack's eyes, he cared about Faye, but he always had difficulty making sure the people he loved know how much he cares for them, so he was hostile towards her.

"Maybe we shouldn't go to Ms. Harper's show," I pronounced to break the tension of Jack and Faye staring daggers at each other.

"No Hayley you and Jack have a good time at the show. Jack is just being a baby as usual," Faye said to me.

"I'm not going," Jack pronounced in a stern tone.

"You said that you wouldn't miss her show for the world," I said to Jack.

"True, but I would miss it in order to keep you two safe," Jack pronounced.

"That is very sweet Jack, but we cannot let those men dictate the rest of our lives. We must live, not under fear of them, but with as much joy in any way we can find it. This musical is a beautiful and life-affirming event and it would be a sin to pass it up," Faye said to Jack.

"We'll flip a coin then," Jack said to Faye.

"Very well, I'll call it," Faye said to Jack.

"Heads I go with Hayley to the show, tails you go," Jack said and then flipped the coin in the air.

"Tails," Faye pronounced, as the coin flipped in the air.

"Tails it is," Jack said with a grin.

"I'm sorry Jack," I said to Jack in a somber tone.

"Don't worry about it kid. I'll catch Dottie's show one way or another," Jack said to me with a dismissive wave.

"Jack, Ms. Harper wants to see you at her show more than us. Are you sure you don't want to reconsider?" Faye inquired as she stood up from the sofa and walked over to Jack who was wiping down the kitchen counter in the same manner he used to do at the speakeasy.

Jack then wrapped his arm around Faye's waist and kissed her forehead. It was as if I was watching a movie and Jack and Faye were the leading roles.

"Jack … was that for Ms. Harper?" Faye inquired in a flirty tone and a smile as she rested her head against Jack's chest.

"No it was for you," Jack replied with a grin.

Jack, Faye and I were different people now than when we all first met last summer. Back then we were all actors performing for each other, afraid to show our true selves. Now we are all bare with our naked fears exposed. My mother was right about Jack.

When I first read the letter she wrote to me before she died telling me that there was good in Jack, I thought that she was crazy. Now I see Jack through my mother's eyes. It was very difficult at times, but Faye and I managed to open up Jack's heart. Jack, Faye, and I are all broken souls, but together we form a whole. Our individual pains complement one another in such a beautiful way I didn't think was possible.

*****

"How many eggs do you want?" Jack inquired as he cooked breakfast, while Faye was playing with Sable.

"Uhm, I'll have two," I replied.

"You should eat more mon chéri. You're looking skinnier," Faye remarked.

"I think she's just getting taller. I would bet you've grown at least an inch over the past year," Jack said to me with a grin as he slid the over easy eggs along with hash browns onto my plate.

I had a family again. I couldn't remember the last time that feeling of a loving family warmed me from within, but I never wanted it to go away. I didn't think about the Five Points Gang when I was with Jack and Faye, and we three were inseparable, so my mind was always at ease. Is this what a normal girl my age feels like all the time?

"Faye is right. We need all the strength we can get," Jack said to me.

"Faye needs the strength more than I do," I said to Jack and then took a small bite of eggs, as he stared at Faye with a sad look in his eyes.

"I hope you two aren't talking about me. I feel stronger today than I have in the past week," Faye said to me.

"That's wonderful Faye," I remarked with a warm smile.

A sudden knock on the door then sparked me Jack, and Faye's attention, as we all stared at the front door of the apartment.

"Who could it be?" I inquired.

"It couldn't be a mobster. They would never knock on the front door," Jack replied as he grabbed his gun from between his belt and slowly walked to the side of the door.

"You know you should really invest in a holster mon chéri. Tucking that weapon right against your manhood could be disastrous," Faye said to Jack.

"Shhh ... who is it?" Jack inquired in a stern tone.

"It's Gracie, Jack. Gracie Bishop. Please for the love of god let me it," a woman's voice replied.

Jack then peered through the peephole of the door with his gun pressed firmly against the door which began to make me nervous again.

"It is Gracie, but how do we know she's alone. That dame is a damn spy for Avery last I recall," Jack said in a whispering tone as Faye and I gathered closely around him.

"All right, I'll unlock and open the door, you two stay behind me," Jack said in a whispering tone.

What I remember about Gracie Bishop was that she was a warm and beautiful woman with a singing voice to match, but could we trust her now. After all we don't know if she's still the same woman I remembered her to be.

"Faye," Gracie remarked with a smile as Jack unlocked and opened the door.

"Gracie it's been too long mon chéri," Faye said to Gracie, but I couldn't see Gracie in the doorway on account of Jack holding me with his free hand, as if Gracie Bishop was an incredibly dangerous woman.

"Don't move Gracie. Hands up, now," Jack said to Gracie in a stern tone.

"Jack, give her—,"

"Shut up. What I remember about Ms. Bishop is that she played me for a fool. She was gathering information on me as I employed her at my speakeasy," Jack interjected in a stern tone. "You played yourself for a fool Jack. Now put the gun down so we can all talk like civilized adults, not like monkeys with guns," Faye remarked with a scoff.

"I'll put my gun down right after you search Gracie for any weapons," Jack said to Faye in a stern tone as he continued to point his gun at Gracie.

"I expected nothing less from you Jack. Our last encounter was rather brief but you're still just as cold as that first snowfall of the year," Gracie said to Jack.

"She has a gun," Faye said to Jack.

"Hand it over," Jack said to Faye in a stern tone.

"Now can we talk Jack, or do you require me handcuffed and chained to the wall," Gracie inquired.

"Let go … Gracie," I remarked with a smile as I broke free from Jack's grasp and hugged Gracie.

"Well I hold all the cards now so sit down and tell me on whose behalf I owe your visit to," Jack said to Gracie.

"I was worried about Hayley and Faye. Jack … I am here on my own behalf. Every day I hear various mobsters mention at least one of you three in the speakeasy," Gracie replied as she took off her black trench coat with a sigh, revealing a crimson blouse and sharp black skirt.

"I knew it! So you do work for them now," Jack said in a stern tone as he pointed his gun at Gracie just as we four were about to sit down.

"Let her explain Jack. Like you said, you hold all the cards right now," Faye said to Jack in a stern tone followed by a series of wrenching coughs.

"Very well, so tell me Gracie, what are they planning? I know Leo is constantly trying to put the fear of god into me, but what that lug head Italian doesn't realize is that I have information on his boss, information I doubt that even you and those smoky eyes of yours managed to gather," Jack said to Gracie with a grin.

"Whatever information you have on Mr. Luciano won't help you. Mr. Luciano is planning a full assault on you three, but if he fails to kill you Jack, then I fear Faye and Hayley will serve as a bargaining chip," Gracie said as she took out a cigarette hesitantly and took a smoke.

"Tell us something we don't know Gracie. We didn't need you to tell us this information," Jack said to Gracie in a stern tone.

"So what's this information you have on Mr. Luciano Jack?" Gracie inquired.

"You must think I'm really stupid. I will only reveal that information when the time is right," Jack replied with a snicker. What information did Jack have on Mr. Luciano, and was it information that could keep us safe? Even though I understood why Jack always had difficulty trusting people, I hope he realizes before the end who his family and who his enemies truly are.

"If I let you go. How do I know you won't report directly back to Mr. Luciano?" Jack inquired in a stern tone.

"You don't. I took that risk coming here, in fear of you shooting me down as you've shot down many mobsters who have tried to kill you over the past year," Gracie replied.

"Don't you dare," I said to Jack in a stern tone as I stepped in front of Gracie with my arms spread out.

"Don't I dare what, protect us from this spy. I know you're smart enough to know what she's capable, kid," Jack said to me in a stern tone.

"We're all capable of evil, but that doesn't mean we are," I said to Jack in a stern tone.

"Hayley's right. Gracie hasn't betrayed us for her own personal gain. If anything she is risking her life all for our safety," Faye said to Jack as she stood up from the sofa and slowly walked over to me.

"So what now Gracie, will you continue to work at the speakeasy that I built for the very man who will stop at nothing to silence me?" Jack inquired.

"I will continue to survive in this man's world Jack, now if you're going to silence me then do it now. I don't want to be shot in the back," Gracie said in a stern tone as she pushed her way through me and Faye.

"Gracie, please be careful," I said to Gracie.

"Gracie …," Faye said to Gracie and then whispered in her ear before she kissed her cheek.

"Already keeping secrets from me huh," Jack said with a scoff.

"Must you always be the center of attention," Faye said to Jack.

"You're lucky these two favor you, Gracie. Or I wouldn't hesitate to silence you," Jack said to Gracie as he lowered his gun and tucked it between the waistband of his pants.

"Take care of yourself Jack, in any way you see fit. Faye, Hayley. I hope you both live long and beautiful lives," Gracie pronounced with a smile.

"Hayley most definitely will, au revoir mon chéri," Faye said to Gracie with a warm smile as she exited the apartment, but Faye's remark left me heartbroken once again as the realization of her illness weighed down on me once again.

"Hayley," Faye said to me in a distressed tone as she reached out her thin, pale arm towards me as I scampered into her bedroom as tears began to stream from my eyes.

I hated it when Faye talked that way. I didn't want to accept it, but Faye always seemed to remind me just when I found myself happy enough to where I forgot she even had such an illness.

"Oh it's you," I remarked in a sobbing tone as I lay in Faye's bed.

"Yes it's me kid, don't look so happy," Jack said with a scoff as he entered Faye's bedroom.

"Why does she have to talk like that?" I inquired, as I sat upright in bed.

"Faye … she's a sharp woman, but she doesn't want to live a lie. She and I have that in common. She knows that sickness of hers will kill her sooner or later, but she always wants to prepare you for when she's gone," Jack said to me as he sat down on the bed beside me.

"Did grandma prepare you when grandpa died in the war?" I inquired in a somber tone.

"No I wasn't lucky enough to have a mother as loving and considerate as Faye is to you, but she tried her best. When my father died, it was like a blow to the head for me, my sister and my mother. During war there is always that possibility of your loved ones not returning, but my mother had me believe that my father would return some day, I just wish it wasn't in a casket," Jack replied as he lit a cigarette and took a smoke.

"I hate imagining her gone. It's like imagining a part of me dying along with her, the very best part of me," I said to Jack as my sobbing rose to a level which made me lie back down in bed and soak the pillow with my tears.

"You've been so strong for Faye, kid. Now you must continue to show her that strength. When her time comes god forbid it be tomorrow or a year from now, you will have no regrets knowing that you were there for her every step of the way," Jack said to me as he placed his hand on my quivering shoulder.

"I'm glad you're here Jack," I said to Jack in a somber tone as I sat upright in bed once again and quickly wrapped my arms around Jack.

"There's nowhere else I want to be kid, trust me I've looked," Jack said to me with a snicker as we continued to hug for a few more precious moments.

*****

It was 7:26 PM as Faye, Jack, and I drove down Broadway to a most heart-warming sight.

"Oh look, it appears that shows are returning to Broadway," Faye remarked with a series of coughs.

"That's a sign of hope for this city if I've ever seen one," Jack remarked.

"Tomorrow is Ms. Harper's big day," I pronounced with a smile as I poked my head up front between Faye and Jack. "Yes opening night. She has rehearsed her entire life for this moment … I wish her luck," Jack said in a somber tone.

I knew Jack wanted to see Ms. Harper perform in her debut musical, despite his brash attitude towards Broadway shows, he cared for Ms. Harper, and I could hear it in the tone of his voice.

"It's not fair," I remarked in a somber tone. "What's not fair?" Jack inquired.

"We all should see Ms. Harper's show together," I replied.

"Life's not fair, kid. I will see Dottie's show come hell or high water, but tomorrow I want you two to have a good time.

"Faye … Faye how are you feeling?" I inquired in a somber tone and wide-eyed stare as Faye began to rest her head on my shoulder.

"Weak," Faye replied in a faint tone.

"Jack we have to go home. Faye is not well," I said to Jack in a distressed tone. Under normal circumstances sleep was always a good thing, but I recognized that look on Faye's pale face, it was the same heartbreaking look she had the day I rushed her to Bellevue just before she went into a coma.

"Hang on Faye," Jack said in a stern tone as he took a sharp turn and sped up southeast towards the apartment.

"Come on stay with us Faye," I said to Faye in a distressed tone as her faint appearance seemed to slip in and out of consciousness.

"Should we take her back to Bellevue?" Jack inquired in a distressed tone.

"No, no, Faye swore to me that she doesn't want to die in that hospital, but could you get more of the medication Dr. Schuster had Faye take when she was in a coma after you drop us off at the apartment?" I inquired as Jack pulled up in front of the entrance of *Magnolia Towers*.

"Sure thing kid, I'll get that medication from that Doctor if I have to beat it out of him," Jack said to me as he picked up Faye in the manner of a princess and rushed her into the apartment.

"Lay her down in bed," I said to Jack as I opened the door of the apartment to the sight of Sable staring out the living room window before he meowed in a concerned tone and walked over to me, Jack and Faye.

"She's burning up. I be right back with that medication," Jack said with a wide-eyed stare as he felt Faye's pale glistening forehead.

Jack then ran out of the apartment as if his life depended on it, but he knew all too well Faye's life was once again hanging in the balance and once again I was left holding her hand as I sat at her bedside.

"Jack is getting more of your medication Faye. Please, please stay with us," I said to Faye in a somber tone as my eyes welled up with tears.

*****

Jack returned in fifteen minutes with medication which we managed to get Faye to take despite her near comatose condition. Faye's fever then soon subsided, but she was still too weak to stand up, so she remained in bed as Jack and I remained at her bedside along with Sable.

"I ... I'm sorry to scare you once again mon chéri," Faye said to me as she sat upright in bed.

"I'm just glad to see you awake and talking to me," I said to Faye with a smile as my face quivered.

"There's the drama queen. How are you feeling Faye?" Jack inquired as he entered the bedroom with a cup of tea which he placed on the nightstand beside Faye.

"You're my hero Jack," Faye said to Jack with a grin.

"Hayley would've done the same thing without threatening the Doctor too," Jack said to Faye with a grin.

"Faye, do you feel well enough to go to Ms. Harpers show tomorrow," I inquired.

"I will let Jack know when the time comes if he should take my ticket, but I don't want to miss that show for the world," Faye replied.

"Then you would be here alone," I said to Faye with a wide-eyed stare.

"We've been over this mon chéri, if those mobsters feel that a sickly French woman is a threat to them then they can put me out of my misery," Faye said to me as her trembling hand grasped the cup of tea. Jack then quickly supported Faye's hand as he guided the cup to her pale chapped lips.

"What a gentleman. Are you sure this is your uncle or a man who looks just like him?" Faye said to me with a grin.

Jack was indeed more gallant than I've ever seen him before, which gave me peace of mind knowing that he would be there for Faye. I've never seen Jack act this way over a woman before. That's when I saw it in his eyes, that warm and nurturing look that is unmistakable even to a young woman like me, Jack loves Faye, and now he's finally showing her that love he's reserved for years.

*****

"I feel much better," Faye remarked as she walked over to me and Jack in the kitchen as we made breakfast of French toast.

"You look much better as well. You have color in your cheeks," Jack remarked with a smile.

"So do you mon chéri," Faye remarked as she pinched Jack's cheek and then kissed him on the mouth.

"Are you well enough to attend Ms. Harper's show tonight at 8PM," I inquired as I dipped a thick slice of bread into the eggs.

"Qui, like my mother always said 'If you're not healthy enough to dance then you're not healthy,'" Faye replied.

"Well far be it from me to criticize your mother," Jack said with a snicker as he playfully shoved me.

"Well who is going to dance with me now, or do I have to dance with Sable?" Faye pronounced with a grin and her hands on her hips.

"All right, all right, I'm coming," Jack said to Faye with a grin as he scampered over to Faye as she put a record on the victrola.

I have never seen Jack dance before. It was as if Faye was bringing out such a beauty from within him, a beauty that was guarded during all those days he worked at the speakeasy, I see that all Jack ever wanted was to be close to Faye. He didn't have that opportunity when she was in good health at the speakeasy flirting with countless men who Jack deemed as 'ignorant aristocrats'. Jack now had Faye all to himself, and the sight of them dancing together in such a clumsy yet beautiful manner brought me to tears.

"What's this dance called?" Jack inquired.

"It's called a waltz mon chéri. Now keep your back straight and your chin up. I don't want your eyes wandering down," Faye replied with a giggle.

I wanted that heartwarming moment in time to last forever. Watching Faye teach Jack how to dance the Waltz was exactly what my heart needed. I don't have any memories of my mother having a heartwarming moment with Johnny or Fernando, it was always fear.

"That's enough. You have much to learn mon chéri, but I commend your effort," Faye said to Jack with a giggle.

"That feels like a high society type of dance. The type that you Europeans do in your castles," Jack remarked.

"I've only ever danced that dance with my mother when I was a child," Faye said to Jack with a smile as she primped her hair in front of the mirror.

Even though Faye's relationship with her mother wasn't the perfect portrait of love, she still finds ways to keep her memory alive. This in turn made me wonder how I'm keeping the memory of my mother alive.

"My sister loved to dance. I remember once Dezerae and I were at a club on the lower east side and she wanted to swing dance with me, but I turned her down and kept drinking shot after shot of bourbon. She then went on to dance with some scumbag who after only a few minutes treated her as if she was his property," Jack said with a scoff as he shook his head.

"Why didn't you dance with her? I inquired in a somber tone as I walked up to Jack as he stared pensively out the living room window.

"I don't know … at the time drinking was just part of my identity. I didn't want to be a part of her world," Jack replied in a somber tone.

"Just look how much you've grown now mon chéri," Faye remarked with a smile.

"Sure and it only took a liquor outlaw and my sister's death. Heavy price to pay just to learn how to dance," Jack said to Faye in a somber tone.

"Faye's right, you're not the same Jack I first met at the hospital the day after my mother died," I remarked.

"Well I just hope this Jack doesn't cower when the chips are down," Jack said to me with a grin as he placed his hand on my shoulder and then entered Faye's bedroom.

Oh we have to get ready for the musical," Faye remarked with a smile as she sprung up from the sofa in such a zealous manner.

"What are you going to wear?" I inquired with a smile.

"I will wear a dress that shows the world I still have plenty of life left to live," Faye replied with a smile.

"May I wear one of your dresses for tonight?" I inquired.

"Of course you may mon chéri. Come now I'll help you pick one out," Faye replied with a smile as she took my hand as we entered her bedroom.

*****

It was 7:58 PM as Faye and I exited the bedroom.

"You two look dressed to kill," Jack remarked with a grin as Faye and I walked up to him in the kitchen. Faye wore a beautiful sheer, low-cut, black dress with a maroon shall which draped over her shoulders and a matching black hat with small maroon feathers. Faye's lipstick and eye shadow were also maroon, which all came together in such a stunning visual that only Faye could portray to the world.

Faye kept insisting for me to wear her dark green dress she bought at a boutique when she was visiting her cousin in Paris. She told me that the contrast of my red hair against the dark green dress will draw all eyes towards me. Faye and I were going to the theatre after all, so now was the time to show the world the measure of women we were.

"We don't want to be late. Let's go mon chéri," Faye said to me as she grabbed her purse and primped her hair.

"Jack, will you be all right," I inquired.

"I'll be just fine kid. Now you two go and have a good time," Jack replied.

I couldn't help but worry for Jack's safety as Faye and I exited the apartment. We were strongest when we were all together, and not having Jack with us as we attended Ms. Harper's musical didn't make the experience feel complete.

"Let's take a taxicab," Faye said to me and then whistled loudly as one drove towards us on the corner of West 10th Street.

"Where are you two beautiful ladies headed?" the taxicab driver inquired.

"To the Cherry Lane Theatre," Faye replied.

"I hope Ms. Harper's musical receives a grand reception," I said to Faye.

"Well this is an off-Broadway show so don't expect it to be anything like a Midsummer Night's Dream," Faye said to me.

"That play was beautiful, but the person I was sharing it with was awful," I remarked as the disgusting thought of Stefano crossed my mind.

"Nous sommes là," Faye pronounced as the taxicab parked in front of the Cherry Lane Theatre which was glowing with such a radiance that rivaled any Broadway show. Faye then paid the fare to the taxicab driver and exited the taxicab.

"Tickets please," a man in a booth at the entrance of the Cherry Lane Theatre pronounced as Faye and I waited in line among the other finely dressed theatre attendees. Faye then reached into her purse and took out the two tickets which Ms. Harper gave to me and handed them to the man in the booth.

"The show will begin momentarily. The man said to Faye with a smile as he handed her back the tickets after he tore off the bottom portions of them.

"I'm so excited for Ms. Harper," I said to Faye with a smile as we walked down the main isle of the theatre to the sight of a closed scarlet curtain.

"Yes It must be nice to fulfill your dream," Faye said to me as she stared pensively at the empty stage as we sat down in our seats.

"Oh my god, look," I said to Faye as I pointed at the seat next to me which had a sign over it that read 'RESERVED FOR JACK DANSBY.'

"How wonderful, Ms. Harper reserved a seat for Jack," Faye remarked.

"I wish he was here with us. Ms. Harper told me that she wouldn't be on that stage if it wasn't for Jack getting her the opportunity," I said to Faye as she lit a cigarette and took a smoke.

"Jack the dream maker. It's a shame that he chose not to attend," Faye said to me.

"I know he will regret it, even if he pretends not to," I said to Faye.

"It's starting," Faye said to me as she tapped me on the arm.

"Ladies and gentleman I present to you Barflies, a tale of three sisters trying to make their way through this turbulent world," a man dressed in a tuxedo pronounced with his arms spread out. The man then bowed and exited the stage.

"Oh that's Ms. Harper," I said to Faye with a smile as the scarlet curtain rose to the sight of Ms. Harper dressed in a wine dress sitting at a bar with her leg stretched out, exposing ripped pantyhose.

"Oh she's beautiful," Faye remarked.

"I think you've had enough Izzy," the barkeep remarked. "It's   never enough Armando," Ms. Harper playing a character name Izzy said to the barkeep in a somber tone. "You just have to come to grips with it darling. He's not coming back," Armando said to Izzy.

"Don't lecture me Armando, and just what makes you such an expert on love?" Izzy inquired in a distressed tone and then finished the last of her cocktail and then placed her head in her hand, propping herself up on the bar.

"I said you've had enough," the barkeep said in a stern tone as he grabbed the cocktail glass away from Izzy's clutches in an aggressive manner.

A spotlight then shown on Izzy as she slowly stood up from the barstool, signaling a most heartbreaking and profound ballad.

"One more glass, one more bout
One more drink to numb the pain.
You men only hear me when I shout!
Oh sure I flout but not in vain!
The memory of him can never be drowned
So within this bottle I'll keep him around."

("You've had enough, Izzy!")

"It's never enough!"

("Go sleep it off Izzy!")

"You think you're so tough.
Just do your job honey-
and keep my glass full.
Here take all this money
and suffer a fool."

"I was told this is my seat," a familiar voice said to me. "Jack, you're here!" I remarked as my face lit up with joy at the sight of Jack standing in front of me with a grin.

"Jack I'm so happy you joined us. Ms. Harper is marvelous," Faye remarked as she pointed to Ms. Harper singing her beautiful and heart-wrenching ballad which was already making my eyes well up with tears.

"So what changed your mind mon chéri?" Faye inquired.

"It's just as you said, 'it would be a sin to pass up this event' and I'm not about to let those mobster bastards dictate my life. We're in this together," Jack replied with a grin. I then wrapped my arms around Jack's waist, as he stared at Mr. Harper on stage for a brief moment of silence, as she stared back at him with a warm smile.

"It's never enough! It's never enough!
My sister told me he couldn't be tamed
Though I loved him dearly-
with a heart unashamed."

("Don't make me do this Izzy!")

"It's never enough!"

("All right let's go Izzy!")

"Damn don't be so rough!"

The barkeep then retrained Izzy in an aggressive manner as she began to cry and then tossed her out the bar. The scarlet curtains then dropped as Jack was the first attendee to rise from his seat and applaud and whistle.

"Go get' em Dottie!" Jack shouted with a smile, as Faye and I joined him as we stood up and applauded.

Ms. Harper was captivating, I could tell she was born to perform, and Jack's selfless act of getting her this role was nothing short of a saintly act. Despite the liquor outlaw act, and the rampant homelessness, I believe there's still so much goodness in this city, a goodness that can prevail and make a woman's dreams come true and Jack and Ms. Harper are a testament to that very goodness.

"I told you Dottie would knock it out of the park," Jack remarked with a smile.

"This is only act one and she's already brought me to tears," Faye remarked, as she wiped the tears from her eyes in a delicate manner not to smear her maroon eye shadow.

"Me too," I said to Faye with a warm smile.

Shhh, act two is starting," Jack said with a smile as he point to the scarlet curtain rising to the sight of two women sitting in a very drab apartment which made Faye's apartment look like a suite by comparison.

"Oh again Izzy, I told you Armando wouldn't stand for the three of us getting feisty in his bar," one woman with curly black hair wearing a beige dress with a tear in the sleeve said to Izzy as she entered the apartment.

"D-Don't act as if you didn't get thrown out of a bar last night Louise," Izzy said to the woman as she stumbled across the living room floor.

"I did no such thing," Louise said to Izzy as she primped her hair in the mirror.

"Then explain that tear in your dress," Izzy said to Louise with a grin.

"Perhaps one of her suitors was rather rough with her last night," a woman with wavy amber hair wearing a white nightgown remarked with a snicker as she lit a cigarette and took a smoke.

"It's an old dress. Don't shame me for not having the finest clothing,

Mable," Louise said to the woman in the white nightgown as she draped her arm over Izzy with a smile.

"None of us have nice clothing. I've made peace with that," Izzy said with a belch.

"You need to sit down, honey. Mable said to Izzy.

"I'm fine Mable. You need to stop treating me like a ...," Izzy said as she slowly fell forward onto the sofa which brought an outburst of laughter all throughout the audience including me, Jack and Faye.

"She's funny too," I remarked with a giggle.

"Oh Izzy what are we going to do with you?" Mable pronounced while shaking her head as she stared at her younger sister passed out face-down into the sofa.

"Let her sleep," Louise said with a dismissive wave.

The scarlet curtain then closed, signaling the end of act two, which left Faye, Jack and I speechless. Once again Jack was the first attendee to rise from his seat and vigorously applaud and whistle in the manner of a proud father watching his daughter perform on stage for the first time.

"Can we smoke in here?" Faye inquired as she took out a cigarette from her purse.

"This is off Broadway Faye, just look around, you may do whatever the hell you please," Jack replied with a grin.

I then noticed many people smoking as I stared at the audience behind me. This atmosphere was much different compared to 'A Midsummer Night's Dream' on Broadway. It was more raw and intimate. There were no pretenses or formalities demanded by the attendees. I found this experience to be most comforting and liberating as I stared with a wide- eyed gaze at the scarlet curtain.

"It's starting," I said with a smile as the scarlet curtain began to rise, signaling the start of act three.

Act three began with Izzy and her two sisters walking down a street backdrop which felt so familiar to me, as if I've walked down the same street many times before.

"Forget about him, honey. Just because you gave him your heart, doesn't mean he owns you. Take back your heart. I know it's in there somewhere," Mable said to Izzy, as men whistled down at Izzy and her three sisters while shouting salacious remarks.

"I'll feel better once I've had at least half a bottle of wine," Izzy said to Mable, as Louise shouted obscenities up at the men to silence them. Like an owner would shout at their dogs to get them to stop barking. This made Jack burst out with laughter, which in turn made me and Faye giggle.

I've never seen women portrayed in such a raw manner in the way that 'Barflies' portrays them, but It felt much more real to me, almost as if I could be friends with any of those woman on the stage.

"Izzy we've been thrown out of every bar within a twenty mile radius. If you need to slake that thirst then you're going to have to buy a bottle of wine at a liquor store," Louise said to Izzy, as she primped her hair.

"Not every bar Louise. After Armando tossed me out of his bar last night like a bag of garbage he told me that the Sapphire Lounge was looking for a woman like me," Izzy said to Louise. "Well let's go then. If the Sapphire lounge is looking for a woman like Izzy then they're also looking for a woman like me," Louise said with a smile.

"Me too," Mable said with a smile as she hailed a cab by sticking her leg out and pulling up her skirt, exposing her stocking covered leg which seemed to glimmer against the streetlights.

"To the Sapphire Lounge my good man," Louise said to the cabdriver as he quickly halted his taxicab at the sight of Mable's exposed leg. The scarlet curtain then slowly closed as the three sisters entered the taxicab, signaling the end of act three.

'Barflies' was as profound as it was humorous. The perfect blend of all those moments which everyday people experience. "Jack, what city is this musical set in?" Faye inquired with a cough.

"It's set in every city," Jack replied.

"It sure looks like Manhattan, maybe even Greenwich Village," I remarked.

"Then for you it's Greenwich Village, kid. What city does it feel like to you, Faye?" Jack inquired with a grin.

"It's just as you said quite eloquently mon chéri. To me it feels like a blend of every city I've ever been to," Faye replied with a smile.

"You know what, kid, these three sisters really remind me of your mother," Jack remarked with a warm smile, as he placed his hand on my shoulder.

This was a side of Jack which brought tears to my eyes. His heart was open when he was with me and Faye attending a musical which his dear friend Ms. Harper was performing in so wonderfully. I couldn't help but cry every time Jack reminisced with me about my mother. Now this musical 'Barflies' will hold an even more special place in my heart.

"Are you all right mon chéri?" Faye inquired as she draped her arm over my shoulder.

"Yes, I'm just … so happy," I replied as I wiped the tears from my eyes with a handkerchief.

"It's starting," Jack said in a zealous tone as the scarlet curtain rose, signaling the start of the final act.

"So what makes you ladies think you can perform at my club?" a sharply dressed man inquired in a stern tone as the three sisters stood with their hands on their hips in front of a backdrop of a club which reminded me of the speakeasy when it was finely furnished by Mr. Luciano's blood money.

"I'll tell you why Mr. Tux. Women like us are the greatest performers. We've been through hell and back and will light up your club with our charm," Louise replied with a grin.

"What experience do you three have performing burlesque?" the man inquired as the three sisters followed him through the club.

"Experience, our lives have been one big burlesque show, Mr. Tux," Mable replied as she scampered up on the stage while the jazz band was playing, signaling a song which I bet will put the pompous club owner known as Mr. Tux in his place.

"I can tell by your eyes you deem us unmeritorious.
Such a bullshit surmise. Women like us are quite glorious."

"Woah lady get off the stage.
Who let your kind in here anyway?"

"We let ourselves in honey-
Just listen to what we have to say.

"If you want a woman who's seen no strife.
A woman so weak in the knees.
Much like this mollycoddled housewife
Now would you hire her, oh please."

"Very well then ladies I've made up my mind
But I can only hire one of you to work at my club"

"No can do honey can't you see
That we three are a packaged deal
We live together, Cry together,
And sure enough we'll die together."

The three sisters continued to sing their empowering anthem about women as they stood on the stage with their arms draped over each other's shoulders while the patrons of the Sapphire Lounge began to cheer and holler including Jack.

Barflies was like no musical I've ever seen before, but it spoke to my heart in such a way that it was as if the three sisters singing at the club knew exactly how I felt and all the hardships I've endured throughout my life. The three sisters were rough, raw, charming, funny and beautiful. Everything a woman is was portrayed so genuinely by Ms. Harper and the two other actresses playing her sisters. I didn't want the anthem the three sisters were singing to end, but I could sense that the musical was about to conclude as I continued to watch with a wide-eyed gaze as Izzy began to sing.

"Listen here Mr. Tux
For I'll say this only once.
No matter where I go in this
World full of misters all your pleading means nothing

To women like us
For I'd rather burn in hell
Than forsaken my sisters!"

"Women like us"
(We are quite glorious!)

"Women like us"
(We are quite glorious!)

"Women like us"
(We are quite glorious!)

"Very well. You three ladies are hired," Mr. Tux pronounced with a smile.

The curtain then closed as the audience began to applaud and cheer. I then stood up from my seat along with Faye and Jack as the curtain rose to the sight of all the actors lined up on the stage. All the actors then began to bow as the audience continued to give them the standing ovation they deserved.

"That was wonderful Jack. Ms. Harper is a true talent," Faye remarked with a smile.

"I expected nothing less from Dottie," Jack said to Faye with a smile.

"Jackie … Jackie!" Ms. Harper shouted as she waved at Jack with a warm smile.

"Dottie!" Jack shouted.

"You and your family get you butts backstage. We have to celebrate," Dottie said to Jack with a smile as she gestured for Jack to follow her backstage as a jazz melody played off the actors as they departed the stage, concluding the beautiful musical named Barflies.

"Jackie, you made it!" Ms. Harper shouted in a zealous tone as she jumped up and down as Jack, Faye and I entered the backstage room.

"I wouldn't miss it for the world. You were fantastic," Jack remarked as Dottie wrapped her arms around Jack and kissed him on the cheek.

"Jackie … I didn't think I would ever see you again, after that night you left with that officer," Ms. Harper said to Jack with a wide-eyed stare.

"Should we give them privacy?" I inquired, as I stared at Jack and Ms. Harper in an intimate embrace while the rest of the actors celebrated.

"Attention, attention everyone. I would like to say a few words," the producer Mr. Calderon pronounced as everyone's eyes became immediately drawn to him.

"When I was a young boy growing up in Barcelona I had a small dream. Although I didn't for sure know exactly what that dream was or how to accomplish it, it was still very precious to me. Then I grew up into the handsome slightly overweight man you see before you. America truly is the land of opportunity, and I want all of you beautiful actors to know that no matter what reviews Barflies gets, what you all have done tonight on that stage is nothing short of magical," Mr. Calderon pronounced with a smile as his eyes began to well up with tears. Those were the kind of tears that you couldn't stop from welling up in your eyes once you've accomplished your dream in life.

I then noticed Faye coughing quite aggressively as everyone in the backstage room smiled except for her.

"Jack, Jack Faye isn't well. We need to go home," I said to Jack in a distressed tone as I tapped him on the shoulder.

"Oh uhm can't she take a taxicab. I mean the after party has just started kid," Jack said to me.

It was at that very moment with a young and beautiful woman like Ms. Harper wrapped around Jack that I began to wonder who Jack loved more. It was callous of him to brush off Faye as her health was once again beginning to diminish, but I also understood why he wanted to celebrate with Mr. Harper. I then noticed that Faye was no longer in the backstage room, as I frantically searched for her throughout the crowd of actors and stagehands.

"Faye ... Faye!" I shouted as I exited the Cherry Lane Theatre. I then noticed Faye sitting on a bench on the street corner as she continued to cough.

"I ... don't belong there mon chéri. That is a celebration of hope and fulfilled dreams," Faye said to me in a somber tone.

"Stop talking like that. I never feel hopeless when I'm around you," I said to Faye in a distressed tone as I sat down on the bench beside her.

"Jack and Ms. Harper are meant for each other. I can see it in their eyes, there is an intense passion burning between both of them," Faye said to me in a somber tone as she lit a cigarette in a shaky manner and took a smoke.

"Stop doing this to yourself. Don't you see how much Jack and I love you," I said to Faye as I took the cigarette out of her mouth and threw it into the gutter.

"He sure has an odd way of showing his love for me. Telling me to take a taxicab rather than—," Faye said to me in a distressed tone as a series of wrenching coughs took her breath away.

"You know how callous Jack can be, but he wanted to celebrate with Ms. Harper," I said to Faye.

"I don't want to be a burden. There was such joy coming from everyone in that backstage room except from me. I used to think that I lit up any room I entered, now I just cast a gloomy cloud of despair wherever I go," Faye said to me in a somber tone while shaking her head.

Tried as I may, Faye seemed inconsolable. Every time I found Faye in the depths of despair I reached out my hand to pull her out. Sometimes I succeeded in doing so, but other times, she was too deep for me to reach her. Those were the times I decided to keep her company in those depths, for whenever Faye hurt, I hurt with her.

"I'll sit with you on this bench all night if you want to Faye, or we can go back home and sit on the sofa with Sable. It's your choice, but just know that whatever choice you make I'll always be by your side," I said to Faye in a somber tone as I wrapped my arm around her.

"H—Haley ... let's go home," Faye said to me with a smile followed by more wrenching coughs.

*****

It was 12:26 AM in the apartment as Faye, Sable, and I sat together on the sofa as a French record played on the victrola.

"I'm sure Jack is having the time of his life right now," Faye remarked with a yawn as she stroked Sable.

"I'm happy for Ms. Harper. She was wonderful tonight. It gives me hope that she fulfilled her dreams to become a Broadway actress," I said to Faye.

"With help from Jack of course, your uncle never ceases to surprise me mon chéri. Just when I think I have him all figured out, he goes ahead and does such an act of benevolence like he's done with Ms. Harper," Faye said to me with a warm smile. "I know what you mean. Jack has surprised me many times as well over the past year, but at least all of those surprising moments have been good surprises," I said to Faye.

"He's suffered so much pain in his life. Jack deserves happiness with Ms. Harper," Faye said to me in a somber tone. "We all have. but just as Jack said, we're all in this together now," I said to Faye.

"Mon chéri … all those memories you have of Jack when you were younger, how do they compare to the man he is now?" Faye inquired.

"Those memories I had of Jack were … snapshots of him during times where he and my mother were fighting. The Jack I know now is the Jack I've read many pages of. I just wish I got to know him as intimately back then as I know him now," I replied.

"That's beautiful mon chéri. Do you know what Jack said to me the first night I walked into the speakeasy nearly three years ago?" Faye inquired with a smile.

"What did he say?" I inquired with a smile. "He said—,"

"You sure know how to light up a room, honey" Jack interjected as he entered the apartment with a grin.

"You heard?" Faye inquired with a warm smile, as Jack placed a bottle of wine on the coffee table.

"Every word and I still stand by that remark," Jack replied with a grin.

"When did you become such a romantic," I inquired with a smile.

"What's that supposed to mean kid? I'm just as romantic as that poet you love so much, what's his name … Shakespeare," Jack said to me as he ruffled my hair in a playful manner as Faye and I giggled.

"What about Ms. Harper?" Faye inquired as she grabbed the bottle of wine from the coffee table and took a swig.

"What about her?" Jack inquired as he sat between Faye and me as he draped his arms over both of our shoulders.

"I thought you would be celebrating with her till dawn's first light and perhaps beyond that," Faye said to Jack with a playful pat to his chest.

"Dottie and her fellow actors are still celebrating. I told them I had to get back home," Jack said to Faye.

"You would really rather be here with us than partying with a Broadway actress?" I inquired with a wide eyed stare.

"Just what do you take me for kid? Yes Dottie is a beautiful and talented young actress that any man with a heartbeat would fall head over heels for, but you two are my family, and no other dame in this world will change that," Jack said to me.

"Mon chéri Jack, I can tell those words are the wine talking. I just hope you feel the same way in the morning.

"Alcohol doesn't speak for me. I speak for alcohol, or at least, I used to. Now ... who wants pancakes?" Jack inquired with a grin as he stood up from the sofa and walked over to the kitchen.

"It's nearly 1 AM," Faye replied.

"I'll have some," I replied in a zealous tone and smile.

"Very well, last chance Faye, or this kid get's the majority of the pancakes," Jack said with a grin as he pointed the spatula at me.

"Yes mon chéri cook up as many pancakes has your heart desires. I suppose I'll have some as well," Faye said to Jack with a warm smile as she walked over to the kitchen with the wine bottle in hand.

Tonight was a beautiful night. One of those nights you wish could last forever in fear of the ever dismal morning after.

Jack's heart was with me and Faye, yet another one of those moments where Jack surprises me in a good way.

*****

It had been months since me, Jack and Faye attended Ms. Harper's musical Barflies and the time that followed felt like an awakening of love and peace for me. I felt as If I was making up for the childhood I never had with my mother and Fernando and Johnny. Those horrible times always make me short of breath when they come to the front of my mind, but now I have new memories living with Jack and Faye. It was what my heart always desired from the first moment I saw them interact with each other in the speakeasy. Back then I always had hopes that Jack and Faye would finally stop playing games and see that they're perfect for each other. Now I believe those two see each other for the first time without all the guises of alcohol or social conformities that were so overbearing in the speakeasy. I continued to write in the morning and afternoon, while Faye did whatever she could to keep her spirits up as her health continued to rise and fall. Jack remained by our side every step of the way, and I could tell by the warm smile of Faye's pale face that she adored all of his emotional support in her most trying times.

"The snow is quite beautiful, is it not," Faye remarked as she stared out the living room window while holding Sable in one hand and a cigarette in the other.

"It makes this city appear magical," I remarked with a smile as I walked up to the living room window and stared out across the street at the snow-laden trees which bordered the women's prison.

"What were you writing mon chéri?" Faye inquired with a warm smile.

"Just my thoughts. I—um, I don't want to tell anybody yet," I replied as I sat back down on the sofa and grabbed my journal.

"Well whatever it is I'm sure it will beguile all those who read it," Faye remarked.

"I'll get it!" Jack shouted from the bathroom as a knock on the front door of the apartment sparked our attention. Jack then grabbed the gun tucked between the waist-band of his pants as he stared through the peephole of the front door.

"Who is it?" I inquired with a wide-eyed stare. "It's our landlord Giovanni," Jack replied.

"Your rent is two days past due! Either you pay me now or I'll have no choice but to evict the three of you. Your name isn't even on the lease Jack, so you should feel grateful I've been allowing you to live here over the past two months" Giovanni said to Jack in a stern tone.

"There's no need for that. I'll be right back with the rent money," Jack said to Giovanni and then scampered into Faye's bedroom.

"Freeloaders, squatters, I have to deal with more of them every day. If this is the American dream then you all need to wake the fuck up," Giovanni said in a stern tone as he pointed to me and Faye. Sable then hissed at Giovanni as Faye put him down the kitchen counter.

"We're trying our best," Faye said to Giovanni in a timid tone.

"There's three of you living here and you still fail to pay rent on time. Your best isn't good enough for me," Giovanni said to Faye in a stern tone, as Sable continued to hiss at him, as if he was an intruder, which in many ways he was.

"Here's your rent money. Don't spend it all in one place," Jack said to Giovanni as he handed him the money.

"Oh and could you take a look at the shower it still takes forever to get—"

Giovanni then stormed out of the apartment with a dismissive wave towards Faye's request. "Putain de salaud!" Faye shouted.

"What she said," Jack said with a sigh as he shook his head and then sat down at the kitchen table.

"I'm almost afraid to ask, but I must, what are our finances, Jack?" Faye inquired.

"We have … twenty-two dollars left," Jack replied.

"What will we do for money?" I inquired with a wide-eyed stare.

"I'll tell you what we're not going to do, and that's resort to our past vices, that goes for you two," Jack said in a stern tone as he pointed at both of us.

"Why take the moral high ground now Jack when in the past you were quite comfortable with those vices which made you decent money," Faye inquired.

"I was an indecent man making decent money and look where that led me, right into the arms of Mr. Luciano and the Five Points Gang," Jack said to Faye in a stern tone.

"I—I could try to find work again, just like I did at the prison library," I said to Jack.

"You really worked at that library kid?" Jack inquired.

"I did, until I got fired for showing too much interest towards the women inmates," I replied.

"How typical that you would be fired for such a bullshit reason, Jack said.

"Perhaps we could pawn something," Faye said to Jack. "Good idea," Jack said to Faye as we both stared at her. "What ... why are you both staring at me? Do I really look so lavish that you think I have so many valuables to pawn?" Faye inquired.

"You're jewelry Faye. We're not asking you to pawn it all, just whatever you haven't worn in awhile," Jack said to Faye. "Ah ... so be it then," Faye said to Jack in a somber tone and then entered her bedroom.

I felt bad about Faye having to pawn her jewelry, seeing as how beautiful she looked wearing it, but the more I thought about it, the more I realized that the jewelry wasn't responsible for Faye's beauty. Faye was the one who made the jewelry sparkle that much brighter just by wearing it.

"All right let's go. I know a pawnshop on the corner of West 12th Street. Let's just hope they're still in business," Jack pronounced.

I noticed many people protesting outside of what appeared to be a factory of some sort. I remember Mickey told me that he used to work in a factory before he started working for Jack at the speakeasy. He told me Jack saved him from the cruelty of the factory. I sure hope he's doing all right now.

"We're here, and it looks like they're still in business," Jack remarked as he parked the car in front of a pawn shop called The Village Voice.

"Are you all right, Faye? You look very pale." I remarked as I helped Faye exit the car.

"I'm always pale mon chéri. You'll have to get used to me looking like a ghost," Faye said to me, as we walked towards the entrance of the pawnshop.

"Let me do the talking. Pawnshop owners are con artists by trade," Jack said to Faye as we walked up to the counter where a somber looking man sat reading the newspaper.

"How may I help you?" the man inquired as he quickly folded the newspaper, stood up from his chair, and put on his wire frame glasses.

I then noticed Faye wipe tears from her eyes as she took out the jewelry from her purse.

"Are you all right?" Jack inquired.

"I'm fine ... here," Faye replied as she extended her trembling pale arm.

"You shouldn't have to do this," Jack said to Faye in a somber tone as he shook his head.

"It's fine mon chéri, just take it," Faye said to Jack.

"No, we shouldn't have to sell a part of ourselves just to survive in this city," Jack said to Faye.

"Jack, we must," Faye said to Jack in a distressed tone. "Well how may I help you?" the pawnshop owner inquired in a stern tone.

"Put your jewelry away Faye. Here, this is a Walther PP 7.65mm. I'll even throw in 7 bullets all for no less than $200," Jack said to the pawnshop owner as he unloaded his pistol on the counter.

"Jack no, we need that gun for protection. Take my jewelry." Faye said to Jack with a wide eyed stare as she placed her jewelry on the counter next to Jack's pistol.

"Ah the German's sure know how to make guns don't they," The pawnshop owner remarked as he examined Jack's pistol.

"Jack you're being foolish once again. Your pistol could keep us alive," Faye said to Jack in a stern tone.

"I know and that's exactly what it's doing now when I pawn it for no less than $200," Jack said to Faye.

"Well ... are you pawning both of these items? If so I could tell you the cost of both items individually or the total of the two items combined?" the pawnshop owner inquired.

"You're not the only one who has a say in this decision," Faye said to Jack in a stern tone followed by a series of coughs. "You're right ... Hayley, you decide, what should we pawn, Faye's jewelry or my pistol?" Jack inquired in a stern tone. "Oh uhm ... please don't make me choose," I said to Jack. "It's all right kid we know you'll make the wise decision," Jack said to me with a grin, as he placed his hand on my shoulder.

"Thank you Jack," I said to Jack as I walked up to the counter and closely examined the two items.

I knew next to nothing about guns and jewelry, but yet another difficult decision was thrusted on me involving the two items. I suppose that's what it means to be an adult, to constantly have to make difficult decisions. As Faye so wisely remarked, Jack's pistol was our protection against any mobster, but if Jack's pistol was worth more than Faye's jewelry, then shouldn't we still pawn the pistol so we could have more money for rent and food? I was trying to be as unbiased as I could when it came to making this decision, but I knew either Jack or Faye would be upset with my decision.

"Uhm ... how much for the jewelry?" I inquired.

"Most of this is costume jewelry, which is worthless. This 12 karat gold necklace however will get you ... $125," the shopkeeper replied.

"Oh, and how much for the gun?" I inquired.

"For this pistol I will pay the price this gentleman requested, plus an additional $25 for the bullets and new condition it's in," the pawnshop owner replied.

"That's $225 right?" I inquired.

"Correct," the pawnshop owner replied.

"Well ... then I suppose we'll take the $225 for the gun and bullets," I said to the pawnshop owner.

"Very well," the pawnshop owner said as he took Jack's pistol and bullets and then took out the money from the register. "You made the right choice kid. I was tired of carrying that pistol anyways," Jack said to me with a grin.

"Sign here," the pawnshop owner said to Jack as he pointed at a document on the counter.

"Worthless costume jewelry eh, well you can va te faire foutre," Faye said to the pawnshop owner in a stern tone as she grabbed her jewelry off the counter and stuffed it into her purse before storming out of the pawnshop.

"Pleasure doing business with you," Jack said to the pawnshop owner as he paid Jack the $225.

"Wait Faye," I said as I exited the pawnshop.

"Ce bâtard. How dare he call my mother's jewelry worthless," Faye said to me in a stern tone.

"I'm sorry, was that necklace also your mother's?" I inquired.

"No the necklace was a gift from a man who I don't even remember the name of," Faye replied as she lit a cigarette and took a smoke with her arms tightly folded over her chest.

"Come on you two lets go get diner. I could really go for a Monte Cristo right now," Jack pronounced with a grin as he gestured for us to enter the car.

*****

"Hayley you've hardly touched your food, are you feeling all right?" Faye inquired as we three sat in a corner booth at a diner named Solomon's Eatery in the upper west side of Greenwich Village.

"Maybe she's just saving room for desert," Jack said with a snicker.

"No I have uhm … cramps," I said to Faye in a timid tone as I wrapped my arm around my stomach tightly.

"You need some antacids kid," Jack remarked.

"No it's not that kind of cramps," I said to Jack.

"Oh say no more mon chéri. We have to get back home now Jack. Hayley is going through something you would never understand," Faye said to Jack.

"All right, this diner is lousy anyways. They don't even have a Monte Cristo on their menu so I had to settle for a burger," Jack said to Faye as he put out his cigarette in the ashtray scoff. Is this what it felt like to be a woman, constantly feeling these painful cramps a couple times a week? I was just grateful that I had Faye to help usher me through this pain which all women experience. Jack was oblivious of course to my womanly progressions, and I didn't want to educate him on the sensitive matter for some things are better left between two women.

It was 5:24 PM in the apartment as Faye showed me what to take and how to take it regarding my womanly progressions. "Remember mon chéri, we women bleed because we feel more than men. You can think of it as a gift and a curse, and I will be there for you whenever you feel this pain," Faye said to me with a warm smile as she placed her hands on my shoulders. "Well, I'm used to being cursed, but I still feel blessed with you and Jack in my life," I said to Faye.

"Allez let's go see what that scoundrel is up to," Faye said to me with a giggle.

"Are you feeling better kid?" Jack inquired as me and Faye exited the bathroom.

"Yes, the pain is going away now," I replied.

"Jack, what are you looking at so intently mon chéri?" Faye inquired.

"That woman prisoner across the street, she was the same woman who tried to swindle me out of a cigarette," Jack said as he pointed out the window with a scoff.

"Oh that's Sidney Seville, she's very nice," I remarked as I opened the window and waved to Sidney, as Jack sat down on the sofa with a sigh, before quickly standing back up and scampering towards the front door of the apartment.

"Where are you going," I inquired.

"I'll be back in a couple of minutes, keep the door locked," Jack replied and then exited the apartment.

I then noticed Jack running across the street to the women's prison. Jack then shouted up at Sidney, but I couldn't quite hear what he was saying to her.

"Jack is talking to Sidney," I said to Faye with a smile as I gestured for her to come over to the window.

"Oh really," Faye said with a smile, as she picked up Sable and walked over to the window.

"Oh she's lowering her cup on a string. Is Jack really going to give her something? I inquired.

"Jack then placed something in the cup as Sidney blew him a kiss, before he scampered back across the street to the apartment.

"That would be Jack," Faye said as a knock averted our attention from Sidney to the front door.

"I'm back you two," Jack shouted. Faye then took a quick peek through the peephole before she unlocked and opened the door.

"What did you give Sidney mon chéri?" Faye inquired with a grin.

"I gave her a pack of cigarettes," Jack replied.

"That is very kind of you. I thought you said she was a swindler," Faye inquired with a smile as she placed her arms on Jack's shoulders.

"She may be a swindler, but I trust this kid's judgment above all else," Jack said to Faye as he pointed to me.

Jack and Faye then entered the bedroom and shut the door.

"No no curious boy, give them their private time," I said to Sable as he meowed and lightly clawed at the bedroom door.

Jack's mood was much lighter ever since he pawned his gun. It was as if an enormous weight was taken off his shoulders. Sure the physical weight of that gun couldn't have been more than 3lbs, but the psychological weight of having to defend your life and the lives of the people you love in fear for every moment a mobster could come out of the shadows and try to kill us was a crushing weight which Jack has had to live with for a year now. I've never seen Jack so happy, light-hearted, and kind as I've seen him now. I wish my mother could see this side of him now, or maybe she is looking down at him with a smile, for she was right all along when she wrote me in her last will that there was 'good in Jack'.

*****

Dear Diary,
November 28th, 9:37 PM,

An English poet named Thomas Tusser wrote 'April showers bring may flowers'. April was a beautiful month of awakening for me, but the month of May along with the six months that followed it had brought nothing but sorrow, for Faye's health seems to be deteriorating day by day, and the medication Jack got for her from Dr. Schuster at Bellevue seems to have no effects anymore. I write to you now because fear is overcoming me once again, the fear that I may lose Faye very soon.

Jack is doing everything he possibly can to help Faye, except take her back to Bellevue of course. She made us promise her to never take her back to that hospital even if she's at death's door. I love Faye so much, I just can't bear it, and now my tears are staining the very pages I write to you on. I now must end this diary entry because someone's knocking at the front door, until we meet again, hopefully during happier times.

"I'll get it," Jack shouted as he scampered to the front door and then stared through the peephole.

"Who is it?" I inquired in a timid tone as I walked up to the front door while holding my diary closely against my chest. "I don't know, some woman. Take a look for yourself," Jack replied. I then stared through the peephole to a most welcome sight.

"That's Virginia. She was the nurse caring for Faye at Bellevue," I said to Jack.

"Are you sure kid?" Jack inquired in an incredulous tone. "I'm positive," I replied.

"All right then," Jack said to me and then slowly opened the door.

"It's wonderful to see you again Ms. Hayley and you must be Jack," Virginia said to me with a warm smile.

"I am, so what business do you have here?" Jack inquired with a stern look.

"Well Mr. Dansby—,"

"Call me Jack," Jack, interjected as he gestured for Virginia to enter the apartment before quickly shutting the door behind her.

"Well, Jack, I owe it to you for bringing to my attention Faye's current condition. I was informed about a month ago from Dr. Schuster that you paid him a visit at Bellevue," Virginia said with a sigh as she put her large leather bag down on the floor.

"Yes he told me that Faye must return to Bellevue or there's nothing he could do to treat her. I then told Mr. Whitecoat that Faye didn't want to be a lab rat in his experiments and if he still wants to help treat her then he will give me more of the medication she was taking at Bellevue," Jack said to Virginia.

"That's not the story Mr. Schuster told me. He told me you threatened him," Virginia said to Jack.

"It was a matter of life or death. Did you come all this way on Mr. Whitecoat's behalf, if so then you can walk right out that door," Jack said in a stern tone as he pointed to the door and then lit a cigarette and took a smoke.

"I'm here for Faye. I believe I can help her. Please may I see her?" Virginia inquired.

"Yes, she's in her bedroom, right this way," I replied, and then walked down the hallway towards the bedroom where the heartbreaking sounds of Faye's wrenching coughs resonated.

"Hello troublemaker," Virginia said to Faye with a warm smile as she entered the bedroom.

"Virginia … is that you mon chéri?" Faye inquired with a smile followed by more wrenching coughs.

"It's me honey, may I take your vitals?" Virginia said as she sat down on the bed and opened up her large leather bag.

"Be my guest. Virginia, if you're here to go out and paint the town red with me and Hayley like I promised you then I'm sorry, I'm in no condition to even get out of bed," Faye said to Virginia.

"Your vitals are very troublesome honey. Please return to Bellevue. Dr. Schuster says that he's—,"

"On the verge of a scientific breakthrough regarding my virus, I know mon chéri, I know, but I also know that the end is drawing near for me, and I want to be surrounded by the people I love in a setting that I love, so my soul may rest in peace," Faye said to Virginia in a somber tone.

If I believed for one moment that bringing Faye back to Bellevue would result in her getting better I would immediately rush Faye back to that hospital against her will, but Faye was right about Virginia and Dr. Schuster, they want to experiment on Faye, but those experiments will be too little too late.

"I see … Is there anything I can get you honey?" Virginia inquired as her face quivered, as she grasped Faye's hand.

"A bottle of red wine, It would make me feel young again as I did when I frequented the speakeasy. I don't feel like … the same woman, just a shadow of her," Faye replied to Virginia as tears began to stream from her bloodshot eyes.

"You're just as beautiful then as you are now, Faye," I remarked in a tearful tone, as I sat down on the bed across from Virginia.

"I'll get you that wine honey, if it's the last thing I do," Virginia said to Faye and then kissed her on the forehead. Please take this medication Dr. Schuster modified for you. The enhanced dosage may help you regain some strength. In the meantime, I want you to remember how much your family and I love you and how much of a precious gift you are in God's eyes," Virginia said to Faye and then exited the bedroom.

"Hayley, please help me up," Faye said to me as tears began to pour from my eyes. Virginia new the end was near for Faye as well and that heartfelt message she gave to Faye before she left the bedroom felt like a final farewell, something I've been far too afraid to say to Faye for the past week.

"That nurse gave me these, she said they might help you," Jack said to Faye as I supported her as we slowly walked towards the sofa.

"Do you want to take the medication Faye?' I inquired as we sat down on the sofa.

"Why not, I'll try anything once," Faye replied as a series of wrenching coughs which sent her hunched over as her frail pale body shook with each cough.

"'You'll try anything once' huh, isn't that why you're in this condition," Jack said to Faye with a grin as he handed her a glass of water and two red and white pills.

"Jack," I said to Jack in a stern tone, before I realized Jack was just trying to make light of the somber mood as he always does, and it worked on Faye, for she giggled and gave Jack a dismissive wave as she always used to do when she would flirt with Jack at the speakeasy. Jack was putting up a brave front for Faye and me, but I could sense how Faye's deteriorating health was affecting him. Jack made the noble decision to be with Faye over Ms. Harper that night of her debut Broadway performance. This was a decision that once again surprised me. This showed me how much Jack truly loves Faye, to be with someone who is dying over someone who is full of life and vigor, in my book there is no greater act of nobility than that.

"What do you two want for dinner?" Jack inquired and then opened the fridge.

Sable then meowed in response to Jack, as if he knew Jack was getting dinner ready.

"We know what you want pampered boy," I said to Sable with a smile.

"Whatever you want to cook mon chéri," Faye said to Jack in a frail voice.

"Coming right up you two, oh Hayley turn on the radio to that French music station Faye listens to all the time," Jack said to me as he pointed to the radio.

"All right," I said to Jack and then turned the radio on to the station which only Faye could understand, but I still enjoyed every French word that graced my ears. I knew what Jack was doing. He was trying to make Faye as comfortable as he possibly could, for he wanted her final moments to be comforting.

"Jack … I must know, what will you do now?" Faye inquired as I helped her sit down at the kitchen table.

"I'm doing what I've always done Faye," Jack replied.

"I mean … what will you do now to support yourself and Hayley?" Faye inquired as her frail voice cut off as if she was being strangled by invisible hands.

"You let me worry about that Faye. You just eat your burger," Jack replied with a grin as he served me and Faye our burgers.

"I'm cold … I need to rest now," Faye said to Jack with a mouthful of burger.

"Can you make it?" Jack said to Faye in a somber tone and wide-eyed stare as her shaking arms couldn't even lift herself up off the chair.

"No I'm too weak mon chéri," Faye replied to Jack in a somber tone as Sable meowed in a sweet manner before rubbing his head against Faye's thin, pale calve.

"All right, legs up," Jack said to Faye and then picked her up off the chair like a princess. Jack then began to limp a little while carrying Faye to her bedroom as her wrenching coughing flared up. The heartbreaking site of Jack limping as he carried Faye as her wrenching coughing seemed to overwhelm her once again brought tears to my eyes.

"She's very weak kid, she wants to talk to you," Jack said to me in a somber tone as he entered the living room.

"No, no I won't say goodbye to her, not now, not ever," I said to Jack in a distressed tone as tears began to stream from my eyes.

"Who said anything about goodbyes, just go and talk to her," Jack said to me.

"All right," I said to Jack in a tearful tone as I wiped the tears from my cheeks.

Jack then patted me on the shoulder as I walked passed him, but I knew the truth of the matter, the truth which Jack's somber eyes told me. Jack eyes only looked like that once before and it was for a brief moment when he stared at my mother's casket during her funeral.

"Hayley … please sit down," Faye said to me as I entered the bedroom.

"Are you in pain right now?" I inquired in a sobbing tone, as I took Faye's pale limp hand and clutched it tightly between my hands.

"No, I can never be in such pain when I'm with you and Jack. You two made me feel at home in this country which used to scare the life out of me," Faye said to me with a warm smile. "I love you Faye. Please don't leave me. I need you," I said to Faye as I leaned over and wrapped my arms around her quivering chest.

"I love you too. You are my sister, daughter, and best friend. Mon chéri … your mother was right what you told me she wrote about Jack in her last will, he does indeed have so much good in him," Faye said to me with a warm smile.

"I know … she was right all along. Even at times when I thought he had no heart," I said to Faye in a sobbing tone. "You're not the first to think that about Jack, but together, you two will do beautiful things for this world. You're in good hands with Jack, and he's in good hands with you," Faye said to me.

"This little guy wouldn't stop scratching at the door so I thought I let him in," Jack said as he entered the bedroom while holding Sable.

"Aw come here my precious boy," Faye said as she outstretched her arms towards Sable as more wrenching coughs began to overwhelm her.

A knock at the front door then averted me and Jack's somber stare from Faye to the hallway

"I'll get it," I said to Jack as I wiped the tears from my cheeks and then exited the bedroom.

I then stared through the peephole to the sight of nobody standing in front of the door, but I know I heard a knock, so I slowly opened the front door and stared down both sides of the hallway but just before I was about to close the door, something caught my eye. It was a bottle of wine on the ground with a letter attached to it with a scarlet ribbon. I then placed the bottle down on the coffee table and began to read the letter.

Dear Faye,

I must get back to Bellevue now. It seems as if this city just keeps getting sicker and sicker, but despite your reservations, I do believe one day the diligent Doctors I work with at Bellevue will find a way to treat or possibly even cure your form of H.I.V. I'm so sorry honey. I wish I could be there to drink this bottle of wine with you but I must continue to care for all the sick at Bellevue, no matter how hopeless it may seem.

Love, Virginia

How Virginia managed to acquire a bottle of Pinot Noir during this liquor outlaw act was beyond me. This was just another testament of the profound effect Faye has on people's lives. Perhaps this will bring a glimmer of joy upon Faye's sickly face.

"Faye, look what Virginia brought for you," I said to Faye with a smile as I entered the bedroom holding the bottle of wine. My eyes then widened at the sight of Jack holding Faye's hand in both his hands as a single tear streamed from his eyes while Sable sat curled up on the bed beside Faye's face.

"She's gone kid ... she's gone," Jack said to me in a somber tone as Sable meowed and rubbed his head against Faye's pale cheek.

The bottle of wine didn't break as I dropped it upon the carpeted floor of the bedroom, but the same cannot be said about my heart as I dropped to my knees and began to cry from the loss of the most beautiful person I've ever known.

*****

One week had passed since Faye's death. Her funeral and wake were respectable, but nowhere near as beautiful as a woman like her deserved in death. I felt cold inside of me once again just as I felt after my mother died and I spent those hopeless days at the hospital waiting for Jack. This coldness inside of me was the result of Faye's warmth. The absence of Faye in my life is something I don't believe I can overcome, nor do I ever want to overcome. Without Faye, I'll never feel warmth in my heart again.

In Faye's last will and testament she had bequeathed her apartment, Sable, and all of her earthly possessions to me and Jack, her last benevolent act to ensure that Jack and I will make it in this cruel world.

The days that followed Faye's death left me as a quivering mass of sorrow.

As Faye told me before she died I was her sister, her daughter and her best friend. So I in turn had lost a mother, sister and best friend all at once. I cried every day from dusk till dawn. I cried so much my eyes were always burning red. I couldn't bear the pain, the mark Faye left on me and this world will forever leave me a changed girl, for I only felt like a strong woman when I was around Faye.

"Do you want a drink," Jack inquired in a somber tone as I entered the kitchen while rubbing my red tear-sodden eyes. "That's the wine Virginia brought for Faye," I said to Jack. "Faye would've wanted us to drink it. How did she know?"

Jack inquired as he stared intently at the bottle of wine. "Know what?" I inquired in a somber tone.

"Pinot Noir was the drink Faye ordered when she first entered the speakeasy. I said to myself, 'This woman is dangerously beautiful, and if I'm to ever have a shot with her then I must get comfortable with danger,'" Jack said with a grin. "All the more reason why we shouldn't drink the wine," I said to Jack.

"I need a drink now more than ever kid," Jack said to me in a stern tone, as he grasped the cork of the wine bottle tightly as his face quivered with sorrow.

"Fine you do what you must," I said to Jack in a stern tone as he struggled to open the bottle of wine as Sable jumped up onto the kitchen counter.

"Damn it!" Jack shouted as he slammed the bottle of wine upon the kitchen counter which made me and Sable recoil.

I saw the sorrow in Jack's eyes at that moment. He wasn't struggling physically to open the bottle of wine, he was struggling emotionally. Jack wanted to preserve those beautiful memories of Faye while also struggling with the lure of alcohol being right in front of him.

I then wrapped my arms around Jack as I began to cry. Jack was now the only shoulder I had to cry on. We all have different ways of dealing with loss, but I for one needed to grieve with Jack, for I knew he was hurting along with me. Even Sable's behavior has changed since Faye's death. I would often find him curled up on the pillow of Faye's bed just as he did when she died.

"I miss her so much," I said to Jack as tears poured from my eyes onto his shirt.

"Me too kid, me too. Come on … let's give Faye her wine," Jack said to me as he grabbed the bottle of wine.

*****

It was 11:06 AM as Jack parked the Chevrolet across the street from the New York City Marble Cemetery where Faye was laid to rest one week ago. A sudden wind then blew as Jack and I walked up to Faye's gravestone, which blew snow from the surrounding trees into my somber face. These New York winters have officially gotten the best of me. I was never the type of girl who could brave the cold weather, but now I feel the cold more than I ever have in my entire life.

"Well Faye … It's too bad we didn't get to share this bottle, but you and I both know you would've ended up drinking most of it anyways," Jack spoke aloud with a grin as his stern face fought hard to hold back tears which came pouring from my eyes as we stood in front of Faye's gravestone. Faye's gravestone read: J'ai vécu comme j'aimais, sans peur. Although I couldn't read the French epitaph on Faye's gravestone, I knew it was a profound and beautiful message.

"We should've brought flowers too," I said to Jack in a somber tone as he placed the bottle of wine down beside Faye's gravestone.

"Next time kid. Your grandmother's grave is pretty close to Faye's. I'm going to check in with her now while you two ladies catch up," Jack said in a somber tone as he placed his hand on my shoulder before walking away.

"Sable misses you. He spends every day at your pillow … I'm so cold now Faye. I know you believed wholeheartedly that Jack and I were in good hands with each other, but without you how can we ever truly feel warm?" I inquired in a tearful tone as I dropped to my knees.

I then noticed that Jack was talking to his mother at her gravestone as I stared at him across the cemetery. I wonder what he could be telling her right now. Is Jack telling his mom the same things I'm telling Faye right now? I thought to myself. "You wanted me to be strong when this day came, but I still want to believe this is just a nightmare I will soon awaken from and then I will see you there at my bedside with your warm smile. Jack and I will continue to live in your apartment. Even in death you continue to support us. I … I keep writing no matter how much pain is overwhelming me every day because I know that's what you would've wanted. It's the only thing I know, it's the only thing I'm good at … I love you," I spoke aloud in a sobbing tone.

"Such high-class wine for such a low-class dame," I voice said with a snicker.

"What did you say, who are you?" I inquired in a stern tone and wide-eyed stare as I looked up at a domineering man dressed in a black pinstripe suit with a matching fedora.

"Take her," the man said in a stern tone as he snapped his fingers and pointed to me. I then found myself restrained by a man who wrapped his arms around me from behind.

"No, no, Jack!" I shouted as I struggled to break free from the other man's arms, but he was much too strong for me. "Take the wine too. It would be a shame to waste that bottle on some lose flapper broad," the man said with a snicker as the other man placed an awful smelling damp rag over my mouth as he dragged me to the car.

"Damn it this doll is putting up a fight," the man remarked, as I flailed my arms and legs has hard as I could.

"Jack, Jack!" I shouted as my vision began to fade

"He wants her unharmed, hurry up you fucking mook," the man said to the other man in a stern tone as he lifted me up in his arms and laid me down in the backseat of the car.

"Hayley!" Jack shouted just as my arms and legs went completely numb and darkness swiftly overwhelmed me.

*****

I awoke in a haze to familiar sounds and smells. I was back. Back in the bed of the kitchen in the speakeasy, back where I spent many nights crying myself to sleep while Jack did anything he could to drown out my pleas. They took me; the Five Points Gang never really gave up on silencing Jack. Over the past year they've been waiting and watching this whole time. Now they believe they can use me as bait to get Jack, but they are terribly mistaken.

I then stood up from the bed but then quickly fell to the floor, as my head spun heavily as if I just drunk a bottle of bourbon all by myself. The dumbwaiter, I could escape without them noticing just as I escaped from this speakeasy before without Jack noticing. I then pushed the storage cabinet away from the wall with a groan, but what I saw crushed my hopes of escaping.

"You're awake. Oh don't bother trying to escape through there. Ever since that Irishman got the jump on us we have learned our lesson to properly fortify this establishment," a mobster said to me with a grin as he entered the kitchen. It was all bricked up this time, not even covered by a sheet of metal, the dumbwaiter, my only hope of escaping the speakeasy, was now gone.

"W—what do you want," I inquired with a wide-eyed stare as the mobster slowly walked closer towards me while the sound of jazz music began to play.

"Looking for this. We couldn't have you sticking one of us with this blade now could we," the mobster said to me as he held my make-shift knife in his hand.

"What do you want?" I inquired in a distressed tone.

"You know exactly what we want, Jack Dansby, your uncle, and Mr. Luciano believes he will arrive very soon," the mobster replied with a snicker.

"If you think you have the upper hand on Jack just because I'm here then you're wrong," I said to the mobster in a stern tone as my face quivered as I slowly stood up from the floor.

"Sit tight sweetheart, the show is about to begin," the mobster said to me with a grin as he pointed to the bed and then exited the kitchen.

I then stuck my head through the doorframe of the kitchen to the sight of about a dozen mobsters sitting at a large round table as they all drunk and smoked with not a care in the world. It was just as Gracie warned us about. The Five Points Gang was plotting this move for a long time now, and even though I was the one being held hostage by them, Jack was the one whose life hung in the balance.

*****

It was 4:15 PM in the speakeasy as I sat on the bed in the kitchen listening to the mobsters cackle.

An hour had passed since they kidnapped me and I felt like a powerless little girl once again by just being around those sinister men. A slow clap then resonated as a familiar mobster entered the kitchen.

"Bravo my doll, bravo. You and your uncle have managed to do what generations of crime families failed to do, and that's get under my uncle's skin, but now you two rats have scurried long enough," Stefano said to me with a grin.

"You're here too huh. So where's your uncle, or have you finally learned to speak for yourself?" I inquired in a stern tone. "Shut your fucking mouth. You belong to me now! Before this day ends your uncle will be nothing but a memory, a smear of filthy blood on the floor, a bloated corpse we will dispose of in the Hudson," Stefano shouted with a wide-eyed stare as he swiftly smacked me in the face.

The sting from Stefano's smack made my eyes well up with tears as he then began to snicker and then gently grabbed a strand of my hair in the manner of a sadistic child playing rough with a doll. I didn't want to speak again in fear of being smacked by Stefano, but at that very moment I felt like I was going down the same path my mother did with Johnny, and I would rather die a valiant woman than live as a mobster's servant.

I then kicked Stefano right in the grown which sent him to his knees groaning.

"Ah goddamn it! I guess you need to be broken in more huh doll," Stefano said to me with a grimace as he slowly stood up and cracked his knuckles.

"Just what exactly am I interrupting here Stefano?" a hulking mobster inquired in a stern tone as he entered the kitchen. I recognized this mobster, he was the one who kidnapped me, and he was also the one who Jack worked with at the bar before they tried to silence him for good.

"Nothing Leo, My doll and I were just catching up on old times," Stefano said to the mobster with a grimace as he continued to clutch his groin.

"Did you hurt her Stefano?" Leo inquired in a stern tone and wide-eyed stare as he walked towards Stefano who coward away from the hulking mobster.

"No, I swear, Leo we were just talking, please," Stefano said to Leo as Leo lifted him up by the collar of his suit and slammed him into the wall of the kitchen.

"Your uncle forbids any of us to lay a finger on Ms. Carmona here!" Leo said to Stefano in a stern tone, as he then let go of his collar, but then threw a series of swift punches to the gut of Stefano.

"I swear please, Leo we were—," Stefano said to Leo as he continued to smack him around over and over again until he fell to the floor, but Leo didn't stop there, he then began to kick Stefano in the gut.

"Stop ... I remember you. You're the mobster who tried to kill Jack," I said to Leo as he stopped kicking Stefano in the gut and grinned at me.

"Wrong Ms. Carmona, If it was me personally your uncle would've been dead before he knew what hit him, but we have this maledetto piccolo fallimento to blame for Jack still defying Mr. Luciano. You see Stefano here was in charge to carry out the hit on your uncle, but once again he did all his thinking with his balls, not his brain," Leo said with a snicker.

"I carried out the plan Leo, just as my uncle ordered. I didn't know about the dumbwaiter or that filthy Irishman who was playing both sides," Stefano said to Leo in a distressed tone as he wiped the blood from his mouth and then slowly stood up from the floor of the kitchen.

"Of course you didn't because you're just a wet behind the ears piccola figo who's going to be the death of your uncle, which brings me to why I came in here in the first place. Mr. Luciano has arrived and he wants Ms. Carmona to join him at the table for the imminent arrival of her uncle," Leo said to Stefano in a stern tone.

They all thought they knew Jack personally, every last one of these horrid mobsters, but they couldn't be more mistaken. The Jack they know is a Jack who knows how to survive around monsters, a Jack of violence, but those monsters in their sharp suits should feel far more threatened by Jack now than they ever have been before, because now he's a Jack of hearts.

Leo then whistled and gestured for me to follow him into the bar to sit with Mr. Luciano at the table full of monsters. I was scared as I entered the bar to the sight of the very man who's brought so much death to this city. Mr. Luciano, he looked just as I remembered him, a suave, finely dressed man who didn't need to raise his voice to strike fear into my racing heart.

"Ah the principessa del villaggio has returned to me. Please sit down my dear," Mr. Luciano said to me with a gesture towards the empty seat beside him as the speakeasy fell eerily silent with nothing but the sounds of the mobster's grunts and coughs resonating as I slowly sat down beside Mr. Luciano.

"Can I get you anything, princess?" Mr. Luciano inquired with a grin.

"No," I replied in a timid tone.

"What about this wine. Top shelf Pinot Noir, this wine is even hard to come by for a man like me. Leo tells me you left it at the grave of that flapper dame who used to frequent this speakeasy," Mr. Luciano said to me.

They wanted to break my heart into even more pieces than it already is, first with Jack and now with the memory of Faye, they were evil men.

"Yes it was for Faye," I said to Mr. Luciano in a somber tone.

"Mementos can have a powerful affect on the heart. Nobody lay a finger on this bottle, comprendere," Mr. Luciano pronounced as he pointed to Faye's bottle of wine as my eyes began to well up with tears.

"Jack 'Wild Card' Dansby, what an individual your uncle is, princess. Do you know one trait me and your uncle have in common … we both laugh in the face of death. Jack and I are cut from the same cloth, but I used that cloth to strangle the life out of those who stand in my way, whereas your uncle uses that cloth to wipe the mouth of powerful men like me," Mr. Luciano said with a snicker and then took a smoke from a cigar as the rest of the mobsters at the table snickered in unison.

"You and Jack are nothing alike. Jack is a loving man and you … you're a monster, a tyrant," I said to Mr. Luciano in a stern tone as my face quivered.

"'Monster' 'tyrant' such big words for such a little princess. Let me educate you my dear. Your uncle is alive right now because of his cunning black heart. Love hasn't kept your uncle alive, his ability to kill my associates has kept him alive," Mr. Luciano said to me as he waved his hand to gesture to all the mobsters at the table.

"Jack isn't a killer. He defends his family and friends from the likes of evil men like you," I said to Mr. Luciano with a wide-eyed stare.

"You're the only family Jack has left, princess, and I have plans for you, and you and I both know that men like Jack have no friends," Mr. Luciano said to me with a snicker.

The front door of the speakeasy then suddenly swung open as the attention of every mobster at the round table was averted from each other to the front door.

"We got him Mr. Luciano. He gave himself up willingly just as you predicted," a mobster said to Mr. Luciano as two mobsters entered the speakeasy as they restrained both of Jack's arms.

"Jack!" I shouted in a distressed tone as the sight of Jack's somber face brought me a sense of comfort and sadness all at once. What would happen now? Would they kill Jack right in front of me? I thought to myself as the two mobsters searched every inch of Jack's body for weapons.

"Ah 'Wild Card' Dansby has returned to the place where he used to reign supreme. We've been waiting for you Jack," Mr.

Luciano said with a grin.

"He's clean Mr. Luciano," one mobster said to Mr. Luciano.

"Well then search him again. I call this man 'Wild Card' for a good reason. The last thing we want to do again is underestimate him," Mr. Luciano said in a stern tone.

"We're positive he's clean Mr. Luciano, he's got nothing on him but the lint in his pockets," one mobster said to Mr. Luciano after he searched Jack once more.

"Oh you're positive are you? Did you hear that everyone, Ricky is positive that Jack has no ace up his sleeve? That's good. Now I'm positive that if Jack does have an ace up his sleeve then Ricky will be the first to suffer the consequences," Mr. Luciano said in a stern tone.

"How do you believe this will all end for you Jack?" Mr. Luciano inquired with a snicker, as the two mobsters sat Jack down across the round table.

"I see myself walking out of this speakeasy with Hayley, while you and your associates seethe in frustration," Jack replied with a grin.

"Is that so mi amico?" Mr. Luciano said with a grin as he swiftly pulled out his handgun and pointed it at Jack.

I couldn't watch Jack die. If this was the moment of the only family I have left dying right before my very eyes then I want to remember Jack as a loving man who stood valiantly against tyrants like Mr. Luciano, so I closed my eyes with a cringe.

"Nothing ... everyone look at Jack. He doesn't flinch in the face of death, but what if I do this," Mr. Luciano said with a grin as he then pointed his gun at my head.

"Is that really how far you've fallen? You would threaten the life of a kid just to get me to blink. Now who's the weak one," Jack said to Mr. Luciano in a stern tone and wide-eyed stare as he stood up slightly from his chair before the two mobsters sitting next to him quickly pulled him back down onto the chair.

"I'm not the weak one Jack. I now hold all the cards in this game. Giving up Johnny, Carlo, and then Nicolai all in exchange for this princess was an even trade in my opinion, because now she has brought you back to me. I've contemplated whether or not to take that flapper dame instead of your niece, but once word caught my ear that her death was imminent, I changed my strategy. I knew you cared deeply for both of them, but your niece here can make you do things you never believed you could do, am I wrong?" Mr. Luciano inquired with a snicker and then took a smoke from his cigar.

"No … you're right, and I thank her for that," Jack replied with a grin.

"Now … you may be incredibly cunning but I've seen that as long as you draw breathe my organization will be in danger," Mr. Luciano said as he snapped his fingers and pointed to Jack. "No," I shouted in a distressed tone as the two mobsters sitting next to Jack pulled out their handguns and pointed them at Jack.

"You hold all the cards huh. Care to bet on that?" Jack inquired.

"Wait … whatever you have in mind Jack, you must know that no outcome will lead to you walking out of this speakeasy with your niece," Mr. Luciano said to Jack.

"Just kill him now and get it over with. Do not play his game," Leo said in a stern tone as he shook his head.

"I agree with Leo. Uncle Charles," Stefano said in a stern tone.

"It appears your associates don't want you to gamble any longer with me, but I know your past, and a certain game of cards was responsible for your rise to power isn't that right Lucky Luciano?" Jack inquired with a grin.

"What do you propose Jack," Mr. Luciano inquired with a laugh. Jack knew indeed how to survive among monsters. I had faith in Jack, even though this could be the last time I see him, I knew Jack would find a way, just as my mother and Faye before me knew, I know in my heart that Jack will find a way.

"A game of Five Card Draw, if I win, then I get the kid and our freedom," Jack replied.

"Then what if I win mi amico?" Mr. Luciano inquired with a grin. I could tell that Mr. Luciano both loved and hated the idea of one poker game that would determine the fate of me, Jack, and his crime organization, but Jack knew this about Mr. Luciano, and he knew how to manipulate a man of power through temptation, just as Mr. Luciano did with Jack when he first arrived at the speakeasy that one night just over year ago.

"If you win then you get the kid and a bullet between these pretty eyes of mine," Jack replied with a grin.

"Only because I respect my enemies' final wishes … you have a deal Jack, but two of my associates will be playing as well in this poker game," Mr.

Luciano pronounced.

"I'll play, and if I win I take control of this organization. Things have gone downhill ever since you let your nephew make decisions," Leo said in a stern tone.

"Oh Leo your delusions of grandeur will be the death of you. Very well mi amico. Who else will join our game?" Mr. Luciano inquired.

"I—I'll play," Stefano replied in a timid tone as he raised his hand up.

"What are you playing for nephew, bigger balls? I'm afraid you have to grow those yourself, Mr. Luciano inquired with a snicker as the rest of the mobsters at the round table laughed in unison.

"If I win, I get my doll Hayley," Stefano replied with a grin. "You're pathetic," I said to Stefano in a stern tone.

"Oh what a prize indeed. Very well Stefano. If she is all your heart desires then far be it from me to deny you," Mr. Luciano said with a snicker.

Stefano was a pitiful child who thought he could win me in a poker game as if I was nothing but an object to him. Why was Stefano still obsessed with me? Was he so twisted in the head that he truly believes that I belong to him? Nevertheless there were now four players in this poker game which made me fear even more for Jack's chances of winning. What could I possibly do to help Jack? I thought to myself as Jack grinned and winked at me from across the round table. I felt an overwhelming sense of helplessness bearing down on me as the nervous mobster known as Ricky began to deal the cards to Jack, Stefano, Leo, and Mr. Luciano. Each player had high stakes in this poker game fueled by their own selfish desires of lust and power, except for Jack. He risked his life coming back to the speakeasy just for me. Mr. Luciano still calls me 'the princess of Greenwich Village' which is a title I no way deserve to have, but Jack is undoubtedly a knight, shinning amongst these monsters which surround him at the table. I couldn't sit idly by for an outcome which I believe will be stacked in Mr. Luciano's favor; I had to help Jack win no matter what the cost.

"Ah you will appreciate this deck of cards Jack. Do you notice the blood stains, well as you mentioned my rise to power did result from me winning a game of poker, and by the end of this game your blood will add to the blood stains of my past enemies," Mr. Luciano said with a snicker and then took a smoke from his cigar.

All four of the players had stern faces with slight grins to perhaps show the other players that they have a good hand. I was close enough to Mr. Luciano to where I could almost see his hand, but the only card I could make out was a nine before he put his hand face down on the table.

"So Stefano, does your uncle know about your plan on his birthday?" Jack inquired with a grin.

"I don't know what you're talking about Jack," Stefano said to Jack with a wide-eyed stare and stern tone.

"Three cards Ricky," Jack said to Ricky. Ricky then dealt Jack three cards in exchange for three cards from his hand. "Two cards. Oh are you planning a celebration for me Stefano?" Mr. Luciano inquired with a grin as he exchanged two cards from his hand for two cards which Ricky dealt to him with shaky hands.

"Not exactly, He plans on killing you on your birthday. Your nephew here will be the death of you, kids am I right," Jack said to Mr. Luciano with a snicker.

"He's lying, Uncle Charles. This filthy rat will say anything to save his skin right now," Stefano said in a stern tone as he pointed at Jack in an aggressive manner.

"Is that so Stefano? I don't doubt Jack is trying to plant seeds of mistrust right now in this crucial moment where his life hangs in the balance of five cards, but I also don't doubt your lust for power my very young and naive nephew. How did this information come to you Jack?" Mr. Luciano inquired with a grin.

The tension at the table was even heavier now that Jack disclosed information about Stefano plotting to kill his uncle on his birthday. Even if this is a lie created by Jack in order to make the mobsters fight among each other so the attention on him and I will be less severe, this sure sounds like something Stefano would do.

"Just as your nephew and his associates plotted to kill me that one night before Samson taught you three a lesson, I heard your associates mention that you were going kill your uncle on his birthday," Jack said to Mr. Luciano.

"I noticed the sweat dripping from Stefano's forehead from across the table as his wide-eyes darted from his uncle to Jack. Jack has always been the kind of man to lie in order to save his own life, but this was no lie, Jack was telling the truth about Stefano, I could tell by the fear in his eyes as his uncle glared at him.

"You too Stefano, Well, well, I must say you three have shown me just how fleeting the word 'loyalty' can truly be in this day and age.

"He's a fucking liar. I swear to you uncle!" Stefano shouted. "Let your cards do the talking now kid," Jack said to Stefano with a snicker.

"Leo, you're being very quiet right now. I know you well enough to know that means one of two things. Either you have a great hand, or you're planning right now how you're going to make it out of this speakeasy alive," Mr. Luciano said to Leo with a snicker.

"One card, Ricky, my hand will be the last hand you ever see, Charles, and as for your nephew, I warned you once before of his intentions," Leo said to Mr. Luciano in a stern tone

"Four cards, you're going to regret all those beatings you gave me," Stefano said to Leo in a stern tone as his face quivered as he exchanged four of his cards for four cards dealt by Ricky. I now felt the attention of the mobsters at the table shift from Jack and me to Mr. Luciano. Still Jack and Mr. Luciano were the only players at the table who remained calm, while Leo and Stefano began to lose their nerve with every passing moment.

"Ah now this is a poker game. A game with no stakes is a game not worth playing, and you three will lose it all. You broke my heart Stefano, after everything I taught you. You are my blood, nephew, but I cannot allow a giovane usurpatore such as yourself to threaten my power, but do not worry, I will tell your mother you died valiantly," Mr. Luciano said to Stefano in a somber tone as he shook his head.

My heart was racing as I wrapped my arms tightly around my chest. Was Jack as scared as I was at this moment? Was he quivering underneath the brash and smug exterior he always wears to protect himself just as a knight would wear a suit of armor to protect himself in battle? Stefano and Mr. Luciano told me they have plans for me, well if the outcome of this twisted poker game leads to Jack's death, then I do not want to live with the monsters who killed him. In life or death, I will go with Jack together.

"All right s—show your hands gentleman," Ricky pronounced.

"Let Stefano reveal his hand first," Mr. Luciano said with a snicker and dismissive wave.

Was it all hopeless, this dire situation Jack and I were in? I thought to myself as I stared into the stern eyes of all the players of this twisted poker game which Jack conceived in hopes to save me and win our freedom from the Five Points Gang. I then stared at Faye's unopened bottle of wine on the table as if I was looking into her warm eyes again. Faye never gave up hope, even when she was bedridden in Bellevue Faye still gave me hope.

*****

"Is it all hopeless, your condition?" I inquired in a sobbing tone as I sat at Faye's bedside.

"'Hopeless' ... I would never use such a word mon chéri. Despite what Dr. Schuster says, as long as there's life ... there's hope, as long as there's a light in your eyes ... there's hope, and as long as there's love in your heart, there's hope for a beautiful future," Faye said to me in a faint tone and warm smile, as tears began to stream from my eyes.

"I want to believe you, but I ...," I said to Faye as I stood up from the bed.

"Mon chéri where are you going?" Faye inquired in a somber tone as she reached out to me as I scampered out of the room.

*****

"Now reveal your hand nephew, We don't have all day," Mr. Luciano said to Stefano with a grin.

"Very well Uncle Charles," Stefano said in a stern tone as he revealed his hand to the table of eager players.

"M—Mr. Stefano Moretti has a full house tens over sixes," Ricky pronounced.

Jack, Leo and Mr. Luciano were grinning in response to Stefano's hand, did this mean that their hands were better, or were they all just masters of projecting smug facades in the face imminent death? I wish I knew more about poker or at least any card games for that matter so I could fully understand the rules, but something tells me that Jack and Mr. Luciano will not be playing by any such rules. I noticed Jack and Mr. Luciano staring daggers at each other as if Leo's hand was of no threat to theirs, but I had no idea what was going to happen next as my heart continued to beat out of my chest.

"I'll go next," Leo pronounced.

"Ah I must admit I'm anxious to see this hand of yours Leo, because my nephew's life now depends on it," Mr. Luciano said with a grin and then took a sip of bourbon poured for him by the nervous mobster dealer known as Ricky 'the Spaz'.

"Very well Charles," Leo said as he revealed his hand.

"M—Mr. L—Leo Calmati has a full house … Kings over nines," Ricky pronounced.

"Arrivederci nephew," Mr. Luciano said to Stefano in a somber tone.

"No please Un—," Stefano said in a distressed tone and wide-eyed stare.

Mr. Luciano then quickly drew his handgun and fired at Stefano, shooting him right in the chest. Nobody at the table except for me flinched at that moment Mr. Luciano killed his own nephew.

"Let my nephew's ambition serve as a lesson to everyone here. The reward of loyalty is life and the cost of betrayal is life, chose wisely i miei amici," Mr. Luciano pronounced as two mobsters carried away Stefano's body. Would Stefano still be alive right now If Jack hadn't of told Mr. Luciano that Stefano was plotting to kill him on his birthday? I couldn't help but feel that Jack was partly responsible for Stefano's death. Yes he was a terrible boy posing as a man, but I still felt remorse for how swiftly his own family killed him.

"Ah the first wise decision you've made in awhile, Charles," Leo remarked with a grin and then took a sip of bourbon poured from the nervous mobster dealer Ricky.

"Good now that there are only men left at the table we can really get down to business," Jack pronounced with a grin. "Good hand Leo. I must admit I'm impressed," Jack remarked with a grin.

"That patronizing tone which I've grown to hate will be the death of you Jack. There's no doubt you're quite a cunning man in the face of death, but that face will continue to peer into your eyes until you finally blink.

"I'm sorry I thought we were playing cards not reciting Shakespeare," Jack said to Leo with a snicker.

"There are now two dead men at this table," Mr. Luciano pronounced with a snicker.

"Oh I agree,"

"As do I," Jack and Leo remarked.

I could tell Mr. Luciano has played these kinds of twisted games before. It's just as Jack mentioned earlier, Mr. Luciano's rise to power was attributed to poker games likes these. He was far too calm as he killed his nephew. That kind of cold- bloodedness was unlike anything I've ever seen in a man.

"Let us reveal our hands at the same time Jack. This game has gone on long enough," Mr. Luciano said to Jack.

"Are you sure. I was just beginning to have fun," Jack inquired with a grin as all the mobsters in the speakeasy laughed in unison to Jack's brash remark.

"Are you ready mi amico?" Mr. Luciano inquired with a grin as he stared intently at Jack.

"Ready when you are," Jack replied with a grin. "Enough!" Leo shouted just as Jack and Mr. Luciano were about to reveal their hands.

Mr. Luciano then flipped up the table as Leo drew his handgun and fired at him.

I then crouched down behind the table beside Mr. Luciano as he fired back at Leo through the table. My arm, I was hit by one of Leo's bullet's intended to kill Mr. Luciano.

My arm was grazed but it still burned so badly along with the devastating sight of Faye's bottle of wine shattered into pieces on the floor.

"Hayley!" Jack shouted in a distressed tone.

"Jack!" I shouted back as Mr. Luciano pulled me up to my feet, as I held my bleeding arm with a grimace.

"You son of a bitch!" Jack said in a venomous tone.

"Your niece suffering this injury was none of my doing mi amico. You can blame Leo for trying to claim what he knew in his heart he could never acquire," Mr. Luciano said to Jack and then whistled and pointed to the up-turned table. Two mobsters then quickly flipped the table upright and began to clean up all the chaos which had just ensued.

Mr. Luciano was winning. One by one each player had fallen to him. Was Jack next, or will he prevail where so many other men have died? The two mobsters then began to sweep away the shattered bottle of Faye's wine, her final momento now being swept away by mobsters.

"I still have my cards in hand, Jack. So let us finish this game una volta per tutte," Mr. Luciano said to Jack with a grin. "Yes let's finish this pal. I'm still holding my cards as well," Jack said to Mr. Luciano with a grin as they both slowly sat back down at the blood and wine stained table.

I could still stop Mr. Luciano. He was far to calm, far too debonair, just as he was when he appeared at the apartment on the night my mother was killed by Johnny. When Mr. Luciano showed up, the entire mood of the NYPD changed. It was as if he instantly commanded them with a few words. He covered up my mother's death, but Johnny and Mr. Luciano's biggest mistake that night was not silencing me as well.

"You were there … I remember, you were there at the apartment when my mother was killed by Johnny," I said to Mr. Luciano as my eyes welled up with tears.

"Your mother's death was never an order carried out by me Princess. Your mother struck fear into Johnny and he acted as any man would act, irrationally. So look at me when I tell you that covering up your mother's death with the NYPD was nothing personal, just an uhm how do you say, business precaution," Mr. Luciano said to me as he stared intently into my tearful eyes.

"Look at me Charles. Don't look at her," Jack said in a stern tone.

"Very well. Go on Jack. Show your hand," Mr. Luciano said to Jack with a grin.

"You and I may both love to gamble Charles, but that's where our similarities end. You see that kid beside you has opened my eyes over the past year," Jack said to Mr. Luciano.

"Mr. Jack Dansby has r—revealed a Jack of Spades," Ricky pronounced as Jack revealed the first card of his hand.

"Oh really, and now that your eyes are opened what do you see mi amico?" Mr. Luciano inquired with a grin and then took a sip of bourbon.

"I see a man who's about to lose it all the same way he won it all. I see a man who once was one of the wealthiest men in the whole damn world now using an injured kid as a poker chip, but most importantly, I see fear in your eyes," Jack replied with a grin.

Mr. Jack Dansby has revealed an Ace of Clubs," Ricky pronounced, as Jack revealed the second card of his hand.

All the mobsters in the speakeasy along with Mr. Luciano then began to laugh at Jack's statement, while I clutched my bleeding arm in agony as tears streamed from my eyes.

"Jack, Jack, Jack, you've made it quite far in this world with your cunning, but my nephew was right in some ways, for a cunning rat is still just a cunning rat. Do I consider you a wiser and more cunning man than most of my associates you see before you? Absolutely, and that is why you must be silenced. The name Dansby leaves a sour taste in my mouth and when you're no longer staining the picture of the grand tapestry that is my empire, I can finally breathe a sigh of relief," Mr. Luciano said to Jack.

They were stalling, both Jack and Mr. Luciano. Was it because they didn't want the poker game to end, or was it because they both feared they would lose?

"Don't worry kid. His reign over this city has come to an end. He just can't admit it," Jack said to me with a grin and then reveled another card from his hand.

"Mr. Jack Dansby has revealed a Jack of Clubs," Ricky pronounced, as Jack revealed the third card of his hand.

"Tell me something Jack. Do you believe this child will flourish under your care?" Mr. Luciano inquired with a grin.

"'Flourish' … I don't even know what that word means pal, but I can tell you that she and I will overcome anything this world throws at us. Even if I lose this game, Hayley has too much of me and her mother in her to ever be tamed by the likes of you and your organization," Jack replied and then revealed another card from his hand.

"M—Mr. Jack Dansby has revealed another Jack of Spades which currently gives him a three of a kind," Ricky pronounced.

Jack had one card left and his current hand didn't shock any of the mobsters gathered around the table, including Mr. Luciano.

"A fool's gambit mi amico. Unlike your sister, I will show this princess the finest things in life and in time, she will learn to love her Uncle Charles," Mr.

Luciano said to Jack with a snicker.

"Your time is over, Charles," Jack said in a stern tone, and then revealed his final card.

"Mr. J—Jack Dansby has revealed a Jack of Hearts. Giving him a four of a kind," Ricky pronounced as Jack revealed the fifth and final card of his hand.

The final card in Jack's hand was met with a reaction of gasps and murmurs from the mobsters gathered around the table, but Mr. Luciano remained stoic as he then took another sip of bourbon.

"Just say the word boss," a mobster said to Mr. Luciano as he drew his handgun and pointed it at Jack.

"Put that fucking gun away Emilio! We are civilized men, playing a civilized game, for civilized courses!" Mr. Luciano shouted as he slammed his fist on the table three times which caused me to recoil from him in such an abrupt manner. Mr. Luciano never lost his temper, did this mean Jack's hand was better than his? Or was he merely offended that one of his associates believed Jack had the better hand?

"I'm in no way a civilized man, but I know it takes far more than dressing in the finest suites money can buy and drinking top shelf liquor to be civilized.

"I will not leave your life in suspense any longer mi amico," Mr. Luciano said to Jack with a grin as he revealed his first card. "Mr. Luciano's first card i s a Five o f diamonds," Ricky pronounced, as Mr. Luciano revealed the first card of his hand. "Mr. Luciano's second card is a Six of Diamonds," Ricky pronounced, as Mr. Luciano revealed the second card of his hand.

Something was wrong. I felt it in the pit of my stomach. Mr. Luciano didn't kill Jack when he revealed his hand. Could this mean that Mr. Luciano wanted the satisfaction of beating Jack in the poker game? Could this mean that Mr. Luciano had the better hand? No, Jack still had me, the mobsters took my make-shift knife from me when they kidnapped me, but there was still something I kept on me that they failed to notice, something far more deadly than a knife, and I would use it now to end Mr. Luciano once and for all, I thought to myself as my eyes widened with a revelatory memory.

*****

"Hayley please come back," Faye said to me in a faint tone, as I scampered out of the ICU room and into another empty ICU room.

I felt powerless, as is the story of my life. A girl like me in this day and age is nothing but a victim of many forces much more powerful than she could ever be. My eyes then widened as I noticed a small phial on a steel tray in the cold and stark ICU room. The bottle read: POTASSIUM CYANIDE 500 MG EXTREMELY LETHAL. No, I could use this poison, with this poison I was no longer a powerless little girl, with this poison I had the power to end a life. I thought to myself as I stared intently at the small phial in my hand.

"What are you doing in here?" a nurse inquired in a stern tone as she entered the ICU room.

"Oh sorry I got lost. Could you show me the way back to the lobby?" I inquired in a sobbing tone as I tucked the phial of poison underneath my bra and then turned to face the nurse with a smile.

*****

I can't believe I forgot about this phial of poison pressed against my chest. I could be the one to stop him. I could be the one to end Mr. Luciano's reign once and for all. All the mobsters' eyes were either focused on Mr. Luciano or Jack at this crucial moment in time. It was as if I was invisible. So I then discretely reached into my bra and took out the phial of poison with a wide-eyed stared.

"Mr. Luciano's third card is a S—Seven of Diamonds," Ricky pronounced, as Mr. Luciano revealed the third card of his hand.

"Mr. Luciano's fourth card is an Eight of Diamonds," Ricky pronounced as Mr. Luciano revealed the fourth card of his hand.

"Emilio, get over here," Mr. Luciano said as he gestured for the mobster standing beside Jack to join him.

I then quickly opened the phial of poison and tipped it over Mr. Luciano's glass of bourbon. I know how much he loves bourbon and now I just need him to take one last sip.

My eyes widened as the drop of cyanide hung on the opening of the phial.

"B—Boss you have to hear this!" a mobster shouted as he turned up the radio.

"Quiet you stammering scemo," Mr. Luciano said in a stern tone.

"Boss it's important!" the mobster shouted.

"I decide what's important. I pull all the strings in this city and I hold all the cards!" Mr. Luciano shouted as he grit his teeth and pointed aggressively at the mobster by the radio.

"Breaking international news! The Twenty-First Amendment has now been ratified which has in turn repealed the Eighteenth Amendment. I repeat, as of this day on December 5th 1933 the nationwide alcohol ban has now ended!" the radio sounded to stone silence in the speakeasy, as I quickly pulled back the phial of poison from Mr. Luciano's glass of Bourbon and tucked it back under my bra.

"Boss what will we do?" Emilio inquired in a distressed tone and wide-eyed stare.

It was as if someone had taken the very life from all the monsters which surrounded me.

It was over. Alcohol was now legal once again. This country would now be able to enjoy alcohol and men who profit from bootlegging like the Five Points Gang will be rendered powerless.

"Thirteen years … now my organization has lost its number one profit," Mr. Luciano said in a somber tone as he stared intently at his glass of bourbon.

"I can't believe it. Is this a dream?" Jack inquired with a wide-eyed stare.

"We must regroup, restructure, and relocate," Mr. Luciano said in a stern tone as he stood up from the table and gestured for every mobster to follow him.

"Boss what about Jack and the girl?" Emilio inquired as he put on his jacket.

"I do not kill for the sake of killing. I've only silenced people as a business operation. Alcohol is now legal in this country, which means are quarrels are no longer relevant in this world. Mr. Dansby, Miss Carmona, arrivederci," Mr. Luciano pronounced.

"Don't call me by that name. I renounce the name Carmona. I am Hayley Dansby," I said to Mr. Luciano with a smile. I then ran over and hugged Jack tighter than I've ever hugged him in my life.

"Charles … it was a pleasure doing business with you," Jack said to Mr. Luciano with a grin as the Five Points Gang exited the speakeasy.

Jack then walked over to the table where Mr. Luciano sat and stared intently at the fifth card laying face down which Mr. Luciano had yet to reveal.

"No," Jack said as he shook his head and then walked over to me with a smile.

"What do you say you and I go west kid?" Jack inquired with a smile.

*****

Jack and I took what we needed from the speakeasy and nothing more before we packed it all up in Jack's Chevrolet and drove west out of Greenwich Village. Part of me will miss New York, but I knew that wherever I was going with Jack, we would be alright. Alcohol was now legal, but Jack didn't immediately try to procure a bottle to numb his pain as he's done most of his life. We had each other and although I've lost so much over the past year, I've also grown a great deal and so has Jack. The journey we were on now would not be one I would take with a fearful heart.

"How's that arm feeling," Jack inquired with a smile as the sun shone through the gray veil of the New York sky.

"It burns, but if you can handle the pain of being shot then so can I, I replied with a smile.

"What are you writing?" Jack inquired with a smile.

'Just my thoughts of a life less lived' is what I thought of telling Jack at that moment. This was the same response I gave to everyone when they asked me what I was writing, but times have changed now.

"My memoir," I replied with a smile.

"You sure have story to tell kid. So what will you call it?" Jack inquired with a smile.

" …'Speakeasy'," I replied as I smiled back at Jack.

ABOUT THE AUTHOR

Greetings, lovers of literature. I am Robert James Allen, and ever since I was nineteen years old, the literary works of Edgar Allan Poe, William Shakespeare, Charles Dickens, and Henry David Thoreau have beguiled me. I consider those renowned writers to be the most prolific writers of all time, and I consider my writing to be wholeheartedly inspired by their work. The art of storytelling is in my blood, and I strive to write about topics that resonate in the hearts and minds of all demographics that are struggling in life and feel like they have no voice. Throughout my entire life, I've only ever felt solace within the deep recesses of my mind. I now share those recesses to the world in hopes that we may better understand and accept each other's demons, rather than stigmatize and forsake them. This is my sophomore novel which I believe will bring people together as this story can be read with someone else in a dualistic literary experience. This story in its essence is a duet of two protagonists during a polarizing time in American history which will shed a light on our past transgressions for the betterment of our future virtues.